Materializing the Middle Passage

Materializing the Middle Passage

A Historical Archaeology of British Slave Shipping, 1680–1807

JANE WEBSTER

Great Clarendon Street, Oxford, OX2 6DP,
United Kingdom

Oxford University Press is a department of the University of Oxford.
It furthers the University's objective of excellence in research, scholarship,
and education by publishing worldwide. Oxford is a registered trade mark of
Oxford University Press in the UK and in certain other countries

© Jane Webster 2023

The moral rights of the author have been asserted

All rights reserved. No part of this publication may be reproduced, stored in
a retrieval system, or transmitted, in any form or by any means, without the
prior permission in writing of Oxford University Press, or as expressly permitted
by law, by licence or under terms agreed with the appropriate reprographics
rights organization. Enquiries concerning reproduction outside the scope of the
above should be sent to the Rights Department, Oxford University Press, at the
address above

You must not circulate this work in any other form
and you must impose this same condition on any acquirer

Published in the United States of America by Oxford University Press
198 Madison Avenue, New York, NY 10016, United States of America

British Library Cataloguing in Publication Data
Data available

Library of Congress Control Number: 2023938973

ISBN 978–0–19–921459–4

DOI: 10.1093/oso/9780199214594.001.0001

Printed in the UK by
Bell & Bain Ltd., Glasgow

Links to third party websites are provided by Oxford in good faith and
for information only. Oxford disclaims any responsibility for the materials
contained in any third party website referenced in this work.

Acknowledgements

This book has taken two decades to write, so I have many people to thank for their support, expertise, guidance, and (not least) patience. At the top of this list are my husband, Rob Young, and our son, Adam. Rob has supported me in countless ways at every stage of the research and writing process. Adam has grown up with *Materializing the Middle Passage*: he was a year old when I began the research and turned 22 as I finished the text. I am sure my boys are mighty glad it is all done at last—but I could not have got there without them.

I am deeply indebted to my friends, who have helped me out in so many ways as this book has taken shape over the years: a huge thank you to Verity Anthony, Julie Evans, Hannah Flint, Sarah Haynes, Julian Haynes, Carsten Heldmann, Mark Jackson, Sophie Moore, Henrik Mouritsen, Caron Newman, Richard Newman, Kirsty Petley, David Richardson, and Debbie Richardson. Thanks also to the allotment that I share with Sarah Haynes—it has been a much-loved sanctuary for the pair of us for a long time, and sometimes we have even managed to grow stuff there.

Materializing the Middle Passage began life with a 2001 Caird Fellowship at the National Maritime Museum. I am most grateful to the Caird Trustees, and especially to Nigel Rigby, who was, at that time, the Director of Research at the NMM. I must thank the museum, first, for letting me loose on their fantastic collections and library resources and, second, for allowing me to spread a one-year fellowship across three years. I asked about that possibility at my interview and was granted it without hesitation; that flexibility allowed me to focus on two works in progress at once (a book and a small boy): I will be forever grateful. My original Caird research project, centred entirely on the NMM's own collection, has snowballed over the years into something roughly the size of the Lambert–Fischer Glacier: I do hope the Caird Trustees and the NMM will feel it was all worth the wait.

Maritime and terrestrial archaeologists from many countries have generously furnished information about their work and provided me with images of their wreck sites and artefacts. I am especially indebted to the *Slavery Images: A Visual Record of the African Slave Trade and Slave Life in the Early African Diaspora* website (http://www.slaveryimages.org), which has been a much-valued source of inspiration, information, and images in the writing of this book. David Moore and Corey Malcom have both shared their expertise on the *Henrietta Marie* shipwreck. Special thanks are also due here to the team at Aust Agder Museum, who curate the finds from the *Fredensborg* wreck, and to Staffin von Arbin, Greg Cook, Karlis Karklins, Michael Cottman, Museum of London Archaeology, and Nigel Sadler. Jerome Handler went to considerable lengths to provide original slides for me from his work at Newton Plantation: I am most grateful to him and to my colleague Mark Jackson, who scanned the Newton images for me. I am also indebted to Adrienne Baron-Tacla for taking me to see Valongo Wharf and the Pretos Novos Institute in Rio de Janeiro, and for facilitating a memorable visit to the finds from Valango. I am grateful also to Helen MacQuarrie, who made it possible for me to see, in Bristol, the artefacts from the Rupert Valley cemetery on St Helena.

This book draws extensively on archive and museum collections, and I have relied throughout on the expertise of a great many archivists, curators, and artefact researchers. Thanks here especially to Bertrand Guillet at the Château des ducs de Bretagne (Nantes), the home of the unique and important images of *Marie-Séraphique*. I am also indebted to Robert Blyth at the NMM, Jeremy Coote and Ashley Coutu at Pitt Rivers, Suzanne Gott, Tony Coverdale, Vibe Martens, Kenneth Kinkor, Liverpool Museums, and Bristol Museum and Art Gallery. Thanks also to Karl-Eric Svardskog and Henriette Jakobsen. Michael Graham-Stewart drew my attention to (and provided a copy of) the entry from the log of HMS *Sybille* discussed in Chapter 10. I am also very grateful to Sarah Coleman, Margarita Gleba, and Malika Kraamer for sharing with me their ongoing work on the cloth samples in Thomas Clarkson's chest, curated by Wisbech and Fenland Museum.

Over the last few years, I have been privileged to collaborate on two digital heritage projects for the *slavevoyages* (Trans-Atlantic Slave Trade Database) website, alongside David Eltis (Emory), Nicholas Radburn (Lancaster), Bertrand Guillet (Château des ducs de Bretagne), and the brilliant creative team at the Emory Centre for Digital Scholarship, who built the digital models of the French slave ships *Aurore* and *Marie-Séraphique* used in the *slavevoyages* videos. My own contribution to these projects has been minor, but my understanding of the appearance and characteristic features of slaving vessels has grown considerably through my involvement with this work.

I have reached out to many other scholars for information about the material world of the slave ship, including Kathleen Murphy (who generously shared her research on the naturalist James Petiver in advance of publication), Stephen Farrell (who in his former role as Senior Research Fellow of the History of Parliament Trust advised me on the workings of eighteenth-century parliamentary committees), Lisa Lindsay (who shared her insights into Robert Norris's time in West Africa), Andrew Lewis (who provided invaluable advice on the terms of the Dolben Act), Deirdre Coleman (who shared her research on Henry Smeathman), and Katrina Keefer (who shared her work on scarification and allowed me to use one of her reconstruction drawings of marks on the face of an African recaptive).

I have always explored slavery from a diachronic perspective, and discussions with colleagues who work on Roman slavery have impacted this book in important ways. I am especially grateful here to Jennifer Baird, Nick Cooper, Simon Corcoran, Sandra Joshel, Franco Luciani, Henrik Mouritsen, Rebecca Redfern, and Ulrike Roth.

My academic home is the Archaeology section of the School of History, Classics, and Archaeology at Newcastle University. Three iterations of the UK's RAE/REF research review system rolled by at Newcastle without this book appearing; but, if my colleagues harboured suspicions that *Materializing the Middle Passage* might never be finished, they did not say so; on the contrary, I have received nothing but encouragement. I would like my co-workers at Newcastle to know that I am truly thankful to be part of such a supportive, inspirational team. I owe a special debt to my friend and colleague Caron Newman for the maps and other images she produced for this book, and for taking on some of the work of organizing image permissions. I have also learned a great deal from former Newcastle graduate students who have shared my interest in slavery, slave ships, West Africa, and postcolonial theory. I am particularly grateful here to Stephanie Moat, Michael Smith, Wendy Smith, and Tom Whitfield. Grants from the School of History, Classics and Archaeology supported the cost of some key images, and indexing.

Colleagues at Newcastle and elsewhere have generously made the time to read and comment in detail on chapters or sections of my draft text. I owe a particular debt to David Eltis and Mark Leone here, but have also benefited from the insights of Katrina Keefer, Lisa Lindsay, and Luis Symanski. I also want to thank Chris Fowler, Diana Paton, Nicholas Radburn, and Rob Young for making time to comment on various aspects and chapters of the book.

A note about images

Every effort has been made to source high-resolution images for this book. In a small number of cases, such pictures did not exist. In these instances, I have elected to include a lower resolution image, rather than leave out important data entirely.

A note on the text

The detailed voyage narratives of greatest service to this book are introduced in Chapter 3 and the authors, ships, and/or dates are thereafter identified in bold throughout (e.g. **Phillips, *Hannibal* 1693–4**).

Contents

List of Figures	xi
List of Tables	xix
List of Boxes	xxi
Abbreviations	xxiii

1. Materializing the Middle Passage: An Introduction in Three Objects	1
2. The British Slave Trade: A Brief Overview	27
3. Voices from the Sea: Documentary Narratives of Middle Passage Voyages	54
4. Artefacts from the Sea: Shipwrecks and Maritime Archaeology	101
5. Guineamen: Materializing the Merchant Slaver	125
6. Witch Crafts: Slave Ships, Sailors, and African Cosmologies	181
7. From Ship to Shore: Some Trade Goods and Their Biographies	211
8. Other Cargoes: Shipping Home the Productions of Africa	256
9. Technologies of the Body on the Floating Pesthouse	283
10. Discipline and Punish: A Material History of Middle Passage Practice	327
11. Surviving the Middle Passage	393
12. The Middle Passage Re-membered: A Conclusion in Three More Objects	439

References	467
Index	499

List of Figures

1.1. *Sandown* in the Floating Dock. From the sea journal of Samuel Gamble (1793–4). LOG/M/21, title page. (National Maritime Museum, Greenwich, London) — 4

1.2. Elizabeth Finch Hatton and Dido Belle. Possibly by David Martin, *c*.1780. (The Earl of Mansfield, Scone Palace, Perth) — 7

1.3. Enamelled porcelain punch bowl depicting *Swallow*, probably painted by William Jackson. C.58–1938. (Victoria & Albert Museum, London) — 9

1.4. Elements of a necklace from grave B72, Newton Plantation, Barbados. (Jerome Handler, Virginia Humanities) — 11

2.1. The 'Guinea' coast, with the West and Central African countries mentioned in Chapter 2. (Created by Michael Athanson, based on drafts prepared by Caron Newman) — 28

2.2. Sketch for the arms and crest granted to John Hawkins, 'The Canton geven by Rob[er]t Cooke Clar[enceux] King of Arms 1568'. (The College of Arms, London) — 29

2.3. Obverse of a 1663 Guinea coin. E1528. (British Museum Images) — 30

2.4. The *Luxborough Galley* on fire, 25 June 1727. John Cleveley, 1760. BHC.2389. (National Maritime Museum, Greenwich, London) — 33

2.5. The jack (knave) of hearts from a set of playing cards marking the collapse of the South Sea Company. (Kress Collection (Bancroft), Baker Library, Harvard Business School) — 34

2.6. The proportions of the 10,480 TSTD slaving voyages undertaken by ships from Britain originating in London, Liverpool, Bristol, and Lancaster. (Image prepared by Caron Newman, using https://(Image prepared by Caron Newman, using https://www.slavevoyages.org/voyages/mOu2kS5A (accessed 21 March 2022)) — 36

2.7. *The Southwell Frigate Trading on ye Coast of Africa*, Nicolas Pocock, *c*.1760. M669. (Bristol City Museums, Galleries, and Archives UK/Bridgeman Images) — 37

2.8. The principal zones from which British ships transported African captives. (Created by Michael Athanson, based on drafts prepared by Caron Newman) — 41

2.9. Locations of the Gold Coast forts (Ghana) and other principal West African trading sites mentioned in Chapter 2. (Created by Michael Athanson, based on drafts prepared by Caron Newman) — 43

2.10. Views of European forts and castles along the Gold Coast. Jan Kip, *c*.1704. PAH2826. (National Maritime Museum, Greenwich, London) — 44

2.11. 'New World' disembarkation sites discussed in Chapter 2. (Created by Michael Athanson, based on drafts prepared by Caron Newman) — 48

xii   LIST OF FIGURES

3.1. Gold weight from the Gold Coast (height 62.5 mm). Af1949,08.2.
(British Museum Images)   57

3.2. Jean Barbot presents himself to the King of Sestro, 1681. Churchill and
Churchill (1732: v, plate G). (British Library Board. All Rights Reserved/
Bridgeman Images)   68

3.3. Lithograph of Hugh Crow (by W. Crane): frontispiece of Crow's 1830
Memoirs. (Private Collection/Bridgeman Images)   72

3.4. Creamware jug (height 242 mm) bearing the transfer-printed image of a
3-masted ship. Below are the words 'SUCCESS TO THE BROOKS CAPᵀ. NOBEL'.
1994,0718.2. (British Museum Images)   80

3.5. Oval silver epergne by Pitty and Preedy, engraved with the arms of the Town
of Liverpool, inscribed: 'This is one of two Pieces of Silver Plate presented TO
JAMES PENNY ESQr by The CORPORATION OF LIVERPOOL 1792'. 1973.278.
(National Museums Liverpool)   86

3.6. Frontispiece of Olaudah Equiano's *Interesting Narrative*, published in 1789.
Based on a painting thought to be the work of the miniaturist William Denton.
British Library Board. (All Rights Reserved/Bridgeman Images)   88

3.7. Ignatius Sancho. Engraving by Francesco Bartolozzi, published by John
Bowyer Nichols in 1781. Based on the portrait of Sancho painted by Thomas
Gainsborough in 1768. (Michael Graham-Stewart/Bridgeman Images)   91

4.1. Locations of the wreck sites discussed in Chapter 4. (Created by Michael
Athanson, based on drafts prepared by Caron Newman)   102

4.2. Model of *Fredensborg*, built by Terry Andersen. Aust-Agder Museum.
(Photo: Karl Ragnar Gjertsen, KUBEN Museum and Archive)   105

4.3. Underwater archaeologist on the site of *Adélaïde*, wrecked on the coast of
Cuba in 1714. (Photo: Christoph Gerigk. Franck Goddio/Hilti Foundation)   107

4.4. Site plan of the Elmina wreck, showing the range of artefacts identified, and
their locations. (Gregory Cook)   108

4.5. Brick stack on the *Havmanden* wreck site. (Staffan von Arbin, Bohusläns
Museum)   109

4.6. Basket (143 × 165 × 165 mm) created in 2015 by artisans in Mossuril,
Mozambique. 2016.168ab. (Collection of the Smithsonian National Museum
of African American History and Culture. Open Access (CC0) http://n2t.net/
ark:/65665/fd5c1dcaef5-0d51-4e34-8df7-27f2ee6dd95a)   110

4.7. *Queen Anne's Revenge* site plan. (Image courtesy of the North Carolina
Department of Natural and Cultural Resources)   113

4.8. Plan of the *James Matthews* shipwreck. (Western Australia Museum)   114

4.9. Plan of the artefact debris field of 'site 35F' (full site name T7a35f-5)
(Sea Scape)   117

4.10. Michael Cottman at the site of the *Henrietta Marie* memorial. (Courtesy of
Michael Cottman)   119

5.1. Creamware punch bowl depicting a three-masted ship with the words 'Success
to the LORD STANLEY Capt. Smale'. 146703. (National Museums Liverpool)   126

LIST OF FIGURES   xiii

5.2. The key structural characteristics of a frigate-built merchant slaver. (Illustration prepared by Caron Newman)   127

5.3. Reconstructed preliminary lines plan of *James Matthews*. (B. Hartley/Western Australian Museum)   127

5.4. *The Practice of Sail Making with the Tools* and *A Sail Loft*, illustrations from Steel (1794: i, unnumbered page preceding 84). (Public domain)   135

5.5. Average (imputed) numbers of captives embarked graphed against TSTD standardized vessel tonnages for British-based vessels between 1680 and 1807. (Data from https://www.slavevoyages.org/voyages/bGGx6qZa (accessed 21 March 2022))   136

5.6. Plan of the profile, hold, and decks of *Marie-Séraphique* made by Jean-René Lhermitte in 1770. (Château des ducs de Bretagnes, Musée d'histoire de Nantes)   138

5.7. William Jackson's painting *A Liverpool Slave Ship*, c.1780. 1964.227.2. (National Museums Liverpool)   140

5.8. The slave ship *Fredensborg II*, commanded by Captain J. Berg. (Privately owned. Photograph: M/S Maritime Museum of Denmark Picture Archive)   143

5.9. TSTD standardized tonnages plotted against average embarkation levels for British slaving voyages, 1787–1807. (Data from https://www.slavevoyages.org/voyages/mOu2kS5A (accessed 20 March 2022))   145

5.10. A Guinea merchant ship, drying sails. William Van de Velde the Younger, c.1675. PAF6918. (National Maritime Museum, Greenwich, London)   146

5.11. Profile view of the likely appearance of *Henrietta Marie* (constructed in 1699). From Moore (1997). ('Henrietta Marie', Slavery Images: A Visual Record of the African Slave Trade and Slave Life in the Early African Diaspora, http://www.slaveryimages.org/s/slaveryimages/item/2617 (accessed May 16, 2022))   148

5.12. *A view of the Blandford Frigate*, Nicholas Pocock, c.1760. M761. (Bristol City Museums, Galleries, & Archives/Bridgeman Images)   150

5.13. *Hall* as illustrated in Hutchinson (1794). (Public domain)   151

5.14. *Description of a Slave Ship*. Broadsheet printed by James Phillips London, in 1789. (Private Collection: The Stapleton Collection/Bridgeman Images)   152

5.15. Cross-section of an eighteenth-century slave ship. (Chris Hollshwander/Division of Work & Industry, National Museum of American History, Smithsonian Institution)   154

5.16. The Anchorage off the Town of Bonny River Sixteen Miles from the Entrance. PAD1929. (National Maritime Museum, Greenwich, London)   159

5.17. Capture of the Spanish slaver *Formidable* by HMS *Buzzard* on 17 December 1834, William Huggin. BHC0625. (National Maritime Museum, Greenwich, London)   161

5.18. Method for separating slaves, accompanying the testimony of Robert Heatley, **HCSP 69: 123**. (Redrawn by Caron Newman)   168

5.19. French slave ship *Marie-Séraphique*, Saint Domingue (Haiti), watercolour by unknown artist. (Château des ducs de Bretagnes, Musée d'histoire de Nantes)   170

xiv LIST OF FIGURES

5.20. Detail from a painting of the slave ship *Fredensborg II*, dated 1788.
(Privately owned. Photograph: M/S Maritime Museum of Denmark
Picture Archive) — 172

6.1. The Mataró ship model. Marietem Museum Collection (Marietem Museum
Rotterdam) — 184

6.2. Detail from the lid of an ivory salt cellar, made by an Edo or Owo artist, Benin
(Nigeria), *c.*1525–1600. Af1878,1101.48. (British Museum Images) — 186

6.3. Drawing of a mermaid as found in the lakes of Angola, by James Barbot Jnr,
from Churchill and Churchill (1732: v, plate 30) (Public domain) — 188

6.4. Sapi–Portuguese salt-cellar lid, with mermaid figure. EDc 67. (National
Museum of Denmark. Photograph by Laila Malene Odyja Halsteen) — 189

6.5. A twentieth-century Ibibio (Nigerian) Mami Wata figure. (87 × 61 × 25 cm).
1994.3.9. (Michael C. Carlos Museum, Emory University. Photograph by
Bruce M. White) — 190

6.6. Copper alloy Akan gold weight in the form of a single-masted European
sailing ship (49 × 88 × 18 mm), eighteenth–nineteenth centuries. nmfa_95-6-3.
(Gift of Ernst Anspach, National Museum of African Art, Smithsonian
Institution. Photograph by Franko Khoury) — 192

6.7. Undated emblem of Agaja (226 × 138 mm). Wooden finial, covered in silver,
depicting a three-masted ship with quarterdeck and two anchors. 1992.40.1
(402.910.001). (Musée Africaine de Lyon. Ji-Elle, CC BY-SA 4.0, https://
commons.wikimedia.org/w/index.php?curid=47162707 (accessed 20 August
2022)) — 193

6.8. Cast of a bas-relief from the Palace of Agaja, Abomey, made by Emmanuel-
Georges Waterlot in 1911. 71.2012.0.4166. (RMN—Grand Palais/Musée du
quai Branly) — 194

6.9. Female figurehead, *c.*1805, attributed to Simeon Skillin Jnr (?1756–1806).
M27185. (Peabody Essex Museum) — 199

6.10. Three nineteenth-century wooden tomb figures from Brass in the Niger Delta. — 200
(Left: 0.4652. Manchester Museum, The University of Manchester.
Centre: Ea7825. Bristol City Museums, Galleries, & Archives. Right:
AF 5122 University of Pennsylvania Museum of Archaeology and
Anthropology)

6.11. Ancestral screen, *duein fubara*, eighteenth–nineteenth centuries, Kalabari,
Nigeria (1140 × 730 × 420 mm). Af1950,45.333.a. (British Museum Images) — 203

6.12. 'Ship-like' instrument. TM-A-11006. (National Museum of World Cultures,
Amsterdam) — 204

6.13. *Nkisi kumbi lipanya*, Cabinda National Museum of Ethnology. AO253.
(Direção-Geral do Património Cultural/Arquivo e Documentação Fotográfica) — 205

7.1. Samples of trade cloth. The West India Company and Board of Directors,
Documents and Letters from Guinea, 1705–1722. (Danish National Archives.
Photo: Vibe Martens) — 217

7.2. European trade knife collected in Senegal in 1787–8 by Anders Sparrman.
1799.02.0083. (Museum of World Cultures, Stockholm) — 217

LIST OF FIGURES xv

7.3. Chokwe pendant, Angola, sixteenth–eighteenth centuries (279 × 375 mm). 1996.456. (Metropolitan Museum of Art) — 220

7.4. Seventeenth-century trade beads from the manufacturing site of Nicholas Crisp, Hammersmith Embankment, London. (MoLA. Photo: Karlis Karklins) — 221

7.5. Glass trade beads collected in Senegal by Anders Sparrman , 1787–8. 1799.002.0090. (Museum of World Cultures. Stockholm) — 222

7.6. Left: powdered-glass bodom bead, probably of nineteenth-century date, made in West Africa. Right: Venetian version of the bodom. 73.3.351 (L) and 73.3.333 (R). Corning Museum of Glass. (Images licensed by The Corning Museum of Glass, Corning, NY (www.cmog.org), under CC BY-NC-SA 4.0) — 222

7.7. One of the 162 block-print designs for *Indiennes* made by Favre, Petitpierre et Compagnie (1800–25). (© François Lauginie / Château des ducs de Bretagne, Musée d'histoire de Nantes) — 227

7.8. Page from a textile sample book made by the Manchester firm Benjamin and John Bower. 156.4 T31. (The Metropolitan Museum of Art/Art Resource/ Scala, Florence.) — 229

7.9. Battery-wares made at Saltford Brass Mill. Left: Lisbon pan (350 × 100 mm). Right: Guinea kettle (300 × 190 mm). (Tony Coverdale, Saltford Brass Mill Project) — 231

7.10. Brass and pewter basin assemblage from the Elmina wreck site. (Gregory Cook) — 233

7.11. A strand of akoso beads dating to the eighteenth–nineteenth centuries. (Suzanne Gott) — 238

7.12. Ijebu-Ode cloth, handwoven local cotton and imported silk, with brocaded imagery. A.716.29. (National Museums Scotland). — 242

7.13. Thomas Clarkson's chest, opened to show its contents. (Wisbech and Fenland Museum) — 243

7.14. A selection of the manillas recovered from the Elmina wreck site. (Gregory Cook) — 245

8.1. A. E. Chalon's portrait of Thomas Clarkson, *c.*1790. (Wilberforce House/ Bridgeman Images) — 258

8.2. Box of shells *c.*1800. Mahogany and pine box with pine trays holding cardboard and glass boxes containing specimens. W.5:1 to 4-2010. (Victoria & Albert Museum) — 269

8.3. The Grotto at Bulstrode Park, as depicted by Samuel Hieronymus Grimm in 1781. King George III Topographical Collection, 11.1d. (British Library Board. All Rights Reserved/Bridgeman Images) — 270

8.4. Mid-nineteenth-century sailor's valentine (shells and mahogany), made in the West Indies. (Christie's Images/Bridgeman Images) — 272

8.5. The four Bambara cowries gifted to Sarah Sophia Banks by Mungo Park in 1797. SSB 155.4. (British Museum Images) — 273

9.1. Mortality rates among captives on British vessels over time—imputed estimate. (TSTD data set https://www.slavevoyages.org/voyages/Neg0nOcp (accessed 20 March 2022)) — 284

xvi LIST OF FIGURES

9.2. Katrina Keefer's reconstruction of the markings of Recaptive 5959, Register of Liberated Africans 1814–15, Sierra Leone Public Archives. (Katrina Keefer) 291

9.3. Medical chest of naval surgeon Sir Benjamin Outram (1774–1856). TOA0130. (National Maritime Museum UK, Greenwich, London) 293

9.4. Left: urethral syringe. Right: apothecary's mortar and pestle. The *Queen Anne's Revenge* wreck site. (Images courtesy of the North Carolina Department of Natural and Cultural Resources) 293

9.5. Cupping instruments in leather case, London, England, 1801–1. A606733. (Science Museum, London/Wellcome Collection Images) 296

9.6. An illustration in *Le Commerce de l'Amerique par Marseille* (1764 : ii). Original copper engraving by Serge Daget, 1725. (Courtesy of the John Carter Brown Library) 304

9.7. Scrubbing brush (16.2 × 6.0 cm) from the *Fredensborg* wreck site. Aust-Agder Museum. (Photo: Karl Ragnar Gjertsen, KUBEN Museum and Archive) 312

9.8. Detail from Résumé du Témoignage Donné Devant un Comité de la Chambre des Communes de la Grande Bretagne et de l'Irelande, Touchant la Traite des Negres, 1814. (Diagram of the Decks of a Slave Ship, 1814, *Slavery Images: A Visual Record of the African Slave Trade and Slave Life in the Early African Diaspora*, http://www.slaveryimages.org/s/slaveryimages/item/2004 (accessed 30 March 2023)) 320

10.1. Snuffbox made from the timbers of HMS *Black Joke*. ZBA 2435.4. (National Maritime Museum, Greenwich, London) 332

10.2. *Wives and Sweethearts, or Saturday Night*, 1792: a broadsheet published in London by John Evans. (American Antiquarian Society) 337

10.3. Brass bell from the Benin Kingdom, sixteenth or seventeenth century. Metropolitan Museum of Art, 1991.17.85. (Metropolitan Museum of Art/Art Resource/Scala, Florence) 339

10.4. Swivel gun, *c.*1750–1770. Mariners' Museum and Park, 1935.0029.000001A. (Courtesy of the Mariners' Museum and Park, Newport News, Virginia) 340

10.5. *Transport des Nègres dans les Colonies*. Lithograph by Prexetat Oursel, second quarter of the nineteenth century. (Musée des Beaux-Arts, Chartres, France/Bridgeman Images) 345

10.6. Items of restraint, punishment, and force-feeding purchased by Thomas Clarkson in Liverpool. From Clarkson (1808: i, between pp. 374 and 375). ('Untitled Image (Iron Shackles)', *Slavery Images: A Visual Record of the African Slave Trade and Slave Life in the Early African Diaspora*, http://www.slaveryimages.org/s/slaveryimages/item/2619 (accessed 13 July 2022)) 348

10.7. Cord-wrapped shackle from the *Queen Anne's Revenge* wreck site. (Image courtesy of the North Carolina Department of Natural and Cultural Resources) 349

10.8. *A Marine & Seaman fishing off the Anchor on board the Pallas in Senegal Road, Jany 75*. Gabriel Bray, 1775. PAJ2013. (National Maritime Museum, Greenwich, London) 350

10.9. Mid-eighteenth-century salt-glazed stoneware dish from the wreck of *Fredensborg*. Aust-Agder Museum. (Photo: Karl Ragnar Gjertsen, KUBEN Museum and Archive) 351

LIST OF FIGURES xvii

10.10. Deck plan of the Danish ship *Rio Volta*, constructed in 1777. Neg. A.3457. M/S Museet for Søfart, Maritime Museum of Denmark. (M/S Museet for Søfart CC-BY-NC-SA) — 353

10.11. Sandstone mortar (400 × 250 × 230 mm) from the *Fredensborg* wreck site. Aust-Agder Museum. (Photo: Karl Ragnar Gjertsen, KUBEN Museum and Archive) — 356

10.12. Colorized version of an archived copy of *Vue du navire la Marie-Séraphique de Nantes au moment de repas des captives. 2e voyage a Loangue 1771*. (Collection Dauvergne, National Maritime Museum, France, Plate No. 9912. Colorization by Ian Burr, Emory University) — 359

10.13. Group of Negroes as Imported to be Sold for Slaves, 1796. Print of an engraving by William Blake for John Stedman. E.1215E-1886. (Victoria and Albert Museum) — 367

10.14. Nineteenth-century naval cat o' nine tails. NMM TOA0066. (National Maritime Museum, Greenwich, London) — 371

10.15. Plan of the slave deck of *Marie-Séraphique* made by Jean-René Lhermitte in 1770. (Château des ducs de Bretagnes, Musée d'histoire de Nantes) — 380

11.1. Colorized reprint of a lithograph from the fold-out sheet ('Plan and sections of a slave ship') included in the cover pocket of Carl Wadström's *An Essay on Colonization*, 1794. (The Library Company of Philadelphia/Everett Collection/Bridgeman Images) — 397

11.2. Illustration by William Butterworth for *The Young Sea Officer's Sheet Anchor*. From Lever (1808: plate facing p. 9). (Public domain, Google Digitized) — 402

11.3. Trade card of the London plane-maker John Jennion. BM, Heal, 118.8. (British Museum Images) — 407

11.4. Illustration by William Butterworth for *The Young Sea Officer's Sheet Anchor*. From Lever (1808: plate facing p. 23*)*. (Public domain, Google Digitized) — 418

11.5. Akan drum acquired by Hans Sloane in Virginia. Am, SLMisc.1368. (British Museum Images) — 421

11.6. Tobacco pipe from grave B72 Newton Plantation, Barbados. (Jerome Handler, Virginia Humanities) — 425

11.7. Left: nineteenth-century Kongo power figure (*Nkisi Nkondi*). Right: *Minkisi Nkubulu*. 1919.01.1162. (L: Dallas Museum of Art, Texas, USA Foundation for the Arts Collection, gift of the McDermott Foundation/Bridgeman Images. R: CC by 2.5, Museum of World Cultures, Stockholm) — 428

12.1. The scarification marks of John Rock recorded 18 February 1820, after Mullin 1994 29). (Redrawn by Caron Newman) — 448

12.2. Scarification marks on the faces of enslaved Africans from Mozambique, Johann Moritz Rugendas, 1835. ('Brazilian Slaves from Mozambique, 1830s', *Slavery Images: A Visual Record of the African Slave Trade and Slave Life in the Early African Diaspora*, http://www.slaveryimages.org/s/slaveryimages/item/1571 (accessed 29 March 2023)) — 449

12.3. Beads found with burial B340, New York African Burial Ground. (Adapted by Caron Newman from Bianco et al. (2006: fig. 299); original drawing by M. Schur) — 457

List of Tables

1.1. Trans-Atlantic Slave Trade Database summary statistics for slaving voyages outfitted in ports in England, Scotland, and Ireland between 1562 and 1807 — 2

2.1. Estimated numbers of captives carried away from Africa (by region) on ships originating in Britain between 1562 and 1807 — 42

2.2. Principal disembarkation points for captives carried away from Africa on voyages originating in British ports between 1562 and 1807 — 47

3.1. Key slaving logs and journals employed in this study — 61

3.2. Key slaving voyage memoirs employed in this study — 66

3.3. Key documents published at the behest of SEAST 1788–9 and containing detailed accounts of the Middle Passage — 74

3.4. Testimonies by sailors with Middle Passage experience recorded in *Substance of the Evidence* (1789) — 77

3.5. House of Commons Sessional Papers (HCSP) containing witness statements made as part of the 1778–92 inquiry process — 78

3.6. Key parliamentary inquiry testimonies made by sailors with Middle Passage experience — 83

5.1. The nine Liverpool vessels measured in 1788 by Captain Parrey — 129

5.2. Characteristics of some of the vessels introduced in Chapter 3, using information drawn from TSTD, *Lloyds Register,* and details provided in sailors' accounts — 131

5.3. Measurements relating to airflow on the ships measured by Captain Parrey — 139

5.4. The metamorphosis of *Duke of Argyle* in 1750, as reconstructed from John Newton's account — 156

6.1. Figureheads of some Liverpool-built slave ships of the eighteenth century, where recorded in the Liverpool Registry of Merchant Ships — 198

6.2. Popular women's names employed for British slave ships, and the number of voyages made by ships so named — 199

7.1. Trade goods in demand at Cabinda, 1700 — 215

7.2. Trade goods carried on *Daniel and Henry,* 1700 — 216

7.3. Trade goods carried on *Henrietta Marie,* 1699 — 223

7.4. Cargo of the East India Company ship *Royal Charles, 1661* — 226

8.1. Individuals with links to the slave trade who collected botanical samples on behalf of James Petiver or transported letters and materials for him — 266

9.1. Crew deaths on Samuel Gamble's *Sandown,* 1793–4 — 299

9.2. Sickness and death on *Duke of Argyle,* 1750–1 — 307

XX LIST OF TABLES

11.1. Documented insurrections on British slaving voyages 395

11.2. Infrapolitical actions on *Duke of Argyle*, 1751 and *African,* 1752–3 404

11.3. Weapons used by captives, with the numbers of times each is mentioned in documentary sources 408

12.1. African-born individuals from selected sites in the Americas 455

List of Boxes

1.1.	The Trans-Atlantic Slave Trade Database (TSTD)	2
3.1.	Slave Ship Crews	55
3.2.	Olaudah Equiano's Middle Passage	89
5.1.	Space 'Enough': Parliamentary Discourse on Tight Packing, 1788–1792	166
9.1.	Claims made in Parliament concerning African Thermotolerance	305
9.2.	'I give and bequeath': Extracts from Wills made on *Hannibal, Don Carlos,* and *Henrietta Marie*	319
10.1.	'Accou Language, used by slaves from the Kingdoms of Haysa and Hio, generally taken in vessels from Ouidah and Badagry' (Extract from Logbook of HMS *Sybille* and HMS *Black Joke* (1827–9)	333
10.2.	Extract from Schedule A appended to 29 Geo. 3 c. 66 (1789), An Act to continue, for a limited Time, and amend an Act, made in the last Session of Parliament, intituled, An Act to regulate, for a limited Time, the shipping and carrying Slaves in British Vessels from the Coast of Africa	358

Abbreviations

BM	British Museum
DRASSM	*Direction des Recherches Archéologiques Subaquatiques et Sous-Marines*
DWP	Diving With a Purpose
EIC	East India Company
GRAN	*Group de Recherche en Archéologie Navale*
HCSP	House of Commons, Sessional Papers
ISA	International Seabed Authority
IZIKO	Museums of South Africa
LRO	Liverpool Record Office
MCC	Middelburgsche Commercie Compagnie
MFMHS	Mel Fisher Maritime Heritage Society
MFMM	Mel Fisher Maritime Museum
MoLAS	Museum of London Archaeology Service
MoLA	Museum of London Archaeology
NABS	National Association of Black Scuba Divers
NCDNCR	North Carolina Department of Natural and Cultural Resources
NMAAHC	National Museum of African American History and Culture
NML	National Museums Liverpool
NMM	National Maritime Museum
NMR	National Monument Record
RAC	Royal African Company
SEAST	Society for Affecting the Abolition of the Slave Trade
SWP	Slave Wrecks Project
TNA	The National Archives of the UK
	CO Colonial Office
	T Treasury
	BT Board of Trade
	PROB Wills 1384–1858
TSTD	Trans-Atlantic Slave Trade Database
V&A	Victoria and Albert Museum
WAPE	West African Pidgin English
WPA	Works Progress Administration

1

Materializing the Middle Passage

An Introduction in Three Objects

Almost 10,500 slaving voyages were undertaken by slave ships outfitted in British ports, forcibly transporting an estimated 2.8 million African men, women, and children into slavery in the Americas (Table 1.1).[1] The British were prolific slaver traders, becoming, by the later eighteenth century, the primary international carriers of captive Africans shipped to European colonies in the Americas.

Since the 1960s, the history of Britain's role in the slave trade has been explored in great depth. Even so, significant gaps remain in our understanding of the voyage that carried Africans to the Caribbean and the Americas—a crossing long known as the Middle Passage.[2] We know a good deal about certain aspects of this experience, not least because important developments in the statistical synthesis and presentation of archival data have produced a much clearer understanding of where captives embarked, where they were taken, the mortality rates on board slaving vessels, and the overall volume of the slave trade (see Box 1.1). As examined in Chapter 3, few detailed autobiographical African accounts of the journey into slavery survive, but many accounts by British sailors have been preserved as sea journals (see Figure 1.1), memoirs, travel narratives, or abolitionist texts. In addition, a mass of testimony regarding conditions on board British vessels was recorded during late-eighteenth-century parliamentary inquiries into the slave trade. The documentary record for British slave shipping is therefore extensive, with the important caveat that this really is a *British* record, not an African one.

Archaeologists have been excavating slave lifeways in the Americas since the mid-twentieth century but have virtually ignored the largest artefact of the trade in slaves: the ship itself. Yet that ship—the 'living, micro-cultural, micro-political system in motion', which Paul Gilroy famously employed as the chronotope or between-space facilitator in *Black Atlantic*—was not simply essential to the slave-trading business; it remains the pivot to heuristic exploration of that trade today.[3] While some pioneering historians have recently focused attention on 'slavery at sea', exploring the Middle Passage experience and its legacies for both captives and crews, archaeologists rarely adopt such a focus.[4] Thanks to recent developments in skeletal analysis, bioarchaeologists are sometimes now able to isolate 'saltwater' Africans (those who crossed the Atlantic on slave ships) among New World slave cemetery populations; but the vessels that transported these individuals remain under-researched. In part this is because only a handful of slaver wrecks have been located; yet historical archaeologists do not normally focus exclusively on excavation data, and, while a lack of wrecks might

Materializing the Middle Passage: A Historical Archaeology of British Slave Shipping, 1680–1807. Jane Webster,
Oxford University Press. © Jane Webster 2023. DOI: 10.1093/oso/9780199214594.003.0001

2 MATERIALIZING THE MIDDLE PASSAGE

hinder archaeological analysis of the Middle Passage, it should not preclude it. As this book will demonstrate, there are other ways to excavate the slave ship and its modalities. Drawing on a wide variety of sources, including voyage narratives, parliamentary records, wreck data, and artworks depicting slave ships, my aim is to rematerialize the British slave ship as a physical and social entity and, in so doing, to write a comprehensive historical archaeology of the voyage into slavery.

Table 1.1 Trans-Atlantic Slave Trade Database summary statistics for slaving voyages outfitted in ports in England, Scotland, and Ireland between 1562 and 1807

Key statistics	Captives	Vessels	Average per voyage
Total number of voyages		10,480	
Captives embarked (imputed)*	2,788,395	10,062	277.1
Captives disembarked (imputed)	2,358,276	9,921	237.7
Percentage of captives embarked who died during voyage			13.3%
Length of Middle Passage (in days)			64.4

* In the absence of sufficient information concerning a voyage, TSTD imputes (infers) some missing data algorithmically. For the methodology underlying the use of imputed variables in TSTD, see https://www.slavevoyages.org/voyage/about#methodology/introduction/0/en/ (accessed 15 August 2022).

Source: All of the statistical estimates concerning slaving voyages employed in this book derive from the Trans-Atlantic Slave Trade Database (TSTD), available online at http://www.slavevoyages.org, or from summary publications by the database authors. Table.1.1 was last generated on 15 August 2022 using the variable 'Place of departure' (checking 'Great Britain', 'England', 'Scotland', and 'Ireland') and using the date range 1562–1807. The url for this search is https://www.slavevoyages.org/voyages/mOu2kS5A. Unless otherwise indicated all statistical estimates for British voyages presented in this book have been generated using this default search, which can be replicated by the reader using the url; but note that the TSTD data set is continuously updated, so totals may differ slightly over time.

Box 1.1 The Trans-Atlantic Slave Trade Database (TSTD)

A great deal of statistical information is now available to those studying the Middle Passage. Close attention to the demographics of slave shipping began in the 1960s, when Philip Curtin published an influential census of the transatlantic trade.[a] Taking Curtin's lead, economic historians in many countries went on to collate unpublished archival data about slaving voyages, developing thereby a better understanding of the volume and nature of the transatlantic slave trade; and of those who profited from it. These scholars built up large data sets, containing information about hundreds or even thousands of voyages. Some converted all the numerical information they had collected into computer-based formats, and, by the late 1980s, sixteen separate machine-readable data sets, containing information on more than 11,000 voyages, had been independently created by scholars across Europe.[b] In the early 1990s, Stephen Behrendt, David Eltis, and David Richardson, three leading statisticians of the slave trade, proposed that a single, multi-source data set should be created, and made available to researchers in CD-Rom format.

This new resource would combine all the information in the data sets noted above, alongside new data obtained via a systematic trawl through unstudied archives. This hugely ambitious project, hosted by the W. E. B. Du Bois Institute for Afro-American Research at Harvard University, came to fruition in 1999 with the publication of *The Trans-Atlantic Slave Trade; A Database on CD-Rom.*[c] This resource (TSTD$_1$) contained information relating to more than 27,000 voyages. Ongoing archival research has swelled the original data set. In 2007 an updated database of 35,000 voyages was made freely available online at http://www.slavevoyages.org. Following further updates, the most recent iteration (TSTD$_3$), last accessed for this book in August 2022, provides information on 36,071 voyages.

TSTD has captured a wealth of data concerning individual British slave ships, their voyages, and the logistics of the British slave trade. These data are the foundation upon which *Materializing the Middle Passage* has been built. To help the reader locate TSTD-derived information about the ships and voyages discussed here, I note wherever possible the unique voyage identification numbers used in the data set (adopting the format 'TSTD 1234').[d] TSTD is in no sense a *complete* record of transatlantic slave shipping. First, because the primary textual sources on which it is based were compiled by Europeans profiting from the slave trade, not by the Africans captives who endured the Middle Passage.[e] Second because many of those archival shipping records are incomplete; often failing to document, for example, the number, sex, and ages of the African captives on board a specific vessel. TSTD employs algorithms to impute (estimate) the missing data.[f] This book is principally concerned with individual British ships, however, and the data for these are among the most complete in TSTD. It is thought that, while there are some gaps in the documentation of British ships before 1700, TSTD includes at least some data on about 95 per cent of all voyages leaving British ports between 1713 and 1779, and probably a full record of voyages made between 1780 and 1807.[g]

[a] Curtin (1969).
[b] Eltis et al. (1999b: 2–4).
[c] Eltis et al. (1999a,b).
[d] For a series of papers based on TSTD as it stood in 2008, see Eltis and Richardson (2008b), and particularly Eltis and Richardson's own contribution (2008a). Eltis and Richardson (2010) present the same data in an Atlas format, using estimates derived from the data set as it stood in January 2008—at which point the database contained details of 34,934 documented slaving voyages (Eltis and Richardson 2010: p. xxv). The overall statistics presented in the present book are drawn from Eltis and Richardson (2008b, 2010), but readers should be aware of two important collections of articles based on the first iteration of TSTD: Eltis and Richardson (1997c) and the papers presented in *William and Mary Quarterly* 58/1 (2001), an issue of that journal dedicated to the TSTD project—for the introduction to which see Eltis (2001).
[e] For the argument that digital black humanities resources including TSTD lack a humanizing perspective (by failing to include the perspective of the enslaved themselves) and can also reinscribe or 'mark up' African bodies in ways that replicate the surveilling actions of slave owners and slave traders, see the recent influential critique by Johnson (2018).
[f] For a recent statement in an ongoing debate concerning the mathematical modelling of captive flows, see Manning and Liu (2020).
[g] Eltis and Richardson (2008a: 26).

4 MATERIALIZING THE MIDDLE PASSAGE

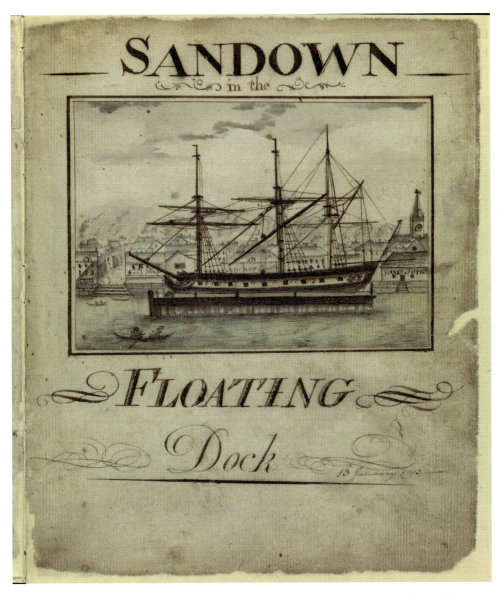

Figure 1.1 *Sandown* in the Floating Dock. From the sea journal of Samuel Gamble (1793–4). National Maritime Museum, Greenwich, LOG/M/21, title page.

This is a book about early modern material culture, written by a historical archaeologist. After such a statement, it is customary for an author to offer definitions of material culture, history, and archaeology, and then to make explicit her own understanding of the interplay between the three. But these categories are of course oversimplified; documents are themselves artefacts, and many artefacts are literate. The sea journal of *Sandown* (shown in Figure 1.1), for example, is both a primary textual source and an artefact of the slave trade. Like many historical archaeologists today, I do not regard texts and artefacts as separate or juxtaposed bodies of evidence: I see my work as involving constant interplay between objects, images, and words.[5] Martin Hall has said of the discipline of historical archaeology that its most prevalent shortcoming has been the failure to marry words and things.[6] This book attempts, for the Middle Passage, just such a marriage. The remainder of this introduction uses three material things—a portrait, a punch bowl, and the components of a necklace—to foreground the themes and issues central to this book, and to outline my own practice as an historical archaeologist. I also discuss some of the scholarship that has informed *Materializing the Middle Passage*. My scholarly debts are many and deep, but I am especially indebted to the work of David Eltis and David Richardson (see Box 1), James Scott, Martin Hall, Edward Kamau Brathwaite, Stephanie Smallwood, Richard Cullen Rath, Homi Bhabha, Alexander Byrd, and Walter Hawthorne.

Transcript and Discourse: Reading between the Lines of Elite Documents

My approach to the interplay between documents and artefacts has been directed by the work of the historical archaeologist Martin Hall. In his brilliant, diachronic analysis of eighteenth-century slavery in South Africa and Chesapeake Bay, Hall was the first archaeologist to make sustained use of a distinction, initially drawn by the anthropologist James Scott, between public transcripts (the overt statements made by those who control resources and hold positions of authority) and hidden transcripts (the covert resistance of ordinary people against the imperatives of those in positions of authority).[7] As both Scott and Hall envisage it, a transcript is a web of relations that entwines both objects and words, producing a new, transdisciplinary form of evidence about the past. Scott defines hidden transcripts as 'discourse that takes place "offstage", beyond direct observation by powerholders'.[8] He has shown that such transcripts comprise not only speech acts but a wide variety of practices, ranging from poaching and pilfering to intentionally shabby work. Scott's exploration of the hidden—that is, low profile or covert—strategies through which power was resisted underpins my own Chapter 11, which focuses on African survival strategies during the Atlantic passage. But throughout this book I make extensive use of the *public* transcripts of the British slave trade, and in interrogating them I am indebted to Martin Hall's application of Scott's anthropological methodology to the archaeology of Cape Colony and the Chesapeake; eighteenth-century social worlds united by what Hall refers to simply as 'the fact of slavery'. One of the aims of Hall's work has been to demonstrate that the experiences of subaltern groups can be found, in part, by identifying dissonances between the public transcripts of a dominant elite and the world of the everyday, as revealed through other verbal and non-verbal transcripts. Hall's methodology has a profound resonance for the present book, in that very few of the texts and artefacts at my disposal were produced and used by captive Africans, while, as will be evident from the discussion of documentary sources set out in Chapter 3, I draw repeatedly on the transcripts of a dominant elite. Yet, by carefully combining multiple lines of analysis, and by articulating the spaces between things and words, the slave ship can be rematerialized as a social space within which the rules and regimes of the Middle Passage—laid down by powerful syndicates of vessel owners and enforced by ships' crews—were experienced by enslaved Africans.

Hall's work on subaltern transcripts has directly informed my own efforts to glimpse African experience of the Middle Passage, but I owe him a further debt. In reading the spaces in and between objects and texts, Hall is not *wholly* concerned with uncovering the experiences of the enslaved. Rather, he reveals that, by understanding the relationships between different kinds of transcript, it becomes possible to write a historical archaeology not just of slave-owning elites, nor even of those they enslaved, but of the historical discourse of chattel slavery as it unfolded around the world in the eighteenth century. The many kinds of transcript explored in the present book, including the slave ship itself, are also statements in that extraordinarily long-lived, racialized discourse, which naturalized the concept that one person could be the property of another. Specifically, the slave ship was a material expression of the idea that humans could be *cargo*. For some three hundred years, British practice, and British law, maintained that slave shipping was indistinguishable from other kinds of maritime trade. Humans, sugar, porcelain, and tobacco crossed the ocean in ships that were, to the uninformed eye, virtually indistinguishable from each other (a point pursued in Chapter 5), and crewed by sailors who had received no specialist training. Africans, like sugar or tobacco, were supposedly simply commodities in transit; yet the public transcripts of British slave shipping reveal that it was never possible to reduce humans entirely to freight. The doomed struggle to do so is perhaps most clearly seen in documents of the later eighteenth century: in the parliamentary inquiries of 1788–92 and in judgments made in the law courts in the same era. In his analysis of eighteenth-century slavery, Hall demonstrated that past truths reveal themselves particularly clearly through the 'constant repetitions of the emblems of domination'.[9] That has also been my experience in writing this book, navigating a route through the ocean of official data relating to 'human cargoes', and teasing out its central patterns, preoccupations, and overdeterminations.

Disputes between slave-ship owners and their insurers are particularly useful in exploring the problem that the human as cargo posed for eighteenth-century maritime insurance law, and several examples are discussed in this book.[10] Most were adjudicated by the Chief Justice, William Murray (1st Earl of Mansfield), and one concerned a notorious incident on board the Liverpool slaver *Zong*.[11] In 1781, Luke Collingwood, the master (captain) of *Zong*, ordered that 132 living Africans be jettisoned overboard as the ship lay off Jamaica. Why he took this decision is unclear, but in 1783 William Murray presided over the second hearing in a dispute between *Zong*'s owners and insurers as to who should bear the cost of the jettisoned captives.[12] As Murray was at pains to point out, this hearing was not a criminal trial. He reminded the court that:

> The matter left to the jury [in the first trial at Guildhall] was, whether it [the jettison] was from necessity for they had no doubt (tho' it shocks one very much) the case of slaves was the same as if horses had been thrown over board it is a very shocking case.[13]

AN INTRODUCTION IN THREE OBJECTS   7

In law, the jettisoning of cargo (even *human* cargo) was allowable on a vessel shown to be 'in peril from the sea'.[14] Despite the fact that it depicts neither a slave ship nor its 'human cargo', the painting in Figure 1.2 helps me to explore this point further, because it contextualizes Mansfield's evident ambivalence about the morality of this point of law. Long attributed to Johann Zoffany (court painter to George III) but now thought to be by another artist, the painting depicts Elizabeth Finch Hatton and her cousin Dido Belle Lindsay, both the great-nieces of William Murray.[15] Both girls were brought up at Murray's home (Kenwood House, Hampstead). Dido was the daughter of Murray's nephew, Admiral Sir John Lindsay, and an African-born woman named Maria Bell. It was once thought that Maria had been on board a Spanish slave ship seized by Lindsay during the capture of Havana from the Spanish in 1762.[16] Recent research has shown, however, that Dido was born in 1761.[17] The child was brought up at Kenwood from a very young age and would later be provided for in Murray's will. As she gazes out at the world in her exotic attire, neither the social equal of, nor servant to, the cousin beside her, Dido Lindsay personifies eighteenth-century social liminality on many levels. As the child of 'cargo', she also explains why it was that the formulation

Figure 1.2 Elizabeth Finch Hatton and Dido Belle. possibly by David Martin, *c.*1780. Scone Palace.

8 MATERIALIZING THE MIDDLE PASSAGE

that slaves, like horses, were simply goods in transit troubled her uncle in his role as Chief Justice. There is another consideration here. Notorious though it was, the *Zong* case was the only one of its kind in British legal history: the sole example of litigation concerning the jettison of living African captives at sea. In other words, even in a world that gave legal and moral sanction to a maritime trade in human beings, very few sailors appear to have contemplated the step that Luke Collingwood took as master of *Zong*. In turn, this would suggest that somewhere within them, even the most hardened slave traders tacitly acknowledged the point so clearly brought to light in the *Zong* proceedings: that their cargo was, indeed, human.[18]

Empathy, Interpretation, and Context: Reading the Material Culture of Slave Shipping

Slave shipping was a brutal business, and many of the documentary sources employed in this book make cruel reading. Brutality, ignorance, and prejudice lace their pages, and to read these accounts is undeniably to feel polluted by the past. Yet one cannot simply decline to engage with such documents in attempting to understand the Middle Passage experience, and the same point applies to the material culture of captive passage. Shackles, whips, and images of slave ships are uncomfortable things to write about or look at, but they reveal crucial information about both the practicalities of slave shipping, and contemporary discourse concerning the slave trade. For many seventeenth- and eighteenth-century Britons, the slave trade was a source of aspiration and pride. The men who built slave ships, the masters who sailed them, and the investors whose hopes sailed aboard them had made both a financial and an *emotional* investment in the slave trade. Contemporary visualizations of the slave ship, like that seen on the enamelled porcelain punch bowl illustrated in Figure 1.3, exemplify these points. The bowl is thought by the Victoria & Albert Museum to date to *c*.1763 and to be the work of Richard Chaffers, whose Shaw's Brow works produced some of the first Liverpool porcelains of the 1750s and 1760s.[19] The ship depicted on the interior is the twin-masted snow *Swallow*, built in Liverpool in 1763.[20] *Swallow* made nine slaving voyages between 1765 and 1777, carrying more than two thousand people into slavery. The hand-painted ship portrait was almost certainly the work of the marine artist William Jackson and is a very accurate portrait of *Swallow*: a point that can be determined by comparing the image on the bowl with the entry for *Swallow* in *Lloyds Register of Shipping*.[21] The portrait was probably commissioned by a member of the Liverpool-based syndicate that owned the vessel. Surviving documentation suggests that the bowl was presented to George Nelson, on completion of his third profitable slaving voyage as master of *Swallow* in 1775.[22] For both owners and master, *Swallow* was a source of pride and affection, worthy of accurate—and expensive— commemoration.

Whilst the notion of celebrating the slave ship repels today, this was clearly not the case for many eighteenth-century viewers of this artefact. This disjuncture, and the

Figure 1.3 Enamelled porcelain punch bowl depicting *Swallow*, probably painted by William Jackson. Victoria & Albert Museum, C.58–1938.

question of how we today, as scholars and as members of the public, should interact with the material culture of slave shipping, has troubled academia in recent years. Since the turn of the century, scholarship on early modern visual images of slavery has been dominated neither by archaeologists nor historians, but by cultural theorists. The seminal study here is Marcus Wood's *Blind Memory*.[23] Wood has argued eloquently that eighteenth- and nineteenth-century representations of slavery are hopelessly compromised by their saturation in racist discourse, and by a voyeuristic obsession with physical suffering. Through critique of a range of images, Wood perceives an intersection between paternalism, pornography, racism, and violence, which, he argues, characterized visual representations of slavery between 1780 and 1865. Further, he suggests that any effort to use these objects to understand 'what happened' in the past is itself compromised: to look upon these works today and to attempt through them to empathize with the trauma suffered by the enslaved is, he suggests, complicity with our eighteenth- and nineteenth-century ancestors.

Wood's work mainly concerns paintings and other images depicting enslaved Africans, but he extends his argument to other artefacts of slavery, including the excavated finds from slave ships discussed and illustrated throughout *Materializing the Middle Passage*. For Wood, any effort to 'rearticulate trauma through empathy with objects' is doomed.[24] There can be no tangible contact with the slave trade, he suggests, even via finds brought up from wrecked slave ships like *Henrietta Marie* (discussed in Chapter 4). Given this pessimism, it is ironic that Wood's reading of the visual culture of slavery—and his analysis of the representation of the Middle Passage in museums—has had such a formative influence on the way the voyage is presented to the public today.[25] Many historians of slavery have taken issue with aspects of Wood's work, pointing out that, whereas *he* might not seek to 'understand' the past, they do. Like archaeologists, most historians keep faith with the idea that a past existed beyond our own cultural imagining of it, and that past is, if not fully 'knowable', at least open to informed, contextualized interpretation.[26] I have suggested above that artefacts, like texts, were transcripts or statements in the discourse of chattel slavery. The object (or text) was framed, and sustained, by a worldview that is, for the historical archaeologist who has written this book, a central point of enquiry. As Felicity Nussbaum expresses it in her discussion of the need for scholars to consider the politics of difference as it emerged in the eighteenth century, the point of that project 'is not simply to display or deconstruct the practices represented by certain narratives of the past, but to locate the *logic* of difference; the structures that were called into place and maintained during the Enlightenment and its legacy'.[27]

The *Swallow* punch bowl, like most of the artefacts encountered in this book, was framed by, and sustained, contemporary discourse on the human as cargo. But, at the same time, porcelain bowls like that in Figure 1.3 would have held entirely different meanings for the master of a slave ship, a Quaker opponent of slavery, and the African 'servant' of an absentee Jamaican planter, mixing punch for his owner in Georgian Liverpool. A contextualized material perspective—that is to say, an *archaeological* focus on the stuff of slavery—has a vital part to play in capturing these polyvalent meanings and exploring what they reveal about the logic of difference in early modern Britain.

Middle Passage Outcomes: Modelling Saltwater Identities

What part did the voyage into slavery play in shaping the identities of Middle Passage survivors, and how was the journey remembered in later life? These questions are central to my book; but they are not at all easy to address. The final of my three objects speaks directly to a point that many documentary historians have been slow to acknowledge, but that archaeologists have long understood: objects have heuristic independence, and can actively challenge, or revise, dominant narratives about the past.[28] In the case of the Middle Passage and its cultural outcomes, the most influential meta-narrative of recent decades can be summed up in the words of one of its leading proponents, Michael Gomez: 'home remained Africa for the African-born.'[29] This book does not seek to overturn that narrative: but it does make a plea for a more complex understanding of the social identities of 'saltwater' Africans in the Americas.

Celebrated as 'the clearest New World archaeological example of African influence on grave goods', the necklace in Figure 1.4 is a good starting point for an exploration of

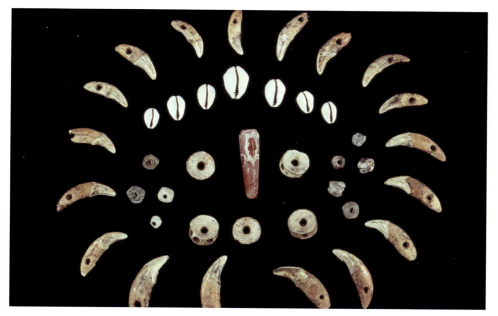

Figure 1.4 Elements of a necklace from grave B72, Newton Plantation, Barbados. Jerome Handler.

saltwater identity in the diaspora.[30] It was found during the first phase of excavation at Newton Plantation, Barbados, in the 1970s, interred with one of 104 individuals recovered from the plantation's slave cemetery.[31] Burial 72, an adult male around 50 years old, had died in the late 1600s or early 1700s.[32] His grave goods included metal jewellery, an iron knife, and a short-stemmed earthenware pipe almost certainly made in Ghana.[33] His necklace is one of a small group of objects supporting the possibility (outlined in Chapter 11) that Africans were sometimes able to retain small artefacts, worn on the body, throughout their Middle Passage.[34] One of his beads is fashioned from powdered European glass and was probably made in Ghana.[35] Another, a cylindrical carnelian bead, appears to have been manufactured in Cambay (Gujarat, India). Traded into East Africa, Indian carnelian travelled through the overland Sahara and Sahel trade to West Africa, where it was present from the first millennium CE.[36] The remaining components of the necklace could readily have been acquired Barbados, but this assemblage points strongly to the maintenance of African traditions in the Caribbean, and it is frequently, and rightly, employed in arguing that case. Jerome Handler, for example, drew on ethno-historical data from West Africa in interrogating the necklace, arguing persuasively that the dead man was revered by the enslaved community at Newton as an obeah man, or healer. Yet even here, in considering one of the best-known excavated artefacts of the diaspora, more than one component of which is of African origin, the Middle Passage itself remains elusive. First, on the evidence available at present, it is not possible to determine whether B72 was born in Africa or had crossed the ocean on a slave ship. Analysis of the lead content in his bones possibly suggests he was born in the New World.[37]

Second, whatever his birthplace, the man may have accumulated some or all of his beads (even those of African origin) as gifts, through barter, or as market purchases, over the course of his life in Barbados. Third, although the glass beads and cowries recovered in plantation burial contexts are regularly framed as exemplifying African practice in the diaspora, both artefact classes had entered Africa, and become embedded in the West African arts, long before this necklace was created. As Barbara Heath has recently demonstrated for Virginia, moreover, some of the surplus cowries entering American ports on slave ships circulated in local economies, and it is likely they were employed as an informal currency by both people of colour and European sailors.[38] Harvested from the Maldives, exchanged for the captives carried by slave ships, embedded in West African and African-American bodily adornment practices, but also in Atlantic port economies, cowrie shells might indeed exemplify the attachment of their owners to Africa: but they are transnational objects, revealing the breadth and complexity of creolization around the Atlantic basin, and the part of the slave ship in that process.

We owe to Ira Berlin the idea of the Atlantic creole—a concept he employed in discussing both the African communities living in coastal towns engaged in the slave trade, and the African-born 'charter generations' whose broad experience of the Atlantic world was so crucial to shaping African America in the seventeenth century.[39] But every generation of captives—indeed every African who endured a slaving voyage—had charter status in the sense that they made a voyage into the unknown, and emerged from the slave ship carrying a body of knowledge and a social persona that differentiated them—often problematically—from enslaved people born in the Americas. As Stephanie Smallwood has emphasized in her ground-breaking study of saltwater slavery, Middle Passage survivors were often viewed negatively in the Americas.[40] In the eyes of both the white minority and of many of those born into slavery, saltwater survivors were *different*. These migrants spoke languages that were not always readily intelligible; they often bore physical markers of African birth, such as dental modification or scarification (discussed in Chapters 9 and 12); they had experienced freedom; and they had all endured an Atlantic crossing.

My book allies itself firmly with the extensive body of historical and archaeological work that has argued, and ably evidenced, the case that the Middle Passage did not constitute a 'social death' that stripped transported Africans of their culture and identity.[41] On the other hand, I do not share the view, appealing though it has evidently been to many scholars in recent years, that the ship was a conduit by which African ethnicities were transferred, virtually unmodified, to the Americas. Inspired by the powerful writing of Africanist scholars including Michael Gomez, Gwendolyn Midlo Hall, and Judith Carney,[42] many historians today regard the Middle Passage as a cultural highway that 'linked the history of transatlantic slave societies to the history of specific peoples of West and West-Central Africa'.[43] This book positions the slave ship as a site in which pre-existing African identities were neither fully retained nor entirely lost, but instead were displaced and reconfigured: as a site, in other words, of mid-Atlantic creolization. I owe a formative debt, in this context, to Stephanie Smallwood's *Saltwater Slavery* and also to Alexander Byrd's *Captives and Voyagers*, published in 2008. Byrd's argument that capture, dislocation, and the extraordinary violence of the Middle Passage all played a formative part in shaping the diasporic identities of Biafran peoples did far more than mark out a middle ground in a fractious dispute about Igbo identity that is still going on.[44] Byrd advanced the case, as I will do here, that the slave ship was more than simply an ethnic conduit: it was 'a forcing house of social change'.[45] In his view, moreover,

> the cultural forms and ethnic identities previous scholars have considered proof of the connections uniting American slaves to their African homelands . . . are not first and foremost evidence of forms that somehow survived the slave trade: rather they must be understood as connections that owe their existence to the disjunction the slave trade effected.[46]

For Byrd, as this passage suggests, the slave ship (like the slave trade) was a site of loss, and diasporic identities should be understood not simply in terms of what survived captivity and transit, but also with reference to what did not.[47] My own viewpoint on the slaving voyage is not dissimilar, but places greater emphasis on the creative outcomes of displacement.[48] In this respect it shares much with, and has drawn direct inspiration from, Walter Hawthorne's *From Africa to Brazil*, a book navigating a careful, persuasive, route between the Scylla and Charybdis of African 'survivals' and New World 'creations' discussed below.[49] But, in advancing my own argument, I have also employed a methodological hybrid inspired by both creolization theory and postcolonial studies.

In some quarters, the concept of cultural creolization is at present not simply unfashionable: it is actively discredited. Many historians and archaeologists (in North America particularly) considered the idea to be 'so elastic and overburdened by decades of debate that using it is sometimes more trouble than it is worth'.[50] Newer interpretative frameworks, claiming to put greater emphasis on African cultural persistence and authenticity in the diaspora, have come to the fore—among them hybridity and ethnogenesis.[51] But, while North American historical archaeology may consider itself post-creole, culture theorists, linguists, creative communities, and indeed many archaeologists in other places whose history has involved plantation slavery (the Caribbean and South America included) still favour creolization as a model for exploring entanglement and transculturation. I unrepentantly identify as one of those whom Stephan Palmié dubs the 'league of creolizers following in the wake of Mintz and Price'.[52] That is to say, I approach cultural creolization as a historicized process (or multitude of processes), not as a generalized meta-narrative.[53] Like many historical archaeologists of the African diaspora before me, I was initially drawn to creolization theory because it facilitates the analysis of entanglement, marginalization, and issues of power in the context of slavery. But I have also come to value its concern with the *translation* of culture. In that context, creolization theory provides an explicit conceptual framework for exploring the relationship that most concerns me in this book: that between words and things in the contingency of the British slaving voyage.

14 MATERIALIZING THE MIDDLE PASSAGE

A brief historical digression is needed to illustrate this point and explore its implications for the present study.

The word 'creole' was first used in a linguistic context in 1685 with reference to speakers of a mixed Portuguese–West African language that emerged in the Gambia as a result of the slave trade.[54] By the late seventeenth century *creole* was commonly employed with reference to languages mixing African and European elements, and the first scholarly studies of these creole languages appeared in the same century.[55] In the early twentieth century, anthropologists investigating the origins of contemporary African-Caribbean and African-American culture also began to take an interest in creole languages. The leading figure here was Melville Herskovits, who in 1941 argued that linguistic 'Africanisms' (African retentions or survivals) in the USA had broader cultural analogues. In *The Myth of the Negro Past* he set out to prove that the social structures, beliefs, and practices of African Americans were rooted in a 'grammar of *culture*' that originated in West Africa and was retained in the diaspora.[56] Herskovits's contention that continuities of cultural practice extended between Africa and the Americas in the era of slavery marked the migration of creolization theory from linguistic into cultural analysis.[57] A second landmark in this context was the publication in 1971 of the historian Edward Kamau Brathwaite's *Development of Creole Society in Jamaica*.[58] Brathwaite presented a sustained case that creolization was a sociocultural process in the Caribbean, extending beyond language to behaviours, traditions, and beliefs. As he put it:

> The single most important factor in the development of Jamaican society was a cultural action—material, psychological and spiritual—based upon the stimulus/response of individuals within the society to their environment and—as white/black culturally discrete groups—to each other. This cultural action or social process has been defined within the context of this work as creolization.[59]

The outcome of this process, Brathwaite argued, was a unique folk culture, explored in his book with reference not only to language, but to religious ideas and practices, music and dance, dress, personal appearance, and so on. Brathwaite also proposed that the cultural creolization of Africans entering Jamaica from slave ships began with several years of 'seasoning'. First, captives were branded, named, and apprenticed. Next, they learned the rudiments of a new language and were initiated into new work routines. For plantation slaves especially, Brathwaite argued, seasoning routines were an important step in cultural adjustment; from participation in the Jamaican sugar cane cutting gang system flowed socialization, facilitated also by communal recreational activities.[60]

In 1976, Sidney Mintz and Richard Price published a seminal study of the origins of African-American culture, very closely echoing Brathwaite's extension of the creolization metaphor to the folk culture of enslaved communities in Jamaica.[61] Mintz and Price contended, as Brathwaite had done before them, that diasporic cultures should not be conceptualized in terms of the transplantation of a (somewhat hypothetical and generic) 'African' culture into the New World, as had long been argued by linguists, and argued instead that scholars needed a clearer sense of the processes by which 'cultural materials that were retained could contribute to the institution-building the slaves undertook to inform their condition with coherence, meaning, and some measure of autonomy' in the New World.[62] The crux of their argument was that direct, linear cultural transfers from Africa to the Americas were the exception rather than the norm. Underlying cultural principles survived the Middle Passage, and were retained, but were subjected to redevelopment and innovation by newly formed collectives of captives, under locally specific conditions. At no point did Mintz and Price suggest that African identities were lost in mid-Atlantic, and in fact they had much to say concerning African survivals in the New World.[63] Most pertinently for the present book, they argued that dyadic relationships forged between 'shipmates' during the Middle Passage 'became a major principle of social organization' among enslaved Africans in many parts of the New World.[64] In this sense the slave ship, for Mintz and Price, was the place in which African-American culture was born.[65] I will return to Middle Passage shipmates in Chapter 11 and in my conclusion; for now it is simply necessary to note that Mintz and Price's essay (reprinted in 1992 as *The Birth of African-American Culture*) was a canonical text for the generation of historical archaeologists who began exploring plantation lifeways in the Caribbean and USA during the 1980s and 1990s. The material world these excavators uncovered was regularly viewed through the creolist lens—though the authors had not used that word themselves— advocated by Mintz and Price. Leading archaeologists pioneered innovative methodologies to recognize African material cultural survivals (dubbed, following Herskovits, as 'Africanisms') in the diaspora.[66] But during the 1990s some influential critiques of Mintz and Price emerged. One of the most important voices here was John Thornton, who argued in *Africa and Africans in the Making of the Atlantic World 1400–1800* that (*contra* Mintz and Price), 'randomization did not occur with the Middle Passage', with most ships acquiring captives at just one or two locations. As a result, the African 'nations' that emerged in the Americas mirrored the ethnic and linguistic groups to be found in West and Central Africa far more closely than had previously been appreciated.[67] Some subsequent historians, and, in turn, some archaeologists, have singled out Mintz and Price for trenchant criticism. Their model, and, with it, the creolist position in general, is now argued to valorize 'newness' or Americanization (New World change) rather than Africanization (Old World continuities), and to ignore or downplay the ability of discrete ethnic groups to maintain their identities and cultural practices in the diaspora.[68] Mintz and Price are now routinely, and entirely egregiously, charged with overemphasizing the ethnic diversity of Africans carried on board slave ships, and positioning saltwater slaves as cultural strangers who, in the absence of commonalities of culture, forged ad hoc social arrangements in the Americas. In short, taking Gwendolyn Midlo Hall's work as an example, Mintz and Price are now held to have suggested 'that the impact of particular African regions and ethnicities on the formation of Afro-Creole cultures in the Americas was nonexistent or insignificant'.[69] With reference to the first of these charges, it may simply be observed that Mintz and Price's position accurately reflected understandings of the

16 MATERIALIZING THE MIDDLE PASSAGE

demography of the slave trade at the time they were writing—the 1970s. With reference to the latter, it is surely obvious that, since they were not at that time able to *observe* dominant ethnic flow channels in the data available to them, Mintz and Price were hardly likely to focus their analysis in that direction.[70]

The Trans-Atlantic Slave Trade Database (see Box 1.1), by anyone's measure a hugely important service to the study of the slave trade, has subsequently demonstrated conclusively that captives *did* flow into the slave trade in dominant ethnic channels. Its creators have also been criticized for their perceived failure to specify the ethnic identities of captives at their point of embarkation.[71] But, as Eltis, Morgan, and Richardson have pointed out, the data that might support this level of analysis are either incomplete, or open to multiple interpretations.[72] Certainly, as Byrd has recently emphasized with reference to captives sourced from the vast Biafran hinterland, it would be a considerable oversimplification to suggest that Africans sharing both a broad regional of origin and an Atlantic crossing were necessarily ethnically *homogenous*.[73]

It is instructive that, in what has become an unproductive stand-off between Africanist and creolist paradigms of culture change in the diaspora, the original Mintz–Price thesis continues to resist easy classification. For example, in the first of two path-breaking critiques of the inclination of the anthropology of the diaspora to valorize the intactness of the old (that is, of the African) in the New World, David Scott positioned Mintz and Price as authors of a 'narrative of *continuities*'.[74] By the second, he had come to regard the pair as advocating a creationist (New World) understanding of the development of African-Caribbean culture, while not entirely rejecting the retentionist (African) model.[75] My own viewpoint is this: Mintz and Price might not have concerned themselves with specific ethnic identities to the extent that some scholars today would prefer, but they recognized as critical the ability of displaced Africans to fold together the old and the new in such a way that the cultural avatars of both—whether languages, practices, beliefs, or objects—always remained consciously, and strategically, present. The outcome was a newness that was neither a mechanical synthesis, nor an attempt simply to recuperate loss, but a unique articulation of African-American experience and identity-making in the diaspora. The challenge Mintz and Price laid down—not simply to *identify* that process, and that newness, but to historicize it—remains as valid today as it did in 1976. When I use the word 'creolization' in this book, it is with specific reference to that challenge, and to the concept of historicized, contingent, cultural creolization as originally outlined first by Brathwaite, and later by Mintz and Price.[76] I am not alone in this endeavour: in their pioneering work on ceramics made by Brazilian slaves, Marcos Torres de Souza and Luis Symanski, for example, have also recently suggested that the historical archaeology of the diaspora needs to 'get back on track with Mintz and Price', and particularly their understanding that the apparent dichotomies separation/interaction and continuity/change were an inherent part in the shaping of slaves' cultural practices.[77]

Edward Kamau Brathwaite certainly regarded the Middle Passage as a pathway between the old and the new, noting in 1981 that 'the middle passage is not, as is popularly assumed, [simply] a traumatic, destructive, experience, separating blacks from Africa, disconnecting their sense of history and tradition, but a pathway or channel between this tradition and what is being evolved, on new soil, in the Caribbean'.[78] My own argument is not dissimilar, but this book will make the case the 'seasoning' of Africans that Brathwaite identified began on that Middle Passage 'pathway' and was continued on the plantations. On the slave ship, it will be argued, captives were exposed for the first time to the technologies of surveillance and discipline, including the bell, the fetter, and the whip, central both to carceral institutions in Britain and to the plantation regimes they would shortly encounter in the Caribbean.[79]

As noted above, creolization theory has not fallen out of favour universally. In the Caribbean in particular, it continues to inform the work of many scholars. Writing in 2002, Michel-Rolph Trouillot influentially proposed four (intentionally abstracted) historical contexts for Caribbean creolization, each characterized by the specific ways in which enslaved labour was mobilized and regimented, and by the frequency and nature of outside contact.[80] Trouillot's contexts—frontier, plantation, enclave, and modernist—are a fruitful tool for thinking; but note that the Middle Passage has no place in his scheme. My own book argues that the voyage into slavery was a further, contingent, context of creolization for all saltwater Africans, prefiguring and shaping what was to come in the diaspora. This point returns me to Mintz and Price, who of course argued explicitly that slave ships were crucibles for change, in which captives forged new and lasting bonds. Their work drew primarily on linguistic data in evidencing these shipmate relationships.[81] The present book has looked for those bonds in a variety of places, and the work of musicologists has been particularly interesting in this respect. Richard Cullen Rath, whose extraordinarily nuanced analysis of the earliest transcription of African music in the Americas is considered in Chapter 11, has this to say concerning creolization:

> Students of cultural creolization have treated it as analogous to linguistic creolization. This analogy is mistaken. Culture is not *like* language; it is integral to language, and language to it. Both are ways in which individuals make sense of their worlds. They are both ways of getting meaning to and from expressible forms. They also make the human landscape comprehensible. Language and culture are two different ways of doing this, each dependent on the other. Thus cultural creolization and linguistic creolization are integral, rather than analogous, to each other.[82]

Rath's understanding that words and things are (and were) integral to each other, and to what Stuart Hall called the 'logics of cultural translation' within displaced societies, resonates deeply with this book.[83] In Chapter 11, in exploring the soundscape of the Middle Passage, and the logistics of shipboard communication, I take methodological inspiration from the work of Rath and other musicologists researching cultural exchanges among enslaved Africans in seventeenth-century North America.[84] As their studies have eloquently demonstrated, music made by first-generation Africans in the Americas provides an excellent basis from which to investigate the earliest stages of inter-African cultural exchanges in the diaspora—a topic of direct interest to anyone exploring cognate processes during the Middle Passage itself. In the course of the Middle Passage, different and unequal groups—captive Africans, who did not invariably speak mutually intelligible languages and British sailors drawn from the working and emergent middle classes—interacted in a nomadic space at once physical and conceptual. In the interstices between these colliding migrant worlds, this book will propose, individual and collective cultural identities were *displaced*.

In framing the Middle Passage with reference to displacement I owe much to the postcolonial theorist Homi Bhabha.[85] His work converges with aspects of creolization theory but opens a new space within it.[86] Bhabha has influentially proposed that encounters between distinct and unequal social groups take place in a conceptual third space—one that occupies a liminal terrain between a dominant public transcript and subalterns' agency in the interpretation of it. This third space can also be understood as existing *between* the public and hidden transcripts of native or subaltern discourse itself.[87] In this liminal space, culture is both disseminated by, and displaced from, interacting groups.[88] As Bhabha puts it: 'The third space displaces the histories that constitute it, and sets up new structures of authority, new political initiatives which are inadequately understood through received wisdom.'[89]

Displacement should not be understood as a gloss for loss or disorientation here: rather, the term articulates that which is *created* in the context of both. Bhabha's third space is not, of course, a physical entity; it is a linguistic one, existing in the now, and displacing the histories that constitute it. Even so, the postcolonial formulation of the third space resonates deeply with my own understanding of the Middle Passage as a physical and conceptual between-space in which nomads 'slip[ped] through the network of classifications that normally locate states and positions in cultural space'.[90] It is noteworthy, here, that the concept of third space (or thirdspace) is beginning to appear in the work of historians of spaces of early modern dissent and popular protest. Katrina Navickas's analysis of the political graffiti used to promote Thomas Spence's radical Plan in eighteenth-century London is a good example here, positioning space as at once material, experienced, and contested.[91] Every slave ship, I would argue, was also a third space, bounded by ocean but material, experienced, subverted, and, at times, temporarily undermined. Its cultural productions—some impermanent, many of them lasting—appear throughout this book.

About the Rest of This Book

Chapter 2 provides contextual information about the British slave trade: it will be useful for readers unfamiliar with this terrain, though others may prefer to skim through it quickly. Chapter 3 introduces the primary documentary sources employed throughout my book. No British slave ship has survived, as Marcus Wood puts it, 'to become a site for memory'.[92] Today, one can visit the remains of Henry VIII's *Mary*

Rose, and even walk on the decks of Nelson's flagship HMS *Victory*, but not a single slave ship has survived the sea in this way. The slaving vessel can, nevertheless, be materialized by drawing on a variety of data sources. Witness testimonies, most of them made by sailors, are the first of these. These documents are artefacts of the trade in human beings, framed within contemporary discourses concerning both Africans and the concept of chattel slavery. At the same time, they provide detailed information about the business of shipping slaves, the physical characteristics of slave ships, and diurnal regimes before and during the Middle Passage. For all these reasons, personal testimonies are an essential starting point for a historical archaeology of the voyage into slavery. The ships encountered in Chapter 3, and the voices of those who sailed aboard them, will be constant companions in this book. A multitude of voyages are referenced throughout, but the detailed voyage narratives of greatest service to this book are discussed in some detail in Chapter 3 and the authors, ships, and/or dates are thereafter identified in bold throughout (e.g. **Phillips, *Hannibal* 1693–4**).

Ships, and the many material things they transported, are themselves statements in the discourse of the slave trade. A handful of wrecks have been identified, and, as discussed in Chapter 4, maritime archaeologists have explored some of them in considerable detail. Only two of the excavated vessels—the English *Henrietta Marie* (1700) and the Danish *Fredensborg* (1789)—were engaged in the slave trade at the time they foundered, but artefacts from these wrecks speak to us about slave shipping with a powerful voice, and, for that reason alone, it is unfortunate that there are no more wreck sites to work with. But witness testimonies and contemporary illustrations also provide invaluable information about the appearance and use of the slave ship, and through careful reading of these sources it is possible to reconstruct its most important features in extraordinary detail. This is the task of Chapter 5, which draws on a multiplicity of data in delineating the key physical characteristics of the ships employed in the British slave trade. On the African coast, merchant ships built to carry inanimate cargoes underwent a metamorphosis that readied them, in the eyes of their owners and crews, for the transportation of human beings. In Chapter 5 British slave shipping legislation, voyage narratives, paintings, ship models, and wreck data are all employed to furnish a better understanding of the routine series of modifications that turned a merchant trader into a 'slaver'.[93] Here, and at other points in the discussion where the surviving evidence is limited, it has been necessary to look beyond the British data to the vessels, and shipping practices, of other nations. Readers will frequently encounter the French vessel *Marie-Séraphique*, for example, because the appearance of this ship and its slave deck were recorded visually in a way that has no equal in the surviving British evidence.

European ships were a familiar site in coastal West Africa for hundreds of years, and the sailing ship impacted upon the arts there in a variety of ways. Even today, merchant ships are depicted on masquerade regalia in some regions, and in others there is evidence to suggest that carved wooden figureheads had an impact on anthropomorphic carving. Ship images have mainly occurred on items used in ceremonial rather than everyday contexts, and, as discussed in Chapter 6, it can be argued that, rather than simply replicating European ships in their art, African artists were appropriating the largest artefact of the Middle Passage and transforming it into something new—something that fitted into a non-European world view and could also be controlled and manipulated ritually. In important ways, then, the reception of the ship image can be seen as a metaphor for the reception of the slave trade itself, at least in its early stages.

On arrival off the coast of Africa, slave ships were laden with manufactured goods carefully selected to meet the localized requirements of traders on different parts of the coast. A selection of these goods, and their complex biographical *chaînes opératoire*, are the subject of Chapter 7. As both historical accounts and recent archaeological fieldwork have shown, West Africans were very selective consumers of European goods, demanding artefacts in media, styles, and colours that accorded with their own traditions and tastes. To better their returns from the slave trade, European merchants and manufacturers made conscious attempts to meet these localized cultural preferences, engaging thereby in a dialogue with African aesthetics and African arts. The opposite is also true: by selecting, using, and often reworking European goods (for example, by cutting down sheet brass vessels to make ritual vessels or by reducing European beads to powder, only to turn them into beads once again), Africans were engaged in their own dialogue with European material things. Out of this dialogue—a conversation in objects rather than words—emerged a unique repertoire of artefacts, some of which are explored in Chapter 7.

The first European ships arrived in West Africa in search of gold rather than slaves, and at the end of the seventeenth century gold, elephant ivory, and pepper remained highly profitable components of the return cargoes of British slave ships. Gold imports declined over time, but interest in other natural resources remained buoyant, feeding the demand at home for melegueta pepper, ivory, hardwoods, dyewoods, resins, and other African products. Chapter 8 focuses on these supplementary cargoes and considers their reception and use in Britain. Through these things, slave ships brought British consumers—many of whom would never come face-to-face with an enslaved African—into regular contact with the bounty of a distant continent. At the same time, many British sailors also engaged in unofficial private ventures in Africa, carrying home gold in dust or scrap form, for example. Some brought back botanical specimens or ethnographic objects at the behest of wealthy collectors for whom Africa was a site of scientific enquiry and prized exotica. Through its official and unofficial cargoes, then, the slave ship played a material part in transforming British engagement with the natural resources of West Africa, and in refashioning the region for home consumption. As the final section of Chapter 8 explores, this understanding, and its potential value to the abolitionist cause, was eventually given material expression in one of the most important artefacts of the anti-slavery movement: Thomas Clarkson's wooden chest containing examples of the 'productions of Africa'.

Chapter 9 turns to the medical and health regimes of the slaving voyage. Many ships of the early modern period made intercontinental voyages, but the slave trade was unique in that it embraced three continents and, thereby, three different disease environments. As a result, the bodies of both captives and sailors acted as carriers of tropical diseases and medical conditions, borne unwittingly into the Americas. These included yaws, yellow fever, and malaria. While slaver crews tended to succumb to yellow fever contracted on the African coast, the principal killer of captives was dysentery—a direct outcome of the filthy, crowded conditions of their Middle Passage. Medical care was always rudimentary on slave ships, but, as Chapter 9 argues, it was firmly contextualized in developing discourses of difference concerning the black body and the white, which the slave trade itself helped to hone into more rigid form in the late eighteenth century.

Chapter 10 focuses upon the modalities of the Middle Passage from the perspective of the British sailors who, for some three hundred years, enacted and enforced the widely shared diurnal routines that characterized a slaving voyage. Drawing princi-pally upon mariners' testimonies, this chapter reconstructs a twenty-four-hour period on a typical British slaving voyage of the later eighteenth century (the era for which we have most detailed documentary evidence) and attempts to identify the key artefacts in the assemblage of Middle Passage practice. A particular focus of this chapter is the role of both words and things in mediating interactions between captives and crews. From the perspective of the latter, the slave ship was a prison in which the behaviour and daily life of the incarcerated could be regulated through established routines of subsistence, surveillance, discipline, and punishment—praxis accrued by generations of sailors over time. As Chapter 10 argues, the slaver was also a locus for creolizing encounters impacting on all those on board. Captains and crews developed some understanding of African foodways, for example, while their cap-tives ate from wooden bowls and spoons fashioned by ships' carpenters. Sailors harpooned exotic fish, ate yams, and flavoured their food with African pepper; captives, meanwhile, smoked (slave-grown) Virginian tobacco from kaolin pipes made in England. These material encounters were in no sense equitable—they could never be that, given the power dynamics involved—but their outcomes reached far beyond the slave ship.

Chapter 11 attempts to explore the same voyage experience from the African perspective. It focuses on coping strategies, exploring the ways in which captives read, endured, and sometimes challenged the rules that the built environment of the slave ship and its diurnal routines attempted to enforce. A slave ship was *designed* to divide and conquer, to foster a culture of fear, and to thwart resistance, yet it was also a place in which Africans found the strength to survive, to develop covert and overt ways to cope and to resist, and to forge new bonds through shared understanding and action. This chapter argues the case for greater consideration of the infrapolitics of the Middle Passage—that is, for the need to focus more effectively on low profile, undis-closed actions that challenged domination without fatal consequences—before going on to materialize the figurative and physical weapons that captives deployed in surviving, and contesting, their enforced Atlantic crossing.

The concluding chapter turns to saltwater identities in the New World and con-siders the ways in which the Middle Passage was, and is, remembered there. Here,

22   MATERIALIZING THE MIDDLE PASSAGE

I draw together several categories of evidence to order to foreground the extraordinary ability of the *African* Middle Passage to evade the direct gaze of the historical archaeologist (and indeed, the historian). I also consider a nuanced body of research grounded in anthropological theory (including creolization theory) exploring localized memorialization of the slave trade through ritual strategies. That body of work has helped me both to crystalize my thinking on the space occupied by the Middle Passage in memory work today, and to understand why this positioning matters, in turn, for articulating African experience in the past.[94]

Notes

1. Table 1.1 concerns only those voyages fitted out in ports in Britain between the first documented voyage in 1652 and the abolition of the British slave trade in1807: it does not include voyages originating in the Caribbean, which comprised about 5% of the British trade. Eltis and Richardson (2010: 23, table 2) estimate the *total* volume of the British slave trade as 3,259,000 embarkations—almost a quarter of the total volume of the transatlantic slave trade. Most British voyages were undertaken between 1680 and 1807, the period with which this book is principally concerned.
2. The term Middle Passage was probably first used by English traders in the eighteenth century (Palmer 2002: 53). It denoted the second leg of the triangular voyage that took ships from England to Africa, from Africa to the Americas, and from the Americas back to England. From the perspective of crews, the Atlantic crossing was thus the middle leg of a three-sided voyage. As Palmer notes, however, the meaning of 'Middle Passage' has shifted over time, so that it is now used to refer, not only to the transatlantic route itself, but also to the captives' ordeal as they crossed the Atlantic. As a result, 'the Middle Passage is now synonymous with the travail of African peoples'. In this book, I use the term in both senses, but take the Middle Passage experience of captives to begin with embarkation, rather than at the point of departure of their ship from the African coast—something that often occurred months after embarkation. This book is thus concerned primarily with slave ships, their crews, and captives while in West Africa and during the crossing to the Americas. Nor do I consider the intercontinental slave trade that transshipped many Africans on a second voyage from the Caribbean to British North America— on which see O'Malley (2014) and the Intra-American database on the slavevoyages website at https://www.slavevoyages.org/.
3. Gilroy (1993: 4): 'Ships immediately focus attention on the Middle Passage, on the various projects for redemptive return to an African homeland, on the circulation of ideas and activists as well as the movement of key cultural and political artefacts.'
4. See, e.g., Christopher (2006), Rediker (2007), Smallwood (2007a), and Mustakeem (2016).
5. Historical archaeologists, like ethnographers and folklorists, study the *lifeways* of their subjects. The total lifeway of a group of people, as John Vlach (1991: p. xv) puts it, includes 'their verbal, material, and spiritual forms of expression'.
6. Hall (2000: 16).
7. Hall (2000: 26).
8. Scott (1990: 4). I have drawn inspiration from Scott's work (1985, 1990).
9. Hall (2000: 38).
10. For a detailed examination of insurance litigation involving slave ships between 1780 and 1807, see Oldham (2007). For a broader meditation on the *Zong* atrocity, slavery, and capital accumulation in the Atlantic world, see Baucom (2005).

11. In 1772, Mansfield had made a well-known judgment in the case of the escaped slave James Somerset, which marked a significant milestone along the road towards the abolition, and which was (wrongly) interpreted by some to suggest that slavery had no legal basis on British soil. The case centred on the legality of the forcible deportation of an enslaved man from England. Mansfield famously ruled that 'no master ever was allowed here [Britain] to take a slave by force to be sold abroad because he deserted from his service . . . and therefore the man must be discharged'. See Oldham (1992: ii. 1225–9).

12. For the background to the *Zong* incident, see Lewis (2007) and Webster (2007), two in a series of papers concerning the *Zong* case published in the *Journal of Legal History*, 3 (2007).

13. *Gregson* v *Gilbert* (1783) 3 Doug. 232.

14. On 'perils of the sea' in relation to losses of captives, see Oldham (2007: 303–7).

15. The artist is possibly the Scottish painter David Martin: see Gerzina (2020: 171).

16. This is the version of events offered in Roulston (2006), for example.

17. Gerzina (2020: 164).

18. On the concept of 'humanity' in the *Zong* trial, as a counterpoint to the Gregson plea of 'necessity', see Walvin (2011: 147). For a reading of the *Zong* case that rejects the argument that later-eighteenth-century maritime law acknowledged, or struggled with, the humanity of captives, see Pearson and Richardson (2019: 421–5).

19. http://collections.vam.ac.uk/item/O278607/punch–bowl–jackson–william/ (accessed 15 August 2022).

20. This and other punch bowls depicting British slave ships are discussed in Webster (2015).

21. *Lloyds Register* 1768, no. 481. At 100 tons, *Swallow* was a smaller than average slaving vessel and was registered as a snauw (a two-masted, square-rigged vessel with a trysail mast to the rear of the main mast), with two guns mounted. The image on the *Swallow* bowl fits this description precisely, strongly suggesting that the artist had made preparatory sketches of *Swallow* at first hand.

22. Watney and Roberts (1993: 21).

23. Wood (2000) and see also Wood (2002).

24. Wood (2000: 300).

25. See Webster (2009) on the display of abolitionist memorabilia in 2007—a year in which many museums staged exhibitions commemorating the bicentenary of the 1807 abolition of the British slave trade.

26. For a historian's view of Wood's *Slavery, Empathy and Pornography* (2002), see Paton (2005: 251–4).

27. Nussbaum (1990: 377); emphasis added.

28. Riello (2009: 30).

29. Gomez (1998: 14).

30. Jamieson (1995: 49).

31. See Handler and Lange (1978). Further excavation was undertaken at Newton in 1997–8. Isotope analysis was subsequently performed on the twenty-five individuals recovered at that time: see Schroeder et al. (2009). The results suggest that most of the people excavated in the 1990s were born on the island, if not on the estate itself. Seven individuals, however, yielded oxygen and strontium ratios in their tooth enamel that are consistent with an African origin, strongly suggesting that they were first-generation captives brought to the island with the slave trade. These people did not all originate from the same part of Africa: the data suggest that they came from at least three different zones, possibly including the Gold Coast and Senegambia.

32. Handler (1997: 98).

33. The likely provenance of this smoking pipe is discussed by Handler and Norman (2007).

34. See Handler (1997: 111) on this possibility in relation to Burial B72's grave goods; and Handler (2009a) for a more general discussion.

35. This is the view of DeCorse (2000: 7), with reference to Handler (1997): but Handler himself does not refer to any of B72's beads as being African made. Powder-glass bead production is discussed in more detail in Chapter 7.
36. See Handler (2007) for a discussion of the two Newton carnelian beads. The second, also from a necklace, was found with Burial B63. These are the only carnelian beads to have been recovered archaeologically from slave cemetery contexts in the New World. Handler (2007: 7) notes that, among some Gold Coast peoples, the bead necklaces worn by priests occasionally contained one long red carnelian bead.
37. Corruccini et al. (1987), summarized in Handler (1997: 100–1).
38. See Heath (2016) for a detailed analysis of 353 cowries recovered from 55 sites in Virginia, only 8% of which were found in plantation contexts.
39. Berlin (1996). Berlin's view (1996: 254) was that the African-born could define themselves in ways that transcended nativity—a view I share.
40. For a discussion of the adjective 'saltwater', see Smallwood (2007b: 6–7). As she points out, it was used by individuals born in the Caribbean to describe—often in a pejorative fashion—slaves born in Africa.
41. On the concept of social death, see Patterson (1982: 38–51); and, in relation to the Middle Passage, see also Christopher (2006: 166–8). For the argument that scholars of slavery (including the Middle Passage) should dispense with the notion that 'social death' was a basic condition of slavery, see Brown (2009: esp. 1231–4).
42. See Gomez (1998), Midlo Hall (2005), Carney (2001).
43. Eltis and Richardson (1997a: 10).
44. This debate began in exchanges between Douglas Chambers (1997) and David Northrup (2000). Chambers (1997: 73) argued that the African Igbo 'were a distinct ethno-historical group who shared a distinctive set of ancestral traditions and drew on the same or very similar material, social and ideological resources in order to adapt to the situations in which they commonly found themselves as slaves'. In contrast, Northrup argued that at the time of the slave trade the peoples of the Niger Delta were too culturally diverse to have embraced, in the diaspora, a single collective identity of the kind envisaged by Chambers.
45. Byrd (2008: 56).
46. Byrd (2008: 56).
47. Byrd (2008: 32).
48. For a similar reading of Byrd, which has also influenced my own thinking, see especially Brown (2009: 1245–6).
49. See Hawthorne (2010: 97–133, esp. 99).
50. Dubois (2016: 52).
51. For a round-up of recent studies, see Weik (2014). For a searching, and often critical, analysis of the use of the concept of ethnogenesis in archaeological research, see Voss (2015). On the blurred boundaries between creolization, hybridity, and ethnogenesis, see Voss (2015: 659), Silliman (2015), and Weik (2014: 301). Sidbury and Cañizares-Esguerra (2011) provide a perceptive analysis of these issues: see especially pp. 181–2 and 184.
52. Palmié (2010: 7).
53. Trouillot's plea (2002) for an ethnographic, historicizing approach to creolization has been a particular inspiration in this context.
54. Baker and Mühlhäuser (2007: 85).
55. These were Van Dyk (c.1765), a study of Sranan (a Dutch creole spoken in Suriname), and Magens and Salicath (1770), a grammar of the Dutch creole Negerhollands, spoken in what is now the US Virgin Islands. The first comparative study was Van Name (1869–70), which considered Negerhollands, Papiamentu, and Sranan (Dutch creoles) and the French creoles of Haiti, Louisiana, Martinique, St Thomas, and Trinidad.

AN INTRODUCTION IN THREE OBJECTS   25

56. Herskovits (1989 [1941]: 81, emphasis added). For a critical discussion of Herskovits's grammar of culture analogy, see Palmié (2007: 182–7).
57. Rath (1993: 705).
58. Brathwaite (2005 [1971]).
59. Brathwaite (2005 [1971]: 296).
60. Brathwaite (2005 [1971]: 296–306).
61. Mintz and Price's 1976 *An Anthropological Approach to the Afro-American Past: A Caribbean Perspective* was republished in 1992 as *The Birth of African-American Culture: An Anthropological Perspective*.
62. Mintz, and Price (1992: 41).
63. Mintz and Price (1992: 52–60).
64. Mintz and Price (1992: 43).
65. Mintz and Price (1992: 44): specifically: 'We believe that the development of these social bonds, even before Africans had set foot in the new world, already announced the birth of new societies, based on new principles.'
66. *Historical Archaeology*, 34/3 (published in 2000), was entirely dedicated to cultural creolization and provides an excellent introduction to the range of archaeological work informed by this concept in the 1990s. For a very influential single study, see Ferguson (1992: esp. pp. xli–xlii).
67. See Thornton (1998: 192) regarding the absence of 'randomization'. His critique of Mintz and Price is principally to be found in Thornton (1998: 129–205).
68. See, e.g., Chambers (2008: 152–4) and Midlo Hall (2010: 139).
69. Midlo Hall (2005: 49). See Price (2010) for a spirited refutation of Africanist charges against the Mintz–Price hypothesis, and a call for anthropologists to keep faith with Trouillot's 'miracle begging for analysis' (2002: 189).
70. See also Palmié (2007: 186). As Palmié observes here, at the time it was written, the Mintz–Price hypothesis appeared neatly to address the problem that, 'although African-American cultures in the United States seemed palpably "different", there was comparatively little that could be directly traced to any specific African source'.
71. See Midlo Hall (2010: 139). This is one of three responses to the paper by Eltis et al. (2007) on the 'black rice hypothesis'.
72. See Eltis et al. (2010: 165).
73. Byrd (2008: 17–31, 50–6).
74. Scott (1991: 261).
75. Scott (2004: 108–10).
76. Stephan Palmié (2007: 187) similarly argues that Mintz and Price (1976) amounted to 'a clarion call for the historicization of African-American anthropology'—undermined, in his view, by the use of linguistic analogy.
77. Torres de Souza and Symanski (2009: 516).
78. Brathwaite (1981: 6–7).
79. 'Discipline' is used here in the Foucauldian sense of 'methods which made possible the meticulous control of the operations of the body, which assured the constant subjection of its forces and imposed upon them a relation of docility-utility' (Foucault 1977: 137).
80. Trouillot (2002: 195–8).
81. Mintz and Price (1976: 42–4).
82. Rath (2000: 100).
83. Hall (2016: 48).
84. I have made particular use of Rath (1993, 2000, 2003, 2008) and Dubois (2016).
85. Bhabha (1985, 1990, 1994).
86. This point is brought out beautifully by Stewart (2007: 19) in an analysis that has greatly informed my own thinking on the relationship between creolization theory and Bhabha's work.

87. This important point is emphasized by Jefferess (2008: 38) in his discussion of the similarities between Scott's theory of public versus hidden transcripts and Bhabha's third space of colonial discourse, and by Johansson and Vinthagen (2020: 128–31) in discussing the between-spaces of everyday resistance.
88. Bhabha (1985, 1990, 1994).
89. Bhabha (1990: 211).
90. Turner (1969: 95); see also Bhabha (1994: 235).
91. Navickas (2015, 2016)—work inspired by the urban theorist Edward Soja (see Soja 1996), for whom the third space is an 'an-Other' space of openness and creativity, populated by the marginalized.
92. Wood (2000: 17).
93. Between 1788 and the 1807 abolition of the slave trade, eleven Acts of Parliament were passed in efforts to regulate the 'shipping and carrying' of slaves in British vessels. Most of these acts (although not the first) also addressed the treatment of slave ship crews. Chapter 5 explores the terms of the most important of these Acts, and their impact on the fitting-out and crewing of slave ships.
94. Apter and Derby (2010b).

2
The British Slave Trade

A Brief Overview

This chapter opens with a summary overview of Britain's part in the transatlantic slave trade. The majority of British-based slaving voyages were undertaken between 1680 and the abolition of the British slave trade in 1807, but to contextualize the rapid expansion of the British trade from the late seventeenth century, the narrative begins with the first documented British voyage in 1562. The primary slave trading ports on the coast of West Africa are then introduced, and the mechanics of slave trading at these sites are detailed. Archaeological work at key African sites is also briefly introduced here, as a preface to more detailed use of information from these important projects later in the book. Finally, brief information is provided on the principal New World disembarkation points for captives carried on British ships. For those readers with a very limited knowledge of the British slave trade, this chapter will introduce it; but the principal purpose of this synthesis—which makes no claims to originality—is to contextualize the voyages discussed in Chapter 3, the wrecks described in Chapter 4, and the primary textual sources and artefacts that appear in all subsequent chapters.

The British Slave Trade, 1562–1807

In 1562, the Elizabethan adventurer John Hawkins undertook a voyage from Plymouth to Sierra Leone with three ships, *Salomon*, *Swallow*, and *Jonas*.[1] Hawkins was not the first Englishman to travel to 'Guinea' (the popular name for West Africa: see Figure 2.1), but he was the first to go there specifically in search of slaves.[2] His voyage marked England's tentative entry into a trading network that (as discussed in more detail in Chapter 6) had been operational in the hands of the Portuguese and Spanish for more than a hundred years. Hawkins acquired some three hundred captives, took them across the Atlantic to Monte Christi (in what is now the Dominican Republic), and, infringing Spain's supposed monopoly on the trade in slaves to the Caribbean at this time, sold his surviving captives at considerable profit. Two further lucrative voyages followed in 1564 and 1567, with Elizabeth I loaning Hawkins the 700-ton *Jesus of Lubeck* in return for a share of his profits. In total, Hawkins and his crews enslaved around 1,200 people, all of whom were sold in the Spanish Caribbean.[3] These voyages brought Hawkins fame and fortune, and marked the beginning of a long maritime trading relationship between England and Africa. The African depicted on Hawkins' crest (Figure 2.2) references the close relationship between the gold and slave trades at

Materializing the Middle Passage: A Historical Archaeology of British Slave Shipping, 1680–1807. Jane Webster,
Oxford University Press. © Jane Webster 2023. DOI: 10.1093/oso/9780199214594.003.0002

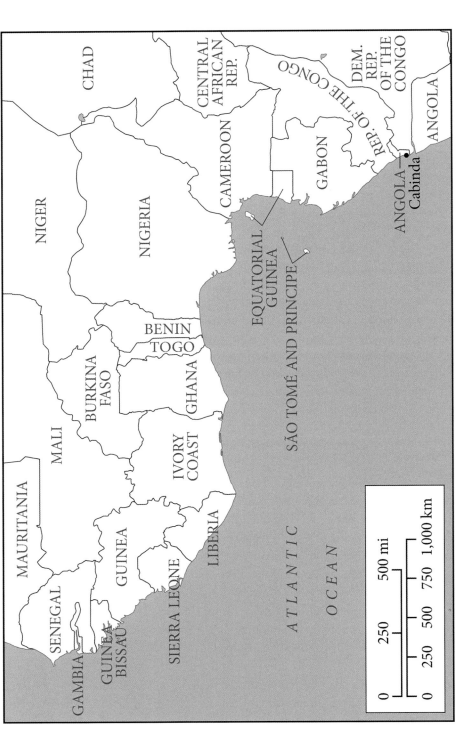

Figure 2.1 The 'Guinea' coast, with the West and Central African countries mentioned in Chapter 2. Cabinda, an enclave of Angola, is also indicated.

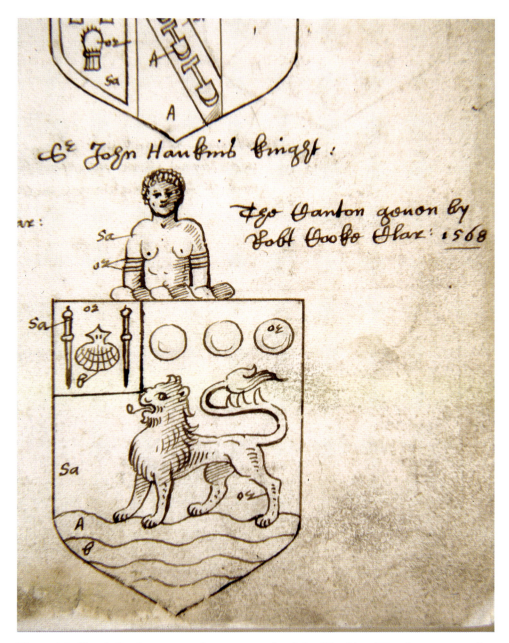

Figure 2.2 Sketch for the arms and crest granted to John Hawkins, 'The Canton geven by Rob[er]t Cooke Clar[enceux] King of Arms 1568'. College of Arms.

this time: he wears a necklace and armlets 'tricked' (indicated by annotated abbreviations) in gold. Despite Hawkins' endeavours, intense Spanish and Portuguese efforts to postpone the entry of the increasingly persistent French, Dutch, and English into the slave trade meant that forty years would pass before English captains once again traded openly for slaves.

As the seventeenth century opened, English settlers established colonies at Jamestown in Virginia (1607), and Bermuda (1609). More colonies quickly followed on the east coast of North America and throughout the Caribbean. Settlers in these new territories, particularly those arriving on Caribbean islands whose indigenous populations had been decimated under Spanish rule, faced problems in securing an adequate supply of labour. It was against this backdrop that, in 1618, James I granted exclusive control over English trade in Africa to the *Company of Adventurers of London Trading to Gynney and Bynney*.[4] The company was primarily interested in gold, but increasing demand for slave labour also stimulated this first monopoly enterprise.[5] The company re-established an English presence in West Africa, and supported some private English slaving ventures on the Guinea coast.[6] But these ad hoc arrangements could not meet the emerging demand for African labour, and in 1631 Charles I granted patents to transport slaves from Guinea to a new syndicate of well-connected entrepreneurs, headed by Sir Nicholas Crisp (or Crispe).[7] The group was given exclusive rights (among English traders) to Guinea, Benin, and Angola for a period of thirty-one years. Slaves are not explicitly mentioned in the patents, but, alongside the acquisition of gold, ivory, redwood, hides, wax, gum, and pepper, the Adventurers were certainly engaged in slave trading.[8] Crisp poured a fortune into constructing the first English fort in West Africa: Kormantin (Cormantine) Castle, sited on the Gold Coast. In 1651, a new Guinea Company was founded, this time headed by Samuel Vassall.[9] Charles I granted Vassall's group a trading monopoly centred on Kormantin and the River Sherbro region in Sierra Leone. Although it failed, this initiative signalled the beginning of regular slave trading by London-based ships.[10] In 1660, shortly after the restoration of the monarchy, Charles II awarded a 1,000–year monopoly on the English trade to a newly founded *Company of Royal Adventurers Trading into Africa*. This venture boasted Prince Rupert as its figurehead, and the shareholders included the king, members of the aristocracy, and numerous leading royalist politicians.[11] From 1663, some of the gold acquired by the Royal Adventurers in 'Guinea' was turned into coins known by that name (Figure 2.3). The elephant illustrated below the royal bust on the

Figure 2.3 Obverse of a 1663 Guinea coin, depicting a bust of Charles II and an African elephant. British Museum, E1528.

guinea coin references another important commodity sought on the West African coast: ivory.

After a series of false starts, a new charter was issued to the company in 1663.[12] At enormous cost, the Adventurers now undertook to restore the trading forts built by their predecessors in West Africa and dispatched forty ships to Guinea in their first year alone.[13] Cape Coast Castle (temporarily seized by the Dutch) was reclaimed and became the headquarters of the English trade. Gold, rather than slaves, initially motivated the *Adventurers*, but the company's agents soon began a sustained trade in slaves, supplying the English Caribbean colonies of Barbados and Jamaica. They also endeavoured to service the requirements of the Spanish.[14] Renewed conflict followed with the Dutch, who were attempting to establish exclusive European rights to the Guinea trade. By the time the war had ended, the Adventurers' finances were in disarray. Crippled by debt, the company finally foundered in 1672, but its collapse did not diminish English enthusiasm for the African slave trade. The Adventurers had for some years been selling licences to independent traders, loosening their own monopoly in exchange for much-needed funds. They had also established a sister company (the Gambia Adventurers), which operated successfully in that region.[15] Both ventures had brought new English investors, and new money, into the African trade. Thus, when the Adventurers fell, a new Royal African Company (hereafter RAC) quickly emerged to fill the void.[16] Receiving its royal charter in 1672, the RAC bought the assets of its predecessor and retained its headquarters at Africa House in London. The new company was once again given a 1,000-year licence to trade across a vast swathe of African coastline, but a monopoly was in this case granted only until 1688. After this date, independent traders would be allowed into the region, in exchange for a fee payable to the RAC. From the start, competition from other quarters was to prove so strong that it was simply impossible for the RAC to enforce a true trading monopoly.[17] Even so, it tried.

The RAC initially focused its attentions on the Gold Coast, establishing numerous fortified trading posts along the shoreline. Cape Coast Castle remained the hub of the RAC network, with a permanent garrison of fifty soldiers and a resident commander. Over time, as the company increased its slave-trading operations, RAC ships became active on the Windward Coast (modern Liberia), and on what became known as the Slave Coast (the Bight of Benin). Between 1672 and 1689, the RAC transported more than 100,000 Africans to New World destinations.[18] The majority were shipped to Barbados, Jamaica, and Nevis in the Caribbean. The remainder went to the English colonies in North America or were sold on to the Spanish from the Caribbean ports.

In 1688, the RAC lost the royal patronage on which its success—and its ability to deal with incursions by interloping vessels—depended. From its earliest days the RAC had been forced to fend off challenges to its monopoly, mainly coming from Bristol-based merchants keen to enter the African trade. Many merchants financed private slaving ventures to Africa, running the risk of seizure by RAC officials, but at the same time avoiding the near-crippling overheads that burdened the RAC itself.[19] By 1688, when the RAC was obliged to sell licences to these independent (or 'separate') traders,

32 MATERIALIZING THE MIDDLE PASSAGE

it was becoming clear that this would not be enough to satisfy the growing demand for a more open trade. Even so, the RAC was able to profit from its fragile monopoly for another decade, trading more than 32,000 slaves between 1690 and 1700.[20] One of the ships encountered in Chapter 3 is *Hannibal*, making a voyage from Gold Coast to Barbados in 1693–4 as part of an RAC convoy during that decade. The watershed came in 1698, when, despite feverish company lobbying, the RAC finally lost its exclusive rights to the African trade. A new, deregulated era was dawning for Britain's slave traders, but more than twenty years were to go by before the floodgates holding back a 'free' slave trade were opened fully. Until 1712, to put it another way, the RAC kept one finger in a very leaky dam.

Although the RAC lost its already shaky monopoly in 1698, the new Act opening up the slave trade to 'interlopers' from Bristol and other ports granted it the right to charge these traders a 10 per cent tax on all the goods they brought to Africa to exchange for slaves.[21] This levy on Guinea-bound cargoes was intended to fund maintenance of the RAC's Gold Coast forts, which were deemed necessary to all English traders in the region. The separate traders who paid this tax, with bitter and vociferous complaint, were known as the 'ten percenters'. *Albion Frigate* (1698), *Don Carlos* (1700), and *Daniel and Henry* (1700), three more vessels whose stories are taken up in Chapter 3, were all 10 per cent ships.[22] The first two sailed out of London, but *Daniel and Henry* was based in Dartmouth, one of the many minor English ports entering the slave trade during these years. This was also the period during which Bristol, by now the major English port servicing the West Indies sugar trade, entered fully into the slave trade.

In 1712, after years of pressure from the separate traders, the 10 per cent tax was finally abolished, and the Guinea trade thrown open to all. By the 1720s, the RAC was unable to make a profit, and in 1730 Parliament voted the company an annual subsidy of £10,000 for the upkeep of its string of West African forts—in effect assuming responsibility for these establishments. The RAC now saw the slave trade pass almost wholly into the hands of independent traders. Despite frequent contemporary charges of incompetence and failure, the RAC had in fact been a very successful company. By 1720, it had dispatched some 600 ships, transporting an estimated 176,000 Africans to the New World, and had exported £1.5 million of European goods too.[23] As discussed in Chapter 7, through its efforts to secure appropriate trade goods, the company had also played a significant part in promoting new manufacturing industries in England and abroad.

With the effective demise of the RAC, the way was now clear for a myriad of merchants, based in ports both large and small, to become traders in humanity. Across Europe, other nations with slaving interests were also abandoning monopolies in favour of a 'free' trade in the unfree. This was happening just as Europe's colonies were becoming increasingly dependent upon slave labour. Then, in 1713, peace broke out between the major European powers, with the signing of the Treaty of Utrecht. Together, these factors led to a massive expansion in slave trading. By the 1720s, an activity that had once been simply a profitable offshoot of a wider European trade in

African goods had become the mainstay of a transatlantic economic system that bound communities in three corners of the world in lasting mutual dependency. The vast majority of those enslaved (around 85 per cent of all Africans transported to the New World) made the journey into slavery after 1700, during the century in which the British slave trade reached its peak.[24]

The Treaty of Utrecht gave Britain a much-coveted thirty-year *asiento* (contract) to supply slaves to the Spanish colonies. The British government promptly sold this privilege to the recently formed South Sea Company (one of whose ships is shown in Figure 2.4), for the astounding sum of £9,500,000.[25] Hope triumphing over experience, the same government then secured a £9,000,000 stake in the company. The hope, of course, was that the *asiento* would wipe out the national debt. Experience was to prove otherwise, but the hordes of investors who clamoured to sink their savings into the new venture were not to know that.

The contract required the South Sea Company to provide Spain with 4,800 slaves annually. The intention was to purchase captives from the still-functioning RAC forts, and to take them to Jamaica and Barbados for onward shipment to the Spanish colonies. From the outset the company was beset by difficulties, not the least being the continued activities of independent traders. In 1720, after a period of frenzied speculation in shares, the South Sea bubble burst (see Figure 2.5).

Figure 2.4 The *Luxborough Galley* on fire, 25 June 1727. John Cleveley, 1760. National Maritime Museum, Greenwich, NMM BHC.2389.

Figure 2.5 The jack (knave) of hearts from a set of playing cards marking the collapse of the South Sea Company. A black domestic servant delivers a message from a ruined 'South Sea Lady' to her slighted love. Baker Library, Harvard Business School.

Many well-connected investors were ruined, but the company itself survived, continuing to supply slaves to Spain.[26] Most of the Africans carried on South Sea Company ships were taken (via Jamaica) to Portobelo in Panama.[27]

The disappointing performance of the South Sea Company did not dampen the enthusiasm of British merchants for the slave trade, which grew extremely rapidly during 1712–20. Most of the British ships engaged in the trade at this time came from

London or Bristol. The decade from 1721 to 1730 witnessed both a growth in the trade to the British colonies in Virginia, Maryland, and the Carolinas, and a gradual eclipsing of London as the premier British slave trading port.[28] In the 1730s—the decade in which the British slave trade really came into its own—this mantle was assumed by Bristol. Within twenty years, however, Liverpool had taken Bristol's place, maintaining this position until the abolition of the slave trade in 1807. The RAC was finally dissolved in 1750, following the establishment of a chartered *Company of Merchants Trading to Africa*.[29] The new company occupied and continued to maintain nine forts on the Gambia River, Gold Coast, and at Ouidah, leaving the separate traders free to expand their operations elsewhere. For the remainder of the eighteenth century, Britain's independent slave traders were a dominant force in the Atlantic slave trade. Chapter 3 considers the voyages of several independently owned ships from Bristol and Liverpool making the Middle Passage between Africa and the Caribbean during the later eighteenth century. These are *Duke of Argyle* (1750–1) on the way to Antigua and St Kitts under the captaincy of John Newton; *Thetis* (1754), undertaking a voyage from the Bight of Biafra to Antigua; and four Caribbean-bound voyages in Bristol ships undertaken by Alexander Falconbridge between 1780 and 1787. Two further voyages considered in this book are those of the London ship *Sandown*, making its way from Rio Nunez (Sierra Leone) to Kingston, Jamaica, in 1793–4; and the 1807 voyage of *Kitty's Amelia* from Bonny to Kingston. *Kitty's Amelia* was one of the last legally authorized slave ships to leave Liverpool, on the eve of the abolition of the British slave trade.

Ports and People of the British Slave Trade

Although many provincial or minor ports sent ships to Africa for slaves, the British trade was dominated by London, Bristol, and Liverpool (as illustrated in Figure 2.6). London led the trade in its earliest years, and, although its share of the trade dipped sharply after 1730, the capital continued to play a significant part in slave commerce throughout the eighteenth century.[30] The great regional port of Bristol, which had been a major importer of tobacco, sugar, and other colonial goods since the 1660s, entered the slave trade in the 1680s.[31] Bristol overtook London as the premier slaving port in the 1730s, ceding that position to Liverpool in the 1750s. Liverpool had not entered the slave trade until the late 1690s, but the port city's share of the trade grew very rapidly, and by 1780 it had become the largest slaving port in the Atlantic world.[32] In the late 1700s, more than 100 ships were clearing the port for Africa every year. In the decade preceding abolition, that figure rose to 123–30 annually.[33] In all, almost 5,000 slave ships cleared Liverpool for Africa, and citizens of the city and its environs owned most of these vessels.

After 1712, the slave trade lay almost entirely in the hands of private traders, who fitted out and crewed ships at their own cost. Putting a ship into the African trade was an expensive business, necessitating expenditure on the vessel and its fittings, the hire

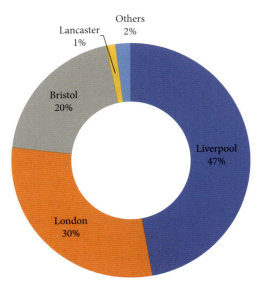

Figure 2.6 The proportions of the 10,480 TSTD slaving voyages undertaken by ships from Britain originating in London, Liverpool, Bristol, and Lancaster: ports with a smaller share of the trade are not identified. (Data derived from https://www.slavevoyages.org/voyages/mOu2kS5A (accessed 21 March 2022)).

of a crew of thirty or forty men, the provision of foodstuffs for both crew and captives, and the purchase of a cargo of trade goods to be exchanged for the latter. It has been estimated that, in the mid-eighteenth century, the cost of putting a Liverpool slave ship to sea would have been around £4,000. This figure rose to as much as £12,000 by the end of the century.[34] Most voyages were funded by syndicates of part-owners—investors who put up a share of the necessary capital to buy or hire, and then fit out, a ship in return for a share of the profits from the venture. Syndicates like these also ensured that the cost of failure, should a ship founder or be captured by an enemy nation, would be spread too. The management of a voyage was usually assumed by one of the partners in the venture, who was known as the ship's 'husband', or agent. David Richardson has traced the names of probable agents for almost 2,000 Bristol voyages between 1698 and 1807, and just 53 agents were responsible for organizing almost three-quarters of all voyages made by Bristol ships in the eighteenth century. The leading men in this group, John Anderson, John Fowler, James Laroche, James Rogers, and Noblet Ruddock, made up the core elite of Bristol agents, with Laroche managing no less than 132 voyages.[35]

Key investors in slaving voyages came from a wide variety of backgrounds, and included merchants, tradesmen, and shipmasters. Although there are many documented instances of individuals risking their savings on a one-off African venture, most of the voyages clearing from the major ports were funded by core groups of regular investors. Some of these men and women grew extremely wealthy from the slave trade, and families such as the Pinneys in Bristol and the Crosbies, Heywoods, and Tarletons in Liverpool saw their fortunes rise very markedly as a result of profits from slaving ventures. These families used their wealth to support consumer spending on a grand scale, and to fund the architectural gentrification of their home cities.[36] In recent years, several excellent histories have appeared, focusing on the wealthy elites at the heart of the slave trade in both Bristol and Liverpool.[37] These were not the only direct beneficiaries of that trade, however. As explored in Chapter 7, the British manufacturing industries also profited, creating artefacts such as brasswares, iron bars, and textiles, for use as trade goods. Large numbers of people were also employed in building and servicing slave ships, and, of course, in crewing them.

Reading *Southwell Frigate*

Thus far, this chapter has focused primarily on documentary history. Nicholas Pocock's pen-and-ink drawing of the Bristol vessel *Southwell Frigate* (Figure 2.7) offers a further way to explore British slave shipping.[38] This drawing is thought to have been made in 1760, during the Seven Years War. At first sight it seems to be a straightforward celebration of a well-armed Bristol privateer—such an image being, as Madge Dresser puts it, 'an emblem of British patriotism'.[39] But in the 1740s *Southwell Frigate*

Figure 2.7 *The Southwell Frigate Trading on ye Coast of Africa*, Nicolas Pocock, *c*.1760. Bristol Museum and Art Gallery, M669.

had also served as a slaver, and the upper register of Pocock's drawing captures the vessel in this role, fully rigged off the African coast. Numerous members of the crew, though no Africans, can be seen on deck. *Southwell Frigate* is depicted again, this time in a view of the stern, in the bottom centre of the painting. On the lower right is a panel showing the vessel at anchor. A well-dressed Englishman, no doubt the master, is being carried to shore from one of the ship's smaller boats. The crew are unloading goods to be used in trading for slaves: the word *Bristol* is printed on the side of the rectangular box (possibly a gun box) held aloft by an African carrying the goods away. The place name is a reminder that the towns and cities engaging in slave trading were also supplying trading goods for that enterprise. The panel on the right-hand side shows three naked, chained captives being loaded into a boat for transfer to *Southwell Frigate*, on whose deck numerous figures can already be seen crowded together. No forts or castles are depicted here, and the Englishmen shown in the picture are negotiating directly with an African partner. Dresser's reading of the three figures observing the slave transfer in the left-hand panel is particularly interesting in this context:

> What makes this such a significant grouping is the relationship of these three figures to one another. The man shaded by the parasol is a cabouceer (a trader imbued with the authority of the local ruler) or possibly even a headman or petty king. He is clasping the hand of the Englishman with one hand and has placed his other hand on the Englishman's shoulder in a gesture which denotes an equitable and friendly relationship between the two. This idealized image of African and Englishman as equal trading partners was not a common one in the period but it is not unique. What this picture admirably demonstrates is that pro-slavery views could coexist alongside relatively favourable characterizations of African trading allies.[40]

The son of a seaman, Pocock (1740–1821) was born in Bristol and went on to captain numerous merchant voyages to the West Indies before becoming a professional marine artist. A prolific and highly regarded painter of naval actions, Pocock also made studies of numerous Bristol merchant vessels, including *Southwell Frigate*. Although registered as a Bristol ship, the 343-ton *Southwell Frigate* (built in 1741) was not constructed for the slave trade but had been captured as a foreign prize at sea. The vessel then made two documented slaving voyages, the first in 1746 and the second in 1748.[41] Details of the first voyage itinerary are sketchy, though the main port of captive sale was certainly Jamaica. On the second trip, *Southwell Frigate* sailed to Malembo (Cabinda, Angola), and from there, with some three hundred Africans on board, to Virginia. The master on both voyages was the same man: John Brackenridge. The key investors in the 1746 voyage were all local merchants: Michael Becher, Martin French, James Laroche, and William Miller. As noted earlier, Laroche was the leading slave ship agent in eighteenth-century Bristol and managed some 132 voyages in that role.[42] Michael Becher was another slaving agent, overseeing twenty-five Bristol voyages, and was principal owner of the 1748 *Southwell* venture. The Becher and Laroche families lived alongside other members of Bristol's slave-trading elite in fashionable Queen's Square, at the heart of the city. William Miller, part-owner of the 1746 venture, served as master on numerous vessels managed by James Laroche. The small, tight-knit syndicate of investors in *Southwell Frigate* is typical of its era.[43] Pocock himself lived (from 1756) in nearby Prince's Street.[44]

Despite the fact that Pocock was only 20 years old when the *Southwell Frigate* sketch is thought to have been executed, his work already seems to have attracted interest. The drawing is one of three very similar studies by this artist depicting slave ships trading off the coast of Africa; the others being pen-and-ink drawings of *Jason* [45] and *Blandford Frigate* (see Figure 5.12).[46] Michael Becher also managed the *Jason* voyage, and, while it is tempting to think that the Becher family commissioned the three works, the single voyage of *Blandford* was managed by another person: James Pearce. The master of both *Southwell* voyages, John Brackenridge, also captained the final (1752) voyage of Becher and Co.'s *Jason*, and *Blandford Frigate's* sole slaving voyage in 1744. It may be that Brackenridge himself commissioned these paintings from the young artist, but this cannot be established with certainty. Whatever the case, the slaving voyages of all three vessels principally took place in the 1740s, when the artist himself was a child. These are not *life* sketches of the African trade then, but, like the *Swallow* punch bowl discussed in my introduction (see Figure 1.3), these artworks visualize—and celebrate—a reality unseen by their creators.

The Abolition of the British Slave Trade

Slavery brought huge profits to some, and employment to many, but others vigorously opposed it. The British abolition movement was founded in 1787, spearheaded by Thomas Clarkson and (in Parliament) by William Wilberforce.[47] As James Walvin has argued, it is important to see their achievements in the context of a broader series of social changes sweeping across Europe and its colonies towards the end of the eighteenth century.[48] Put another way, abolition would have been literally inconceivable before 1770, but in 1787 the British anti-slavery lobby found itself in the right place at the right time. The 1770s and 1780s were decades of social unrest and radical politics in Europe, and important changes were also afoot in the American and Caribbean plantations on which most enslaved Africans laboured. Many plantation owners recognized that slave ownership was morally questionable, even as they claimed it to be economic necessity. Ever fearful of slave insurrections, and seeking for ways to justify their actions, those with a vested interest in slavery argued that the practice was defensible on racial (not simply economic) grounds. Racism, segregation, and ever-more brutal surveillance regimes resulted. The British abolition movement grew up in part because the evidence emerging from the Caribbean and the now independent United States was becoming impossible to ignore. Some of these reports directly concerned conditions and events on the Middle Passage; the case of the slave ship *Zong*, discussed in Chapter 1, is a good example here.

40 MATERIALIZING THE MIDDLE PASSAGE

The abolition movement did not initially seek to put an end to slavery itself. Rather, its leaders reasoned that the way to achieve emancipation was first to bring about the demise of the *trade* in slaves from Africa to the Americas. To this end, they produced pamphlets and tracts spelling out the horrors of the Middle Passage and submitted petitions to Parliament. In 1788 Parliament responded by setting up a committee to investigate the British slave trade. The evidence gathered by this and subsequent committees is central to the present book and is introduced in Chapter 3. An early outcome of the inquiry process was the 1788 Dolben Act, regulating for the first time the number of slaves carried on British ships.[49] Almost a decade passed, however, with many false starts and setbacks, before Parliament finally voted to end the Atlantic slave trade. The new law came into effect on 1 May 1807, from which date it was illegal for British ships to transport African captives.[50]

West Africa at the Time of the Slave Trade

While the complex economic systems of the slave trade touched countless people across Africa, most captives were shipped from major trading centres located on the Gold Coast (Ghana), the Bight of Benin (Togo and Dahomey), the Bight of Biafra (the Niger Delta and Cameroon), and in West Central Africa.[51] Sierra Leone and the Windward Coast were also important procurement zones for British ships. These zones are all indicated on the map in Figure 2.8. The estimates for the numbers of Africans carried away from each zone shown in Table 2.1 are derived from the Trans-Atlantic Slave Trade Database (TSTD), for more information on which see Box 1.1.

As Table 2.1 indicates, the Gold Coast was very important to the British trade (see Figure 2.9). Most of the ships arriving here came from London and Bristol, the principal ports of origin for British vessels before 1760. The Portuguese were almost always the dominant presence in the Bight of Benin, but Britain played a major role here too. British-based vessels dominated trade with the Bight of Biafra, with many of the ships trading at Bonny and Old Calabar originating from Liverpool, the major slaving port for English ships after 1760. During the latter part of the eighteenth century, British departures from the Bight of Biafra exceeded those from both Benin and the Gold Coast. The extent of the British slave trade in West Central Africa is often under-appreciated, but in fact the number of captives taken from this region exceed that from the Bight of Benin, and Loango and Cabinda were particularly important procurement zones for Liverpool-based vessels.

I will now turn to these regions in more detail, beginning with the Gold Coast and its fort-based trade. The Portuguese had first established a fortified trading post on the Gold Coast in 1482, ten years before Columbus reached the Americas.[52] This was São Jorge da Mina (or Elmina), which would much later be occupied by the British. Between 1631 and the 1890s, British companies built or occupied more than fifty outposts in West Africa—many of them along the 300-mile stretch of the Gold Coast.[53] These European outposts were, to borrow a phrase from John Osei-Tutu, tenuous possessions: built on land controlled by African rulers, and with their trading activities dependent upon careful

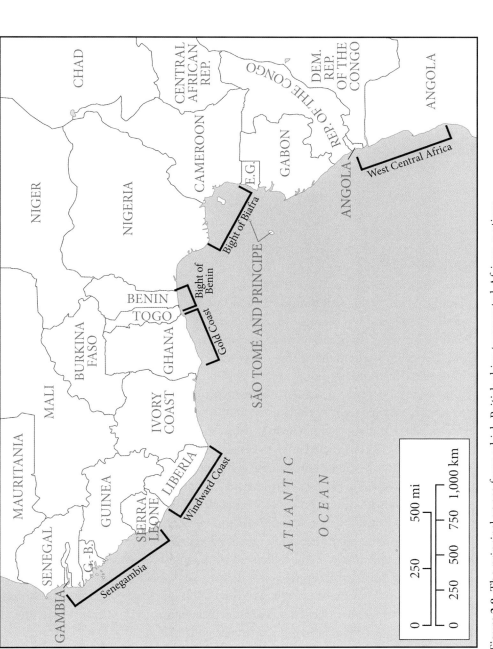

Figure 2.8 The principal zones from which British ships transported African captives.

Table 2.1 Estimated numbers of captives carried away from Africa (by region) on ships originating in Britain between 1562 and 1807

Region	Estimated total embarkations
Senegambia and offshore Atlantic	122,225
Sierra Leone	120,125
Windward Coast	138,351
Gold Coast	404,225
Bight of Benin	209,590
Bight of Biafra and Gulf of Guinea islands	730,150
West Central Africa and St Helena	366,220
SE Africa and Indian Ocean Islands	11,427
Other Africa	697,170
TOTAL	2,781,663

Source: Figures derived from TSTD, https://www.slavevoyages.org/voyages/mOu2kS5A (search generated 15 August 2022).

localized negotiations and the payment of often considerable dues.[54] Inland from the forts themselves, which were built right up against the shoreline, lay a series of small, independent African states, which controlled (and so made revenue from) the trade routes from the interior of West Africa along which slave traders brought their captives. For much of the eighteenth century, the most powerful of the hinterland states bordering the Gold Coast was Asante, which periodically engaged in warfare with its neighbours and rivals.[55] All of these states struggled to control the trade routes that brought gold, ivory, and slaves to the European buyers waiting at the forts.

The forts themselves were generally positioned overlooking important harbours. Firepower, in the form of cannon, allowed the forts to exclude or penalize ships that did not have a legal right to trade there. In this way, companies, or nations, enforced their exclusive trading rights. The first British fort was Kormantin, built in 1631, but the majority were constructed after 1672, under the RAC.[56] The company established its main base at Cape Coast Castle (Fetu) and built many more Gold Coast fortifications, including Komenda, Anomabu, Tantumquerry, Winneba, Accra, Dixcove, and Sekondi. (Figure 2.10 shows a contemporary etching of eleven English, Dutch, and Danish forts, based on plates in Bosman's *New and Accurate Description of the Coast of Guinea*.)[57] Archaeological work on the European fort sites has been relatively limited, but extensive work has been undertaken on the settlement surrounding Elmina, and the findings from this site will be discussed at several points in this book.[58] Fieldwork has also been carried out at Komenda and more recently at Kormentin/Fort Amsterdam and the British-owned Fort Metal Cross (Dixcove), and its settlement quarter.[59] There is currently an ongoing project at Christiansborg (now known as Osu).[60]

Following common practice among European monopoly trading companies in Africa, the RAC maintained a permanent staff at its forts (known as 'castles'), which served both as trading centres and as holding places (*barracoons*) for captives awaiting sale to incoming vessels.[61] Many captive Africans were brought to the forts from smaller, inland or up-river, trading posts. The British referred to these as factories,

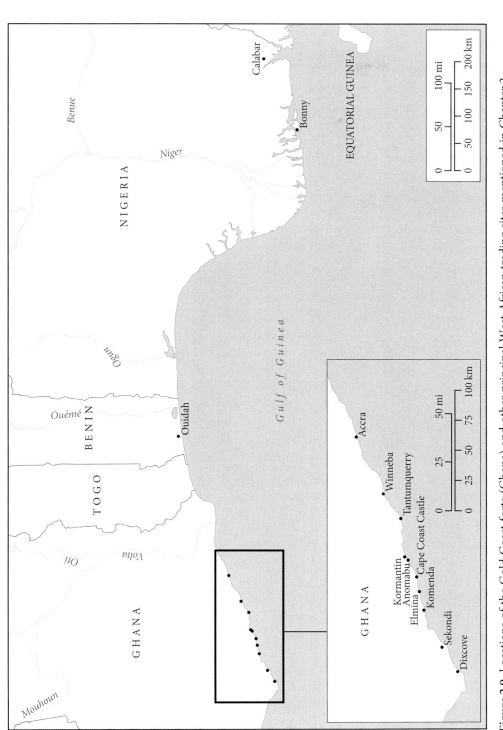

Figure 2.9 Locations of the Gold Coast forts (Ghana) and other principal West African trading sites mentioned in Chapter 2.

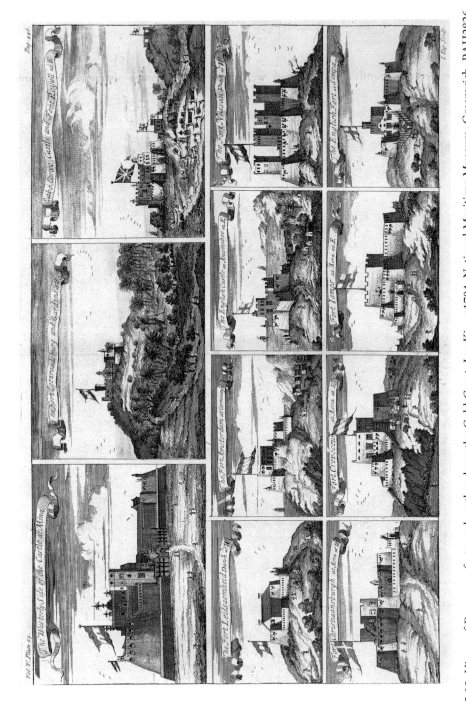

Figure 2.10 Views of European forts and castles along the Gold Coast. Jan Kip, c.1704. National Maritime Museum, Greenwich, PAH2826.

and to the company business agents who staffed them as factors. The fort/factory system helped monopoly companies to minimize the time that their ships lay at anchor in African harbours. Crews, not captives, were the consideration here: for many European sailors, a lengthy sojourn on the West African coast was the equivalent of a death sentence. Company ships arriving at a fort or factory holding large numbers of captives could acquire captives quickly by negotiating with the factor, then leave the coast relatively speedily. But captives were not always readily available, entailing delays, and necessitating journeys to other company forts. In areas where the company did not maintain forts (such as the Windward Coast and Sierra Leone), RAC captains traded directly with African merchants, engaging thereby in 'ship trade' rather than 'fort trade'.[62] Before 1698, the masters of interloping vessels, who had no option other than to trade directly with African suppliers, were also engaged in ship trade and could be on the coast for many months before meeting their quota. After 1698, when the slave trade was opened to all-comers, fort trade and ship trade existed side by side, and many venture syndicates and masters built up close working relationships with private slave dealers, some of whom created sizable personal empires.[63]

By the 1720s, the expansion of the slave trade and the decline of monopoly companies like the RAC were already lessening the need for forts.[64] Many of the British forts had fallen into disrepair, and the financially stretched RAC struggled to maintain the buildings, even with the aid of government subsidies granted from the 1730s.[65] After the dissolution of the RAC in 1752, Parliament established the *Company of Merchants Trading to Africa* to oversee the forts, and significant modifications were made to certain of them, including the creation of the large subterranean 'slave holes', which are today the best-known features of the Gold Coast forts.[66] The slave containment areas at Cape Coast Castle, which remained the centre of British Gold Coast operations, were enlarged, and the company also built a new fort at Anomabu in 1753.[67] These changes were effected to increase a growing demand among independent traders who had also begun to explore regions further to the east.

In 1701, after the French had won the coveted *asiento* (contract) to supply slaves to Spain, European attention began to focus more tightly on the region of the Bight of Benin, which became known as the Slave Coast.[68] The English had constructed their first factory at Ouidah in 1681, and three years after this built a site later known as William's Fort.[69] By the late 1600s, Ouidah had become a major focal point for the slave trade. The number of captive departures from this and neighbouring ports rose dramatically at this time. Between 1675 and 1725, more than 40 per cent of all those taken forcibly from Africa departed from the Bight of Benin, and the majority of these were shipped from Ouidah itself; but, following incorporation into the Kingdom of Dahomey, the number of captives leaving Ouidah dipped, and never rose to the same heights again.[70] Like their counterparts on the Gold Coast, the rulers of Ouidah achieved their dominant position in the slave trade thanks to their ability to control trade routes coming into their territory from regions much further inland. Many of those who were sold at Ouidah had arrived there after lengthy overland journeys. The same was true, of course, for captives held at entrepots throughout West Africa.

Ouidah was so named by Europeans because until 1727 it was part of the Hueda kingdom, the capital of which lay at Savi, a few kilometres further inland.[71] Ouidah was the region's only major point of departure on a coastline that, like many parts of West Africa, lacked natural harbours. Ships of all nationalities could come and go in the open roadstead as they pleased: but, in the absence of harbours, slave ships needed seagoing canoes and experienced canoemen (generally hired on the Gold Coast) willing to brave the pounding surf and gain access to the shore. The vast majority of the personnel staffing the establishments built here by the French, British, and Portuguese were gromettoes (hired or enslaved Africans): in the 1700s the English fort was manned by 20 white men, and 100 gromettoes and slaves.[72]

As Robin Law has stressed: 'In Ouidah there was never any question that the European establishments were in the final analysis subject to local control, rather that representing independent centres of European power.'[73] Savi, furthermore, remained central to the conduct of trade: by 1716, the French and English had established lodges at Savi and negotiated for captives from these: Ouidah at this point was effectively a place of storage (for trade goods) and transit. In 1727, the Hueda kingdom was conquered by Dahomey, and Savi was destroyed, but the coastal town retained the name Ouidah and, under Dahomian rule, was a major centre of the Atlantic slave trade. Trade was now focused at Ouidah itself, with ships gaining the right to trade by paying customs in the form of trade goods to a local official (the Yovogan) based there. As explored later in the book, valuable archaeological work has been undertaken at Savi, the pre-Dahomian Hueda capital,[74] but very limited excavation has been undertaken at Ouidah.[75]

Until the 1780s, Ouidah remained the pre-eminent slaving outlet in West Africa. By 1750, however, the British and other European traders were already showing an increasing interest in Bonny and Old and New Calabar, located in the Bight of Biafra. Overall slave exports from the Bight of Biafra began to outnumber those from the Bight of Benin in the 1770s, with the massive rise in departures appearing to coincide with the rise to power of the Aro, a people from the Niger Delta region.[76] The Aro, who originally came from the town of Arochuku, had built up extensive commercial networks in the interior of south-eastern Nigeria, and now dominated the region's slave trade. Shipments from Biafra rose in tandem with the increasing involvement of ships from Liverpool in the region, especially after 1780, and the Bight of Biafra remained of crucial importance to the Liverpool-based slave trade until 1807.

New World Destinations: Disembarkation Points for British Captives

The TSTD data set contains information on the New World disembarkation points for more than 80 per cent of the saltwater captives who survived a Middle Passage on British ships.[77] Table 2.2 provides a summary; see also Figure 2.11.

For much of the seventeenth century, demand for slave labour in the British colonies was at its highest in the Caribbean, where, following the settlement of Barbados (1627), Nevis (1628), and Monserrat and Antigua (1632), labour-intensive sugar-cane cultivation was widely adopted. By 1655, when Oliver Cromwell's men wrested Jamaica from Spain and secured the dominance of the English in the Caribbean, sugar had already become the economic mainstay of the British territories. As plantations emerged across the island landscape, the use of indentured labour declined and reliance on slave labour increased. Until 1680, many of the captives arriving in the British Caribbean to feed this growing demand were transported in British-owned ships and disembarked at Barbados.[78] After this, Jamaica became the principal point of entry, with Barbados and the British Leeward islands taking a lesser but still important role. Figures for the number of captives arriving in Jamaica during the eighteenth century are simply staggering.[79] It should be noted, however, that many were then re-exported, making a second journey by sea either to different Caribbean islands or (in smaller numbers) to mainland North America.

North American settlers made use of African labour from the earliest stages of colonization.[80] Until the 1650s, the Dutch dominated the trade in slaves here, but, after this date, British and North American merchants met the demand. As Table 2.2 indicates, the proportion of captives carried to North America on British ships was relatively low. This was because North American owners generally acquired their African-born slaves independently. At first this was via the Caribbean, trans-shipping newly arrived captives to the mainland from Barbados and other key ports of entry. As early as the 1640s, however, merchants in colonial

Table 2.2 Principal disembarkation points for captives carried away from Africa on voyages originating in British ports between 1562 and 1807

Broad region	Specific region	Estimated no. of captives embarked	Estimated no. of captives disembarked
British West Indies	Jamaica	1,003,387	864,820
	Barbados	331,716	274,792
	St Kitts	128,500	106,876
	Grenada	126,923	112,043
	Antigua	115,310	97,220
	British Guiana	71,793	65,444
	St Vincent	58,010	52,033
North America	South Carolina	126,558	108,360
	Virginia	92,680	75,897
	Maryland	23,393	19,102
	Georgia	7,499	6,555
	Florida	1,765	1,486
	North Carolina	1,308	1,130

Source: https://www.slavevoyages.org/voyages/mOu2kS5A (search generated 19 August 2022).

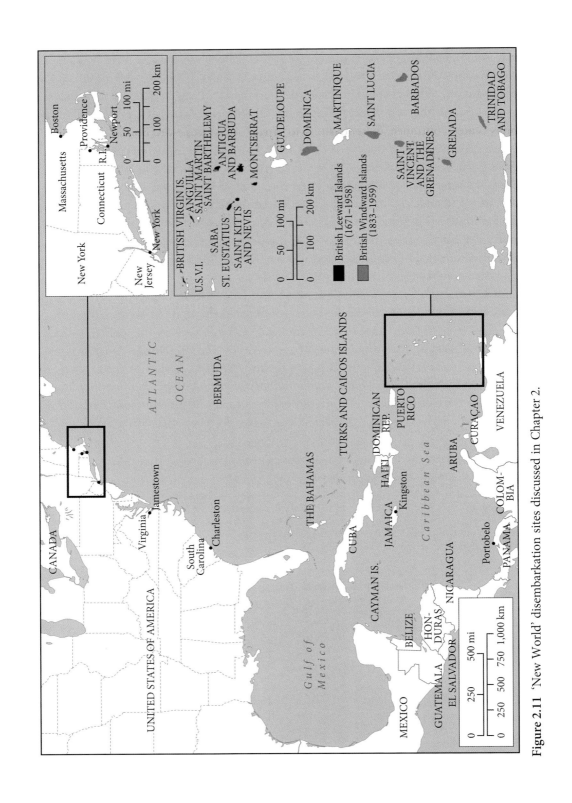

Figure 2.11 'New World' disembarkation sites discussed in Chapter 2.

New England began to express an interest in importing slaves directly from Africa. Between 1698 and the outbreak of the American War of Independence in 1775, a flourishing independent slave trade built up in the ports of Boston, New York, Newport, and Providence. By the mid-1700s, Newport (on Rhode Island) had become a major slaving port, selling captives mainly to buyers in the southern states of the USA and the Caribbean. Following independence from Britain, the Unites States continued to send ships to Africa for slaves. Key ports of this era included Newport, Boston, and Charleston. In the British Caribbean, meanwhile, Barbados similarly developed a significant independent slave trade (especially before 1720): some 11 per cent of captives arriving in Barbados did so on ships based on the island.[81]

The TSTD project has facilitated increasingly fine-grained studies of demographic trends in the trade in West African slaves, and it is now very clear that dominant channels can be identified along which people flowed across the Atlantic and entered the British Caribbean. Thus, the data set indicates that two out of three captives entering Jamaica before 1720 came from the Bight of Benin and the Gold Coast, while, from 1720 to 1807, up to 40 per cent of arrivals came from the Bight of Biafra.[82] A large proportion of captives entering Barbados, meanwhile, came from the Gold Coast and the Bight of Biafra.[83] The Windward Coast (stretching southwards from Sierra Leone) also supplied a significant number of captives to the British Leeward Islands, particularly in the later years of the trade.[84]

Rapid advances in the study of DNA in modern populations are providing further insights into these patterns, and sometimes complicate the picture provided by TSTD. Thus, while the TSTD data set suggests that the Bight of Biafra was the dominant procurement zone for captives entering Jamaica, a recent DNA project has revealed the primary importance of the Gold Coast to the maternal ancestry of the Jamaican population, demonstrating that women from this region gave birth to the highest proportion of children born into slavery in Jamaica. This finding, interestingly, supports the assertion, often made in the eighteenth-century literature, that the majority of saltwater slaves resident in Jamaica were 'Coromantees' from the Gold Coast.[85] The apparent discrepancy between the TSTD and DNA data can perhaps be resolved by acknowledging that many of the Africans who entered Jamaica were quickly transhipped elsewhere, and that more Africans from the Bight of Biafra were sold off the island than was the case for Africans from the Gold Coast. Whatever the answer here, Newman and co-workers' Jamaican DNA study is a fitting place to conclude this brief overview of the British slave trade. It is a model of interdisciplinary research, combining the science of origins with careful use, and critique, of primary historical sources. It also foregrounds the increasingly important role that science is playing in the study of both the history and the contemporary legacies of the slave trade: a point picked up again—and not without some concerns about the essentializing tendencies of genomic historicization—in my concluding chapter.

Notes

1. TSTD 98836–8.
2. The first English voyage to Guinea took place in the 1530s (Thomas 1997: 154). Between 1553 and 1565 nine voyages undertaken by English merchants (including those of Hawkins) were recorded in Hakluyt's 1589 collection of voyage narratives. A good introduction to these and other sixteenth-century Guinea voyages can be found in Hair (1997a,b). See also Habib (2008: 66–118) for Tudor voyages, and archival data concerning Africans in London before 1603. Hakluyt (1965 [1589]: 97) records that in 1554 *John Evangelist* brought 'certain black slaves' back to England on the return voyage from Guinea. However, as Hair and Alsop (1992: 56, n. 32) have pointed out, this pre-Hawkins reference to slaves is 'misleading (if ideologically significant), since the evidence of later voyages shows Africans returning from England and acting as agents for the English'. Merchants prior to Hawkins seem to have been more interested in melegueta pepper, ivory, and gold, than in slaves.
3. 1564: TSTD 98839–42. 1567: TSTD 998846–51.
4. Porter (1968: 57–8); Blakemore (2015). By the late fifteenth century, it was common practice for European monarchies to grant trading monopolies (to traders of their own nation) in West African locations.
5. Robert Rich, later Earl of Warwick, fronted the Company of Adventurers. He was both a royal favourite and the owner of a Virginia plantation. As Thomas notes (1997: 174), the desire for plantation labour no doubt prompted Rich's interest.
6. As early as 1607 there is a record of an English vessel carrying slaves from São Tomé to Elmina (Thomas 1997: 174–5). In 1629, Nicholas Crisp complained of the seizure of his ship *Benediction*, taken by the French with 180 captives on board (Thomas 1997: 175–6).
7. The life and fortunes of Crisp (1598–1666), who lost control of the company in 1644, are charted by Porter (1968). See also Thomas (1997: 175–8).
8. Porter (1968: 62); Thomas (1997: 176).
9. Crisp's syndicate had been denounced by Vassall and other rivals in 1649: Thomas (1997: 176).
10. For an account of a failed, London-based, private slaving venture undertaken by *Swan* in 1651 (TSTD 99025), see Appleby (1995).
11. Thomas (1997: 199); Pettigrew (2013: 22–3).
12. This was the first Adventurers' charter to reference the slave trade.
13. In total, TSTD lists 105 voyages by ships owned by the Adventurers. These voyages (the first in 1662 and the last in 1672) carried an estimated 27,489 individuals into slavery. https://www.slavevoyages.org/voyages/YJXX4sLI (search generated 19 August 2022).
14. As Borucki et al. (2015: 444) note, both the Royal Company of Adventurers and its successor, the Royal African Company (RAC), usually refused to deliver captives directly to the Spanish colonies. Instead, captives were sold through the company factories in Barbados and Jamaica. Using TSTD data, the authors estimate a total flow of 247,500 captives from British to Spanish jurisdictions.
15. James Fort, the key British trading post in the Gambia, was established in 1661. Some archaeological survey was undertaken here in the 1960s (Lawrence 1963: 250–61). A new project was initiated at the fort and its environs in 2004: see DeCorse et al. (2010).
16. The standard history of the RAC is Davies (1957), but see also Pettigrew (2013) and the excellent overview by Mitchell (2020: 9–50). For an assessment of the economic functioning and impact of the RAC, see Galenson (1986).
17. Galenson (1986: 14–21). On the RAC's struggle against interlopers, see also Carlos and Brown Kruse (1996) and Mitchell (2020: 51–91).

18. Thomas (1997: 202). TSTD records 352 RAC voyages between these dates, embarking an imputed 105,739 captives. Of these, 81,284 are estimated to have survived the crossing (https://www.slavevoyages.org/voyages/1QNOty2W (search generated 4 March 2022); includes voyages not originating in Britain).

19. The RAC was responsible for the establishment and maintenance of British outposts and forts in West Africa. The company was constantly in debt as a result: Thomas (1997: 202).

20. TSTD lists 91 documented RAC voyages between 1690 and 1700, carrying an imputed 32,040 individuals into slavery (https://www.slavevoyages.org/voyages/3GaYFSRU (search generated 19 August 2022); includes voyages not originating in Britain).

21. The 1698 *Act to settle the trade to Africa* (9 Will. 3c. 26) also imposed a 10% tax on imports to Britain from all locations on the African coast between Capo Blanco and Capo Monte. The levy on Guinea-bound cargoes was to be paid to the Director of Customs at the port from which a vessel cleared. The money would then (in theory at least) be passed on to the RAC.

22. Mitchell (2020) discusses the career, and ships, of the prolific London-based slaving merchant Humphry Morice, whose first ventures into the slave trade took place in the 10% era.

23. By 1731, the date of the last documented RAC voyage, the TSTD data set indicates that these totals had risen to 652 and 187,133 respectively (https://www.slavevoyages.org/voyages/RibGyfaC (search generated 19 August 2022); includes voyages not originating in Britain).

24. Harms (2002: p. xvii). In all, 8,821 of the 10, 480 British-based voyages documented in TSTD left Britain between 1700 and 1800.

25. Dale (2004: 49–50) sets out the provisions of the 1713 *asiento*. For the British *asiento* trade, and the operations of South Sea Company, see also Palmer (1986) and Borucki et al. (2015).

26. Dale (2004: 125–39) provides the details.

27. TSTD contains information on 118 South Sea Company slaving voyages, transporting an estimated 41,923 captives (https://www.slavevoyages.org/voyages/A4Vpo2HZ (search generated 19 August 2022); includes voyages not originating in Britain).

28. Bristol merchants pioneered a trade in slaves to Virginia, which had hitherto received few slaves from British ships: Thomas (1997: 245).

29. See Brown (2007: 37) for discussion of these developments.

30. See Rawley (2003: 18–38). As Rawley suggests, London's share in the eighteenth-century trade was greater than is sometimes suggested, and in overall terms London sent a third more ships to Africa than did Bristol.

31. The first documented Bristol voyage is TSTD 21049 (vessel name unknown); an unsuccessful voyage of 1686.

32. The first documented Liverpool voyage is that of a vessel of unknown name clearing Liverpool for Africa in 1696 (TSTD 21236).

33. Figures here are taken from Richardson (1994). As Richardson (1994: 75) notes, there is still much debate about the causes underlying Liverpool's success as a trading port.

34. Richardson (1994: 75).

35. Richardson (2001 [1985]: 16–17). For a study of the ultimately unsuccessful business of James Rogers, see Morgan (2003).

36. Morgan (2016) provides an excellent overview of the urban infrastructure of Bristol and Liverpool in the eighteenth century, exploring harbour and dock developments, and the townhouses and public buildings funded by investors in the slave trade.

37. David Richardson's seminal work *Bristol, Africa and the Eighteenth-Century Slave Trade to America* (published in four volumes between 1986 and 1996) remains the essential text for Bristol. Richardson's books cover the period 1698–1807. Dresser (2001) also provides an excellent social history of the port and its slave trading elite. See also Richardson et al. (2007).

38. See Dresser (2001: 54–8) for a discussion of representations of race in Pocock's paintings.

52 MATERIALIZING THE MIDDLE PASSAGE

39. Dresser (2001: 54). See Otele (2012) for a critique of the use of this painting in the Transatlantic Slavery Trade Gallery in the Bristol Industrial Museum (which closed in 2006 and reopened as M Shed in 2011).
40. Dresser (2001: 55).
41. TSTD 17160 and 17217.
42. Richardson (2001 [1985]: 29).
43. See Dresser (2000, 2001) for the interconnections between Bristol's merchant elite.
44. Dresser (2000: 30).
45. TSTD documents five voyages for *Jason*, or *Jason Gally*, between 1744 and 1752 (TSTD 17108, 17157, 17207, 12268 and 17319). The master on the last of these was John Brackenridge, master of both *Southwell Frigate* voyages.
46. TSTD 77559: a voyage undertaken in 1743.
47. Properly titled the Society for Effecting the Abolition of the Slave Trade (SEAST).
48. Walvin (2001: 67–76).
49. *An Act to regulate, for a limited Time, the shipping and carrying of slaves in British Vessels from the Coast of Africa* (28 Geo. III c. 54). The bill was brought before Parliament by Sir William Dolben, hence the common short-hand term Dolben Act. The Act became law in 1788.
50. The last slaving voyage from Bristol was undertaken by *Alert*, in February 1807 (TSTD 18272). Some Liverpool vessels cleared for passage before the May deadline departed as late as July and August 1807. *Kitty's Amelia*, whose voyage is followed in this book, was one of these. The ship left Liverpool on 25 July 1807. The final legal slave ship to clear Liverpool was *Eliza*, departing 16 August 1807 (TSTD 81195).
51. West Central Africa broadly encompasses the modern regions of Congo and Angola. An estimated 5.7 million people (45% of all those carried from Africa) began their journey here: Eltis and Richardson (2008a: table 1.7). The West Central African trade was strongly dominated by the Portuguese, and the majority of African peoples removed from this region crossed the Atlantic to South and Central America.
52. In the vast majority of cases, Europeans became tenants on West African soil, constructing buildings and conducting trade with the permission of local rulers and paying revenues (generally in the form of trade goods) to those elites. Europeans thus claimed sovereignty only inside their fort walls.
53. For an excellent summary overview of these tools of empire see DeCorse (2016).
54. Osei-Tutu (2018: 15).
55. Shumway (2011) is a study of one of their main rivals, the Fante,
56. DeCorse (2016: 172–5) covers the earliest forts.
57. Bosman (1705); for a discussion of this and other eighteenth-century illustrations of the Gold Coast forts, see Mann (2018).
58. For the earliest archaeological interventions, see Lawrence (1963). The more recent archaeological work undertaken at Elmina is summarized in DeCorse (2001).
59. For Komenda, see Calvocoressi (1975a). Investigations at Kormentin 1, the settlement adjacent to Fort Amersterdam, is discussed in Boachie-Ansah (2008, 2015); see also Agorsah and Butler (2008). For the recent work at Dixcove, see Biveridge (2018, 2020).
60. Engmann (2019) discusses preliminary findings from the community-based field project at Christiansborg. See also Merkyte and Randsborg (2012) for a summary of work on the Danish forts.
61. Harms (2002: 125–32); DeCorse (2016). The disgusting conditions in which slaves were kept in the 'slave holes' beneath European coastal forts were a significant factor in pre-embarkation deaths among those awaiting shipment to the New World. For further information on estimates of loss of African lives before embarkation (that is, at the point of enslavement, or in transit to the coast and in barracoons), see Klein and Engerman (1997: 38–9).

THE BRITISH SLAVE TRADE   53

62. The distinction was first made by Davies (1957). In the fort trade, slaves were obtained via RAC middlemen, employed at company settlements large and small. In the ship trade that characterized slaving at Bonny, Calabar, Cameroon, Upper Guinea, much of the Bight of Benin, and the Angolan coast, the British lacked permanent factory complexes. In these circumstances, ships' officers acted in effect as supercargoes, choosing where and from whom to purchase slaves, and working directly with African partners.

63. Some of these traders were African or Euro-African; others were European or American. Some Europeans, like the former ship's surgeon James Walker, who was based at Nunez (Sierra Leone), traded successfully in slaves for decades. See Mouser (2002: 47) for an account of Walker's dealings with Samuel Gamble, captain of *Sandown*.

64. Walvin (2001: 31).

65. See Brown (2007) for a detailed study of the relationship between Parliament and the RAC after 1713, and the granting of public subsidies for the Gold Coast forts. The latter commenced in 1730 and continued until the early nineteenth century.

66. Nelson (2014: 101) comments on the addition of slave containment chambers to some RAC-built British forts at this time. More information on the dimensions of the dungeons at Cape Coast can be found in Wellington and Oppong (2018: 257–60).

67. Nelson (2014: 102).

68. The river Volta marked the boundary between the Gold Coast and the Slave Coast. The latter extended from Togo to modern-day western Nigeria.

69. Law (2004: 33); for more on William's Fort see Law (2018).

70. Eltis and Richardson (2010: 121–2, maps 79, 80).

71. The name for Ouidah in the Fon language is Glehue: Law (2004: 19).

72. Law (2004: 39).

73. Law (2004: 36).

74. Kelly (2001, 2004, 2010); Norman (2009, 2010, 2014); see also Monroe (2014: 47–62).

75. Kelly (2009: 166–9) summarizes the work undertaken to date. Monroe (2014) is a vital source on the archaeology of the Slave Coast under Dahomey, and also considers the Hueda.

76. Eltis (2001: 34).

77. Eltis (2001: 35).

78. Eltis and Richardson (2010: 235, map 155).

79. Eltis and Richardson (2010: 234, map 154) estimate that numbers peaked at 16,000 new arrivals per year in the 1790s.

80. In 1619, settlers at Jamestown (Virginia) purchased '20 and odd Negroes' from a Dutch ship— the first documented account of the purchase of Africans by English New World colonists. For discussion of the Angolan origins of these Africans, and their removal from the Portuguese slave ship *San Juan Bautista*, see Newby-Alexander (2019). On their status as Atlantic creoles, see Berlin (1996: 276, n. 60).

81. Eltis and Richardson (2010: 235, map 155).

82. Eltis and Richardson (2010: 234, map 154).

83. Eltis and Richardson (2010: 235, map 155).

84. See Eltis and Richardson (2010: 247, map 163) for Antigua, for example.

85. Deason et al. (2012); Newman et al. (2013). Y-chromosome (patrilineal) DNA analysis has also been employed to determine the patrilineal ancestry of the modern populations of six Bahamian islands: see Simms et al. (2011). While this study clearly demonstrated that the strongest genetic affinities on most islands lie with West and Central Africa, the breadth of these relationships was extremely wide, reflecting not only the points of origin of captives entering the archipelago from Africa itself, but the transportation of both African-born and New World-born slaves into the region by British Loyalists following the American Revolution.

3

Voices from the Sea

Documentary Narratives of Middle Passage Voyages

Throughout this book, primary sources such as sea journals and parliamentary testimonies are excavated repeatedly for data about British slaving voyages undertaken between 1680 and 1807. To help set these documents in context, this chapter provides background information concerning how, and by whom, slave ships were crewed. It also highlights the different contexts in which first-hand accounts of the Middle Passage were produced, paying detailed attention to parliamentary inquiries conducted into the British slave trade between 1788 and 1792, and to publications sponsored by the nascent abolition movement during the same period. Finally, the chapter turns to the few surviving African narratives describing a Middle Passage on a British ship.

Each of the primary sources introduced in Chapter 3 will be encountered again, often many times. The sources are listed in the tables in this chapter, and **bold** is used throughout this book for references to author or commander, title or ship's name, and date, as appropriate. This strategy allows the reader to appreciate where, when, and in what context, the textual evidence employed in *Materializing the Middle Passage* was generated. Almost all the documents discussed in this chapter were produced by white British mariners of senior rank (masters, mates, surgeons), most of whom came from the middling social classes. To address why this is so, it is necessary to begin by examining the make-up of slaver crews, and to ask why some sailors, but not others, made records of their experiences at sea.

Slave Ship Crews

The muster rolls or crew lists survive for many (mainly eighteenth-century) British merchant voyages, and these reveal a great deal about the composition of crews on slave ships at that time.[1] Recent synthetic work by historians has also improved our understanding of the composition of slave ship crews, which varied according to the nature of the trade in different African regions.[2] Pulling all such information together, it becomes possible to offer a snapshot of the crew of a British slave ship (see Box 3.1 and, for a rare African depiction of one of the mariners who will have been such a familiar sight in the era of the slave trade, Figure 3.1).[3]

Materializing the Middle Passage: A Historical Archaeology of British Slave Shipping, 1680–1807. Jane Webster,
Oxford University Press. © Jane Webster 2023. DOI: 10.1093/oso/9780199214594.003.0003

Box 3.1 Slave Ship Crews

THE MASTER

The master (captain) had overall charge of the crew, the vessel, and all trading operations.

THE SPECIALISTS

First Mate

The First Mate was the second in command and would assume command if the captain was incapacitated or died. Mates were ranked by seniority, and some ships carried between two and four.

Surgeon

Prior to the Dolben Act of 1788, slave ships were not obliged to carry a surgeon, though most did.[a] Some surgeons were assisted by mates, or apprentices.

Supercargo

The supercargo supervised the influx and outflow of the ship's cargo (primarily trade goods on the outward leg; humans on the Middle Passage; sugar, rum, and other New World staples on the homeward leg) and recorded all business transactions relating to the voyage. Supercargoes were regularly employed on seventeenth-century vessels, but, in the eighteenth century, masters generally took over their role.

Boatswain

The boatswain was both a foreman over the crew, and a craftsman responsible for maritime maintenance duties, including care of the sails, rigging, anchors, and cables.

Carpenter

The carpenter was a highly trained craftsman, qualified (after a lengthy apprenticeship) to work as a shipwright ashore or as a carpenter at sea. Many slave ships also had one or more carpenter's mates, serving apprenticeships with the senior man.

Cooper

The cooper assembled, trimmed, and repaired the many wooden barrels and casks containing water and spirits. Coopers were employed on all transatlantic voyages but were especially important to slave ships because the captives (as well as the crew) required fresh water.

Gunner/Armourer
The gunner was responsible for the ship's armaments. The post was common before the early 1700s, but less frequent thereafter.

Cook
Cooks were at the bottom of the specialist hierarchy and generally poorly paid.

THE FOREMASTMEN
Foremastmen made up the bulk of the crew. They were so named because they berthed 'before the [fore]mast' (that is, they slept below the raised deck built over the fore part of the ship's main deck). The majority would have been able seamen—experienced sailors with basic maritime skills. Next in rank came a smaller number of less experienced ordinary seamen, and others serving apprenticeships. Slave ships sometimes also carried stewards, musicians, and other specialist crew.

BOYS
Merchant vessels usually shipped a small number of boys, generally aged between 11 and 13. These children often worked as personal servants to the captain and other officers. Many of them came from impoverished backgrounds, as did their counterparts on naval vessels.[b]

[a] The 1788 Dolben Act (28 Geo. III 54. Cap. 13) obliged every slave ship to carry at least one qualified surgeon, who must be able to prove that he had passed a recognized examination. Surgeons had been active in the African trade from its outset (see, e.g., Alsop 1990 on sea surgeons between 1553 and 1660), but the Dolben Act made their presence on slave ships a legal obligation for the first time.
[b] See Pietsch (2004) for a study of boys who joined the British navy during the Seven Years War.

Crew sizes on merchant ships were generally determined in relation to the tonnage (carrying capacity) of vessels. Put simply, the bigger the ship and its cargo hold, the more work there was to do. Thus *Thetis,* with the lowest tonnage of the case study vessels discussed below, had the smallest crew, and *Hannibal,* the largest vessel discussed in this chapter, the largest. But manpower requirements in the slave trade were also informed by the topography of the region of trade and by the differing demands of the fort and ship trades. Behrendt has used the TSTD data set to calculate that between 1750 and 1807 ships trading at Senegal, Gambia, and Sierra Leone mustered an average of fifteen to twenty-five hands, while those trading to Bonny recruited thirty-eight men.[4]

At this point, it will be helpful to look in a little more depth at the status and aspirations of the men crewing Guinea ships. What was their social standing, and what drew them to the African trade? Throughout the period considered in this book, there were two principal paths to a working life at sea: the Royal Navy and the merchant marine.[5] In the latter, though not in the former, social class was less of a barrier to advancement

Figure 3.1 Gold weight from the Gold Coast (height 62.5 mm). This rare example is perhaps intended to represent a sailor: the double-breasted, buttoned jacket and hat certainly recall the 'uniform' of contemporary mariners. British Museum, Greenwich, Af1949,08.2.

than might be assumed, and it was possible for a youth of humble origins to work his way up through the ranks from ship's boy to mate. Only when surmounting the final hurdle—the jump from mate to master—would a man require financial capital as well as experience.[6] Some would-be masters looked to their families or connections for that money; others found it by putting profits aside from earlier voyage earnings. Put simply, then, the merchant marine consisted in large part of men from modest backgrounds; in Ralph Davis's words 'sons and nephews of seamen, paying apprentices and paupers, farmhands attracted by the pay in peace and artisans by the prospects in war'.[7] They advanced by serving apprenticeships either on land, at sea, or both: thus carpenters, the most important of all the slave ship's specialists, served apprenticeships with shipwrights on land before putting to sea as carpenters' mates.[8]

Experience, then, counted more than class. The major exceptions to this generalization were well-connected masters (the sons of shipmasters or merchants, for example) with family or friends prepared to speed their advancement; surgeons, who tended to come from families wealthy enough to sponsor their expensive medical training; and supercargoes, who were often related to lead members of owning partnerships—thus literally keeping a ship's business transactions in the family. But why would any of these men choose to sail on slavers? The first point to emphasize here is that many seamen did not make a permanent choice between the navy or the merchant marine; they simply signed on for specific voyages, moving frequently

58   MATERIALIZING THE MIDDLE PASSAGE

between merchant vessels in different trades, and indeed between the merchant service and the navy.[9] There is some evidence to suggest that, by the late eighteenth century, many sailors (foremastmen in particular) had become reluctant to sign on for slaving voyages, but the carriage of African captives was not the principal sticking point here.[10] Rather, seamen were by this point more aware of the health hazards of African voyages, and of the notorious ill treatment meted out to Guinea crews by some masters.[11] Yet, despite knowing the hazards, men signed on anyway. Some, perhaps, had a desire to see the world; others were drawn by the prospect of shore time in Barbados or Jamaica. But the key factors putting ordinary sailors aboard slave ships were financial need, and the desire for increased experience. The latter, most commonly to be gained through a period of apprenticeship at sea, was the key to career progression, and ambitious men seized whatever work experience came their way.[12]

This brief background helps to explain why many foremastmen would spend some time on slave ships. But the factors drawing in the senior crewmen, particularly the masters, mates, supercargoes, and surgeons, were more complex. What brought these men to Guinea ships?

Much was required of the master of a slaver. As Hugh Thomas puts it, he was

> the heart and soul of the whole voyage, and had to be able, above all, to negotiate prices of slaves with African merchants or kings, strong enough to survive the west African climate, and to stand storms, calms and loss of equipment. He had to have the presence of mind to deal with difficult crews who might jump ship, and he had to be ready to face, coolly and with courage, slave rebellions.[13]

To fulfil these roles, a man needed a reasonable level of education and a good deal of prior sea experience. Most masters of slavers were therefore men in their thirties who had already spent many years at sea.[14] Many had gained their first sea experience in the West Indies trade, entering the slave trade as mates in their mid-twenties, and attaining their first command at around the age of 30.[15] The importance of experienced command was formally recognized in the 1788 Dolben Act, which required slave ships to carry a master who either had formerly captained a slave ship, or had 'served as chief mate or surgeon during the whole of two voyages, or either as chief or other mate during three voyages'.[16] Rates of pay for masters and other specialists were competitive, reflecting the difficulties of attracting experienced specialists and the risks the voyage entailed. Behrendt's detailed analysis of the wage scale in the Bristol trade during 1789–94 indicates that (before the bonuses discussed below) masters earned £5 per month, chief mates, surgeons, and carpenters £4, second mates £3 10s., coopers £3 6s, and third mates £3, while able seamen received 30s. per month—the latter wage being broadly comparable with other British overseas trades.[17]

The hazards of African voyages were such that few seasoned masters regarded slave trade captaincy as a *permanent* career move. Most slave ship captains made fewer than four voyages as master,[18] even though the handful of elite commanders—men with at least five captaincies to their name—could command very high wages and, with bonuses, earn up to £2,000 per voyage.[19] In general, a captain's aim was to make money, to quit the sea, and often to invest in the trade he had just left. It was not uncommon for seventeenth-century masters and supercargoes to own a share in the vessel or venture they commanded; Thomas Phillips, for example, was a part-owner of *Hannibal* (see Table 3.1); and James Barbot had a similar stake in *Albion Frigate* (see Table 3.2).[20] Part-ownership of slave ships by masters was less common in the eighteenth century,[21] but, in order to maintain as close a tie as possible between the men at sea and an owning group on land, most owners offered masters and specialist crew a series of potentially very lucrative bonuses. The rationale here was that these men would be more likely to perform well if they had a vested interest in the successful outcome of a voyage. Masters, first mates, and surgeons often carried a small stock of trade goods to and from Africa as a private venture. Similarly, many owning syndicates granted masters a right to one or two 'privilege slaves'—captives personally chosen in Africa and often branded with an officer's own initials. These captives were transported to the Americas at the owning group's expense and sold there by the master for personal profit. Privilege slaves could greatly supplement a master's income: thus James Fraser, master of the 1783 voyage of *Emilia*, landed 306 captives in 1784 and received two privilege slaves per hundred carried, selling these individuals (free of sale and import duty) for a total price of £340.[22] As explained in Chapter 10, some masters would put their privilege slaves into informal apprenticeships on board ship, in an effort to maximize their profits at the point of sale.

During the eighteenth century, it also became customary to pay masters a coast commission (or head money)—an agreed bonus for each healthy slave sold.[23] These commissions could be very lucrative, with masters earning £4 on every £104 of gross sales.[24] The 1788 Dolben Act formalized this incentive system, stipulating that masters who kept the slave mortality rate low on their voyages should receive fixed bonuses.[25] As a result of this package of incentives, a master putting to sea on his first slaver command in the later eighteenth century could reasonably hope to generate enough money from around four successful voyages to buy his own vessel, join a syndicate of investors, or, like Hugh Crow (see Table 3.2), retire in comfort. Some would go on to become wealthy merchants, often with a continuing interest in the slave trade.[26]

Slave ships thus had their attractions for masters. The same was true, looking down the ranks, for mates and supercargoes. Many of these men aspired to become captains.[27] Some set their sights considerably higher. One of these was William Boys, the son of a woollen draper.[28] Boys first went to sea in a merchantman commanded by a friend of his father, and later joined the Royal Navy as a midshipman. He subsequently sailed as mate on *Luxborough Galley*, a slave ship destroyed by fire during its passage home from the West Indies (see Figure 2.4). At the age of 28, Boys re-entered the navy, and this time stayed there. His humble origins did not impede his rise, and when he died in 1772, he was Lieutenant Governor of Greenwich Hospital, London.

As these anecdotes suggest, mates and supercargoes signing up for slavers might reasonably aspire to captaincy or better things. But what of surgeons? The life of a slave ship surgeon was nasty, brutish, and, all too often, short. The work was onerous and

60 MATERIALIZING THE MIDDLE PASSAGE

unpleasant, and mortality rates among medical men were appalling.[29] Indeed, the turnover rate for surgeons was higher than for all the other specialist positions in the slave trade.[30] Why would well-educated men, often, though by no means always, with some degree of expensive medical training under their belt, be attracted to this 'loathsome profession'?[31] As a generalization, the work tended to attract people in financial or personal difficulties or in need of funds to make further headway in the medical world.[32] Bristol surgeon Alexander Falconbridge, for example (Tables 3.3 and 3.6), lacked the capital necessary to set up a medical practice of his own, and hoped to make enough money to do so by working on slave ships. This was a potentially lucrative option: like masters, surgeons usually had a right to privilege slaves and/or head money.[33] Falconbridge was certainly granted a privilege slave (valued at £53) on his *Emilia* voyage, for example.[34] Most Guinea surgeons were hoping, like Falconbridge, to quit the sea after a few African runs, but some aspired to captaincy.[35] A few, like Patrick Renney, who served as a surgeon on both whalers and slavers, went on to successful careers in the Royal Navy.[36] The most eminent among this group was undoubtedly Thomas Trotter (see Table 3.6), who in 1790 recounted before Parliament the details of his 1783 voyage as surgeon on *Brooks*. Trotter had joined the navy as a surgeon's mate in 1779, at the age of 19. After his unhappy experience on *Brooks*—his sole slaving voyage—he returned to the Royal Navy, rising to the post of Physician of the Fleet.[37]

In summing up this brief look at slaver crews, it may be remarked that, in the most general terms, an ambitious man aspired to be the man above him in the chain of command, and slaving voyages were made if they were likely to forward that aim. Captains wanted to become owners, or investors backing voyages; mates and super-cargoes aspired to become masters; some surgeons also hoped to be masters, but the majority hoped that a brief spell at sea would further their medical careers on land. As for foremastmen, most wanted to make a little money, and gain the experience that might help them to become specialists. Many were illiterate or semi-literate, and their stories are often as hard to reconstruct as those of the Africans they carried into slavery.[38] The loudest voices from the sea, for all the reasons explored above, were those of their shipboard superiors.

Sea Journals

Detailed primary data relating to shipboard routines, outward cargoes, crewing arrange-ments, captive numbers, and crew and captive mortality rates are all central to the needs of this book. In this context, the foremost category of document concerning the Middle Passage is the daily journal, kept at sea as a voyage progressed.[39] Sea journals invariably provide more detail than any other type of slave trade narrative, and five have been selected as case studies for sustained analysis in this book (see Table 3.1). Among these, the journals of Walter Prideaux, John Newton, and Samuel Gamble stand out as providing the day-by-day *minutiae* that make it possible to build up a clear picture of shipboard routines on their voyages, particularly during the Middle Passage.

VOICES FROM THE SEA   61

Table 3.1 Key slaving logs and journals employed in this study

Account	Author	Ship and date	Edition used	TSTD
A Journal of a Voyage Made in the *Hannibal* of London Ann. 1693, 1694 ... By Thomas Phillips, Commander of the Said Ship	**Phillips**	*Hannibal* 1693–4	Churchill and Churchill (1732: vi. 173–239)	9714
Journal of Walter Prideaux, Supercargo, *Daniel and Henry* of Exeter	**Prideaux**	*Daniel* 1700	Tattersfield (1991	21298
The Journal of a Slave Trader (John Newton) 1750–4	**Newton**	*Argyle* 1750–1	Martin and Spurrell (1962: 1–62)	90350
Log of *Unity* 1769–71	**Norris**	*Unity* 1769–71	Unpublished MS: D/EARLE/1/4, Merseyside Maritime Museum	91567
A Journal of an Intended Voyage ... in the Good Ship *Sandown* by me Samuel Gamble, Commander	**Gamble**	*Sandown* 1793–4	Mouser (2002)	83502

Some journals were kept simply because masters and supercargoes were required, by their venture owners, to maintain them. Other men kept records of their voyage voluntarily, both as training exercises in navigation, and as mental aids for putative future voyages. This would appear to be the case with Walter Prideaux (***Daniel*** 1700), for example. His journal contains detailed descriptions and illustrations of the coast-line of Africa and documents at length the patterns and terms of trade in the regions he visited. Some masters and specialists in the African trade simply wrote things down for their own use, never intending their journals for publication. Numerous examples in this category have survived, passed down through families over the years and some-times bequeathed to libraries and museums. Two manuscript journals in my case study sample, those of Newton and Gamble, are in the care of the National Maritime Museum (NMM). Newton's fame as a hymn-maker and friend of the poet Cowper ensured that his maritime journal was edited for publication some years ago.[40] Samuel Gamble's journal, in contrast, remained unpublished until 2002.[41] A scattering of manuscript journals survive in museums and libraries throughout Britain. Unsurprisingly, most are preserved in collections in former slaving ports such as London, Liverpool, and Bristol. Robert Norris's unpublished *Unity* journal is one of these. Extracts from others have been published in syntheses of primary data on slave shipping, and elsewhere.[42]

Thomas Phillips on *Hannibal* (1693–4)

On 25 October 1693, the London ship *Hannibal* cleared London for Africa, in an RAC fleet making its way to Ouidah and the Gold Coast to trade for ivory, gold, and slaves. The master, Thomas Phillips, kept a journal at sea.[43] *Hannibal* successfully fought off a

62 MATERIALIZING THE MIDDLE PASSAGE

French man of war in the Canaries, and arrived off the Cape Verde islands on 2 December.[44] Phillips then began a slow progress eastward along the Gold Coast and on to Ouidah, where he arrived 20 May 1694, trading at first for gold and ivory, and latterly for slaves. By 27 July 1694, Phillips had purchased 684 captives, but he did not leave African waters until 25 August. *Hannibal's* Middle Passage crossing from São Tomé to Barbados stretched from 25 August to 4 November, and the mortality rate on this voyage was very high: more than 300 captives perished.[45] The ship began its return journey to London on 2 April 1695.

Little is known about Thomas Phillips beyond the details available from his own journal. This reveals that he was a native of Brecknock in Wales, and an experienced but unlucky maritime commander—his previous ship having been captured in the 'last war' with France.[46] Phillips was thereafter unemployed but was wealthy enough to join a syndicate of merchants headed by Sir Jeffery Jeffreys, an influential London-based member of the RAC. Phillips refers to himself as both co-owner and captain of *Hannibal*, which he purchased on Jeffreys's instruction. The vessel entered RAC service in 1693.[47] It is not clear whether Philips had captained a Guinea ship before this; indeed, it is not certain that he had been to Africa before.[48] Phillip's journal makes it clear that he never again made such a voyage: he was incapacitated by deafness following an illness contracted in Africa, and retired to Wales, never to put to sea again. In 2010, both Phillips and *Hannibal* were memorialized on a plaque erected at the Captain's Walk, a promenade close to Phillips's former home in Brecon. The town council's decision to commemorate Phillips in this way was widely criticized, not least because the text made no reference to the slave trade.[49] In 2020, the plaque was removed by unidentified objectors.[50] The ship made at least one further voyage to Guinea: an RAC-owned *Haniball* (under William Hill) departed London for Africa and Barbados in November 1696.[51]

Walter Prideaux on *Daniel and Henry* (1700)

In Chapter 2, it was explained that from 1698 a 10 per cent tax was levied on private traders by the RAC. Among the new breed of entrepreneur entering the slave trade in the era of this levy were two Exeter-based tobacco merchants named Daniel Ivy and Henry Arthur. They did so with *Daniel and Henry*, employed until this point in the tobacco trade with the American colonies.[52] On 24 February 1700, just two years after the slave trade had officially been opened to private investors, *Daniel and Henry* cleared Dartmouth for the Gold Coast, undertaking its first, and only known, slaving voyage under Roger Mathew.[53] The venture was financed by Daniel Ivy, Henry Arthur, and their fellow merchant James Gould.

Walter Prideaux, supercargo, kept a journal at sea. It was edited for publication by Nigel Tattersfield, who carried out extensive research on the background to the Dartmouth-based voyage, and on the slave trade from this and other minor ports.[54]

Prideaux came from Ermington to the west of Dartmouth, and from a family both ancient and financially secure. His father, Walter Jago, was a wealthy merchant, and his mother (who died at the child's birth) came from another influential merchant family dealing in New England timber and Caribbean sugar. His maternal kin also had strong plantation links. Walter Prideaux was thus a man with connections, and, setting to sea on *Daniel and Henry* at the age of 23, he served as supercargo to a master who was also his uncle. This family link probably helps to explain why a young man on what appears to have been his first long-haul voyage should be entrusted with such a senior post. The venture began well. Arriving off Alampi on 11 April 1700, Mathew traded successfully for 458 captives over the course of five months. *Daniel and Henry* remained in African waters until 6 September, finally departing from São Tomé for Jamaica on that day. The Middle Passage lasted until 19 November 1700, on which date *Daniel and Henry* entered Jamaica carrying 250 captives.[55] Walter Prideaux was to put to sea again, but not with great frequency. Over the next twenty years he made only five more voyages, including one to Barbados in 1717. Prideaux married in 1705, fathering thirteen children, and ended his days on dry land, as a maltster. He died in 1757.[56]

John Newton on *Duke of Argyle* (1750–1)

John Newton, sometime slave ship captain, later minister of the Church of England, composed many popular Christian hymns, including 'Amazing Grace'. As a result, he is undoubtedly the best known of the sailing men discussed in this chapter. Newton was born in London in 1725. His father, a master of ships in the Mediterranean trade, always intended to send his son to sea, but these plans were pre-empted in 1744 when the boy was impressed into service on HMS *Harwich*. After numerous adventures, Newton entered the slave trade at Madeira, as a foremastman on a slave ship bound for Sierra Leone. After a period of captivity in Sierra Leone, Newton returned to England on the African trader *Greyhound*. On board this ship he underwent an intense religious experience, which prompted him to embrace evangelical Christianity.

In 1748, still only 23 years old, Newton sailed as first mate on *Brownlow*, a Liverpool slaver bound for Africa and thence to Charlestown, South Carolina.[57] He went on to captain three slaving voyages, the first on *Duke of Argyle* and the second and third on *African*. All three are described in Newton's journal of 1750–4.[58] *Duke of Argyle* left Liverpool in August 1750, heading for the Bananas Islands, Sherboro, and the Windward Coast. Newton began bartering for captives in October and, by his own calculation, embarked 174 Africans in all. Eighteen of these people died before the ship had left Africa, setting sail for Antigua on 22 May 1751. A further ten deaths occurred on the Middle Passage, with the ship arriving in the Caribbean on 3 July 1751.[59]

Newton brought *Duke of Argyle* back to Liverpool in October 1751 and was soon back at sea; his next slaver, *African*, cleared Liverpool for Sierra Leone and the Windward Coast on 30 June 1752. The ship arrived off Sierra Leone on 12 August,

64   MATERIALIZING THE MIDDLE PASSAGE

and quickly began buying slaves. Newton calculated that he bartered for 207 Africans on this run, 167 of whom disembarked in St Kitts.[60] The Middle Passage crossing lasted from 26 April to 2 June 1753. *African* returned to Liverpool on 29 August 1753, putting to sea again just two months later, on 27 October. Once again, the ship was bound for the Windward Coast, arriving off Sierra Leone on 3 December. On this voyage, Newton acquired eighty-seven captives. They began their Middle Passage to St Kitts on 7 April 1754, arriving there on 21 May. Not a single person—captive or crew—died during the crossing. As Newton was later to point out to the Privy Council, this was largely because he had set out to acquire 220 captives but left Africa with only a third of that number.[61] *African* returned to Liverpool in August 1754, but Newton was to make no further slaving voyages. He will be encountered again in discussing the parliamentary inquiries of 1788–92.

Robert Norris on *Unity* (1769–71)

Unity, constructed in Liverpool in 1683, was owned by a syndicate of Liverpool merchants including John Dobson and James Moneypenny. The latter captained *Unity*'s sister ship, *Society*. Robert Norris, making his first voyage as master of a slaver, maintained a sea journal that survives among the Earle family papers in Liverpool Maritime Archives and Library.[62] On 21 July 1769, *Unity* and *Society* departed from Liverpool in tandem. Their first stop was Hellevoetsluis, Holland, where Norris shipped a large cargo of cowrie shells. *Unity* was heading for Ouidah, which lay within the cowrie 'currency' zone stretching from the eastern edge of the Gold Coast to the western Niger Delta, and the cowries would be used in bartering for captives.[63] *Unity* left Holland on 26 August 1769, arriving at Cape Coast Castle on 16 November, and at Ouidah shortly after. On 2 December 1769, Norris went on shore at Ouidah to trade at the 'English Castles', and no further details are recorded until 10 February 1770, when the captain notes that he travelled to Abomey (the capital of Dahomey) for an audience with the King. Norris's published memoir suggests that many of the captives taken on board *Unity* over this period contracted smallpox.[64] The ship finally left Ouidah on 28 April 1770 carrying 227 Africans. Norris then called at São Tomé to receive 200 more captives by transfer from *Society*. The Middle Passage crossing to Kingston, Jamaica, was a difficult one, and on four occasions (as discussed in Chapter 11) the captives on board attempted to rise against the crew. Seventeen Africans died during this crossing, which ended on 24 July 1770. The ship arrived back in Liverpool on 24 May 1771, after a voyage of 368 days. Just three months later, Norris and *Unity* were back at sea, heading once again to Ouidah. In total, Norris would make five voyages as master (see Table 3.6), ploughing his profits back into the trade by becoming part-owner of six ventures, some of which he captained himself. By the time of his death in 1791, Norris was a slaving merchant of some note. As a specialist in the Ouidah trade, he built up considerable expertise in the history of Damoney, and in 1789 published an account of the reign of Tegbesu (Bossa), who ruled Dahomey in 1740–4.[65] Like his contemporary John Newton, Norris testified in the parliamentary inquires of 1788–92; but Norris spoke on *behalf* of the slave trade, as one of three witnesses recruited in Liverpool to promote the interests of the town's slave trading elite. His parliamentary testimony is considered in more detail below.

Samuel Gamble on *Sandown* (1793–4)

In 1793, an investment syndicate of merchants, mariners, and shipbuilders charted the London-registered *Sandown* from its owners, Cameroon and Company, and sent it to Guinea to buy slaves.[66] Details of the journey of *Sandown* are preserved in a record maintained by the master of *Sandown*, Samuel Gamble (see Figure 1.1).[67] In the year the voyage began, Gamble was only 30 years old, but several strands of evidence suggest he had built up considerable experience of slaving voyages.[68] A Samuel Gamble appears on the muster roll for the October 1787 voyage of *Fisher* (master Isaac Nixon),[69] and TSTD also names a Samuel Gamble—surely the same man—as second captain of the Liverpool ship *Jemmy* crossing the Atlantic from the Bananas Islands to Montego Bay, Jamaica, in 1790.[70] In 1792, he captained *Lively* on its voyage to Sierra Leone.[71] Gamble thus seems to have had several years of African experience behind him by 1793, but the *Sandown* voyage was beset by sickness, crew unrest, and insurrection. Gamble records that he purchased 280 slaves in Africa, 242 of whom, by his own account, were brought to market in Kingston, Jamaica.[72] The Middle Passage crossing from Rio Nunez (Upper Guinea) to Barbados and Kingston lasted from 27 March to 30 April 1794.[73]

The protracted stay of *Sandown* on the African coast and the resultant deaths, sickness, and crew desertions meant that, by the time it reached Barbados, the vessel was, in the master's own words, in great distress.[74] Facing legal action by his own absconded crew, Gamble and his few remaining men took what was left of the captives to Jamaica. On arrival in Kingston, Gamble, now ailing with gout, was discharged to sick lodgings, and control of the vessel passed to Samuel Apsey. Gamble returned to England as a passenger on *Benson*, leaving Kingston on 24 July 1794. The ill-fated *Sandown,* making its own way home, was seized as a prize by the privateer *Guillotine* on 18 July and carried to Havana.[75] There, the vessel was driven on shore during a hurricane, and condemned.[76] Thus ended an entirely unsuccessful voyage beset by problems from start to finish. Despite this, Gamble went on to captain the Sierra Leone slaving voyage of *Brothers* in 1796, and a will in the Lancashire archives, made in 1799 before a voyage to Angola, suggests that he remained in the trade until the turn of the century.[77]

Gamble may have struggled as a master of *Sandown*, but his journal is a remarkable document, meticulous in terms of both its content and its execution. And, while *Sandown* was built in 1781, the voyage post-dates the 1788 Dolben Act, the first piece of legislation impacting upon slave shipping.[78] A further value of this text lies in *Sandown's* itinerary, which centred on the Windward Coast, to the west of the heartland areas of West Africa identified in Chapter 2.

66 MATERIALIZING THE MIDDLE PASSAGE

Memoirs Based on Sea Journals

A second category of Middle Passage writing comprises memoirs written, in most cases, some years after the events described, but almost certainly with the aid of sea journals. Again, I have selected a representative sample of important texts from this group to serve as case studies in this book (Table 3.2).

These accounts were produced for a wide variety of reasons, one of which was undoubtedly financial gain. Vessel owners and masters were willing to pay for up-to-date information about the African trade, and some of those engaged in slave trading kept sea journals in the hope of profiting from their publication. The Barbot family (discussed below) would have been keenly aware of the value of eyewitness information, and this is probably why all the seagoing members of that family kept journals. The demand for trading information also helps to explain the enormous popularity of narrative accounts of voyages to Africa, which first began to be published in England in the sixteenth century.[79] From that time onwards, publishers actively sought out new and previously unpublished accounts of travels to the West African coast, and several of the logs and journals discussed in this book first appeared in print as part of edited collections of early voyage narratives.[80] The writings of Jean (John) Barbot, which appeared in the early eighteenth century, are particularly important in this context.[81]

Table 3.2 Key slaving voyage memoirs employed in this study

Account	Author	Ship/short title and date	Edition used	TSTD
An Abstract of a Voyage to New Calabar River, or Rio Real, in the Year 1699	James Barbot	*Albion* 1699	Hair et al. (1992: ii. 681–700)	20173
An Abstract of a Voyage to Congo River, or the Ziar, and to Cabinde, in the Year 1700	James Barbot Jnr	*Don Carlos* 1700	Churchill and Churchill (1732: v. 497–522)	20207
On the Treatment of Slaves Aboard Ship	John Barbot	*Treatment* 1712*	Hair et al. (1992: ii. 778–83)	
The Unfortunate Shipwright, or, Cruel Captain, being a Faithful Narrative of the Unparalleled Sufferings of Robert Barker, Late Carpenter on Board the Thetis *Snow of Bristol*	Barker	*Thetis* 1754–5	Barker (1758)	17380
Oeconomy of a Slave Ship	Smeathman	*Oeconomy* c.1775	Coleman (2007)	75405?
Three Years Adventures, of a Minor	Butterworth	*Hudibras* 1786–7	Butterworth (1831)	81890
Memoirs of the Late Captain Hugh Crow of LiverpoolCrow	Crow	*Kitty's* 1807–8	Crow (1830)	82203

* Barbot's account of the treatment of slaves was first published in Churchill and Churchill (1732: v), but was probably written around 1711 or 1712, shortly before his death.

John Barbot and His Family (Writing 1678–1712)

The Frenchman Jean (John) Barbot was born in the Ille de Ré (La Rochelle) in 1655, growing up as part of a large, Protestant, mercantile family.[82] In his twenties, he gained a reputation as a commercial agent, and worked for La Rochelle traders with interests in Africa. He later went on to become a merchant in his own right. Barbot fled to England as a Huguenot refugee in 1685 and spent the remainder of his life building up a mercantile business first in London and later in Southampton. There is some evidence to suggest that he may also have dabbled in passing intelligence about French shipping to the British government. He died in Southampton in 1712, at the age of 57. Barbot's writings on Guinea are not, of course, the work of a Briton, but he lived in England for many years, and the level of detail he provides on the seventeenth-century slave trade is unparalleled.

Educated, intelligent, curious, and an enthusiastic lover of the written word, Barbot was engaged for much of his life upon a lengthy textual description of West Africa. The first version of this work was compiled, in his native French, between 1683 and 1688. Thwarted in his efforts to publish the manuscript, Barbot spent the best part of a decade translating his text into English, making many additions and enlargements as he did so.[83] The account was finally published in 1732, twenty years after his death.[84]

Historians have long mined Barbot's writings on Guinea for information on the Atlantic slave trade in the late seventeenth century.[85] As a result, much has been written on the ways in which Barbot and other travel writers, to whom Barbot himself was often heavily indebted, reflected and shaped contemporary perceptions of Africa and Africans.[86] The slave trade was not a *central* focus of Barbot's work, but a man writing about West Africa in the 1680s could hardly have avoided the theme. Not that Barbot wished to do so: he had considerable experience of slaving and had made substantial investments in the trade. Barbot recounts that in 1678–9 and 1681–2 he had made two slaving voyages to Guinea, acting as an agent for the activities of La Rochelle traders belonging to the Compagnie Royale d'Afrique.[87] Figure 3.2 depicts him at work in 1681, appearing before the King of Sestro (in what is now Liberia). Some years later, and by now based in England, Barbot joined forces with other merchants to finance two private slaving ventures. That of *Griffin* (1697) was a disaster, ending in shipwreck.[88] *Albion* (1699) fared better financially, but almost half of the captives on board this 10 per cent ship perished during the Middle Passage from New Calabar to Barbados. A good deal is known about the voyage of *Albion*, because Barbot's brother James sailed as supercargo, and Barbot reproduced material from James's sea journal in his Guinea writings.[89] *Albion* left England on 1 January 1699 and traded for 648 captives along the Gold Coast, at Bonny and New Calabar.[90] The 600 people who survived the vessel's stay in Africa began the Middle Passage from Bonny on the 29 August 1699, entering Barbados on 22 November of that year.[91] Only 250 Africans disembarked in the New World.

In 1700 Barbot's nephew (James junior) made a slaving voyage on *Don Carlos*, captained by William Esterson. This was another 10 per cent ship, bearing captives

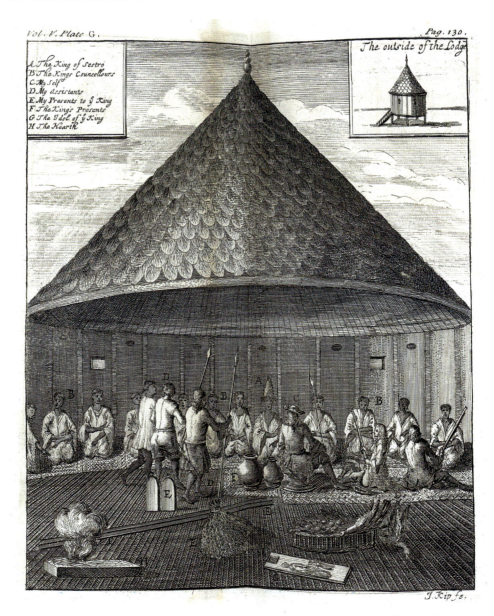

Figure 3.2 Jean Barbot presents himself to the King of Sestro, 1681. Barbot is the seated figure facing the king. Churchill and Churchill (1732: v, plate G).

from Cabinda and the Congo River to Jamaica. Barbot's account of Guinea incorporates material from two journals made on board this slaver, which left England on 13 January 1699 and departed from African waters with 417 captives on board on 1 January 1701.[92] The Middle Passage crossing ended on 22 March, with 373 Africans being disembarked in Jamaica. Details for this journey are fewer than for the *Albion*, but Barbot gives an account of an insurrection on the *Don Carlos*, prompting the inclusion of this narrative here. Finally, while reworking his French manuscript into

English in the early 1700s, John Barbot wrote some 'general observations' on the shipboard management of slaves. I have also drawn on this important series of observations, which are based in part, at least, on the personal experiences of Barbot and his relatives.[93]

Other memoirs were produced for quite different reasons. Robert Barker (see Table 3.2) was a man with a very specific axe to grind, publishing his pamphlet as part of a campaign to obtain financial compensation for permanent injuries received during his 1754 voyage on *Thetis*.

Robert Barker's 1774–5 Voyage on *Thetis* (published 1758)

Robert Barker was a carpenter by trade. Born in Wigan in 1729, he was apprenticed to Thomas Holland of Liverpool at the age of 14. He went on to work as a barge-builder for some years, eventually moving to Bristol, where he was engaged in building the slave ships *Trial* (1751) and *Thetis* (1754). When work on *Thetis* was complete, Barker signed on as the carpenter for the ship's maiden voyage to Guinea, under the command of John Fitzherbert. The ship cleared Bristol in December 1754 and traded for captives along the Bight of Biafra. *Thetis* then made the Middle Passage to Antigua, arriving on the 30 October 1755. An imputed 276 Africans were boarded, with 209 reaching their destination alive.

Following the death of the master in Africa, Barker suffered abuse at the hands of the chief mate, Robert Wabshutt, and the ship's surgeon, John Roberts. Permanently blinded because of his treatment, he was nevertheless one of three men charged with piracy. He was imprisoned in Antigua, finally returning to England aboard HMS *Advice*. On his return, Barker was granted a disability pension of 3s. 6d. per week by the Seamen's Hospital in Bristol and began a lengthy battle for redress against Wabshutt and Roberts.[94] *The Unfortunate Shipwright* was part of that campaign. Upon its publication in 1758, the Society of Merchant Venturers promptly withdrew Barker's pension.[95] Barker lived into his 80s, when an extended version of his memoir was published on his behalf.[96] Despite—indeed, because of—its lack of objectivity and its very specific central focus upon crew relationships, *Unfortunate Shipwright* is an unusual and important testimony: an illuminating source of information on the relationships between officers and men aboard slavers, and on the cruelties that officers sometimes inflicted upon sailors under their command.

Henry Smeathman (Writing *c.*1775)

In 1771 a prominent group of naturalists including Joseph Banks, John Fothergill, and the entomologist Dru Drury sponsored Henry Smeathman to undertake a collecting expedition to the Bananas Islands, off the coast of Sierra Leone. Born in Scarborough, Yorkshire, in 1742, Smeathman had a lifelong interest in insects, particularly ants and termites. As discussed in Chapter 8, he was one of a surprising number of eighteenth-century naturalists whose collecting activities brought them into contact with slave ships and the slave trade. Smeathman remained in Sierra Leone for three years, then in 1774 travelled to the Caribbean as a passenger on board the slaver *Elizabeth*, which was bound for Barbados and subsequently condemned as unseaworthy in Tobago.[97] Smeathman corresponded regularly with his patrons and at some point between 1775 and 1777 penned a brief essay, *Oeconomy of a Slave Ship*, describing a day in the life of a slave ship during the Middle Passage.[98] He sent a fair copy of this document to the ornithologist Marmaduke Tunstall, but the essay was not published and remained largely unknown until 2007, when it was transcribed in full by Deirdre Coleman.[99]

Oeconomy is a difficult piece to categorize, in that it is based on the personal experience of a slaving voyage made by a passenger, not a sailor.[100] While very detailed, it is also intentionally impressionistic: Smeathman cultivated the pose of a whimsical, educated commentator on the unusual, penning numerous letters to his patrons concerning the peculiarities of life in Africa, all employing a similar, patronizing tone to that found in *Oeconomy*.[101] But, if Smeathman's text is difficult to classify, so too is his attitude to slavery and the slave trade, which vacillated at different stages in his own life experience. *Oeconomy* was written after a lengthy stay in Sierra Leone, which led him to retract his broadly anti-slavery sympathies, but at a time when he was witnessing the realities of the plantation slave system in the Caribbean. In terms of the interests of the present book, Smeathman's *Oeconomy* is a particularly useful document. The author was no sailor, and as a result wrote about aspects of slave ships, such as sleeping arrangements and sounds, that most seamen took so much for granted that they failed to mention them. Smeathman also had a naturalist's eye for minutiae: his focus on the small things of the diurnal routine is most unusual and has greatly informed Chapters 10 and 11 of this book. Smeathman went on to write a well-received treatise on West African termites in 1781, but never returned to Africa. He was, however, one of the earliest promoters of the idea of a free black colony in Sierra Leone. Shortly before his death in 1786, he wrote a pamphlet that set out a contractual scheme to encourage 'blacks and free people of colour' to settle as free men in Sierra Leone.[102]

William Butterworth's 1786–7 Voyage on *Hudibras* (published 1823)

William Butterworth was the son of a Leeds copperplate engraver.[103] In 1786, at the age of 16, he ran away from home in search of adventure at sea. Arriving in Liverpool, he was persuaded to sign articles for the Guinea voyage of *Hudibras*, owned by Thomas Earle and captained by Jenkin Evans.[104] Butterworth spent three years at sea, eventually returning home to follow his father into the copperplate trade. More than thirty years later, he wrote *Three Years Adventures, of a Minor, in England, Africa, The West Indies, South Carolina and Georgia*, a narrative of his time at sea.[105] While his account was much embellished in the telling, Butterworth has nevertheless been shown to be an accurate and informative source, corroborated elsewhere, on the conduct of the slave trade at Calabar.[106] Butterworth also documented his youthful experience on the Middle Passage of *Hudibras*, which purchased 360 captives at Calabar, and transported them to Grenada, arriving there 26 February 1787. His is one of very few accounts of a slaving voyage written by an ordinary seaman: in fact, as ship's boy, Butterworth was on the very lowest rung of the crew hierarchy on *Hudibras* and suffered accordingly.[107] Butterworth probably maintained a diary at sea, but it should be noted that even this is unclear. Whatever the case, in *Three Years Adventures* he was looking back, after a considerable passage of time, on things he had witnessed and interpreted as a naive teenager. Ultimately, Butterworth was telling a story with himself as hero, and some of his assertions are highly questionable. Notwithstanding, his comments on a range of issues—from enslaved women and oral culture to insurrection—have been accepted as valid by leading scholars, and on that basis alone he cannot be ignored here.[108] Even so, I draw on his narrative with some misgivings. Butterworth has a further role in the present study, because he engraved the plates for Darcy Lever's *The Young Sea Officer's Sheet Anchor, or, A Key to the Leading of Rigging, and to Practical Seamanship*. Illustrations from this hugely popular reference work for the aspiring sailor, first published in 1808, appear in Figures 11.2 and 11.4.

Hugh Crow 1807–8 Voyage on *Kitty's Amelia* (published 1830)

Published posthumously in 1830, Hugh Crow's memoirs detail an eventful and unrepentant life.[109] (For a portrait of the author, made in later life, see Figure 3.3) Born in Ramsey on the Isle of Man in 1765, the son of a respectable tradesman, Crow was initially apprenticed to the boat-building trade, but at 17 he headed for Whitehaven and a career at sea. After an adventure-filled apprenticeship in the West Indies and Americas, he made his first (non-slaving) voyage to Africa at the age of 25. He sailed as mate on his first slaver in 1795, and on his return to Liverpool in July 1798 was appointed captain of *Will*. Thus began his successful career as a slave ship master—a trajectory that finally came to an end in 1807 with the voyage of *Kitty's Amelia*. Crow cleared Liverpool on 25 July 1807 and, having successfully traded for captives at Bonny, made the Middle Passage to Jamaica, arriving at Kingston on 25 January 1808. Here, an imputed 233 Africans were disembarked. Crow took *Kitty's Amelia* home to Liverpool and retired from the sea, using the profits from his voyages to buy a small estate near Ramsey.

Crow returned to Liverpool in 1817 and died there in 1829. His life and the voyages he made with *Will*, *Ceres*, *Mary*, and *Kitty's Amelia* are commemorated on an Adam-style chest tomb at Maughold's Church, Isle of Man. Other Crow family members are commemorated here too; one is Hugh's brother William, who died at Bonny, Nigeria, in February 1799. William Crow was the first captain of the Liverpool slaver *Charlotte*

Figure 3.3 Lithograph of Hugh Crow (by W. Crane): frontispiece of Crow's (1830) *Memoirs*.

(TSTD 81717), which left Liverpool for Nigeria in 1799; his was one of fifteen crew deaths on the ship.

Hugh Crow's memoirs (and indeed his tombstone) reveal a blunt self-publicist little given to introspection or regret. Unlike John Newton, to whom he provides an obvious contrast, Crow remained unapologetic about his former career, and his memoir closes with a robust defence of a now illegal trade. As one of the last captains to clear Liverpool with a legal slaver, Crow also offers useful insights into the dying moments of the slave trade.

The Parliamentary Inquiries of 1788–1792

Important though they are, logs and memoirs are not the only categories of Middle Passage testimony. Another genre is the witness statement made in the context of parliamentary inquiries into the slave trade. The flurry of parliamentary (and abolitionist) activity between 1788 and 1792 was such that a large proportion of the British documentary evidence available today dates from those few years. Put simply, more first-hand information about the Middle Passage was collected between 1788 and 1792 than at any other point in the history of the British slave trade. Written towards—and stimulating the demise of—the British slave trade, this body of testimony heralded the beginning of the end.

Yet for much of the period considered in this book, Parliament had barely concerned itself with slave shipping.[110] Little at all was said on the topic between 1713 and 1788, and this lack of political debate, as Christopher Brown has noted, reflects the peculiar place of the Atlantic slave trade in eighteenth-century British culture, as well as in Hanoverian politics.[111] Brown suggests that for much of the eighteenth century, slave trading

> elicited few public reflections, discussion, or comment. It never became a regular subject of praise or condemnation among novelists, or poets, or chroniclers. It did not become enmeshed in narratives of imperial greatness or, until the very end of the period, fears of national decline. That absence from the cultural imagination stands in contrast to the treatment of colonial slavery, which inspired verse, fiction, and song in Britain by the middle decades of the eighteenth century. By comparison, in the cultural realm, the Atlantic slave trade almost seemed not to exist. One could savour the fruits of slave labour, witness the wealth generated by slaving fortunes, count the ships headed to African waters, and encounter Africans on the street, and yet not muse at all upon the international trade in African labour that made such experiences possible. For most of the British nation, as well as for most members of parliament, the African slave trade was at once fundamental and almost entirely invisible.[112]

As noted in Chapter 1, slave shipping was not *entirely* absent from the cultural imagination, but many of the artefacts produced to commemorate or refute it (for example, commemorative ceramics, as in Figure 1.3, and the earliest abolitionist propaganda, as in Figure 5.14) precisely elucidate Brown's point: they are the product of a world in which slave shipping was an *absent* presence.

Organized abolitionism began in Britain in May 1787, with the formation of SEAST in London (discussed in Chapter 2). From the moment of its creation, the London Committee of SEAST set about soliciting eyewitness testimonies, recognizing clearly that the best way to establish a constituency for abolition was through the written word.[113] Some of these accounts were subsequently collated and published as pamphlets and short books. Key examples are set out in Table 3.3 and discussed in more detail below.[114] All owe their existence to the indefatigable efforts of Thomas Clarkson, bloodhound of the abolition movement.

Born in Wisbech, Cambridgeshire in 1760, Thomas Clarkson was one of the driving forces behind the campaign for abolition. He was one of the twelve founding members of the London committee of the SEAST and its most dedicated seeker of personal testimonies.[115] At his urging, SEAST commissioned pamphlets detailing the slave trading experiences of both Alexander Falconbridge and John Newton, both of

74 MATERIALIZING THE MIDDLE PASSAGE

Table 3.3 Key documents published at the behest of SEAST 1788–9 and containing detailed accounts of the Middle Passage

Author	Title	Short title and date
Alexander Falconbridge	*An Account of the Slave Trade on the Coast of Africa*	*Account* 1788
John Newton	*Thoughts upon the African Slave Trade*	*Thoughts* 1788
James Stanfield	*Observations on a Guinea Voyage*	*Observations* 1788
Thomas Clarkson (collating testimonies from various witnesses)	*The Substance of the Evidence of Sundry Persons on the Slave-Trade*	*Substance* 1789

whom would also appear in the parliamentary inquiries of 1788–92 (see Table 3.6).[116] Clarkson became the principal broker for the abolition movement during the enquiry process, procuring numerous witnesses and testifying in person.

Alexander Falconbridge, *An Account of the Slave Trade* (1788)

Falconbridge was a native of Bristol.[117] Having spent a year as a student at the Bristol Infirmary, he began his medical career as a slave ship surgeon, making four African voyages in the 1780s (see Table 3.6). These took Falconbridge from the Gold Coast and the Niger Delta to Angola, though most of his descriptions focus on Bonny and New Calabar, and on Middle Passage voyages from those regions to Jamaica and Grenada. Many of his most vivid passages concern the difficult voyage of *Alexander*, which cleared Bristol for Bonny on 28 April 1785. The master, John McTaggart, purchased an uncertain number of captives, who made the Middle Passage to Grenada between 15 September and 14 November 1785. Of these 307 Africans survived the crossing.[118]

Disturbed by what he had seen, Falconbridge nevertheless made one further voyage (on *Emilia*) perhaps because he was able to sail once again under James Fraser, a master in whom he placed considerable trust.[119] In the spring of 1787, he returned home to practise medicine in Bristol. In debt to his father and hoping to continue his studies, Falconbridge now came to the attention of Thomas Clarkson, who visited Bristol in the summer of that year to gather evidence about the slave trade. Falconbridge gave Clarkson a detailed and unflinching account of the shipboard care of slaves and was among the first of his interviewees to agree to testify before Parliament—a break-through for which the abolitionist remained deeply grateful.[120] Clearly feeling he had met a kindred spirit, Falconbridge volunteered to accompany Clarkson to Liverpool on the next leg of the latter's fact-finding tour. There, this 'athletic and resolute looking man' acted as Clarkson's assistant and bodyguard.[121] Clarkson passed the surgeon's testimony on to the London committee of the SEAST, which resolved to publish it.[122] Falconbridge travelled to London and, with the editorial assistance of the Quaker lawyer Richard Phillips, put his recollections into publishable form. The *Account* was published by James Phillips, the abolitionists' favoured printer, in 1788. It is almost certainly based on Falconbridge's voyage logs: a surgeon's pay was closely tied to the percentage of slaves delivered alive, so it was important to keep records, and many did so either voluntarily or as a term of their employment.[123] Shortly after the *Account* was published, Falconbridge made his first appearance in Parliament, testifying before the Privy Council inquiry (see Table 3.6).

The initial print run of 3,000 copies of *An Account of the Slave Trade* was circulated as anti-slavery propaganda and sold well. The six pence per copy Falconbridge received for the first edition (rising to seven pence for the second) helped him to set up a medical practice in Lodway. The year 1788 was eventful in other ways too, because Falconbridge married Anna Maria Horwood, a young Bristol woman who, at this point at least, shared his radical and anti-slavery sympathies. The couple's close association with Clarkson and the abolition movement continued, with Falconbridge facing extensive questioning by the House of Commons Committee in March 1790 (see Table 3.6). A year later, Clarkson persuaded the surgeon to become governor of the Province of Freedom, the free black trading settlement established in Sierra Leone through the efforts of the abolitionist Granville Sharp. This troubled venture was now in the hands of the Sierra Leone Company, which counted Sharp, Clarkson, and Wilberforce among its directors. Falconbridge set sail for Sierra Leone in January 1791, accompanied by his wife and his brother, William. Samuel Gamble, who passed through Freetown with *Sandown*, noted that 'one white lady of consequence' lived there (**Sandown 1793–4: 95**). He was referring to Anna Maria Falconbridge, who subsequently published a narrative of her travels to West Africa.[124] In that account, she recorded the death of her husband in December 1792. His final months were plagued by alcoholism and disappointment in both the Sierra Leone Company and his evidently unhappy marriage. Within a few weeks of his death Anna Maria had remarried, leaving Africa on board the slaver *Nassau*, captained by her sister's husband, Matthew Morley, in June 1793.[125]

John Newton, *Thoughts upon the African Slave Trade* (1788)

In 1750, John Newton (whose journal from *Argyle* is described above) had married his childhood sweetheart, Mary Catlett. Marriage, coupled with illness, prompted a career change. In 1755, a year after the journal ends, Newton left the sea to become a Tide Surveyor for HM Customs in Liverpool. Here, he taught himself Greek, Hebrew, and theology, and came under the influence of the leading Methodists George Whitefield and John Wesley. At 39 Newton was ordained and appointed curate at Olney, Buckinghamshire. In 1767, the poet William Cowper settled there too, and the pair collaborated on the *Olney Hymns*, published in 1779. In 1780 Newton became rector of St Mary Woolnoth in London. His preaching drew large numbers of people, William Wilberforce among them. By this time, Newton had repented of his former calling as a slave ship master and was lending his support to the abolition campaign. In 1786,

76 MATERIALIZING THE MIDDLE PASSAGE

he was interviewed by Thomas Clarkson, and, in 1788, wrote the pamphlet *Thoughts upon the African Slave Trade*, published at the behest of SEAST.[126] Newton was by now firmly committed to the anti-slavery movement and went on to give evidence to both the 1788 and 1790 parliamentary inquiries (see Table). He died in London in 1807.

Newton wrote about the slave trade over a long period and changed his mind about it along the way. The sea journal, compiled 1750–4 (see Table 3.1), was the work of a captain who did not question the morality of his trade. But the much later reflections contained in *Thoughts upon the African Slave Trade* (see Table 3.6) were penned by a cleric who had come to regard his former career with revulsion and were published in an anti-slavery context.

James Stanfield, *Observations on a Guinea Voyage* (1788)

Born in 1749, James Field Stanfield was educated for the priesthood, but in 1774–6 he was a sailor on a slaving voyage from Liverpool to Benin. The name of the vessel is not stated, but while in Africa Stanfield spent eight months ashore, trading for captives at the port city of Gwato (Ughoton). His narrative, like that of Barker, is one of few detailed testimonies written from the perspective of the ordinary seaman. That said, Stanfield was clearly of a higher social standing and had been better educated than most jobbing sailors; some series of events must have pushed him to sign on to a slave ship, but he does not elaborate. By 1788, when the account was written, Stanfield had established himself as an actor, and would go on to a (failed) career as a wine merchant before returning to acting. His *Observations* was set out in a series of letters addressed to Thomas Clarkson, and again printed by James Phillips.

Thomas Clarkson, *Substance of the Evidence* (1789)

In 1787, Clarkson toured Bristol and Liverpool, collecting eyewitness statements from sailors directly involved in the trade. These findings were synthesized in very truncated form in his 1788 *Essay on the Impolicy of the African Slave Trade*. In the same year, Clarkson travelled to ports along the south coast, from Kent to Cornwall, collecting further testimonies, but this time in a more systematic way.[127] The twenty-two testimonies collected at this time were collated in *Substance of the Evidence* (see Table 3.4), printed in April 1789 in readiness for a parliamentary debate on the slave trade which opened on 12 May.[128] *Substance* is one of the most important documents employed in the present book. In part, this is because some of the testimonies are by ordinary seamen; as noted above, the viewpoints of these men were rarely sought and recorded. As explored below, before setting out on the data-gathering exercise that resulted in *Substance*, Clarkson attempted to systematize his method for interviewing witnesses. This may have had a significant impact on the parliamentary inquiry process as it opened in 1788.

Table 3.4 Testimonies by sailors with Middle Passage experience recorded in *Substance of the Evidence* (1789)

No./Name	Rank	Voyage(s) described	TSTD	Parliamentary testimony (HCSP = House of Commons Sessional Papers)
I George Millar	2nd mate	*Canterbury* (London) 1766	77918	HCSP 73: 391–5
II William James	3rd mate	*Britannia* (Bristol) 1769	17717	HCSP 69: 48–9. 96–8, 137–40
III Mr Henderson	Unstated	*Tryal* (Liverpool) 1768	91405	No
IV Mr Thompson	Unstated	*Pearl* (date recollected as 1762)	90812?	No
V Mr Dove	Unstated	*Lilly* (Liverpool)	91436	No
VI John Douglas	Boatswain	*Warwick Castle* (London) 1771	78040	HCSP 82: 121–5
VII Henry Ellison	Unstated	*Upton* (Liverpool) 1761 *Briton* (Liverpool) 1762	90773 90983	HCSP 73: 367–77
VIII James Bowen	Master	*Russel* (London) 1776	77184	No
IX Mr Town(e)	Boy, carpenter	*Peggy* (Liverpool) 1760 *Sally* (Liverpool) 1768	90856, 91464	HCSP 82: 14–32
X Mr Janverin	1st–3rd mate	*Catherine* (London) 1767 *Tartar* (London) 1769	77916 78276	No
XI James Morley	Boy, foremastman, gunner, boatswain, mate	*Eagle Gally* (Bristol) 1758 *Venus* (Bristol) 1771	17435 17795	HCSP 73: 131–77
XII Mr Ponton	Foremastman	*Sally* (Liverpool) 1770 *Polly* (Liverpool) *African* (Liverpool) 1772	91466 Untraced 91880	No
XIII Mr Bell	2nd mate	*Nelly* (Lancaster) 1777	24013	No
XXI Isaac Parker	Foremastman	*Black Joke* (Liverpool) 1764	91135	HCSP 73: 123–39

78 MATERIALIZING THE MIDDLE PASSAGE

Each interview has roughly the same structure: the sailor describes how slaves are acquired in Africa, then goes on to describe the conditions for the captives and crews on board the ship. As Warren has rightly emphasized, *Substance* is a co–authored document; the testimonies are written in the third person and were recorded by Clarkson himself.[129]

Testimonies before the House (1788–92)

On 11 February 1788, William Pitt commissioned a report on the slave trade by the Privy Council Committee for Trade and Plantations. The committee, a precursor of the Board of Trade, was presided over by Charles Jenkinson, Baron Hawkesbury (later the first Lord Liverpool), who would later prove a strong parliamentary opponent of the abolitionist cause. The committee obtained its evidence by interviewing witnesses who could give first-hand accounts of the trade.

The Privy Council began collating data in June 1788 (**HCSP 67**; see Table 3.5). At the same time, the House of Commons resolved itself into a Committee of the Whole to hear evidence in relation to Sir William Dolben's bill to regulate the slave trade, brought in formally on 26 May 1788 (**HCSP 68**).[130] The African merchant interest in Liverpool dispatched five individuals, including the sailors Robert Norris (whose

Table 3.5 House of Commons Sessional Papers (HCSP) containing witness statements made as part of the 1778–92 inquiry process

Series	Volume title	Identifier
House Commons Sessional Papers of the Eighteenth Century, vol. 67	*Slave Trade 1788–90* (12 June 1788 to 17 March 1790)	HCSP 67
House Commons Sessional Papers of the Eighteenth Century, vol. 68	*Minutes of Evidence on the Slave Trade 1788 and 1789* (20 April 1789 to 22 June 1789)	HCSP 68
House Commons Sessional Papers of the Eighteenth Century, vol. 69	*Report of the Lords Committee of Council appointed for the consideration of all matters relating to Trade and Foreign Plantations . . . concerning the present state of the trade to Africa, and particularly the Trade in Slaves*, Part 1 (25 April 1789)	HCSP 69
House Commons Sessional Papers of the Eighteenth Century, vol. 70	*Report of the Lords Committee of Council appointed for the consideration of all matters relating to Trade and Foreign Plantations . . . concerning the present state of the trade to Africa, and particularly the Trade in Slaves*, Part 2 (25 April 1789)	HCSP 70
House Commons Sessional Papers of the Eighteenth Century, vol. 71	*Minutes of Evidence on the Slave Trade 1790,* Part 1 (5 February 1790 to 15 March 1790)	HCSP 71
House Commons Sessional Papers of the Eighteenth Century, vol. 72	*Minutes of Evidence on the Slave Trade 1790,* Part 2 (19 March 1790 to 1 April 1790)	HCSP 72
House Commons Sessional Papers of the Eighteenth Century, vol. 73	*Minutes of Evidence on the Slave Trade 1790* (4 April 1790 to 9 June 1790)	HCSP 73
House Commons Sessional Papers of the Eighteenth Century, vol. 82	*Slave Trade* (1 March 1791 to 14 May 1792)	HCSP 82

voyage with *Unity* is discussed above), James Penny, and James Matthews, to support the case that slave shipping was conducted humanely (see Table 3.6).[131] Thomas Clarkson produced the first of many counter-witnesses on behalf of SEAST, among them John Newton and Alexander Falconbridge. James Arnold, a surgeon who had served with Falconbridge on *Alexander*, made two very detailed written submissions concerning the 1786–7 voyage of *Ruby*. The Privy Council report was finally laid before the House of Commons in April 1789 (**HCSP 69–70**), and a month later, after lobbying by opponents of abolition, the Commons appointed a committee to investigate the slave trade further.[132] This and subsequent Select Committees were more supportive of abolition, being dominated by pro-abolition MPs, including William Wilberforce (**HCSP 71–3 and 82**). Newton and Falconbridge were once again among the many individuals interviewed. Captain James Fraser, under whom Falconbridge had served on three slaving ventures, also testified, as did Thomas Trotter, surgeon aboard *Brooks* on its 1783–4 voyage. The experienced Liverpool-based master Clement Noble, who commanded Trotter's *Brooks* voyage, also gave a lengthy account of his own experiences.

The creamware jug shown in Figure 3.4 is an important artefact associated with both *Brooks* and Noble. It bears the transfer–printed image of a 3–masted ship flying the red ensign and a pennant. Below are the words 'SUCCESS TO THE BROOKS CAP$^\text{T}$. NOBEL'. The ship, its flags, and the sea are enamelled in several colours. On the opposed side of the jug is a second image, depicting rope-makers with their coat of arms in a shield; in the background are several sailing ships. The foreground carries the inscription 'behold our support'. Below the pouring lip are the words 'king/ and/ constitution'. The jug also bears the monogram 'wh', above the date 1793. Finally, below the rope-makers' scene, are the words 'success to the rope makers and the glorious 10th. of march. may it never be forgotten.' While the *Brooks* broadsheet plan discussed in Chapter 5 is undoubtedly the best-known icon of both the British slave trade and its abolition, the jug shown here–which beyond doubt depicts the same vessel—has received surprisingly little scholarly attention. Noble captained *Brooks* five times and part-owned three of its ventures, but his formal relationship with the ship had ended long before 1793. The precise circumstances surrounding the production of the jug are unclear, but it is surely no coincidence that two visualizations of the same slave ship, one employed by the abolition movement and the other celebrating a former captain and prominent witness in the 1788–92 parliamentary inquiry process, should appear within a few years of each other.[133]

Asking Questions about the Slave Trade: The Clarkson Factor

The later eighteenth century was a period of enormous growth for parliamentary inquiry, particularly involving the interrogation of witnesses. It was only from the 1770s that the reports resulting from Select Committee inquiries were routinely published, and, as noted by Joanna Innes, the history of parliamentary inquiry in this period has 'yet to be written'.[134] As Diana Paton has emphasized:

Figure 3.4 Creamware jug (height 242 mm) bearing the transfer-printed image of a 3-masted ship. Below are the words 'SUCCESS TO THE BROOKS CAP^T. NOBEL'. British Museum, 1994,0718.2.

In their structure, such committees appeared to subscribe to a highly empiricist understanding of knowledge production, in which each witness was taken as a bearer of truth. At the same time, the actual process of questioning reveals the participants' awareness of the contested and politicized nature of the knowledge they were producing, as committee members and witnesses struggled to control the message they were creating. Thus, the questions asked, as well as the answers given, provide significant evidence. In the process of establishing its existence, calling witnesses, questioning them, recording the questions and answers, and publishing this information, the committee, composed entirely of male property-holding members of Parliament, claimed for itself the right and the ability to produce and propagate knowledge about slavery. Effectively, it defined the qualities required to speak with authority about the subject.[135]

Surprisingly little is known about how the eighteenth-century committees put together an appropriate list of witnesses. MPs often had their own contacts, but they also relied on 'opinion brokers', who would travel the country to collect evidence and source witnesses: Thomas Clarkson certainly played this role for supporters of abolition throughout the slave trade inquiry process.[136] Even less is known about the ways in which committees decided upon the *range* of questions to put to witnesses, though it is likely that in most cases the chair of a committee would have the most say here, in what would have been a fairly informal (and unrecorded) decision-making process.[137]

In terms of knowing what to ask, the slave trade, and the Middle Passage in particular, must have presented some significant challenges, given that very few Britons, and even fewer MPs, had direct experience of the realities of slaving voyages. The abolition movement was rather better placed in this respect, not least through the efforts of Thomas Clarkson. In my view, the basic framework of questioning adopted by the Privy Council in 1788 (and also by subsequent inquiries) owes a good deal to that developed earlier in the same year by Thomas Clarkson, just before he set out on the testimony-gathering exercise later published as *Substance of the Evidence* (1789).

In June 1788, Clarkson drew up a series of six 'tables' of queries to put to all his interviewees, as he toured the ports of Britain speaking to slave ship sailors.[138] At almost the same moment, the Privy Council began hearing evidence in the first parliamentary inquiry into the slave trade. Clarkson was in regular contact with the Privy Council committee between February 1788, when it was first commissioned, and June 1788, when witness hearings began. It seems at least possible, despite the pro-slavery sympathies of the committee's chair, that Clarkson's method had some influence on the pattern of questioning employed by the Privy Council. Clarkson later spoke of his tables of queries thus:

> I was at Teston, writing a long letter to the Privy Council on the ill usage and mortality of the seamen employed in the slave-trade, which it had been previously agreed should be received as evidence there. I thought it proper, however, before I took my departure [to collect information for *Substance*], to form a system of questions upon the general subject. These I divided into six tables. The first related to the productions of Africa, and the disposition and manners of the natives. The second, to the methods of reducing them to slavery. The third, to the manner of bringing them to the ships, their value, the medium of exchange, and other circumstances. The fourth, to their transportation. The fifth, to their treatment in the Colonies. The sixth, to the seamen employed in the trade. These tables contained together one hundred and forty-five questions. My idea was that they should be printed on a small sheet of paper, which should be folded up in seven or eight leaves, of the length and breadth of a small almanac, and then be sent in franks to our different correspondents. These, when they had them, might examine persons capable of giving evidence, who might live in their neighbourhoods or fall in their way, and return us their examinations by letter.[139]

There is a striking correspondence between the pattern of questioning outlined here, and that adopted by successive parliamentary committees. Arguably, there is a simple logic to much of that questioning, following the trajectory of captives from Africa to the Americas. The treatment of sailors could be discussed at any point, however, and yet questions on this topic are generally left—just as in Clarkson's tables—to the last. It is intriguing to think that in 1788 a leading abolitionist may have helped to frame the terms of reference for the inquiry process simply by virtue of refining, through his own early interviews with sailors in the trade, exactly *what* might be asked concerning a trade so unfamiliar to most parliamentarians.

A great many individuals were called before the parliamentary committees during these inquiries, which addressed everything from the circumstances of captive acquisition in Africa, through conditions on the Middle Passage, to the treatment of slaves in the Americas. In making my own selection from the mass of data generated by the inquiry process, I have prioritized the most detailed of the testimonies made by sailors with personal experience of the Middle Passage (Table 3.6: and see also Table 3.4 for parliamentary testimonies by sailors also interviewed for Clarkson's *Substance of the Evidence*). I have largely focused on the inquiries themselves, rather than on related debates in both the Commons and Lords, because the latter generally summarized information from the former, or generated briefer and less informative new testimonies. Most of the men listed in Table 3.6 were ship's officers: masters or surgeons on slave ships. Their accounts relate to voyages made over a period of more than thirty years, from 1752 to 1788.

Some appeared at the behest of the abolition movement, and others, of course, spoke in favour of the trade. As noted above, John Matthews, Robert Norris, and James Penny were recruited in Liverpool to represent that town's slave-trading interests.[140] The silver epergne presented to Penny in 1792 (Figure 3.5) was gifted in explicit recognition of his role in the inquiry process. Differences of emphasis and tone by witnesses on opposing sides of the abolitionist fence are inevitably marked, particularly when interviewees are answering questions relating to the four most basic lines of questioning concerning slaving voyages: overcrowding (sometimes known today as 'tight packing'); captive and crew mortality and the factors leading to high death rates; daily regimes on the passage, and violence towards both captives and crews. These differences are most explicit in cases where two witnesses shared a voyage: the testimonies of Clement Noble and Thomas Trotter, and similarly of Alexander Falconbridge and James Fraser (see Table 3.6), are particularly valuable in this context.[141]

Testimonies by witnesses in favour of the trade can also be especially revealing in their overdetermined eagerness to portray slave shipping in favourable terms. Thus Robert Norris, who was singled out by William Wilberforce for the biased nature of his testimony, went to considerable efforts to portray slave ships as uncrowded spaces, and in so doing revealed aspects of the sleeping arrangements for children that have had a formative influence on arguments developed later in this book concerning the liminal position of children on slaving vessels.[142]

Table 3.6 Key parliamentary inquiry testimonies made by sailors with Middle Passage experience

Name	HCSP principal testimony	Experience	TSTD voyages traced	Pro/anti slave trade	Notes
Arnold, James*	Vol. 69: 50–5, 125–36	Three voyages as surgeon's mate and surgeon	17948 *Alexander* (1785)** 17955 *Little Pearl* (1785) 18006 *Ruby* (1787)	Anti	-
Claxton, Ecroyde*	Vol. 82: 32–9 (10–11 Feb. 1791)	One voyage as surgeon's mate; joined a second ship as surgeon on African coast	81550 *Garland* (1787) 84092 *Young Hero* (1788)	Anti	-
Dalziel/Dalzel, Archibald	Vol. 68: 29–35 (9 and 12 June 1788); Vol. 69: 14–18, 43, 45–7, 60, 69–70, 121–2	One voyage as supercargo, three as master Governor of the fort at Whydah, 1762–6	72602 *Hannah* (1775) 81323 *Europa* (1783) 83454 *Saint Ann* (1783) 83725 *Tartar* (1785) Also: 81632 *Gosport and Havre Packet* (1789)	Pro	-
Ellison, Henry*	Vol. 73: 367–77 (7–8 June 1790)	Ten voyages, serving as naval gunner at time of testimony	Ten voyages pre 1770, including: 90773 *Upton* (Liverpool) 1761 90983 *Briton* (Liverpool) 1762	Anti	Also *Substance of the Evidence:* Table 3.4
Falconbridge, Alexander*	Vol. 69: 13, 21, 31, 48, 50, 57; 120–1; Vol. 72, 293–344, 354 (8–11 Mar. 1790)	Four voyages as surgeon (first did not reach Africa)	17913 *Tartar* (1782)** 17920 *Emilia* (1783)** 17948 *Alexander* (1785)** 17967 *Emilia* (1786)**	Anti	Also *An Account of the Slave Trade on the Coast of Africa* (1788): Table 3.3
Fraser, James	Vol. 71: 3–58 (29 Jan. and 1–4 Feb. 1790)	Twenty years in the trade: master of numerous voyages from 1772	17800 *Catherine* (1777) 17830 *Catherine* (1773) 17888 *Alexander* (1776) 17895 *Valiant* (1777) 17902 *Tartar* (1780) 17913 *Tartar* (1782)** 17920 *Emilia* (1783)** 17933 *Emilia* (1784) 17952 *Emilia* (1785) 17967 *Emilia* (1786**) 17990 *Emilia* (1787)	Pro	-

Continued

Table 3.6 Continued

Name	HCSP principal testimony	Experience	TSTD voyages traced	Pro/anti slave trade	Notes
Hall, John Ashley	Vol. 69: 19–20, 49–50, 71, 122; Vol. 72, 513–61 (1 June 1790)	Two voyages as 3rd, 2nd, and then 1st mate	78098 *Neptune* (1772) 77124 *Neptune* (1774)	Anti	-
Heatley, Robert	Vol. 69: 123–24; 30–1	Numerous voyages 1763–88, three as master	81444 *Ferret* (1783) 80085 *Africa* (1785) 80086 *Africa* (1786)	Pro	-
Henderson, David*	Vol. 69, 55–6, 139–40	Two voyages in the African trade. naval gunner at time of testimony	90405 *Tryal* (1768) *Richey* (untraced)	Anti	Also *Substance of the Evidence*: Table 3.4
Knox, John	Vol. 68: 145–82 (9 June 1789)	At least nine voyages, including six as surgeon and three as master	*Tartar* (1782) (untraced) 81257 *Fairy* (1783) 82240 *Lark* (1785)	Pro	-
Littleton, William	Vol. 68: 283–312 (18 June 1789)	One voyage to Gambia, as mate: several more as passenger Africa–Carolina and West Indies	Vessel not named	Pro	-
Matthews, John	Vol. 68: 19–20, 23–7, 41–3 (3 June, 16 June 1788) Vol. 69, 34–6, 83–6	Three voyages 1770–87. naval lieutenant at time of testimony.	Vessels not named	Pro	One of the delegates sent from Liverpool to speak on behalf of the trade.
Morley, James*	Vol. 73: 151–77 (12 May 1790)	Six: role unstated, but naval gunner at time of testimony	17454 *Eagle Gally* (1759) 17538 *Amelia* (1761) 17555 *Marcus* (1763) *Tom*—untraced voyage 17795 *Venus* (1771) 91747 *Whim* (1775)	Anti	Also *Substance of the Evidence*: Table 3.4
Newton, John*	Vol. 69: 12, 36, 60, 67, 118; Vol. 73, 139–51 (11–12 May 1790)		90350 *Duke of Argyle* (1750) 90418 *African* (1752) 90419 *African* (1753)–	Anti	Journal: Table 3.1 *Thoughts upon the African Slave Trade* (1788): Table.3.3
Noble, Clement	Vol. 73: 100–20 (8–10 May 1790)	Two voyages as mate, seven as master	91898 *Corsican Hero* (1772) 91899 *Corsican Hero* (1773)	Pro	-

			92522 *Brooks* (1775)		
			92521 *Brooks* (1776)		
			80663 *Brooks* (1781)		
			80664 *Brooks* (1783)**		
			80665 *Brooks* (1785)		
Norris, Robert	Vol. 68: 1–19 (2–3 June 1788); Vol. 73: 51–66 (1–4 May 1790)	Five voyages as master	91567 *Unity* (1769) 91568 *Unity* (1771) 91969 *Unity* (1773) 91970 *Unity* (1775) 92002 *Britannia* (1775) 92729 *Society* (1777)	Pro	Author of *The Memoirs of the Reign of Bossa Ahadee, King of Dahomy* (1789) and *A Short Account of the African Slave Trade* (1788) One of the delegates sent from Liverpool to speak on behalf of the trade.
Parker, Isaac*	Vol. 73: 123–39 (21 May 1790)	Three voyages	91134 *Black Joke* (1764)	Anti	Also *Substance of the Evidence*: Table 3.4
Penny, James	Vol. 68: 37–41 (13 and 16 June 1788); Vol. 69: 116–18	Two voyages as mate, eleven as master	90120 *Jupiter* (1764) 90121 *Jupiter* (1765) 91485 *Cavendish* (1768) 91486 *Cavendish* (1770) 91856 *Wilbraham* (1772) 91919 *Wilbraham* (1773) 91921 *Wilbraham* (1775) 91921 *Wilbraham* (1776) 92482 *Nicholson* (1777) 80735 *Carolina* (1781) 80917 *Comte du Norde* (1783)	Pro	One of the delegates sent from Liverpool to speak on behalf of the trade.
Towne, James*	Vol. 82: 14–32 (8–10 Feb. 1791)	Two voyages: first as boy, second as carpenter.	90856 *Peggy* (1760) 91461 *Sally* (1768)	Anti	Also *Substance of the Evidence*: Table 3.4
Trotter, Thomas*	Vol. 73: 80–100 (5–7 May 1790)	One voyage as surgeon	80664 *Brooks 1783***	Anti	-
Wilson, Isaac	Vol. 72: 273–93 (5–6 Mar. 1790)	One voyage as principal surgeon	81202 *Elizabeth* (1788)	Anti	-

* A witness sourced by Thomas Clarkson.

** Voyages shared by more than one witness

Figure 3.5 Oval silver epergne by Pitty and Preedy, engraved with the arms of the Town of Liverpool, inscribed: 'This is one of two Pieces of Silver Plate presented TO JAMES PENNY ESQr by The CORPORATION OF LIVERPOOL 1792'. National Museums Liverpool, 1973.278.

African Voices

An estimated 2.42 million Africans survived the voyage into slavery on British ships but only a tiny handful of African accounts of that experience exist today.[143] First-person accounts by women are especially rare, and the recent rediscovery of the fragment of the 'Memoirs of the Life of Florence Hall', an Igbo woman who endured a Middle Passage crossing to Jamaica as a child, offers a rare glimpse of the experiences of a young girl on board a slave ship. Hall says of her voyage:

> The white people received, and stripped us of all our beads and shells, and while the naked children were permitted to walk about the ships, the men and women were chained and kept in darkness below. Our food was sparing, and ever bad. Our punishment was frequent and severe, and death became so frequent an occurrence, that at last it passed on, without fear on the dying, or grief on those left behind, as we believed that those who died were restored to their people and Country. A long voyage at length brough the ship to Jamaica.[144]

For reasons having much to do with New World Africans' lack of access to education, but also informed by cultural preferences for oral history, no surviving examples of transatlantic black writing on any subject predate the late eighteenth century. The first 'slave narratives' emerged in England in the 1760s, most taking the form of spiritual autobiographies.[145] Between this date and the end of slavery in British territories in 1838, a small number of British-based black writers produced autobiographies and narratives of captivity and travel. All were written in English, and the majority appeared, like so many commentaries on the trade in slaves, between 1780 and 1807.[146] The most famous, and contentious, of these writers was Olaudah Equiano, who by his own account was born in Nigeria around 1745, kidnapped for the slave trade at the age of 11, and shipped to the West Indies. His autobiography, *The Interesting Narrative of the Life of Olaudah Equiano, or Gustavus Vassa, the African*, was published in London in 1789 (see Figure 3.6 for the frontispiece, depicting the author holding a copy of the Bible in his right hand. It is open at Acts 4:12, a text stated in the narrative to have been central to Equiano's spiritual awakening). This book contains a much-reproduced account of Equiano's Middle Passage experience, an abridged extract from which can be found in Box 3.2.

Since Vincent Carretta's discovery of baptismal and naval records suggesting that Equiano was born a slave in South Carolina, doubt has been cast on the veracity of this account of the Middle Passage.[147] Carretta's findings have caused dismay among many, and generated considerable academic debate.[148] I make limited use of Equiano's Middle Passage narrative in the present book, but that is not because it is a source of debate. Rather, my use of Equiano is limited because his narrative so closely echoes other testimonies generated in 1788–9 that it provides very few *unique* points of detail about the materiality of the slaving voyage. But I will return to Equiano in my concluding chapter, by which point the striking parallels between the extract in Box 3.2 and those of sailors testifying in the parliamentary inquiries will have become clear to the reader.

Whatever the truth regarding Equiano's origins, it is certain that upon his arrival in England he joined a growing number of people of colour, some of whom were living as 'servants' in wealthy households. Some of these individuals came directly from Africa; others were the property of New World planters visiting the home country.[149] According to a brief biography written by Joseph Jekyll in 1782, the composer, writer, and grocer Ignatius Sancho (Figure 3.7) was born on a slave ship in 1729. In his letters, however, Sancho referred to his birthplace as Africa.[150] Brought to England from Granada at the age of 2, Sancho was the valet of the first Duke of Montagu. He later opened a grocery store—a surviving trade card from which advertises 'Sancho's best Trinidado', and depicts a native American smoking tobacco and an African harvesting it.[151] Sancho became the first black person to vote in parliamentary elections in Britain (in 1774 and 1780).

Quobna Ottabah Cugoano, a contemporary and friend of both Olaudah Equiano and Ignatius Sancho, was born on the Gold Coast in the 1750s. Cugoano was kidnapped into slavery as a child and shipped to Grenada. After a period of plantation labour, he was brought to England, where he worked as a servant to the artist Richard Cosway. His *Thoughts and Sentiments on the Evil and Wicked Traffic of*

Figure 3.6 Frontispiece of Olaudah Equiano's *Interesting Narrative*, published in 1789. Based on a painting that is thought to be the work of the miniaturist William Denton. British Library Board.

the Slavery and Commerce of the Human Species was published in 1787.[152] This work—the first substantial anti-slavery text written in English by an African—was in part autobiographical, and included a very brief account of Cugoano's Middle Passage experience, which began off Cape Coast:

> When we were put into the ship we saw several black merchants coming on board, but we were all drove into our holes, and not suffered to speak to any of them. In this

Box 3.2 Olaudah Equiano's Middle Passage

The first object which saluted my eyes when I arrived on the coast was the sea, and a slave ship, which was then riding at anchor, and waiting for its cargo. These filled me with astonishment, which was soon conveyed into terror when I was carried on board. I was immediately handled, and tossed up to see if I were sound by some of the crew; and I was now persuaded that I had gotten into a world of bad spirits, and that they were going to kill me. Their complexions too differing so much from ours, their long hair, and the language they spoke, (which was very different from any I had ever heard) united to confirm me in this belief... When I looked round the ship too and saw a large furnace or copper boiling, and a multitude of black people of every description chained together, every one of their countenances expressing dejection and sorrow, I no longer doubted of my fate; and, quite overpowered with horror and anguish, I fell motionless on the deck and fainted. When I recovered a little, I found some black people about me, who I believed were some of those who brought me on board... I asked them if we were not to be eaten by those white men with horrible looks, red faces, and loose hair... I was soon put down under the decks and there I received such a salutation in my nostrils as I had never experienced in my life: so that with the loathsomeness of the stench, and crying together, I became so sick and low that I was not able to eat, nor had I the least desire to taste anything. I now wished for the last friend, death, to relieve me; but soon, to my grief, two of the white men offered me eatables; and, on my refusing to eat, one of them held me fast by the hands, and laid me across I think the windlass, and tied my feet, while the other flogged me severely. I had never experienced anything of this kind before; and although, not being used to the water, I naturally feared that element the first time I saw it, nevertheless, could I have got over the nettings, I would have jumped over the side, but I could not; and, besides, the crew used to watch us very closely who were not chained down to the decks, lest we should leap into the water; and I have seen some of these poor African prisoners most severely cut for attempting to do so, and hourly whipped for not eating... for I had never seen among any people such instances of brutal cruelty; and this not only shown towards us blacks, but also to some of the whites themselves. One white man in particular I saw, when we were permitted to be on deck, flogged so unmercifully with a large rope near the foremast, that he died in consequence of it; and they tossed him over the side as they would have done a brute... The closeness of the place [below decks] and the heat of the climate, added to the number in the ship, which was so crowded that each had scarcely room to turn himself, almost suffocated us. This produced copious perspirations, so that the air soon became unfit for respiration, from a variety of loathsome smells, and brought on a sickness among the slaves, of which many died... This wretched situation was again aggravated by the galling of the chains, now become insupportable; and the filth of the necessary tubs, into which the children often fell, and were almost suffocated. The shrieks of the women and the groans of the dying, rendered the whole a scene of sorrow almost inconceivable. Happily perhaps for myself I was soon reduced so low here that it was thought necessary to keep me almost always on deck; and from my extreme youth I was not put in fetters... One day, when we had a smooth sea and moderate wind, two of my wearied countrymen who were chained together (I was near them at the time), preferring death to such a life of misery, somehow made through the nettings and jumped into the sea; immediately another quite dejected fellow, who, on account of his illness, was suffered to be out of irons, also followed their example: and I believe many more would very soon have done the same if they had not been prevented by the ship's crew, who were instantly alarmed. Those of us that were the most active were in a moment put down under the deck, and there was such a noise and confusion amongst the people of the ship as I never heard before, to stop her, and get the boat out to go after the slaves. However two of the wretches were drowned but they got the other, and afterwards flogged him unmercifully for thus attempting to prefer death to slavery... Many a time we were near suffocation for the want of fresh air, which we were without for whole days together. This, and the stench of the necessary tubs, carried off many.

Source: Extracted from Equiano (1789: 70–83).

situation we continued several days in sight of our native land... and when we found ourselves at last taken away, death was more preferable than life, and a plan was concerted amongst us, that we might burn and blow up the ship, and to perish all together in the flames; but we were betrayed by one of our countrywomen, who slept with some of the head men of the ship, for it was common for the dirty filthy sailors to take African women and lie upon their bodies; but the men were chained and pent up in holes. It was the women and boys which were to burn the ship, with the approbation and groans of the rest; though that was prevented, the discovery was likewise a bloody scene.[153]

This account reveals valuable information about such aspects of the Middle Passage as sexual violence and attempted insurrection (discussed in greater detail in Chapter 11) but is very brief; indeed, terse. Again, I reserve further discussion of this point for my concluding chapter. For now, I need simply emphasize that, in the absence of detailed African eyewitness commentaries, it is possible to gain some understanding of African experiences from sailors' testimonies. Moreover, when one excavates *between* the lines of those accounts, reading against the grain in the spaces in which what was *not* said in the past awaits discovery in the present, some illuminating findings are revealed. Finally, as Chapters 4 and 5 will go on to show, it is also possible to look beyond written accounts to other kinds of source in searching for African experiences of the voyage into slavery.

Figure 3.7 Ignatius Sancho. This engraving by Francesco Bartolozzi, published by John Bowyer Nichols in 1781, is based on the portrait of Sancho painted by Thomas Gainsborough in 1768. Michael Graham-Stewart.

Notes

1. Muster rolls became the norm in 1747, when parliament ordered customs houses to record crew lists in *An Act for the Relief and Support of maimed and disabled Seamen and the Widows and Children of such as shall be killed, slain or drowned in the Merchants Service* (20 Geo. I c. 38). Muster rolls report the names of all the crew sailing on voyages, and record such information as dates of discharge, desertion, imprisonment, or death. Some also list rank, and cause of death. The 1789 amendment to the Dolben Act (29 Geo. III c. 66) re-enforced the requirement for slave ship masters to update their muster rolls at sea, and stipulated that they should also maintain log books noting penalties, forfeitures, and charges against officers and seamen. Musters survive for four out of five Liverpool slaving voyages between 1770 and 1807, and for some Bristol voyages dating from 1748 to 1794 (Behrendt 1997: 50). Details from the muster rolls of 2,120 Liverpool voyages have been integrated into the TSTD data set (Behrendt 1997: 50).
2. For a detailed analysis of the personnel on Liverpool voyages from 1750 to 1807, see Behrendt (2007).
3. The ranking system in the merchant marine was considerably simpler than that employed by the Royal Navy. In this book I have taken my lead from Davis (1962) and employ three basic crew categories: master, specialists, and foremastmen.
4. Behrendt (2007: 70–1, table 3.1).

5. A third option, during wartime, was privateering. Privateers were privately owned vessels commissioned (by the Crown) to seize and plunder enemy ships. Put simply, they engaged in legalized piracy.

6. That is, the money necessary to become part-owner of a ship, or to purchase a share in a trading venture.

7. Davis (1962: 116–17).

8. Davis (1962: 120).

9. In times of peace naval men (including officers furloughed at half pay) would often sign on for merchant ships. In times of war, by contrast, the navy frequently exercised its right to impress (draft) merchant crewmen. All those aboard merchant vessels were liable for impressment, with the supposed exception of the master, chief mate, boatswain, carpenter, and boys: see Mouser (2002: 11, n. 45). Naval vessels were authorized to impress slaver crewmen in both British and Caribbean waters, but not in Africa or during the Middle Passage. Merchant ships were able to obtain written approval to recruit a crew of a specified size, who were by this means protected against impressment. However, many Guinea captains were forced to recruit before their approval arrived, and sometimes lost crewmen to the Impress Service as a result. Samuel Gamble's voyage (*Sandown* 1793–4, 10–12) took place during a time of war with France, and ten of his crew, including his boatswain and carpenter, were impressed before *Sandown* sailed.

10. Clarkson's collection (1789) of sailor's testimonies includes numerous references to the practice of crimping, whereby landlords and others 'sold' drunken and indebted men to the masters of Guinea ships: see Christopher (2006: 31–2) for a discussion of this practice in relation to slavers. There was always intense competition for manpower between the navy, the merchant service, and privateering, and this intensified during wartime. At such times, masters throughout the merchant marine made use of crimps: Rodger (1988: 183).

11. Abolitionists were careful to document the conditions endured by slave ship crews, as well as by enslaved Africans. Thomas Clarkson made a damning study of mortality rates among Guinea crews, based on analysis of 188 muster rolls from slave ships leaving Liverpool and Bristol. The data were presented before Parliament (via a letter from Clarkson) in 1788 (**HCSP (House of Commons Sessional Papers) 69: 144–56**). It is a measure of the success of this approach that almost every piece of British slave ship legislation passed after 1788 included clauses designed to improve the working and living conditions of slaver crews. The most important of these was the 1793 Act (33 Geo. III c. 73), which allowed slaver crews river pay (an extra payment above regular wages) to be made during a ship's sojourn off the coast of West Africa. The 1793 Act made further crew provisions reflecting the very specialized nature, and dangers, of slaving voyages. These included specified quantities of 'sufficient and wholesome food', and amenities and shelter while in Africa.

12. Christopher's suggestion (2006: 28) that penniless seamen regarded slave trading as an 'uncommonly abhorrent occupation' needs temporal qualification: while this may have been the case by the very end of the eighteenth century, thanks, in no small part, to the parliamentary inquiry process, the picture is more clouded for earlier periods.

13. Thomas (1997: 305).

14. Behrendt (1990) is an invaluable source of information on the social background and maritime careers of later-eighteenth-century slave ship masters.

15. Behrendt (1990: 91, 115). Hugh Crow's early career (*Kitty's* 1807–9) followed precisely this path.

16. 28 Geo. III c. 54 XI.

17. Behrendt (2007: 72–3, table 3.2).

18. Behrendt (1990: 87).

19. Behrendt (2007: 74).

20. *Hannibal* **1693–4: 173;** *Albion* **1699: 681.**

VOICES FROM THE SEA 93

21. A list of 423 Liverpool, London, and Bristol voyages made between January 1789 and May 1792 (TNA: T 64/286) shows that forty-two captains had partnership shares in their voyage: Behrendt (1990: 107).

22. A list of the privilege slaves and bonuses awarded to officers on *Emilia* (1783) is to be found in **HCSP 72: 349–50**.

23. Behrendt (1990: 94 and n. 45).

24. Behrendt (1990: 94 and n. 45).

25. 28 Geo. III c. 54 XIV: £100 was to be awarded if the mortality rate did not exceed two slaves per hundred, and £50 if mortality did not exceed three slaves per hundred.

26. See Behrendt (1990: 112–13) for Liverpool slave ship masters (1785–1807) moving on to merchant careers.

27. Barbot relates that John Grazelier, one of the supercargoes sailing on **Albion 1699**, later went on to captain three slaving voyages: Hair et al. (1992: ii. 698).

28. Rodger (1988: 271).

29. Behrendt's analysis of a sample of late Liverpool voyages has shown that one in four surgeons died on slaving voyages from that port between 1801–7: Behrendt (1997: 60). For a study of some of the surgeons who testified in the 1788–92 parliamentary hearings, see Boog Watson (1969).

30. Behrendt (2007: 74).

31. Walvin (2001: 47).

32. Note that a significant proportion of surgeons (and captains) in the British trade came from Scotland and the Isle of Man: see Schwarz (2015) for more on the careers of five of these men: James Currie, Archibald Dalzel, James Irving, James Irving Jnr, and Thomas Trotter.

33. The rate varied, but eighteenth-century surgeons were commonly paid 1*s.* for each slave delivered into port (Boog Watson 1969: 207; Mouser 2002: 30–1, n. 129). The 1788 Dolben Act stipulated that surgeons should receive a bonus of £50 for keeping mortality rates below two slaves per hundred, or £25 if deaths did not exceed three per hundred (28 Geo. III c. 54 XIV). The Dolben Act also required new slave ship surgeons to pass a qualifying examination. The role of the Royal College of Surgeons of Edinburgh in examining aspiring slave ship surgeons is discussed by Boog Watson (1969: 211–13).

34. **HCSP 72: 349–50**.

35. Behrendt (1990: 98) has identified thirty-six surgeons who became captains between 1785 and 1807. As he points out (1990: 99), the practice of promoting surgeons to command became more common after the Dolben Act of 1788, as these men were often the most experienced officers available to merchants.

36. For more on surgeons becoming captains, see Fyfe (2000: 193). Patrick Renney is discussed by Rodger (1988: 269).

37. Boog Watson (1969: 209); Sheridan (1985: 112). For a detailed study of Trotter's life, see Vale and Edwards (2011).

38. Ship's Articles (documents setting out the terms and conditions under which crew were hired) provide a useful indication of literacy among merchant seamen. All members of a ship's crew were required to sign Articles, with illiterate men simply making a mark against their name. On its voyage of 1775, the Bristol slaver *Hungerford* (TSTD 17859) carried a crew of fifty-one. Most of the officers and specialist seamen were able to write their own names, while nineteen seamen made marks against their name, suggesting that they could not write. For the Articles from Hungerford, see **HCSP 69: 165–6**. Crewmen were also required to sign muster rolls. On the 1781 muster roll of *Sally* of Bristol (**HCSP 69: 173–4**), all the specialist crew could write their own names. Nineteen of the remaining thirty seamen were not able to do so. As these examples illustrate, many (but by no means all) foremastmen were illiterate, while skilled crewmen were often literate. With reference to the latter, see Dresser (2001: 66–7) on written accounts of slave ship careers by two skilled Bristol seamen. Silas Told, the son of a physician fallen on hard times,

94   MATERIALIZING THE MIDDLE PASSAGE

first went to sea at the age of 12. He subsequently became a Methodist preacher in London, and in 1786 published a pamphlet detailing his time on slave ships between 1726 and 1733. Joseph Banfield, the son of a cordwainer from Falmouth, Cornwall, first went to sea on a whaler at the age of 12. He arrived in Bristol in 1765 and served on Bristol Guineamen from 1767–78. His manuscript remains unpublished.

39. I have used 'sea journal' in preference to 'logbook' in categorizing these accounts. At its most basic, a logbook was a navigational aid that kept track of a ship's location by noting its speed and direction, though, on many ships, a great deal of additional information was recorded in them (Gilje 2016: 67). Robert Norris's *Unity* log was a navigational record of this kind, as was the 'journal' maintained by Gamble. Prideaux's 'journal', in contrast, did not contain navigational details and was one of several records maintained on *Daniel and Henry*. But in all cases, as Gilje (2016: 65–8) emphasizes, these documents were 'logbooks of memory': the written records of voyages, reflecting a certain view of time and place, and—because they were expected to be accurate—also perceived to be truthful records.

40. Martin and Spurrell (1962).

41. Mouser (2002).

42. Donnan (1930–5) is a key source here, reproducing extracts from a large number of sea logs and journals.

43. TSTD 9714. Phillips's journal first appeared in print in Churchill and Churchill (1732: vi. 173–239 (187–255 in later editions), but it must have been known to the publishers for many years before this, since Phillips's name appears among those on the Royal Licence granted to the Churchill brothers in 1700: see Hair et al. (1992: i. p. xxix). Extracts from the Churchill text appear in Dow (2002 [1927]: 31–7) and Donnan (1930–5: i. 392–410), but no independent critical edition has appeared in print.

44. The attack is reported in correspondence sent to Cape Coast by Thomas Buckridge, RAC factor at Dixcove, in January 1694 (Law 1997–2006: no. 37, part 3); the incident is also noted in a letter written by Phillips on board *Hannibal* at Montserado in January 1694 (Law 1997–2006: no. 1395, part 3).

45. Phillips says he purchased 700 Africans (*Hannibal* 1693–4: 230) and buried 320 (*Hannibal* 1693–4: 236); yet he elsewhere notes that 372 survived to Barbados (*Hannibal* 1693–4: 237). TNA: T70/12, 58 (Abstract of letters received by the RAC from the West Indies) records Phillips arriving with 'but 376 negroes', suggesting 324 deaths overall.

46. Phillips is presumably referring here (*Hannibal* 1693–4: 173) to the War of the League of Augsburg (or Grand Alliance), still being fought in the colonies in 1693, although the Anglo-French naval war in Europe had more or less ended with English victory at the battle of La Hogue in 1692.

47. The RAC both owned and hired ships for the African trade. The owners of hired vessels like *Hannibal* entered into detailed contracts (known as charter parties) with the RAC. These contracts specified the size of the crew, the number of slaves to be purchased, places of purchase and disembarkation, and so on.

48. There are no other seventeenth-century captains of same name in TSTD, so this may well have been Thomas Phillips's only African voyage, at least as a master.

49. The plaque read: 'Brecon Town Council/CAPTAIN THOMAS PHILLIPS/Havard House, Brecon/First made this/Captain's Walk/author of/A Journal of a Voyage/Made in the Hannibal 1693–94/to Africa and Barbadoes.'

50. The controversy prompted the Bristol Radical History Group to initiate a new project centred on *Hannibal*: see https://www.brh.org.uk/site/project/the-hannibal-slave-ship/ (accessed 31 August 2022).

51. TSTD 15024.

VOICES FROM THE SEA 95

52. All background information on Prideaux and *Daniel and Henry* is drawn from Tattersfield (1991).
53. TSTD 21298 is the only documented voyage for *Daniel and Henry*.
54. Tattersfield (1991). The original journal is now lost, but a version of it was copied out in 1857. As we now have it, the 1857 text ends abruptly on 20 October 20, midway through the Middle Passage. In 1920, F. C. Prideaux Nash published edited extracts from his ancestor's journal in the *Mariner's Mirror* (Prideaux Nash 1920: 3–9), and his version of the text carries on to 27 November, when *Daniel and Henry* arrived in Jamaica. Prideaux Nash omits navigational information but appears to preserve Walter Prideaux's other main observations. Tattersfield's edition (1991) draws on both the 1857 fair copy (to 20 October) and Prideaux Nash's abridged text (for 21 October–17 November). Throughout this book, all page numbers for **Prideaux, Daniel 1700** refer to Tattersfield (1991).
55. TNA: T70/175, 176.
56. Tattersfield (1991: 32).
57. TSTD 90226. Martin and Spurrell (1962: pp. xi, xvi, 22, 81, 111).
58. The journal covers the voyages of *Duke of Argyle* 1750–1 (TSTD 90350), *African* 1752–3 (TSTD 90418), and *African* 1753–4 (TSTD 90419). The original manuscript is in the NMM (NMM LOG/M/46) and has been published by Martin and Spurrell (1962), who reprint the full text of the *Duke of Argyle* journal but provide only selected entries for later voyages. I have selected only the fully published *Duke of Argyle* journal as a key case study. Throughout this book, all page numbers for **Newton, Argyle 1750–1,** refer to Martin and Spurrell (1962).
59. The imputed figures in TSTD (156 embarked, 146 disembarked) are different from those that can be reconstructed from the journal text.
60. Martin and Spurrell (1962: 95).
61. **HCSP 69: 118**. This information appears in a letter of 23 May, sent to the committee shortly after Newton's personal appearance.
62. D/EARLE/1/4. The document is currently on display in the International Slavery Museum in Liverpool. All material herein has been transcribed from the digitized copy in the *Slavery, Abolition & Social Justice* primary source collection.
63. On the cowrie currency zone, see Hogendorn and Johnson (1986: 102–9).
64. Norris (1789: 117–18).
65. Law (1989) analyses the strengths and weaknesses of Norris's account, to which was appended a brief defence of the slave trade, first published by Norris in 1788. The tone and content of the latter have much in common with Norris's parliamentary testimony.
66. TNA: BT 107/9 London Foreign Trade, 159, records *Sandown* as registered under charter to a syndicate of brokers: see Mouser (2002: 2, n. 3).
67. Gamble's original manuscript is in the NMM (NMM MS/LOG/M21). The journal entries (but not the daily navigational details) were edited by Bruce Mouser (2002). Throughout this book, all page numbers for **Gamble, Sandown 1793–4** refer to Mouser (2002).
68. Gamble's age was determined by Behrendt (2004: 147) using annotations in the journal.
69. **HCSP 69: 189**. This voyage does not appear in TSTD.
70. TSTD 82004.
71. TSTD 83993.
72. These figures, suggesting 38 captive deaths in total, appear on the title page of the journal, and were no doubt added at the end of the voyage. There is some discrepancy between these totals and the numbers that can be calculated independently from the pages of the journal itself. The latter indicate ten deaths as a result of insurrection and 34 as a result of disease: 44 deaths in all.

96 MATERIALIZING THE MIDDLE PASSAGE

73. **Gamble,** *Sandown* **1793–4: 101**. The ship departed from Cape Verga.

74. **Gamble,** *Sandown* **1973–4: 109**.

75. *Lloyds List,* Friday, 17 October 1794.

76. *Lloyds List,* Friday, 28 November 1794.

77. *Brothers*: TSTD 26060. A Samuel Gamble made a will on *Goodrich*, Master, H. Kennedy, bound out to Angola on 8 October 1798 (TSTD 87624). He left all his worldly goods to his 'friend' (common-law wife) Sarah Hyde: Lancashire County Archives WCW/Infra/C1452/73.

78. 28 Geo. III c. 54. *Sandown* cleared England on 7 April 1793, two months before another important Act was passed to regulate the slave trade (33 Geo. III c. 73).

79. The very earliest published account of an English overseas long-haul voyage in fact concerned a voyage to Guinea, undertaken by Richard Eden in 1555: Hair (1997b: 3).

80. One of the first such collections was Hakluyt (1965 [1598]), which incorporated several accounts of voyages to Guinea. These included Eden's travels and those of the first English slaver, John Hawkins. A second important collection was organized and published by Awnsham and John Churchill in 1704. The complex publishing history of *Churchills' Voyages* is detailed by Hair et al. (1992: i. pp. xxviii–xxxi). Two of the narratives followed in the present book (Thomas Phillips on *Hannibal* and the first English-language version of Barbot's writings on Guinea) appeared in the extended 1732 edition of Churchill and Churchill. It is important to note that they took editorial liberties with manuscript and published sources. Because of this I have relied on Churchill and Churchill only for Phillips's *Hannibal* voyage, and for James Barbot Jnr's account of *Don Carlos*, which is not included in Hair et al. (1992).

81. Interest in Africa expanded even further in the early eighteenth century. Almost four times as many books about Africa appeared in the first half of that century as in all of the previous one: Wheeler (1999: 15).

82. Background information on Barbot is drawn from Hair et al. (1992: i. pp. ix–vix). All page references for works by John Barbot refer to Hair et al. (1992).

83. Barbot's manuscript was accepted by the Amsterdam publisher M. Savouret, but the latter died soon after the deal was struck: Hair et al. (1992: i. p. xxv).

84. The French version remains unpublished. The English text first appeared in Churchill and Churchill (1732: v). This contained a good deal of supplementary material, with which Barbot had enlarged his French manuscript of 1688. For a detailed discussion of the composition of the English text, see Hair et al. (1992: i. pp. xxvii–xxxvi). The editors are of the opinion that Barbot began reworking the French text in 1703, completing the English version around 1711 or 1712, the year of his death. The definitive edition of Barbot's writings on Guinea edited by Hair et al. in 1992 is a translation of the original French text but incorporates most of the significant additions from the 1732 English text.

85. Hair et al. (1992: i. p. ix).

86. See, e.g., Hair (1974) and Law (1982).

87. Hair et al.1992: i. p. xlii. The journal of Barbot's 1678–9 voyage on *Soleil D'Afrique* (BL Add. MS 28788) was published by Debien et al. in 1978. This voyage (TSTD 21953) took Barbot to the Gold Coast and Ouidah.

88. TSTD 21874. Since this voyage began a year before the RAC opened up the slave trade to the ten percenters, *Griffin* would appear to have been an interloping vessel. Departing after the new 10% tax was imposed, *Albion* and *Don Carlos* were certainly 10 per cent ships.

89. Hair et al. 1992: i. p. xlii. The journal of Barbot's 1678–9 voyage on *Soleil D'Afrique* (BL Add. MS 28788) was published by Debien et al. in 1978. This voyage (TSTD 21953) took Barbot to the Gold Coast and Ouidah.

VOICES FROM THE SEA 97

90. The TSTD entry for this vessel is confusing. The departure date in TSTD is given as 8 December 1698, rather than 13 January 1699, as recorded in Barbot's text. TSTD also records an insurrection, which is not noted by Barbot. There would appear to be some confusion here with the voyage of *Don Carlos*.
91. TNA: CO 33/13: see Tattersfield (1991: 185).
92. Churchill and Churchill (1732: v. 497–522). The account of the voyage of *Don Carlos* draws on the journals of both James Barbot Jnr and that of the ship's first mate, John Casseneuve: Hair et al. (1992: i. p. cv1). John Barbot does not specifically say so, but it is likely that he part–financed this voyage: Hair et al. 1992: i. p. xvi.
93. Churchill and Churchill (1732: v. 546–548) = Hair et al. (1992: ii. 778–83).
94. Barker (1758). See Dresser (2001: 90, n. 58) for a summary of legal documentation relating to Barker's case.
95. The trustees of the Seamen's Hospital, to whom Barker had applied for relief, were members of the Society of Merchant Venturers: the SMV thus administered his pension. See Dresser (2001: 90, n. 52).
96. Barker (1809).
97. Smeathman's voyage from Sierra Leone to the Caribbean was probably TSTD 75405.
98. Coleman (2018: 176) determines that Smeathman's *Oeconomy* was written between mid-1775 and May 1777.
99. The circumstances surrounding the production of the document are detailed in Coleman (2007: 134–5). Smeathman asked Tunstall to accept the essay as a draft towards a planned volume of voyages and travels, which was never completed. The essay is reproduced in Coleman (2007: 130–47). Coleman (2018: 176–86) discusses the voyage itself in greater detail. The fair copy of Smeathman's document about his slave ship voyage is now in the collection of Michael Graves-Johnston, London. Extracts are cited throughout as **Smeathman, *Oeconomy c.1775***, following the original pagination, as noted in Coleman's 2007 transcription.
100. For discussion of another supposed 'passenger' memoir (Riland 1827), see Burstein (2020). As Burstein demonstrates, Riland's account is without doubt a fiction, and I have elected not to use his descriptions of the Middle Passage in this book.
101. These included a letter to Dru Drury describing the deck of a slave ship as seen from the vantage of the barricado (see Fyfe 1964: 76–7 and Coleman 2007: 115).
102. Coleman (2018: 230–7).
103. Butterworth was long thought to be the pseudonym of the Leeds printer Henry Schroeder, but this has now been shown to be a mistake originating in an obituary of Schroeder: see Butterworth's entry in the Dictionary of National Biography https://doi.org/10.1093/ref:odnb/101073 (accessed 18 August 2022).
104. TSTD 81890.
105. Butterworth (1823). I have used a slightly later edition, published in 1831.
106. See, e.g., Behrendt et al. (2010: 36–8).
107. Another example of a memoir by a former ship's boy, again embellished long after the events described, is Robinson (1867). The author states that he sailed on *Lady Nelson* (TSTD 82216) in 1801 (though he remembers the vessel as *Lady Neilson)* and on *Crescent* in 1802: the latter voyage may be TSTD 80934, but that vessel is thought to have sailed from Liverpool, not (as stated by Robinson), from London.
108. Butterworth's memoir is cited repeatedly, for example, in Rediker (2007), and Brown (2009) employs it as the jumping-off point for his refutation of the metaphor of social death. A comparable memoir is that of Thomas Smith, who made voyages as an ordinary seaman on *Anne Galley* (TSTD 75063) and *Squirrel* (TSTD 91025) in 1762 at the age of 20. Many years

98   MATERIALIZING THE MIDDLE PASSAGE

later, he wrote (or perhaps dictated) an account of his experiences that was edited and then published for the author in his home town of Arbroath in 1813: a surviving copy was recently digitized by the National Library of Scotland and can be read at https://digital.nls.uk/antiquarian-books-of-scotland/archive/120564108#?c=0&m=0&s=0&cv=0&xywh=-852%2C-106%2C2849%2C2112 (accessed 22 August 2022). I have employed Smith's memoir at several points (particularly in Chapters 10 and 11), but with the caveat that I have reservations about the validity of certain of his recollections.

109. Crow (1830). The edition used here is the facsimile reprint of 1970 by Frank Cass & Co. A further edition appeared in 2007: it is reviewed by Law 2007. As Law (2007: 484) notes, the relationship between what Crow wrote and what his executors caused to be published was not straightforward, and in the absence of the original manuscript it is necessary to rely on the statements of the original editors, who acknowledge retrenchment in cases of verbosity and the omission of personal attacks on leading abolitionists but have clearly added some material post-dating Crow's slave shipping experience.

110. See Paley et al. (2010) for the (abortive) bills concerning slavery discussed in Parliament between 1660 and 1710. In the decade leading up to the final expiry of the RAC's monopoly on the slave trade in 1712, the fate of company's forts was a matter of national debate, with the Board of Trade launching an inquiry into the organization of the slave trade in 1708: Mann (2018: 113).

111. Brown (2007: 27).

112. Brown (2007: 28).

113. Oldfield (2003: p. xiii).

114. For a recent summary of the HCSP volumes, and an index of names and places, Lovejoy and Oliveira (2013). The authors emphasize both the importance of these data, and the limited use made of them by historians of the slave trade.

115. See Jennings (1997: 34–51) for a useful summary of the formation of the London committee.

116. Clarkson (1808: i. 463). The committee commissioned publication of 3,000 copies of both Newton's and Falconbridge's memoirs in January 1788.

117. Details on the life of Falconbridge are drawn from Fyfe (2000) and Clarkson (1808).

118. TSTD 17948 imputes 335 captives purchased, but Falconbridge later recalled (**HCSP 69: 120**) that the ship had carried 380 Africans, and that 'upwards of 100' died. Richardson (1996: 100) notes that the agents for their sale were Campbell, Baillie & Co., who reported selling 273 slaves for an average of £35 5s. 5d. each. Campbell, Baillie & Co. went on to report that the vessel had had 'the Misfortune to bu[r]y a great many' and that they had had to sell 'at Vendue 34 so meagre & sickly as to produce very little'.

119. Between 1780 and 1787, Frazer captained at least seven Guinea voyages (TSTD 17902, 17913, 17920, 17933, 17952, 17967, 17990), transporting an imputed 2,369 Africans. Of these, 2,018 are estimated to have disembarked in the Caribbean (a mortality rate of 9%). Falconbridge (**HCSP 72: 310**) described Frazer as 'one of the very best men in the trade'.

120. 'Never were words more welcome to my ears,' Clarkson (1808: i. 348) was later to recall.

121. Clarkson (1808: i. 388).

122. 6,025 copies of the *Account* were produced—one of the largest print runs for a SEAST text: Swaminathan (2016: 100).

123. From 1788, surgeons were obliged by law to keep a journal recording slave numbers, along with deaths and causes of death among both slaves and crew. The Dolben Act (28 Geo. III c. 54) required that surgeons keep 'a regular and true Journal' and should deliver this to a British port official upon arrival at the ship's first port of call in the Americas.

124. Anna Maria Falconbridge, *Narrative of Two Voyages to the River Sierra Leone during the Years 1791-1792-1793*, can also be found in Fyfe (2000). Anna Maria was one of the first European women to write about Africa, and her *Narrative* has thus received considerable attention. An

interesting discussion of the text, and the author's attitude to the slave trade, can be found in Thomas (2000: 43–5).

125. TSTD 18159.

126. Two versions of Newton's pamphlet appeared in 1788: I have used the twenty-four-page version printed for, among others, J. Phillips.

127. Clarkson (1789: 182–3).

128. *Substance* was originally published without the names of the witnesses or ships: both have been identified using the annotated version of the text in Oldfield (2003: 181–320).

129. Warren (2013: 201).

130. Two main forms of commons committee existed at this time: the Committee of the Whole House and the Select Committee. The latter included only a subset of MPs, meeting outside the main debating chamber: see Innes (2005: 122). The slave trade inquiries were conducted at various points by both kinds of committee. See LoGerfo (1973 for a detailed account of events leading up to the passage of the Dolben Act.

131. See Waldman (1965: 187–8) for Liverpool Council's vote of thanks to these men in June 1788.

132. The inquiry that opened in May 1789 was initially conducted by a Committee of the Whole, but in January 1790 was turned over to a Select Committee (Jennings 1997: 58).

133. For further details on this and other late eighteenth–century ceramics depicting British slave ships see Webster (2015).

134. Innes (2005: 121).

135. Paton (1996: 165).

136. Innes (2005: 129).

137. I am grateful to Stephen Farrell (in his former role as Senior Research Fellow of the History of Parliament Trust) for discussing the inquiry process with me. Farrell suggested that the chairman of a committee would have had the most say in how the committee was run, who was examined, the questions to be asked, and by whom. Generally speaking, this would have occurred in a fairly informal fashion. Sometimes committees would have discussed and even voted on who to call and what line of questioning to take, but that would almost certainly not have been recorded formally.

138. Clarkson (1808: ii. 3).

139. Clarkson (1808: ii. 3).

140. Matthews was appointed as a delegate at some point after the inquiry process began; **see HCSP 69: 12** and Sanderson (1972: 64).

141. See Rediker (2007: 331–5) for a brief discussion of discrepancies in the Noble–Trotter testimonies.

142. Cobbett (1816: 46), reporting comments by Wilberforce during a debate of 12 May 1789. Wilberforce stated that 'the situation of the slaves has been described by Mr Norris, one of the Liverpool delegates, in a manner which, I am sure will convince the House how interest can draw a film over the eyes, so thick that total blindness could do no more.'

143. Handler (2002) painstakingly draws together the handful of surviving autobiographic accounts by individuals making the Middle Passage on British ships. Of the fifteen accounts he has traced, only six make any reference to the voyage itself; in most cases, these references are very brief indeed.

144. Hall's 'Memoirs' is preserved in the papers of the Jamaican plantation-owner Robert Johnson (1739–1839) and was written, in Johnson's own hand, at some point between 1810 and 1830. The document is discussed, and transcribed in full, in Browne and Sweet (2016).

145. I use this term (following Thomas 2000: 158) to refer to texts published in England and composed, dictated, or co-edited by slaves and ex-slaves. These texts were usually accompanied by an engraved portrait of the subject of the narrative, passages of biblical text, poetic epigrams, authenticating testimonials, certificates of manumission, letters and dedications to benefactors, and so on.

146. Innes (2005: 17–55) and the papers in Carretta and Gould (2001) provide an overview of eighteenth-century black Atlantic writing.
147. Carretta (1999, 2005).
148. See, e.g., Byrd 2006, Lovejoy (2006a, 2007), Carretta (2007).
149. Other African and African-Caribbean arrivals in eighteenth-century Britain included sailors, soldiers, musicians, actors, prostitutes, princes, scholars, students, and professional beggars: Fraser (1993: 52–4). It is estimated that by the late eighteenth century, 10,000–20,000 black people were resident in Britain: Innes (2005: 11).
150. See Carey (2003: 6) on the likelihood that Sancho's birth story is a posthumous fabrication by Jekyll.
151. Victoria & Albert Museum F.118:194.
152. Cugoano (1787).
153. Cugoano (1787: 9–10).

4

Artefacts from the Sea

Shipwrecks and Maritime Archaeology

Ships are big things; so big that it is hard to consider them as artefacts of the human past as we would ceramic sherds, coins, or post holes. But slave ships *are* of course artefacts: physical statements both articulating the discourse of chattel slavery and enabling one of its outcomes: the forced migration of captive Africans. There are many ways to materialize these vessels today, from the eyewitness accounts introduced in Chapter 3, to the paintings, ship models, and other objects examined in Chapters 5 and 6. The present chapter focuses on another strand of evidence: the wreck data uncovered by maritime archaeologists. Had it been written twenty years ago, this would have been a very short chapter indeed, but the millennium ushered in several new archaeological initiatives, stimulated by the imminent bicentenaries of the abolition of the British, American, Dutch, and French trades. Much has happened in the period since I last attempted a synthetic account of work on slaver wrecks in 2008, yet it remains the case that few slaving vessels have been located, and fewer still have been explored in any detail by maritime archaeologists.[1] Excavated wrecks are still too few to confine myself to British examples in this chapter, so all known examples, whatever their port of origin, are discussed below. Two ships stand out here: the British *Henrietta Marie* (lost in 1700) and the Danish *Fredensborg* (lost in 1768). They remain the only active transatlantic slavers to have been subject to both extensive excavation and detailed archival research.

Having considered *Henrietta Marie*, *Fredensborg*, and other located wrecks, this chapter then moves on to ex-slavers—ships once used in the slave trade but employed in other ways at the time of their loss. The final section considers wrecked vessels that may have been involved in the slave trade, but whose identities remain uncertain. Figure 4.1 shows the locations of the ships discussed. The overall purpose of this chapter is to offer a broad overview of known and potential slaving wrecks, and to introduce the range of the material recovered from them. The details these sites have furnished concerning the construction of slave ships are set out in Chapter 5, and, as the book progresses, I will consider the artefacts recovered from these wrecks in greater detail.

Materializing the Middle Passage: A Historical Archaeology of British Slave Shipping, 1680–1807. Jane Webster, Oxford University Press. © Jane Webster 2023. DOI: 10.1093/oso/9780199214594.003.0004

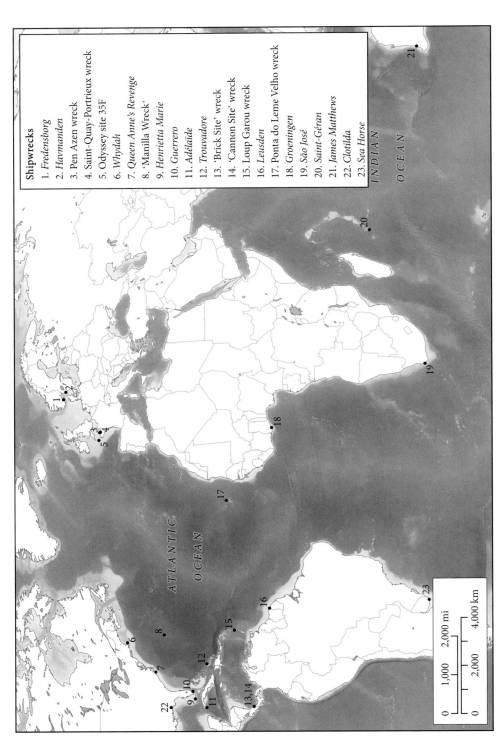

Figure 4.1 Locations of the wreck sites discussed in Chapter 4.

Maritime Archaeology and Slave Shipping

Few floating eighteenth- and nineteenth-century wooden ships survive today, and certainly no former slave ships. The only way to examine the extant physical remains of slaving vessels is, therefore, to locate wrecks. In theory, this should not be overly difficult to do, because many vessels were lost at sea during the slave trade. More than one thousand such losses are currently recorded in the TSTD data set, and further, undocumented, examples must also be envisaged.[2] Yet only a handful of slaver wrecks have been located to date, and, before going further, it is important to ask why.

Before the present century, few maritime archaeologists showed an interest in slave shipping, and even fewer made a deliberate effort to locate slaver wrecks.[3] This helps to explain why, even today, the slave ship still tends to be overlooked in general texts on maritime archaeology.[4] Why have so few slaver wrecks been found, and why has the work that has been done failed to find its way into mainstream academic publishing? In part, the answer lies in the difficult relationship between commercial salvage companies and maritime archaeologists working in the heritage and academic sectors. Despite the rapid growth of maritime archaeology as a discipline, underwater search and excavation was (and still is) so costly that many historic wrecks were (and still are) discovered, not by heritage professionals, but by salvors who target treasure ships. It is no accident that two of the slaver wrecks identified thus far, *Henrietta Marie* and *Adélaïde*, were discovered by private companies investigating Caribbean routes plied by Spanish treasure fleets, while two of the located ex-slavers, *Whydah* and *Queen Anne's Revenge*, were also found by salvors in search of pirate gold. The bicentenary of the abolition of the British slave trade fell in 2007, and the Netherlands and France marked similar anniversaries in 2014 and 2015 respectively. These bicentenaries stimulated a new academic interest in slaver wrecks and saw the establishment of numerous projects, discussed below. Yet *Fredensborg*, located in 1974, and *Clotilda*, found in 2018, remain the only transatlantic slaver wrecks to have been deliberately and successfully sought for non-commercial reasons.

The discovery in 1972 of *Henrietta Marie* highlights the issues that arise when a private company locates and obtains legal title to a slaver wreck. What remains of *Henrietta Marie* lies on New Ground Reef, 35 miles west of Key West (Florida) and was located by Treasure Salvors Incorporated, a commercial salvage company. The discovery was an accidental one, the company's primary goal being the *Nuestra Señora de Atocha,* a Spanish treasure galleon. It became clear in 1973 that the newly discovered ship was not *Atocha*, and the company's attention shifted elsewhere.[5] The *Atocha* wreck was finally located in 1985, and, in the interim, the anonymous English wreck of 1972 remained largely unexplored.[6] In 1983, salvor Henry Taylor began work on the wreck site, under an agreement with a second salvor, Mel Fisher. One of the team employed by Taylor and Fisher was a professional archaeologist, David Moore, and one of his divers made a fortuitous find that clinched the ship's identity—a cast bronze bell etched at the waist with the words 'THE HENRIETTA MARIE 1699'. Thanks to this discovery, the wreck was quickly identified as a London-registered slave ship.

104 MATERIALIZING THE MIDDLE PASSAGE

Moore returned to the site in 1984 and 1985, but, after that, no further work took place for some time. In 1988 the Mel Fisher Maritime Heritage Society (MFMHS) assumed responsibility for the wreck, and in 1991 a team led by MFMHS archaeologist Corey Malcolm returned briefly to *Henrietta Marie*. After another hiatus, more work was undertaken in 2001–2. This phase included a detailed re-examination of the condition of the surviving portion of the ship's hull.[7]

In 1993 Mel Fisher donated his claim to the wreck site and all the artefacts he had retrieved from it to the Mel Fisher Maritime Heritage Society (now the Mel Fisher Maritime Museum (MFMM)). This is a not-for-profit organization, funding ongoing research and conservation on the *Henrietta Marie* material. A small number of research reports have been made available online, and via the internet and its touring exhibition, *A Slave Ship Speaks*, the MFMHS can be credited with having taken pioneering steps in bringing the archaeology of slave shipping to a wide public audience.[8] But, as this summary will have made clear, in the forty years since its discovery, work on the *Henrietta Marie* has been sporadic, with the findings princi-pally disseminated not through academic papers, but via the MFMM website. Partly for this reason, but also as a result of the fraught relationship between commercial salvors and heritage professionals, information about the *Henrietta Marie* has taken a long time to find its way into mainstream academic writing on the archaeology of slave shipping.[9] But after a long period in which only two slaver wrecks have been available for study, several new finds have been made in recent years, and the future for maritime archaeology in this field looks more promising. The remainder of this chapter explores these wrecks and the finds from them. In each of the sections below the wrecks are presented in chronological order of their date of discovery.

The Excavated Wrecks

Henrietta Marie (1700)

Henrietta Marie was a London-registered ship, making its second documented slaving voyage.[10] The first, in 1697, had been as an interloper, circumventing the monopoly still help by the RAC at that time. That monopoly ended in 1698, and *Henrietta Marie* became one of the first generation of ten percenters, paying a tax to the RAC in order to participate legally in the slave trade. Having cleared Jamaica in June 1700, shortly after selling 190 captives, the ship struck New Ground Reef off the southern tip of Florida.[11] The lower stern portion of the slaver, which had been torn away from the (unlocated) remainder of the hull, was discovered by Treasure Salvors Inc. in 1972.

Henrietta Marie was a ship of 120 tons and is unlikely to have been built specifically for the slave trade. Indeed, it is likely that the vessel was built in France for use in the English Channel trade and was captured as a prize during the Anglo-French King William's War.[12] The ship was then bought up by a consortium of London-based traders, renamed, and entered the slave trade. The varied interests of the owning syndicate are clearly reflected in the trade goods recorded as being loaded on board the *Henrietta Marie* from July to September 1699.[13] These included 282 lb of Great Bugles (a tubular form of trade bead), a large quantity of cloth, 14.5 cwt of pewter, and 1,200 copper bars.[14] In total, 28 iron bars, some 13,000 glass beads, and 328 pewter basins, spoons, tankards, and bottles have been recovered from the *Henrietta Marie* wreck site. The ship's trade goods are considered in detail in Chapter 7. Additional finds from the *Henrietta Marie* wreck site provide valuable information about the daily routines of a slave ship. They include medical equipment, eighty sets of shackles, two copper cooking stoves, a grindstone, and two cast-iron cannons. These artefacts are discussed in Chapters 9 and 10.

Fredensborg (1768)

Fredensborg, a vessel belonging to the Danish West-India Guinea Company (the Danish equivalent of the British RAC), ran aground at Tromøy, an island outside Arendal in southern Norway, in 1768. The slaver had almost made it home to Copenhagen following a voyage from the Gold Coast to St Croix in the Danish West Indies, where 265 Africans had been sold.[15] The wreck was discovered in 1974 by diver Leif Svalesen (Figure 4.2). The circumstances of this discovery differ from that of

Figure 4.2 Model of *Fredensborg*, built by Terry Andersen. Aust-Agder Museum.

Henrietta Marie in one very important respect. Put simply, Svalesen was looking for *Fredensborg*. Armed with archival data, including the records of the Court of Inquiry held after the shipwreck, he also had a good idea where to find it. The wreck was successfully located within a month of the first dive.[16]

Archaeological work was carried out in 1975 and 1977, and again in 1995–7.[17] Svalesen spent more than twenty years researching this ship, and the Danish slave trade in general, and published a detailed account of the voyage and excavation of *Fredensborg* in 2000.[18] The ship sank in shallow water, and every life on board was saved. Remarkably, three logbooks were rescued along with the crew, and *Fredensborg* thus has the unique distinction of being the only located slaver wreck for which sea logs or journals survive. The first of these journals was maintained by the Captain, Espen Kiønig, the second by the Chief Officer, Peder Christian Lundberg, and the third by the Ship's Assistant (supercargo), Christian Hoffmann.[19] These and other documents now in the Danish National Archives provide an unparalleled level of detail about the construction, cargo, crew, and slaving voyages of *Fredensborg*.[20]

Most of the hull was crushed when the ship sank, but some timbers and iron fittings survive, along with elements of the rigging, armaments, and tools. *Fredensborg* was carrying a varied homeward cargo, incorporating elephant and hippopotamus ivory from the Gold Coast and large quantities of mahogany and dyewood from the Caribbean: as discussed in Chapter 8, many slave ships carried supplementary cargoes such as these. Personal possessions of the crew recovered from the seabed included a wooden box containing writing equipment, sealing wax and seals; book bindings; and items of clothing including shoes, buckles, and buttons. The finds from the *Fredensborg* excavations are curated by the Norwegian Maritime Museum (Oslo) and the Aust-Agder Museum (Arendal). Staff at the latter have complied a digitized catalogue of the *Fredensborg* material, and images of some of the finds recovered from the wreck site can be seen on the DigitaltMuseum website.[21] Even though the ship's captives had been disembarked, significant traces of their experiences remain. Iron objects such as shackles and other restraints had rusted away in the salt water, but clear imprints of shackles were found on the seabed. Other finds included African mortars (grindstones) used to prepare meals, and clay pipes distributed to captives during the Middle Passage. These finds are considered in Chapters 10 and 11.

Sea Horse (1728)

In 1713, as discussed in Chapter 2, the British South Sea Company won the coveted *asiento* to supply the Spanish colonies with slaves. *Sea Horse* was one of the ships fulfilling that contract. Having disembarked 225 captives from Madagascar at Buenos Aires, the 230-ton ship was wrecked off Gorriti Island, Uruguay in 1728.[22] The wreck site has been located, but very little information has appeared concerning it.

All that seems to remain are some of the ship's cannon and ballast stone, spread over a 400 m² area of the seabed.[23]

Adélaïde (1714)

The French slaver *Adélaïde* was excavated during the summer of 2003 by maritime explorer Franck Goddio, better known for his work on the Egyptian port of Alexandria. A private researcher whose work is funded by the Hilti Foundation of Lichtenstein, Goddio has worked on more than fifty underwater sites since the 1980s. Since 2003 he has worked closely with Oxford University, overseeing underwater fieldwork for the University's Centre for Maritime Archaeology.[24] *Adélaïde* was discovered during a survey mission off the south-west coast of Cuba, and as yet no publications have appeared on the work carried out there.[25] The 400-ton ship was the property of Louis XIV of France, and had been chartered by the *Compagnie de l'Assentio*, a French company supplying slaves to Spain. The vessel had sailed from Lorient in Brittany to Ouidah in the Bight of Benin, purchasing 300 captives, who then made the Middle Passage to Léogane in Haiti.[26] The ship encountered a hurricane after departing Haiti, and was thrown onto a reef.[27] *Adélaïde* was extensively damaged, and most of the surviving remains comprise heavy, structural elements of the vessel itself. But human remains were reportedly also located, along with parts of the rigging, navigational instruments, ceramics, shackles, and two anchors (Figure 4.3).

Figure 4.3 Underwater archaeologist on the site of *Adélaïde*, wrecked during a hurricane (10 October 1714), on the coast of Cuba. FranckGoddio/Hilti Foundation.

The Elmina Wreck (Mid-Seventeenth Century)

No archaeological shipwreck survey of any sort was undertaken in sub-Saharan West Africa until 2003, when archaeologists from Syracuse University initiated a survey project focused on the approaches to Elmina (Ghana), the earliest and largest European trading entrepôt on the West African coast. In that one year, seventy potential wreck sites were located, and three targets have subsequently been investigated in more detail. The assemblage from one of these sites spans the entire slave trade and beyond, and is clearly mixed, but much of the material is of mid-seventeenth-century date and derives from a single wrecking episode (Figure 4.4). This was almost certainly the loss of the Dutch West India Company's *Groeningen*, which sank off Elmina when one of its

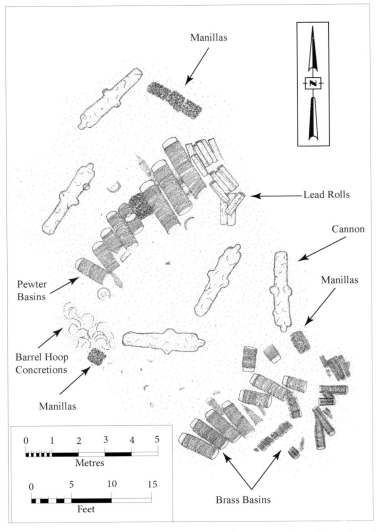

Figure 4.4 Site plan of the Elmina wreck, showing the range of artefacts identified, and their locations. Gregory Cook.

guns exploded as it saluted the castle upon arrival in 1647.[28] This wreck is a very important source of the kinds of artefact routinely employed in bartering for captives and provides a wealth of information on the carriage of such goods. The trade beads and brass basins recovered from the wreck site are discussed in Chapter 7.

The vessels described above are the only working slave ships to have been excavated to date. One further vessel remains to be noted here, however. In 2000–1, archaeologists from Bohuslän County Museum, Sweden, carried out a limited programme of reconnaissance on the wreck of *Havmanden*, a Danish West India Company ship wrecked off Björkö Island (Göthenborg, Sweden) in 1683, and discovered by sport divers in 1999.[29] *Havmanden* was travelling from Copenhagen to the Danish colony of St Thomas (West Indies), carrying building materials, colonists, and prisoners sentenced to plantation labour, but it was intended that, having arrived in St Thomas, the ship would then undertake a slaving voyage to Africa.[30] A mutiny in the early stages of the voyage put paid to these plans. The colonists and prisoners were put ashore in the Azores, and the ship turned home for Copenhagen. After suffering storm damage, *Havmanden* foundered off the west coast of Sweden on 30 October 1683. Only a handful of artefacts have been recovered from the wreck site. They include the remains of the ship's bell, two grindstones, and two ceramic jugs. Other finds include bricks—presumably some of the building materials being carried out to St Thomas—and the anchor (Figure 4.5).

Figure 4.5 Brick stack on the *Havmanden* wreck site. Attempts are being made to protect the site by covering it with geotextile, as seen in the foreground. Bohusläns Museum.

São José

The search for slaver wrecks today is spearheaded by the Slave Wrecks Project (SWP), a collaborative initiative launched in 2008 by the Smithsonian's National Museum of African American History and Culture (NMAAHC), with partners including IZIKO (Museums of South Africa).[31] One of the partnership's key successes to date has been the excavation of the wreck of the Portuguese *São José*, wrecked off Cape Town in 1794 while transporting captives from Mozambique. The wreck was initially located (and misidentified) in the 1980s. In 2010 the SWP uncovered archival information that stimulated new underwater work, which continued until 2015. Hull timbers, a pulley, and iron ballast from the ship are currently on display at the Smithsonian's NMAAHC, which opened in 2016 (Figure 4.6). The choice of this vessel—whose captives were shipped from Mozambique to South Africa and did not make a transatlantic crossing to the Americas—speaks to the relationship between NMAAHC and the SWP but also to the continuing reluctance of publicly funded institutions to display artefacts derived

Figure 4.6 Basket (143 × 165 × 165 mm) created in 2015 by artisans in Mossuril, Mozambique. The soil it contained was poured into the ocean at the site of the *São José* shipwreck, symbolically reconnecting the deceased with their homeland. Smithsonian Institution, 2016.168ab.

from the transatlantic slaver wrecks excavated by salvage companies. The *São José* wreck remains unpublished at the time of writing.[32]

Clotilda (1860)

The schooner *Clotilda* was the last documented vessel to carry captive Africans to North America, transporting 100 captives from Ouidah to Mobile, Alabama, in 1860.[33] In 2018, The Smithsonian NMAAHC, the SWP, the Alabama Historical Commission, and SEARCH Inc. joined forces to locate the remains of the ship, which upon completion of its (illegal) voyage was burnt to the waterline and sunk in the Mobile River. In May 2019, it was announced that the vessel had been found, and its identity authenticated.[34] This is a truly remarkable discovery, but at the time of writing little information has appeared concerning this very new find.[35] Documentary evidence shows that the 121-ton twin-masted schooner was built in Mobile, and the limited information available at present suggests that timbers and metalwork from the vessel have survived both its burning, and long submersion in the river.

The Ex-Slavers

This section examines excavated ships that were not actively engaged in the slave trade at the time they were wrecked, but that had formerly been employed as slavers. Three ships fall into this category, and the identity of one of them, the purported *Queen Anne's Revenge*, is much debated.

Whydah (Wrecked 1717)

Whydah is a contentious ship of firsts: the first pirate ship to be excavated, during the first major commercial salvage project in the USA to involve the direct participation of professional maritime archaeologists.[36] The wreck was located in 1982 by salvor Barry Clifford, who has given it pride of place in a pirate-themed heritage attraction at Yarmouth, Massachusetts.[37] *Whydah* was a London-built slaver, but was captured in the Bahamas by the pirate Samuel Bellamy in February 1717, shortly after selling its captives in Jamaica.[38] Bellamy was not to be master of *Whydah* for long: as he was returning to Cape Cod in April 1717 the ship was wrecked in a storm off Marconi Beach, and he and most of his crew were drowned.

Thousands of artefacts have been recovered from the 300-ton *Whydah*.[39] Among the most important, with reference to the ship's slave trading past, are fragmentary gold ornaments from the Gold Coast. They comprise the oldest known group of reliably dated Akan gold artefacts in the world.[40] Small gold ornaments (sold by weight, in the same way as gold grains) were often acquired in the course of slaving

112   MATERIALIZING THE MIDDLE PASSAGE

voyages to the Gold Coast, and, like many vessels, the *Whydah* had traded for both gold and slaves while in Africa.[41] Gold items were not purchased for any perceived artistic merit; they would simply be melted down for bullion. Many of the pieces from *Whydah* are chopped, flattened, folded, or show other signs of wear, and it is possible that they were acquired as scrap metal when the ship was trading for slaves. Pirates menaced merchant shipping on the African coast, as well as the Caribbean, however, and a member of Bellamy's crew may conceivably have acquired these items at another time. The *Whydah* gold is discussed in more detail in Chapter 8.

Unlike most of the vessels discussed in this chapter, *Whydah* was built specifically for the slave trade. Contemporary accounts referred to the ship as a galley (a term that denotes the shape of the hull, which was designed for speed as well as for carrying capacity). Even though the remains of *Whydah* are very widely scattered on the seabed, excavation, in conjunction with the examination of historical documents, has revealed some important details of the architecture and components of the ship.[42] These features are discussed in Chapter 5.

Queen Anne's Revenge (1718)

In 1996, the salvage company Intersal Inc., under contract with the state of North Carolina, discovered the remains of a wreck off Beaufort Inlet. The ship was quickly identified as *Queen Anne's Revenge*, the flagship of the notorious pirate Edward Teach (Blackbeard), and one of two ships he deliberately grounded on the shoals off Beaufort Inlet in June 1718.[43] Since its discovery, the state of North Carolina has led the excavation of the site through the North Carolina Department of Natural and Cultural Resources (NCDNCR) Underwater Archaeology Branch with collaboration from East Carolina University and North Carolina Marine Fisheries (Figure 4.7).[44] The fact that the ship was discovered by treasure salvors who retain some commercial rights relating to the finds has undoubtedly led to some animosity towards the project.[45] The vessel's identity is also questioned by some scholars.[46] This debate matters here, because *Queen Anne's Revenge* had begun its career as a French slave ship, *La Concorde de Nantes*. *Concorde* made three documented slaving voyages,[47] and, when captured by Blackbeard in November 1717, had not yet completed the last of these. Having purchased an imputed 516 captives at Ouidah, the vessel was nearing the end of the Middle Passage but was seized 60 miles south of Martinique.[48]

Over 400,000 artefacts have been recovered from the wreck site, many of them referencing the ship's French origins.[49] Among these are a range of implements and containers used by *Concorde*'s surgeons, discussed in Chapter 9. Artefacts suggestive of a slaving voyage to Africa include 798 tube-drawn glass beads, and a single African-made powder-glass bead, discussed in more detail in Chapter 7. *Concorde* had purchased gold in Africa, and the 15,000 gold grains (20 g in weight in total) recovered from sediment may represent all that is left of the 20 lb of gold

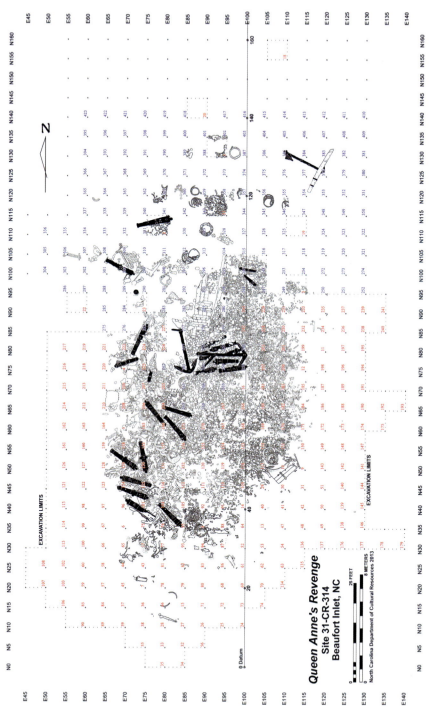

Figure 4.7 *Queen Anne's Revenge* site plan. North Carolina Department of Natural and Cultural Resources.

reportedly confiscated by the pirates who seized the ship.[50] Shackle components have also been found on the wreck site.

James Matthews (1841)

During the 1830s, Britain made efforts to persuade other governments to permit condemned vessels to be broken up before resale, and a break-up clause was successfully inserted into the Anglo-Spanish anti-slave trade treaty of 1835.[51] Both Portugal and Brazil resisted the break-up of slave ships, however. In 1837 HMS *Griffon*, a British anti-slavery vessel patrolling the coast of Dominica, captured *Don Francisco*, a Portuguese-owned slaver *en route* from Whydah to Havana. Built in Bordeaux in the late 1700s, *Don Francisco* was a single decked, fast, shallow-draft, 107-ton snow brig.[52] The vessel was captured as a 'prize' by HM Brig *Griffon* in 1837 and condemned by the Court of Mixed Commission at Sierra Leone. It should have been broken up, yet this already very elderly ship was later re-registered in London for general trading purposes, as *James Matthews*.[53] In 1841, having carried settlers and roofing slates to Fremantle, Western Australia, *James Matthews* foundered after grounding in a storm.

The wreck was excavated between 1973 and 1977 by staff from the Department of Maritime Archaeology at the Western Australia Maritime Museum and is well published.[54] The wreck site was totally exposed during the 1975–6 summer season, when the detailed site plan in Figure 4.8 was completed.

The hull of *James Matthews* is very well preserved, and the ship's final cargo of roofing slates and other constructional materials survived largely intact.[55] More than eight hundred additional artefacts were recovered from the wreck, ranging from fittings and cordage to personal effects of the crew.[56] As might be expected given the ship's history, none of the manufactured goods found on this vessel relates directly to *James Matthew*'s slave trading past. As will become clear in Chapter 5, however, the wreck provides a wealth of information about the construction and components of a shallow-draft slaver from the latter stages of the slave trade.

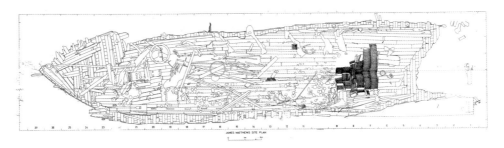

Figure 4.8 Plan of the *James Matthews* shipwreck. Western Australia Museum.

Possible Slaver Wrecks

Into the group of possible slaver wrecks fall several seventeenth- and eighteenth-century wrecks that have produced artefacts indicative of a voyage to Africa but cannot be shown with certainty to have been engaged in the slave trade. The difficulty here is that, while the glass beads, copper-alloy manillas, and other trade goods recovered from these wrecks were things regularly used in bartering for captives (as detailed in Chapter 7), such goods were also carried by bilateral trading vessels exchanging European manufactures for African resources other than slaves. Similarly, African elephant ivory was frequently carried home to Europe by slavers (as seen in Chapter 8) but arrived on other vessels too. The identity and function of the vessels discussed below are thus uncertain, but some of them may well have been slave ships.

Little remains of the first of these vessels, discovered in 1973 off Ponta do Leme Velho, Sal Island, Cape Verde. It, or the assemblage that survives today, was revealed by the explosives employed in salvaging cargo from a modern vessel. The material comprises faience plates, bowls, glass, and other artefacts suggestive of a Portuguese vessel dating 1680–1700. The ship was also carrying glass beads and manillas, which might suggest involvement in the slave trade. Most of the Portuguese slavers servicing Brazil stopped at Cape Verde to take on supplies, and it is perhaps no coincidence that two of the bowls in the assemblage bear the coat of arms of a leading Brazilian family (the de Negreiros). The bead concretions are discussed in Chapter 7.[57]

Another site yielding manillas—the largest number yet recovered from a wreck—was discovered 6 miles north-east of Bermuda in 1975.[58] By 1977 salvors had recovered a cannon embossed with the logo of the Dutch West India Company and a significant collection of items commonly used as slave trade 'currency'. Among these were approximately 10,000 glass trade beads, and many manillas. The latter prompted the name Manilla Wreck, by which the site has been known ever since (see Figure 4.10).[59] A two-phase programme of professional archaeological fieldwork was carried out in 1998–9, under Clifford Smith of the Bermuda Maritime Museum.[60] No traces of ships timbers were located, but twenty cannons were found. Although the recovered artefacts were concentrated in a small area (20 × 25 m), they included ceramics and bottle glass with a date range centred on 1720–60. On the basis of their 1998–9 work, the excavators concluded that the Manilla Wreck is not a wreck at all but comprises a scatter of debris cast overboard from a ship damaged on the Bermuda reef system.[61] They have conjectured that *Amazon*, a distressed French ship arriving in Bermuda in 1739, may have jettisoned these finds. *Amazon* had been making its way from St Domingue to Nantes. It is not certain either that the ship was engaged in the slave trade (it is not in the TSTD), or that the excavated finds can be traced to it.[62] The wreck site produced many Dutch-made items, from the cannon mentioned above to trade beads and case (square) gin bottles. Analysis of the beads and some of the other finds has suggested that the material derives from a Dutch ship, dating to the mid-eighteenth century.[63]

116 MATERIALIZING THE MIDDLE PASSAGE

Another possible slaver wreck lies at Saint-Quay-Portrieux, off Brittany.[64] As in the case of *Fredensborg*, ivory tusks comprised the first finds to be brought up from this wreck—some being found as early as the 1930s. These finds indicate that the ship traded in Africa, and it may have been a slaver. More than a hundred African elephant tusks have been recovered since the 1980s, along with forty glass trade beads and a single brass manilla. One of the most interesting finds from this wreck is a portion of a cross-staff, used for astronomical navigation, and stamped with a date of either 1719 or (more likely) 1711.[65] This artefact suggests *a terminus post quem* for the wreck event, but it is impossible to determine whether the ship was engaged in slave trading, or traded directly with Africa for ivory and other goods. Many of the closest parallels for artefacts recovered from the wreck site are of Dutch manufacture, but it is by no means certain that this is a Dutch ship. Other possible (but unidentified) slaver wrecks include an unidentified vessel at Pen Azen, France, explored by DRASSM (*Direction des Recherches Archéologiques Subaquatiques et Sous-Marines*) in 1994 and 1995. The site is known to have produced manillas and other finds, but this wreck remains unpublished. In 1991, an elephant tusk was recovered from a wreck at Loup Garou (Martinique), the find again pointing to a ship involved in trade with Africa, if not the slave trade. The wreck of *Saint-Géran*, a ship belonging to the French Compagnie des Indes, has also been briefly examined by divers. *Saint-Géran* was wrecked off the island of Maurice (Martinique) in 1744, with thirty captives on board.[66]

In 2003–5 the MFMHS and RPM Nautical Foundation initiated a search for the wreck of the Spanish slaver *Guerrero*, which foundered off Turtle Harbour, North Key West (Florida), in 1827 while under fire from a British anti-slavery patrol vessel.[67] This quest was in part stimulated by archival research carried out on the *Guerrero* tragedy by local writer Gail Swanson.[68] *Guerrero* was in transit to Cuba, with more than five hundred captives on board: most were taken off the foundering vessel and subsequently sold in Cuba, but forty-one perished in the wreck event. The 2003–5 magnetometer survey identified multiple anomalies, including traces of a shipwreck (Site 2–04), which is thought to be *Guerrero*. None of the material recovered from the wreck site from 2004–15 is indicative of the slave trade, however.[69]

In 2005 the salvage company Odyssey Marine Exploration initiated a project in the Western Approaches of the English Channel, and in the same year discovered the poorly preserved remains of a heavily armed vessel dating to the period 1660–1700.[70] The ship was carrying a cargo, almost all of it now lost, which included ivory tusks, brass basins, and manillas, all of which are indicative of trade in West Africa (Figure 4.9). Only fifty-eight artefacts have been recovered from the site, and it cannot be established with certainty that the vessel was engaged in the slave trade. Even so, the working hypothesis that Odyssey site 35F may be all that is left of a late-seventeenth- century RAC ship is plausible.[71] Unfortunately, the wreck lies in heavily fished waters, inhibiting the prospect of further work and exposing what is left to displacement and damage.

ARTEFACTS FROM THE SEA 117

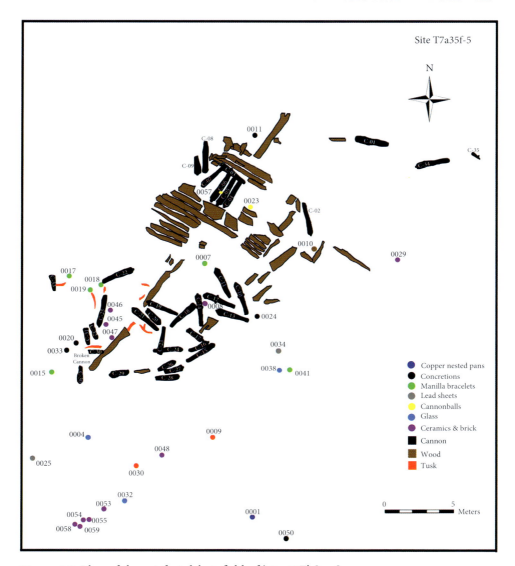

Figure 4.9 Plan of the artefact debris field of 'site 35F' Sea Scape.

In the Bahamas region, a search was initiated in 2004 for *Trouvadore*, grounded on a reef at Breezy Point on the Caicos Bank (Turks and Caicos Islands) in 1841.[72] Sailing with a crew of twenty under Spanish papers, *Trouvadore* had purchased captives at São Tomé. When the ship foundered, the crew were seized and most of the 193 Africans who struggled ashore were liberated. The majority (168 in all) were distributed among salt proprietors on Salt Cay and Grand Turk and were given one-year 'apprenticeships' in salt production. What happened to these Africans after this period is uncertain, but it would appear possible that many of the group were relocated to the less populated Caicos Islands. Much of what was left on board appears to have been salvaged and sold shortly after the wreck.[73] Survey work hoping to locate *Trouvadore* began in 2004, and the remains of a wooden ship were located in September of that year.

118   MATERIALIZING THE MIDDLE PASSAGE

The *Trouvadore* project continued until 2008 but did not produce dating or other evidence to confirm the identity of this wreck.[74] A second vessel falling into the sought but not found category is the Dutch West India Company's *Leusden*, which hit a sandbank at the mouth of the Marino River, Paramaribo (Surinam), while transporting captives from the Gold Coast in 1738. The crew survived, but 664 Africans perished because the hatchways to the slave decks had been nailed down to prevent their escape to shore. Magnetometer survey was conducted at the river mouth in 2013, but no further work has taken place.[75] *Leusden* is a maritime graveyard and, should what remains of it one day be found, the wreck will undoubtedly become the subject of a fierce ethical and legal debate concerning the disturbance (or not), and appropriate treatment thereafter, of the many hundreds of African bodies potentially awaiting discovery.

The two most recently claimed candidates for slaver wrecks are located at Cahuita National Park on the Caribbean coast of Costa Rica. The two wreck sites were in fact first explored in 1981 by Stephen Gluckman of the University of Florida, and, during his reconnaissance, one small piece of manilla was recovered from what is now known as the Brick Site: one of Gluckman's informants also reported having seen eight to ten more.[76] East Carolina University returned to the area in 2015–16.[77] The first location they explored, the Brick Site, encompasses a spread of scattered and stacked yellow bricks, each 210 × 110 × 40 mm. These are clearly part of the cargo or ballast of a vessel. Two cannons, three grindstones, and a bottle and kettle of nineteenth-century date were recorded here in 2015. The second location, known as the Cannon Site, is 1 km to the south of the first, and the finds here include an anchor, ten complete cannons, and fragments of three more. The 2015–16 excavators have hypothesized that these sparse finds represent the remains of the Danish West Indian Company slave ships *Christianus Quintus* and *Fredericus Quartus*, wrecked in 1710, but, in the absence of further evidence, this suggestion must be considered speculative.[78]

Conclusion: Wrecks as Sites of Memory

None of the handful of excavated vessels encountered in this chapter foundered in the course of its Middle Passage. Even where wrecks exist, then, the captives they carried are missing. In their absence, one wreck in particular serves as a site of memory today. In May 1993 the National Association of Black Scuba Divers (NABS) held a memorial service on a boat above the wreck of *Henrietta Marie*.[79] At the end of the service, a plaque was lowered into the sea (it can be seen in Figure 4.10). Bolted to a concrete stand, there it remains. Inside it is a steel case listing the names of the thirty men who made the dive on that day. Marcus Wood has said of this object—and others through which efforts are made today to empathize with the traumas of the slave trade—that they work in precisely the opposite way we want them to do, revealing our *inability* to make such a contact.[80] But a very different viewpoint is offered by Michael Cottman, who was among the divers that day. [81] What is evident from Cottman's account of his

Figure 4.10 Michael Cottman at the site of the *Henrietta Marie* memorial. Michael Cottman.

'spirit dive' is the affective quality of both the wreck site and the plaque. The relationship between object, touch, and memory is brought out movingly, as every diver touches the monument, with one 'running his hands gently over the inscription as if he were stroking the face of an old friend'.[82]

The captives of *Henrietta Marie* were sold before the ship foundered. No bodies were recovered from the wreck site, and the plaque is not a marker of the dead; it is, as Cottam puts it, a memorial for lost lives.[83] In all, some 12 per cent of the Africans carried on European slave ships perished at sea, and, until a ship wrecked during its Middle Passage is finally located—as it surely will be one day, bringing with it both research opportunities and enormous ethical challenges—captives lost to the sea will remain an absent presence, remembered, mourned, but beyond the reach of archaeological enquiry.[84] But it is also the case that more than 88 per cent of those who endured the Middle Passage survived it. Every time a team of bioarchaeologists in the Americas confirms that an individual recovered from a former plantation cemetery or segregated burial ground had been born in Africa, they also materialize the slave ship's 'human cargo'. Through the work of terrestrial excavators and bioarchaeologists, the corporeal remains of a handful of Middle Passage survivors *are* now within archaeological reach, but, as the concluding chapter of this book will go on to explore, much remains to be done to determine the changes that their ocean crossing wrought to both self and collective identity.

Notes

1. See Webster (2008) for a summary of maritime archaeological work on slaver wrecks before 2007.
2. 1,019 ships in TSTD are currently recorded as being shipwrecked or destroyed at sea, https://www.slavevoyages.org/voyages/bGGx6qZa (search generated 26 October 2020). In 253 cases, the loss occurred after embarkation or during slaving, and most of these vessels must have had some Africans on board. British vessels make up a very high proportion of the overall number of slave ships lost at sea: the default query (https://www.slavevoyages.org/voyages/mOu2kS5A) for voyages fitted out in British ports between 1562 and 1807 returns 562 examples of British-based ships wrecked or destroyed, with 95 of these losses occurring after embarkation or during slaving (search generated 26 October 2020). The high proportion of British wrecks may simply reflect the quality and quantity of contemporary shipping returns. After 1734, British shipping casualties and losses were routinely recorded in *Lloyds List*, for example.
3. An important exception here has been the work of the French *Group de Recherche en Archéologie Navale* (GRAN), which began collating information about known slaver wrecks in southern Africa, former French West Africa, and the French West Indies in 1982. GRAN is a not-for-profit organization set up by the French government to supervise underwater excavations and undertake research into maritime history. Its members include professional archaeologists and historians. In 1994 GRAN's slave shipping project (*The Sunken Memory of the Slave Trade*) was incorporated into the UNESCO programme *The Slave Route* (1994–2014). GRAN's work on slave shipping can be accessed online at http://www.archeonavale.org/slaveroute/ (accessed 26 October 2022).
4. Slave ships are largely (or entirely) absent, for example, from recent syntheses including Gould (2011), Adams (2013), and Catsambis et al. (2013).
5. Sullivan (1994: 45–50) outlines the discovery.
6. The *Atocha* wreck yielded 40 tons of silver and gold and 70 pounds of emeralds, worth $200 million–400 million. Title to (ownership of) the *Atocha* wreck site was bitterly debated in the 1970s (see Elia 2000 on the landmark judgment of 1978), and the wreck remains a *cause célèbre* in the battleground between treasure hunting and professional archaeology.
7. In conjunction with the RPM Nautical Foundation, MFMHS has continued to conduct magnetometer surveys on New Ground Reef, in part with the aim of recovering 'missing' elements of the *Henrietta Marie*.
8. The website for *Henrietta Marie* is https://www.melfisher.org/henrietta-marie-1700 (accessed 26 October 2020). A number of general audience books have also appeared on the wreck, including Sullivan (1994) and Cottman (1999).
9. For scholarly publications on *Henrietta Marie*, see Burnside (2002), and Moore and Malcom (2008).
10. The first voyage took place in 1697 (TSTD 15131 London–Bight of Biafra–Barbados).
11. TSTD 21285.
12. Burnside (2002: 84).
13. TNA: T70/349, ff. 52, 71, 72, 75; Malcom (2000/2003: 4).
14. Images and brief notes on artefacts from the wreck site can be found on the MFMHS Florida Slave Trade Portal database, https://www.floridaslavetradecenter.org/Browse/Objects (accessed 26 October 2020). See Malcom (2000, 2003 and 2021) for short research articles on the ship's trade goods, bilboes (shackles), and cooking cauldrons.
15. TSTD 35181.
16. Svalesen (2000: 13–20) describes the archival detective work leading to the discovery of the wreck.
17. Under Norwegian Law (The Law for Protection of Cultural Heritage), the cargo on board sunken ships is the property of the state. The 1975 fieldwork was directed by the Norwegian Maritime

Museum, with a further exploration of 1977 taking place in cooperation with the Aust-Agder Museum (Svalesen 2000: 173–4). The Aust-Adger Museum directed additional work in 1995–7.

18. Svalesen (2000).

19. Danish National Archives, Copenhagen: Archives of the Guinea Company no. 88 (Kiønig), no. 89 (Lunberg), and no. 109 (Hoffmann). All extracts from these journals are taken from Svalesen (2000).

20. Digitized copies of the logbooks from *Fredensborg* can be found on the Danish National Archives website at https://www.virgin-islands-history.org/ (accessed 26 October 2022). *Fredensborg* (formerly the *Cron Prindz Christian*) had made one earlier slaving voyage, in 1755: see Svalesen (2000: 23–4). This voyage is not in TSTD.

21. I am greatly indebted to Tanja Røskar Reed, Conservator at the Aust-Agder Kulturhistoriske Senter, Arendal, for providing me with a copy of the *Fredensborg* inventory in advance of its publication online, and for sharing information about the *Fredensborg* finds. A sample of finds from the wreck can be viewed at https://digitaltmuseum.no/search/?q=Fredensborg&aq=owner %3F%3A%22AAK%22 (accessed 26 October 2022).

22. TSTD 90557.

23. Guérout (2014: 136).

24. Goddio's relationship with Oxford has proven a controversial one, with some maritime archae-ologists arguing that the university should not be contracting out fieldwork in this way (Lawler 2005: 1192). Others, who point to both the costs of underwater survey and excavation and Goddio's widely acknowledged field skills, argue that the arrangement gives Oxford scholars access to data they could not afford to generate themselves (Lawler 2005: 1193).

25. The only available information is contained in a brief statement, accompanied by ten photo-graphs, on Frank Goddio's website, http://www.franckgoddio.org/projects/others/adelaide.html (accessed 31 August 2022).

26. The Treaty of Utrecht of 1713 terminated the slave shipping *asiento* (contract) between France and Spain and probably explains why *Adélaïde* sold its slaves at Léogane, and not in a Spanish colony.

27. TSTD 33343. The data set records a crew of 130, but, according to the Franck Goddio Society press release, 106 men died when the ship went down, and a further 45 survived.

28. Cook et al. (2016: 375). A Dutch West India Company ship named *Gronigen* made a slaving voyage to Luanda in 1642 (TSTD 11327), but no slaving voyage is documented for a ship of this name in 1647. Whatever the case, it is a likely hypothesis that the wrecked vessel was trading for slaves: Cook et al. (2016: 379). For further discussion of maritime Archaeology in Ghana, including the Elmina Wreck Project, see Cook (2014).

29. A brief report on the history and exploration of *Havmanden* can be found in von Arbin and Bergstrand (2003). I am indebted to Staffan von Arbin for answering my queries about *Havmanden*, and for patiently summarizing his findings in English.

30. von Arbin, pers. comm.

31. https://nmaahc.si.edu/explore/initiatives/slave-wrecks-project (accessed 26 October 2020). See Sharfman et al. (2012) for more on the evolution of the Slave Wrecks Project (SWP). The other four partners in SWP are the US National Park Service Submerged Resources Centre and its Southeast Archaeological Centre, the George Washington University Capitol Archaeological Institute, IZIKO Museums of South Africa, the South African Heritage Resources Agency, and Diving With a Purpose (DWP). Initially focusing on South Africa, the second phase of the SWP has seen the development of work in Cuba, Brazil, and elsewhere.

32. *Meermin*, a further example of a slaver employed in the East African slave trade, is discussed by Boshoff (2018).

33. TSTD 36990.

34. https://nmaahc.si.edu/about/news/statement-discovery-slave-ship-clotilda (accessed 26 October 2020).

35. https://www.nationalgeographic.com/culture/2019/05/finding-clotilda-the-last-american-slave-ship/ (accessed 26 October 2020). For the story of *Clotilda*, the people the ship carried, and their descendants in Africatown, Alabama, see Diouf (2007). Durkin (2020) discusses the life of Matilda McCrear, the last survivor of *Clotilda*.

36. For the excavation, see Clifford (1999) and Hamilton (2006). For the use of professional archaeologists, see Elia (1992) and Ewen (2006: 6–7).

37. The museum website is *https://www.discoverpirates.com//* (accessed 26 October 2020). Critiques of the ethics of this pirate-themed museum and its treatment of slavery include Johnston (1993) and Rodley (2012).

38. TSTD 78954. The former slave ship master William Snelgrave, who was himself captured by pirates in 1718, documented the 1716 seizure by Palgrave Williams of *Whidaw Galley*: Snelgrave (1734: 258).

39. Clifford (1999: *passim*) illustrates numerous artefacts from the wreck. Publications detailing some of these finds include Hamilton (2006).

40. See Ehrlich (1989: 52) and Clifford (1999: 206–7) for the seventy-nine pieces recovered in the first phase of fieldwork. Two pieces discovered more recently are discussed in Ehrlich (2012).

41. Contemporary accounts suggest that *Whydah* was carrying between £20,000 and £30,000 in silver and gold when wrecked: Hamilton (2006: 132). Much will undoubtedly have come from vessels robbed by Bellamy, but some is clearly of African origin.

42. See Hamilton (2006: 135–6) on the formation of 'discontinuous' wreck sites, such as that of *Whydah*.

43. Wilde-Ramsing (2006: 160–4) gives the background to this event.

44. Wilde-Ramsing and Ewen (2012: 115).

45. Wilde-Ramsing and Ewen (2012: 111).

46. See Rodgers et al. (2005: 25), who suggest that 'no single piece of evidence, or trend of circumstantial evidence, indicates that this wrecked vessel is actually *Queen Anne's Revenge*.' Moore (2005) and Miller et al. (2005) address technical issues raised by Rodgers et al. (2005), and support the identification with *Queen Anne's Revenge*. Two papers on this wreck also appear in Skowronek and Ewen (2006). One (Wilde-Ramsing 2006) refers to the wreck as *Queen Anne's Revenge*. The other (Lusardi 2006) prefers the designation 'Beaufort Inlet Shipwreck'. The most recently published works making the case that the wreck is indeed *Queen Anne's Revenge* are Wilde-Ramsing and Ewen (2012), and Wilde-Ramsing and Carnes-McNaughton (2016, 2018).

47. TSTD 30028 Nantes–Whydah–Martinique (1713), TSTD 30059 Nantes–Congo–Haiti (1715–16), and TSTD 30090 Nantes–Whydah–Martinique (1717).

48. TSTD 30090. Reports filed in 1719 by Pierre Dosset and Francois Ernaut, commander and lieutenant of *Concorde*, reported that after capture the ship was taken to the island of Bequia (St Vincent) and systematically plundered. The pirates gave the French crew a 40-ton Bermuda sloop, in which they completed their transport of most of their African captives to Martinique: Moore (1997: 31–5).

49. Wilde-Ramsing and Carnes-McNaughton (2016: 35–54). A quarter of the artefacts from the wreck are of French manufacture.

50. Pierre Dosset, master of *Concorde*, later claimed that Blackbeard and his pirates stole more than 20 lb of gold dust from his officers and crew: Rodgers et al. (2005: 33–4). See also Wilde-Ramsing (2006: 191). Rodgers et al. (2005: 34) state that the gold grains recovered from the wreck are of European or Mediterranean origin, a claim strongly contested by Miller et al. (2005: 339–40).

51. British and Foreign State Papers XXIII, 343–74.

52. Henderson (1978: 73).

53. The Mixed Commissions were tribunals set up to adjudicate upon vessels seized on suspicion of slave trading. They existed from 1819–71 and were responsible for the condemnation of over 600 slave vessels: see Bethell (1966) for an introduction, and Lovejoy (2016) for more on the Registers of Liberated Africans, which were maintained by the Havana Slave Trade Commission and which we will meet later in the book.

54. Henderson (1975, 1976, 1980, 2008). See also Barker and Henderson (1979) and Henderson and Stanbury (1983).

55. Although a conservation survey undertaken in 2000 indicates that the most exposed areas of the hull are in relatively poor condition, http://museum.wa.gov.au/research/research-areas/maritime-archaeology/treasures-from-the-deep/james-matthews/conservation-report (accessed 27 October 2020).

56. An online database of 878 artefacts (unfortunately not illustrated) is available at http://museum.wa.gov.au/maritime-archaeology-db/artefacts/search (accessed 27 October 2020).

57. Gomes et al. (2015) provide a recent reassessment of the assemblage from this wreck.

58. Information on this site is taken from Smith and Maxwell (2002).

59. Smith and Maxwell (2002: 57).

60. See Smith and Maxwell (2002: 58–63) for the excavation history of the wreck.

61. Smith and Maxwell (2002: 61–2). The authors go on to discuss the possibility of a slave-smuggling nexus operating out of Bermuda.

62. Smith and Maxwell (2002: 80–3).

63. Karklins (1991: 40–1).

64. Details on this site are taken from Herry (2004).

65. Herry (2004: 98–9).

66. Details on these three wrecks are taken from the GRAN website, http://www.archeonavale.org/slaveroute/retrouvees.htm (accessed 27 October 2020).

67. TSTD 654.

68. Swanson (2010).

69. Malcom (2017) details recent work in the hunt for this ship.

70. For a balanced discussion of the legal and ethical complexities surrounding two other ships located by Odyssey Marine Exploration—*Black Swan/Mercedes* and HMS *Sussex*—see Henn (2012). Both Neil (2010) and Henn (2012) consider the pros and cons of the bilateral partnership model (the so-called Sussex Agreement) entered into by the British Government and Odyssey Marine Exploration in 2002 concerning HMS *Sussex*. This vessel sank in 1694 carrying an estimated $4 billion in gold and silver coins.

71. The exploration of the wreck site, and the artefacts recovered, are discussed in Cunningham and Kingsley (2011).

72. Information on *Trouvadore* is taken from Sadler (2008).

73. Sadler (2008). Archival research has shown that a comprehensive salvage operation was carried out. Finds including sails, rigging, and chain cables were all recovered and sold.

74. Sadler (2008) outlines the story of *Trouvadore* and the effort to locate the wreck. See also https://slaveshiptrouvadore.org/ (accessed 27 October 2020). The website does not appear to have been updated since 2008.

75. TSTD 10221. Balai (2011) charts the voyage of *Leusden* and explains the circumstances leading to the murder of its captives. The appendix to Balai (2014) (the English-language version of Balai 2011) contains brief details on the 2013 survey.

76. Gluckman (1998: 462).

77. The 2015–16 work is discussed by Harris and Richards (2018).

78. TSTD 35157–8.

79. The monument was originally scheduled to be dedicated in 1992, but weather conditions prevented the dive.

124 MATERIALIZING THE MIDDLE PASSAGE

80. Wood (2000: 300–1).
81. See in particular Cottman (1999: 166–7).
82. Cottman (1999: 166).
83. Cottman (1999: 172).
84. As Turner et al. (2020) note, the ongoing quest for mineral resources in the Atlantic Basin will inevitably disturb, or traverse, underwater cultural heritage from the slave trade. They propose that virtual memorial ribbons be placed on International Seabed Authority (ISA) maps as a way to respect and memorialize those who lost their lives as a result of the slave trade.

5

Guineamen

Materializing the Merchant Slaver

Introduction

For much of the period covered by this book, the ships that carried captive Africans were popularly known in Britain as Guineamen—a term that spoke to their itinerary (Guinea being a descriptor for West Africa), not their purpose. It might be reasoned that this term was favoured because it euphemized an ugly reality, but it more likely gained traction because the British 'slave ship' was generally neither purpose-built for the slave trade, nor employed exclusively in it; most slaving vessels were second-hand merchant ships that had already seen service elsewhere. Until at least the 1740s, ship design—whether in a royal dockyard or a merchant yard—was the prerogative of the shipwright concerned.[1] As a result, the slave ships of the later-seventeenth and early eighteenth centuries varied considerably in size and form. It was only from the middle of the eighteenth century that vessels began to be built specifically for the British trade, and most of those purpose-built ships were constructed in Liverpool. Even at the height of the slave trade, three in four British slavers comprised conversions from other activities: they were merchant vessels before they were employed as slavers, and many would be redeployed after one or more slaving voyages. It is helpful to think of these vessels not as slave ships but as *merchant slavers*.[2] *Lord Stanley* (the three-masted, 240 ton ship shown in Figure 5.1) is an excellent example here, having been constructed in Liverpool in 1775 but not making its first slaving voyage until 1786. The bowl was probably commissioned to celebrate the first of this merchant slavers' eleven trips to Africa.[3]

This chapter uses a wide variety of source materials to materialize the shared characteristics of the ships employed in the slave trade. It also provides a series of short portraits of examples constructed between *c.*1680 and 1807, tracing the small but significant changes to the merchant slaver over the course of that period.[4] Particular attention is paid to the impact of the 1788 Dolben Act and subsequent legislation upon slave ship design. Figure 5.2 introduces some of the key terminology employed in this chapter and indicates the location of the most important features of a ship modified to carry African captives.

The merchant slavers departing for Africa from British ports were barely distinguishable from other long-haul merchantmen, but when they arrived off the coast of Africa, they underwent a metamorphosis transforming them from merchant ships into *slave* ships. Platforms, bulkheads, and other new features were erected above and below

Materializing the Middle Passage: A Historical Archaeology of British Slave Shipping, 1680–1807. Jane Webster,
Oxford University Press. © Jane Webster 2023. DOI: 10.1093/oso/9780199214594.003.0005

Figure 5.1 Creamware punch bowl depicting a three-masted ship with the words 'Success to the LORD STANLEY Capt. Smale'. National Museums Liverpool, 146703.

decks, creating the spaces, at once physical and social, of the Middle Passage. The second part of this chapter details these temporary changes, which were largely built from timber and were dismantled upon the ship's arrival in the Americas. The impermanence of these key features means materializing a ship in the act of transporting captives is particularly challenging. Some of the excavated wrecks introduced in Chapter 4 are of considerable value in examining hull design (as can be seen from Figure 5.3), but, simply because none of these ships was lost during the Middle Passage itself, they are less useful when considering temporary modifications such as platforms and bulkheads. Even if a Middle Passage wreck is one day found, these features may no longer be in evidence, because the upper structural remains of wooden ships do not always survive well underwater.

To visualize the modifications that transformed merchant ships into slave ships, then, it is necessary to turn to non-archaeological sources. Contemporary artworks, and in particular the very detailed watercolours produced during voyages undertaken by the French *Marie-Séraphique* and the Danish *Fredensborg II*, have been an essential source of information for this chapter.[5] I have also made use of detailed plans of the English *Henrietta Marie* and the French *Aurore*, drawn up in the twentieth century using seventeenth- and eighteenth-century evidence.[6] Digital renderings of the French slavers *Aurore* and *Marie-Séraphique* and the Dutch *Unity* are now available online,

GUINEAMEN 127

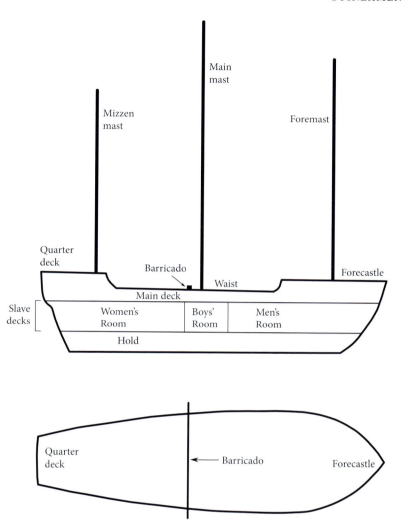

Figure 5.2 The key structural characteristics of a frigate-built merchant slaver.

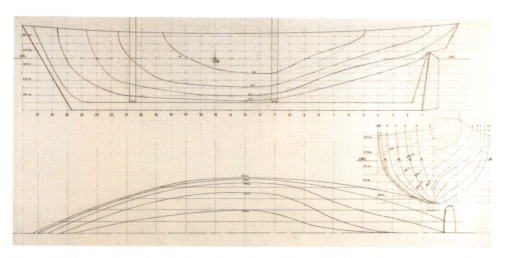

Figure 5.3 Reconstructed preliminary lines plan of *James Matthews*. Western Australian Museum.

128   MATERIALIZING THE MIDDLE PASSAGE

and have been enormously helpful to my own efforts to materialize a British slaving vessel.[7] But perhaps the most important source for this chapter has been a non-visual one: the parliamentary inquiry data of 1788–92. The hearings generated an astonishingly detailed body of data through which it is possible to rematerialize important features of the built environment of the Middle Passage in the mid–late eighteenth century, and, as will quickly become clear below, many of the sailors questioned in Parliament provided important points of detail about features of their ships. Many such testimonies have been useful here, but one source stands out among them. In 1788, a naval officer named Captain Parrey was dispatched to Liverpool, at Parliament's request, to inspect slaving vessels there. Parrey visited twenty-six ships in all and made detailed measurements on nine of them (Table 5.1). On 12 June 1788, the Controller of the Royal Navy, Sir Charles Middleton, presented Parrey's measurements to Parliament.[8] They are preserved in tabular form in volume 67 of the Sessional Papers of the House of Commons.[9] The document provides very detailed insights into the dimensions of slavers fitted out in the most prolific slaving port in Europe, at the high point of the British slave trade. Parrey's data are referred to at many points in this chapter.

Some basic details about the size, tonnage, and features of many of these ships were already available, because all existing British merchant ships had recently been re-registered to comply with a new 1786 General Act of Registry. But Parrey wanted much more information than was available via the Liverpool Registry. On each of the nine vessels included in Table 5.1, he made forty-three separate measurements, or calculations based on measurements. He noted the hull form, recorded the height between decks (measurements which in some cases, as can be seen in Table 5.1, differed slightly from the dimension recorded in the 1786 Liverpool Registry), counted the number of guns mounted, and made numerous measurements on the gratings, hatchways, air ports (portholes), and other features employed to enhance air flow through the lower decks.[10] But many of his calculations related to features he could *not* see: the temporary platforms and partitions that would not have been *in situ* at the time he inspected the ships. These temporary features—essential to the business of shipping slaves—are the subject of the second half of this chapter. Parrey will have been able to identify where on these recently used vessels these fittings were positioned, and from this determine their precise dimensions; but in effect he was measuring shadows. Here, as so often happens when documentary evidence promises to facilitate a clearer view of the Middle Passage, it remains elusive: visible, but through a glass, darkly.

General Characteristics of Merchant Slavers

Ships from the age of sail were floating bodies of wood, and shipbuilding itself was essentially a specialized form of carpentry. The major structural features of sailing ships, including the hull and masts, were all fashioned from timber.[11] Oak—and preferably English oak—was the only option for the framing elements of the hull,

Table 5.1 The nine Liverpool vessels measured in 1788 by Captain Parrey

Vessel name	Built	Voyages	TTSD	Standardized tonnage	Profile	Height between decks (ft/in)	Height between decks in Liverpool Registry (ft/in)
Brooks	Liverpool 1781	4	80663–6	297	Frigate-built (but no forecastle)	5 8	5 6
Bud	Liverpool 1783	5	80704–8	97	Galley-built	5 0	4 2
Golden Age	Havana 1779	5	81606–10	377	Frigate-built	5 4	5.0
Betty	Lancaster 1783	3	80551–3	200	Frigate-built	5 8	7.2 (single-decked, so measured as depth of hold)
Kitty	Spain, year unknown, but taken as prize in 1780	2	82181–2	137	Galley-built	4 4	4.0
Venus	Taken as prize from the Americas in 1781	4	83938–41	146	Galley-built	4 2	4.2
Brothers	Liverpool 1787	6	80685–90	325	Frigate-built	6 0	6.0
Rose	Lancaster 1783	4	83397–40	147	Galley-built	5 1	5.0
Jane	Liverpool 1766	10	81987–96	242	Galley-built	5 5	5.4

130 MATERIALIZING THE MIDDLE PASSAGE

until larch was accepted as a suitable alternative in the 1790s.[12] Elm tended to be used for keels, and Scots pine (fir), much of it from the Baltic, was employed for masts, spars, underwater cladding, decking, and inner partitioning. The tree trunks were squared and cut into planks by sawyers, working in pairs in a sawpit, then converted (cut roughly to shape) by the shipwrights.[13]

For most of the period discussed in this book, wooden sailing ships were characterized according to three factors: hull form, rig, and tonnage. Shipping records only occasionally mention specific hull forms, but a good deal of evidence is available about how vessels employed as slavers were rigged and the profile of their upper decks (for example, whether they were frigate- or galley-built). Table 5.2 summarizes the principal characteristics of some of the vessels introduced in Chapter 3, and it will be obvious that, whilst standardization was lacking, some common characteristics, and temporal patterns, do emerge.

Profile (Hull and Upper Deck)

The profile of any ship's hull determined its carrying capacity, sailing performance, stability, and manoeuvrability, and in slave shipping the balance between these factors was especially important. A broad hull increased carrying capacity but slowed down the vessel; conversely, a slimmer, faster vessel ensured a rapid Middle Passage, but restricted carrying capacity. As an additional consideration, slave ships also needed cannon to defend themselves again enemy warships, privateers, and their own human 'cargoes'. In short, the slave trade demanded well-armed ships with specific sailing qualities: neither so broad nor bluff that the ship was overly slow, nor so slimline that carrying capacity was deemed too low for profit. These qualities might also help explain why, as became clear in Chapter 4, pirates often commandeered slave ships for their own use.[14] Figure 5.3 shows the reconstructed preliminary lines plan of *James Matthews*. This 178-ton, two-masted snow-brig was built in Bordeaux in the late 1700s, and as discussed in Chapter 4 was wrecked off Western Australia in 1841, some years after its last deployment as a slaving vessel. A great deal is known about the hull of this former slaver, because the timbers were preserved by the cargo of roof slate that sank with the ship. So much of the hull was preserved that the excavators were able to produce a 1:10 scale site plan, along with cross sections of the hull at every metre of its length. The site plan provides valuable information on the ship's iron deck supports, indicating the position of the main deck. A photo-mosaic of each 6 m × 1 m grid section of the hull was developed by a specialist archaeological photographer. This information, along with all available historical documentation and comparable lines plans, was then used to develop preliminary lines and sail plans for *James Matthews*. The lines indicate a sharp-built vessel, designed for speed.

Specific hull profiles were not routinely recorded in merchant shipping registers, but, where information is available on the side-on profile of the upper deck (or, as is the case for several vessels in Table 5.1, where it can be reconstructed from details

Table 5.2 Characteristics of some of the vessels introduced in Chapter 3, using information drawn from TSTD, *Lloyds Register*, and details provided in sailors' accounts

Vessel	Built	Date of construction	Profile	Rig	Standardized tonnage	Previous use
Hannibal (1693–4)	? London	?	Frigate-built	Ship	337	Formerly a 4th-rate naval vessel
Albion Frigate (1699)	France: formerly *Le Beaulieu* captured by HMS *Dover* in 1693	1682	Frigate-built	Fregata	299	Naval vessel, *Dover-Prize*; bought from the Royal Navy in 1698
Daniel and Henry (1700)	? (registered Exeter)	?	?	?	305	?
Don Carlos (1700)	England, port unspecified	?	Frigate-built	?	293	?
Duke of Argyle (1750–1)	Liverpool	1729	Frigate-built	Snow	182	?
Thetis (1754–5)	Britain, port unspecified	?	Frigate-built	Snow	110	?
Unity (1769–71)	Liverpool	1763	Frigate-built	Ship	182	Merchant vessel, formerly *Nancy*
Sandown (1793–4)	France	1781	Galley-built	Ship	150	Merchant vessel, lengthened in 1787
Kitty's Amelia (1807–8)	France	1802	?	Ship	272	Merchant vessel, captured as a prize

132 MATERIALIZING THE MIDDLE PASSAGE

provided in sea logs or other sources), the majority of British slaving vessels appear to have been frigate-built.[15] That is, they had a raised afterdeck (usually termed a half- or quarterdeck, depending on its lateral extent) and many also had an elevated forecastle or foredeck (see Figure 5.2). The ship's wheel and compass were located on the quarterdeck, and the officers' quarters immediately below it, and this was where the captain and senior crew would spend much of their time. As discussed more fully below and again in Chapters 10 and 11, the raised quarterdeck facilitated the confinement and surveillance of male captives while they were on deck during the day and gave the crew a defendable space should the Africans on board try to take the ship. Elevated forecastles also facilitated defence and the management of captives providing spaces for the containment of younger captives or the sick during the day, and a second vantage point for the crew. Not all slavers were frigate-built, however: the trade also employed flush-decked vessels lacking a forecastle, and these were generally referred to as galley-built ships. Tables 5.1 and 5.2 include several examples of such vessels. All nine of the ships measured by Parrey in 1788 (Table 5.1) were frigate- or galley-built, and, while six were constructed in Britain, three were of foreign origin, and were probably taken as prizes.[16] The average lapse between the launch and first major repair of a naval ship at this time was between twelve and seventeen years, but only one of the slave ships measured by Parrey (*Jane*) was over a decade old.[17] This observation supports recent work, suggesting that vessels employed in slaving generally needed to be replaced every four years.[18]

Hull Sheathing

Timber vessels required very significant maintenance and were especially vulnerable to damage from marine boring molluscs, including the teredo worm. From the late seventeenth century, the hulls of all vessels sailing in the tropics were provided with an outer layer of sacrificial planking that could be replaced whenever worm damage became too severe. Excavation revealed that the sacrificial planking on *Henrietta Marie* (1700) was covered in a layer of animal hair and pitch, applied to the underside of the planks before attachment to the hull.[19] One of the few major changes to British merchant ship design in the later eighteenth century was the introduction of the copper-sheathed hull, a development first trialled by the Royal Navy in 1761, and rapidly thereafter adopted for merchant ships sailing in the tropics.[20] In the earliest trials, the copper plates were fastened to the hull using iron bolts, but it was rapidly realized that galvanic action (iron corrosion) occurred when copper sheathing was used below the waterline on iron-fastened ships.[21] Specially strengthened copper alloy bolts were first patented in 1783 and gradually replaced iron bolts. The first known commercial vessel to be coppered was *Little Will* in 1772.[22] Some 150 vessels surveyed by Lloyds in the first four years after diffusion of the practice had already been coppered.[23] In 1786, *Lloyd's Register* recorded 125 vessels in the African trade as being so treated.[24] As a 1791 advertisement for the sale of the Liverpool ship *Iris* suggests, coppering was regarded as particularly advantageous for slavers, because they spent protracted periods in tropical waters and their hulls were thus expensive to refit and repair. *Iris* was advertised as being sold 'with all her materials as she arrived from Africa, copper bolted and sheathed, has made two voyages to Africa, for which trade she was purposely built, and remarkably well calculated'.[25] In addition to reducing worm damage, copper sheathing had the additional advantage of inhibiting seaweed growth on the hull. Trailing weed slowed a vessel considerably, and significantly reduced manoeuvrability: the only way to get rid of it was to scrape it off by hand in dry dock. Coppered slave ships trailed far less weed, thus increasing their sailing speeds—an important factor in reducing death rates. It has also been suggested that the presence of copper sheathing lowered humidity below decks, again helping to improve survival rates.[26] A recent statistical analysis has calculated that, on coppered slave ships of the late eighteenth century, death rates were 50 per cent lower than on vessels that had not been sheathed.[27]

Rig

Rig refers to the arrangement of a vessel's masts, spars, and sails. By the eighteenth century most large merchant vessels were rigged as ships—a term used specifically for three-masted vessels—or as twin-masted brigs and snows.[28] From reference to *Lloyd's Registers of Shipping* and other sources, it has been possible to determine rig for many of the ships included in the TSTD.[29] Almost half of the documented voyages originating in Britain took place using vessels rigged as ships, with snows (the largest of the two-masted vessels, carrying a larger spread of sail than brigs) also popular.[30] TSTD indicates that the proportion of British slaving vessels rigged as ships increased significantly after 1750, and even more markedly after 1788. The key factor here was that ships could carry a greater burden, and therefore a larger number of captives. The preference for larger, three-masted vessels was notable even in the case of slavers destined for Ouidah, where, from the late eighteenth century, customs, or fees for permission to trade, were graduated according to the size of the ship, as measured by the number of its masts.[31] Most eighteenth-century slave ships were square-rigged— that is to say, the principal sails were carried on horizontal spars (yards) perpendicular to the keel. In most cases, fore-and-aft triangular sails were also attached to the boom, and hinged to the masts.[32] These sails were easy to adjust and could be used to change direction without sending men aloft—an important consideration on ships that, as discussed below, were effectively cut in two by a wall of timber, inserted before captives were boarded. The eighteenth century also brought an increase in sail area, achieved using extended masts (called topmasts) carrying topgallant and royal sails above the standard main and topsails.[33] It has been suggested that slave ships actively pioneered the use of taller rigging and additional sails, in the hope of making better speed in the steady, south-easterly trade winds blowing ships from Africa to the Americas.[34]

134 MATERIALIZING THE MIDDLE PASSAGE

Archaeological excavations rarely yield detailed evidence about the rigging of ships, but the unusual circumstances of the loss of the Portuguese ex-slaver *James Matthews* (see Figure 5.3) favoured the preservation of rigging.

The vessel heeled to starboard after striking a sand bank. The masts were cut away to lessen the force of the wind, but the mainmast fell through the main hatch and served as a lever, pulling the vessel over. The rigging associated with the lower sections of that mast became jammed under the starboard side of the vessel and lay well protected in an anaerobic environment until the site was excavated. More than 75 metres of cordage has subsequently been treated in the laboratory.[35]

The sails of all merchant vessels were made from canvas, a tightly woven linen cloth made from hemp or flax. Canvas had many uses and came in many forms, but in the seventeenth century the types employed for making sails included medrinacks, polda-vis, noyalls, and Ipswich sailcloth. Much was imported from Brittany, Holland, and Gdansk, but Ipswich emerged as a centre for sailcloth production in the sixteenth century. Foreign sailcloth, while always available, was regarded as far inferior, and from 1735 legislation obliged all British ships to carry one set of British-made sails. Manufacturers were also obliged to stamp their canvas, to prove it had been made in Britain.[36] With this new stimulus, British manufacturing centres grew up in Lancashire, Cumbria, and Scotland in the eighteenth century.[37] Their sailcloth was manufactured in standard bolts, a bolt being 38 yards long and 24 inches wide and classified according to weight: Canvas No. 1 weighed 44 lb, whereas Canvas No. 10 weighed only 15 lb.[38] Sails were difficult things to cut and sew, and the work was undertaken in specialized sail-lofts (Figure 5.4). Fragments recovered from the *Queen Anne's Revenge* wreck site employ the double-round seam, which was used in stitching vertical seams on square sails in the first half of the eighteenth century; flat seams were employed in the second half.[39]

Tonnage

Tonnage does not describe the *weight* (or displacement) of a vessel, which could vary significantly from one voyage to another according to the cargo carried. Instead, tonnage describes the volume of a vessel available for stowing cargo or accommo-dating passengers: its *burden*. This is the origin of the commonly used term 'tons burden/burthen'.[40] Unfortunately, tonnage is one of the most difficult things to determine for vessels built before 1786. Until that year, when Parliament introduced a Registration Act to standardize the way vessel tonnages were computed, the RAC, the Naval Office, the Royal Navy, and *Lloyd's Registers of Shipping* all measured tonnages differently. As a generalization, the commercial world favoured measure-ments of 'tons burthen' (an estimate of carrying capacity), with the government and shipbuilders favouring 'measured tons' (calculated from dimensions including length of keel, breadth, and depth of hold). TSTD has attempted, where possible, to convert pre-1786 registered vessel tonnages to the 1786 British measured ton,

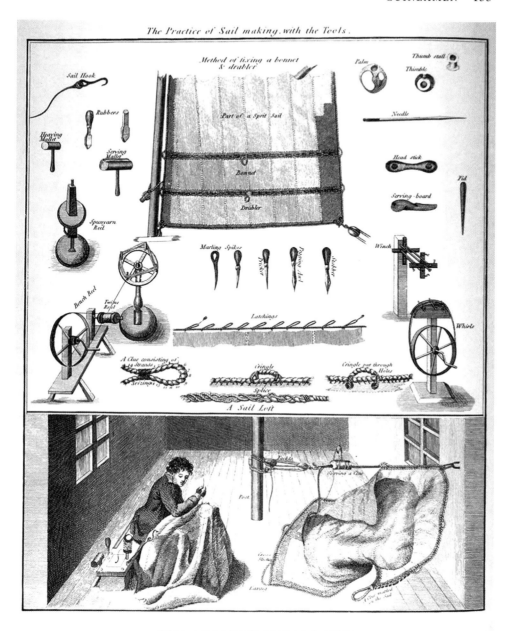

Figure 5.4 *The Practice of Sail Making with the Tools* and *A Sail Loft*, illustrations from Steel (1794: i, unnumbered page preceding 84).

and, while these TSTD 'standardized' tonnages are employed throughout this book, it should be emphasized that these figures offer at best crude indices as to pre-1786 tonnages for individual ships.[41] This said, TSTD is a useful tool in exploring slaving vessel tonnages over time. As Table 5.2 shows, the tonnage of the average later-eighteenth-century British slaver lay in the 150–225-ton range, which was somewhat smaller than for ships in other trades.[42] The general trend over time, following the opening-up of the slave trade in 1712, had been for a gradual, incremental rise in average tonnage until the 1780s. As Klein's work has emphasized, however, increasing tonnage did not necessarily increase the space available for captives. To quote Klein:

> What is the difference in space available for each slave in a vessel of 4,000 tons taking on 600 slaves (or 1.5 slaves per ton, which was close to the average), and a 100-ton vessel carrying 300 Africans for a very high ratio of 3 slaves per ton? The latter ratio of slaves per ton would seem to indicate very crowded conditions. But in fact, the 4,000 ton vessel contained only two-and-a half times more deck area (not four times the deck area) than the 100-ton vessel. This the smaller ship was able to carry 3 slaves per ton compared to just 1.5 slaves per ton with little significant difference between actual space available.[43]

Tonnage was nevertheless the rule of thumb by which slaving quotas tended to be calculated, and, in that context, it can be noted that from the late seventeenth century, when significantly more slaves were carried per ton than throughout the rest of the trade, the slave to ton ratio remained relatively steady at around 1.6 slaves per ton, until the decade in which the Dolben Act was passed (Figure 5.5). It may be that parliamentary interference, coupled with speculation about abolition, caused merchants actively to *increase* slave numbers on their ships in the late 1780s. That trend was, however, finally reversed in the late 1790s, when legislation began to impact more directly upon slave to ton ratios. If we look back to Table 5.1, the disparity in carrying capacity (tonnage) across the nine ships measured in 1788 appears anomalous, but, in a doomed effort to establish a clear relationship between tonnage, hull profile, and carrying capacity, Parrey is likely to have actively sought out vessels with divergent tonnages.

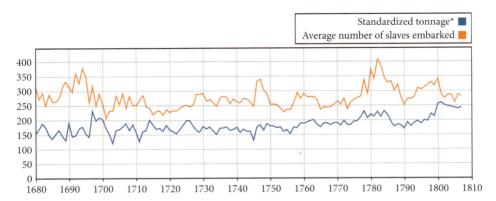

Figure 5.5 Average (imputed) numbers of captives embarked graphed against TSTD standardized vessel tonnages for British-based vessels between 1680 and 1807. (Data from https://www.slavevoyages.org/voyages/bGGx6qZa (accessed 21 March 2022)).

Hatchways and Gratings

I have frequently seen them fainting away through heat, and the steam coming
through the gratings like a furnace from their breath; we have been obliged to
get many of them up for fear they would die in the rooms.

(Testimony of Henry Ellison, **HCSP 73: 374**)

On every merchant ship, rectangular hatchways (or scuttles) facilitated vertical
access, via ladders, from one deck to another. On slave ships, these hatches tended
to be covered by open-work timber gratings, which allowed air to penetrate below
decks. The date at which the practice of using open-work gratings began is unclear.
Writing in the early 1700s, John Barbot referred to Dutch West India Company
ships as having gratings and scuttles (small hatchways) that could be covered with
tarpaulins in wet weather (**Treatment 1712: 778**). He was clearly contrasting this
with the practice of other nations, including Britain. But gratings were certainly in
regular use on British ships by the mid-eighteenth century: John Newton, for
example, makes numerous references to gratings on *Argyle*, and indicates (**Argyle
1750–1: 21**) that bars were attached to these, presumably to render them more
secure. In his *Universal Dictionary of the Marine* (1769), Falconer refers to gratings
as being

formed by several small laths or battens of wood, which cross each other at right
angles, leaving a square interval between. They are formed to admit the air and light
from above into the lower part of the ship, particularly when the turbulence of the sea
or weather renders it necessary to shut the ports between the decks.[44]

Ships built or modified for the slave trade appear to have had more hatches and
gratings than other vessels, but these tended to be smaller than on standard merchantmen.[45] A surviving drawing of the main deck of the French ship *Marie-Séraphique*,
made in 1770, provides a very clear view of the ship's many gratings—a long row of
which are positioned directly above the men's room, with two more sets directly above
the women's room (see Figure. 5.6, far right). One of the gratings above the men's
room is open and appears to be hinged at the rear.

Gratings on the Measured Ships of 1788

When Captain Parrey visited Liverpool in 1788 to take measurements of vessels
engaged in the slave trade, he made numerous careful measurements relating to the
length (L.) and breadth (B.) of gratings and bulkheads on the lower and upper decks of
these slave ships. Parrey also recorded the number of air ports (portholes) inserted on
the lower deck. His findings are summarized in Table 5.3.

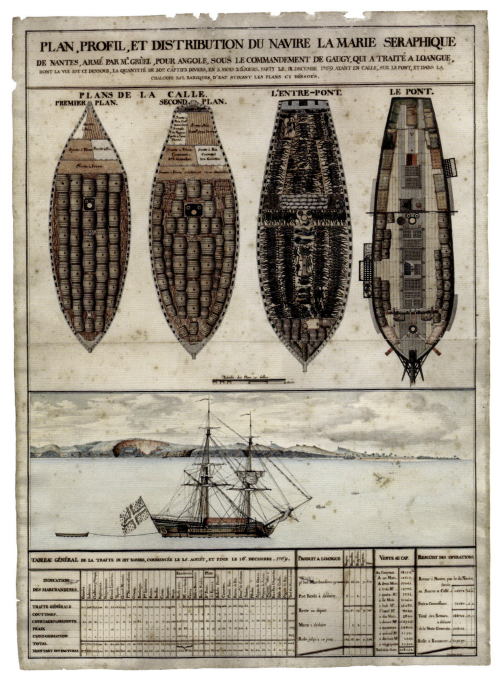

Figure 5.6 Plan of the profile, hold, and decks of *Marie Séraphique* made by Jean-René Lhermitte in 1770. Château des ducs de Bretagnes, Musée d'histoire de Nantes.

It is surely revealing that, despite making so many measurements relating to gratings of one form or another, Parrey made no effort to record the dimensions of the *apertures* through which air passed—that is, of the size of the holes within the

Table 5.3 Measurements relating to airflow on the ships measured by Captain Parrey

Ship	Columns										
	1	2	3	4	5	6	7	8	9	10	11
	L. of main gratings lower deck (ft/in.)	B. of main gratings upper deck (ft/in.)	L. of two gratings foreside the windlass for air (ft/in.)	B. of two gratings foreside the windlass for air (ft/in.)	L. of the after gratings on the main deck(ft/in.)	B. of the after gratings on the main deck(ft/in.)	L. of grating on quarterdeck (ft/in.)	B. of grating on quarterdeck (ft/in.)	No. of grating bulkheads between decks	Thickness of each grating bulkhead (in.)	No. of air ports on lower deck
Brooks	31 6	10 8	8 4	3 6	19 6	6 6	7 9	6 3	4	4	14
Bud	21 0	6 0	2 4	4 0	11 0	5 0	—	—	4	4	2
Golden Age	30 6	7 6	5 0	3 0	20 0	5 7	5 8	4 9	4	4	16
Betty	28 0	6 0	3 0	3 0	16 0	5 8	14 8	5 6	4	4	22
Kitty	19 9	6 6	2 1	2 8	11 6	5 6	—	—	4	4	18
Venus	12 6	6 2	4 6	2 6	10 3	4 6	—	—	4	4	4
Bros.	23 4	6 9	9 3	3 1	9 6	6 10	14 6	5 7	4	4	14
Rose	25 8	6 3	4 0	3 0	12 4	6 1	—	—	4	4	16
Jane	28 0	7 6	8 0	3 11	19 8	5 6	14 7	6 7	4	4	10

Notes: Columns 1–8 concern the gratings above the slave decks, 9–10 the vertical partitions separating the 'rooms' in which captives were confined, and 11 the portholes on the slave decks. L. = length; B. = breadth.

latticework of timbers that made up an open-work grating. Gratings have been recovered from the wreck of the former slaver *James Matthews*, and the apertures of these were extremely small (57 mm × 42 mm).[46] While the gratings on this ship were made of iron rather than timber and cannot be compared directly with their timber counterparts on British ships, they foreground the point that the most important of all measurements relating to airflow on British ships was never taken.

Air Ports

Most slaving vessels were also equipped with air ports—sub-circular portholes inserted into the side of the hull, below decks. A close look at the Liverpool ship in the painting in Figure 5.7 reveals four ventilation holes, just above the waterline on the vessel. Air holes at this depth on a hull are a likely indicator of the presence of slave decks, and this ship's previously uncertain status as a slaver was confirmed when recent cleaning of the background to the painting revealed the coast of West Africa, with longboats ferrying slaves to the vessel for embarkation on the Middle Passage.[47] John Barbot noted (***Treatment*** 1712: 778) that some Dutch ships were fitted with portholes (he called

Figure 5.7 William Jackson's painting *A Liverpool Slave Ship*, c.1780. National Museums Liverpool, 1964.227.2.

them lights), secured with iron bars, to let in air. His comment appears to indicate that air ports were not a common feature of ships of other nations at this date. Yet, by the late eighteenth century, air ports were a near-ubiquitous feature of British slavers, and each of the nine Liverpool ships measured by Parrey (Table 5.1) were furnished with some.[48] What is striking here is the variation in practice: *Bud* had only two air ports on its 63-foot lower deck, whereas *Kitty*, at 65 feet, had eighteen. As described by Alexander Falconbridge, air ports were also very small, measuring approximately 6 × 4 inches (*Account* **1788: 24**).

In poor weather, both air ports and gratings would be covered over to prevent seawater being washed below decks. Mr Janverin (*Substance* **1789: 64**), who sailed on several London ships in the 1760s–70s, noted that, when gratings were covered, the tarpaulin was laid over a 4-foot high pole at the centre of the grating (rather like a tent) to make it possible to admit some air.[49] Such methods had very little effect, and, as discussed in more detail in Chapter 9, the temperatures reached on the slave deck were often extremely high.

An Opportunity Largely Ignored: Hales's Ventilator

In the 1740s, Stephen Hales developed a manually operated ventilator, based on the design of organ bellows.[50] This device was intended for use on ships, and was supposed to replace bad (disease-causing) air with good air.[51] Hales's invention was trialled extensively by the Navy Board, but was initially felt to be both cumbersome and (at 10 × 5 × 2 ft) space consuming. The navy persevered with the basic principle, nonetheless, and eventually adopted a portable, mechanical (windmill-powered) version of the original in 1756.[52] Ventilators were introduced into the French slave trade in 1753 but were not widely adopted in the British equivalent.[53] Hales noted optimistically in 1756 that some British slave ship owners had tried out his invention:

> Mr Cramond also informs me, that he found the good effect of ventilators on board a slave ship of his with 392 slaves, twelve of which were taken on board, just before they sailed from Guinea, ill of a flux; which twelve all died; but the rest, with all the Europeans in the ship, arrived well at Buenos Ayres.[54]

Hales also records a letter, this time from Henry Ellis of Bristol, who had tried out ventilators very successfully on a slaving voyage, and who advocated their use on ships carrying 'passengers, slaves, cattle and other perishable commodities'.[55] Captain Ellis cheerfully noted that slave ships had a unique labour supply to hand, and 'even the exercise [working the bellows] had advantages not to be despised, among people so much confined'. It is clear from the 1788–92 inquiry data that vessels built for the trade after 1750 did occasionally carry ventilators, but there are inconsistencies in sailors' testimonies concerning this issue.[56] Compare, for example, the statements of two experienced Liverpool masters, both of whom gave evidence in support of the trade before the 1788 Privy Council inquiry. James Penny reportedly stated (**HCSP 69: 116**) that

142 MATERIALIZING THE MIDDLE PASSAGE

slave ships at Liverpool are built on purpose for this trade and are accommodated with air ports and gratings for the purpose of keeping the slaves cool—great improvements had been made at Liverpool within these 20 years, in the construction of these ships—the space between the decks is sufficiently large to contain the number of negroes above-mentioned (500–600) and is planed very smooth and painted—that they are also provided with wind sails and most of them have ventilators.

On the other hand, upon being asked whether he was aware of Hales's invention, Robert Norris answered in the affirmative but stated that he had never served on, nor even seen, a ship carrying ventilators. The principal objection to their use, he suggested, was that they took up much-needed space (**HCSP 68: 11**). Only a handful of sailors reported service on a vessel carrying ventilators, which suggests that on a British merchant slaver space came first and air supply to the captives a poor second.[57] Sir William Dolben was fully persuaded of the merits of ventilators, nonetheless, and his bill to regulate the slave trade initially proposed that two ventilators be installed on every slave ship. This recommendation did not survive the debate stage, however, and it was not included in the Dolben Act of 1788. As a result, the device that the pioneer of naval medicine James Lind regarded as 'the most beneficial invention for mariners, which this age has produced' was very rarely installed on British slave ships.[58]

Windsails

In place of a ventilator, many eighteenth-century slave ships carried canvas tubes known as windsails, which were used to funnel air down to the slave deck. Windsails were not unique to the slave trade and were widely used on other merchant ships and naval vessels. In his *Universal Dictionary of the Marine*, Falconer described the windsail thus:

WINDSAIL a sort of wide tube or funnel of canvas, employed to convey a stream of fresh air downward into the lower apartments of a ship. This machine is usually extended by large hoops situated in different parts of its height. It is let down perpendicularly through the hatches, being expanded at the lower end like the base of a cone; and having its upper part open on the side which is placed to windward, so as to receive the full current of the wind; which, entering the cavity, fills the tube, and rushes downwards into the lower regions of the ship. There are generally three or four of these in our capital ships of war, which, together with the ventilators, contribute greatly to preserve the health of the crew.[59]

Steel's detailed description of the naval example is also of considerable value in materializing the windsail:

Figure 5.8 The slave ship *Fredensborg II*, commanded by Captain J. Berg. This painting, dated 1788, does not depict the *Fredensborg* wrecked in 1768, but a later ship of the same name and design. M/S Maritime Museum of Denmark Picture Archive.

> Four breadths are sewed together, and the outer selvages joined, with an inch seam, leaving one cloth four feet short of the top. A three-inch tabling goes around the top and bottom. It is distended by circular hoops, made of ash, sewed to the inside; one at the top and one at every six feet distance. The upper part, or top, is covered with canvas, and a small rope sewed around the edge; into which are spliced, at the quarters, the ends of two pieces of rope, that are sewed up to the middle, and an eye formed by seizing the bights. The length of a windsail is taken nine feet above the deck to three or four feet below the lower hatchway.

Figure 5.8 depicts windsails in use on the slaver *Fredensborg II*, successor to the excavated vessel discussed in Chapter 4. Three canvas windsails, opened to face towards the oncoming wind, are clearly visible on this painting, made in 1788. The windsails were placed over the grating hatches above the slave deck. The two forward funnels will have provided fresh air down to the male slaves, while the smaller funnel closest to the stern sent air to the women and children. It is clear from the 1788–92 inquiry data that windsails were the *only* form of ventilation employed on most British slave ships by the later eighteenth century. While many owners and masters appear to have persuaded themselves of the efficacy of this rudimentary technology, most sailors testifying on behalf of the abolition movement spoke of windsails as having little practical value.

144   MATERIALIZING THE MIDDLE PASSAGE

Like open-work gratings, these ineffectual canvas tubes could be employed only in good weather, and, even then, only in the daytime. They were hoisted up at night, and the hatches were secured, even in the best of weather. Much of the time, therefore, those confined below decks breathed the hot, fetid air unique to the slave hold, and so carefully described in 1788 in a well-known passage by Alexander Falconbridge (*Account* 1788: 24):

> The hardships and inconveniences suffered by the negroes during the passage, are scarcely to be enumerated or conceived. They are far more violently afflicted by the sea-sickness, than the Europeans. It frequently terminates in death, especially among the women. But the exclusion of the fresh air is among the most intolerable. For the purpose of admitting this needful refreshment, most of the ships in the slave-trade are provided, between the decks, with five or six air-ports on each side of the ship, of about six inches in length, and four in breadth: in addition to which, some few ships, but not one in twenty, have what they denominate wind-sails. But whenever the sea is rough, and the wind heavy, it becomes necessary to shut these, and every other conveyance by which the air is admitted. The fresh air being thus excluded, the negroes' rooms very soon grow intolerably hot. The confined air, rendered noxious by the effluvia exhaled from their bodies, and by being repeatedly breathed, soon produces fevers and fluxes, which generally carries off great numbers of them.

Falconbridge's testimony serves as a powerful reminder that features designed to bring air into the sleeping quarters of slaves were far less efficient that some commentators have supposed.[60] Moreover, new technologies for ventilation were ignored in a trade that might have valued such developments more than any other. As discussed in Chapter 9, the failure to employ ventilators was not simply related to concerns about space; it was also in part linked to contemporary understandings of the African body, and its perceived ability to withstand higher temperatures than the European body could endure.

Legislation and Slave Ship Design after 1788

Slave shipping—and slave ships—remained entirely unregulated until 1788, when, for the first time, Parliament sought to set limits on the number of captives a vessel could transport. Britain can hardly be said to have been a pioneer here; the Portuguese Crown had regulated slave-to-ton ratios on its ships as early as 1684.[61] The 1788 Dolben Act stipulated that, after 1 August 1788, it would be unlawful for the masters of slaving vessels clearing British ports

> to have on board at any one time, or to convey, carry, bring, or transport slaves from the coast of *Africa*, to any parts beyond sea, in any such ship or vessel, in any greater number than in the proportion of five such slaves for every three tons of the burthen

of such ship or vessel, so far as the said ship or vessel shall not exceed two hundred and one tons; and moreover, of one such slave for every additional ton of such ship or vessel, over and above the said burthen of two hundred and one tons; or male slaves who shall exceed four feet four inches in height, in any greater number than in the proportion of one such male slave to every one ton of the burthen of such ship or vessel, so far as the said ship or vessel shall not exceed two hundred and one tons, and (moreover) of three such male slaves (who shall exceed the said height of four feet four inches) for every additional five tons of such ship or vessel, over and above the said burthen of two hundred and one tons...[62]

In other words, ships could carry 1.66 slaves per ton up to 201 tons burden, and one slave per ton over 201 tons. Stephen Behrendt has calculated that in effect this reduced the number of slaves loaded onto British ships by 13 per cent.[63] At first sight, the new legislation appears to have had some impact on vessel sizes: the average (standardized) tonnage of British slavers rose from c.180 in 1787 to c.300 in 1801 (Figure. 5.9). While it is tempting to think that this happened because shipbuilders were forced to improve the spatial allocation for captives, the reality is more complex.

The extent to which legislation had a positive impact by increasing personal space and decreasing mortality has been a matter of some debate among historians.[64] Here, it is only necessary to note that legislation had very little impact indeed upon slave ship *design*. The reason may be simply put: the earliest legislation centred upon slave-to-ton ratios, and, while owners might be obliged to carry fewer captives per voyage, they were not required to modify their vessels in any way. It was not until 1797 that consideration was given in law to the *aerial* space allocated to captives below decks.[65] Even then, the standards imposed were so minimal as to have little impact upon existing practice. It was only with the passage of the 1799 Act, discussed above, that newly built slave ships began to take on a consistent form. Put simply, vessels built in the final decade of the trade were deeper of hold than many of their predecessors, and all were fitted with

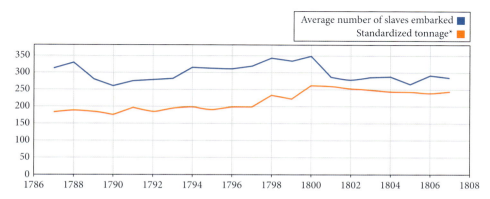

Figure 5.9 TSTD standardized tonnages plotted against average embarkation levels for British slaving voyages, 1787–1807. (Data from https://www.slavevoyages.org/voyages/mOu2kS5A (accessed 20 March 2022)).

platforms.[66] The Act of 1799 had a further influence on the appearance of slaving vessels, obliging vessel or venture owners to letter their ships, as follows.

> And be it further enacted, That every such Ship or Vessel, previous to her being cleared out, shall have painted in White or Yellow Letters, of a Length not less than four Inches, upon a Black Ground, on some conspicuous Part of her Stern (provided there shall be Sufficient Space for that Purpose, but if not, in Letters as large as the Space will admit) the Words 'Allowed to carry Slaves', the Number of Slaves expressed in the Licence annexed to the Clearance of the said Vessel being added thereto, in Figures of the same Length and Colour.[67]

Thus, for the first time, in the dying years of the trade, a British slave ship was immediately recognizable as such—an advertisement of its purpose painted on the stern for all to read.

Snapshots: Some British Slave Ships through Time

The Seventeenth-Century Slaver

The sketch in Figure 5.10 is one of very few visualizations of a seventeenth-century slave ship. It was produced by William Van de Velde, the son of a well-known Dutch maritime artist, who moved to England with his father in 1672. From the spritsail

Figure 5.10 A Guinea merchant ship, drying sails. William Van de Velde the Younger, c.1675. National Maritime Museum, Greenwich, PAF6918.

topmasthead, this twin-decked English vessel is flying the RAC's *Guinea Jack*—a flag with a red cross at the centre of a red chequered border, on a white background. This image aside, we know very little about the appearance of seventeenth-century British slave ships: a particularly frustrating point, since, as Figure 5.5 suggests, the vessels with the largest carrying capacity (tonnage) in the history of the British trade, and transporting the largest numbers of slaves, were at sea between *c.*1690 and 1700.

There would appear to be some correlation between the declining fortunes of the RAC and the sharp rise in vessel tonnage around 1690. As discussed in Chapter 1, the RAC lost its monopoly on the slave trade in 1698 and subsequently attempted to impose a 10 per cent levy on private Guinea trading—an effort abandoned in 1712. It might be that the rise in carrying capacity reflects attempts by private traders to offset levy payments by using bigger ships, but some of the largest ships of the period were owned by the RAC themselves: the 337-ton *Hannibal* is a case in point. It might be that the decline of RAC also meant that there were fewer really big ships at sea. It is, however, difficult to explain why tonnages should drop sharply around 1705, only to rise again.

Visualizing *Hannibal*: Excavating Thomas Phillips's 1693–4 Voyage Journal

Neither plans nor wreck of *Hannibal* survive, but by careful reading of Thomas Phillips' voyage journal of 1693–4 it is possible to visualize the key features of this very large RAC charter-party vessel. *Hannibal* was bought by Phillips, on behalf of Sir Jeffrey Jeffreys, in 1693. The ship measured 450 RAC tons (337 standardized tons) and carried 36 guns (cannon). Phillips mentions that the vessel was purchased in London and had formerly been 'a 4th rate in his majesty's service' (*Hannibal* 1693–4: 239). This does not necessarily mean that *Hannibal* was built as a ship of the line in a British naval dockyard, since it might have been hired, or a captured foreign prize, but this statement does suggest that *Hannibal* was twin-decked and square-rigged. It is clear from Phillips's text that *Hannibal* was three-masted and rigged as a ship. Like many seventeenth-century merchantmen, *Hannibal* had a spritsail topsail—a small square sail set on a vertical mast at the outer end of the bowsprit. *Hannibal* was also not in the best of repair: during a storm on the outward run to Africa, the foremast sprung (cracked), ripping through the forecastle deck, and the timber was found to be rotten to the heart.

Hannibal was clearly frigate-built, with a stepped profile, and a waist (see Figure 5.2 for the features of a frigate-built slave ship). Guns were mounted on the elevated quarterdeck, and a door gave access to steerage, where more guns were present, trained on the captives held in the waist of the ship during the day. Women remained on the quarterdeck (along with the crew), and the children were confined to the poop: a short additional deck at the stern present on many naval vessels of this period. The captain had his own private quarters in a roundhouse constructed on the poop deck. The space below decks is harder to visualize. Phillips refers to the use of 'partitions and bulkheads' to separate male and female captives but makes no mention of the construction of temporary decks or platforms. He refers to a lazaretto, a term sometimes used in the seventeenth century for a storeroom for provisions, and usually located in the after part of the hold. On some late-seventeenth-century vessels, this was converted into a sickroom. John Barbot (*Treatment* 1712: 781) refers to the lazaretto under the forecastle being used as a 'sort of hospital'.[68] Openwork gratings were employed on *Hannibal*: Phillips notes that, to fumigate below decks, it was necessary to cover these gratings with tarpaulins.

Henrietta Marie (constructed before 1697)

The wreck of *Henrietta Marie* was introduced in Chapter 3. This ship was almost certainly built in France in the 1690s and the visualization in Figure 5.11, based on excavation data and documentary sources, offers a glimpse into the appearance of a small, frigate-built, three-masted slaver at the end of the seventeenth century.[69] On entry into Barbados during its first slaving voyage in 1696, the ship was recorded as a 114-ton vessel carrying 14 guns.[70] A 6.1 × 3.7 metre section of the stern survives underwater today, and has been discussed in detail by David Moore, one of the

Figure 5.11 Profile view of the likely appearance of the wrecked frigate-built slaver *Henrietta Marie* (constructed in 1699). From Moore (1997).

archaeologists who excavated *Henrietta Marie*.[71] His work provides important information on the framing and planking components of this square-sterned slaver.

The major structural components of *Henrietta Marie* were made of white oak, and the planking of pine. Surviving framing elements from the stern section include six floors of crutch (or rising) timbers, fastened to the futtock ends (the inboard frame) using iron spikes. The surviving bottom planks are 6 centimetres thick, and three have burned or scorched inboard faces, revealing that the builder used fire or heat in bending the planks to fit the curve into the stern. The hull of *Henrietta Marie*, like other vessels of the time, was sheathed with sacrificial planking to protect it from wood-boring organisms. These 1.3-centimetre planks were attached to the exterior planking with small iron tacks, in random patterning. While the stern structure of *Henrietta Marie* is not extensive, it provides important clues as to the design and construction of the vessel and was employed by David Moore in producing the hypothetical reconstruction of the ship's appearance shown in Figure 5.11.

Blandford Frigate (constructed 1719)

The work of the Bristol maritime artist Nicholas Pocock was introduced in Chapter 2, in discussing his painting of *Southwell Frigate* (see Figure 2.7). Pocock also illustrated the 270-ton *Blandford Frigate*, built in London in 1719 for the navy, as a sixth-rate frigate (Figure 5.12).

Having been condemned as unfit in 1741, this 270 (310 standardized) ton, 20-gun ship was sold on and refitted for the slave trade, undertaking a single slaving voyage in 1743.[72] As considered in Chapter 2, Pocock was not born until 1740, and cannot have painted his slave ship portraits from life, but representations of early–mid-eighteenth-century British slave ships are few, and Pocock's very detailed drawing allows some insights into the appearance of a repurposed naval vessel from that era. His portrait of *Blandford Frigate* is particularly useful for its depiction of sailors at work on the main deck of the ship, which seems to be depicted prior to its departure: certainly, it has undergone none of the physical changes that, as considered later in this chapter, turned a merchantman into a slave ship on the African coast. This painting does not reveal it, but *Blandford Frigate* was also one of the tiny handful of slaving vessels fitted with Hales's ventilators. The *Daily Advertiser* reported on 10 December 1743:

> We are inform'd, that a large pair of such ventilators as are describ'd in a treatise on that subject, are fix'd on board the Blandford, on the lower deck, near the main mast, which being eight feet long, and each three feet and a half wide, they draw at the rate of nearly sixty thousand tons of air out of the hold in twenty-four hours, and convey it above deck thro' a trunk a foot square, under the gang-way or steps that lead up to the quarterdeck; by which means a likely quantity of foul air being drawn down into the hold, from among the slaves who are between decks, they, who will be five or six hundred, will thereby be greatly refresh'd.[73]

Figure 5.12 *A view of the Blandford Frigate*, Nicholas Pocock, c.1760. Bristol City Museums, Galleries and Archives, M761.

Hall (built 1785)

William Hutchinson's description and plan of the 375 (standardized) ton *Hall*, built in Liverpool in 1785 for William Ward (Figure 5.13), gives us a good idea of the appearance of a later-eighteenth-century Atlantic cargo ship. *Hall* was designed by Hutchinson himself and, in his view, was a vessel 'as perfect as can be expected'.[74] The engraved sheer (profile), half-breadth (waterline curvature) and body (section) plans at the base of the plate in Figure 5.13 are reduced versions of the original sheet draught, drawn up by Joseph Elliot of the King's Yard, Deptford, to demonstrate Hutchinson's method for determining the shape and rake (inclination) of the stern and stern-post on the ideal vessel Principally employed in the bilateral West Indies trade ferrying goods between Britain and Jamaica, the ship carried slaves on its sixth voyage in 1790.[75] Hutchinson describes the vessel as frigate-built, with a waist four and a half feet deep, and a long quarterdeck and (elevated) forecastle. The ship is praised for another essential characteristic: stability in the water. Hutchinson reports that, on meeting a violent tornado on the Middle Passage, *Hall* lost its mainmast and all three topmasts, but was stiff (steady) enough in the water not to be overturned.

The dimensions of *Hall*, as preserved in the Liverpool Registry are length 103 feet, breadth 29 feet 7 inches, and depth of hold 5 feet.[76] The dimensions of the near-

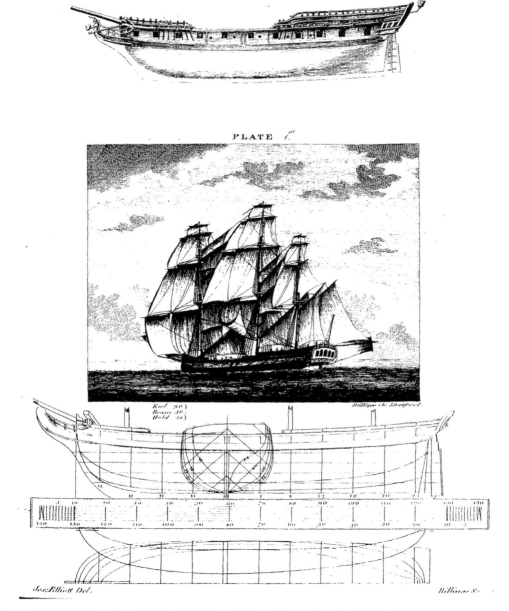

Figure 5.13 *Hall* as illustrated in Hutchinson (1794). (Public domain).

contemporary, frigate-built *Brooks* were very similar: length 99.8 feet, breadth 26.7 feet, and depth of hold 5 feet 6 inches.[77]

Visualizing 'Human Cargoes': *Brooks* (1787)

The *Description* of the Liverpool slaver *Brooks* shown in Figure 5.14 is today undoubtedly the best-known eighteenth-century realization of any British slaving vessel. This is

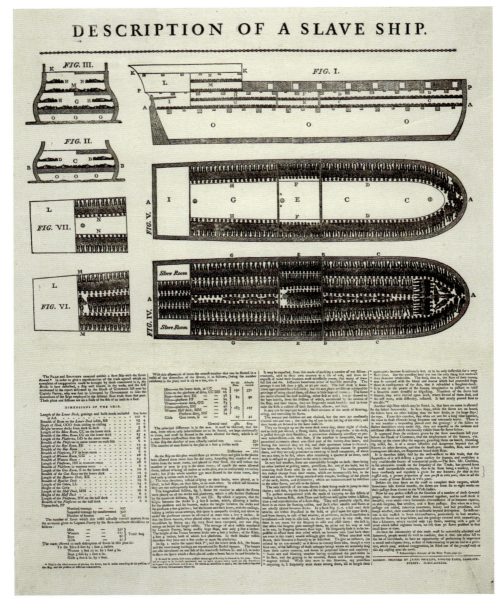

Figure 5.14 *Description of a Slave Ship*. Broadsheet printed by James Phillips London, in 1789. The Stapleton Collection.

because, unlike every other British image considered thus far, it attempted to look *inside* the slave ship, to its captive cargo. As emphasized in my Introduction, much of the population of a nation that had shipped almost three million people into slavery over three hundred years remained largely ignorant of the realities of that trade until its final two decades. As a result, when the time at last came to attempt it, the visualization of a ship carrying captives proved extraordinarily challenging.

In the spring of 1789, the year after the Dolben Act had been passed to reduce the carrying capacity of slave ships, five leading abolitionists, the SEAST committee members Thomas Clarkson, James Phillips, George Harrison, Joseph Woods, and Samuel Hoare, took the first of the nine sets of dimensions obtained by Captain Parrey for Parliament (Table 5.1) and produced a stowage plan for the first of these, *Brooks*.[78] The 297 (standardized) ton, three-masted ship was built in Liverpool in 1781, and named after its co-owner Joseph Brooks Jnr.[79] The ship had made four slaving voyages to the Gold Coast between 1781 and 1786.[80] The upper portion of the *Description* presents a series of diagrammatic plans and overviews of *Brooks*'s slave decks to illustrate the point that, even under the new regulations imposed by the Dolben Act, captives would be confined in appalling conditions. In all, 442 individuals are shown packed onto the slave decks.

The rendering of the African captives themselves, lying in neat rows on their backs, and wearing identical loin cloths, is both simplified and stylized. The men, women, boys, and girls are distinguished as such simply by altering their heights as a group, and by adding breasts to the women and shackles to the ankles and wrists of the men.[81] The *Description* quickly became the most widely disseminated, and most frequently reproduced, of all British slave ship images. As the text accompanying this engraving points out, the number of captives carried on the *Brooks* on the four voyages made before the 1788 Dolben Act far exceeded the 442 depicted in this rendering. On each of those trips *Brooks* had carried over 600 people, and in 1785 the figure reached 704.[82] On these voyages, Africans had been stowed 'spoonways'—lying on their sides rather than their backs, tightly pressed up against their neighbours.[83]

In preparing their illustration, Clarkson and his colleagues had used as a guide a stowage plan drawn up by the Plymouth branch of SEAST some months before, combined with Parrey's measurements, mathematical reasoning, and more than a little guesswork. The guesswork was necessary, because none of these men had ever seen a slave ship laden with African captives. While it is clearly a flawed, compromised realization, the *Description* thus marks a significant moment in the visualization of British slave shipping: the first attempt to visualize not simply the slave ship itself, but its captives below decks. The *Description* is certainly not an *accurate* representation of the stowage of 'human cargoes', then, but it is not entirely without value as a source on information on eighteenth-century understandings of the slave ship, and I return to key features of the *Brooks* diagram below, particularly its visualization of platforms and slave rooms.[84]

The Metamorphosis

As they set out from Liverpool, Bristol, and other British ports, ships that would be employed in slaving were barely distinguishable from merchantmen engaged in other trades. As they approached their destination, however, these ships began to take on a new appearance. Figures 5.2 and 5.15 illustrate the key changes made. Figure 5.15, the

Figure 5.15 Cross-section of an eighteenth-century slave ship, built by Chris Hollshwander for the Smithsonian Institution.

cross-section model of an eighteenth-century slave ship, built by Chris Hollshwander, depicts several of the key features discussed below. The 'slave deck' is located ''tween decks' (that is, in the space between the upper deck and the hold). Some captives lie on platforms inserted laterally on either side of the slave deck. Legislation passed in 1797 set a minimum between-deck height of 4 feet 1 inch on a British ship with (as here) a partial platform inserted above the lower deck: this would provide a minimal 'headroom' of only 2 feet and 0.5 inches for those sleeping on or below the platforms. The model also illustrates the timber *barricado* running across the main deck. It has a single doorway. The principal way in which slave decks were ventilated is also illustrated here: a canvas wind sail, placed above the grating over the central hatchway, funnels fresh air to the slave deck below.

An excellent sense of the changes wrought to a ship in advance of the Middle Passage can also be gleaned from the very detailed account of the process provided by John Newton (*Argyle* 1750–1), as set out in Table 5.4. Newton had set sail from England in August 1750 and sighted the Canary Islands on 21 September. Work began almost at once and continued long after the first captives were purchased at the end of October.

Newton's men were engaged in preparations common to every slaving voyage by at least the early eighteenth century. One of first tasks noted by the captain is the raising of the gratings in what would become the ship's women's room. This process involved elevating the grating above the deck level to let in more air. In his parliamentary testimony, James Morley mentioned that timber 'bannisters' could be used to raise gratings several feet above the coaming (frame) of a hatchway, to increase air flow (**HCSP 73: 160**). Next, Newton's crew began to put together a temporary shelter on the deck (Newton calls it an awning); they cleared out the between-deck space so that it could accommodate captives; they built additional sleeping platforms; and they constructed vertical bulkheads that would partition what was now the slave deck into separate compartments. These comprised a men's room, a women's room, and—although its construction is not explicitly detailed by Newton—a boys' room.[85] A substantial timber partition, known to slave shippers as a barricado, was inserted laterally across the main deck, isolating the elevated quarterdeck from the remainder of the vessel. The barricado is discussed in more detail below, but some sense of its position and appearance can be gained by looking back at Figures 5.2, 5.6 and 5.15. In Figure 5.6, the barricado of *Marie Séraphique*, can be seen extending over the sides of the ship in the plan of the upper deck (far right).

Many of these tasks, including making ready the ship's smaller boats, were undertaken or supervised by the ship's carpenter. A similar programme of carpentry work to that set out in Table 5.4 is described, though in less detail, by Robert Barker, carpenter aboard *Thetis* in 1755 (*Thetis* 1754–5: 9). The coast of Africa was sighted in March 1755, and from that point, Barker notes, he was

> fully employed at my own business, in caulking [making watertight] the decks, making bulkheads, barricadoes &c. for the reception of the slaves, and doing other necessary things in the ship, so that in short my work was completed, except caulking the sides, which is never done till about a week before the ship's departure from the coast.

Every carpenter would have had at his disposal a significant quantity of timber shipped from home. He also required tools: things that, as discussed in Chapter 10, required careful storage because some could be weaponized by captives. A rare, surviving example of a slave ship carpenter's rule was recovered from Odyssey site 35F, which, as discussed in Chapter 4, may be the wreck of a late-seventeenth- century RAC ship.[86]

156 MATERIALIZING THE MIDDLE PASSAGE

Table 5.4 The metamorphosis of *Duke of Argyle* in 1750, as reconstructed from John Newton's account

Date (dd/mm/yyyy)	Crew used	Activity	Number of captives now on board
25.09.1750	Carpenter	Raising the gratings of the [intended] women's room	—
26.09.1750	??	Unbent the MTG sail [main topgallant sail] for a quarterdeck awning	—
04.10.1750	?? Carpenter	Awning coated with resin and oil for second time, and covered with old canvas Fitting up the stateroom [master's quarters] to use as a shop on the coast	—
08.10.1750	?? Carpenter	Clearing out between decks. Slaves' rooms marked out Began to build the bulkheads	—
10.10.1750	Carpenter	Having completed the fore bulkhead, began preparing the deck and powder room of the yaul	—
18.10.1750	Carpenter	Work on yaul completed	—
24.10.1750	Carpenter	Began work on the longboat	—
03.11.1750	Carpenter	Work on longboat completed	3, purchased 25.10.1750
19.11.1750	Carpenter	Barricado completed (and, later, two carriage guns placed upon it)	?
26.111750	The people [crew] Carpenter	Making waroning [?] for a netting on the awning At work on the bulkheads	13
30.11.1750	Carpenter	Completed the men's room Began to build place for women to wash between the main chains and the barricade	26
01.12.1750	Carpenter	Completed the washing place	?
03.12.1750	Carpenter Gunner Boatswain	Building the bulkheads in the women's room Cleaning the small arms Making a netting for the awning	?
04.12.1750	Boatswain Carpenter	Continued to make netting Closed up the women's room	?
05.12.1750	Boatswain Gunner Carpenter	Finished netting Loaded small arms Completed women's room and fixed bars on the gratings	?
06.12.1750	Carpenter	Built platform in the men's room	?
07.12.1750	Gunner/ crew	4 swivel blunderbusses placed in the barricado	?
18.01.1751	Crew	Sheathed [with metal] the forepart of the main mast and the deck between it and the barricado in order to set up the [cooking] furnace	46
19.01.1751	?	Bricked and plastered the furnace	?
21.01.1751	Crew	Finished the platforms in the women's room	?
29.01.1751	?	Fixed the nettings upon the awning	?

The Saint-Quay-Portrieux wreck, another ship involved in trade to Africa, has also produced a possible carpenter's aid; in this case a small rotary grindstone probably used by the carpenter in sharpening his tools.[87] The quantity of both timber and nails required to build bulkheads, a barricado, and temporary decks was astounding. Deal (pine) planks were used to lay in platforms and build bulkheads, and these were brought out to Africa ready cut.[88] The demand for timber was such that, as domestic supplies declined throughout the eighteenth century, wood, and indeed the people to work it, were increasingly sourced from the Baltic.[89]

Ships' carpenters thus played a vital part in effecting the slave ship's metamorphosis—a fact that was reflected in their pay. Behrendt's analysis of a sample of forty-five Bristol slave voyages made between 1789 and 1794 shows that carpenters were the fourth highest-paid Bristol crewmen, after masters, chief mates, and surgeons.[90] Many ships carried a carpenter's mate, both to aid in what were onerous tasks, and as an insurance policy should the carpenter become ill or die. Samuel Gamble (*Sandown* **1793–4: 63, 77, 79**) reveals the enormous difficulties occasioned by the sickness and eventual death of a ship's carpenter. When *Sandown* began purchasing slaves, his carpenter, Marshall-Fair, was laid low by illness. Gamble was therefore forced to hire three replacements from shore to put up *Sandown's* barricado and build the slaves' rooms.

Now that we have gained a clear understanding of the many processes involved in the metamorphosis of a merchant vessel into a slaver, some of these steps can be explored in more depth.

Longboat, Pinnace, and Yawl: The Smaller Boats Carried by Slave Ships

Formal ports or harbours were a rarity on the West African Coast, and bars (barriers of sand) across the mouth of many harbours or sheltered bays prevented access by deep draft, ocean-going vessels. Slave ships therefore tended to find anchorage some way offshore (in what was known as the roadstead, or road), and their smaller boats, the hulls of which had been hoisted aboard and stowed on the main deck throughout the crossing from England, would then be lowered into the sea. Before that could happen, keels needed to be fitted, the hull weather-proofed, masts cut and inserted, and sails made. As Table 5.4 indicates, John Newton's carpenter and crew devoted considerable time to these activities. Once completed, the boats would be employed in a variety of ways. They guided or towed the parent ship through often treacherous waterways; laid out or weighed anchors, and ferried people, goods, and drinking water across the bar (and its often-treacherous surf) between ship and shore. (The yawl of *Blandford Frigate*, with a crew of four, can be seen making is way back to the ship in the upper image on Figure 5.12.) On the Gold Coast and in other regions where European forts were constructed, captives would be carried from the forts to the waiting ships in the roadstead in both local canoes and in the largest of the European ships' boats: the

158   MATERIALIZING THE MIDDLE PASSAGE

longboat. In regions where forts were lacking, but where navigable rivers offered access into the interior, boats would play a particularly important role in captive acquisition. Able to travel where the deeper-drafted parent vessel could not, longboats and pinnaces would traverse the inland waterways for weeks or months at a time, seeking out captives for sale. These smaller vessels were, in such cases, slavers in their own right.

All ships' boats had one or more sails, and were manned with oars.[91] Longboats, in use from the fourteenth century, generally had eighteen oars. For centuries they were fitted with a single sail, but by the 1740s longboats carried a mainsail, staysail, and jib. The pinnace was introduced in the seventeenth century (replacing the twelve-oared cokkeboate), and the smaller yawl was first introduced in the eighteenth century. Large naval vessels could carry as many as six different boats, but the majority of merchant-men employed only a longboat and a yawl. On Guinea voyages to regions with navigable inland waterways, however, many also carried a pinnace, or another small boat. For use on the Sherboro River estuary and the Windward Coast, Newton (*Argyle* 1750–1) employed a longboat, yawl, and punt. On his voyage to the waterways of the Rio Nunez in Sierra Leone, Gamble (*Sandown* 1793–4) carried a longboat and pinnace.

Temporary Deckhouses and Awnings

One of the first actions undertaken as slave ships arrived in Africa was to create temporary accommodation for captives, who would be boarded as the lengthy process of building the bulkheads, slave decks, and platforms required for the transatlantic crossing were all completed. The solution to this difficulty was to create a temporary structure on the upper (main) deck, often known as a house. The house was generally built from a latticework of criss-crossed timbers or canes, with apertures between the timbers providing ventilation. Houses were constructed from African timber, generally felled by shore parties made up of members of the ship's crew. James Stanfield, employed in the trade in the 1760s, wrote memorably of the calamitous effects of timber procure-ment upon slaver crews (*Observations* 1778: 16). Indeed, Stanfield regarded the fabri-cation of the house as one of the greatest causes of crew deaths, stating:

> This enclosure helps the stagnation of air and is, in that point of view dreadful: but it is more fatal in the act of its preparation. I know nothing more destructive than the business of cutting wood and bamboe, for the purpose of erecting and thatching this structure. The process is generally by the river-side. The faces and bodies of the poor seamen are exposed to the fervour of a burning sun, for a covering would be insupportable. They are immersed up to the waist in mud and slime; pestered by snakes, worms and venomous reptiles; tormented by muskitoes, and a thousand assailing insects; their feet slip from under them at every stroke, and their relentless officers do not allow a moments intermission from the painful task.

Figure 5.16 *The Anchorage off the Town of Bonny River Sixteen Miles from the Entrance.* The 'deck houses' on the ships shown here, in an image dating from the 1820s or 1830s, are similar to those used previously on slave ships. National Maritime Museum, Greenwich, PAD1929.

The timber and bamboo having been cut and carried to the ship, the framework was erected, and the structure roofed. The house on Newton's *Duke of Argyle* was effectively a giant tent, created by laying a canvas awning, formed from one of the ship's spare sails, over a central ridgepole. Other commentators refer to houses being roofed with bamboo or with rush matting, much like the examples shown in Figure 5.16. Alexander Falconbridge (*Account* 1788: 5) provides a detailed account of the construction of a house roofed with matting:

> On arrival of the ships at Bonny and New Calabar, it is customary for them to unbend the sails, strike the yards and topmasts, and begin to build what they denominate a *house*. This is effected in the following manner: The sailors first lash the booms and yards from mast to mast, in order to form a ridge-pole. About ten feet above the deck, several spars, equal in length to the ridge-pole, are next lashed to the standing rigging and form a wall-plate. Across the ridge-pole and wall-plate several other spars or rafters are afterwards laid and lashed, at the distance of about six inches from each other. On these, other rafters or spars are laid length-wise, equal in extent to the ridge-pole, so as to form a kind of lattice, or net-work, with interstices of six inches square. The roof is then covered with mats, made of rushes of very loose texture, fastened together with rope-yarn, and so placed, as to lap over each other like tiles. The space between the deck and the wall-plate is likewise enclosed with a kind of lattice, or net-work, formed of sticks lashed across each other, and leaving vacancies of about four inches square... The design of this house is to secure those on board from the heat of the sun, which in this latitude is intense, and from the wind and rain, which at particular seasons, are likewise extremely violent. It answers these purposes

160 MATERIALIZING THE MIDDLE PASSAGE

however but very ineffectually. The slight texture of the mats admits both the wind and the rain, whenever it happens to be violent, though at the same time, it increases the heat of the ship to a very pernicious degree, especially between decks... Another purpose for which these temporary houses are erected is, in order to prevent the purchased negroes from leaping overboard. This, the horrors of their situation frequently impel them to attempt; and they now and then effect it, not withstanding all the precautions that are taken, by forcing their way through the lattice work.

There is nothing explicit in the primary sources to suggest that African men, women, and children were separated from each other while they were located in the house. That is an important observation, because it may have been possible for captives to build up relationships there in a way that was not possible on the segregated slave decks that would come into use thereafter. The house was not especially sturdy and— simply because it was on deck—will have been easier to escape from than any below-deck space. In this context, many commentators speak of the use of netting, which was employed to enclose both the house and the entire main deck once captives began to be boarded. The only way off the ship, for African captives, was to find a way through this netting. In his 1791 parliamentary testimony, Ecroyde Claxton (**HCSP 82: 36**) noted a successful escape attempt of this type:

> All the main deck was netted, and one part of the netting was lashed to the bulk-head [i.e. the barricado] which separated the main deck from the quarter deck, and one of the tubs was unfortunately next to where the netting was lashed; some of the slaves had premeditated their escape... and while they were sitting upon the tub they were secretly unloosing the lashings, which fastened the nettings to the bulkhead.

Newton's account (Table 5.4) suggests that the production of netting was a major task, undertaken by as many of the crew as could be spared. The mesh was presumably made from twisted hemp yarn, or marline. The gunner's inventory for *Fredensborg* included three hundred netting nails, indicating how netting was attached.[92] Strung around the sides of the vessel, it will have enclosed the ship much as a web circles a spider—detecting and hampering the movements of the crew and of the captives crowded into the house. Falconbridge is again our most detailed source here (*Account* **1788: 6**). He notes that

> [a] door is made in the lattice or net-work at the ladder, by which you enter the ship. This door is guarded by a sentinel during the day, and is locked at night. At the head of the ship there is a third door, for the use of the sailors, which is secured in the same manner as that at the gang-way. There is also in the roof [of the house] a large trap-door, through which the goods intended for barter, the water casks &c. are hoisted out or in.

While the ship was on the African coast, as Ecrodye Claxton again explained (**HCSP 82: 35**), netting would be untied only to empty the necessary tubs, containing human waste, over the side of the ship. Although it is nowhere stated explicitly, it seems likely that part of the netting shrouding the main deck will have been pulled down, with the house, before leaving Africa. Full netting would have been both highly impractical and easily damaged at sea and would have hampered both the work of the crew and their surveillance of the captives.[93] Although there are few references to netting in the British trade, it is likely that some was retained around the quarterdeck where the unchained women and children spent the day. The clearest evidence for this comes from John Fountain, former governor of the British fort at Tantumquery, Ghana, who made two voyages on slave ships. He explained to Parliament in 1789 that, once boarding of captives was completed, netting 'above the railing' was removed. He also suggested that, on ships with high railings, netting was not employed at all.[94] Fountain may have been referring to the narrow quarter-rails that edged an elevated quarterdeck, but is perhaps more likely that he was speaking of the railings that ran all along the sides of the upper deck, where it was exposed to the sea. The painting of the Spanish slaver *Formidable* in Figure 5.17 provides a very detailed illustration of the tattered netting still in place at the time of the ship's capture in 1834, shortly after emerging from the Calabar River into the open sea; here, however, the remnants of the full netting still seem to be in place.[95]

Figure 5.17 William Huggin's painting of the capture of the Spanish slaver *Formidable* by HMS *Buzzard* on 17 December 1834 provides a detailed illustration of the use of netting by ships engaged in slave trading. National Maritime Museum, Greenwich, BHC0625.

162 MATERIALIZING THE MIDDLE PASSAGE

The Slave Decks and Their Platforms

> We build a sort of half-deck along the sides with deals and spars provided for that purpose in Europe, that half-deck extending no farther than the side of our scuttles. (John Barbot, *Treatment* 1712: 778)

While captives sweated in the heat of the deckhouse, the rooms below decks in which they would pass much of the coming Middle Passage were erected by the carpenter and his team. In these spaces, the act of bondage was given material expression in the form of spatial confinement: a new relationship was forged, as Gikandi puts it, between (African) bodies and (European) spaces.[96] The majority of English merchant ships had both an upper (main) and a lower deck.[97] Wherever possible, vessel owners sought to maximize carrying capacity by inserting temporary sleeping platforms in the between-deck space—that is, in the area between the upper deck and the hold. These platforms created the 'half-decks' described by John Barbot in the passage above (and illustrated in Figure 5.15). On frigate-built vessels, further platforms would also be constructed below the raised half- or quarterdeck, permitting additional tiers of captives to be accommodated there. Figure 5.14 depicts these platforms as used on *Brooks*, which was frigate-built and thus had a raised quarterdeck but lacked an elevated forecastle. Additional sleeping platforms were therefore inserted into the space below the quarterdeck to extend the women's room on this vessel. Thus, in addition to the platform (H) inserted on the slave deck (G), which runs the length of the vessel, captives were also stowed on the deck (M) below the quarterdeck (K), and on a platform inserted above it (N).

Platforms could be constructed, as Newton (Table 5.4) makes clear, only once the space between decks had been cleared of everything stored there, and that included people. On the voyage out to Africa, the 'tween deck, as sailors called it, belonged to the ordinary seamen, but, once building work began, the crew were usually obliged to sleep on the upper deck. On some ships, the men were given a temporary platform of their own on the upper deck: on others, sleeping arrangements were more ad hoc, with sailors effectively competing for space with young captives. But, with the crew ousted from their quarters, sleeping platforms could now be inserted between decks to hold African captives. Fixed to the inner hull planking, these shelves ringed the between-deck space laterally, leaving a gangway at the centre, as seen in Figure 5.15. The ends of the platforms were left open: Robert Norris noted (HCSP 68: 8) that oars were lashed to the supporting stanchions in order to prevent captives sliding off in bad weather.

Platforms were inserted on vessels with a between-deck height as low as 4 feet, giving captives sleeping on or below the platform an aerial space (known as headroom) of only 2 feet. But it was widely accepted that, to admit platforms, a slaver should have a between-deck height greater than 5 feet. In 1707, the Secretary of the RAC, Colonel John Pery, expressed the opinion that the intended charter-party vessel *Golden Frigate*, with a between-deck height of 4 feet 5 inches, was 'far too low to carry 2 tier of negroes without stifling', later noting that: 'tis morally impossible that two tier of Negroes can be stowed between decks in 4 foot 5 inches. Would she four or five inches more they would venture, but as the case stands tis neither fit for you nor them to undertake it.'[98] Writing in the early 1700s, John Barbot (**Treatment** 1712: 778) stated that, on a ship with a platform, the between-deck height should be from 5 feet 6 inches to 6 feet.[99] And, in 1788, Robert Norris asserted that a between-deck height of 5 feet 4 inches– 5 feet 7 inches was 'looked on as a proper height to admit a platform'.[100] Norris added that on ships without platforms—though he had never been aboard one himself—the height between decks was generally between 4 feet 4 inches and 4 feet 6 inches.[101] The between-deck height on the nine ships measured for Parliament by Captain Parrey ranged from 4 feet 2 inches (*Venus*) to 6 feet (*Brothers*). Venus was not fitted with platforms, but *Kitty,* with a between-deck height of just 4 feet, had platforms fitted in both its men's room and its boys' room. On most vessels, then, the aerial space for captives was extremely restricted: for those on the platforms of later-eighteenth-century ships, somewhere around 2 feet 9 inches. It would have been possible to lie down, but not to sit up fully.

The axial space allocation for captives was equally pitiful. A recent analysis of Liverpool register data for 251 Liverpool voyages undertaken before 1789 suggests that the median degree of crowding on these ships was 6 feet, 4 inches square, with captives on 114 of the voyages crammed into spaces measuring less than 6 square feet per person.[102] The parliamentary witness testimonies present a similar scenario, suggesting that most captives lay in a space at best 5 feet 10 inches long and (as repeatedly asserted in Parliament) only 14–18 inches wide, an average deck area of 6.8 square feet per person.[103]

To appreciate what this pitiful personal spatial allowance *felt* like, it is only necessary to find a desk around 0.8 metres high (you may be seated at one as you read), crawl under it and mark out a space 1.78 metres × 0.36 metres. Orlando Patterson famously defined the slave as a socially dead individual; whether or not one agrees with that assessment, it is surely the case that the saltwater captive, lying on a platform, enclosed above and below by timber, and pressed in upon by human bodies, was entombed alive.[104]

Legislation and Its Impact on Platform Construction after 1788

The 1788 Dolben Act stipulated that, after 1 August 1788, it would be unlawful for the masters of slaving vessels clearing British ports

> [t]o have on board, at any one time, or to convey, carry, bring, or transport slaves from the coast of *Africa*, to any parts beyond sea, in any such ship or vessel, in any greater number than in the proportion of five such slaves for every three tons of the burthen of such ship or vessel, so far as the said ship or vessel shall not exceed two hundred and one tons; and moreover, of one such slave for every additional ton of such ship or vessel, over and above the said burthen of two hundred and one tons; or male slaves who shall exceed four feet four inches in height, in any greater number

164   MATERIALIZING THE MIDDLE PASSAGE

than in the proportion of one such male slave to every one ton of the burthen of such ship or vessel, so far as the said ship or vessel shall not exceed two hundred and one tons, and (moreover) of three such male slaves (who shall exceed the said height of four feet four inches) for every additional five tons of such ship or vessel, over and above the said burthen of two hundred and one tons.[105]

In other words, ships could carry 1.66 adult slaves (an 'adult' male being one over 4 feet 4 inches tall); per ton, up to 201 tons burden, and one adult slave per ton over 201 tons. As noted earlier, this reduced the number of slaves loaded onto British ships by 13 per cent.[106] Through their analysis of Liverpool Registry data for 895 voyages undertaken between 1789 and 1799, Radburn and Eltis have determined median crowding to have been 7 feet 4 inches: a slight improvement on the period before the Dolben Act became law.[107] A factor here will have been a further *Act for regulating the Height between Decks of Vessels entered outwards for the Purpose of carrying Slaves from the Coast of Africa*, coming into law in 1797.[108] This Act defined space allotments for captives more exactly, stipulating:

That, from and after the passing of this Act, no *British* Ship or Vessel shall clear outwards from any Port in his Majesty's Dominions for the Purpose of shipping or carrying Slaves from the Coast of *Africa*, in which the Space between the Decks allotted for the Reception of Slaves, under the Provisions of any former Act, shall not be, in every Part throughout the whole Length and Breadth thereof, of the full and complete perpendicular Height of four Feet one Inch at least, measuring from the upper Surface of the Lower Deck to the under Surface of the Upper Deck.

This was the first time at which any consideration was given in law to the *aerial* space allocated to captives below deck. The stipulation that between-deck space for captives below decks should be no less than 4 feet 1 inch might at first sight be thought to have had a significant impact on slave ship design, in that an increase in height below decks could only have been achieved by deepening the profile of slaving vessels. Yet, as is indicated by the measurements made by Captain Parrey in 1788 (see Table 5.1), the height between decks on most slaving vessels, whether purpose-built or converted from other trades, was in fact already well over 4 feet 1 inch by 1788. Ships with a between deck height around 4 feet were certainly not unknown by 1788, but they were uncommon.[109] It would appear, then, that the 1797 legislation imposed a minimum standard well below existing norms.

In 1799 a further *Act for better regulating the Manner of carrying Slaves, in British Vessels, from the coast of Africa* increased aerial space for slaves below deck to 5 feet, and for the first time specified (if only formulaically, as a proportion of the overall between-deck space) the length, headroom, and *breadth* of the space to be allocated to each slave below decks:

And be it further enacted, That in every such Ship or Vessel, the said Space between Decks so allotted for the Reception of Slaves shall be, in every Part throughout the whole Length and Breadth thereof, of the full and complete perpendicular Height of Five Feet, measuring from the upper Surface of the Lower Deck to the under Surface of the Upper Deck.

And be it further enacted [that] the Height between Decks, and also the extreme Length and Breadth, in Feet and Inches, of the Lower Deck of the said Vessel; which Length and Breadth being multiplied together, the Product shall be deemed and considered to be the true Superficial Contents of the said Deck; and the said Contents so obtained, being divided by Eight, the Quotient in Whole Numbers shall express the greatest Number of Slaves which the said Vessel shall be permitted to have on board at any one time.[110]

In real terms, the 1799 Act prescribed a minimum of 8 square feet per captive, and, as Stephen Behrendt has noted, this reduced loading levels to about one slave per ton: a 47 per cent reduction on pre-1799 levels.[111]

Bulkheads below Decks: The Rooms

As Newton's account (Table 5.4) makes clear, sturdy timber transverse partitions known as bulkheads were erected on a slaver to divide the between-deck space into separate 'rooms', with the women's room running from the mizzen mast to the main mast, and the men's room terminating at the fore of the ship. The boys' room, if the ship had one, was sandwiched between the two. References to the use of bulkheads can be found in the earliest British accounts. Phillips notes (*Hannibal* 1693–4: 218): 'we separate the men and women aboard by partitions and bulk-heads.' In some cases, these partitions appear to have been solid walls of timber, but there is much to suggest that by the later eighteenth century a bulkhead was fashioned from solid timber stanchions, to which was attached a timber lattice rather like that used on the gratings that covered the ship's hatchways. In his parliamentary testimony, Robert Norris refers to this kind of partition (**HCSP 69: 202–3**), noting that 'the space between decks is divided by grating partitions into three rooms, which are allotted solely to the use of the slaves'. When Captain Parrey made his measurements on board nine Liverpool slave ships (Table 5.3) he noted the number of 'grating bulkheads between decks' (in each case, four) and the thickness of each of those bulkheads (in all cases, 4 inches). Parrey cannot have seen these bulkheads himself, since they were only ever in place during the Middle Passage, but the terminology, like that of Norris, suggests a lattice-like timber frame, fastened to sturdy wooden uprights. Such an arrangement was presumably intended to improve airflow, but, as discussed in Chapter 11, grating bulkheads will also have facilitated communication between those incarcerated below decks, and even made it possible to transfer objects: a young woman was caught smuggling gunpowder through a hole in the

Box 5.1 Space 'Enough': Parliamentary Discourse on Tight Packing, 1788–1792

In the 1788–92 inquiries, parliament was greatly preoccupied with quantifying the parameters of 'enough' space per slave on the slave decks. What allowance of space, it was repeatedly asked, was adequate for a slave to lie down in? One of the most interesting features of the earliest hearings (**HCSP: 68**), and their bearing on the Dolben Act and subsequent legislation is the way that an 'adequate' *breadth* of space to be allotted to each captive was determined. This is all the more revealing given that 'tight packing' (the cramming in of as many individuals as possible) was achieved not simply by building upwards (inserting additional platforms) but also by squeezing as many bodies as possible onto these temporary shelves.

Slave ship masters and owners were of course well aware of this, and the fact that pro-slavery witnesses tended to be imprecise regarding breadth allocation for slaves can hardly be co-incidental. The merchant James Jones, asked to explain how traders calculated the number of slaves a vessel could carry, remarked: 'I have never calculated in that manner—but I should suppose a full-grown slave takes 16 inches in width—the small slaves in proportion 12–14 inches, according to the size of them—The captain is never directed to go to a precise number, it must be left to his own discretion'. (**HCSP 68: 46**). This is precisely why breadth allocation *should* have been an important consideration in parliament's deliberations, and yet it was not. Having specified the length of the platforms on his ships (5 ft 10 in), Robert Norris added: 'I never measured the inches for breadth, but . . . the white people whose business it was to attend to the negroes and administer to their wants, could step among them without putting them to any inconvenience'. (**HCSP 68: 6**). Surgeons—unlike masters—were obliged to traverse the slave decks daily, and Norris' assertion was contradicted by numerous witnesses in subsequent Parliamentary hearings. Alexander Falconbridge would state in 1790 that:

> They had not so much room as a man has in his coffin, neither in length nor breadth, and it was impossible for them to turn or shift with any degree of ease. I have had occasion very often to go from one side of their rooms to the other; before I attempted it I have always taken off my shoes, and notwithstanding I have trod with as much care as I possibly could to prevent pinching them, it has unavoidably happened that I did so; I have often had my feet bit and scratched by them, the marks of which I have now (**HCSP 72: 301**).

To explain the Parliamentary Committees' limited consideration of *breadth* allocation as a factor in overcrowding, it is necessary to consider the contemporary allocation of space on naval vessels. The examination of the naval Lieutenant John Matthews, on 3 June 1788 (**HCSP 68: 25**) is particularly revealing regarding the latter. Matthews had formerly made three slaving voyages (see Table 3.6) and was one of several pro-slave trade witnesses to maintain that a breadth allocation of 14–18 inches was perfectly acceptable for an adult captive. He was asked: 'Do you think that a full-grown Negro can lie on his back in a less space than 15 inches?' He replied: 'I do not suppose that a full-grown Negro can lie on his back in a less space than a full-grown white man of the same dimensions'. The question being repeated (presumably because the witness's equation of white and black bodies was regarded with incredulity), Matthews said: 'Impressed as I am with awe and respect to this Committee, it is impossible I could mean to answer anything ludicrously; and I can only answer the question by saying I do not know.' The question was then rephrased as: 'Have you been on board a Man of War?' and 'What space is allotted to the sailors?' This allowed Matthews to confirm that in the navy, sailors were allocated: 'For their hammocks 14 inches between each clew [metal ring].'

As this line of questioning makes clear, when the Committee addressed whether 14–18 inches was 'adequate' for human cargoes, naval practise was explicitly raised as a comparator. Warships certainly were crowded below decks, and 14 inches was indeed the standard width allocated for the hammocks of the 600–700 men berthed on the lower (gun) deck of a large warship.[112] But this bears little comparison to the situation on a slave deck: the crew on a warship did not all share their sleeping space at the same time, and with hammocks being slung alternately by starboard and larboard watches, each man in practice had 28 in of sleeping space. Moreover, a hammock suspended the body above the deck, protecting it from both the hard timbers below, and from the pitch and toss of the vessel. This carefully phrased line of questioning regarding space, clearly framed to demonstrate that Africans were accommodated within the limits of white, naval, tolerance effectively obliterated further consideration of breadth. This helps to explain why no reference was made to axial (or indeed aerial) space in the Dolben Act of 1788, or in any Act of Parliament until 1797.[113]

bulkhead separating the men's room and women's room on *Industry* in 1729, for example.[114]

A visual representation of room allocation is found in **HCSP 69: 123,** as part of the testimony of Captain Robert Heatley, who had made numerous slaving voyages between 1763 and 1788.[115] This sketch is presented in Figure 5.18.

Heatley's diagram depicts the four rooms of a slave deck, separated by bulkheads, and housing women, men, boys, and a hospital space. But the accompanying wording confuses matters by suggesting that the diagram depicts the *upper* deck and its barricado (which was a single, vertical palisade). Vertical partitions were in fact in place on the upper deck of slavers, as discussed below, and it is possible that this rendering conflates information provided by Heatley concerning the separation of captives on both the upper and slave deck. Whatever the case, the diagram visualizes boys—in contrast to girls—as a discrete group, with their own designated space.

Figure 5.18 Method for separating slaves, accompanying the testimony of Robert Heatley, **HCSP 69:** 123.

It is unclear when, and why, boys' rooms emerged in the British trade. They are not mentioned at all in accounts predating the mid-eighteenth century, but a boys' room was certainly constructed on Newton's *Argyle* in 1750 (see Table 5.4). Newton in fact makes the earliest reference, to my knowledge, to such a space. Careful analysis of the 1788–92 parliamentary testimonies suggests that similar rooms were in use on some, but not all, slave ships by the 1760s, and were near-ubiquitous after 1780.[116] Boys' rooms were certainly a feature of all nine of the ships that Captain Parrey measured for Parliament in 1788 (see Table 5.1). It is far from clear why boys' rooms were introduced, or even what the age range of their occupants might have been, but it is highly likely that this development was related to the problems that older male children (that is, boys from around 10 to 13 years of age) presented for slaver crews. This point is taken up again in Chapter 11, in considering the liminal status of the unshackled male child.

To summarize thus far: between decks on every British slave ship, women and girls were confined at one end of the vessel and men at the other, sometimes with boys between. That separation was also maintained above deck. As captives came up from their separated rooms by ladder, and passed through a hatchway into the fresh air, the women would emerge onto the elevated quarterdeck, where the majority of the ship's crew would also spend the day. The male captives, in contrast, would climb up into the waist of the ship, where perhaps the single most important feature of a slaver at work— the barricado—would ensure that they could not access, or even see, the quarterdeck. It this way, above decks as below, male captives were entirely isolated from both their female counterparts, and the majority of the ship's crew.

Changes on the Main Deck

By the eighteenth century, a near-universal feature of the slave ship was a wooden *barricado* (barricade) running athwart the vessel, and projecting beyond the sides (as shown on Figure 5.2). The barricado was essentially a defensive structure; positioned close to the main mast, and against or forward of the (usually elevated) half- or quarterdeck, it gave the crew a defendable palisade from which to observe the male captives who, in good weather conditions, would spend the daylight hours of the Middle Passage on deck. Like the platforms inserted below decks, the barricado was built from pre-cut deal (pine) planking, carried from Britain for that purpose. Falconbridge (*Account* 1788: 6) provides a detailed description:

Near the main-mast, a partition is constructed of inch deal boards, which reaches athwart the ship. This division is called a *barricado*. It is about eight feet in height, and is made to project near two feet over the side of the ship. In this barricado there is a door, at which a sentinel is placed during the time the negroes are permitted to come upon deck. It serves to keep the different sexes apart, and as there are small holes in it, wherein blunderbuses are fixed, and sometimes a cannon, it is found very convenient for quelling the insurrections that now and then happen.

Smeathman (**Oeconomy c.1775, 2**) travelled on a vessel with a very similar barricado, nine or ten feet high and projecting three or four feet over the sides 'so that people cannot go around it'. Paul Erdemann Isert, a passenger on the Danish slaver *Christianborg* in 1786, remarked: 'A slave ship is equipped amidships with a strong high wooden partition called the bulwark [a term here for the barricado] whose side facing forward must be extremely smooth, without any open grooves in which the slaves might get a fingerhold.'[117]

It is difficult to be certain when the barricado was first introduced into the slave trade, but no explicit mention is made of this feature in the earliest sources. Phillips noted at the end of the seventeenth century that, on his ship, the door to steerage was kept 'shut and well barr'd' (**Hannibal 1693–4: 229**) and that guns were mounted both here and on the quarterdeck: but he makes no direct reference to a barricado. Writing in the early 1700s, John Barbot noted (**Treatment 1712: 778**): 'As to the management of our slaves aboard, we lodge the two sexes apart, by means of a strong partition in the main mast; the fore part is for the men, the other behind the mast for the women.' This would seem to suggest that, on the French-built vessels on which Barbot has sailed, the barricado had come into being by the turn of the eighteenth century: see Figure 5.19 for an excellent visualisation of the barricado on a later eighteenth-century French vessel (*Marie-Séraphique*). A similar partition was certainly present on some British ships by the middle of the eighteenth century: William Snelgrave describes captive attempting to 'force the barricado' in his 1734 description of an attempted insurrection on a slave ship.[118]

The barricado remained in use until the very end of the British trade. Looking back on a voyage made on *Lady Nelson* of Liverpool in 1800, Samuel Robinson remembered that:

Just before the slaves come aboard, a very strong wooden barricade is fixed across the deck, just before the mainmast, projecting over the sides, and twelve feet high, on the top of which sits two men with loaded muskets all the time the slaves are on deck—from eight in the morning to four in the afternoon—while through a port on each side of the deck a cannon, laded with grape, stands ready for use should a rising take place ... All the crew—except the second mate and the boatswain—are also kept on the quarter deck during the day, with an arm chest full of loaded muskets, pistols and cutlasses ... There is a small door through the barricade which is kept shut during the day.[119]

Note the height of barricado in this description: at 12 feet, it is considerably higher than that described by Falconbridge. Clearly, the barricado was built to a greater height

Figure 5.19 French slave ship *Marie-Séraphique*, Saint Domingue (Haiti), watercolour by unknown artist. The caption (translated) reads 'View of Cap Français and the Marie Séraphique of Nantes/Captain Gaugy/the day of the opening of its [slave] sale [after] its third voyage from Angola, 1772, 1773'). (TSTD 30968). Château des ducs de Bretagnes, Musée d'histoire de Nantes.

on some vessels than on others. Samuel Gamble refers, on arrival off Barbados, to cutting down 'the upper part' of *Sandown's* barricado (*Sandown* 1793–4: 103), but, while it is tempting to think that taller versions would be employed on frigate-built ships with elevated quarterdecks (to raise the barricado well above the quarterdeck height), *Sandown* was flush decked.

The principal role of the barricado was to segregate the adult male captives from both the crew, and from the remainder of the Africans on board. Witness testimonies repeatedly assert that, when captives were 'aired' on deck during the daytime, adult males would, without exception, be contained fore of the barricado in the waist or 'pit' of the main deck, and possibly also on the forecastle. Women and younger children were invariably kept behind the barricado, on the half- or quarterdeck. Guns, in the form or blunderbusses and swivel guns, or small cannon, were mounted on the barricado and aimed towards the male captives, who, from the perspective of sailors, represented the greatest potential threat to crew safety. William James, who served on *Britannia* (1768), told Thomas Clarkson (**Substance 1789: 15**) that on his ship the barricado was furnished with 'loopholes with musketry near them, as well as portholes for a four-pounder on either side, loaded with a canister of musket balls, to rake the main deck, if there should be any occasion for it'. The only way to pass from one side of the barricado to the other was via one, or sometimes two, closely guarded hinged doors built into the structure itself (as seen in Figure 15.5). A very detailed description of such a door, and its use, is provided by Henry Smeathman (**Oeconomy c.1775, 2**). As Smeathman's account makes clear, barricado doors often had two separate sections, rather like a stable door:

> There are two doors in this Barricado, always on the star board or right hand side. They are both together not so large as a common house door, and only permit one person to go through it at a time. The uppermost is only about the size of a small window where the Captain or any other person can stand and lean at ease to view the men upon the main deck. Buckets of provisions, and other necessary and useful things, can be delivered through it. The large door is immediately under the small one, and it is opened, the latter being shut, to let any of the crew pass. The whole partition is strong and the doors fasten on the afterside with strong bolts.

The barricado was the principal, but not the only, temporary partition employed on the main deck of an eighteenth-century British slave ship. Additional deck partitioning is, however, one of the most difficult aspects of the appearance of a slave ship to reconstruct, because witness testimonies are either brief on this point, or difficult to interpret. In particular, while common sense might suggest that that frigate-built ships would employ a second barricado or bulwark, built up against the forecastle to ensure that male captives could not escape the waist of the ship by moving either fore or aft, evidence for such a structure is very limited indeed in British sources. This arrangement can, however, be seen on in the painting of the Danish ship *Fredensborg II*, where, in addition to the principal barricado positioned just in front of the main mast, a smaller bulwark is clearly visible against the forecastle, offering some protection and enabling sailors to be stationed there (see Figure 5.20; the same arrangement is shown on the model of *Fredensborg* in Figure 4.2). It is highly likely, in my view, that this arrangement was also in place on those frigate-built British ships with both a forecastle and a quarterdeck.

Why would such an additional barrier be useful? First, because ships had to be sailed, and the principal barricado, projecting over the sides of the ship (and any gangways there), cut a slave ship in two. On a three-masted vessel with a barricaded quarterdeck, the only fully accessible yards and sails would have been those of the

Figure 5.20 Detail from a painting of the slave ship *Fredensborg II*, dated 1788, showing both the barricado (aft) and a second timber partition (fore) closing off the forecastle. M/S Maritime Museum of Denmark Picture Archive.

mizzenmast, which rose from the quarterdeck itself. Depending on the length of the half- or quarterdeck (which in turn determined the position of the barricado), it may also have been possible for mariners to access the mainmast. Much of the handling of the sails could be done from the deck, using clewlines and buntlines, and the lateen sails on the aft-most mast facilitated directional change without the need to send men aloft, but there must have been occasions on which sails fore of the barricado needed immediate attention (or stowing). How did the crew move forward from the quarterdeck when this was required? The obvious option was via the rigging: the boatswain and other men on *Ann Galley* saved their lives during a shipboard insurrection in 1762 by 'climbing between the two masts, as nothing could save them but coming behind Barakheada (barricado) to join the rest of the crew.'[120] Movement through a hold filled with water barrels and much else would have been impracticable. Potentially, sailors might have descended to the slave deck and traversed that: but it is most unlikely that the temporary rooms on the slave deck were furnished with the doors to facilitate this. Bulkhead doorways on the slave deck would have presented a significant security risk and appear to have been avoided: rather, each room was accessible individually, via a ladder descending from grated hatchways on the upper deck.[121]

For mariners to move fore of the barricado on many ships, then, it would have been necessary for them to work forward through the rigging, or to return the male captives to their 'room' below decks. As discussed in Chapter 10, moving the male captives from one deck to another was an especially laborious process, and it seems unlikely that this will have been a preferred option. On frigate-built ships, a second barricado against the forecastle (of the type employed in Figure 5.20), would have reduced these logistical problems by giving a skeleton crew, protected by a forecastle bulwark, direct access to the foremast, jib, and staysails. This would have made the ship easier to sail, and would also have safeguarded the gunroom and powder magazine, which on most merchant ships was probably positioned under the forecastle, as was the cooking hearth for the crew. This arrangement might also have provided a separate space (as explored in Chapters 10 and 11) for older children when on deck.

Despite the evident merits of a forecastle barricado/bulwark, it remains the case that explicit references to such features are lacking for the British trade, and multiple testimonies appear to indicate that, other than at meal times, the entire crew were stationed on the quarterdeck. It is perhaps significant that in the mid-eighteenth century, as discussed in Chapter 10, the leg shackles of male captives on British ships were reeved to long chains whenever they were on the upper deck. It seems reasonable to suggest that this practice evolved, in part at least, to facilitate safer crew movement fore of the barricado.

Better evidence is available for two other key spaces created during the ship's metamorphosis: a 'washing' space for women, and temporary platforms elevated above the main deck for the use of the off-duty crew and child captives who were not designated as boys. On Newton's *Argyle* (see Table 5.4) a closed-off space was created between the main chains and the barricado for the women to wash, and presumably also to use dedicated rudimentary toilet facilities, out of sight of the crew. On the Danish *Fredensborg* and the Dutch *Unity*, box-like latrines projecting off the side of the quarterdeck were constructed for women.[122] Smeathman noted similarly (***Oeconomy** c.1775*, **6**, emphasis added) that on his voyage the women took it in turns to wash 'in a scaffold built on the side of the half deck on purpose for them to retire to; and the boys do the same *on the forecastle*'. This important passage supports the suggestion, above, that, on frigate-built ships with boys' rooms fitted below deck, those same boys may have been confined on the forecastle during daylight hours.

Once the slave decks were in place and captives had begun to be boarded, the off-duty crew could no longer find shelter below decks. Until the first amendment to the Dolben Act in 1789 only the captain, surgeon, and first mate were guaranteed a sheltered sleeping space on most ships, and, in some cases, they shared these spaces with captives: specifically, small children.[123] As a 10-year old, Archibald John Monteith was one of twelve Igbo boys accommodated in this way during a Middle Passage crossing to Jamaica. He says that he

> and 11 other boys were taken by the captain into the cabin. We were happy; skipped about, eat [*sic*] and drank, and yet I felt very sorry when I saw the other slaves come up from the hold of the ship daily, into the air, and heard their heartrending cries of anguish; fathers & mothers longing for their homes and children, and often would neither eat nor drink, and were so strictly watched and held in such rigid confinement.[124]

Robert Norris's detailed discussion of the arrangements on his crowded ships (**HCSP 68: 16**) is invaluable in demonstrating how small boys like Monteith were accommodated:

> There is the [Captain's] Cabin holds Forty or Fifty or more; a long Half Deck under which the sailors sleep; they receive among them a portion of those people;—there is from the Mainmast to the Foremast, a space probably of Thirty or Thirty-five Feet, perhaps (that is an assumed Number) called the Booms, under which, and over the

Boat, is suspended a temporary deck or platform, which will accommodate thirty or forty; it is protected by a canvas awning and in cold Weather one of the old Sails is thrown over them.

The 'long half deck', as clarified a little later in Norris's testimony, was erected over the upper deck and was used by the off-duty sailors, along with 'twenty or more slaves'. The platform between the booms (that is, in the space between the mainmast and the foremast, in which the ship's boats were also stored) was about 5 feet in length and in Norris's view was 'broad enough to take a double range of those small Boys, for their feet and legs went under these booms'.[125] This platform was located directly over the full length of the gratings supposedly funnelling air below.[126] Norris's testimony is unique for the level of detail it provides on the extra platforms that were probably to be found on the upper decks of many crowded slaving vessels, but are rarely mentioned in other primary accounts. It also brings to the fore the astonishing extent to which captive children shared sleeping spaces with the ship's crew. The Middle Passage was a liminal zone full of between-spaces; and African children slept in some of the worst of them. I return to this point in Chapters 10 and 11.

Conclusion

It has sometimes been suggested that the British slave trade was conducted by a specialized fleet of purpose-built ships.[127] As this chapter has demonstrated, however, most of the ships employed in the trade were second-hand merchant vessels that had not been designed to carry an animate cargo. Even in the decade preceding abolition, it was still the case that a significant proportion of Guineamen were still foreign prizes or converts from other trades.[128] Likewise, some 20–50 per cent of the 'slave fleet' comprised ships that were not solely used in slave trading.[129]

While some ships were certainly constructed explicitly for the slave trade after the mid-1700s, these new vessels were no more suited for the purpose of transporting human beings than their predecessors had been. The emergence of the purpose-built slaver has sometimes been put forward as a factor in explaining mortality decline on British vessels after 1750, but, as this chapter has shown, the few improvements ameliorating overcrowding had to be forced upon the trade through legislation, while innovations such as the ventilator were widely resisted. Many of the vessel owners, captains, and surgeons appearing before Parliamentary Committees in the 1780s and 1790s attempted to persuade themselves and the nation that slave ships were fit for the purpose of transporting human beings, but the fundamental needs of those captives—space, air, water, food, sanitation—were in practice as poorly and unwillingly met in 1790 as they had been a century earlier. For as long as the notion of the human as cargo endured, that would remain the case.

Notes

1. Lavery (1984: 7).
2. See Stammers (1994: 40) on the multiple usages of eighteenth-century merchantmen, and Postma (1990: 142–7) on the very similar situation that prevailed in Holland, where many vessels employed in slaving, including more than half of those owned by the Dutch monopoly company, made only one such voyage each. Essentially, as Postma notes, any cargo ship could readily be modified into a slave ship, and just as readily redeployed elsewhere after having made a Guinea voyage.
3. *Lord Stanley's* first slaving voyage was TSTD 82467. For this and other ceramics depicting British slaving vessels, see Webster (2015).
4. For a similar exercise, focused on later-eighteenth-century ships, see Rediker (2007: 41–72). Rediker includes here (pp. 50–3) a detailed analysis of ships built in Rhode Island in 1745 for Joseph Manesty, co-owner of John Newton's *Duke of Argyle*.
5. *Marie-Séraphique* (originally *Dannecourt*) made five slaving voyages between 1765 and 1773: TSTD 30806, 30910, 30941, 30968, and 31003. Two watercolour paintings, both probably completed during the first of these voyages, and now in the Musée d'Histoire de Nantes, are the subject of a detailed analysis by Guillet (2009). The first (Figure 5.6 in this book) signed by Jean-René Lhermitte, provides four deck plans and a profile of the ship prior to its departure from Angola in 1769, with 307 captives. Lhermitte was a member of the crew, in charge of the ship's boats, and the third of his deck plans provides a unique and exceptionally important visualization of the stowage of human captives on board a slave ship: it is discussed in detail by Radburn and Eltis (2019). The second image (Figure 5.19) is unsigned but clearly the work of a different (and technically rather better) artist who was possibly the ship's captain, Jean-Baptist Fautrel-Gaugy. Itdepicts *Marie-Séraphique* at Cap Français, Haiti, on the opening day of the sale of its captives during its third voyage, in 1772. A third, unsigned, painting of *Marie-Séraphique*, depicting the feeding of captives off the coast of Angola in 1771, is discussed and depicted in Chapter 10 (Figure 10.12). The painting of *Fredensborg II* (Figure 5.8), dated 1788, depicts the ship during one of its four crossings from the Gold Coast to St Croix (TSTD 35002, 35008, 35035, 35049).These voyages took place between 1779 and 1789. As discussed by Svalesen (2000: 104–5), the original *Fredensborg* and its successor were very similar in terms of tonnage and appearance.
6. Plans of *Henrietta Marie*, based in part on excavated data, can be found in Moore (1989). A detailed set of conjectural plans of the La Rochelle slaver *Aurore*, which made a slaving voyage from Angola to Haiti in 1784 (TSTD 32359), is provided by Boudriot (1984). The author drew on sketches and construction estimates for several ships in preparing these plans: see Boudriot (1984: 6–13).
7. For *Aurore and Marie-Séraphique,* rendered by a team at the Emory Centre for Digital Scholarship for slavevoyages.org (the TSTD website), see https://www.slavevoyages.org/voyage/ship#slave- (accessed 31 August 2022). The key textual source for *Aurore* is Boudriot (1984), and, for *Marie-Séraphique*, see Guillet (2009), with Gualdé (2022: 166–86). For the reconstruction of the Dutch snow *Unity* (*Enigheid*), rendered by DPI Amination House (Hague) for the Zeeland Archives' 'MCC Slave Voyage The Unity 1761–63', weblog project, see https://eenigheid.slavenhandelmcc.nl/verantwoording-bronnen-en/reconstruction-ship/?lang=en (accessed 31 August 2022). The Middelburgsche Commercie Compagnie archive contains numerous documents concerning *Unity's* third voyage in 1761–3 (TSTD 10543), and these were used in compiling the weblog. But no plans of this ship survive, and the rendering of the vessel is based on information drawn from a wide variety of sources.
8. Parliamentary Archives HL/PO/JO/10/3/280/6.

176 MATERIALIZING THE MIDDLE PASSAGE

9. *Dimensions of the Following Ships in the Port of Liverpool, employed in the African Slave Trade*; **HCSP 67: 1.**

10. See Craig and Jarvis (1967) for transcriptions of the Liverpool Registry of Merchant Ships for 1786–93. For *Brooks*, see Craig and Jarvis (1967), 19, no. 62; for *Bud*, 33, no. 113; for *Golden Age*, 86, no. 136; for *Betty*, 28, no. 96; for *Kitty*, 106, no. 219; for *Venus*, 106, no. 219; for *Brothers*, 55, no. 10; for *Rose*, 66, no. 53; and for *Jane*, 82, no. 116.

11. On the origins of the 'skeleton' building technique (which dates from *c.*1450), see Stammers (1994: 35).

12. Dodds and Moore (1984: 18).

13. Lavery (1984: 30).

14. Moore (1989: 116).

15. Thus, for the vessels detailed in Table 5.2, Joseph Lyne, master of HMS Fowey, noted that *Daniel and Henry* was a hagboat: Tattersfield (1991: 175). *Don Carlos* is stated by Barbot to have both a foreyard and forecastle door (Churchill and Churchill 1732: v. 497), and, from the description of an attempted insurrection, it also appears to have had a raised quarterdeck (Churchill and Churchill 1732: v. 513). Newton refers many times to both a quarterdeck and a forecastle on *Argyle*, and Barker to the same on *Thetis*. For the lengthening of *Sandown*, see *Lloyd's Register* 1793, S-151, and Mouser (2002: p. xxii). The majority of ships employed in the eighteenth-century Dutch slave trade were also frigate-built: see Postma (1990: 144).

16. Parrey also made very brief notes on the origins of seventeen other slaving vessels in port at Liverpool. Of these, four are described as British-built 'for the trade', and four more as 'British-built'. The remainder were built in Bermuda, America, France, and the East Indies.

17. On the lapse between launch and repair, see Wilkinson (2004: 76, table 4.2).

18. Behrendt (2001: 177) estimates that the destructiveness of the slave trade to shipping required merchants to purchase sailing vessels every three to four years. Timber deterioration was one factor here; all timber ships were subject to both wet and dry rot, as discussed by Wilkinson (2004: 80–1). Dry rot, a fungal growth that flourishes in warm, damp, and poorly ventilated conditions, was a particular threat to any ship operating in the tropics.

19. Moore (1989: 94). The combination of hair and pitch was common from the 1560s onwards. As Moore notes, John Hawkins (who, as discussed in Chapter 2, was Britain's first successful slaver) is usually credited with development of the method.

20. For detailed background to the introduction of copper sheathing, see Harris (1966) and McCarthy (2005: 102–14).

21. Harris (1966: 552).

22. Solar and Rönnbäck (2015: 810) (*contra* Rees 1971: 94, who noted *Hawke* as the first coppered Liverpool ship, in 1777).

23. Rees (1971: 86–7).

24. Rees (1971: 89); Minchinton (1979: 350).

25. *Liverpool General Advertiser*, 21 January 1791.

26. Haines and Shlomowitz (2000: 263).

27. Solar and Rönnbäck (2015: 821). As the authors note, other factors, including a reduction in crowding, also played a part here.

28. Minchinton (1989: 58).

29. *Lloyd's Registers*, the first of which were published 1764–6 and 1768–71 and have appeared annually since 1775, provide a mass of information on ships insured by the company, including details on tonnage, age, rig, ownership, draft, and condition.

30. Details on rig are not always known, but the default query https://www.slavevoyages.org/voyages/mOu2kS5A (accessed 22 August 2022) reveals 4,218 of 10,845 British-based ships rigged as ships, 1,213 as snows, and 836 as brigs. Minchinton's work on Naval Office records for slave ships entering North America has similarly shown that the majority of British vessels entering

Virginia between 1725 and 1769 were rigged as ships or snows: see Minchinton (1989: 59, table 4, and 60).

31. On this practice, introduced *c*.1777, see Law (2004: 127–8). Rig can be determined (via TSTD) for thirty-nine British vessels trading principally at Ouidah after 1777, twenty-four of which were three-masted (https://www.slavevoyages.org/voyages/mOu2kS5A (accessed 29 October 2020), (checking date range 1777–1807 and principal place of purchase as Whydah).
32. Cook (2012: 85).
33. MacGregor (1985: 344).
34. See here Van der Vliet (2017: 247–8), arguing the case that the model of *De Witte Oliphant* in the Rijksmuseum collection may represent a slave ship.
35. Henderson and Stanbury (1983).
36. 9 Geo. II c. 37 *Manufacturing of Sail-Cloth Act.* Also 19 Geo. II c. 27.
37. Morris (1998) discusses the rise of the Ipswich sailcloth industry. On the sailcloth industry at Zaanstreek, Holland, see Kleij (2017). For Lancashire's sailcloth industry, see Schofield (1986).
38. Steel (1794: 86).
39. Focht (2008: 24) discusses the transition to flat-seamed sails.
40. This useful description is taken from Tattersfield (1991: 49).
41. Because it is so difficult to make meaningful comparisons between the various definitions of tonnage used before 1786, TSTD employs mathematical formulae to adjust tonnages to a single standard: the British measured ton (as defined from 1775–1835): see https://www.slavevoyages.org/voyage/about#methodology/tonnage/18/en/ (accessed 31 August 2022), for an explanation of this process. Solar and Duquette (2017) are highly critical of the standardization methodology employed by TSTD, but in the interests of consistency I have elected to employ TSTD standardized tonnages for all the British vessels discussed in this book.
42. Klein (2010: 142–4) suggests that, for all European slave trading nations, the optimal slave ship measured 150–250 tons, a modal range unique to the slave ship, designed both to trade along coasts and rivers in Africa and to ensure a swift passage to the Americas.
43. Klein (2010: 135).
44. Falconer (1769: Goo–Gri).
45. Henderson (2008: 46).
46. Henderson (2008: 46).
47. Tibbles ed., (1994: 141); See Quilley (2000) for further discussion of this painting.
48. Air ports could be cut into any merchant vessel lacking them: Gamble (**Sandown 1793–4: 8**) mentions his carpenter 'cutting out ports in the waist' of *Sandown* while fitting out the ship prior to the voyage. As Mouser (2002: 9, n. 38) notes, this could be a reference to gun ports, but it is possible that Gamble is referring to air ports.
49. Robert Norris (**HCSP 68: 7**) also refers to the use of a canvas awning, 9–10 ft above the deck.
50. Hales (1743, 1756). See also Allan and Schofield (1980: 84–90) for a summary of Hale's impact on ship ventilation. His ventilators were also employed in prisons and gaols.
51. It was widely believed that confined air—and particularly the vapours and perspiration expelled by the human body—were a cause of infection: Wilkinson (2004: 83).
52. Allan and Schofield (1980: 84).
53. See Klein and Engerman (1979) for discussion of the use of ventilators in the French slave trade. Following introduction of the new equipment in 1753, mortality rates fell.
54. Hales (1756: 41).
55. Hales (1756: 42–5). Henry Ellis was master of three voyages of the Bristol slaver *Halifax* (TSTD 17263, 17314, 17365) in the 1750s.
56. Riley's assertion (1987: 132) that Hales's ventilators were widely used on slave ships is not borne out by the parliamentary data.

178   MATERIALIZING THE MIDDLE PASSAGE

57. One of the men who had served on a slave ship with a ventilator was Mr James, who sailed on *Britannia* in 1768 (*Substance* **1789: 14**).
58. Lind (1762: 44).
59. Falconer (1769: Win–Wor).
60. Klein (2010: 150), for example, regards the gratings and air ports as a supply on slave ships as creating an unusual but 'reasonably efficient' air circulation arrangement on slave ships.
61. Klein (2010: 150).
62. 28 Geo. II c. 54.
63. Behrendt (1997: 63).
64. Cf., e.g., Garland and Klein (1985), and Klein (2010: 132–61); with Duquette (2014).
65. 37 Geo. III c. 118.
66. 39 Geo. III c. 80. See the discussion in Garland and Klein (1985: 240).
67. Recollecting a voyage made on *Lady Neilson* in 1800, Samuel Robinson (1867: 13) remembered that the words 'Lady Neilson of Liverpool, allowed to carry 294 slaves' were painted in large letters on the stern. This is presumably TSTD 82216—a vessel taken as a Spanish prize.
68. The fire that sank the slaver *Luxborough Galley* in 1727 began in its lazaretto: Boys (1787: 1).
69. On the likely French origins of *Henrietta Marie*, see Moore (1989: 128).
70. Moore and Malcom (2008: 26).
71. See Moore (1989: 83–109). My account of the ship's features is taken entirely from Moore's work.
72. TSTD 77559. For the naval history of this ship, see Winfield (2007b: 763).
73. This voyage was TSTD 77559. The information that *Blandford* had been fitted with ventilators was uncovered by the *British Tars 1740–1790* website, https://www.britishtars.com/2017/03/a-view-of-blandford-frigate-c1760.html (accessed 31 August 2022).
74. Hutchinson (1794: 33).
75. Hutchinson (1794: 40–5) (TSTD 81687). *Hall* carried more than 200 slaves from the Cameroons to Kingston, Jamaica, on this, its only documented slaving voyage.
76. Craig and Jarvis (1967: 19, no. 61). The dimensions given by Hutchinson are slightly different: length 90 ft, maximum breadth 30 ft.
77. Stammers (1994, 40); see Craig and Jarvis (1967: 19, no. 62).
78. The process was later described in detail by Clarkson in his 1808 *History* of the abolition movement: see Clarkson (1808: ii. 112). See Webster (2008) and Radburn and Eltis (2019) for more information on the creation of the *Description*.
79. See Craig and Jarvis (1967: 19, no. 62) for the details about *Brooks* recorded in the *Liverpool Registry of Merchants Ships*.
80. These voyages are TSTD 80663–6.
81. See Wood (2000: 25–9) and Radburn and Eltis (2019: 540) for discussion of these depiction of *Brooks*'s captive cargo.
82. This voyage was TSTD 80665.
83. The term 'spoonways' was employed by Thomas Trotter (**HCSP 73: 84**), who had made a voyage as surgeon on *Brooks* in 1783–4.
84. See Radburn and Eltis (2019: 539–41) for a detailed consideration of what is missing from the *Brooks* image, and a comparison with the more realistic contemporary visualization of the slave deck of *Marie-Séraphique*.
85. Some months later, in April, Newton refers to clearing one side of the boys' room to use as a hospital (*Argyle* **1750–1: 49**).
86. The exploration of the wreck site, and the artefacts recovered, are discussed in Cunningham and Kingsley (2011).
87. Herry (2004: 99).
88. Small planking fragments found on the *Henrietta Marie* wreck site (ranging in size 1.9–3.2 cm deep and 7.6–15.2 cm wide) might potentially represent the remains of temporary platforms: Moore (1989: 96).

89. Behrendt (2001: 175). The Royal Navy also, of course, required enormous quantities of timber.
90. Behrendt (2001: 177, n. 20).
91. These details are taken from May (1978).
92. Svalesen (2000: 52).
93. Tattersfield's suggestion (1991: 156) that 'gigantic net flounces supported by spars' stayed in place on *Daniel and Henry* is speculative.
94. **HCSP 68: 193**. Svalesen (2000: 106) refers to the remaining netting as 'quarter-netting'.
95. TSTD 2489.
96. Gikandi (2011: 210).
97. On single-decked vessels, a false deck would usually be laid in above the hold to serve as the temporary slave deck. From 1797 it was illegal for single-decked vessels to accommodate captives without laying in a false deck, the Act of that year stipulating: 'That in all such Vessels a Floor or False Deck shall be fixed in the Hold, for the Reception of the Slaves, which shall be taken and considered as her Lower Deck, for the Purposes of this Act' (37 Geo. III c. 118).
98. TNA: T.70/43, cited in Tattersfield (1991: 18).
99. John Barbot (***Treatment*** 1712: 778).
100. **HCSP 68: 11**.
101. **HCSP 68: 17**.
102. Radburn and Eltis (2019: 540).
103. For estimates given in Parliament, see, e.g., Norris, **HCSP 68: 11, 16–18,** and Jones, **HCSP 68: 46**.
104. See Patterson (1982: 38–45) for the concept of social death.
105. 28 Geo. III c. 54.
106. Behrendt (1997: 63).
107. Radburn and Eltis (2019: 540–1).
108. 37 Geo. III c. 118.
109. Samuel Gamble's *Sandown*, built in France in 1781, was galley-built (flush-decked) and had a between-deck height of just 4 feet: see Mouser (2002: p. xxii, n. 2).
110. 39 Geo. III c. 80.
111. Behrendt (1997: 63).
112. Rodger (1988: 61).
113. 37 Geo. III. *c.* 118.
114. *Weekly Journal or: The British Gazeteer* (London) 5 July 1729. TSTD 92391.
115. For Heatley's voyages, see Table 3.6.
116. A boys' room appears in the testimony of James Towne, concerning his voyages on *Peggy* in 1760, and on Sally in 1768: **HCSP 82: 19–20**. George Millar mentions a boys' room on *Canterbury* (1767): **HCSP 73: 392**. Similar spaces are noted in the testimonies of Elroyde Claxton (**HCSP 82: 33**), Robert Heatley (**HCSP 69: 123**), William Littleton (**HCSP 68: 293**), James Fraser (**HCSP 71: 47**), Clement Noble (**HCSP 73: 121**), James Morley (**HCSP 73: 168**), Robert Norris (**HCSP 68: 16**), and John Matthews (**HCSP 68: 20, 43**). But many testimonies are silent on the matter, and it is clear that boys' rooms were not invariably employed.
117. See Axelrod Wisnes (2007: 234).
118. Snelgrave (1734: 190; see also 183).
119. Robinson (1867: 54).
120. Smith (1813: 22).
121. I have not found a single reference in any testimony studied for this book to doors in the bulkheads separating the 'rooms' used by captives.
122. For the women's toilets on *Fredensborg*, see Svalesen (2000: 106). The latrines ('slave house') for the women on board the Dutch ship *Unity* were constructed on the day the first African

180 MATERIALIZING THE MIDDLE PASSAGE

woman was purchased, 10 December 1761, and that for the men erected on the side of the waist two days later (as noted in the first mate's logbook for 10 December 1761 and 12 December 1761: see https://eenigheid.slavenhandelmcc.nl/introductie-en/het-verslag-van-de-dag/?lang=en (accessed 22 August 2022)).

123. The Articles of Agreement appended to 29 Geo. III c. 66 (1789) required masters to provide 'a Space reserved for two third Parts of the Ship's Company to shelter themselves while the Slaves are on board; if a Frigate-built Ship, it shall be under the Half Deck, or in the Steerage, or under a standing Awning of Wood, well caulked, in any other Ship or Vessel'.

124. Monteith (1990: 104).

125. **HCSP 68: 17.**

126. Norris insists (**HCSP 68: 17**) that the platform did not impede air flow, being suspended 6 ft above the gratings, and supplied with an awning that, when laid horizontally, allowed a draft of air. But, given that the ship's boat was generally carried on the main grating, the air reaching the slave decks must have been minimal.

127. See, e.g., Inikori (2002: 282)—an analysis certainly overstating the case for a specialized fleet of British Guinea vessels.

128. Behrendt (2001: 178, n. 27). An 1801 advertisement for the French prize *La Venus* (*Gore's Advertiser*, 1 August 1801) is a good illustration of this point, describing the vessel as 'suitable for either a voyage for rice or a compleat Guineaman'.

129. Williams (2000a: 6, and table 2).

6

Witch Crafts

Slave Ships, Sailors, and African Cosmologies

How did the African communities supplying the slave trade conceptualize the enormous wooden vessels anchored off their coastlines? And in what ways did African understandings of European slave ships and their sailors change with the passage of time? These questions are asked in the present chapter, but they have proven surprisingly difficult to address, because, although the body of work exploring the impact of the slave trade on West Africa is enormous, very little attention has been paid to cultural—or, more specifically, aesthetic and cosmological—aspects of West African encounters with European slave *ships*.[1] Admittedly, representations of European ships do not appear to have been a common feature of African representational practices at any point in the history of the slave trade, so surviving African-made images are few. And yet the contexts in which these ship images appear are very significant, in that they were produced mainly by coastal communities directly involved in trade with Europeans and occur principally in courtly and ritual settings. It will be argued below that, in such contexts, Africans controlled and manipulated the European ship image for their own purposes. As this chapter also aims to show, the slaver, as a carrier away of people and a traverser of the water between the two worlds of the living and the dead, was embedded in African thought and practice in other, less direct ways than those involving use of the ship image itself. Most important of these, in terms of the interests of this book, was the understanding of the slave trade as a form of witchcraft—a term employed here, following James Sweet, to refer to 'religious malevolence, tied to temporal misfortune, especially misfortune caused by hidden human powers'.[2]

The best-known early modern first encounter between indigenes and British sailing ships had nothing to do with shipping captive Africans, but offers a useful starting point for this chapter, nonetheless. In 1779 Captain Cook explored Hawai'i. His arrival there, as brilliantly reconstructed by Marshall Sahlins, coincided with Makahiki (the New Year festival), marking the annual return of the god Lono, a deity whose wooden effigy was borne clockwise round the Hawaiian Islands annually by boat.[3] Appearing from the sea with his two ships (*Resolution* and *Discovery*), Cook made his own clockwise tour of the 'Big Island' and was welcomed rapturously by communities who regarded him as the embodiment of Lono. The fact that the Makahiki image of Lono was a tall wooden crosspiece covered with white cloth—not unlike the masts and sails of British ships—might well have played some part in facilitating the identification of Cook as Lono.[4] Cook's death came about a few months later because, returning unexpectedly to

Materializing the Middle Passage: A Historical Archaeology of British Slave Shipping, 1680–1807. Jane Webster, Oxford University Press. © Jane Webster 2023. DOI: 10.1093/oso/9780199214594.003.0006

182 MATERIALIZING THE MIDDLE PASSAGE

the island to repair *Resolution's* broken mast, he was perceived to have transgressed the ritual status that had been afforded to him.

This example highlights two points of direct concern to the present chapter. First, wherever, and whenever, indigenes first encountered Europeans and their ships, both were understood in terms of, and bent to the needs of, indigenous cosmologies. Second, as the anthropologist Wyatt MacGaffey emphasizes in his exploration of the fifteenth-century encounter between the Portuguese and the people of the Kongo Kingdom (where Christianity was adopted by the elite within a few years of first contact), the processes by which Europeans and Africans arrived at the mutual intelligibility that made this adoption possible were largely 'dialogues of the deaf', involving fundamental misunderstandings on both sides.[5] To recall one of the concepts introduced in Chapter 1, these misunderstandings opened up a new conceptual terrain: a third space of cultural enunciation. In Bhabha's terms, the colonial (or in this case, precolonial) encounter with the new was always more than simply a dialectical play of recognition, wherein two cultures found some common ground: reading the new created uncertainty, and opened up between spaces that became innovative sites of collaboration, and also arenas for contestation.[6] For the first Central and West Africans to encounter them, as will become clear below, slave ships were firmly located in a liminal metaphysical zone between the land and the sea, the living and the dead, and the spirit and human worlds. In short, they were *witch* crafts. Even after Guineamen had been arriving off African coastlines for hundreds of years, this was still to some extent the case; and understandings of the slave ship as a manifestation of witchcraft were, of course, carried on board slaving vessels by many captives. This point will be revisited in some detail in Chapter 11, because their understanding of the voyage into slavery as (malevolent) bewitchment directly informed the decisions and actions of captives during the Middle Passage. But in the present chapter, my aim is to chart the evolution of understandings of European ships in West and Central Africa, both before and during the time period that most directly concerns this book (1680–1807). That story begins in the late 1400s.

Dead Ancestors Walking: African Understandings of the Portuguese and Their Ships, *c.*1480–1550

In the early 1400s, well before Columbus had discovered a 'new' world for Europe, Portuguese sailors had begun a detailed exploration of a little-known part of the old one: the coastline of sub-Saharan Africa. In 1444, captives were carried away from Africa on European ships for the first time, and a year later a Portuguese trading fort was constructed at Arguin, Mauritania. The Cape Verde islands were settled in the same period, and in 1462 Portuguese ships arrived at Sherbro Island, off Sierra Leone. By 1471 the Portuguese were trading off the coast of Ghana, and by 1482 they had encountered Kongo, in what is now south-western Angola.[7] In 1486, meaningful contact was established with the Benin Empire.[8] In 1482, as noted in Chapter 2, the

Portuguese built the first of what would be many European trading fortresses on the Gold Coast, at Elmina.

As Africans encountered European ships and sailors for the first time, they made two fundamental observations concerning the strangers in their midst: the newcomers were white, and they came from the sea. As Henry Drewal has noted, their ships played a material part in shaping how foreign sailors were conceptualized: 'Early European travellers reported that Africans associated them with the sea and water spirits, an impression that would have been reinforced by the sight of their large sailing vessels coming into view from below the horizon.'[9] Many West and Central African peoples shared a belief that the dead travelled across water to reach the place of the ancestors.[10] As Robin Law has shown, while most reports of crossing water to the land of the dead concerned lakes and rivers, some accounts attached the story to the Atlantic Ocean, and on the Slave Coast (though not in West Africa as a whole) a belief grew up in the era of the slave trade that the land of the dead lay beyond the Atlantic.[11] Many Africans also regarded whiteness as indicative of the spirit world and of death.[12] Within this framework, the Portuguese ships that appeared in Sierra Leone, the Benin Empire, and the Kongo kingdom in the late fifteenth century were carrying the dead. As MacGaffey explains with reference to BaKongo cosmology, the strangers

> exhibited the principal characteristics of the dead: they were white in colour, spoke an unintelligible language, and possessed technology superior even to that of the local priestly guild of smiths...The first Portuguese, like their successors to the present day, were regarded as visitors from the land of the dead.[13]

As assimilated into pre-existing understandings, these visitors were traffickers from the occult, and, as transatlantic contact grew, the slave trade would come to be understood as carrying away people prematurely to a land of the dead that, in some readings, was identified with the Americas.[14] I will return to African understandings of the slave ship as a site of bewitchment in Chapter 11, in discussing evidence for counter-witchcraft during the Middle Passage.

What were these traffickers from the land of the dead using for transport? The Portuguese explored the Atlantic using the carrack or *nau* (Figure 6.1), the earliest versions of which were single-masted. The *nau* eventually acquired additional masts and become considerably larger.[15] In 1492, Columbus crossed the Atlantic in just such a developed *nau*: *Santa Maria*. African coastal peoples were experienced sailors: lagoon, river, and ocean-going canoes employed in warfare, fishing, and trade long predated European contact.[16] Some canoes were 80 ft in length, and carried more than a hundred people, but the newly arrived European ships dwarfed even the biggest of these craft, and were constructed and manoeuvred using techniques unfamiliar to Africans, including the use of sails.[17]

Alvise Cadamosto, a Venetian explorer in the employ of Henry the Navigator, provides the earliest eyewitness voyage testimony concerning African responses to Portuguese sailing ships.[18] Cadamosto made two voyages to Upper Guinea in 1455 and

Figure 6.1 The Mataró ship model. Made in the Catalonian town of Mataró in the fifteenth century, this medieval votive object is thought to depict a single-masted cog, or its successor, the Iberian *nau*. Marietem Museum Rotterdam.

1456, visiting the Gambia, and the Senegal and Rio Grande rivers, and claiming discovery of the Cape Verde islands. In his travel narrative he made several observations concerning reactions to European ships on the Upper Guinea coast and in Sierra Leone. For example, he noted:

> It is asserted that when for the first time they saw sails, that is, ships, on the sea (which neither they nor their forefathers had ever seen before), they believed that they were great sea-birds with white wings, which were flying, and had come from some strange place: when the sails were lowered for the landing, some of them, watching from far off, thought that the ships were fishes. Others again said that they were phantoms that went by night, at which they were greatly terrified... Thus, as they did not understand the art of navigation, they all thought that the ships were phantoms.[19]

Elsewhere, Cadamosto reported: 'They were also astonished at the ingenuity of our ship with its equipment, its masts, sails and anchors. They also thought that the eyes that were painted on the prow of the ship were real eyes and that in this way the ship could see where it was going at sea.'[20] Cadamosto's account does not really tell us what indigenes thought, of course: it merely tells us what European adventurers *surmised* onlookers thought when faced with a new technology. His words nevertheless suggest a duality, in that Africans appear to have perceived the sailing ship to belong to both the natural and the spirit worlds. The custom of painting eyes (oculi) on a ship was an ancient and long-lived one, employed by the Greeks and Romans and still to be found in Portugal at the turn of the twentieth century.[21] In the fifteenth century, this tradition may have played a part in shaping indigenous understandings of European ships as living beings.

It has been argued since the seventeenth century that Kongo peoples regarded European ships as *ntele* (whales), and that this understanding gave rise to the term *mindele*, employed for the Portuguese themselves.[22] As MacGaffey rightly stresses, early European etymologies need to be treated with caution, but this example suggests, at the very least, that Portuguese traders perceived themselves and their ships to be closely allied in Kongo thought.[23] It is worth noting that a similar conflation was made centuries later, in another part of West Africa entirely. In the eighteenth and nineteenth centuries, Efik traders at Old Calabar (Nigeria) 'identified the ship in the captain'.[24] That is to say, they used a captain's name to designate his vessel. Antera Duke, an Efik trader who in 1785–8 recorded his dealings with Liverpool ships in a diary written in pidgin English, provides many examples of this practice. On 28 January 1785, for example, he wrote 'wee two go Bord Captin Smale with 3 slave', indicating that he and a companion boarded Captain John Smale's ship *Perseverence*.[25]

If we turn back to the fifteenth century, a further glimpse into early local readings of Portuguese ships comes from the Benin Empire, where white was associated with both the dead and Olokun, god of the sea.[26] Bini people regarded the Portuguese as liminal beings, able to move freely between this world and that of the dead. It was their ships that made the journey possible, allowing the Portuguese to traverse Olokun's waters laden with luxury goods.[27] The people carried away in the same Portuguese ships were regarded as travelling to join the dead: for Kongo peoples, then, 'the slave trade was, and is, thought of as a trade in souls taken prematurely to the land of the dead'.[28] An additional belief, among some Kongo, was that, once on board slave ships, captives would be killed and eaten by 'white cannibals'.[29] In Central African thought, cannibalism—as the ultimate form of human exploitation—was regarded as a manifestation of witchcraft, and it has been argued by several scholars that the belief that those carried away on slave ships would be eaten, either literally or spiritually, helped to cement an understanding of the slave trade as witchcraft.[30] James Sweet has emphasized that, for Central Africans, crossing the Atlantic Ocean in slave ships represented 'a premature death at the hands of witches, who nourished themselves on black bodies in the land of the dead (the Americas)'.[31] But it is interesting to note that some captives believed they would be feeding the slave ships themselves. For example, Jose Monzolo, an enslaved man born at the edge of the Kongo Kingdom, said in 1659 of his own passage across the Atlantic that his fellow slaves believed the Spanish 'bought them to kill them and make flags for their ships from the remains, for when they were red it was from the blood of the Moors'.[32]

Art historians use the name 'Afro-Portuguese ivories' to designate a group of early ivory artefacts (salt cellars, boxes, spoons, forks, dagger handles, and horns) that were commissioned from local artists by Portuguese elites, missionaries, and traders and fuse African and European figurative elements. Afro-Portuguese ivories were first made by Sapi artists from Sierra Leone in the 1490s, and subsequently (from *c*.1520) by artists in Benin.[33] This important corpus of ivory work provides insights into the first stages of a dialogue between African artisans and European material culture that, as explored further in Chapter 7, would continue throughout the era of the transatlantic slave trade. These objects also provide the earliest instances of African renderings of European traders, who are depicted as bearded, long-haired, hooked-nosed, gaunt, and unsmiling: the land of the dead clearly took its toll on those who walked there. Images of Portuguese men are often juxtaposed with those of the sea creatures associated with Olokun: fish, snakes, and crocodiles. Visualizations of their ships are extremely rare, but two surviving ivories from the Benin Empire do depict sailing vessels (see Figure 6.2 for an illustration of one of these).[34]

It is open to question whether the stylized, single-masted ship depicted in Figure 6.2 is an independent, indigenous visualization of the Portuguese *nau* or is based on

Figure 6.2 Detail from the lid of an ivory salt cellar, made by an Edo or Owo artist, Benin (Nigeria), *c*.1525–1600, depicting a Portuguese sailor on the main top of his ship. British Museum, Af1878,1101.48.

drawings or designs, perhaps European heraldic images, provided by the trader who commissioned this object. Some art historians favour the latter view, even while suggesting that the ship may have been observed from life by the artist.[35] Whatever the case, the artist who created the ship whose main top (crow's nest) is detailed in Figure 6.2 reveals a keen interest in the materials from which European ships were constructed, detailing the timbers of the main top (or crow's nest); the planking of the hull; and the fibres twisted to make the ropes on the rigging and anchors. The Portuguese sailor in the main top, clutching the hailer that allowed his voice to travel further than that of any mortal being, was a dead man; but his ship was constructed from familiar, organic materials.[36]

Arts for Water Spirits: Mermaids and Mami Wata

Ships and sailors were not the only European maritime subjects to be depicted on ivories. The Portuguese carried with them to Africa images and folk tales concerning a variety of mythical creatures, such as dragons and centaurs.[37] Mermaids—beautiful but treacherous creatures, believed to lure mariners to a watery death—held a particular fascination for European sailors, particularly those charting unknown waters. Many of these men believed firmly that mermaids were real: in 1493, Christopher Columbus recorded the sighting of three mermaids off the coast of Haiti, noting that they were 'not so beautiful as painted, though to some extent they have the form of a human face'.[38] James Barbot Jnr's account of the slaving voyage of *Don Carlos* (**Don Carlos 1700: 517**) includes both an image (Figure 6.3) and a lengthy discourse on European beliefs surrounding mermaids, occasioned by his observations on mermaid-like fish living in the lakes of Angola:

> The lakes also breed several creatures, especially those of Angola, Quihite, and Anglom, in the province of Massingan; where, among others, is taken a fish, by the inhabitants, called Ambisangalo and Pesiengoni; by the Portuguese, Peixe Mother, or woman-fish; by the French Syrene and by the English the mermaid; both male and female, some eight foot long with short arms, and hands, and long fingers, which they cannot close together, because of the skin growing between them, as is in the feet of ducks and geese. They feed upon grass on the sides of lakes and rivers, and only hold their heads out of the water. Their heads and eyes are oval, the forehead high, the nose flat, and the mouth wide without any chin or ears. The males have genitals like horses, and the females two strutting breasts, but in the water there is no distinguishing the one from the other, being both of a dark grey.

On at least one occasion, a Portuguese trader or sailor commissioned an ivory salt cellar from a Sapi artisan and provided that artist with a European mermaid image, which was faithfully replicated on the object (Figure 6.4).

Figure 6.3 Drawing of a mermaid as found in the lakes of Angola, by James Barbot Jnr, from Churchill and Churchill (1732: v, plate 30).

Among African peoples, beliefs in water spirits—often depicted as part human, part aquatic beings—are both widespread and ancient. Semi-anthropomorphic fish-figures are frequently depicted in Benin and Yoruba art and are found on some of the earliest surviving bronzes and ivories. Among these images, which also include beings with human bodies and legs in the form of mudfish, are others that have human bodies but grasp one end of a forked or double fish tail in either hand. As art historians have long recognized, these figures are not unlike a European variant on the mermaid image, which shows her grasping her forked tail with either hand. Some scholars, including Douglas Fraser, have argued that, while African fish-figures bear a superficial resemblance to mermaids, they predate European contact, and were among a series of related symbols employed in Benin and by the Yoruba to denote the mastery of divine kings over the natural world.[39] Others see self-dompting fish-figures (that is, those grasping their own forked tails) as Africanized renderings of European mermaid images, brought to the attention of African artists by the Portuguese via marine carving (ships' figureheads), flags, books, heraldry, and trade items. The leading proponent of the latter argument is Henry Drewal, who has written extensively on the possible interplay between West African beliefs in water spirits and European mermaid imagery.[40] Drewal locates the genesis of one of modern West Africa's most popular

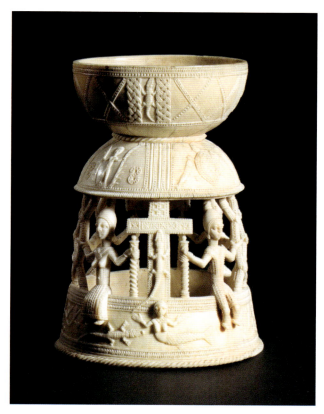

Figure 6.4 Sapi–Portuguese salt-cellar lid, with mermaid figure. National Museum of Denmark, EDc 67.

divinities, Mami Wata (Mother Water), in the dialogue between Portuguese traders and Sapi sculptors in the late fifteenth century. Mami Wata (seen in Figure 6.5) is very much a deity of the twentieth and twenty-first centuries, and Drewal's suggestion is not, therefore, without its critics.[41] But the protagonists in this fascinating debate are really focused on different things. One of these themes (the one of most interest to postcolonial anthropologists and scholars of modern African art) is Mami Wata worship *today*; multifaceted, heterogeneous, and drawing on a vast range of imported visual referents including Hindu art. The other (the one that interests more traditional art historians) is possible European influence upon the centuries-old water-spirit imagery that informed the concept of Mami Wata. Some scholars appear to feel that to focus on the latter is somehow to detract from the agency and creativity of today's Mami Wata devotees. This is not the case: it is simply to explore one moment in an aesthetic dialogue that began the second Europeans arrived in West Africa and is still going on today. The key point here is that, whether for reasons ancient or modern, Mami Wata is frequently depicted emerging from the water combing her long hair and gazing at her reflection in a mirror, just as mermaids do. The mirror is central to Mami Wata belief and ritual practice: as Drewal puts it, worshippers 'construct an image of the exotic, supernatural entity of Mami Wata and then reflect it in their own lives in

Figure 6.5 A twentieth-century Ibibio (Nigerian) Mami Wata figure. (87 × 61 × 25 cm). Mami Wata is generally depicted as she is here: pale skinned, long-haired, and wreathed in snakes. Michael C. Carlos Museum, 1994.3.9.

order to define themselves and to assert control over their world'.[42] Mami Wata is sometimes, though by no means always, depicted with a fishtail, but it is perhaps significant that, when rendered three-dimensionally, the divinity almost always lacks a lower body. This observation has led Drewal and others to suggest that Mami Wata imagery specifically, and water spirit depictions more generally, may have been inspired by the timber prow figures on European sailing ships, many of which depicted real, allegorical, and mythical females (mermaids included).[43] Figureheads are discussed in more detail at a later point in this chapter.

Shifting Understandings: Ships and Ship Motifs after *c.*1700

The Whidawers [people of Ouidah] much admire white men, and say, that God loves them, because they have such plenty of all sorts of commodities; are much puzzled to think how we find our way thro' the sea into their country... [*The sea being too rough to come ashore to trade*] The old king desired me to be easy and that he would make the sea quiet the next day. Accordingly he sent his *Fatishman* with a jug of palm-oil, a bag of rice and corn, a jar of pitto [*beer*], a bottle of brandy and a piece of painted callicoes, and several other things to present the sea to appease it. When the *Fatishman* came to the sea-side (as I was informed by men that were there and saw the ceremony) he made a speech to it, assuring the sea that his king was its friend, and lov'd the white men; that we were honest fellows; and come to trade with him to supply his country with what he wanted, and that he requested the sea not to be angry, nor hinder us to land our goods; and told it; That if it wanted palm-oil his king had sent it some; and so threw the jar with the oil into the sea, as he did with the same complement the rice, corn, pitto, brandy, callicoe &c.

(**Phillips,** *Hannibal* **1693–4: 226)**[44]

By the time the RAC's monopoly of the British slave trade was opened up to interlopers in the late 1600s, slave ships and their smaller boats had become a familiar sight on the coastline of West and Central Africa. The belief that white people lived under the ocean remained strong, nevertheless, and in the Kongo, at least, not only is well attested in missionary reports of the seventeenth century but is current even today.[45] Long after slave ships had been a familiar sight to generations of coastal dwellers, Guineamen continued to be interpreted in terms of local cosmologies. In 1700, André Brüe, Director of the French Royal Company of Senegal, described what he called an 'odd ceremony of sacrificing a cock', witnessed on a voyage to Guinea-Bissau:

[A] canoa approached with five negroes; one of whom came on deck, holding a cock in his left hand, and a knife in his right. After kneeling a minute before the Sieur Brüe, without speaking, he rose; and turning to the east, cut the cock's throat, and placing himself on his knees again, let some drops of blood fall on the Sieur Brüe's feet. He did the same to the mast and pump of the ship, and returning to the general, presented him the cock. The general, ordering him a bumper of brandy, asked him the reasons of this ceremony: he replied, that the people of his country looked on the whites as the gods of the sea; that the mast was a divinity that made the ship walk, and the pump was a miracle, since it could make water rise up, whose natural property is to descend.[46]

The mainmast was one of the most obvious features of a sailing ship, but the bilge pump, used to expel the seawater that inevitably seeped in below the water line, was located in the hold—a place to which only the crew had access. A conduit or dale made of canvas, planking, or lead directed the foul-smelling bilge water directly over the side of the ship, however, and this expulsion of water would have been visible to external observers.[47]

As this example indicates, European ships remained objects of cosmological speculation to African observers at the start of the eighteenth century. Was this speculation given material expression? Slave ship images do occasionally figure on the gold weights employed by the Akan along the Gold Coast, and it has been suggested that '[s]ailing ships supporting the gold and slave trade during the seventeenth and eighteenth centuries made a dramatic impression on the Akan as evidenced by their depiction in goldweights, often complete with rigging, flags, and cannons'.[48] But in fact, I have been able to locate only two gold weights in the form of European ships, both now in the Smithsonian collections (one of these is illustrated in Figure 6.6).

In early eighteenth-century Dahomey, the image of the slave ship was actively appropriated to the courtly arts and harnessed as a symbol of African royalty. The Kingdom of Dahomey was established around 1600 by the Fon and was centred on Abomey in what is today southern Benin. Dahomey was one of several powerful regional polities supplying the demands of European trade on the Slave Coast. In 1724, the Dahomean king Agaja conquered the neighbouring kingdom of Allada and, in 1727, he subdued the Hueda kingdom and its slaving entrepot at Savi. The defeat of the Hueda gave Agaja control, by 1733, over the important slaving port of Ouidah.[49] Dahomian traders at Ouidah paid close attention to the appearance of slave ships, introducing a system for the payment of customs (that is, permission to trade, bought with trade goods) graduated according to the size of a ship, which was measured by the number of its masts.[50] The Dahomian elite understood well that their identity as a

Figure 6.6 Copper alloy Akan gold weight in the form of a single-masted European sailing ship (49 × 88 × 18 mm), eighteenth–nineteenth centuries. Smithsonian Institution, nmfa_95-6-3.

sovereign trading state was inextricably entwined with the presence of European traders in their territory—a presence they nevertheless sought to control to their advantage. As Kenneth Kelly notes, this double understanding was celebrated in Agaja's choice of personal iconographic symbol: the European sailing ship. 'To this day', Kelly notes, 'the European sailing ship is associated with Agaja because it was he who brought the power of trade control to the Kingdom of Dahomey'.[51] No surviving examples of Agaja's icon can be securely dated to the eighteenth century, but see Figures 6.7 and 6.8 for two undated depictions.

Figure 6.7 Undated emblem of Agaja (226 × 138 mm). Wooden finial, covered in silver, depicting a three-masted ship with quarterdeck and two anchors. This object would have surmounted a wooden shaft. Musée Africaine de Lyon, DE 1992.40.1.

Figure 6.8 Cast of a bas-relief from the Palace of Agaja, Abomey, made by Emmanuel-Georges Waterlot in 1911. Musée du quai Branly, Paris, 71.2012.0.4166.

It is beyond doubt, as Robin Law has noted, that the Dahomian elite 'had an informed understanding of where it was that slaves were sent and what fate awaited them when they got there', not least because Dahomian officials had travelled to America and Europe on diplomatic missions.[52] The ship image was not adopted by Agaja in blissful ignorance of the fate of the enslaved, therefore, and part of its power lies in precisely this point.

The regularity with which African trading partners were able to observe slave ships at close quarters should not be underestimated. Africans routinely boarded slavers in the course of their transactions with the supercargoes or captains. Ships were an important focus for social rituals in this context; convivial but also formal spaces in which eating and drinking oiled the wheels of commerce. As explored further in Chapter 7, captains often converted their own cabins into showrooms where African partners could browse the range of trade goods offered in exchange for slaves. In Senegambia and on the Slave Coast, waged African canoe men, mariners, and navigators came and went from slave ships on a regular basis, and in some regions, including the Gold Coast and Calabar, dependants of important African brokers spent time on board slave ships as pawns—living surety against the supply of European goods advanced to their kin.[53] On the Gold Coast, captains secured the services of

African intermediary agents known as gold-takers, who would remain on board a ship throughout its lengthy coastal stay.[54] Skilled canoe men were also hired on the Gold Coast and transported to Ouidah and other sites with hazardous sand bars: here they would pilot the canoes employed to ferry people and goods over the bar from shore to ship (**Philips, Hannibal 1693–4: 228**). It is interesting to note, in the latter context, that one physical manifestation of local familiarity with the slaver was the modification of indigenous canoes in ways that referenced European sailing ships. By 1600, African fishing canoes on the Gold Coast were being propelled by sails (made from rush or straw mats) as well as by paddles, but it was explicitly noted by European observers that this technology had been learned from the Portuguese.[55] All slavers were armed with cannon to protect them against external threat, and, as discussed in Chapter 11, they also employed more portable armaments such as swivel and carriage guns, used to maintain control over captives. By the later eighteenth century, war canoes in some parts of West Africa were similarly being armed with small brass or iron cannon.[56] Archibald Dalzel described an attack on Ekpe by Dahomey and Ardra in 1778–82, during which the fire from two Ardran canoes, each armed with a pair of brass guns, enabled the Ardra to make a successful retreat.[57] Dalzel's account of this action implies that the guns were mounted on swivels, which would have enabled them to be fired at an angle to the direction of the canoe. According to Dalzel, swivels had been introduced on the West Coast by Antonio Vaz Coelho, a Brazilian-born former slave who became a successful trader.[58]

Some traders furnished their canoes with sails and flags, again referencing European practice. In Senegambia, *grumetes* experienced in the use of Portuguese vessels developed the pirogue, a composite craft derived from both African and Portuguese traditions. The pirogue was a small, flat-bottomed boat with sails: it transformed shallow-water fishing throughout the region.[59] The most expensive single item carried to Calabar on board *Dobson* in 1769 was a red ensign, purchased along with 360 yards of bunting, and made by the Liverpool sailmakers Joshua Rose and James White.[60] The flag and bunting were not items for barter; they were clearly gifts for a leading Efik trader. In 1773, one such trader, Ephraim Robin John, listed 'canvas to make sails for my canoes' among the many items requested in writing from the leading Liverpool merchant (and former slave ship master) Ambrose Lace.[61]

An invaluable collection of documents written by the Efik trader Antera Duke provide fascinating insights into the material world of the African merchants at Old Calabar, where leading British syndicates and their captains built up very strong individual partnerships.[62] These relationships were materialized in a unique range of custom-made, personalized artefacts, some of which still survive today. A brass bell (just like those used to toll the watch on slave ships), now the property of the Society of Merchant Venturers, Bristol, is inscribed: 'THE GIFT OF THOMAS JONES OF BRISTOL TO GRANDY ROBIN JOHN OF OLD TOWN OLD CALABAR 1770'.[63] Handsome gifts such as this cemented the close relationship between slave ship owners and the local partners with whom they built, through their ships' captains, a mutually beneficial trading relationship.[64] Less expensive ivory bracelets or disks, designed to be worn on the body,

196 MATERIALIZING THE MIDDLE PASSAGE

served as testimonials to the reliability of the African trading partners who wore them, thereby encouraging other Europeans to do business with these men. Several such testimonials survive in museum collections, among them an ivory example engraved with the words 'Tom Buck of Grandy Bonny, an Honest Trader, he sold me 20 slaves'.[65] Another, inscribed 'The Gift of Captain Trousdall to Young West India of Grandy Bonny', was acquired by the abolitionist Thomas Clarkson, and is discussed in Chapter 8.

Other kinds of bespoke artefact materialize from a careful reading of British and African textual sources. Thus in 1769 John Potter's *Dobson* carried out to Calabar twelve bass basins engraved 'Antera Duke', and in 1771 *Hector* shipped eighteen manillas engraved with 488 letters (some 27 per object), which were probably the names of a Liverpool merchant and his African partner.[66] Liverpool slave ships even transported the component parts of English furnishings including tables, chairs, and beds, which their ships' carpenters then put together in the homes of favoured partners. On 30 December 1785, Antera Duke recorded in his diary that Thomas Charles, mate on *Quixote*, visited his house to nail a base onto a wooden bed.[67] Ephraim Robin John's correspondence with the Liverpool trader Ambrose Lace also included a request for a 6 feet × 6 feet looking glass with a sturdy frame; also a table and six chairs and two armchairs.[68] The ultimate status symbol for some leading Efik merchants was an entire English-style two-storey wooden house, brought out from England in pieces and assembled with the help of ships' carpenters and crews. Egbo Young Ofiong possessed such a house and named it Liverpool Hall.[69] Antera Duke appears to have owned another, noting in his diary on 18 August 1787 that thirty-five sailors from the slaver *Ned* assisted in putting up two sides of a house.[70] In 1785, the senior British trader at Old Calabar, Patrick Fairweather, transported another house from Liverpool for Duke Ephraim. It was still standing in 1805 when Henry Nicholls, accommodated there as a representative of the African Association, described the building as being 'about twenty yards long, and thirty feet high, with a ground floor, a first floor, and a kind of cock-loft'. Nicholls was much amused by the elaborate European furnishings in his chamber and described them in condescending detail to his correspondent:

> I have two large-pier-glasses, seven feet by four, elegantly gilt and ornamented; twenty five ditto, from two and a half to four feet; three large sophas, twelve chairs. Two handsome escritoire desks, six tables, two large garde vines, one handsome marble side board, and an immense quantity of glasses, china and earthenware; six paintings, and twenty large engravings, five clocks, and two musical ditto; and a pretty jumble of furniture it is.[71]

Nicholls's description provides a fascinating glimpse into the material world, and aspirations, of Efik traders. The point that every single item on this lengthy list must have been carried to Old Calabar by slave ships, and where necessary reassembled by ships' carpenters, bears repeating: slave ships impacted on the aesthetics of African traders' homes in surprising ways, and the carpenters who constructed slave decks and barricados on board ship were also building relationships on land.[72]

African Engagement with Ships' Figureheads

> Most of us know that sailors refer to a ship by the feminine pronoun. But the extent of the metaphor of the ship as a living, feminine and anthropomorphic being, is not, I think, appreciated.
>
> (Rodgers 1984: 2)

The feature of the slaving vessel that most interested African communities was undoubtedly the figurehead. Wood was a commonly employed medium for figurative sculptures and masks in West and Central Africa throughout the era of the slave trade. At the same time, most European sailing ships were embellished with carved and painted wooden figureheads, the majority of which depicted animals or anthropomorphic figures (see Table 6.1 for details of figureheads from Liverpool slave ships). Various strands of evidence indicate that figureheads excited local interest and impacted upon indigenous practice. The first of these is textual and comprises an anecdote concerning one of the ships whose voyage is central to this book: *Sandown*. On 8 December 1793, Samuel Gamble was being rowed around the exterior of his ship, with a 'slave boy' at the oars of the yawl. As they rowed, Gamble records, the boy

> paid great attention to the Head, an excellent piece of carved work, being the figure of the unfortunate Louis 16 King of France and fresh painted. He was silent, till we came under the stern, where he saw the image (he then broke out in a kind of rapture, shaking his head exclaim'd whiteman savey every thing, no more that time man dead he can't make him rise again).   (*Sandown* 1793: 89)

Sandown was a French-built vessel, hence the choice of subject for the head. As discussed below, French figureheads were highly ornate, and much admired in Britain: this newly painted example will have been especially eye-catching.[73]

From the seventeenth century until the mid-eighteenth, the most common subject for both naval and commercial figureheads was the lion.[74] (For a lion head, see Pockock's illustration of *Blandford Frigate* in Figure 5.12.) Other animal subjects were also popular: Falconer's *Universal Dictionary of the Marine* illustrates an eagle head that, the author suggests, would be 'suitable for a frigate'.[75]

From the 1760s, human figures largely supplanted animal subjects on the figureheads carved for the merchant marine. French figurehead forms, with highly ornate carving styles, were extremely influential by the later eighteenth century, and one of the key subjects favoured by French artisans was a woman in a flowing gown.[76] Female figureheads were certainly a very popular choice for British merchant ships, in part because many sailing vessels were given women's names. Detailed information on

198 MATERIALIZING THE MIDDLE PASSAGE

British figureheads is hard to obtain; even after the introduction of the 1786 Registry Act, the precise details of figureheads were not systematically recorded when ships were surveyed and registered. But, by extracting figurehead details, where given, from the Liverpool Registry (Table 6.1) and by interrogating the information on British vessel names provided in the TSTD data set (Table 6.2), some clear trends emerge.

First, a figurehead generally complemented the name of the vessel: a *Neptune* would usually sport a figurehead depicting the god of the sea, for example. Second, personal names—of ship owners, of members of their families, of biblical and mythical figures, and of members of the royal family—were all popular choices when slave ships were named. Male Christian names were frequently used (among the most popular being *John, William, Will, George*, and *Thomas*), but female names were even more popular, as Table 6.2 indicates.

One in every thirty-seven British slaving voyages was undertaken by a ship whose name included the female Christian name *Mary*. Exactly how many of the ships thus named sported female figureheads is unknowable, but the pattern shown in Table 6.1 suggests that most will have done so, and that painted carvings depicting women will have been viewed time and time again by coastal communities and traders in West Africa. Very few eighteenth-century figureheads survive today, but an American example from *c*.1805 provides some indication of the appearance of female figureheads at the turn of the century (Figure 6.9): the elaborate coiffure, flowing dress, and carefully detailed jewellery were common features of figureheads depicting women.

Table 6.1 Figureheads of some Liverpool-built slave ships of the eighteenth century, where recorded in the Liverpool Registry of Merchant Ships

Ship name	Date constructed	Figurehead	TSTD voyages
Searle	1756	Bust	83542
Jane*	1766	Woman	81987–96
Gascoyne	1772	Man	81559–62, 81564
Neptune	1774	Neptune	82917–21, 82925
Will	1777	Vulture	84015–6, 84018–24
Garland	1778	Lion	81549–54
Elizabeth	1784	Woman	81206–8
Kitty	1784	Woman	82189–99
King Pepple	1785	Man	82153–63
Philip Stephens	1786	Lion	83081–5
Dick	1786	Negro	81028
Hawke	1786	Hawk	81755–7
Ann	1787	Female	80254–9
Brothers	1787	Man	80685–90
Peggy	1787	Woman	83039, 83041–3
Anne	1788	Woman	80309–12
Squirrel	1788	Squirrel	83612–4
Martha	1788	Woman	82490–93

* *Jane* was one of the ships measured by Captain Parrey in 1788; see Table 5.1.

Source: Craig and Jarvis (1967).

Table 6.2 Popular women's names employed for British slave ships, and the number of voyages made by ships so named

Vessel name (or name element)	Number of voyages by ships so named	Date range for voyages (departures)
Mary	286	1644–1807
Ann, Anne	241	1707–1807
Nancy	156	1710–1800
Betty	147	1677–1786
Elizabeth	131	1657–1807
Sarah	103	1656–1804
Molly	102	1725–1806
Betsey	77	1735–1804
Sally	72	1696–1806
Jane	57	1657–1807
Peggy	54	1737–1799
Fanny	50	1747–1805

Source: TSTD data derived from interrogation of https://www.slavevoyages.org/voyages/mOu2kS5A (last accessed 22 August 2022).

Figure 6.9 Female figurehead, *c.*1805, attributed to Simeon Skillin Jnr (?1756–1806). Peabody Essex Museum, M27185.

Remarkably, the female figurehead from one vessel employed in the closing years of the slave trade may have survived. It is thought to come from the enormous American-built clipper *Nightingale*, constructed in 1851 and captured by the Union Navy in 1861, carrying more than 900 captives. The figurehead depicts a woman argued by some to be the famous Swedish soprano, Jenny Lind.[77]

How would Africans have conceptualized these figureheads depicting women? As noted earlier, Drewal and others have speculated that prow figures, alongside the mermaid imagery discussed above, might have influenced the depiction of female water spirits in some parts of West Africa. A group of nineteenth-century tomb figures from the Niger Delta clearly reference both female prow figure imagery and European carpentry techniques. These figures represent members of the family of the Ijo King Ockiya (Figure 6.10). The faces are naturalistically styled and bear signs of having been painted white. Two wear wrappers made from trade cloth and are adorned with necklaces fashioned from other trade goods carried by European ships: cowries and metal bells. The third was probably also once similarly dressed and adorned.[78] The arms of these figures were made separately and then pegged into place—a European joinery technique.[79] The lower bodies and legs are much truncated: these are essentially seated torso figures, again echoing eighteenth-century female figureheads, many of which were torso figures characterized by a vertical posture, with the legs (if present) truncated and bent at the knee.

Figure 6.10 Three nineteenth-century wooden tomb figures from Brass, Niger Delta. Left: Manchester Museum, 0.4652. Centre: Bristol City Museums, Galleries & Archives, Ea7825. Right: University of Pennsylvania Museum of Archaeology and Anthropology AF 5122.

The example on the far right of Figure 6.10 closely resembles a Kalabari figure in the Pitt Rivers Museum, to which a revealing oral tradition is attached. The relevant entry in the Pitt Rivers Accession Book identifies the figure as the divinity Awomekaso (formerly Owamekaso) and notes:

> This goddess or spirit is said to have come to the tribe 'floating up out of the sea by her own power'. She was found in the form of a beautiful woman, very pale coloured, sitting alone in a small canoe, during the reign of King Owerri Daba (i.e. about 250 years ago). According to Chief Obenibo of Abonnema, whose testimony was corroborated by several other chiefs, 'we think that she may have been a shipwrecked white woman. This was before other Europeans came to our land.'[80]

Awomekaso, the national deity of the Kalabari, is to this day understood to be a shipwrecked Portuguese nun of the sixteenth century: an identification that, once again, points to an interplay between ships, women of foreign origin, and wooden sculpture.[81]

It is interesting to speculate, in this context, on indigenous readings of the near absence of women from European ships, and on the habitual feminization of the same vessels by British sailors. From the fourteenth century, all ships—whatever their names—were referred to by British sailors as 'she', despite the fact that the presence of women on board was regarded by many as a guarantee of ill fortune. Thomas Phillips's use of gendered terminology with reference to *Hannibal* offers a particularly interesting example of the habitual metaphor of the ship as a fictive woman.[82] In his text *Hannibal* is always personified as 'she', while the main and foremast are generally referred to as 'he': thus, facing action from a French ship, Phillips reports (***Hannibal*** **1693–4: 180**): 'we defended the ship, tho' she was most miserably shatter'd and torn in her mast and rigging, having had eleven shot in our main mast, three quite thro' him and several lodg'd in him and gaul'd him.' Presumably Phillips spoke about his ship in the hearing of African trading partners in much the same terms as he wrote about it in his voyage narrative: *Hannibal* was always 'she'. To add another layer of complexity, while *ships* were always female, sailors frequently described *women* using a vocabulary of maritime terms. The double meanings of words such as 'vessel' and 'port' were played upon in many ways in British maritime discourse.[83] A young woman, disguised as a male RAC employee, was discovered on board *Hannibal* on the voyage out to Africa. Phillips noted in his journal that the surgeon's mate had uncovered her identity when, sent to administer medication to the sick 'John Brown', he discovered 'more sally ports than he expected' (***Hannibal*** **1693-4: 179**). 'John Brown' spent the remainder of her voyage taking care of the captain's laundry. She was, Phillips, noted 'a likely black girl'—a phrase perhaps suggesting she was a woman of colour.[84]

As considered in greater detail in Chapter 10, maritime speech (or 'Ship English') had a considerable part to play in the versions of English that developed in coastal west Africa, so it is interesting to contemplate what indigenes might have made of these complex British linguistic practices and allied beliefs: of 'female' ships, penetrated by

202 MATERIALIZING THE MIDDLE PASSAGE

'male' masts, and seemingly interchangeable with, or standing for, women.[85] It is possible, perhaps, that carvings like those in Figure 6.10, and indeed the torso figures of Mami Wata like that shown in Figure 6.5, are the outcome of localized efforts to navigate these concepts.

Kalabari Ancestral Screens

Many of the themes discussed above coalesce in Figure 6.11, a Kalabari funerary screen (*duein fubara*, or 'forehead of the dead') made in the New Calabar region, Nigeria. They also meet in the following observation about such screens and their makers, by Nigel Barley:

> I am aware that to ascribe all change in Africa to external European influence is yet another pernicious cultural myth, but I suggest that we should sympathetically consider this possibility for the Kalabari case. The screens, after all, appear as part of a more complex rite of burial involving European foods, clothes, weapons and language. In addition, it should not be forgotten that European ships were floating ateliers of artisanal skills: brasscasting, ivory carving, joinery and patchwork quilting. On the west coast of Africa such 'traditional' African skills still show a high correlation with areas of western nautical contact to the present day.[86]

The Kalabari Ijo were important middlemen in the Atlantic trade in Nigeria, importing European brass, gunpowder, alcohol, and luxury goods into the interior and exporting slaves, ivory, palm oil, and pepper westwards to the coast.[87] Many Kalabari trading houses contained large numbers of foreign slaves who, simply because they were foreign, were not able to approach traditional sources of ancestral power. These individuals and their descendants were obliged to shape new identities, and in so doing drew on the European objects (themselves also foreign) that had helped to bring them to prominence as traders. The Kalabari believed that each person is born with an unchanging spirit (*teme*) located in the forehead. When the leader of a Kalabari trading house died, a screen was commissioned as a vessel to contain his spirit, and to serve as a medium through which the living could communicate with their ancestor. The first person to be commemorated with a screen of this form was Amachree I, a member of a trading house of slave origin who assumed the kingship in the late eighteenth century. Kalabari screens depict a particular ancestor in a masquerade outfit, accompanied by flanking figures. They clearly draw inspiration from two-dimensional framed portraits—prints, paintings, and photographs—of European origin. The portrait-like tableau in Figure 6.11 is set within a western-style mitred frame, and employs numerous European joinery techniques, including mitre, mortise, abut fitting, and pegging. Kalabari screens are constructed from multiple pieces of wood that are attached together using joinery, ties, pegs, and nails. The limbs of the central figure, for example, are tied to its torso, which in turn is mounted on horizontal strips of wood. Pegs hold

Figure 6.11 Ancestral screen, *duein fubara*, eighteenth–nineteenth centuries, Kalabari, Nigeria (1140 × 730 × 420 mm). British Museum, Af1950,45.333.a.

the projecting feet to the screen's base.[88] At the centre of the screen sits an important house head, flanked by two attendants. All three figures are wearing wrappers made from imported textiles, and the house head holds a European silver-tipped cane. He is also wearing a masquerade outfit known as *Bekinarusibi* ('white man's ship on head'), which incorporates a model of a two-masted, fully rigged sailing ship, and celebrates the wealth generated from trade. Versions of the *Bekinarusibi* mask can be traced back to the eighteenth century, and it is perhaps significant, in this context, that *Bekinarusibi* is also the name of a water spirit: Barley reports that informants describe the spirit as shimmering in the water like a jellyfish, only to disappear as a man approaches.[89] This interesting combination of associations returns us full circle, and three hundred years later, to the reading of the earliest Portuguese ships to arrive in Central and West Africa as *ntele* (whales), discussed above. Masquerade, as Barley notes, has always been open to the new, because 'it brings the power of outsiders, foreigners, monsters, the dead into contact with the human sphere'.[90] At the same time, as middlemen in the slave trade, the Kalabari shaped their own identity with direct reference to imported goods and—in this case—the vessels that transported those goods. The ship-on-head masquerade is still employed today: modern versions depict ocean liners.[91]

'Shiplike' Harps from Sierra Leone

One fascinating group of objects remains to be discussed in this chapter. These are vertically strung harp-lutes, relatives of the modern kora, which bear a striking resemblance to European sailing ships. Eight of these objects survive today (see Figure 6.12 for an example), and a strong case can be made that all of them were manufactured in Sierra Leone, by the Mende people.[92] Either by accident or by design, these instruments resemble full-bellied sailing ships with rudders, keels, prows, bowsprits, masts, rigging, and figureheads. While their 'shiplike' appearance was first noted in 1973, little has been written about them since, and the authors of the few published studies rather evade the question that most concerns me here: was the form of these instruments directly inspired by that of European ships?[93]

In my view, a good case can be made that the artisans who fashioned these instruments drew direct inspiration from European marine architecture. Longitudinal bands have been carved in relief along the body of the example in Figure 6.12, giving the appearance of hull timbers; and the scroll on the 'prow' below the figurehead—which has no functional purpose—closely echoes the profile of the knee and head on the prow of an

Figure 6.12 'Ship-like' instrument. National Museum of World Cultures, Amsterdam, TM-A-11006.

Figure 6.13 *Nkisi kumbi lipanya*. Cabinda. National Museum of Ethnology, Lisbon, AO253.

eighteenth-century sailing ship.[94] The subjects of the figureheads, all of which face away from the body of the instrument, just as a ship's figurehead faces outwards from the prow, are familiar ones from maritime architecture: animals (antelopes), birds, and humans. It is also certain that most of these objects were collected at the end of the eighteenth century: William Hart's investigation into the provenance of the two examples in the Hunterian Museum, Glasgow, suggests that they were collected by Thomas Winterbottom, physician to the Sierra Leone colony in 1792–6.[95] Winterbottom was a friend of the Swedish scholar Adam Afzelius, who almost certainly collected the harp-lute now in Stockholm.[96]

At the End of Things: The Ngoyo *nkisi*

It is important to remember that, while Britain abolished slave shipping in 1807, the trade persisted in other hands far into the nineteenth century. One of the regions first involved in the trade (the former Kongo Kingdom) was also among the last. An extraordinary artefact from Cabinda, an enclave at the mouth of the Zaire River, speaks to this point perfectly: it is shown in Figure 6.13. This is a blood red, boat-shaped, clay and wood *nkisi* (ritual container) in which two anthropomorphic figures lie side by side.[97] A piece of broken mirror is placed on top of the pair: medicines must lie underneath the glass (as they do with other Kongo *nkisi*),[98] and a cord has been nailed to the wooden base, binding the figures below it. The name of this *nkisi* is *kumbi lipanya*: the meaning of the second word is obscure, but *kumbi* means 'European ship'.[99] Cabinda was actively involved in the slave trade until 1865, and the slave ship was the likely reference for this boat, in which two constrained figures lie.[100] This is a rare artefact—as we have seen, slave ships themselves have rarely been depicted in Africa at any period—but it is an object of extraordinary power and poignancy.

One final, nineteenth-century, object may be noted before leaving slave ship imagery and turning to trade goods (and with them, another series of African–European cultural dialogues) in Chapter 7. This is not, at least directly, a depiction of a slave ship, and it survives only as a description. Like the Ngoyo *nkisi* seen in Figure 6.13, this example foregrounds the point that, from the Kongo kingdom in the fifteenth century to North America in the nineteenth, the voyage into slavery and the journey into death would be jointly understood by many Africans as ocean crossings. This point is revisited in Chapter 11 in discussing African understandings of the Middle Passage and the use of *minkisi* and other objects of power in countering an experience that, in James Sweet's words, 'must have been understood as the most virulent form of witchraft'.[101] In 1837, Charles Ball, born a slave in Maryland in the late eighteenth century, published an account of his life. There he recorded details of the burial of an infant, at which he had assisted the child's parents. Ball notes that the child's African-born father interred him

> with a small bow and several arrows; a little bag of parched meal; a miniature canoe, about a foot long, and a little paddle (with which he said it would cross the ocean to his own country); a small stick with an iron nail, sharpened and fastened into one end of it; and a piece of white muslim [*sic*] with several curious and strange figures painted on it in blue and red, by which, he said, his relations and countrymen would know the infant to be his son, and would receive it accordingly, on its arrival amongst them.[102]

Borne by his little white-sailed canoe, the child would journey to a home he had never seen, crossing in reverse the ocean his father had once traversed into slavery. There, he would take his place among the ancestors, in the kingdom of the dead beyond the sea.

Notes

1. For a similar point, with specific reference to African understandings of the Atlantic, and for a summary of work in this area to date, see Law (2011: 9–10).
2. Sweet (2003: 162).
3. Sahlins (1987: 105–35; 1995: 17–84).

4. For an illustration see Sahlins (1995: 28).
5. MacGaffey (1994: 251–2; 260–1). On the adoption of Christianity in the Kongo kingdom, see also Thornton (2013).
6. Bhabha (1994: 2).
7. These initial voyages of discovery charted in Thomas (1997: 68–96) and by Newitt (2010: 43–54). See also Thornton (2018) and MacGaffey 2018 on the early history of the kingdom of Kongo, located in what is now south-west Angola. It was one of the largest polities in sub-Saharan Africa at the time the Portuguese arrived in 1483 and was interpreted by Europeans as constituting a 'kingdom' (Thornton 2018: 40). The 'Kongo' constructed by historians of the Diaspora is critiqued by MacGaffey (2018).
8. The Benin Empire was a precolonial Edo state in what is today southern Nigeria and was an entirely separate entity from the modern-day country named Benin.
9. Drewal (1988b: 161).
10. For an excellent summary of these beliefs, and on understandings of interment as embarkation, see Law (2011: 11–12).
11. Law (2011: 13).
12. On the interpretation of sailors as dead men, see Blier (1993: 380) and MacGaffey (1986: 19).
13. MacGaffey (1986: 199).
14. Thornton (2003: 281–2); Schuler (2005: 186–7); Law (2011: 10).
15. Gould (2011: 191).
16. Law (2011: 2–3) discusses the use of coastal canoes in Atlantic West Africa.
17. See Smith (1970: 518) for discussion of larger African canoes. As Law (2011: 4) notes, the evidence is explicit that sails were not known in West Africa prior to European contact.
18. On the importance of Cadamosto's narrative, see Newitt (2010: 55).
19. Crone (1937: 20–1).
20. Newitt (2010: 73).
21. In a 1923 survey of the contemporary use of marine oculi, Hornell illustrated numerous examples from Portugal: Hornell (1923: 310–13 and figs 21–5).
22. MacGaffey (1974: 425).
23. MacGaffey (1974: 425); see also Bontick (1995: 138). Bontick argues that *mindele* may be translated as 'hommes d'éttofes' (men of cloth), reflecting the fact that the Portuguese were clothed from head to foot.
24. This phrase is discussed by Behrendt, Latham and Northrup (2010: 69). It was first used in 1823 by the British adventurer James Holman.
25. Behrendt et al. (2010: 136, n. 18). Smale's voyage on *Perseverence* is TSTD 83063.
26. Blier (1993: 380).
27. Blackmun (1988: 131).
28. Biebuyck and Herreman (1996: 248).
29. For further discussion of African beliefs concerning 'white cannibalism', see Piersen (1977), Thornton (2003), and Sweet (2003: 162–3).
30. On Central African thought, see MacGaffey (1986: 62), Thornton (2003: 273), and Sweet (2003: 162–3). Rosalind Shaw (1997, 2002) has shown that the slave trade was similarly understood in the idiom of witchcraft in Sierra Leone and Cameroon. Shaw was among the first scholars to argue that the slave trade was at once assimilated to pre-existing understandings of witchcraft, and a *producer of* new understandings of witchcraft and divination.
31. Sweet (2003: 162).
32. Thornton (2003: 273).
33. 'Sapi' was a name used by the sixteenth-century Portuguese to refer generally to a number of ethno-linguistic groups in Sierra Leone, including the Bullom and Temne. Ivories produced in the Kingdom of Benin are sometimes known as Bini-Portuguese artefacts. Ivory olphants (side-

208 MATERIALIZING THE MIDDLE PASSAGE

blown horns) were also produced in the Kongo Kingdom in this period, and perhaps from as early as 1482 (Bassani 2000: 277), but were not produced specifically at the request of European traders or to European designs and are not usually referred to as Afro-Portuguese (Blier 1993: 375). Given their lack of explicit reference to Portuguese sailors and ships, the Kongolese artefacts are not considered further here.

34. For a very similar example, see Bassani (2000: 255, no. 793); a European single-masted ship again serves as the finial of the lid of this salt cellar, complete with a crow's nest, rigging, and anchors.

35. The carver of Figure 6.2 was dubbed 'Master of the Heraldic Ship' by Bassani et al. (1988: 180). Bassani (2000: 298–9) suggests that the model for the ship may have been engravings such as woodcuts by Volgemuth, printed in Nuremburg in 1493; but it is perhaps more likely that the single-masted ships on the salt cellars are stylized depictions of *naus*. For discussion of the idea that artists may have observed ships from life, explored with relation to both the British Museum and Belgian examples, see Bassani (2000: 299).

36. The object held by the sailor resembles a telescope, but this instrument had not yet been invented; it is probably a hailer, using to communicate from ship to shore.

37. Drewal (2013: 29).

38. Markham (2010: 154).

39. Fraser (1972); see also the discussion of Fraser in Drewal (2013: 31–2).

40. Drewal has written extensively on this topic: see, in particular, Drewal (1988a: 38; 2013: 31–5).

41. For a recent collection of papers on Mami Wata, see Drewal (2008b) and the introduction by Drewal (2008a). As a number of the contributors to this volume are at pains to point out (particularly Coote 2008: 269–72; Nevadomsky 2008: 351–9; see also Gore and Nevadomsky 1997), Mami Wata cannot be conceptualized entirely in terms of the European historical antecedents that have shaped her image, nor in terms of an untroubled syncretism between African beliefs and European images: her cult is far too heterogeneous, widespread and long-lived for that to be possible. It is beyond doubt, nevertheless, that mermaid imagery and ships' figureheads played some part in shaping pre-nineteenth-century images of African water spirits, and the analysis presented in the present chapter owes much to Drewal's arguments in this context (Drewal 1988a,b, 2008a: 9–12).

42. Drewal (1988a: 38).

43. A possible link between Mami Wata and mermaid figureheads was suggested by Salmons (1977: 8).

44. Law (2004: 22) cites this passage as evidence both that the cult of Hu (the god of the sea) was established at Ouidah by the seventeenth century, and that the cult was enhanced by the development of the slave trade.

45. MacGaffey (1994: 257).

46. See Drewal (1988b: 161–2), discussing a passage from A New General Collection (1745: ii. 105).

47. Oertling (1996: 30).

48. Ross (1981: 173).

49. Law (2004: 50–9).

50. Law (2004: 127).

51. Kelly (2010: 111).

52. Law (2004: 148).

53. For the Gold Coast, see Sparks (2014: 28–9), and, for Calabar, Lovejoy and Richardson (1999).

54. Sparks (2014: 145–7).

55. Law (2011: 4).

56. Smith (1970: 526).

57. Dalzel (1793: 169). For Dalzel's slaving voyages, parliamentary testimony, and career at Ouidah and Cape Coast, see Table 3.6.

58. Dalzel (1793: 169).

59. Brooks (2003: 54).
60. Behrendt et al. (2010: 63).
61. Lovejoy and Richardson (2001: 106, letter no. 8). Lace had captained seven Liverpool slaving voyages between 1754 and 176 8 (TSTD 90529, 90463, 90734–5, 90829, 891100, 91767) and was an investor in fifty-five voyages between 1759 and 1786.
62. These documents comprise the diary of Antera Duke (1785–8), the definitive scholarly edition of which was compiled by Behrent et al. (2010). There are also fourteen letters dating from 1760–89 collated by Lovejoy and Richardson (2001).
63. For this and similar bells, see Lovejoy and Richardson (2001: 95 and n. 33). Writing in the 1930s, Stewart-Brown (1932: 49) stated that the Calabar Bell was in his possession and had been 'purchased many years ago at a sale in Liverpool of ships stores'.
64. A similar bell inscribed 'Effywatt Captain Calabar 1799', gifted by Peter Cumberbach, a slaving merchant and former master of *Gasgoyne* (TSTD 81559–60), is discussed by Behrendt et al. (2010: 149).
65. For additional examples, see Lovejoy and Richardson (2004: 375, n. 44).
66. Behrendt et al. (2010: 57).
67. Behrendt et al. (2010: 173).
68. Williams (1897: 546).
69. Behrendt et al. (2010: 139, n. 35).
70. Behrendt et al. (2010: 207).
71. Letter from Henry Nicholls to the African Association, Old Calabar, 15 February 1805, in Hallett (1964: 207–8).
72. American ships also carried furniture to West Africa: in the 1740s the slave dealer Nicholas Owen worked on a Rhode Island slaver whose cargo included 'household furniture' (Owen 1930: 38).
73. See Olsen (1979: 124) for admiration of the French figurehead in Britain.
74. Olsen (1979: 321): from 1703–27, naval vessels were obliged by law to employ only lion heads. From 1740, naval ships were allowed to carry individual figureheads, most of which represented the name of the ship: Lavery (1984: 62).
75. Falconer (1769: entry for 'Head', and plate 4g).
76. Olsen (1979: 124).
77. Jenny Lind (1820–87) was known as the Swedish Nightingale. The clipper *Nightingale* (TSTD 4955) made one slaving voyage. The Lind identification is postulated by Karl-Eric Svärdskog (2005). *Nightingale* was re-employed as a blockade vessel during the American Civil War and resold several times subsequently. The clipper was eventually bought by a Norwegian captain and refitted as a freighter. It was wrecked in 1893 off the coast of Norway. Svärdskog theorizes that the figurehead was removed (and thus preserved) during a refit in 1885.
78. This piece is discussed by Anderson and Peek (2002: 20), who note that, while Ockiya may have borrowed the idea of royal portraiture from the nearby Kalabari or the more distant court of Benin, the figure's naturalism contrasts markedly with the strict geometry of other Ijo carvings, and Ockiya's carvers here seem to have been inspired by the figureheads of European ships.
79. Willett (1971: 89).
80. Pitt Rivers Museum 1916.45.162. Details recorded in Accession Book entry.
81. Barley (1988: 39).
82. Rodgers (1984: 4).
83. See, e.g., McCreery (2000) for a discussion of Isaac Cruikshank's 1802 caricature *British Vessels, Described for the use of Country Gentlemen*, which depicts seven women who are linked through their involvement in prostitution and/or their association with ports.
84. As Murdoch (2004) has suggested. But 'black' was also used at this time to refer to demeanour: one of the definitions of 'black' in Samuel Johnson's *Dictionary* (1755–6) is 'cloudy of countenance; sullen'.

210 MATERIALIZING THE MIDDLE PASSAGE

85. On maritime terminology in the commercial languages that emerged in coastal West Africa, see Behrendt et al. (2010: 2, 187, n. 184). On 'Ship English' and its impact on West African Pidgin English (WAPE) languages more generally, see Hancock (1986), Bailey and Ross (1988). For 'Ship English' in Caribbean contexts, see Delgado (2013, 2019). 'Ship English' is discussed in more detail in Chapter 10.

86. Barley (1988: 40).

87. Picton (1996: 392).

88. Barley (1988: 22–3).

89. Barley (1988: 54).

90. Barley (2000: 109).

91. Barley (2000: 120).

92. Hart (1994) discusses two harp-lutes from the Hunterian Museum Glasgow and collates information on the other known examples. See also Bassani (2000: entries 573–4, 633, 679). A ninth harp (whereabouts unknown) was collected in the nineteenth century by the missionary Daniel Flickinger: see Hart (2006: 15, figure 5).

93. The term 'shiplike' was first employed for these instruments by Wachsmann (1973), in a study that focuses on the example in the Museum of Ethnology, Stockholm (1874.1.368). As Wachsmann's drawing and maritime architectural terminology suggest, the harp-lute bears a strong resemblance to a European sailing ship, and each of its key components might be considered as analogous to a characteristic feature of a sailing ship.

94. Wachsmann (1973: 50).

95. Hart (1994: 83–4). Alexander Falconbridge (whose voyages on slave ships are outlined in Chapter 3) was governor of the colony at the start of this period. Winterbottom was the unnamed physician whom Anna-Maria Falconbridge credited with her recovery following a period of ill health: Fyfe (2000: 85).

96. Wachsmann (1973: 53).

97. In Kongo thought, *nkisi* is a personalized force from the land of the dead that has chosen, or been induced, to submit itself to a degree of human control (MacGaffey 2000: 37). *Nkisi* (pl. *minkisi*) are at once ritual procedures and the material things employed in those procedures, *Nkisi* objects are essentially containers for relics of the dead and medicines. The act of containment harnesses the forces within to achieve a desired end: Biebuyck and Herreman (1996: 248); MacGaffey (2000: 43–4).

98. The mirror serves as the eyes of the *nkisi*, allowing it to see things concealed from normal view: Biebuyck and Herreman (1996: 248).

99. MacGaffey (2000: 48).

100. Biebuyck and Herreman (1996: 248, cat. no. 4.11); MacGaffey (2000: 49, cat. no. 30).

101. Sweet (2003: 162).

102. Ball (1837: 265).

7

From Ship to Shore

Some Trade Goods and Their Biographies

On Thursday, 4 October 1750, John Newton's *Argyle* was approaching the Bananas islands, off Sierra Leone. Although nearing the end of a long crossing from Liverpool, his crew had no time to rest. The ship's carpenter was busy 'fitting up the stateroom to serve as a shop on the coast', and, on the next day Newton reported that his men undertook 'a rummidge in the hold, removed most of the India cloth and a sortment of other goods into the cabbin' (*Argyle* 1750–1: 10). In this way, the captain's quarters were transformed into a showroom for the trade goods carried out from Liverpool, and *Argyle* was readied for the business of barter. Textiles, metals (raw and manufactured), glass beads, alcohol, and a host of other commodities from hats to guns were decanted from slave ships like *Argyle* into the arms of local partners all along the West African coast. This chapter centres on some of these material things, exploring a range of issues concerning their life courses. Where had they been manufactured? How had they been selected and purchased? How were they shipped? How were they exchanged, and, finally, in what ways were they used in Africa?

Most of these questions, of course, return the discussion to the notion of Atlantic creolization outlined in Chapter 1. How so? First, because the slave trade was a barter trade, involving material dialogues that impacted on the practices of both the Europeans who bartered for captives and the Africans who supplied them. Second, because trade goods entered the redistributive networks, markets, and lifeways of communities along the Atlantic coast of Africa; and some proportion of these items also gravitated inland, far from the coastal centres. As a result, many of the people carried away from Africa on slave ships had already acquired at least some familiarity with the exogenous artefacts that they would meet on board, from firearms to bells and beads. That familiarity, as explored in Chapters 10 and 11, could in turn inform individual and collective experiences, and strategies for survival at sea.

The volume, purchase price, and profitability of the goods bartered from slave ships has received considerable scholarly attention, and the contemporary textual evidence underlying these studies is equally compendious.[1] Some selectivity is clearly necessary in a chapter-length archaeological treatment, and three artefact classes especially important to the British trade—glass beads, cotton cloth, and sheet brass-wares—are my chosen focus here. They are considered through the lens of object biography; a relational approach to material culture that explores the interactions between people and things, and considers how the meanings of objects accumulate and are transformed over time and context.[2] This type of analysis is particularly suitable for

Materializing the Middle Passage: A Historical Archaeology of British Slave Shipping, 1680–1807. Jane Webster, Oxford University Press. © Jane Webster 2023. DOI: 10.1093/oso/9780199214594.003.0007

commodities manufactured for the slave trade: material things with well-recorded documentary histories, whose relational stories were written on two, sometimes even three, continents and whose biographical chapters include manufacture, purchase, shipping, entry into indigenous economies as bartered goods, and finally African reception and recontextualization.[3] A tiny proportion of these objects also have biographical epilogues, in that they have been excavated, or collected, and are today curated by museums and private collectors. The biographical technique is therefore used in the present chapter to explore the life courses both of artefact classes (Newton's 'Indian cloth', for example), and of individual objects within those categories, such as the important fabric wrapper shown in Figure 7.12.

Colleen Kriger has woven a fascinating history of cloth in West Africa around detailed narrative histories of three individual textile products. Her artefact-centred methodology interlaces archaeological data, museum collections, and primary documentary sources in writing a textured, material history of indigenous textile production and use.[4] The present chapter takes a similar approach. It begins by drawing on some of the voyages, wrecks, and witness testimonies followed throughout the course of this book, using them as a lens through which to see the manufacture, purchase, and shipping of beads, cotton cloth, and brasswares over time. The second section of the chapter concerns the reception of these artefacts in West Africa, focusing primarily on Elmina in Ghana (formerly the Gold Coast) and Ouidah in the Republic of Benin (formerly Dahomey). Both are places where recent archaeological fieldwork has shed nuanced light on the reception of trade goods borne out to Africa on slave ships. As I aim to show, many of these things were entirely repurposed by African consumers. Imported beads and textiles were certainly valued as finished products and in many areas became—and remain—firmly embedded in local strategies for bodily adornment; but trade beads were just as likely to be modified, or ground down to powder and reformed. Similarly, imported cotton cloth could be worn as purchased, but was also unravelled and incorporated into local textiles. Brasswares were especially likely to be used as raw materials: manillas (open-ended, bracelet-shaped ingots), basins, kettles, and other hollowwares produced in British foundries were recut, or melted down and recast, in African workshops. And every one of these objects, however employed, had been part-exchanged for a human being. On multiple levels, then, trade goods, like the slave ships that carried them, were at once embedded in, and transformative of, African lives.

Assortment Bargaining

Most slave ships carried an astonishing variety of goods, commonly traded in 'sortments', or mixed batches. Virtually every European transaction in West Africa involved 'assortment bargaining' using an array of goods, some of which were seen as going at a loss, but without which no trade could be done: the loss was compensated for by more profitable items.[5] All of these goods were exchanged, not sold. Currency in the form of 'shell money' (cowries) was widely used in the West African coastal zone stretching from the eastern edge of the Gold Coast to the western Niger Delta, but even here assortment bargaining was the rule: European traders very rarely acquired captives by exchanging them solely for cowries.[6] One exception to that rule was *Unity* 1769–71: Robert Norris's cargo largely comprised cowries, collected from Hellevoetsluis (Holland), before crossing to Africa.

The range of goods making up sortments increased considerably over time. By the early eighteenth century more than 150 different categories of artefact were available—a much broader range than at the start of the seventeenth century.[7] The goods most in demand by African partners fell into just a few broad classes, however. Textiles, iron, copper, brass, glass, and alcohol made up the bulk of the primary raw materials and manufactured goods exchanged for slaves by British ships between 1680 and 1807.[8] The vast majority of these goods were well made and durable: the 'gewgaw myth'—the notion that Africans were gullible, indiscriminate trading partners, exchanging captives for trinkets, defective firearms, and cheap drink—has long since been debunked.[9]

Textiles were particularly important to the British slave trade: cloth made up 68 per cent of all commodities exported to Africa in the period 1699–1808.[10] Home-produced woollens dominated until the 1720s, after which Indian-made cotton fabrics took their place.[11] By the later eighteenth century, British- and Indian-made cottons comprised 70–80 per cent of the cloth carried to the Guinea coast on British ships.[12] This most important category among British trade goods is unfortunately also the least visible to the archaeologist. Organic fabrics break down quickly in the ground, particularly in humid climates, and excavated examples of traded textiles from pre-nineteenth-century African contexts are very few. Because the majority of the fabrics sent to West Africa were inexpensive and utilitarian, moreover, few examples have found their way into museum collections.[13] As so often in this book, therefore, it is necessary to turn repeatedly to the documentary sources in order to materialize a key component of a slave ship's cargo.

Glass trade beads, in contrast, are extremely durable and also have a lengthy history as collectors' items. As a result, many historical examples from West Africa survive today, either as curated objects in private hands, in museum collections, or in excavated assemblages. Brass was traded both in ingot form and as manillas, kettles (cauldrons), and neptunes (bowls or basins). The hollow-ware vessel forms were generally known as battery-wares, because they were fashioned from sheet brass that had been hammered, or battered, into shape. Brass is a durable medium and generally survives well in archaeological contexts in Africa. As explored below, exogenous brass was often recast locally to produce artefacts that, since the nineteenth century, have excited considerable interest among western collectors, ethnographers, and art historians. As a result, many objects fashioned in West Africa from British brass are today curated by private collectors and museums. I return to this point at the end of the chapter.

Materializing Trade Goods

What do we know about the trade goods carried on the voyages that are central to this book? In the earliest years of the British trade, as noted in Chapter 3, vessel owners and masters were willing to pay for up-to-date information about local preferences, and the demand for trading information from insiders helps to explain the enormous popularity of narratives concerning voyages to Africa. Thomas Phillips's account of the voyage of *Hannibal*, published in volume six of an enormous compendium of travel tales, falls into this category. Phillips recorded very specific details regarding goods in demand on the Gold Coast in the late seventeenth century (***Hannibal*** 1693–4: 206):

> The commodities that are most in demand upon the Gold Coast, are blue and red perpetuannas, pewter basins of several sizes, from one to four pound weight, old sheets, large Flemish knives, iron bars, cases of spirits, blue sayes, if well dyed, and coral, if large and of a good colour. I also carried there on account of the African company muskets, nicanees, tapsails, baysadoes [baize], brass kettles, English carpets, Welsh plains, lead bars, firkins of tallow, powder &c. None of which did answer expectation, being offr'd to bring back to England a great part of them; and those we sold were at a very low rate.

Meanwhile at Ouidah, in the heart of the cowrie currency zone (***Hannibal*** 1693–4: 227):

> The best goods to purchase slaves here are cowries, the smaller the more esteem'd ... the next in demand are brass neptunes or basins, very large, thin and flat; for after they have bought them they cut them into pieces no make anilias or bracelets, and collars for their arms and legs.[14]

James Barbot Jnr, supercargo on *Don Carlos* in 1700, similarly made very careful notes on the merchandize most in demand much further to the east at Cabinda (Angola). Fabrics, principally in shades of blue, or with blue stripes, were especially popular here (Table 7.1).[15]

Many seventeenth- and early eighteenth-century slave ships employed supercargoes like James Barbot—specialist traders responsible for the transactions that saw goods exchanged for slaves. These men devoted considerable time to recording both the goods on their ships and the levels of local demand for them. Bound out to the Gold Coast, Walter Prideaux, supercargo on the voyage of the Exeter ship *Daniel and Henry*, copied out a lengthy invoice itemizing and costing all of the trade goods on board (***Daniel*** 1700: 41–5; summarized in Table 7.2). Textiles, metals including 354 'Guinea brass pans', glass beads, and spirits made up almost the entire cargo. Prideaux also carefully detailed every single chest, hogshead, barrel, case, and cask in which these goods were protectively encased within the hold. Figures 7.1 and 7.2 illustrate textiles and a trade knife very similar to those carried on this ship. Figure 7.1 illustrates a

Table 7.1 Trade goods in demand at Cabinda, 1700

Fabrics	Metals	Other
Annabasses—*fustian*	*ARMS*	Coral
Black-bays (baize)—*fine woollen fabric made in Holland and England*	Muskets	
Blue-basts—*dyed cotton from Gujarat*	(Gun) Powder	
Blue-perpetuanas—*hard-wearing woollen cloth from the south-west of England*	Dutch cutlasses	
	Knives with	
Blue-paper Slessia—*fine linen fabric from Silesia*	horn hafts	
Guinea stuffs—*low-cost cottons made in Western India: striped or checked with coloured threads*	*OTHER METAL*	
	Brass basins	
Nicanees—*low-price striped cotton from India, loom patterned*	Pewter basins	
Painted calicoes –*Indian cotton*		
Tapsails—*striped cotton cloth from Gujarat*		

Source: **James Barbot Jnr, *Don Carlos* 1700: 513.**

remarkable survival in the Danish National Archives: samples of the trade cloth shipped to Ghana by the Danish West India and Guinea Company in the early eighteenth century. The knife in Figure 7.2 is 'slope pointed', just like those carried on *Daniel and Henry*. It was collected by Anders Sparrman, a correspondent of Thomas Clarkson and witness in the parliamentary inquiry process discussed in Chapter 3. Both men will be encountered again in Chapter 8.

By the eighteenth century, the task of negotiating for captives in Africa fell mainly to ships' captains, but the selection, purchase, lading, and accounting of the trade goods at their disposal had usually been undertaken by one of the managing owners of the vessel or tasked to an agent (known as a ship's 'husband').[16] Neither owners nor agents travelled out to Africa with their cargo. The eighteenth-century masters whose journals are used in this book, including John Newton and Samuel Gamble, provide very detailed information on many aspects of their voyages, but they record very little about the trade goods they carried. Newton reveals, as already seen, that he stocked his makeshift shop on *Argyle* with 'Indian cloth and a sortment of other goods' (***Argyle*** 1750–1: 10) and in his journal he refers many times to 'ships' bars'—a term employed simultaneously for bar iron and as a denominator for a locally recognized unit of account (the bar).[17] Thus, on his first slaving voyage with *African* in 1752–3, Newton recorded incredulously that the price demanded for slaves on the Mano River (Sierra Leone) was '7 guns, 7 cags of powder, 4 whole and 5 cut cloths, 4 pans and basons, 2 or 3 kettles, 2 large cases and from 4–10 iron bars upon every slave, besides knives, beads and other small articles which together can be little less than 90 ship's bars'.[18] In 1793, Samuel Gamble committed the entire (unspecified) cargo of *Sandown* to a single deal with James Walker at Nunez (***Sandown*** **1793–4: 47**).

While later eighteenth-century captains may not have recorded precise trading information in their logs, detailed account books and cargo invoices are available for some English ships of this era. Richardson's pioneering 1979 study of eighteenth-century West African consumption patterns drew on ninety-three invoices of cargoes

Table 7.2 Trade goods carried on *Daniel and Henry*, 1700

Textiles	Metals	Other	Alcohol
Basts—*white or dyed cotton from Gujarat, India*	*ARMS*	Rangoes—*red carnelian beads*	English brandy
Brawles—*blue and white striped Indian cloth*	Fuzees—*light muskets*	Assorted beads	Malt spirits
Crocus—*strong sailcloth used in making wrappers (wrap skirts)*	Carbines	Currell—coral	
Darnicks—*woollen fabric from Tournai*	Superfine pistols	Looking glasses	
Ends—*half lengths of cloth*	Hangers—*straps for swords/ scabbards*	Gunflints	
Guinea stuffs—*low-cost cottons made in Western India: striped or checked with coloured threads*	Gunpowder	Tallow	
Hounscott says—*worsted cloth from Devon*	Negro knives		
Nehallaware—*cotton from India*	Knives		
Nikanees—*low-price striped cotton from India, loom-patterned*	Sheaths		
Perpetuanas—*hard-wearing woollen cloth from the south-west of England*	Slope pointed knives		
Salempore (salampuris)—*cotton from India with red borders*	Rapiers		
Sheets—*cotton bed sheets (often second hand)*	*OTHER METAL*		
Slessia—*fine linen fabric from Silesia*	Iron bars		
Topsails (or tapseils)—*striped cotton cloth from Gujarat*	Small cases of lead		
Ticking—*cheap cloth used for mattress covers*	Guinea brass pans		
	Pewter tankards, quarts and basins		

Source: Synthesized from Tattersfield (1991: 41–5).

Figure 7.1 Samples of trade cloth from the correspondence of the Danish West India and Guinea Company. The textiles shown include Indian-made brawles (No. 2), nikanees (No. 4), chello (No. 5), and gingham (No. 6).

Figure 7.2 A European trade knife collected in Senegal in 1787–8 by the Swedish naturalist Anders Sparrman. Museum of World Cultures, Stockholm, 1799.02.0083.

for Bristol and Liverpool ships during the period 1758–1806, calculating the percentage of textiles, bar iron, metal manufactures, beads, and other goods laded on each of them. Richardson calculated that beads made up 7.7 per cent of the value share of the eight main slave-trading cargoes from this period, with textiles comprising 27.9 per cent and brassware 14.3 per cent.[19] The records of one of the leading later eighteenth-century Liverpool merchants, William Davenport, contain particularly detailed information of the outfitting of over seventy of his ships between 1757 and 1785; and the papers of James Rogers, allied with the surviving accounts from additional Bristol

218   MATERIALIZING THE MIDDLE PASSAGE

vessels, permit a detailed analysis of the cargoes and profitability of twenty-seven Bristol ships between 1772 and 1790.[20]

Information about the goods traded to Africa was also collated during the parliamentary inquiries into the trade towards the end of the eighteenth century. In March 1788, shortly after the Privy Council inquiry had been ordered, the House of Commons requested detailed information from the customs houses in London, Liverpool, Bristol, Lancashire, and Poole concerning trade goods carried out to Africa from these ports from 1772–6 and 1783–7. These data are to be found in volume 67 of the sessional papers of the House of Commons.[21] Parliament requested information on foreign-made goods, such as Indian cotton, and the cowries brought back from the Maldives by the Dutch or English East India Companies for re-export into the slave trade. Domestic products were also quantified. Woollen textiles, iron, and brass made up the bulk of these, but the full range of British-made goods listed in these returns was very wide, comprising: Allum, Apothecary Ware, Apparel (parcels), Bags, Beer, Books, Brass (wrought), Bricks, Cabinet Ware, Candles, Cards, Coals, Colours for painters, Confectionary, Copperas, Cordage, Corn, Cyder, Cotton, Drugs (Sal. Ammoniac), Fish, Flax, Glass, Gloves, Grindle [grind]stones, Gunpowder, Gunflints, Haberdashery, Hats, Hoops, Horns (ram), Iron (cast, nails, ore, wrought), Lead, Leather, Lime, Linen, Molasses, Pewter, Pictures or Prints, Plate (wrought), Provisions, Salt, Silk, Slates, Soap, Spirits, Sugar, Starch, Stationary, Stockings (thread), Tiles, Tin, Tobacco pipes, Toys, Vinegar, Woollen goods, and Miscellaneous Articles. The data synthesized for Parliament in 1788 accord very well with a detailed modern analysis of more than a thousand commodity exchanges taking place on the Gold Coast between 1772 and 1780.[22] George Metcalf's study isolated twenty-eight staples of the trade in this period, half of which were textiles manufactured in India and England.[23]

Manufacturing for the Slave Trade

In November 1686, Ralph Hassell, chief factor at the RAC's fort at Anomabu, wrote to his employers in London to complain that the 369 brass pans he had just received by ship

> are not of the sorte that last was, which they doe not like by reason they are bright within and turnd in streaks on the outside and are to weighty. I have sent a sample of the sort and size they would buy; if they be a very little size bigger and lesser it matters not much.[24]

Hassell's peeved but precise letter exemplifies a point evidenced repeatedly below: Africans were not indiscriminate consumers of European goods picking randomly from floating department stores anchored off their coastlines. They were, on the contrary, discerning customers. Factors, slave ship owners, and captains acknowledged this fact by working hard to anticipate local preferences. But, while many European traders understood local demand very well, they met it for the most part from a repertoire of goods also widely used at home: very few commodities were produced *uniquely* for the slave trade. There were some important exceptions to this rule, as discussed below with reference to textiles and metal ingots, but, rather than creating entirely new ranges destined only for the slave trade, European manufacturers generally sought to identify shapes, colours, and finishes that were particularly favoured by African consumers, and then modified their existing outputs accordingly. David Evans's work on the Welsh copper industry provides a fascinating example of this process.[25] Copper was generally sent out to Africa in ingots, sometimes in the form of cigar-shaped bars, and sometimes as rods (known as Guinea rods). Both were manufactured in dimensions, and with a finish, that satisfied African consumers. Visiting the Greenfield works on Deeside in the 1750s, the Swedish metallurgist Reinhold Angerstein was surprised to see copper rods being drawn out under a trip hammer, rather than through the more usual iron plate, and was told that a trip hammer increased ductility. Enhanced pliability was important because, as Angerstein was aware, the rods would be repurposed in African ways: 'Negroes in Guinea use the rods as ornaments and wind them around arms and legs.'[26] But it would be an overstatement to suggest that producers always understood *why* such things as ductility mattered to their target market: for the most part, empiricism, not ethnography, guided the actions of manufacturers attempting to make a profit by anticipating African preferences. As ever with generalizations there were exceptions, and Figure 7.3 illustrates one of them. Dating to the sixteenth–eighteenth centuries, this raffia and wood necklace incorporates a ceramic disk, probably made in Germany, which resembles the cross-section of a white snail shell. European manufactures showing an informed understanding of African cosmological concepts are rare: but the Portuguese traders who commissioned disks like this one were clearly aware that the snail was an important symbol of spirituality and leadership among the Angolan Chowke.

Beads for the Slave Trade

Glass trade beads were a ubiquitous feature of Europe's encounter with others, from the Americas to West Africa and the Pacific. Billions of glass beads were produced for trading purposes, but before the nineteenth century there were only two basic ways to make them: by winding and by drawing. Glass itself is made from silica, an alkali, a stabilizer, and a colouring agent fired into a liquid.[27] In the production of wound beads, a cane (length) of molten glass without a central hole was wound around a wire or mandrel and was then either rolled or pressed into shape. Colours could either be incorporated into the molten glass or applied later. Drawn beads were made by trapping an air bubble inside molten glass. The glass was then rapidly drawn out into a long tube or cane that could be decorated by applying coloured glass, or by

Figure 7.3 Chokwe pendant, Angola, sixteenth–eighteenth centuries (279 × 375 mm). Metropolitan Museum of Art, 1996.456.

twisting. When cooled, the tube was chopped into shorter lengths. The beads were finished off by tumbling them in sand to remove the sharp edges, or by grinding facets.[28] The majority of the trade beads carried by British ships were drawn 'seed' beads (known as *conterie*) and wound or 'lampworked' beads (known as *perle a lume*) manufactured in Venice and its island of Murano. These were imported to England, by ship, in barrels and chests. Venice had begun manufacturing beads for export in the eleventh century and by the fourteenth was Europe's leading maker—a position it would hold right through the era of the slave trade. But trade beads were also manufactured in the Netherlands, Bohemia, and, for a brief period in the seventeenth century, in London also.

In November 1631, as discussed in Chapter 2, Charles I granted patents to transport slaves from Guinea to a syndicate of well-connected entrepreneurs, headed by Sir Nicholas Crisp (or Crispe). In *c.*1635, Crisp secured a patent for making and vending beads, some of which were destined for the colonial (North American) market and others for the slave trade. The site of Crisp's glassworks on the Hammersmith Embankment in London was excavated by the Museum of London Archaeology Service (MoLAS) in 2001 and 2005. This is a very significant site, yielding the first recorded evidence for the manufacture of glass beads in England during the post-medieval period.[29] The excavators recovered examples of tubular, circular, and barrel-shaped beads in eighteen colours and in fifteen main varieties. Some examples are shown in Figure 7.4. Correlatives for some of Crisp's beads have been found at excavated Mohawk sites in New York State, but none thus far in West Africa.[30] This may be because Crisp's venture was very short-lived: Parliament obliged him to surrender his monopolies in 1640. His endeavour does not appear to have been repeated, and from 1680 to 1807 English traders relied heavily on Venetian beads, alongside others sourced from the Netherlands and Bohemia. The examples shown in Figure 7.5 were collected in Senegal by Anders Sparrman, who described them in his 1799 inventory as 'Glass beads being brought by Europeans'.[31]

As Ajmar-Wollheim and Molà have shown, a truly global market for Venetian beads developed during the Renaissance.[32] From the outset, Venetian producers made efforts to meet local tastes, and even to replicate them. The earliest such efforts in an African context, documented in 1504, attempted to copy the West African akori, a dichroic glass bead worth its weight in gold in local markets, and now believed to be a product of southern Nigeria's early glass bead-making industry.[33] As Suzanne Gott explains, certain highly valued beads have traditionally been regarded in West Africa as gifts from deities residing in the earth, heavens, or sacred waters. These 'precious' beads

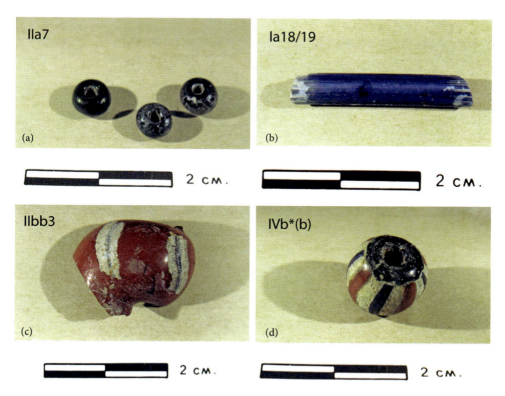

Figure 7.4 A selection of seventeenth-century circular, tubular, and globular trade beads from the manufacturing site on the estate of Nicholas Crisp, Hammersmith Embankment, London. MoLA/Karlis Karklins.

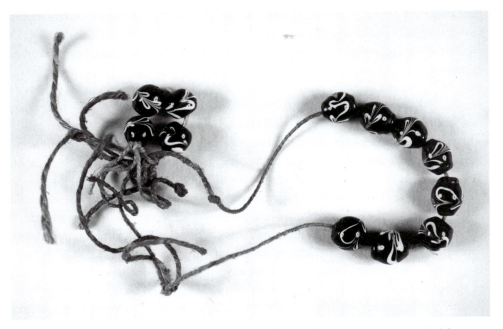

Figure 7.5 Glass trade beads collected in Senegal by Anders Sparrman, 1787–8. Museum of World Cultures. Stockholm 1799.002.0090.

Figure 7.6 Left: Powdered-glass bodom bead, probably of nineteenth-century date, made in West Africa. Right: Venetian version of the bodom, Corning Museum of Glass, 73.3.351 (L) and 73.3.333 (R).

were viewed as both living and life-giving forces.[34] Figure 7.6 shows the bodom, another important category of precious bead, manufactured in Ghana from powdered glass, which was placed in a mould, or shaped by hand. The second bead shown in Figure 7.6 is a Venetian attempt to imitate the shape size, colour, and decoration of the bodom. European copies like this one tended to be a brighter yellow colour, and have a smoother surface, than their African counterparts. The central eyespot is a common feature of bodom beads, and in the Venetian example is made from a chevron cane slice with extra trailing.

FROM SHIP TO SHORE   223

Table 7.3 Trade goods carried on *Henrietta Marie*, 1699

Owner of goods (investor in voyage)	Commodity	Value `(£ s. d.)
Thomas Starke	282 lb great bugles	18.15.4
Anthony Tournay	33 tons of iron	448.12.6
Daniel Jamineau for William Deacon	1,792 lb great bugles	192.00.0
	60 short gurrahs (*Indian muslin*)	
	3½ cwt short linen	
	2½ cwt broad Germany (*linen*)	
Thomas Winchcombe	6 cwt pewter	36.04.6
Robert Willson	1,200 copper bars	152.05.2
	7½ cwt pewter	
	4 doz. felts (*hats*)	
	70 half cases spirits	

Source: After Moore and Malcom (2008: table 1), utilizing TNA: T 70/349, fos 52, 71, 72, 75.

Various British-based merchant houses specialized in the importation and sale (for re-exportation) of Venetian beads; the London-based Huguenot bead dealers Jamineau & Rousseau had an effective monopoly on the Venetian bead trade between 1698 and 1725.[35] In the early eighteenth century, beads for the slave trade were often freighted to the Isle of Man, where they were warehoused, duty free, until collected by slave ships on the outward leg of their journey. In 1765, the Isle of Man's free port status was terminated, and in the following year two of Liverpool's most important slaver traders, William Davenport and Thomas Earle, established a company importing beads from Venice. The William Davenport and Co. Bead Company became the leading middleman in the supply of Venetian beads to England's merchant slavers, and for a few years between 1766 and 1773 half of all the Venetian glass beads re-exported to Africa from England were supplied by this one Liverpool-based company.[36] In 1776, Davenport handed control of his bead business to John Copeland, another leading merchant with interests in the slave trade.

Shipping Beads: Evidence from the Shipwrecks

Henrietta Marie, as noted in Chapter 4, was wrecked off the coast of Florida in 1700. Like *Albion Frigate*, *Don Carlos*, and *Daniel and Henry*, this vessel was one of the first generation of ten percenters—private ventures paying a tax to the RAC in order to participate legally in the slave trade. The trade goods laden on *Henrietta Marie* in 1699 (Table 7.3) included 14.5 cwt of pewter, 1,200 copper bars, a large quantity of cloth, and 2,074 lb of great bugles (a tubular, faceted form of drawn bead) between 1 inch and 4 inches in length.[37] The major investor was Anthony Tournay, a wealthy trader in iron, who supplied both naval and merchant vessels. Tournay provided 33 tons of iron for *Henrietta Marie*'s second voyage, much of it probably in the form of bars marked with the recognizable personal stamp that African partners demanded as an assurance of provenance.[38] The beads committed to this cargo had been purchased by William Deacon and Thomas Starke, both of whom part-owned several slaving voyages in the first decade of the eighteenth century.[39] William Deacon's beads were sourced from the Huguenot bead dealers Jamineau & Rousseau, mentioned above. Daniel Jamineau was heavily involved in slave shipping and had a stake (presumably again in the form of beads) in James Barbot's *Albion Frigate* venture.[40] When Deacon's cargo was laden on *Henrietta Marie*, it was James Barbot who signed for the beads in Deacon's stead.[41]

Goods that were not exchanged for slaves were simply shipped home again, and *Henrietta Marie* thus sank with an unwanted stock still on board. Twenty-eight iron bars, 328 pewter items ('basons' (bowls), tankards, spoons, plates, bottles, and a large flagon) and more than 11,000 glass beads have been recovered from the wreck site.

Although large numbers of cylindrical bugles were carried out to Africa on *Henrietta Marie*, only one has been found on the wreck site; perhaps suggesting the popularly of bugles at the point of barter.[42] *Albion Frigate* had also visited Calabar in 1699, and James Barbot reported that the king and his retinue 'objected much against our wrought pewter and tankards, green beads, and other goods which they would not accept of' (*Albion* **1699: 689**). Most of the surviving beads from the *Henrietta Marie* wreck are of exactly the type described by Barbot as unwanted at Calabar: small, drawn, green and yellow seed beads between 1 mm and 6 mm in diameter. The *Henrietta Marie* beads were made in at least eight colours, but the majority are opaque green.[43] The 798 seed beads recovered from the *Queen Anne's Revenge* wreck site have also been plausibly interpreted as unsold trade beads, left over from the voyage that this former French slaver (*Concorde*) had been undertaking at the time of its capture off Martinique in 1717.[44] Most of these small, drawn, monochrome (mainly yellow) beads were recovered from a section of the stern in association with barrel staves and other materials, suggesting they were stowed as cargo.

How were beads transported? Some of those carried on *Henrietta Marie* were strung with what appears to be iron wire. It is likely that a large number were originally strung in this fashion, as many of the beads have been extracted from extremely hard concreted masses. Although it is not a slaver, the *La Belle*, wrecked off the Texas coast in 1686, provides a useful comparison here. Archaeologists recovered many beads *in situ*, still in the wooden box in which they had been stored in the aft hold. The beads were strung by colour and laid in rows on top of hay, with each group of colours held together by a cord.[45] In the twentieth century, seed beads were still strung together when packaged for shipping.[46]

An estimated 10,000 glass beads were found on the site of the Manilla Wreck, which, as indicated in Chapter 4, may or may not comprise the jettisoned cargo of a Dutch vessel lost off Bermuda in the mid-eighteenth century. The beads, concentrated in pockets in one section of the wreck, comprised sixteen varieties of drawn bead and seventeen wound types. They were possibly all of Dutch manufacture.[47] The seventeenth-century Elmina wreck provides further information about the mechanics of shipping beads. Divers found an estimated 35,256 beads, either concreted together or loose on the wreck site here.[48] As with *Henrietta Marie*, the majority of the assemblage was found in discrete concretions, with only one bead type visible within each of the concretions. Three of these contained yellow beads (26,349), one had blue beads (4,931), and one held striped beads (191). They appear to have adhered *in situ*, suggesting that the beads were shipped in containers that no longer survive, and in separate colour groups. In all, sixteen identifiable types of bead were recovered from the Elmina shipwreck assemblage; all of them drawn.[49] Most were in blue, green, yellow, orange, and white, and originated from Venice or Bohemia.[50] They had been finished by the *a ferrazza* (or *a ferraccia*) method, which involved rounding the ends of beads by placing them in a copper pan held over a heat source; sand and ash were used to fill the perforations to prevent collapse and also to keep the beads from sticking to each other.[51] Similar bead concretions were found on the wreck of a seventeenth-century Portuguese ship, evidently engaged in the Guinea trade, at Ponta do Leme Velho, Cape Verde.[52]

Cotton Cloth for the Slave Trade

Cotton cloth, as Giorgio Riello argues, was perhaps the first truly transcontinental manufactured product: the outcome of a commodity chain that brought together capital, labour, land, technologies, and consumers on different continents.[53] Cotton was first cultivated in India around 3,200 BCE. It was not until the tenth century that its cultivation spread to sub-Saharan Africa and southern Europe, however.[54] It was only possible to produce cotton in small ecological niches in Europe at this point: the Mediterranean islands, and Cyprus in particular. Raw cotton was imported into Western Europe from the Middle East by Italian (particularly Venetian) merchants, and was spun locally. By the fifteenth century, the spinning and weaving of cotton had extended from Lombardy to some parts of France, Flanders, and southern Germany. But this expanding industry was hampered by inadequate supplies of raw materials and lacked the technological mastery of the more developed Asian textile industries. From the mid-1600s until the later eighteenth century, the highly fashionable calicoes, chintzes, and muslins so much in demand for domestic consumption in Britain were largely imported from India by the East India Company (EIC), which in 1612 established the first of its Indian factories (trading posts) at Surat in Gujarat. By 1660, the EIC had become the major importer of Indian cottons into London.[55] In that year, the English-based Guinea and Asian trades were *both* in the hands of the EIC—a little-known aspect of the EIC's history uncovered by Margaret Makepeace and deserving greater attention, not least for the light it sheds on the EIC's considerable efforts to meet already exacting African demands.[56]

In 1657, the EIC had purchased the remaining fifteen years of the monopoly on the African trade that in 1631 had been granted to the Guinea Company (headed, as indicated earlier, by Sir Nicholas Crisp). The EIC needed gold to support its operations in India, and where better to find it than the Gold Coast? The EIC held the lease for three short years (until the formation of the Company of Adventurers into Africa),

226 MATERIALIZING THE MIDDLE PASSAGE

Table 7.4 Cargo of the East India Company ship *Royal Charles*, 1661

Commodity	Amount	Value (£)
Iron	12,095 bars	3,676
Sletia	46 chests containing 1373 pieces	2,608
Old Sheets	174 chests containing 11,310	2,137
Pewter	41 casks	670
Muskets	6 chests containing 324	129
Hats	1 dry fat containing 12 dozen	18
Knives and sheaths	13 chests and 2 fats	250
Blue say	6 bales containing 180 pieces	600
Long cloth	200 bales containing 3000 pieces	4,926
Taffeta	3 bales containing 722 pieces	411
Fine pintado	1 bale	30
Muskets	3 chests containing 189	72
Provisions	(not listed)	249

Source: Makepeace (1989: 267–8).

but between 1657 and 1664 sent fifteen company ships from England to the Gold Coast laden with £111,000 in trade goods, principally English and Indian textiles, to be exchanged for gold, ivory, and a small number of African labourers. The latter were destined for the company's factories in India. Table 7.4 details the cargo of one of these ships, *Royal Charles*.

Royal Charles sailed from London to the Gold Coast in December 1661. The ship left Africa for Madras (now Chennai) in January 1662, laden with 3,776 oz of gold and fifteen captives intended for Bantam. The textiles carried by *Royal Charles* comprised European manufactures (hats, linen from Silesia, old bed sheets, and says, which were made from twilled wool) alongside Indian-made long cloth (cotton in plain white, or piece-dyed, usually *c*.37 yards long), taffeta (silk), and pintado (painted calico). These materials were packed into chests (presumably made of wood), dryfats (large baskets used to hold dry goods), and bales and casks—only some of which were fully watertight.

The EIC went to considerable efforts to anticipate and shape local demand for Indian cloth. In 1661, the company ship *Coronation* carried out fifty pieces of coloured gingham, two pieces of 'fine paintings of yellow grounds', and four pieces of brawle to see how well they would sell on the Gold Coast. If they proved popular, small pieces of the favoured fabrics were to be sent with *Coronation* along with a note of the quantities required.[57] Such efforts clearly paid off: Thornton has estimated that by the mid-seventeenth century the Gold Coast was already acquiring 20,000 m of European and Indian cotton annually.[58] English-made woollens dominated the African market until the 1720s, but after this African consumers, like their British counterparts, increasingly demanded lightweight, colourful—and colourfast—Indian-made printed fabrics.[59] In the 1740s, at the peak of their popularity at home, Asian textiles accounted also for some 60 per cent of all the textiles exported to Africa. In the last decade of the eighteenth century, a quarter of all the cottons imported into London by the EIC were then re-exported to West Africa.[60]

As might be expected, European manufacturers were keen to replicate Indian techniques, and in the mid-seventeenth century a cotton textile printing industry began to develop in France. Calicoes printed using Asian dyeing techniques were first made in Europe (in Marseilles) in 1648.[61] In the eighteenth century, Nantes established itself as a centre for making block-printed calicoes known as *Indiennes de traites*, the first of which were produced in 1759. These fabrics were produced almost exclusively for the African trade. A remarkable survival, now in the Musée d'Histoire de Nantes, is an album containing 162 block-print designs for *Indiennes* made by Favre, Petitpierre et Companie (1800–25). These fabrics were printed in red and blue, using madder and indigo dyes. Some of the designs were drawn from contemporary maps of Africa, or (as in the example in Figure 7.7) were embellished with images of African animals.

In 1701, in an effort to protect the domestic wool and silk industries, the import and use of printed or painted cotton was banned in England by Act of Parliament. The Act did, however, permit cotton to be imported and warehoused for re-exportation; it also allowed *plain* white calicoes from India to be imported and printed in England, both

Figure 7.7 One of the 162 block-print designs for *Indiennes* made by Favre, Petitpierre et Compagnie (1800–25), depicting four African animals. Château des ducs de Bretagne, Nantes.

228 MATERIALIZING THE MIDDLE PASSAGE

for the domestic market, and for export.[62] This first prohibition against imported cotton actively stimulated the growth of a domestic calico printing industry, which had begun in London in the 1670s and was reliant on imported Indian white calico. In 1722, a more draconian Calico Act came into force: once again prohibiting the consumption in England of printed, painted, stained, and dyed calicoes. Printed East India calicoes could still be imported for re-export, and plain calicoes could still be imported and printed, but only for export.[63] The result was a dramatic increase in the domestic production of cotton cloth, using raw cotton fibres imported initially from India. By the 1750s, a buoyant cotton industry, centred on Manchester, was producing not only cotton cloth for domestic use, but also mixed cotton and linen cloth for export. As Joseph Inikori has demonstrated, a high proportion of the would be turned into low-cost garments for plantation slaves in the colonies.. Figure 7.8 shows samples of checked fustian (cotton warp, silk weft) made by the Manchester firm Benjamin and John Bower. In 1771, as inscribed on its cover, this book of samples travelled from Liverpool to New York with Captain Nicholson on the brigantine *Havannah*.

Mixed cotton and linen checks like these imitated the Indian piece goods that were popular with West African trading partners, and as Inikori's work has shown, Africa also became a very significant market for English cotton checks after 1750.[64] Several of the leading Manchester manufacturers had close financial ties to the slave trade: Sir William Fazackerly and Samuel Touchet, for example, were both members of the Company of Merchants Trading to Africa.[65] Touchet was also owner or part-owner of four slaving voyages documented in TSTD.[66]

In 1769, the English textile entrepreneur Richard Arkwright patented a new invention, the water frame. His water-powered spinning machine mechanized the production of yarn and, allied with other technological innovations, rapidly revolutionized textile production. By the late eighteenth century, imported cotton was being spun into yarn in a new generation of water-powered textile mills in northern England, and woven into cloth on handlooms either in loom shops or in the homes of thousands of workers, paid by the piece for their labours. The raw cotton for these new ventures was imported from the West Indies and, towards the end of the eighteenth century, also from the US, which in 1811 sold 43,000 tons of cotton to England—over half of all the cotton used by British mills.[67] It was all grown, of course, by the enslaved.

The cottons sent into the British slave trade were known collectively as Guinea cloth but had a host of more specific names. Despite the huge variety, some were enduringly popular. Indian textiles included chelloes, cullanees, guinea stuffs. pulicats, romauls, and striped satin; while the most popular English-made textiles were plain cottons and chinzes.[68] West Africans also produced cotton textiles locally, and eighteenth-century English manufacturers put considerable effort into replicating some of that output. For example, samples of 'Ashantee and Whydah cloth' were demanded from Cape Coast Castle in the mid-eighteenth century to facilitate replication.[69] By the 1790s, some loom-patterned and printed textiles made in both India and England were being adapted to consumer preferences at points all along the Guinea coast.[70] Thus, John Adams, trading in West Africa from 1786 to 1800, recommended Indian-made romals

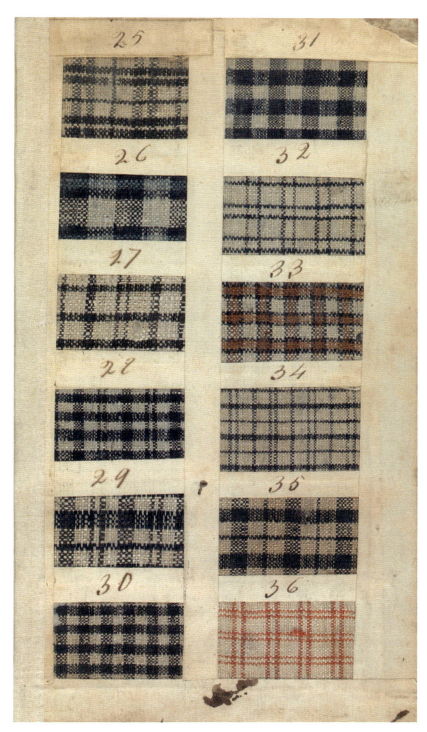

Figure 7.8 Page from a textile sample book made by the Manchester firm Benjamin and John Bower. The page open here shows samples of checked fustian (cotton warp, silk weft). Metropolitan Museum of Art, 156.4 T31.

of a type known as 'Bonny Blue' as being most suitable for barter at Bonny. Even more precisely, these should be 'small pattern, red border best'. Chinz, in contrast, should be 'English, large pattern, blues best'.[71]

Cloth does not generally survive on wreck sites, but invoices and ships' accounts provide considerable detail on how it was shipped. Prideaux's invoice of the trade goods on *Daniel and Henry*, for example, indicates that many fabrics were bought by the piece and shipped in wooden chests. Thus, one chest contained eighty pieces of ticking, 9 yards in a piece, bought for 6*s.* 8*d.* per piece; and another held 114 pieces of 'Guinea stuffs' bought for 7*s.* 8*d.* a piece. Some fabrics were bought by the ell (that is, around 17 inches, or the length of a cubit), and shipped in packets, to be cut into pieces suitable for wrappers: rectangular lengths of cloth draped around the body and secured under the arm, over the shoulder or at the waist (*Daniel* **1700: 40–2**).

Brass for the Slave Trade

Brass is an alloy of copper and zinc, and in the early stages of the slave trade the copper used in its manufacture was sourced from northern Europe.[72] But by the end of the seventeenth century British slavers were shipping home-produced copper, manufactured using a coal-fuelled, reverberatory furnace method developed in Bristol in the 1680s. Copper was produced thereafter in Bristol itself and, increasingly, in the Swansea–Neath district in Wales. Seaborne access to ores from Cornwall, and abundant coal from the Wales coal measures, gave Wales a huge advantage in the copper industry: by 1800 Welsh copper works were smelting some 40 per cent of the world's copper.[73] Chris Evans's pioneering work has foregrounded the symbiotic relationship between Britain's copper industry and slaving, showing that slave traders took shares in copper works because they gained thereby privileged access to the supplies they needed for trading on the Guinea coast, while copper masters invested in slaving ventures because they were aware of the African appetite for their products. It is no accident, then, that the earliest copper works in the Swansea valley (Llangyfelach and White Rock) were established by partnerships led respectively by Richard Lockwood, a director of the RAC, and Thomas Coster, a Bristol MP with links to the Carolina slave trade.[74]

Bristol was another important producer of brass throughout the eighteenth century. The region was an attractive choice for manufacturers: copper ore was readily sourced from Cornwall, and calamine (the carbonate ore of zinc, necessary for the production of brass) was available from the nearby Mendip Hills. Coal was available locally, and water power for the machinery could be sourced from the rivers Avon and Frome.[75] The Bristol Brass and Copper Company, founded in 1702 by a syndicate of Bristol Quakers, became one of the most important brass manufacturers in Britain.[76] The works were located at Baptist Mills on the River Frome. Abraham Darby, the so-called father of the industrial revolution, was the first 'active man' (manager) here, working at the site in 1702–8.[77] Darby's presence foregrounds the close relationship between industrialization and the slave trade that Joseph Inikori has done so much to uncover.[78] Similarly, Isaac Hobhouse, one of Bristol's most prolific slave ship agents in the quarter century after 1720, was also a partner in one of the Bristol copper concerns, sending his own copper out to Africa on his own ships.[79] Abraham Darby employed Dutch workers who understood how to transform brass ingots into hollow battery-wares. The molten brass produced by the melters at Baptist Mills was cast into slabs, approximately ¼ inch thick. These were then hammered into flat sheets, known as naps, which were next beaten into shape using large water-powered hammers.[80] To produce hollow-ware of desired specifications, the blows of the hammer radiated from the centre of the vessel to its desired circumference as the nap revolved, and the vessel would be heated or annealed to prevent cracking. These steps would be repeated, often using different hammer weights, separated by numerous episodes of annealing. Once the desired size and depth were achieved, the rim was finished, and the vessel was complete.[81] Darby also developed and patented a method for casting hollow-wares using expendable moulds formed from wet sand.[82]

By 1712, Baptist Mills needed two hundred tons of raw material per year and the Bristol Brass and Copper Company brought in two thousand cartloads of coal per week to fuel its operations—a staggering quantity for this period.[83] In 1754, Reinhold Angerstein visited Baptist Mills on his tour of English metal manufactories. His travel diary records forty-eight brass furnaces here, all belonging to the Bristol Brass and Copper Company. Angerstein reported that the company expended 80–90 tons of copper every year in producing some fifty or sixty varieties of 'Guinea pans', ranging in diameter from 4 feet to 1 foot.[84] Bristol's Saltford battery mill, the last remaining battery-ware manufacturer in England, closed in 1908. In 1968, Joan Day interviewed three elderly former workers from Saltford. Among the manufacturing terms they recalled were 'Guinea kettle' and 'Lisbon pan'—two names for hollow-wares that were once commonly exchanged for slaves.[85] Examples of both can still be found in the Salford Mill's collection (Figure 7.9).

Figure 7.9 Battery-wares for the slave trade, made at Saltford Brass Mill. Left: Lisbon pan (350 × 100 mm). Right: Guinea kettle (300 × 190 mm). Saltford Brass Mill Project.

Shipping Brass: Metals from the Elmina Wreck

Chapter 4 introduced an unnamed seventeenth-century Dutch wreck (likely to be *Groeningen*), discovered off Elmina in 2003. This find sheds extraordinarily nuanced light on the manufacture and shipping of European trade goods to the Gold Coast. Artefacts are always powerful things, but there are moments when—just because they are *there*, to touch, inspect, put under a microscope, or simply ponder—objects really do say more than a thousand words. The story of the production and barter of European trade goods in West Africa has been painstakingly recovered and retold by documentary historians, but the small things brought to the surface from the murky waters of the Elmina roadstead—glass beads, cowrie shells, glass bottles, ceramics, manillas, bricks, brasswares, pewterwares, and brass pins—materialize tiny, tactile, and sometimes overlooked details of that story in a particularly effective, and affective, way. The brass basins from this wreck, my subject here, are heavy objects and were found on the ocean bed in nested rows, just as they would have been stored in the ship's hold. In all, seventy brass and pewter trade items were found on the wreck site, fifty of which were initially catalogued by Nicole Hamann.[86]

Brass basins were the very first objects recovered from the Elmina wreck site, and provided an immediate indicator of its significance. Archaeologists went on to record thirty-four nested stacks of brass basins, some of the stacks being several metres long. (These are visible on the wreck site plan in Figure 4.4.) Further individual basins were scattered on the sea floor, and, while many more could be detected through probing or hand excavation of the sediment, the overall number and variety of brasswares were impossible to estimate. The pewter bowls laden on *Henrietta Marie* were similarly stacked, and even retained their original straw and paper packing material.[87] Careful examination of the Elmina basins, comprising kettles and pans or four different types (Figure 7.10), has revealed many details concerning their manufacture. Some exhibited compression marks indicative of the battery process, while others had smooth surfaces with no obvious hammer marks.[88] But all exhibited concentric circles on their interior and exterior surfaces (Figure 7.10), which are suggestive of lathe finishing.[89]

Several of the Type 3 basins from the Elmina wreck site exhibit dents, cuts, and other damage unlikely to have occurred during shipment (since they were recovered in a single nested stack, and the damage varies between individual pieces). This is an intriguing discovery, which, as Greg Cook has plausibly suggested, provides material support for the historically documented practice of importing damaged brasswares to the Gold Coast, presumably with the intent that they would be recast locally.[90] Finally, two of the excavated basins bear touchmarks (manufacturer's marks). They are not fully distinguishable but may represent a fleur-de-lis or a stylized cross with the letters M and/or W legible on each side.[91] The presence of such marks on early brass pieces implies continental manufacture: English coppersmiths rarely stamped their wares prior to the nineteenth century.[92]

Figure 7.10 The brass and pewter basin assemblage from the Elmina wreck site. Type 1 (left): kettles with two riveted rolled handles; Type 2 (bottom): basins with slightly convex sides and flat rims; Type 3 (top): vessels with rolled rims and straight sides sloping into round bases; Type 4 (right): vessels averaging 41.87 cm diameter and 8.5 cm depth. Gregory Cook.

African Lives: Trade Goods at Elmina and Savi/Ouidah

> Reaching beyond trade lists and artefact inventories to understand how indigenes used and transformed artefacts is basic to an anthropological perception of cultural contact, continuity and change.
>
> (DeCorse 2001: 15)

There is considerable debate regarding the precise motives for African interest in European goods, and the extent to which foreign manufactures were acquired for their novelty value.[93] For some scholars, including the influential historian John Thornton, Europe offered nothing that Africa did not already produce, and Africans desired exogenous trade goods largely for motives of 'prestige, fancy, changing taste, and a desire for variety'.[94] Certainly, it is clear from both historical and archaeological evidence that West Africans produced beads, wove excellent wool and cotton cloth, and smelted copper well before the era of the slave trade. But local manufacturers often lacked the precise technological skill set or natural resources to match the range of textiles, metalwares, and so on offered by Europe, and, in that sense, some communities were reliant upon slave ships for goods that they could not make themselves. Two examples should suffice to evidence this point. First, while iron smelting was widespread in Africa, smelters without access to imported metal were restricted to small batch production: Bassar (Togo), a leading centre for iron production, produced an annual maximum of 80 tons in the eighteenth century.[95] Similarly, imported red wool was highly prized among the Yoruba and in Benin, even though local dyers could produce red dyes; what they could not match was the intensity and saturated quality of the colour found in wool cloth, which absorbs dyes very deeply.[96]

Exploring how beads, textiles, and brasswares were received in West Africa necessarily involves a broader consideration of the role of exogenous artefacts within local political economies, power structures, and cosmologies. These are, of course, questions that archaeologists have asked many times regarding past societies but that also apply to goods entering West Africa via the slave trade: what part did these things play in creating, maintaining, and reshaping indigenous systems of authority and belief? Did they fundamentally alter local behaviours, or simply supplement existing repertoires? Did they impact significantly upon existing technologies and social practices? These questions will be addressed by focusing on just two places, selected in part because of their importance to the slave trade, but also because extensive archaeological projects have been undertaken at both.

In 1482, the Portuguese built the first European fortified trading post sited in West Africa. This was Castelo de São Jorge da Mina, founded adjacent to an existing Fante settlement. The Dutch captured the Portuguese stronghold in 1637, undertaking extensive redevelopment of what would become the centre of Dutch operations on the Gold Coast until the British took control of the site in 1872.[97] Under the Dutch, the town's population increased substantially, numbering in the thousands or even tens of thousands as large numbers of people from other parts of the Gold Coast, and beyond, sought Dutch permission to reside there.[98] By the eighteenth century, the population of Elmina town was notably heterogeneous, comprising not only Fante but also Ewe and small numbers of Mande and Dyula. 'Mulattos' and resident slaves, including *translaven*, or company slaves in the service of the Dutch, made up a significant proportion of the population. Evidence for the political structure of the town is somewhat difficult to decipher, but it would appear that trade, whether in gold or in slaves, was not controlled by any one individual or social group. The trade goods bartered for both commodities were, as a result, widely available. For much of the era of the slave trade Elmina town was a self-governing enclave with more than one ruler.[99] The royal court appears to have been undistinguished, at least until the nineteenth century. Even then, *asafo* (associations based on patrilineal descent) were as important to the sociopolitical balance of the town as the paramount king (*ɔmanhen*)—a role that appears to have evolved in the eighteenth century. Fifteen years of archaeological fieldwork exploring this complex settlement have produced extensive insights into local responses to the

Portuguese, Dutch, and British trade goods flooding into Elmina as ownership of the forts changed hands over several hundred years.[100] Imports may have been widely available at Elmina itself, and no doubt at other fort sites, but the extent of their use further inland is less clear. For example, trade goods appear to have played a limited part in the lives of the Banda people living at Makala Kataa (West Central Ghana) in the eighteenth century.[101]

As noted in Chapter 2, Ouidah was the second most important embarkation point in all of Africa, exporting over a million captives.[102] Until its conquest by Dahomey in 1727, Ouidah was part of the Hueda kingdom, with its capital lying at nearby Savi. Archaeological work undertaken in and around Savi by Kenneth Kelly and Neil Norman has provided illuminating insights into the uses of trade goods by the Hueda.[103] The rich documentary evidence for the history of Ouidah under both the Hueda and Dahomey has recently been synthesized in a major study by Robin Law, while two major field projects (the Abomey Plateau Archaeological Project and the Benin–Denmark Archaeology initiative) have greatly enhanced our knowledge of eighteenth-and nineteenth-century Dahomey and its material world.[104]

Kenneth Kelly's programme of excavation at Savi has shown that—in strong contrast to the situation at Elmina—the European presence here was tightly controlled. Small groups of Europeans lived, not in imposing, fortified 'castles' built in the European style, but in 'lodges' constructed some miles inland, and in the vernacular style.[105] Moreover, these lodges were adjacent to, yet separate from, the Huedan palace complex. This strategy enabled the Hueda to do two things at once: limit interaction with the Europeans in their midst, while also preventing those traders from distancing themselves socially. The Hueda elite also tightly controlled access to the imports entering Savi via Ouidah, distributing some as gifts at ritualized activities such as feasts and parades, and restricting others entirely to their own use.[106] Nine rooms in the palace compound at Savi were floored with European bricks, for example, publicly demonstrating (as Mitchell puts it) privileged royal access to an import denied to local people and European residents alike.[107] Neil Norman's work at Savi and its nearby secondary palace complexes added significantly to our understanding of the use of trade goods by the Huedan elite. But some items, such as glass beads and tobacco pipes, have also been excavated from 'commoner' residences at Savi. This is a reminder that, even where royal officials or powerful trading families dominated the slave trade and the goods it brought, not all trade goods were 'parlayed into political action'.[108] That is to say, not all imported commodities were 'prestige goods' operating above the level of local economies and employed principally to create or maintain elite social distinction.

As discussed further below, Norman's work has shown that, in the hinterland of the Hueda trading centre at Savi, imported artefacts became structurally embedded in *vodun* religious sites and practices.[109] But the extent to which trade goods entered local economies after Ouidah was incorporated into the kingdom of Dahomey in 1727 is a matter of some debate. Under Dahomey, Ouidah was a centre for fishing, salt production, and local trade, and also a seat of provincial administration and a garrison town; but its central function was trade with Europeans.[110] Once a year, the king of Dahomey formally distributed customs (trade goods) at his capital, Abomey, as a mark of his largesse, and, since the 1960s, it has generally been accepted that the effective state monopoly over trade goods meant that these imports did not enter local markets.[111] In contrast, Robin Law argues that the lifestyle of Ouidah was marked by widespread consumption of imported goods, readily available from local marketplaces. The slave trade itself was not a royal monopoly, Law points out, and many captives were supplied to Europeans by private merchants whose earnings (in the form of trade goods) were expended within the local economy. The personnel from the European forts and ships' captains and crews purchased goods and services in the local market too, again using trade goods. Law draws persuasively on documentary evidence concerning the many European goods available at the main market in Ouidah in support of this case.[112] But archaeological fieldwork paints a rather different picture. Monroe's view, based on his work on the Abomey plateau, is that, '[a]lthough historical sources suggest some of these items [trade goods] made it into regional markets for sale, imported trade goods were a closely guarded source of symbolic power for kings in this period'.[113] Kelly's (admittedly limited) fieldwork in the European fort 'quarters' at Ouidah certainly suggests that European imports made up a very small proportion of the artefacts in daily use here: in all time periods from the 1660s to the early nineteenth century, locally manufactured materials predominated, with the only exceptions being the use of imported tobacco pipes and beads.[114] So there is good reason to think that access to, and reception of, European goods at Ouidah did not work in the same ways as at Elmina.

The Afterlives and Impact of Trade Beads

As Marcus Wood notes, beads 'were symbolically, religiously, economically and aesthetically central to the lives of every sub-Saharan African society involved in the processes of the slave trade'.[115] African peoples were very familiar with glass beads long before the slave trade. Some 165,000 glass and carnelian beads have been found at the important site of Igbo-Ukwu in Nigeria, for example, imported via Muslim-controlled long-distance trade, and probably predating the end of the first millennium CE.[116] It is not surprising, therefore, that the beads available from slave ships rapidly became embedded in bodily adornment strategies. John Barbot noted at the end of the seventeenth century that Gold Coast peoples

> adorn their necks, arms, legs and even feet with many strings of glass beads, coral and Venetian *rassade*. I have seen some who had whole bunches of 4ct. of this *rassade* hanging aslant from their neck, intermixed with an abundance of their small gold ornaments and bark from the fetish tree.[117]

But it is important to recognize that exogenous glass beads were so desirable in part because they were entering communities that already had their own well-established traditions of bead manufacture.

Nigeria provides the most extensive evidence of early West African bead-making, with a renowned glass bead-making industry emerging at Ile-Ife between 1000 and 1500 CE and producing dichroic beads which appeared blue in reflected light and green in transmitted light.[118] It was believed for many years that the Ife-Ife industry was based wholly on the use of imported Islamic and European glass, but it is now thought that primary production of glass was taking place at Igbo Olókun in the eleventh century, if not earlier.[119] Portuguese traders became aware very early on of locally made dichroic beads (which, as noted earlier, were known as akori, or cori). By the late fifteenth century, Portuguese ships were transporting African-made beads along the coast to Elmina, most probably from Ile-Ife.[120] This trade was also developed by Africans, with indigenous Gold Coast merchants using ocean-going canoes to trade independently with the Slave Coast in akori, in competition with the European traders: indeed, it was reported in the 1650s that the akori trade had been 'taken over' by African merchants.[121] As noted above, large quantities of European-made glass beads also began to be shipped to West Africa, and Venetian manufactures also attempted to copy some African-made beads (as illustrated in Figure 7.6). Venetian and other European beads were, as John Barbot suggests, restrung and amalgamated with other local materials, but African expertise was also rapidly applied to repurposing some of these imported commodities entirely. From the sixteenth century, bead-making in sub-Saharan African was concentrated in Nigeria and Ghana. Much—though, as already suggested with reference to Ife-Ife, not all—bead production involved reworking imported glass (as seen in Figure 7.11), and the Gold Coast became an important centre for this technology.

With the introduction of European goods, bead artists had a steady supply of glass at their disposal, and the indigenous bead industry boomed. Some idea of the range and quantity of beads imported can be gleaned from a list of proposed merchandise, compiled by Dutch West India Company agents stationed at Elmina in 1653, and requesting almost 19,000 pounds of Venetian beads. Specifically, they asked for 4,000 lb lemon-coloured *past*, 3,000 lb white *quispel*, 1,000 lb red *quispel*, 2,000 lb torquyn *quispel*, 2,000 lb blue lavender *quispel*, 1,200 lb straw-yellow lemon *quispel*, 2,000 lb black *rosados* with white stripes, 1,200 lb striped crystal, 500 lb violet *quispel*, 1,000 lb *roo madrigette* with white and blue stripes, and 1,000 lb blue-violet *madrigette* with white stripes.[122]

Archaeological evidence supports the contention that most, if not all, Gold Coast bead-making practices were probably dependent on imported glass sources. Some thirty thousand European and locally made beads were recovered during DeCorse's fieldwork at Elmina, where an industry based on modifying European beads developed in the sixteenth century.[123] Subsequently, Ghanaian artisans began to manufacture beads by crushing European glass beads to a powder, then heating the powder and pouring it into moulds, thereby creating new beads. The first European to comment on this practice was John Barbot, who noted that the natives of Mina 'also recast crystal and glass, taking considerable pains'.[124] This industry grew rapidly; indeed, recent research suggests that, by the end of the seventeenth century, imported Venetian

Figure 7.11 A strand of akoso beads dating to the eighteenth–nineteenth centuries, displaying some of the earliest dated mould-form powder-glass bead designs from Ghana. These beads were acquired by Suzanne Gott from a Hausa trader at the biweekly bead market at Agomanya, Krobo, in July 1999. Suzanne Gott.

monochrome beads were being used primarily as colouring agents for the art of powder-glass bead-making. The seeds in the monochrome concretions from the Elmina wreck were almost certainly intended for use as colouring agents, for example.[125] This technique was by no means restricted to the coast. At New Buipe, a seventeenth-century site north-east of the important entrepot of Begho, archaeologists have also found evidence for local artisans using clay moulds to produce beads of powdered glass.[126]

DeCorse did not find direct evidence of the powder-glass manufacturing process at Elmina, but he excavated reworked beads that had been made by heating glass fragments and then perforating them. Most were made from broken European beads.[127] Ghanaians also used abraders in shaping local beads of stone, shell, or glass, and the technique was also applied to imported glass beads.[128] Venetian pipe-beads, or short pieces of glass cane, also from Murano, were broken into smaller pieces and abraded at the ends to make a starlike pattern from the stripes.[129] In this context, it is interesting that DeCorse found evidence for bead abrading at Elmina, recovering grooved sandstone blocks that had probably been used as abraders, along with some types of glass bead with abraded ends. Many of the beads found at Elmina will have been worn on the body, but David Calvocoressi's excavation in 1970s at Fort Veerche Schanns (a nineteenth-century Dutch fortification at the western edge of Elmina) provided additional information about the use of beads in funerary contexts. Calvocoressi identified thirty structures containing artefacts of fifteenth–nineteenth century date, many of which came from burials within houses. Some 5,238 beads were recovered, 5,199 of which were associated with just two skeletons.[130] All but thirty-one of these beads were of European origin. The vast majority were seed beads of opaque greenish-yellow, though some white beads with longitudinal blue stripes were also recovered.[131] Recent fieldwork at the settlement quarters neighbouring the British fort at Dixcove has also produced many European-made beads, among an artefact assemblage in which European-made artefacts comprised some 71 per cent of the total number of objects recovered. Most of these beads were monochrome examples from Venice and Bohemia. Bauxite beads constituted the only locally manufactured examples found at Dixcove.[132]

European beads were imported into Ouidah in similarly huge quantities and became a constituent element of material culture at Savi and Ouidah. Kelly notes that just a handful of the great numbers of beads excavated at the Savi palace compound were of African origin.[133] Unfortunately, all of the imported beads he recovered from both Savi and Ouidah were in contexts of discard or accidental loss, making it difficult to determine exactly how they were used; although they were found in both elite and commoner districts, suggesting that they were widely accessible to, and accepted by, the bulk of the population. The RAC established a factory at Savi in 1682, relocating it to Ouidah in 1684.[134] The correspondence generated by the RAC factors at Ouidah and Offra (Allada) sheds more detailed light on bead use here at the end of the seventeenth century, indicating a demand for small beads (particularly in white), including broken ones.[135]

Neil Norman's pioneering work in the environs of Savi since 1999 has cast nuanced light on the ways in which trade goods, including small numbers of beads, were integrated into vodun, the Huedan religious system. Vodun was associated, as Norman expresses it, with an 'unselfconscious accumulative aesthetic', amassing both artefacts and new deities from the multinational communities surrounding Savi and Ouidah.[136] This acquisitive principle was driven by a powerful religious rationale: vodun was (and is) a religion embracing the unfinished and the new, and it was believed that the inclusion of previously foreign objects in vodun 'assemblages' (from altars to amulets) ensured that the religion remained vibrant and powerful.[137] Thomas Phillips visited Savi, and noted in 1694 both the number of temples and the technology used to represent vodun, observing: 'I have often seen little figures of clay about their houses with oil, rice, corn and other offerings before them' (*Hannibal* 1693–4: 223–5).[138] Local ceramics played a central part in vodun worship, but Norman's excavation of a 'spirit house' at a site 2 kilometres from Savi reveals the extent to which trade goods were incorporated into vodun in the pre-Dahomian era. The excavation produced Huedan-era ceramics and imported items, including a

240 MATERIALIZING THE MIDDLE PASSAGE

yellow-and-black striped trade beads, iron fasteners, and pipe fragments.[139] At a second site (interpreted as a settlement centre) 1.5 kilometres north of the palace, a small test excavation inside a temple or ritual complex produced a cache of faceted colourless trade beads alongside a large locally made ceramic vessel (gozin). A similar deposit was recovered from a secondary palace complex 3 kilometres to the north-west of Savi.[140] Norman's work reveals the extent to which Vodun shrines aggregated items such as trade beads and smoking pipes from across the Atlantic world, and confirms that costly trade items tended to be concentrated in religious spaces in the Savi countryside. He concludes that 'Huedans who profited directly or indirectly from trans-Atlantic trade in war captives, lavished a portion of these gains on Vodun and ancestral members', thereby maintaining the affluence flowing from the slave trade.[141]

The Afterlives and Impact of Imported Textiles

What was the impact of exogenous cloth within West Africa? It is fair to say that this is a much debated question, with arguments centring on the accessibility of foreign textiles—which was far from even geographically, and often restricted to specific status groups—and the extent to which imports impacted upon local production. Archaeological evidence for textiles is, as already noted, very limited. No garments were recovered at all from Elmina, for example. As early as 1617, the Portuguese traded 15,000 pieces of 'Guinea cloth' through Elmina.[142] Yet a single Dutch bale seal, from the Leiden wool industry, is the sole piece of excavated evidence for the well-documented cloth trade here.[143]

Some scholars, including Colleen Kriger, have argued that the imported textiles that flowed into Elmina and other points on the Gold Coast thereafter were worn, albeit with some restrictions according to class and gender, by most of the Gold Coast population.[144] Others suggest that, throughout West Africa, access to foreign cloth was in fact more limited. Having calculated that the 9.5 million yards of cloth imported into West Africa in the 1780s amount to no more than 0.4 yards per person, David Eltis concluded that only a small proportion of Africans could have worn imported cloth.[145] But, as Kriger and others have demonstrated, a significant proportion of this material was not worn as acquired: a considerable amount of imported cloth was unravelled into its constituent threads and rewoven into cloths meeting African sensibilities.[146]

Cotton, wool, wild silk, raffia, and bast are all indigenous to West Africa, and cloth was being woven there from cotton, wool, and other fibres many centuries before the slave trade. The earliest dated examples (of a bast-fibre cloth) come from ninth-century contexts at Igbo-Ukwu and were probably woven on an upright single heddle loom. Fragments of cotton and wool textiles, using indigo dye, have been recovered from eleventh–twelfth century contexts in Mali, and had been woven on a horizontal double-heddle loom.[147] By the fourteenth century, cotton was being cultivated, spun into thread, and woven on a vertical loom in the Bight of Benin.[148] Cloth from this region would in fact later be exported into the slave trade elsewhere.[149] Early Portuguese traders made frequent references, from the 1450s, to cotton production on the Senegal and Gambia rivers and in Sierra Leone.[150] In the late seventeenth century, the RAC exported cloth made in Allada and Ouidah for resale on the Gold Coast.[151] The blue stripes in blue-and-white Ouidah cloth, as Thomas Phillips noted, (*Hannibal* 1693–4: 220) were made by unravelling imported says and pertetuanas. Drawing on descriptions of the visual features of African cotton textiles, Kriger argues persuasively that the Indian-made cottons that were the most successful trade items on the Guinea were cottons very much like those already being produced in West Africa.[152] As was also the case with glass beads, however, the availability of imports stimulated developments in local production, particularly in terms of enhancing the local repertoire of patterns and designs. In some Yoruba areas, for example, scarlet cloth was unravelled and the red threads woven into ceremonial cloths, for display at funerals and in masquerade costumes.[153]

Imported cloth became a particularly important vehicle in the development of local textiles on the Gold Coast. The Asante were producing cloth from processed bark and bast fibre before the slave trade, and in the fourteenth century the weaving of narrow strip cloth on a treadle loom developed, using locally produced cotton. In the eighteenth century, this technology was harnessed to produce a new cloth: kente. Imported silk, acquired from the Dutch, was unpicked and woven into kente, inspiring a huge elaboration of traditional designs.[154]

Archaeological evidence for the impact of exogenous textiles is as limited at Savi as at Elmina. Here, too, a single lead bale seal serves as material testimony to a very extensive trade in imported textiles, evidenced in the documentary record.[155] In the Bight of Benin, imported cloth was favoured by the unmade yard rather than made up into garments, because 'long cloth' spoke to the local tradition of wearing the wrapper.[156] Kriger has drawn on RAC correspondence to assess imported cloth most in demand at Ouidah in the late seventeenth century, and her analysis shows growing demand for painted or printed fabrics from India.[157] Kriger has demonstrated that, although there seem to have been innumerable types of cloth yardage entering the Bight of Benin from Britain and elsewhere, a coherent set of consumer preferences can be identified: woollens not available in local workshops (perpetuannas, says, kerseys) but also cottons and linens that closely resembled local vertical loom products in colour and pattern—for example, loom patterned stripes and checks.[158] The only true 'novelties' were painted and printed calicoes and chintzes, which were very highly prized.

In the nineteenth century, women in the Igbo town of Akwete (Nigeria) began producing wrappers made from a type of cloth that, according to oral tradition, was invented by a woman who wove new designs using threads from imported cloth.[159] Akwete cloth has antecedents in the ceremonial cloth from Ijebu-Ode, known as aso olona (cloth with patterns). A surviving eighteenth-century example, incorporating European silk into local cotton cloth, is illustrated in Figure 17.12. Heavily embellished with brocade, this piece will have been worn draped on the shoulder of a local ruler.

Figure 7.12 Ijebu-Ode cloth, handwoven local cotton and imported silk, with brocaded imagery. National Museums Scotland, A.716.29.

This rare survival is an important object for the study of the history of the textile industry in Nigeria, but it also speaks powerfully to the theme of the slave ship, having been acquired in the course of a slaving voyage. The cloth was donated to the National Museum of Scotland in 1861, and the register entry for the piece states: 'Cotton cloth, brought from interior of Africa about 70 years ago by Capt. William Corran, snr.'[160] The TSTD data set shows William Corran to have been a Liverpool captain who made eight slaving voyages between 1785 and 1801. These voyages were all to the Gold Coast and Bonny in the Bight of Biafra, but John Corran (probably William's son) captained three slaving voyages to Ouidah in the 1790s.[161]

This piece is one of very few examples of eighteenth-century African-made textiles surviving in British museums today. It is no accident that a uniquely important source of further examples, with equally close links to the slave trade, is the famous wooden chest in which the abolitionist Thomas Clarkson kept his 'productions of Africa' (see Figure 7.13). In advance of the 1788 parliamentary inquiry into the slave trade, as discussed in more detail in Chapter 8, Clarkson toured British ports collecting both witness testimonies about conditions on board slave ships, and samples of African manufactures. Clarkson was well aware of indigenous cloth production in West Africa and also of the incorporation of unravelled European thread into local cloth, and sought out examples of both for his chest. Division three of the chest eventually contained 'an African loom and an African spindle with spun cotton round it. Cloths of cotton of various kinds, made by the natives, some white, but others dyed by them of different colours, and others, into which they had interwoven European silk'.[162] These cloth samples—some of the earliest known textile samples from West Africa—were procured from Clarkson's many contacts: a Mr Biggs furnished some small pieces of dyed cloth, while Thomas Bonville, who was engaged in the bilateral

Figure 7.13 Thomas Clarkson's chest, opened to show its contents. These include numerous samples of African cloth. Wisbech and Fenland Museum.

produce trade with Africa, furnished further samples.[163] Another possible source was the former Bristol slave ship surgeon Alexander Falconbridge, who, as his parliamentary testimony states, had acquired numerous pieces of dyed cloth in West Africa.[164] Falconbridge probably passed these on to Clarkson, whose chest contains several blue-and-white cloth samples. Malika Kraamer has tentatively identified one of the samples in the chest as probably coming from Falconbridge, and two others from the bilateral trader *Lively*, which Clarkson had visited while in port at London: here, he persuaded the mate to sell him two pieces of cotton cloth.[165]

While the textual evidence has little to say on the specific provenance of Clarkson's textiles, ongoing scientific analysis of seven pieces, all made on a horizontal double-heddle loom, suggests most were produced in the region between Ghana and Ouidah, with three most likely coming from the Ewe-speaking region in Ghana. This new work is also providing important new information about late-eighteenth-century weaving practices and cultural dialogue in West Africa. For example, Mexican cochineal had been used as a red dye source in the Clarkson samples containing red yarn—again, suggesting that imported cloth was unravelled, and repurposed, locally.[166]

In May 1787, Clarkson took some of his recently acquired African cloth samples to the dinner party, hosted by Bennett Langton, at which William Wilberforce was persuaded to become the parliamentary figurehead for the abolition movement.[167] The chest contained many other things, but it is likely that the cloth samples were chosen for this propitious event because, as is evident from Clarkson's acquisition of cloth incorporating European silk, he clearly understood the appeal of these samples,

244 MATERIALIZING THE MIDDLE PASSAGE

not simply in terms of evidencing African ingenuity, but in foregrounding the extent of the African market for European manufactured goods.[168] The slave trade would not fall without something to replace it: through these fragments of fabric, Clarkson was materializing new possibilities, building on centuries of trade.

Red Gold Reworked: The Afterlives and Impact of Brasswares at Elmina

Copper embodied three characteristics—colour (red), luminosity, and sound—that, long before the slave trade, embedded the metal firmly in indigenous ritual practices and mythological systems throughout West Africa.[169] The long history of precolonial copper working in the region has been studied extensively, particularly since the publication in 1984 of Eugenia Herbert's seminal book *Red Gold of Africa*. As with cotton production, some of the earliest evidence comes from Igbo-Ukwu, where radiocarbon dates suggest copper-working by the end of the first millennium CE.[170] The celebrated brass industries of the Kingdom of Benin, and of Ife, have both been studied in depth by art historians, but the Gold Coast also had an extensive brass industry prior to European contact, centred on the forested region near Elmina.[171] Excavations at Begho in 1975 revealed well over five hundred crucibles and several small brass smiths' furnaces at an atelier in the Dwinfuor quarter. Local production was generally on a small scale, however, and dependent upon trans-Saharan supply. From 1470 to about 1520, copper became the most popular metal purchased from the Portuguese station at São Jorge, Elmina.[172] A ledger kept by Esteveo de Barradas, the Portuguese agent there, reveals that, in a period spanning just over two years between 1529 and 1531, some 216,700 manillas and 9,000 brass and copper vessels were exchanged for gold at Elmina.[173] In 1602, the Dutch trader Pieter de Marees provided an exceptionally detailed account of the local uses to which imported brasswares were being put on the Gold Coast, noting that

> all sorts of basins are brought there, such as small and large Neptunes, Barber's Basins, cooking Basins, fater-basins, chased basins, big Scottish pans not less than 2 fathoms in circumference, and small rimless Cups. These Basins they use for various purposes: they use the small Neptunes to store Oil with which they rub themselves; the big Neptunes to immure in Tombs on the graves of the dead, and also to carry something or other in. They use Barber's basins to wash and shave; Fater-Basins as lids, to cover other basins, so that no dirt may fall into them; on chased Basins they put their ornaments and trinkets; those big Scottish pans they use for slaughtering a Goat or Pig and cleaning it in, instead of a tub; small rimless cups to cook in; for them, these are quite convenient and they do not want handles on them, like those we use in our Country. Such Brass Basins, which the Ships bring there in large quantities, have become so common in the Country that people often sell brass-ware as cheaply (to the Negroes or their Landsmen) as it is bought in Amsterdam. Although these Basins

are brought there in such quantities and are not as perishable a commodity as Linen, one does not see much old brass-ware there; so there must be a huge population in the Interior which uses and employs such quantities of imperishable goods. Furthermore great heaps of Cauldrons are brought there, which they use a lot for fetching water from Wells and Valleys, as well as red copper stewing pots, coated with tin on the inside, which they use to store water, instead of putting a beer Barrel in their house.[174]

This is a fascinating glimpse into the afterlives of brasswares, but concerns only hollow-wares (basins and bowls). De Marees does not mention manillas, nor does he refer to the local recasting of imported brass, although his observation that little 'old' brass was in evidence might be interpreted as suggesting that this was taking place. The Dutch capture of Elmina in 1637 brought a boom in access to artefacts manufactured from Flanders brass, including some not mentioned by de Marees. Documentary evidence shows that, in December 1645, Dutch traders at Elmina had a stock of more than 360,000 copper alloy fishhooks to hand; yet DeCorse excavated just a handful of examples of these.[175]

The dialogue in metal that developed between European traders and their African partners is perhaps best exemplified by the bracelet-like brass manilla (Figure 7.14), described by Nigel Barley as 'simply a European version of a very old African design'.[176] When Portuguese explorers began exploring the West African coast, they

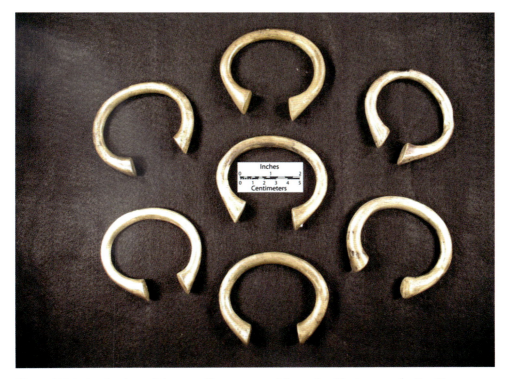

Figure 7.14 A selection of the manillas recovered from the Elmina wreck site. Gregory Cook.

246 MATERIALIZING THE MIDDLE PASSAGE

encountered 'ring currencies', in the form of horseshoe-shaped arm- and leg-bands with flared ends, which were used as a means of exchange. They gave these objects the name 'manillas'—a term derived, perhaps, from the Spanish word for bracelet (*manella*) or the Portuguese for hand-ring.[177] The Portuguese did not manufacture copper themselves, but they quickly began to source manilla-shaped ingots from producers in Flanders and elsewhere, always imitating the forms encountered in West Africa. A contract made with the Fugger company in Antwerp in 1548 (a surviving example of many such triennial contracts let by royal agents in Flanders) provides details on the supply of 6,750 quintals of brass rings for the commerce of São Jorge da Mina. These items were required to 'correspond to the accustomed weight which was: the Manillas of Mina, 160 in each 100 arrates [the Portuguese pound] just about, smooth and with well-filed heads which are called tacoais; and those of Guinea of 190 or 200 manillas in each arrates'. The manillas destined for the trade at Elmina weighed around 10½ oz and were slightly heavier than those required for 'Guinea' (presumably, the Bight of Benin), at around 8 oz.[178] The commercial salvage company Arqueonautas recovered 238 manillas from a sixteenth-century wreck in Getaria Bay, northern Spain—most likely a Flemish vessel chartered by Portugal to ship its cargo to São Jorge da Mina.[179] Almost seven hundred manillas have been found on the Elmina wreck site (Figure 7.14).[180] Some were concreted in the circular shape of the casks in which they had been stored for travel.[181] The Elmina wreck manillas are very similar to those from Getaria Bay, despite their later date.

The rise of the Bristol brass trade in the seventeenth century meant that production of manillas for the British slave trade was largely a domestic affair. The Cheadle family's White Rocks Copper works in Swansea boasted a dedicated 'Manilla House' before 1744, and the Cheadle Brass Wire Company built another in 1790.[182] In the eighteenth century, Birmingham specialized in manilla production, and most patterns and weights of manilla were made there. One particular form, crescent-shaped and flared ended, was known specifically as the Birmingham manilla. These weighed about 90 grams, though some weighed as much as 300 grams.

As noted earlier, sheet brass was particularly important to the British trade. By the eighteenth century very large quantities of hollow 'battery-wares', made by hammering brass sheets into the required shape, were arriving on the Gold Coast. Some were repurposed to create ritual vessels known as *forowa*. These were long regarded as a nineteenth century phenomenon, but several fragments from burial contexts at Elmina suggest they were being produced by the mid-eighteenth century.[183] *Forowa* were made from separate pieces of sheet metal, carefully joined with copper rivets.[184] They were then stamped or punched with Akan motifs. The numerous examples now in British museums were collected during the nineteenth and twentieth centuries, but some, resembling the squat, flat-lidded, mid-eighteenth-century example from Elmina, may be considerably earlier in date than was once thought.[185]

Sheet brass was also repurposed to facilitate the gold trade, with Akan goldsmiths cutting the sheet brass and forming it into spoons, gold-dust boxes, sieves, scoops, and scale pans. Another essential component of the Akan goldsmith's trade was the gold weight, cast from brass using the *cire perdue* (lost-wax) method (see Figures 3.1 and 6.6). Both gold-dust boxes and weights—several million of the latter, perhaps—were made on the Gold Coast between the fifteenth and nineteenth centuries, principally using repurposed, imported brass.[186] Very few have been recovered from securely dated archaeological contexts, but Garrard has argued, largely on stylistic grounds, for a phased typology in which early geometric weights (1400–1700) are supplemented by more naturalistic, figurative examples (1700–1900). Nine weights were excavated from nineteenth-century archaeological contexts at Elmina. Two of these are early types; the remainder appear to belong to Garrard's late period.[187]

Conclusion: Curated Lives

I began this chapter with Marshall Sahlins, and it also seems fitting to conclude it with him. Writing about Pacific indigenes, Sahlins once famously suggested that '[t]he first commercial impulse of the people is not to become just like us, but more like themselves. They turn foreign goods to the service of domestic ideas, to the objectification of their own relations and notions of the good life.'[188] As the archaeologist Ann Stahl noted, picking up on this statement in her account of the lives of Banda villagers at Makala Kataa in West Central Ghana, there were times in those lives when Sahlins's point may have been more applicable than at others, but, in the eighteenth century at least, exogenous trade goods tended to be used in familiar ways. Even so, as Stahl's careful analysis shows, demand for European goods gradually increased inland, bringing subtle changes in local practice.[189] Makala Kataa was a long way from the sea, and thus from day-to-day engagement with the Atlantic slave trade, but, even at important coastal hubs like Elmina and Ouidah, as evidenced repeatedly above, the vast majority of the goods for which human lives were bartered either supplemented or expanded, rather than replaced, existing material repertoires. The commodities decanted from slave ships were contextualized within, and informed by, existing technological, political, and social practices.

As this chapter has indicated, while some categories of exogenous beads, brass, and cotton cloth were restricted to social elites, and played a notable part in their social and political lives, others were widely embedded in non-elite bodily adornment strategies. As a result, the possessions that sailors stripped from the bodies of captives boarding slave ships would routinely have included wrappers made from Indian or British cotton; strings of Murano seed beads; other beads fashioned from powdered Italian or Dutch glass; and recut, coiled sheet brass from Bristol, Birmingham, or Swansea, reworked into bracelets and anklets. There were also occasions, as explored further in Chapter 11, when a handful of beads, secreted on the person of an African captive, would make the Middle Passage to the Americas, adding a second Atlantic voyage to one those beads had made some years before in the hold of a different slaver. Such were the material ironies of slave shipping; and the complexities of the life courses of commodities bartered for African captives.

A further implication of this point, but one often overlooked, is that some of the West African artefacts now in British museums are undoubtedly made from repurposed trade goods once exchanged for children, women, and men. This is particularly likely for brasswares. Most of the thousands of gold weights now in English museums were acquired by military personnel who took part in wars with the Asante kingdom from 1824 to 1900.[190] The earliest examples will certainly have been made from brass imported into Africa by slavers. The same point applies to *forowas*. Manillas—commonly collected as examples of African currency—were, of course, cast as ingots specifically for the slave trade. Examples of all three artefact categories can readily be founded in British museums today. In recent years, some of the larger museums have been revisiting and 'unpacking' their ethnographic collections, writing new (online) chapters in the biographies of some of these artefacts, and bringing into the public domain the complex circumstances of the production, use, and acquisition of material things implicated in the slave trade.[191] The *Rethinking Pitt Rivers* initiative is a case in point here: among the online artefact biographies generated by the project is a case study on a manilla salvaged off the Cork coast in 1836, employed as a launch point for an exploration of the relationship between European brass and slaving.[192] The British Museum has similarly undertaken a detailed reanalysis of 2,000 of the 3,500 Akan gold weights in its collection, although its detailed online catalogue still says virtually nothing about the sources of the brass used to make them, or indeed about the slave trade.[193] Much remains to be done in writing the current, curatorial chapter in the life course of some of the objects discussed above. The Ijebu-Ode cloth in Figure 7.12, for example, rightly celebrated by historians of the African arts and textile manufacture, is described on the National Museum of Scotland's website, rather misleadingly, as 'trade cloth of handwoven cotton and silk, imported from Europe'. The object is noted as being associated with Captain William Corran, but Corran's links to the slave trade are not made explicit.[194] Finally, there is the pre-nineteenth-century African trade bead: so difficult to date, and so rarely to be found (or at least acknowledged) in European museum collections. Marcus Wood has recently argued that there is considerable scope for ethnographers and others to explore in greater depth the part that trade beads continue to play in the cultural lives of Africans and African-Americans.[195] Wood's argument—essentially about the need to uncover the continuing biographies of trade beads—should rightly extend to museum collections too. The beads collected by the naturalist and abolitionist Anders Sparrman, for example (see Figure 7.5), are nested in bigger stories: of European exploration, expansion, and biological imperialism, but also in the parliamentary inquiries into the British slave trade (at which Sparrman testified), and in the 'collecting' and display, for the eighteenth-century public, of Africa. That is a story surely worth the telling: and this point carries us forward to Chapter 8, where the other (that is, non-human) cargoes that made the Middle Passage on British ships are explored in greater detail.

Notes

1. Comprising, as Alpern (1995: 5) notes, 'many thousands of surviving bills of lading, cargo manifests, port records, logbooks, invoices, quittances, trading-post inventories, account books, shipping recommendations, and orders from African traders. English customs records of commerce with Africa during the eighteenth century, when the slave trade peaked, alone contain hundreds of thousands of facts'.

2. Gosden and Marshall (1999: 169). This paper introduced a pioneering volume of papers on the cultural biography of objects, comprising *World Archaeology*, 31/2. As this volume demonstrated, artefact biography is particularly valued by archaeologists working in colonial and precolonial contexts, and by museum curators charting the collection and curation histories of ethnographic artefacts. For the object biography approach in museum studies, see Gosden and Knowles (2020) and the object biographies created for the Rethinking Pitt Rivers project at https://web.prm.ox.ac.uk/rpr/index.php/objectbiographies.html (accessed 25 November 2022).

3. Some trade goods moved between three continents: textiles made in India and cowrie shells from the Indian Ocean were shipped to Europe before being loaded onto slave ships for re-export to Africa.

4. Kriger (2006). Kriger notes (2006: 6–7) that her approach might be considered both as material culture studies and as historical archaeology.

5. Hogendorn and Johnson (1986: 143). For a detailed regional analysis, see Metcalf's study (1987) of assortment trading on the Gold Coast in the 1770s.

6. For further discussion of the parameters of the cowrie zone see Hogendorn and Johnson (1986: 102–9).

7. Herbert (1984: 124).

8. Alpern (1995: 7); Inikori (2007) also demonstrates the gradual increase in the proportion of firearms imported on British ships.

9. The 'gegaw myth' was discussed and debunked by Curtin (1975: 312). A pioneering study for the British trade was Richardson (1979), based on an analysis of ninety-three cargo invoices for English vessels from the period 1758–1806.

10. Kriger (2009: 125); Riello (2013: 138).

11. Klein (2010: 89); Inikori (1992: 160–4).

12. Kriger (2009: 123). For British cotton production, see Riello (2013: 211–37), Inikori (1992: 164–5), Eltis and Engerman (2000: 133–4), and Alpern (1995: 8–10).

13. For African cloth entering European collections before 1800, the essential source is Bassani (2000). Kriger (2006) is very useful for the nineteenth century, bringing together numerous examples of textiles from Nigeria.

14. From the seventeenth century, as Hogendorn and Johnson (1986) have demonstrated, the British East Indian Company carried staggering quantities of cowries to England for re-export by slave ships, and, while both Barbot and Phillips refer to cowries in their narratives, only one the eighteenth-century ships employed as case studies in this book (*Unity*) was trading in the 'cowrie zone' centred on Ouidah; the others are therefore unlikely to have been carrying cowries.

15. Throughout this chapter, trade goods terminology is drawn from the glossary of trade terms in Tattersfield (1991: 389–94). For textiles, I have also relied on the glossary in Riello and Parthasarathi (2011: 409–20) and Alpern (1995: 6–10).

16. 'Husband' in the sense of master, rather than spouse.

17. For a detailed discussion of the trade in voyage (or bar) iron, and its reception in West Africa, see Evans and Rydén (2018).

18. Martin and Spurrell (1962: 70).

19. Richardson (1979: table 12.2).

250 MATERIALIZING THE MIDDLE PASSAGE

20. Richardson (1976, 1996).
21. **HCSP 67: 53–68.**
22. Metcalf (1987).
23. Goods leaving Liverpool for Africa in the year 1770 were also quantified by Enfield (1774: 84–5). Enfield's lengthy list includes many varieties of textile, including 27,286 yards of British linen, 4,130 yards of square-printed cotton, and 500 pieces of calico, along with 134½ tons of wrought brass.
24. Law (1997–2006: pt 2, p. 179).
25. Evans (2010: 31–41).
26. Berg and Berg (2001: 324); Evans (2010: 35).
27. Kidd and Kidd (2012: 40).
28. Sprague (1985) provides a very detailed discussion of glass bead manufacture.
29. The beads are discussed in Karklins et al. (2015: 16–24).
30. Karklins et al. (2015: 20).
31. Bassani (2000: 195, no. 585).
32. Molà and Ajmar-Wollheim (2011: 13).
33. Gott (2014: 19).
34. Gott (2014: 13). The discussion of bead-making in Ghana presented in the present chapter draws extensively on Gott (2002, 2014).
35. Tattersfield (1991: 222).
36. Robinson (2016: 51). Robinson provides a detail account of the business partnership between Davenport and Thomas Earle. Guerrero (2010) also analyses the role of Liverpool in supplying Venetian beads for slave ships between 1750 and 1800.
37. Sprague (1985: 92).
38. Evans and Rydén (2018: 239).
39. Deacon: TSTD 20228, 20285 (*Henrietta Marie*), 21307, 21320, 21338; Starke: TSTD 21218, 21220, 20276, 21301, 21412.
40. Alongside a further fifty-eight slaving ventures between 1699 and 1712. None of these voyages was part-owned by Anthony Tourney, whose iron was carried by *Henrietta Marie*.
41. Moore and Malcom (2008: 27; citing TNA: T 70/349, fo. 72).
42. The only beads listed on the manifest are bugles—tubular beads. It is possible that the seed beads were left over from an early voyage by *Henrietta Marie*. They may also have been intended for 'recreational' use by the ship's captives. This point is explored in Chapter 10.
43. Moore and Malcom (2008: 29–30).
44. Urban (2017: 39); Price (2016: 161–2).
45. Hopwood (2009: 107).
46. Sprague (1985: 92).
47. Karklins (1991) provides an analysis of the beads and other finds from this site. In his view (1991: 40), the wreck was of Dutch origin.
48. In her detailed analysis of the beads, Hopwood (2009: 42) estimated the total number of beads present by breaking off a small section of one of the bead concretions, removing the beads from the sediment, and counting the number of beads contained within that section of concretion. The section weighed 35 grams and contained 605 beads; therefore, the bead count per gram was 17.3 beads. That number was then multiplied by the weight of each large concretion to find the total estimate of beads.
49. Hopwood (2009: 42–3).
50. Hopwood (2009: 64); though note that glass beads were also produced in Amsterdam during the seventeenth century: Karklins (1974).
51. Hopwood (2009: 65).

52. Gomes et al. (2015: 167). Glass trade beads have also been recovered from two English wrecks post-dating the slave trading era: *Douro*, lost in 1843 (NMR878697), and *Custos*, lost in 1856 (NMR 878729). Both wrecks lie off Scilly.
53. Riello (2016: 135).
54. The summary provided here draws extensively on Riello (2013: 41–8).
55. Riello (2013: 92).
56. Makepeace (1989).
57. Makepeace (1989: 241).
58. Thornton (1998: 49).
59. Kriger (2009: 123). Linen was also a regular component of textile-based cargoes. Much of it came from the Prussian province of Silesia. Steffen and Weber (2016) provide a discussion of the eighteenth-century linens produced in Silesia for the slave trade.
60. Riello (2013: 139, 148).
61. Raveux (2009: 292).
62. Inikori (1989: 352).
63. Inikori (1989: 352–3).
64. Inikori (1989: 355–8).
65. Riello (2013: 152).
66. These ships were *Terrible* (TSTD 77616), *Earl of Halifax* (TSTD 77617), *Lydia* (TSTD 90647), and *Favourite* (TSTD 90893).
67. Riello (2013: 203).
68. Kriger (2009: 123–4).
69. Kriger (2009: 123–4).
70. Kriger (2009: 123–4).
71. Adams (1822: 111). Romals (or ramauls) were small, thin squares of silk or cotton, usually decorated with painting or embroidery.
72. Evans (2010: 31).
73. Evans (2010: 39).
74. Evans (2010: 33–4). Thomas Coster part-owed five voyages in TSTD: 16831, 16835, 16879, 16925, and 16973.
75. Hamilton (1967: 107–10).
76. The definitive history of the Bristol trade is Day (1973).
77. The name of the Bristol Brass and Copper Company changed numerous times during the company's existence: see Dresser and Giles (1999: 98).
78. Particularly in Inikori (2002).
79. Richardson (1986: p. xxiii).
80. Day (1988: 30).
81. Day (1973: 167–8).
82. Cox (1990: 129).
83. Dresser and Giles (1999: 98).
84. Berg and Berg (2001: 144).
85. Day (1968).
86. Hamann (2007); for subsequent discussions, see Pietruszka (2011), Cook (2012, 2014), and Cook et al. (2016). Hamann's very thorough typological analysis was completed before the date of the wreck had been determined.
87. Moore (1989: 56).
88. Cook (2012: 187).
89. Cook (2012: 191).
90. Cook (2012: 185). De Marees mentions the import of badly cracked and repaired brasswares to Elmina in the seventeenth century: van Dantzig and Jones (1987: 55).

252 MATERIALIZING THE MIDDLE PASSAGE

91. Pietruszka (2011: 112).
92. While the Elmina wreck is a most important source of nested brass basins, it is not the only one: a nest of four heavily damaged copper basins was also recovered from Odyssey Marine site 35F, a possible RAC wreck in the English Channel: Cunningham and Kingsley (2011: 35; see Figure 4.9).
93. For a good summary of arguments concerning the impact of European commodities in West Africa, see Monroe (2014: 26–8).
94. Thornton (1998: 44–5).
95. Evans and Rydén (2018: 61). In Dahomey, there is now considerable evidence for extensive iron production, beginning long before the slave trade, but for a variety of reasons iron production appears to have ceased on the Abomey plateau by 1600, and (with textiles) iron became a primary import in the era of the slave trade: Monroe (2014: 39–41).
96. Kriger (2006: 36).
97. The account of the history of Elmina given here draws extensively on DeCorse (2001: 18–43).
98. DeCorse (2001: 35).
99. No reference appears to kingship here until 1732, at which point three 'kings' are noted: DeCorse (2001: 40).
100. The work at Elmina is set out in DeCorse (2001). Further glimpses into local use of trade goods have come from fieldwork at Ntwarkro and Daazikessi, the oldest settlement quarters at Dixcove: see Biveridge (2018: 218).
101. Stahl (2001: 184–5).
102. Eltis and Richardson (2010: 90, table 5). The premier embarkation point was Luanda in Angola.
103. See Kelly (2001, 2004, 2009, 2010); and Norman (2009, 2010, 2014).
104. The documentary synthesis is provided by Law (2004): a detailed social history of Ouidah centred on 1727–1892, but also covering the period before the conquest of the Hueda kingdom by Dahomey in 1727. The work of the Abomey Plateau Archaeology project is summarized in Monroe (2014). For the Benin–Denmark initiative, see Merkyte and Randsborg (2009) and Randsborg and Merkyte (2009).
105. Kelly (2009: 63) provides a good summary of these points, noting also that the lodges occupied by European traders were built for them by the Hueda.
106. Huedan ritualized gifting is discussed by Norman (2010).
107. Mitchell (2005: 191).
108. Norman (2009: 190).
109. Norman (2009).
110. Law (2004: 123).
111. This influential argument was first put forward in Polanyi and Rotstein (1966).
112. Law (2004: 147–8). A small group of graves from Abomey City, discussed by Merkyte and Randsborg (2009), might appear to support Law's contention, in that they contain significant quantities of imported beads; but these graves were located in the Dahomean capital, where greater access to such goods is to be expected (and had also been opened/plundered prior to archaeological examination). Merkyte and Randsborg discuss additional graves from Kana and its environs, and the quantity of European beads in these instances is notably lower.
113. Monroe (2014: 45).
114. Kelly (2009: 166–8).
115. Wood (2016: 251). Wood provides a fascinating account of the use of trade beads, principally of nineteenth century or later date, in contemporary Brazil. But his suggestion that the place of trade beads in African perceptions and cultures has been 'overlooked' or 'trivialized' (Wood 2016: 249) does not do justice to the enormous body of scholarship on trade beads and their reception and repurposing within West Africa, on which the present chapter has been fortunate to draw.
116. For discussion of the likely origin of the beads at Igbo-Ukwu, and the possible routes by which they arrived at the site, see Insoll and Shaw (1997).

117. Hair et al. (1992: ii. 494). This passage first appears in the 1732 English edition of Barbot's text. Rassade were small coloured glass beads.
118. Ogundiran (2002: 432–3). For a more recent survey of local glass bead production in Nigeria and elsewhere, see Koleini et al. (2019).
119. In the 1970s, Frank Willett (1971: 22) suggested that glass-bead-making in Ife-Ife consisted of reworking imported glass and glass beads by drilling or melting them in crucibles, with the imports probably coming from both Europe and the Islamic world. For more recent evidence for primary production at Ife-Ife, see Babalola (2017) and Babalola et al. (2017).
120. Ogundiran (2002: 434); Law (2011: 7).
121. Law (2011: 8).
122. Jones (1995: 179–80); Gott (2014: 12). Quispels and madrigettes are small, transparent glass beads.
123. DeCorse (2001: 136, 145).
124. As Gott (2014: 17) notes (drawing on Hair et al. 1992: ii, 389, n. 36), this is the earliest European account of coastal bead manufacture in Ghana. Earlier authors such as De Marees had stated that Venetian beads were broken and polished before being resold. But Barbot's use of the term 'recast' is highly significant, because it appears to refer to the development of new mould-form techniques for producing powdered glass beads.
125. Gott (2014: 17). A single powdered glass bead has also been found on the *Queen Anne's Revenge* wreck site: Urban (2017: 39).
126. Gott (2014: 16).
127. DeCorse (2001: 137). DeCorse uncovered several examples of these fired beads, which were made from chips of mostly white and blue or blue–green glass, but he also found examples with yellow and brick-red glass fragments too, many of which were ground after cooling: DeCorse (1989: 48).
128. DeCorse (1989: 48), discussing abraders discovered at Elmina.
129. Jones (1995: 53, n. 8).
130. Calvocoressi (1977: 130).
131. Calvocoressi (1977: 132).
132. Biveridge (2020: 202).
133. Kelly (2001: 91; 2004: 229).
134. Law (2004: 33, 43–4). The factory at Savi was destroyed in two episodes of fire in 1684. The purchase of slaves was always negotiated at Savi, however, and by 1716 an English lodge was being maintained there, in addition to the factory at Ouidah.
135. There are several references to broken beads in the correspondence sent by the factors at Ouidah and Offra (Allada): see, e.g., Law (1997–2006: pt 2, nos 478, 487). It is possible that broken beads were being imported for reworking; but it is equally likely, given the contexts in which these references occur, that the small quantities of broken beads noted by the Ouidah factors had been damaged in transit or storage and were proving difficult to offload.
136. Norman (2009: 190).
137. Blier (2004); Rarey (2018: 29).
138. Barbot similarly noted white 'fetishes' made of wood or earth: Hair et al. (1992: ii. 638).
139. Norman (2009: 201).
140. Norman (2009: 211).
141. Norman (2009: 212–13; 2014: 11).
142. Riello (2013: 90).
143. DeCorse (2001: 14).
144. See Kriger (2006: 37).
145. Eltis (1991: 108).
146. Kriger (2009: 124–5).

254 MATERIALIZING THE MIDDLE PASSAGE

147. Picton (1996: 341).
148. Kriger (2006: 26–9).
149. Kriger (2009: 102).
150. For a synthesis of these fifteenth-century references, see Kriger (2006: 99–102).
151. Law (1997–2006: pt 1, pp. 447, 450; pt 2, nos 22, 812).
152. Kriger (2009: 112).
153. Kriger (2006: 36).
154. Barley (2000: 108); Kriger (2009: 124); Kraamer (in press).
155. Kelly (2004: 227).
156. Kriger (2006: 19).
157. Kriger (2006: 140–4) principally using the correspondence transcribed in Law (1997–2006).
158. Kriger (2006: 38–9).
159. Kriger (2006: 46).
160. For these details, see Bassani (2000: 185, no. 568).
161. John Corran's Ouidah voyages are TSTD 83274, 80341, 80519.
162. Clarkson (1808: i. 14–16).
163. Clarkson (1808: i. 303).
164. See **HCSP 72: 314 and 320** for Falconbridge's acquisition of African cotton cloth on the Windward coast and at Bonny. Some of this was 'dyed with a very beautiful and permanent blue'.
165. Clarkson (1808: i. 237). Kraamer (in press) has researched the cloth from Clarkson's chest in considerable detail and sets it in the context of the abolition movement. I am most grateful to Malika Kraamer for sharing this work with me in advance of its publication.
166. For a summary of findings from this ongoing research, see Coleman et al. (2022).
167. Clarkson (1808: i. 252).
168. Similarly, the chest also contained 'knives and daggers made by them from our bar-iron' (Clarkson 1808: ii. 16).
169. Herbert (1984: 277–82).
170. Herbert (1984: 116–17) on the dating controversy here—like most scholars today, Herbert accepts the radiocarbon dates indicating early production.
171. Herbert (1984: 88–9).
172. Herbert (1984: 126).
173. Herbert (1984: 126–7); Garrard (1979: 38).
174. Van Dantzig and Jones (1987: 51–2).
175. DeCorse (2001: 109).
176. Barley (2000: 97).
177. This information is taken from the object biography created by Eric Edwards for a nineteenth-century manilla in the Pitt Rivers Museum: https://web.prm.ox.ac.uk/rpr/index.php/objectbiographies/78-manilla.html (accessed 2 September 2022).
178. Herbert (1984: 127–8).
179. Cook (2012: 108).
180. Pietruszka (2011: 100).
181. Hamann (2007: 66).
182. Herbert (1984: 150).
183. DeCorse (2001: 133). The earliest *forowa* found at Elmina was associated with the mid-eighteenth-century burial of an adult male. Other, better-preserved, examples were excavated from late-eighteenth- and nineteenth-century contexts.
184. Garrard (1979: 44).
185. See, e.g., British Museum (BM) Af1947,13.36.a.
186. Garrard (1980: 2) estimates that three million such weights may have been produced.

187. DeCorse (2001: 128–30).
188. Sahlins (1993: 17).
189. Stahl (2001: 182–5).
190. This was certainly the case with most of the 3,500 gold weights in the British Museum collection; see https://webarchive.nationalarchives.gov.uk/20190801111218/https://www.britishmuseum.org/research/online_research_catalogues/agw/african_gold-weights.aspx (accessed 26 November 2022).
191. Byrne et al. (2011) provide an excellent overview of the process of 'unpacking' museum collections. For case studies relating specifically to West African objects in museum collections, see Finden's brief discussion (2013) of the Akan drum in the founding collection of the British Museum (discussed in Chapter 10); Basu (2011) on artefacts from Sierra Leone in the global museum-scape, and Poulter (2011) on nineteenth-century African 'souvenir' art in the Manchester Museums collection.
192. https://web.prm.ox.ac.uk/rpr/index.php/objectbiographies/78-manilla.html (accessed 2 September 2022).
193. https://webarchive.nationalarchives.gov.uk/ukgwa/20190801111218/https://www.britishmuseum.org/research/online_research_catalogues/agw/african_gold-weights.aspx (accessed 2 September 2022).
194. https://www.nms.ac.uk/explore-our-collections/collection-search-results/trade-cloth/332729 (accessed 2 September 2022). It is, however, clear from Bassani (2000: 184) that curator William Hart undertook research on Captain William Corran on the Museum's behalf some years ago, and uncovered his links to the slave trade.
195. Wood (2016).

8

Other Cargoes

Shipping Home the Productions of Africa

On 25 August 1694, after eight months in African waters, Thomas Phillips's *Hannibal* turned towards the open sea at São Tomé, carrying 684 captives purchased with some of the trade goods that were the subject of Chapter 7. *Hannibal* was a crowded ship, but human beings were not its only cargo. Safely stowed in the captain's cabin was a leopard skin, presented to Phillips by King Andreo at Cape Mount (*Hannibal* 1693–4: 193) and worth, as he cheerfully noted, '3 or 4 *l.* in England'. Caged on the quarterdeck was a living big cat: Phillips considered it to be a tiger with spots, but it was almost certainly a cheetah. The animal was a gift from an English trader at Cape Corse (Accra). Also caged on the deck were two civets and several monkeys, baboons, and parrots purchased from a Dutch slaver 'for a piece of eight each' (*Hannibal* 1693–4: 213). Phillips had also taken on board five hundred parakeets at São Tomé (*Hannibal* 1693–4: 233). Many of his crew probably also acquired things in Africa, making small 'ventures' (private trades) for everything from scrap gold to seashells. In short, *Hannibal* was carrying both Africans and what the abolitionist Thomas Clarkson would later come to call the 'productions of Africa'.[1]

The captives whose Middle Passage will be detailed in Chapters 9–11 would end their journey in the Caribbean, but supplementary cargoes, ranging from gold and pepper to parakeets and ivory, remained on board and were shipped home to Liverpool, London, and Bristol. The metropolitan consumption of slave-grown commodities such as sugar and tobacco has been widely documented,[2] but, as this chapter will demonstrate, Britons also routinely consumed West African produce. The affective properties of some of these things, notably gold and ivory, were far greater than others, but together they had a lasting impact on consumer practices, foodways, and other facets of daily life in Britain, particularly among the middle and upper social strata. In short, the slave ship played an important part in the circum-Atlantic movement of Africa's things, as well as of its people.

It was explained in Chapter 2 that, when European ships first arrived in West Africa in the 1400s, they were in search of gold, not slaves. The later seventeenth-century ships encountered in this book, including the RAC vessel *Hannibal* (1693–4) and the private trader *Daniel and Henry* (1700) were still trading extensively for gold, some of which was later used elsewhere in purchasing slaves.[3]

Materializing the Middle Passage: A Historical Archaeology of British Slave Shipping, 1680–1807. Jane Webster, Oxford University Press. © Jane Webster 2023. DOI: 10.1093/oso/9780199214594.003.0008

Indeed, RAC ships normally carried two types of trading cargo: one used to barter for captives, the other intended for the purchase of commodities such as gold and/or ivory.[4] As the eighteenth century progressed, the gold trade declined significantly, but elephant tusks (or 'teeth') and melegueta pepper remained important, highly profitable, components in the return cargoes of slave ships of all nations.[5] The independent merchants who dominated the British slave trade from the early 1700s routinely maximized the returns from their voyages by importing African products, helping to feed the demand at home for melegueta pepper (the 'grain' that gave its name to the Grain Coast), ivory, hardwoods, dyewoods, and resins, which were used in a variety of ways by British consumers. When the Dolben Act was passed in 1788, restricting the number of captives a vessel could carry in relation to its tonnage, slave traders began to take even greater interest in these alternate—and of course non-restricted—African goods. Palm oil began to feature prominently in return cargoes from *c*.1750, with imports tripling in value between the 1750s and 1790s, and nearly doubling again between the 1790s and the 1800s. In 1790, the quantity of palm oil imported into Britain was 2,299 cwt; by the 1830s, well over 200,000 cwt was being imported annually.[6]

These official return cargoes are only one part of the story told in this chapter, however. British sailors from all social classes also engaged in private ventures in Africa, carrying home gold in dust or scrap form, and a host of artefacts, either for their own or for others' use. Some mariners brought back botanical specimens or ethnographic objects at the behest of collectors, certain of which were subsequently gifted to museums. Many more sailors carried home a pocketful of scrap gold to sell on for personal gain. The activities of sailors who contributed to the development of botanical collections, wills and inventories made at sea, and the biographies of artefacts bequeathed to museums by former slave ship sailors are all important sources of information here. Together, they provide new insights into the ways in which sailors, and the collectors whose activities they supported, remembered and refashioned West Africa for home consumption.

The final section of this chapter focuses on the wooden chest in which the abolitionist Thomas Clarkson housed his own collection of the 'productions of Africa'. Assembled in 1786–7, the chest and its contents were of great personal significance to Clarkson: the box is positioned at his feet in the portrait painted by Alfred Chalon (Figure 8.1). Clarkson's remarkable showcase is also particularly important to the present chapter. First, it was specifically created to materialize eighteenth-century British engagement with the *other* cargoes of the slave ship, and (though this is rarely acknowledged) it contains a significant number of mundane pre-nineteenth century African artefacts: something of a rarity in British museum collections. Second, as this chapter will show, the chest and the men who contributed objects to it were also deeply embedded in the parliamentary slave trade inquiries of 1788–92. In this sense, Clarkson's chest is an object that materializes both the nascent abolition movement and its strategies.

Figure 8.1 A. E. Chalon's portrait of Thomas Clarkson (c.1790), seated beside his box of African 'productions and manufactures'. Wilberforce House, Hull.

Sixteenth- and Seventeenth-Century 'Ventures' in Gold

Many slave ship sailors undertook private 'ventures' on their own behalf, carrying out to Africa a stock of manufactured goods and exchanging them on the coast for items to be sold in the West Indies, or in England, for personal profit. Sailors' wills can provide evidence concerning African goods acquired through private ventures. Captains and surgeons—many of whom had quite substantial estates to dispose of—tended to plan ahead, making a will in advance of a first voyage to Africa. Ordinary sailors had far fewer possessions, but those who sickened at sea frequently dictated wills, naming the beneficiaries who were to receive their personal effects and any wages owed them. Ninety-three wills made by the first British sailors to travel to Guinea (between 1553 and 1565) have been studied intensively by Hair and Alsop.[7] While these sailors were trading for gold and ivory rather than slaves, their testaments provide a fascinating glimpse into the material world and shipboard economy of the Tudor seamen who first ventured to Africa. In terms of the interests of the present chapter, these early wills reveal that goods acquired in Africa were being shipped home by individual sailors who were engaged in personal trading ventures. Thus, Justin Goodwin (*John the Baptist* 1565) bequeathed 'one oliphant's tothe wayinge ffortie pounds' and 'twoo oliphantes teethe wayinge threescore pounds, and six peases of gold' to the master of his ship.[8] Several men on *Primrose* (1553) bequeathed gold and 'Beny clothe' (cloth acquired on the Benin River). Gold objects also appear in the wills, with several men bequeathing rings that must have been acquired in Guinea.[9]

Among the many thousands of wills proven by the Prerogative Court of Canterbury between 1680 and 1807 are hundreds written or dictated by sailors in the course of slaving voyages, a handful of which (discussed in more detail in Chapter 9) were made on ships discussed repeatedly in this book. Many maritime wills were nuncupative, dictated by sailors on their deathbeds, and unfortunately these men rarely went into real detail concerning specific possessions. Frequently, an ordinary seaman simply left 'all that I own and is due to me' to a messmate or to kin in England. Even so, it is clear that some mariners left Africa with private caches of gold. Among these was Alexander Mackcersie, a sailor on the RAC's *Dragon* at Ouidah in 1685, who left his brother George 'a marke of gold'.[10]

John Barbot was particularly interested in African gold-working, carrying home numerous examples of Akan origin that were then illustrated in his writings on West Africa.[11] It is interesting to note in this context that more than 350 fragments of worked Akan gold have been recovered from the wreck of *Whydah*, the London-built slave ship that, as discussed in Chapter 4, was captured by the pirate Samuel Bellamy in 1717.[12] Some of these pieces are very similar to those illustrated by Barbot, but most of the gold fragments from *Whydah* are chopped, flattened, and folded, and the few pieces that are intact show signs of wear. It is likely that these items were acquired as scrap metal, either as part of the official return cargo, or as a private venture of a member of the crew. Two clipped or chopped fragments of gold and a clasp were also recovered from the *Queen Anne's Revenge* wreck site.[13] Subsequent analysis of the sediment removed from the ocean floor during excavation has yielded a further 14,329 gold grains, weighing 20.8 grams.[14]

Walter Prideaux, supercargo on *Daniel and Henry* (1700), and an inveterate list maker, compiled detailed inventories of the personal possessions of two sailors who died at sea in 1700 (**Daniel** 1700: 164). John Fort, the ship's gunner, died on 27 June 1700 on the African coast. His son Nicholas took custody of his possessions, which included personal 'goods of adventure' in the form of cloth brought out from England to be traded in Africa, and the gold (valued in ackeys) that Fort had received in exchange for some of this cloth. This little store of gold would ordinarily have found its way home to England, and, having been sold on to a goldsmith, it would have been amalgamated with other small 'ventures', melted down in a crucible and cast into bar form. Unadulterated gold was extremely pure, but

260   MATERIALIZING THE MIDDLE PASSAGE

African traders frequently 'cheated' by mixing gold dust with brass or rock dust. Fort seems to have fallen foul of this practice: some of his store was deemed by Prideaux to be 'bad or false' gold, and the remainder only 'indifferent good'. Gold valuing two ackeys was deducted from the total of 56½ ackeys and used to bury Fort on shore.[15] John Chapman, chief mate on *Daniel and Henry*, died en route to Jamaica on 9 October 1700. As a senior member of the crew, he was freighted to transport a substantial personal venture, again mainly comprising cloth, and to ship two privilege slaves to the Caribbean at the RAC's expense. Chapman's slaves, a man and a girl, had been branded with the initials J:C. He had also purchased nineteen small elephant ivory tusks in Africa, some marked J.C. and others marked J.C.A. and J.C.P.[16]

Gold dust was the currency employed in most transactions along the Gold Coast and the eastern sector of the Ivory Coast, and, as noted in Chapter 7, the paraphernalia required for those transactions was extensive. Necessary items included scales, sieves, scoops, spoons, gold-dust boxes, and brass gold weights (*abrammuo*) cast using the lost-wax technique. The earliest gold weights were influenced by Islamic art and tended towards geometric abstraction, but during the seventeenth century they became increasingly figurative, referencing in miniature both the natural and the material worlds of the Akan. While there is no suggestion that gold weights—even those depicting European things—were produced specifically for a 'tourist' market, large numbers of them can be found in the African collections of many British museums today. As noted in Chapter 7, most of the examples in British museum collections were acquired in the nineteenth century; but it is surely likely that, long before this, some of these light, inexpensive, and easily portable objects (most are only a few centimetres high) found their way home in the pockets and sea chests of mariners engaged in the slave trade.[17] Sadly, evidence in support of this suggestion is lacking: I am not aware of a single gold weight that can be shown with certainty to have arrived in Britain before 1800.[18] But perhaps this is simply because such humble artefacts did not grace the cabinets of curiosity of early elite collectors, and their routes into museum collections are therefore often poorly documented.

Africa in the British Home

Some West African commodities were an everyday sight in elite and middle-income British homes. Chief among these was elephant ivory, which, as Stahl has emphasized in her study of the circulation of African ivory in Georgian and Victorian England, was 'bound up in the social actions through which raced, classed, and gendered bodies were produced' in the long eighteenth century.[19] Ivory had long been valued as a luxury raw material, but during the era of the slave trade it was imported in huge quantities and put to a host of usages. In the first quarter of the eighteenth century alone, the RAC imported almost 639,000 lb of ivory to England.[20] Ivory was easy to work and polish and, being difficult to fracture, was ideal for making fine-toothed combs for the hair. Some of these combs were decorative, and some functional: the lice comb was a much-needed commodity in an era in which hair was rarely washed. In the seventeenth and eighteenth centuries, ivory was also used for knife handles, toys, gaming pieces, billiard balls, grooming implements, fans, knitting and sewing equipment, hand mirrors, and various components of musical instruments. It was also demanded for scientific instruments, because it was easy to clean, and high-contrast notation and numbering could be engraved or inked on its white surface.[21] Ivory was also used to make dentures.[22] The lengthy *chaîne opératoire* by which the raw material moved from ship to shore and was transformed into artefacts can be glimpsed via the periodic auctions through which the RAC sold on tusks of varying sizes, and in a 1777 receipt indicating payment to one Sarah Walker for the cleaning of ivory tusks that had arrived in Liverpool on William Davenport's slaver *Badger*.[23]

Like ivory, melegueta (*Afromomum melegueta*) had been known to Europeans long before the slave trade began. The peppery spice was obtained by grinding the seed of the plant, and from the Middle Ages was prized in Britain both for its pungent taste and as a flavouring and supposed strengthening agent for beer and gin.[24] It was also used in veterinary medicine: Bartlet's *Pharmacopaeia Hippiatrica* is one of many eighteenth-century works for the farrier/veterinarian to contain recipes employing melegueta. Bartlet recommends for fatigued horses a cordial powder made from crushed aniseed, bay berries, grains of paradise (yet another popular name for melegueta) nutmeg, cloves, and ginger.[25] Women suffering 'obstructions of the menses', deemed to be one of many causes of 'hysteria', could subject themselves twice daily to two spoonsful of a globally sourced decoction whose ingredients included melegueta, the root of common sweet flag (*calamus aramaticus*), bay berries, mace, galangal, penny royal, water, and wine.[26]

A significant proportion of the imports from West Africa were employed not in dosing horses and hysterics but in furniture production. Resources in this group include several varieties of hardwood and numerous resins that formed the base for varnishes used on wooden furniture and paintings. Copal, a very hard resin found in Mesoamerica and both East and West Africa, was turned into varnish by melting it into drying oil that could be thinned with turpentine.[27] The best-known copal varnish, *Vernis Martin*, could be made at home, notwithstanding some very unpleasant fumes and an ever-present danger of combustion, using a widely available recipe.[28] Copal varnish was particularly favoured for 'japanning'—the production of finishes that mimicked the high-gloss oriental lacquer found on Japanese furniture.[29] Ebony, ivory, and tortoiseshell were all used in marquetry (veneering). Beeswax was employed as a polish for timber furniture, as well as in making candles. Among the many material complexities engineered by the slave trade is this one: West African trading partners demanding that slave ships bring out to them English-made furniture (as discussed in Chapter 6) may well have dined at 'English' tables finished with varnishes of African origin.

262 MATERIALIZING THE MIDDLE PASSAGE

Collecting Africa

Global collecting became a particularly fashionable pursuit among the Georgian elite, but a market for curiosities from Africa had flourished in Europe from the earliest years of the slave trade. In 1456, Alvise da Cadamosto presented Henry the Navigator with an ivory tusk and an elephant foot, collected on the coast of Senegal—the first of many such exotica to be sent home to Portugal.[30] During the seventeenth and eighteenth centuries Africa was never 'collected' to the extent that was true of the Pacific or the East, but, while the vast majority of the African artefacts to be found in European museum collections today were acquired in the nineteenth century and later, a steady trickle of objects did find their way into Europe long before this. Most fell into three principal categories: items valued primarily for their material (goldwork, for example); ethnographic items; and 'souvenir' items produced specifically for European customers.[31] As a rule, most of these artefacts were also easily portable. Items entering Europe from the Gold Coast, for example, included weapons, textiles, musical instruments, ornaments, stools, and perhaps also gold weights.[32]

Carved ivory salt cellars, spoons, and other items, first discussed in Chapter 6, were among the most sought-after items arriving in Europe from Africa in the sixteenth and seventeenth centuries.[33] These 'Afro-Portuguese' objects, commissioned from local artisans by Portuguese traders, were the first African-made artefacts to be produced solely for Atlantic export: for this reason they are sometimes referred to as an early example of what is now known as 'airport art'.[34] Many ivories found their way into the cabinets of curiosities of the European Renaissance aristocracy, and from these into the great private collections that formed the nuclei of major public museums throughout Europe. British collectors certainly showed an early interest in Afro-Portuguese pieces. In 1625, the naturalist John Tradescant the elder, one of the first men in England to establish a cabinet of curiosities (known as The Ark), wrote to the 'Marchants of the Ginne Company and the Gouldcost Mr Humfrie Slainy Captain Crispe & Mr Clobery & Mr John Wood Cape marchant' requesting, among a lengthy and rather eclectic list of *desiderata*, 'instruments of their long ivory long fluts'.[35] The 'Captain Crispe' addressed in Tradescant's letter is probably Sir Nicholas Crisp (1598–1666), who, in 1628, as discussed in Chapter 2, became the controlling stockholder in the *Company of Adventurers to Guinea* (the forerunner of the RAC) and who, in the earliest written references naming him, was described as 'Captain Crispe'.[36] It seems very likely, therefore, that Tradescant's African instruments were imported on ships belonging to the *Company of Adventurers*. Charles I, one of the greatest collectors of the seventeenth century, similarly owned two Sapi oliphants (side-blown horns), unfortunately now lost.[37] Hans Sloane, whose collection helped to create the British Museum, had acquired another.[38]

While ivory salt cellars and spoons were particularly sought after by elite collectors in the opening decades of the slave trade, other objects were imported too. From the outset, plant-fibre mats and baskets—objects that were at once botanical specimens (ecofacts) and ethnographic curios (artefacts)—excited European interest. The records of the *Casa de Guiné* in Lisbon (the customs office where goods imported on ships from overseas were recorded) were almost entirely destroyed in the Lisbon earthquake of 1755, but one book survived, for 1504/5. Analysis of these records reveals a steady trickle of African artefacts arriving on ships returning from Elmina, among which were wooden spoons, and a range of baskets, small sacks, and mats, all made from plant fibres.[39] Similar objects interested later traders too. John Barbot acquired numerous mats on his West African travels, specifying that they were of various colours and 'very handsome'. He remarked of these mats: 'You may have seen one laid out in a small apartment in my house'—a reminder that for Europeans, as for Africans, such items could serve a purpose at once functional and decorative.[40]

Exotic Animals: The Live Animal Trade

For the earliest explorers and slavers such as Cadamosto, coastal West Africa was a store of wonders: around every corner, something new to see and describe. By the eighteenth century, that sense of wonder had been tarnished by familiarity; not only had West Africa been visited and described many times over, but the shipping of slaves had become so intensive that little time was left simply to marvel. Sandwiched between the sixteenth-century seekers of the exotic and the eighteenth-century big business-men, however, were the slavers of the late seventeenth century. For traders such as the Barbot family and Thomas Phillips, Africa was still able to excite an almost childlike curiosity—and to foster an acquisitive habit. John Barbot was one of many French slave traders who transported small birds from Africa and the Caribbean on his ships.[41] He drew attention in his writing to the availability of grey and green parrots on the Bissago islands (Guinea); monkeys and parakeets at Principe and on the Gold Coast, and blue parrots and monkeys at Calabar.[42] Barbot also acquired a monkey in Boutroe, which, he suggested, would fetch 20 louis d'or (480 livres) in Paris. The animal later took a case containing Barbot's silver handled knife, fork, and spoon, and tossed it overboard.[43]

As note at the start of this chapter, the quarterdeck of Thomas Phillips's *Hannibal* was crammed with exotic animals: it was practically a floating zoo. And this on a vessel in which space was clearly at a premium. The transport of live animals entailed other inconveniences: Phillip's captive 'tiger' was housed in a wooden cage and had to be fed on 'guts of fowls, and other garbage, for he would eat nothing but flesh' (**Hannibal 1693–4: 213**).[44] During the Middle Passage the animal broke out of its cage and mauled one of the female captives. A stronger cage was built, but, on the journey home to England from the Caribbean, Phillips' cabin boy lost his hand in a second mauling incident (**Hannibal 1693–4: 238**).

Where did the animals and birds carried on slave ships end up? Some will have gone to aristocratic menageries and aviaries, and others will have been put on show in travelling animal spectacles.[45] Noting that parrots were to be had 'for three or four knives a-piece; and a monkey for half a piece, and sometimes for less' at Cabinda,

James Barbot Jnr remarked (***Don Carlos*** 1700: 512) that baboons and 'orang-utans' were sometimes shipped to England from Africa to be employed as exotic spectacles. John Casseneuve (first mate on *Don Carlos*) had seen an 'orang-utan' in London, 'publickly show'd behind the Royal Exchange' (**James Barbot Jnr, *Don Carlos* 1700: 512**). If one had the money and inclination, parrots and other exotic birds could be purchased with ease from numerous establishments in London by the mid-eighteenth century: the influential naturalist and bird illustrator George Edwards bought specimens variously from Bartholomew Fair, a shop called the Parrot and Cage, and a public house on the Strand, whose landlord traded in exotic species.[46]

The carriage of exotic quadrupeds and birds continued even on the business-like slave ships of the later eighteenth century.[47] Robert Barker (***Thetis*** 1754–5: 38) reported that mate (and later captain) Robert Wabshutt's extensive private venture on *Thetis* included not only 700 lb of ivory but 'a large quantity of parrots'. Captains who refused to carry ventilators, giving lack of space as their reason, could apparently still find room to transport cages full of birds. The parliamentary inquiry data reveal that parrots and parakeets continued to be carried on slave ships, probably as private trading ventures of their captains, in the 1780s. Thomas Trotter noted in 1790 (**HCSP 73: 88**) that, on a former voyage, Clement Noble, captain of *Brooks*, had transported twelve parakeets to the West Indies, all of which died on the Middle Passage.[48] In 1801, the slaver *Bolton*, returning to Liverpool from Demerara (Guyana), was attacked by a French privateer and plundered of a cargo that included a 'tiger' and a large collection of birds and monkeys.[49] In the dying days of the British trade, Hugh Crow carried home several monkeys, presented to him by the governor of São Tomé (***Kitty's*** 1807–8: 155–6). Documentary sources like these have long been cited in support of the suggestion that African green monkeys (*Cercopithecus aethiops*), a common sight on the islands of Barbados, St Kitts, and Nevis today, first arrived in the Caribbean as the pets of slave ship sailors.[50] Genetic evidence from faeces has conclusively demonstrated the African origin of the modern-day Caribbean monkey population, making this scenario very likely.[51]

Collecting Nature: The Slave Ship and the Naturalists

In her discussion of the collecting activities of sailors who travelled to the Pacific on Captain Cook ships between 1768 and 1779, Beth Fowkes Tobin notes that '[s]hip's crews, from officers down to common seamen, knew all about the natural history business, and hoped to profit from whatever they could lay their hands on, trade for, and transport back home'.[52] Her analysis brings to the fore two important general points concerning the relationship between long-distance voyages and the highly fashionable interest in global natural history among the eighteenth-century British upper classes. First, whether they were seeking exotica from the South Seas, Caribbean, or West Africa, collectors relied, in part at least, upon sailors to collect them. Second, collectors depended entirely on ships to transport home their specimens. Cook's first voyage in 1768 was a collaborative venture between the Admiralty and the Royal Society, underscoring the point that science, collecting, and maritime exploration went hand-in-hand in the eighteenth century. Historians have long shown an interest in the flora, fauna, and artefacts brought into England on Cook's ships, because many of these specimens entered, and indeed inspired, some of the earliest museum collections in Britain; but a growing body of scholarship is now focusing on the part played by slave ships in the collection and transportation of natural specimens from another part of the world: the African coast.

The apothecary and naturalist James Petiver (c.1665–1718) provides an excellent illustration of the routes by which an eighteenth-century British naturalist was able to obtain specimens from distant West Africa. Central to Petiver's endeavour was an assiduously cultivated network of international contacts. Like many collectors, Petiver was careful to acknowledge his benefactors in print whenever the occasion arose: as James Delbourgo puts it, the acknowledgement of suppliers in this way helped a collector to 'advertise his status as a global specimen broker in the Republic of Letters'.[53] Petiver's vast network of contacts has been carefully detailed by Kathleen Murphy, who has identified 106 individuals in the Atlantic world (including British North America, the Caribbean, West Africa, and Spanish America) who participated in Petiver's collecting activities between 1690 and 1718.[54] Twenty-seven of these people were captains or surgeons on ships, and fifteen of them had made slaving voyages. A further ten individuals were involved in the slave trade in other ways—principally as employees of the South Sea Company (Table 8.1).

The natural curiosities that mariners presented to Petiver were usually specimens found on or close to the shore. As a result, shells, butterflies, and other insects predominated among the apothecary's West African collections. Slave ship surgeon Richard Planer, for example, sent Petiver a yellow butterfly from Mesurado (Liberia), a 'Pompom' lizard from 'Guinea', an insect from 'the *Guinea* Coast', and a finely toothed moss from Mount Serrado, as well as a black butterfly and 'very *curious Insects*' from the coast of Cartagena. Meanwhile, ship surgeon James Skeen provided a butterfly and African grasses from Cape Three Points on the Gold Coast, a butterfly from Ouidah in the Bight of Benin, a shell from Jamaica, and 'three or four Books of *Plants*, with ... *Shells* and *Insects*' from Ouidah and Cape Three Points.[55] Slave ships also played an important part in transporting Petiver's specimens and delivering his correspondence. George Jesson not only collected a large number of butterflies off the coast of Buenos Aires for Petiver, but, as captain of the South Sea Company's *William and Sarah*, also delivered letters and collecting supplies to the naturalist's correspondents in Jamaica before delivering slaves to Buenos Aires in 1716.[56] After delivering slaves to Portobelo for the South Sea Company, Captain Edward Noll Coward of the *John Gally* took charge of the three-toed sloth sent to Petiver by John Burnet, the company's surgeon in Portobelo.[57]

Petiver's collection eventually passed to the renowned physician and scholar Hans Sloane, and it is likely that some of the forty-eight ethnographic objects of African origin owned by Sloane derive ultimately from Petiver's network of correspondents.[58]

266 MATERIALIZING THE MIDDLE PASSAGE

Table 8.1 Individuals with links to the slave trade who collected botanical samples on behalf of James Petiver, or transported letters and materials for him

Last name	First name	Occupation	TSTD	Further details
Barcklay	Robert	Ship surgeon	15235	1710 voyage on *New Providence*
Bartar	Edward	Slaving agent at Cape Coast		Collected matice-weed at Cape Coast
Bond	William	Captain	?21307 and 15,115	Collected specimens near Cape Coast. Possibly captained *Cecelia* (1700) and *Companion/Defiance* (1701)
Bruce	Michael	Ship surgeon		Contributed insects from the coast of Guinea
Burnet	John	Ship surgeon; factory surgeon at Portobelo	76318	On *Wiltshire* voyage (1714) collected a shell and five kinds of fish while in Africa
Child	John	Captain	9725	1695 voyage on RAC-owned *Kendall*; delivered letters to Smyth for Petiver
Cooke	?	Surgeon		Surgeon to South Sea Company at Panama
Coombs	Charles	Ship surgeon		Collected plants from Calabar
Coward	Edward Noll	Captain	75696	1718 voyage on South Sea Company-owned *John Gally*; Burnet sent home specimens to Petiver on this ship
Daniels	?	Ship surgeon	7922	1697 voyage on RAC-owned *Prince George*; delivered letter from Petiver to Bartar in West Africa
Dover	Thomas	Physician and chief agent		Chief agent to South Sea Company at Buenos Aires
Fraser [Frazer]	James	Ship surgeon	21162	1703 slaving voyage on *Mayflower*
Jesson	George	Captain	76521	In 1715 worked for South Sea Company commanding a packet boat; in 1718 slaving voyage on the RAC-owned *Sarah Gally*
Kirckwood	John	Ship surgeon		Collected insects at Old Calabar, and Angola, and plants from Cabenda
Mabbot	William	Captain	75656	Plants collected at Ouidah?
Mason	?	Ship surgeon		Contributed specimens from Angola
Patton	David	Ship surgeon; supercargo	76479	1714 slaving voyage on South Sea Company-owned ship *Elizabeth*; by 1716 employed as surgeon at Vera Cruz
Planer	Richard	Ship surgeon		Collected plants and fungi at Mesurado
Skeen	James	Ship surgeon		Collected in West Africa
Smyth	John	Clergy		Clergy to RAC at Cape Coast; later in Jamaica
Toller	William	Surgeon		Surgeon at Buenos Aires
Tunnell	James	Captain	9702	1693 voyage on RAC-owned *Kendall*; delivered letters to Bartar for Petiver
Walker	William	Captain		Specimens from South Carolina and Guinea
Watt	William	Ship surgeon		Collected in West Africa
Wingfield	George	Ship surgeon		Collected specimens at Mesurado

Sources: collated from Murphy (2013, 2020), with additional data supplied by Kathleen Murphy (pers. comm.), and my own use of TSTD data.

A fibre bag in Sloane's collection is documented as having been 'given by Mr Burnett': this is undoubtedly the John Burnet noted in Table 8.1.[59] Following his slave ship experience, Burnet was employed by the South Sea Company at Cartagena, and provided Sloane with natural curiosities from South America too.[60] Sloane did not visit Africa, and like Petiver relied on contacts with links to the region in order to obtain specimens. One of these men was Job ben Solomon (Ayuba Suleiman Diallo), a Fulbe Muslim from Senegal who in 1731 was captured while trading on the Gambia River, and sold into slavery. Following his capture, Diallo made the Middle Passage to Maryland on the London-registered slaver *Arabella*.[61] He was taken to Britain in 1733 and later (as a free man) employed by the Royal African Company in Gambia.[62] Hans Sloane was acquainted with Diallo, having employed him to translate his collection of Arabic texts, and Sloane's collection includes two artefacts gifted by him: the bowl of a tobacco pipe and a poisoned arrow from the Gambia River.[63]

Sloane acquired one African object—a drum—that foregrounds an important point: artefacts, like people, were in constant motion in the maritime Atlantic economy. As a result, some botanical specimens and ethnographic objects originating in Africa were actually collected in the *Americas*, having arrived there aboard slaving vessels.[64] Thus Sloane's drum, discussed in greater detail in Chapter 11, was collected in Virginia, but had probably arrived there from the Gold Coast, on board a slave ship.

In 1695, Sloane's former servant James Salter founded Don Saltero's Coffee House in Chelsea. Sloane donated a number of curiosities to this very popular establishment. Salter died in 1728, but catalogues listing Don Saltero's many curiosities were advertised regularly for many years thereafter, and the donors were named and thanked therein. Among the individuals listed in the twenty-fifth edition of the catalogue, published in *c*.1756, are thirteen 'Captains', at least two of whom—Capt. Flower and Capt. Tublay—were involved in the London-based slave trade.[65] Henry Flower captained nine slaving voyages between 1724 and 1737, and James Tublay took *Prince Clause* to West Central Africa in 1749.[66] Perhaps it was one of these men who gifted to Salter's establishment the elephant's teeth, 'negro boys cap', and 'large worm that eats into the keel of ships in the West Indies' on show in the coffee house.

Plants, seeds, birds, and insects were still being transported to England on slave ships by, or at the behest of, naturalists in the late eighteenth century. The collector William Bullock, who was for some time based in Liverpool, acquired a number of African curiosities from sea captains, some of whom may well have been engaged in the slave trade. These items are inventoried in Bullock's *Companion* to his collection. Among the objects described there are an African amulet ('fetish') 'taken from the breast of a black man, engaged in battle, by Captain Clarke, of the ship *Roebuck*, of Liverpool' and a hammock, presented to the museum by Captain Roberts of Liverpool.[67] Two artefacts in the National Museum of Scotland were originally collected by William Corran, who had served as master of the Liverpool slaver *Port au Prince* in 1797.[68] These are the Ijebu cloth discussed in Chapter 7 (see Figure 7.12) and a cap, decorated with feathers and manillas, which had been presented to Corran by King Pepple.[69]

268   MATERIALIZING THE MIDDLE PASSAGE

Another important late-eighteenth-century collector was Henry Smeathman. His important voyage memoir is one of the key sources employed in this book (see Table 3.2), and, before making his own slaving voyage home from Africa, Smeathman regularly returned samples to England via slave ships. Among the specimens transported by this means were many botanical samples and two (dead) Colobus monkeys gifted to Sir Ashton Lever for his museum, the Holophusikon, which opened in Leicester Square in 1775.[70] As Deirdre Coleman has noted, Smeathman's wealthy patrons were uneasy concerning the Middle Passage of the secondary cargo they had commissioned from him. Dru Drury fretted about his insects 'sweating their way across the middle passage', and in a letter to Linnaeus, John Fothergill—a man whose Quaker sympathies made him far more wary of the slave trade than most collectors—complained that not a single seed or plant had reached him from Smeathman in three years.[71] Smeathman certainly collected most of the West African insects illustrated in Drury's *Natural History*, and gifted termites (as well as monkeys) to Ashton Lever. He also sent more than six hundred West African plant samples to Joseph Banks, one of which (the Passion Flower, *Smeathmannia*) was later named in his honour.[72]

Smeathman's funds did not last long in Sierra Leone, but in 1773 Drury persuaded Margaret Cavendish Bentinck, the dowager Duchess of Portland, to support the insect collector's venture, promising that 'the things he [Smeathman] will send over in less than a twelve month will be more than sufficient to discharge' the £100 she provided.[73] The duchess was one of the wealthiest women in Britain and a well-established collector of fine art. The 'things' she sought from Smeathman were not antiquities, however, but African seashells and insects. Over a twenty-year period before her death in 1785 the duchess built up the largest collection of shells in Britain, using, like Petiver and Sloane before her, the services of an extensive network of specialist collectors, dealers, travellers, and sailors to obtain specimens from around the world.[74] She bought, or was gifted, samples collected by sea captains, and acquired others from London-based dealers such as George Humphrey, who in turn acquired much of his stock from sailing men.[75] Most of the duchess's shells came from the Caribbean and the South Seas, but, as her patronage of Smeathman suggests, she also coveted examples from the Guinea coast. The Duchess of Portland's shells were displayed in a very similar manner to the cabinet shown in Figure 8.2, with playing cards being adapted for use as specimen trays. It is no accident that Thomas Clarkson's chest of the 'productions of Africa', discussed at the end of this chapter, similarly employed compartmentalized trays to show off the items he had collected (see Figure 7.13): Clarkson's assemblage spoke directly, and intentionally, to the collecting practices of the elite. The Duchess of Portland's West African shells, along with numerous insects from Sierra Leone, were eventually sold in assorted lots in the spectacular auction through which the Portland Museum collection was dispersed in 1786.[76]

Seashells were of great interest to naturalists but were also sought for their use in craftwork. The creation of 'shellwork' (that is, ornamental pieces incorporating sea-shells) was a very fashionable pastime in the eighteenth century, particularly among wealthy women. One of the most celebrated practitioners of this art was Mary Delany,

Figure 8.2 Box of shells c.1800. Mahogany and pine box with pine trays holding cardboard and glass boxes containing specimens. Victoria & Albert Museum, W.5:1 to 4-2010.

a close friend and confidant of the Duchess of Portland, who employed shells to decorate ornate picture frames and a chandelier at Delville, her Dublin home. Like the Duchess of Portland, she sourced some of her shells via sea captains—rejoicing in one of her letters that she had been introduced in Bath to 'a seafaring captain called Edwards who has promised me a box of shells from Guinea, Jamaica etc.'[77] Delany also used shells to cover the walls of the room at Delville that served as a chapel—a variant on the extremely fashionable shell grotto or cave created in, or below, the grounds of some of the most important and influential houses in Britain.[78] The earliest known example is the indoor shell room at Woburn Abbey, Bedfordshire, designed by Isaac de Caus in 1626.[79] A celebrated early eighteenth-century grotto, created before 1721, survives today in the former grounds of Carshalton House in the borough of Sutton, London. This example dates from the early 1720s and was commissioned by Sir John Fellowes, a director of the South Sea Company. Mary Delany and the Duchess of Portland together created a grotto in the grounds of the latter's Buckinghamshire home, Bulstrode House (Figure 8.3).[80] Grotto-making was a time-consuming and expensive project: the Duchess of Richmond's version at Goodwood House, Chichester, took seven years to complete between c.1738 and 1748.[81] Some families hired in specialists like John Castles, who had designed a grotto for Sir Robert Walpole's house in Chelsea, and whose shop and showground were based in Grotto Passage in Marylebone.

Figure 8.3 The Grotto at Bulstrode Park, as depicted by Samuel Hieronymus Grimm in 1781. British Library: King George III Topographical Collection, 11.1d.

Many grottoes were built or commissioned by families whose fortunes were tied up with the slave trade. The Bristol merchant Thomas Goldney III is a good example here. Following the death of his industrialist father in 1737, Goldney diversified into banking and metals manufacturing. Among the outputs from his copper, brass, and iron works were pig and bar iron for the West African trade and cast-iron components for plantation machinery. In 1739, Goldney made plans to construct a new landscape garden at his Bristol home, Goldney Hall. The crowning glory of this scheme was to be an underground shell grotto in the Rococo style. This edifice took many years to create and was not completed until 1764. Dan Hicks, who has conducted an archaeological exploration of Goldney's garden, provides a fascinating account of this eclectic, hybrid, underground space. Here were juxtaposed the products, colours, and textures of the new industries (the grotto roof, for example, was coated in black copper slag, and the floor was lined with Coalbrook tiles), with statues of classical deities, and thousands of shells of African and Caribbean origin. As Hicks persuasively argues, Goldney's eclectic style was a local manifestation of the hybrid creative impulse that characterized elite house and garden landscapes throughout the eighteenth-century mercantile Atlantic world. From Bristol to the Caribbean and from London to North America, the Georgian elite were creating spaces in which 'the complexities of wider Atlantic worlds were imagined, enacted and worked out'.[82] These artificial grottoes, mimicking yet controlling the natural world and accessible to, and readable by, a select few, were constructed on two of the three continents bound together in the Atlantic trading

OTHER CARGOES 271

nexus, and decorated using seashells whose collection was facilitated by global mercantile trade. On all of these levels, grottoes perfectly embodied the complex place-making of the Atlantic Georgian elite.

Made at Sea: Sailors' Shell Craft

Many of the British sailors undertaking lengthy voyages devoted a portion of their leisure time to craft activities. Some forms of maritime craftwork—the creation of knot displays, for example—employed materials available on all sailing ships, and thus were not linked to specific voyage experiences. But other craft activities utilized materials such as baleen, elephant ivory, and seashells that spoke more directly to a sailor's personal voyage experience. One fascinating piece of evidence demonstrates that eighteenth-century slave ship sailors were producing shellwork artefacts which, while less refined than those produced by Mrs Delany and other wealthy English women, belonged to the same craft tradition. Nicholas (Nics.) Owen, an Irish trader resident in Sierra Leone in the mid-eighteenth century, maintained a diary, spasmodically, through the years 1746 to 1758/9.[83] From 1754 until his death in 1759, Owen was settled permanently on the Sherboro coast. Here he repeatedly met British ships' captains, and in January 1758 noted: 'I have been on board Capt. Engledo today, where I found him employ'd in making a curious piece of shellwork in his cabbin upon an old picture. Tomorrow I entend to imitate him as nigh as my abilities will alow, as we have great numbers of shells upon the beetch.'[84]

Owen had called upon William Engledue, experienced master of the Bristol slaver *Mercury*, who in May 1758 would arrive safely in St Kitts with captives purchased in part from Owen himself.[85] The diarist set to work and completed his own shellwork piece just a day later, noting:

> I have just finish'd my shell work and I think it's just shuteable for my dwelling. It's of a round form with a looking glass in the middle; I have wrought it into divers figures with various kinds of shell and moss taken from the bark of old trees and shrubs, which I have laid on with turpentine and bees wax boiled well together into a hard substance.[86]

By the nineteenth century the 'sailor's valentine' had become a popular maritime souvenir. It comprised an ensemble of seashells mounted onto a wooden backboard (usually octagonal in shape), covered by a glass panel and enclosed in a mahogany or cedar frame. Sailors' valentines like the one shown in Figure 8.4 were reputedly first produced in Barbados in *c*.1830, and were generally made for sailors, not by them. Even so, they provide some clues as to the objects crafted almost a century earlier by Captain Engledue and Nics. Owen.[87] We cannot know how many sailors practised a similar craft, but it is worth noting here that shells were found on the wreck on the

Figure 8.4 Mid-nineteenth-century double octagon shellwork sailor's valentine (shells and mahogany), made in the West Indies. Christie's.

Danish slaver *Fredensborg*, and the excavators concluded that sailors must have been transporting them home as souvenirs.[88] Perhaps these shells were intended for use in shellwork of the type discussed here, or would have been sold to either a private collector or a more genteel practitioner of the shellworker's art.

The Extraordinary Biography of Mungo Park's Cowrie Shells

The most extraordinary story concerning shells and slave ships is surely that of the cowries gifted to Sarah Sophia Banks (sister of Joseph Banks) by the Scottish explorer Mungo Park in 1797 (see Figure 8.5). In 1794, Park was hired by the African Association, at the prompting of Joseph Banks, to discover the course of the Niger River. In December 1795, he set out for the interior from the Gambia River, and in July 1796 he arrived at Ségou, capital of the Bambana Empire. Mansong Diara, the king, refused Park a personal interview but gave him five thousand cowrie shells with which to purchase provisions on his journey inland. A year later, after many adventures, Park arrived back at the coast having lost all of his possessions except the hat under which he stowed the notes from his journey. As Catherine Eagleton has noted, there must also have been 'four cowry [cowrie] shells under his hat, since on returning to London in December 1797 he gave those shells to Sarah Sophia Banks, who recorded their remarkable provenance'.[89] Park must have carried these cowries with him from Africa to Antigua on the American slaver *Charleston*, on which he began the first leg of his return journey to England. Since the ship had no surgeon, he took on the role himself.[90] From Antigua he then took passage to Falmouth on the packet *Chesterfield*.[91] But these shells were well travelled even before they left Africa. As noted in Chapter 7, cowrie shells were not native to West Africa: they were found in the Indian Ocean, and from the early 1500s were being shipped from the Maldives to

Figure 8.5 The four Bambara cowries gifted to Sarah Sophia Banks by Mungo Park in 1797. British Museum, SSB 155.4.

Portugal, where they were loaded on to slave ships bound out to the Bight of Benin, to be exchanged for captives.[92] From the seventeenth century the British East Indian Company carried staggering quantities of cowries to England for re-export by slave ships.[93] It is estimated that the Dutch and English together shipped more than ten billion cowries to West Africa from 1700 to 1799, with English ships carrying on average 50.1 tonnes of shells every year.[94] Park's cowries, in short, had travelled the world—and may well have made not one but two slaving voyages by the time they arrived in Falmouth.

Sarah Sophia Banks, like her better-known brother Joseph, was a member of the social elite and a 'global' collector. Joseph collected nature; Sarah collected coins, tokens, medals, prints, and books. Her coin collection, comprising more than nine thousand examples from around the world, was one of the most impressive in England. Following her death in 1818, Joseph Banks donated his sister's coins to the British Museum, which retained seven thousand examples and handed the rest to the newly founded museum of the Royal Mint.[95] Mungo Park, one of many explorers to benefit from the patronage of Joseph Banks, had acknowledged his debt in a particularly sensitive way, gifting his benefactor's much-loved sister with a handful of the 'shell money' he had personally received from an African ruler. At the same time, however, Park had used these shells to answer some of the key questions the African Association had asked him to address in his travels. As Eagleton explains:

> Mungo Park had not only been to Africa to find the course of the Niger River, but also to find out about trade, including the currencies used inland. The aim, ultimately, was to bring to Britain, and to the African Association, the necessary know-how that

274 MATERIALIZING THE MIDDLE PASSAGE

would allow them to trade inland in Africa. The notion of 'legitimate' trade as a potential replacement for the slave trade had been seen before...and it was also a powerful force in the change in public opinion in Britain that finally enabled Parliament to pass the bill outlawing the slave trade, on 25 March 1807. The collecting of these four cowry shells, therefore, can be seen...as an activity linked to these debates about the future nature of trade in West Africa, and the possibility of free trade with free Africans.[96]

At the centre of the debates Eagleton mentions, of course, was the abolitionist Thomas Clarkson, who in 1787 devised a means to showcase the 'legitimate' productions of Africa for his contemporaries. Artefacts from Clarkson's wooden chest have already been discussed at several points in this book, but the collection merits particular attention in the present chapter, both as an important source of African-made artefacts predating 1807, and for the light it sheds on the materialization of Africa itself during the 1788–92 parliamentary inquiry process.

Thomas Clarkson, Abolition and the 'Productions of Africa'

I wished the [privy] council to see more of my African productions and manufactures, that they might really know what Africa was capable of affording instead of the slave trade, and that they might make a proper estimation of the genius and talents of the natives.

(Clarkson 1808: ii. 13)

In advance of the initial parliamentary hearings into the slave trade in 1788, as outlined in Chapter 3, Thomas Clarkson toured the ports of England collecting witness testimonies about conditions on board slave ships, and collating statistics concerning crew mortality on long-haul voyages. He also acquired samples of African artefacts and natural resources that were carefully arranged in a customized timber box (see Figure 7.13). With its echoes of Renaissance cabinets of curiosity,[97] and, more pertinently, its strong resemblance to the compartmentalized cases that housed the specimen collections created by many professional and amateur naturalists in the eighteenth century (compare Figure 8.2 and Figure 7.13), this chest was a travelling showcase, hawked by the abolition movement's tenacious head salesman.[98]

Clarkson's chest was presented to the Wisbech and Fenland Museum in 1870 and is still curated there.[99] Some of the original contents are now missing, but Clarkson provided a detailed description in his 1808 *History* of the abolition of the slave trade:[100]

The first division of the box consisted of woods of about four inches square, all polished. Among these were mahogany of five different sorts, tulip-wood, satin-wood, cam-wood, bar-wood, fustic, black and yellow ebony, palm-tree, mangrove, calabash, and date. There were seven woods of which the native names were remembered: three of these, Tumiah, Samain, and Jimlaké, were of a yellow colour; Acajoú was of a beautiful deep crimson; Bork and Quellé were apparently fit for cabinet work; and Benten was the wood of which the natives made their canoes. Of the various other woods the names had been forgotten, nor were they known in England at all. One of them was of a fine purple; and from two others, upon which the Privy Council had caused experiments to be made, a strong yellow, a deep orange, and a flesh-colour were extracted. The second division included ivory and musk; four species of pepper, the long, the black, the Cayenne, and the Malaguetta: three species of gum; namely, Senegal, Copal, and rubber astringents; cinnamon, rice, tobacco, indigo, white and Nankin cotton, Guinea corn, and millet; three species of beans, of which two were used for food, and the other for dyeing orange; two species of tamarinds, one for food, and the other to give whiteness to the teeth; pulse, seeds, and fruits of various kinds, some of the latter of which Dr. Spaarman [sic] had pronounced, from a trial during his residence in Africa, to be peculiarly valuable as drugs.[101] The third division contained an African loom, and an African spindle with spun cotton round it; cloths of cotton of various kinds, made by the natives, some white, but others dyed by them of different colours, and others, in which they had interwoven European silk; cloths and bags made of grass, and fancifully coloured; ornaments made of the same materials; ropes made from a species of aloes, and others, remarkably strong, from grass and straw; fine string made from the fibres of the roots of trees; soap of two kinds, one of which was formed from an earthy substance; pipe-bowls made of clay, and of a brown red; one of these, which came from the village of Dakard,[102] was beautifully ornamented by black devices burnt in, and was besides highly glazed; another, brought from Galàm[103] was made of earth, which was richly impregnated with little particles of gold; trinkets made by the natives from their own gold; knives and daggers made by them from our bar-iron; and various other articles, such as bags, sandals, dagger-cases, quivers, grisgris, all made of leather of their own manufacture, and dyed of various colours, and ingeniously sewed together.[104]

Clarkson made a very careful effort to acquire samples of the principal imports from West Africa, which by the later eighteenth century comprised ivory, melegueta pepper, beeswax, palm oil, gums, resins, and timber: principally redwood, camwood, and ebony. Lesser imports included rice, almonds, and copper. It is estimated that, in the 1780s, the value of African imports into Britain—almost all of which came from West Africa—amounted to around £31,700,000.[105] All of this produce arrived, of course, by ship. Clarkson's samples of these various goods came from a variety of sources, but it is noticeable that many of his donors were directly involved in the 1788–9 parliamentary inquiry process. In his *History*, Clarkson first mentions obtaining specimens of African products from the master and mate of the London-based bilateral trading ship *Lively*— an encounter that appears to have sown in his mind the idea of developing a collection of similar samples.[106] The first reference to the chest itself is made in the context of Clarkson's visit to Bristol in July 1787, where he says one of his aims was to 'ascertain what were the natural productions of Africa and, if possible to obtain specimens of

276 MATERIALIZING THE MIDDLE PASSAGE

them with a view to forming a cabinet or collection'.[107] In Bristol, he obtained numerous samples from merchants whose ships traded on the African coast. One of these was Sydenham Teast, a Bristol shipbuilder and ivory trader, who provided Clarkson with gum copal and two kinds of wood. Teast subsequently appeared before the Privy Council Committee (**HCSP 69: 72**). A Mr Biggs furnished gum Senegal, yellow wood, two kinds of pepper, and some small pieces of dyed cloth, while Thomas Bonville provided samples of wood, rice, and additional cloth samples.[108] Further specimens were sourced from abolitionist allies who had travelled to Africa and would later testify before parliamentary committees. Among these men (as noted in the passage quoted above) was the naturalist Anders Sparrman, who also provided evidence to Parliament. Another likely source was the former Bristol slave ship surgeon Alexander Falconbridge, who (as his own parliamentary testimony states) had acquired numerous pieces of dyed cloth in West Africa.[109] As noted in Chapter 7, Falconbridge probably passed these on to Clarkson, whose chest contains blue-and-white cloth samples. In Liverpool, finally, the abolitionist was gifted a sample of pepper by Captain Robert Norris, who, much to Clarkson's indignation, would later testify in Parliament on behalf of the Liverpool pro-slavery lobby (see Table 3.6).[110]

Clarkson's fascination with the productions of Africa was undoubtedly stimulated by Parliament's interest in the same topic. In March 1788, shortly after the Privy Council inquiry had been ordered, the House of Commons requested detailed information from the customs houses in London, Liverpool, Bristol, Lancaster, and Poole concerning trade goods carried out to Africa from these ports between 1771 and 1788. At the same time, data were requested concerning African products entering England via the same ports (**HCSP 67: 53–68**). It is instructive that this information was being sought in the context of an inquiry centred on the *slave* trade. It was widely appreciated that alongside the lucrative bilateral (England–Africa–England) trade that brought West African produce directly into English ports, slave traders routinely maximized their returns by importing products from Africa alongside slave-grown sugar from the Caribbean. The full extent of the African produce trade and the part played in it by the country's major slaving ports was something the Privy Council Committee was evidently keen to quantify; but customs officers were not at this time asked to distinguish between vessels employed in shipping slaves and those returning directly to England from Africa, so the exact proportion of African produce being carried on slave ships remained very unclear in the final report.[111] But, as Clarkson and his contemporaries were well aware, slave ships were deeply embedded in the African produce trade. Sydenham Teast, a bilateral trader who (as above) was also the source of some of the items in Clarkson's chest, informed Parliament in his testimony (**HCSP 69: 73**) that '[a]bout half the quantity of ivory now imported, is imported in slave ships, but it could not be imported in any other way to profit, for there is no demand for the bulky articles, which must make up the cargo'.

The data compiled for Parliament were subsequently published in volume 67 of the Sessional Papers of the House of Commons—the volume of the slave trade inquiry proceedings that also contains the set of measurements upon which the Society for

Effecting the Abolition of the Slave Trade based its famous broadsheet of the Liverpool slaver *Brooks* (see Figure 5.14). It would appear, then, that the data collated for **HCSP 67** impacted upon the abolition movement in more ways than one, and actively shaped SEAST's early visual propaganda strategy. As I have suggested elsewhere, this was certainly the case in terms of the production of the famous *Brooks* placard.[112] This parliamentary data set and Clarkson's chest were equally closely entwined: in essence, the latter materialized the former.[113] In fact, the contents of divisions one and two of Clarkson's chest and those listed in *An Account of the Value and Amount of the Productions of Africa Imported into Great Britain from the Year 1771 to 1788* correlate extremely closely. The full range of African goods recorded in **HCSP 67** was enormous—there are over fifty separate categories recorded in the summary table for London, Liverpool, Bristol, Lancaster, and Poole collectively—but Clarkson's chest contains examples of virtually all of the most significant products recorded in these tables, in terms of both the quantities of each resource being imported and its financial value. These key products, as noted above, included ivory; Guinea grains/pepper; various forms of cordage; gum Seneca; gum Copal; palm oil; various species of redwood; camwood; ebony; rice; cotton wool, and cotton. The only significant products missing from the chest are at once the least exotic and the most likely to spill or melt: oil and beeswax.

The histories of the chest and of the parliamentary inquiry process are woven together in other ways. In May 1787, Clarkson took some of his African cloth samples to the dinner party at which William Wilberforce was persuaded to become the parliamentary figurehead for the abolition movement.[114] In February 1788, as the Privy Council inquiry was announced, Clarkson paid his first visit to William Pitt in an effort to persuade the Prime Minister to support the abolitionist cause. Clarkson took his 'African productions' with him, and Pitt, as Clarkson reported in the *History*, was

> astonished at the various woods and other productions of Africa, but most of all at the manufactures of the natives in cotton, leather, gold and iron, which were laid before him. These he handled and examined over and over again. Many sublime thoughts seemed to rush in upon him at once at the sight of these, some of which he expressed with observations becoming a great and dignified mind.[115]

In Clarkson's eyes, clearly, the chest played a material part in drawing Pitt to the abolitionist cause. Shortly thereafter its contents were shown to Pitt's cousin, William Grenville: in 1807, as Prime Minster, Grenville would champion the second reading of the Act to abolish the slave trade.

Clarkson's collection subsequently made two physical appearances in Parliament. The abolitionist testified before the Privy Council Committee shortly before the summer recess in 1788, noting at the time that he had acquired certain specimens in Liverpool and Bristol: indigo, rice, cotton, malegueta pepper, cayenne pepper, long pepper, black pepper, tulip wood, yellow wood, musk, gum Copal, gum Seneca, Gum rub. astringens, mahogany, and cotton cloth. The pepper, Clarkson told the

278 MATERIALIZING THE MIDDLE PASSAGE

Committee, came from Ouidah and the cotton from the River Gambia. His *History* records that, the Lords having consented, Clarkson presented 'several things for their inspection, out of my box'.[116] It is thus quite certain that Clarkson employed his specimens directly during this appearance: he seems to have offered the Committee an artefact handling class not at all unlike those favoured in teaching children about the transatlantic slave trade today. The report goes on to note that, '[a]t a subsequent attendance upon the Committee on the 24th January last, Mr Clarkson delivered in further specimens of African productions, viz. a specimen of cotton wool, the growth of Senegal'. Several of the specimens he produced were, 'by their Lordships order', sent on to leading manufacturers of the day for analysis and testing. The findings of these experiments are also reported in **HCSP 69: 74**. Here it is reported that the Senegalese cotton was tested by John Hilton, a Manchester cotton manufacturer. A sample of yellow dye wood was reported on by a representative from the Society for the Encouragement of Arts; and several specimens of potential cabinet wood were examined by the fashionable furniture makers Chippendale, Haig & Co.

In summary, the contents of Clarkson's chest, and the manner in which they were displayed, spoke directly to the long-established practice of acquiring and displaying natural curiosities and manufactured goods from far-flung corners of the world. The chest was carefully designed to furnish Parliament with a showcase (via divisions one and two) of Africa's bounty and (via the ethnographic artefacts presented in division three) of the ingenuity of its people. At the same time, the box gave visual expression to the mass of data on African produce that had been summarized for the House of Commons in the Customs Houses of London, Liverpool, Bristol, Lancaster, and Poole. The appeal of the 'legitimate' (non-human) cargoes championed by Clarkson was clearly already evident to merchants who were not directly involved in the slave shipping business. By 1805, no less than 30 per cent of the return cargoes of Liverpool slave ships would comprise items freighted for merchants and brokers who were based in the city but were not themselves members of these vessels' owning syndicates.[117] Following the abolition of the British trade in 1807, former slave ships would continue to make regular voyages to Africa to purchase 'legitimate' cargoes, particularly palm oil, which, while edible, was widely employed in candle-making, as a lubricant for machinery, and as an ingredient in soap.[118] Several of the most prominent slaving merchants of Liverpool turned their attentions to the palm oil trade after 1807, among them James Penny, who had testified in Parliament in 1788.[119] In assembling his 'cabinet', then, Clarkson was undoubtedly aware that he was nudging at a door ready to open.

While Africa would never exert the same fascination for elite eighteenth-century collectors as did the Pacific and Orient, the buoyant demand for ivory and pepper, and the steady trickle of objects arriving in Britain between 1680 and 1787, had helped to shape growing understandings of West Africa as a place with more to trade in than slaves. Clarkson's chest did not simply illustrate the productions of Africa: just as the present chapter has sought to do, it reminded his contemporaries of the extent to which African commodities were *already* part of their world.

Notes

1. Clarkson (1808: ii. 13).
2. See Walvin (2017) for excellent summary overviews concerning the domestic consumption of the sugar, tobacco, and other goods produced by the enslaved in the British colonies.
3. On the reuse of traded gold in the acquisition of captives on *Daniel and Henry*, see Tattersfield (1991: 123–40).
4. Eltis (1994: 242).
5. On the factors informing the decline of the gold trade, see Metcalf (1987: 380–1).
6. Lynn (1997: 12–13; see in particular table 1.1).
7. Hair and Alsop (1992); Alsop (2012); for wills of sea surgeons 1553–1660, see Alsop (1990).
8. Hair and Alsop (1992: 320), citing TNA: PROB 11/48, f. 162.
9. Alsop (2012: 99).
10. TNA: PROB 11/396; the voyage is TSTD 15038. Some sailors also carried silver coinage that had not been acquired in Africa. John Beale, mariner on the RAC ship *Providence*, made a will in 1674 on the middle passage from the Gold Coast to Barbados (TNA: PROB 11/343). He bequeathed 'sixtie pieces of eight to be equally divided between them' to his fellow sailors Robert Seaman (master) and Thomas Woodfine. Presumably Beale had acquired these silver reals (coins of Spanish origin but widely used across the Caribbean) in the course of his sailing career.
11. Hair et al. (1992: ii. 499, n. 9) discuss the various iterations (1679, 1688, and 1732) of Barbot's illustration of Akan goldwork. See Bassani (2000: 68, no. 261) for the 1769 drawing, and, for the 1732 version, Churchill and Churchill (1732: v, plate 22).
12. For the wreck, see Hamilton (2006). For the gold ornaments, see Clifford (1999: 206–7) and Bassani (2000: 220, no. 681).
13. Wilde-Ramsing and Ewen (2012: 127).
14. Price (2016: 162).
15. Tattersfield (1991: 115).
16. Tattersfield (1991: 164–5).
17. See Jones (1994: 352) for the suggestion that gold weights were among the portable objects imported into Britain from the Gold Coast before the nineteenth century.
18. No gold weights are included in Bassani's catalogue (2000) of African objects entering European collections before 1800.
19. Stahl (2015: 74).
20. As calculated by Feinberg and Johnson (1982: 445, table IV-A), the RAC imported 5705.34 cwt of ivory between 1699 and 1725.
21. Chaiklin (2010: 6).
22. Stahl (2015: 78).
23. Stahl (2015: 77), citing NML: D/DAV/10/12. *Badger* (TSTD 92536) traded for captives, and ivory, at Cameroons River.
24. While numerous commentators (including van Harten 1970: 209) speculate that a bill passed in the reign of George III to prevent the use of melegueta as an adulterant in beer will have led to a collapse in imports of the spice, this Act was not passed until 1809 and related specifically to Ireland (49 Geo. III c. 57).
25. Bartlet (1764: 223).
26. Bullman (1789: 34).
27. Kirby Talley (1997: 43).
28. This recipe is to be found in Anon. (1773).

280 MATERIALIZING THE MIDDLE PASSAGE

29. Ballardie (1998) reproduces numerous seventeenth- and eighteenth-century varnish recipes including copal.
30. Bassani (2000: 171): these passed from Henry to his sister Isobel and onwards to her son, Charles the Bold.
31. Bassani and McLeod (1985: 246); Jones (1994: 352).
32. Jones (1994: 352).
33. See Bassani (2000) and Bassani et al. (1988). Mark (2007) discusses the continued importation of ivories from Sierra Leone (as well as Benin) into the seventeenth century.
34. Barley (2000: 90).
35. MacGregor (1983: 20). The Tradescant collection eventually passed to Elias Ashmole and, through him, to the University of Oxford's Ashmolean Museum. The collection includes a West African ivory horn, which may have come to Tradescant as a result of this written appeal: Bassani (2000: 51, no. 203). There are also two ivory spoons, possibly of Sapi manufacture, in the Tradescant collection: Bassani (2000: 51–2, nos 204–5).
36. Porter (1968: 57).
37. Bassani (2000: 38, nos. 137–8).
38. Bassani (2000: 43, no. 158). Sloane also acquired two ivory horns from Calabar (Bassani 2000: 42, nos 156–7).
39. Summarized in Bassani (2000: 180–1).
40. Hair et al. (1992: i. 186). See also Bassani (2000: 69, no. 262).
41. Robbins (2002: 27): parrots, parakeets, finches, and also monkeys were regularly transported by French traders. The French naturalist Buffon described the importation of rose-ringed parakeets on slave ships returning to France from Senegal and Guinea: Buffon (1779: 152).
42. Hair: et al. (1992: ii. 319 (Bissago), 362, n. 40, 416 (Gold Coast), 477 (Principe), 694 (Calabar))
43. Hair et al. (1992: ii. 474, n. 10), citing an additional passage from Barbot's 1732 text (= Churchill and Churchill 1732: v. 212).
44. These proved difficult to keep alive: only a dozen made it to Barbados (*Hannibal* **1693–4: 233**).
45. For more on Georgian menageries and exotic pets, see Plumb (2015).
46. MacGregor (2014: 40).
47. A leopard destined for the Versailles menageries was transported from Mozambique to St Domingue by slave ship in 1787. It was then shipped to Lorient and transported by coach to Versailles: Robbins (2002: 58).
48. Noble boasted to Trotter and others that the sailor he deemed responsible for the death of his birds was lashed for twelve days to one of the topmastheads and forced to eat one of the dead parakeets each day (**HCSP 73: 87**).
49. Williams (1897: 384). This voyage is TSTD 80605.
50. Scholarly work on the origins of Caribbean green monkeys is summarized in Denham (1981).
51. Van del Kuyl and Dekker (1996).
52. Fowkes Tobin (2014: 149).
53. Delbourgo (2012: 735).
54. Murphy (2013: 643, n. 14). See Murphy (2020: 270–3) for further discussion of some of Petiver's contacts. I am very grateful to Kathleen Murphy for sharing with me her findings, both published and unpublished, on Petiver's slave-trading contacts. My discussion of Petiver and the summary provided in Table 8.1 has drawn extensively on her research.
55. Murphy (2013: 643).
56. Murphy (2013: 645).
57. Murphy (2013: 645–6).
58. Bassani (2000: 41).
59. Bassani (2000, 47, no. 182 = Sloane, *Miscellanies*, no. 876). For more information on Sloane's dealings with Burnet, see Delbourgo (2017: 236–8).

60. Delbourgo (2017: 236–7).
61. TSTD 75094.
62. For details of Diallo's life and relationship with Sloane, see Delbourgo (2017).
63. Bassani (2000: 48–9, nos 186, 196).
64. For a fifteen-month period during 1687–9, Sloane spent time in Jamaica as the physician to the newly appointed governor of the island, the Duke of Albemarle. During his stay he collected and shipped home over 800 botanical specimens. Among these was a sample of kola (*Cola nitida*) taken from a tree whose origins are particularly interesting. Sloane notes that, '[a]ltho' this tree was but seven Years old, rais'd from Seed, which was brought from *Guinea*, yet it was twenty Foot high . . . The Seed brought in a *Guinea* ship from that Country was here planted by Mr *Goffe*, in Colonel *Bourden's* plantation beyond *Guanaboa*' (Sloane 1707: ii. 60–1).
65. Don Saltero's Coffee-house (*c*.1756).
66. Flower's voyages were TSTD 75944, 76656, 77018, 25903, 76699, 76714, 76701, 76951–2. Tublay made a second voyage in 1765 (TSTD 77818).
67. Bullock (1810: 11); see also Bassani (2000: 33, no. 95; 35, no. 116). TSTD documents one Liverpool *Roebuck* (TSTD voyage ID 84108 for 1796), but none of the three named masters was called Clarke. Two Liverpool-based slave ship masters named Roberts can be found in TSTD. Both were active *c*.1800–7 (TSTD voyage ID 80414, 81117, 81330–2).
68. TSTD 83153.
69. Bassani (2000: 184, no. 568; 186, no. 572). 'Pepple' was the name adopted by one of the leading slaving dynasties at Bonny.
70. These are now in the Vienna Natural History Museum: the story of their rediscovery is recounted by Coleman (2013).
71. Coleman (2013: 124).
72. Smeathman correspondence with Fothergill, reproduced in Fothergill (1783: i. 191). The small group of West African shells in Joseph Banks's shell collection were almost certainly also provided by Smeathman: Wilkins (1955: 112–13).
73. Dru Drury, Letter Book 1761–83, Natural History Museum London; cited in Fowkes Tobin (2014: 73). Smeathman himself later recorded that the greater part of his shell collection was lost through a series of misfortunes: see the correspondence with Fothergill reproduced in Fothergill (1783: i. 192).
74. The story of the Duchess's collection, and its eventual dispersal in 1786, is told by Fowkes Tobin (2014).
75. In 1762, George Humphrey opened a shell warehouse in St Martin's Lane, Strand, selling shells, corals, fossils, and other natural curiosities: Fowkes Tobin (2014: 31–2).
76. Skinner and Co. 1786.
77. Fenneteaux (2009: 103), citing Delany's Correspondence, iii. 367, 1755 letter to Mrs Dewes.
78. Jackson (2001: 16).
79. Jackson (2001: 3).
80. Jackson (2001: 15).
81. Fenneteaux (2009: 96).
82. Hickes (2005: 385).
83. Owen's diary was published by Eveline Martin: see Owen (1930). Owen's use of dates (1930: 18–19) is perplexing, but entries were still being made by the author until at least the end of 1758.
84. Owen (1930: 91).
85. Mercury's voyage is TSTD 17423.
86. Owen (1930: 91).
87. Wertkin (2004: 550).
88. Svalesen (1995: 476).
89. Eagleton (2013: 32).

90. See Park (1799: 360–2) for the explorer's voyage on *Charleston*, which transported 120 captives from Goree to Antiqua, and was condemned as unseaworthy upon return to Charleston, South Carolina: TSTD 25406.
91. Park (1799: 362–3).
92. Hogendorn and Johnson (1986: 19, 30–6).
93. Hogendorn and Johnson (1986: 40–63).
94. Hogendorn and Johnson (1986: 58–61, table 5.1). Each tonne contained some three-quarters of a million shells (Walvin 2017: 42).
95. Eagleton (2013: 24).
96. Eagleton (2013: 33). Sarah Sophia Banks's collection also included a penny struck at the Soho mint in Birmingham for the Sierra Leone Company in 1792 (though dated 1791), presented to her by the Swedish botanist Adam Afzelius. Banks notes that he 'brought it from Sierra Leone' (Eagleton 2013: 30).
97. Wood (2007: 218). Wood (2007: 222) also notes that the chest makes metaphoric reference to the seachests used by British sailors.
98. The idea of Clarkson as travelling salesman is beautifully brought out in Wood (2007: 218–19). For a detailed discussion of Clarkson's chest in the context of the parliamentary inquiry process, see Webster (2017).
99. For a description of the contents as they stood at that time, see Devenish (1994: 84–9).
100. Clarkson (1808: ii. 14–16).
101. The Swedish naturalist Anders Sparrman collected the trade beads from Sierra Leone discussed in Chapter 7.
102. Presumably Dakar, Senegal.
103. Also in Senegal: the location of the French slave trading establishment Fort St Joseph.
104. The fourth 'division' contained a very different category of artefact, discussed in Chapter 10.
105. Eltis and Jennings (1988: 939).
106. Clarkson (1808: i. 237); see also Kraamer (in press).
107. Clarkson (1808: i. 295).
108. For Mr Biggs and Thomas Bonville, see Clarkson (1808: i. 303).
109. **HCSP 72: 314, 320.**
110. Clarkson (1808: i. 379). See also Clarkson's testimony concerning Norris in **HCSP 73: 67.** For Norris's parliamentary testimony, see Table 3.6.
111. See Inikori (2002: 240–1) for a discussion of the difficulties here.
112. See Webster (2009).
113. This is the argument advanced in more detail in Webster (2017).
114. Clarkson (1808: i. 252).
115. Clarkson (1808: i. 474).
116. Clarkson (1808: ii. 14).
117. Drake (1976: 94–5).
118. Drake (1978: 92): some seventeen of the twenty-two Liverpool ships engaged in the African trade in 1809 were former slave ships, trading mainly for palm oil.
119. See Table 3.6.

9

Technologies of the Body
on the Floating Pesthouse

The black body—the *raison d'être* of a slaving voyage—was one of the two most significant impediments to its success. The other was the white body. While at sea, captives and crews sweated, overheated, dehydrated, defecated, urinated, bled, sickened, and died.[1] What were the contemporary understandings and technologies employed to mitigate the physical frailties of these many bodies; to deal with the multitude of substances that flowed from them and, despite all, to keep the majority of those on board alive? These questions are the concern of the present chapter, which tracks the British slave ship and its medical regimes from the African coast to the Caribbean.

On any slave ship, staying alive presented a formidable challenge. Three geographically remote disease environments—northern European, Africa south of the Sahara, and the sub-tropical Americas—were embraced in every voyage.[2] As a result a toxic soup of global diseases including dysentery, diarrhoea, ophthalmia, malaria, smallpox, yellow fever, scurvy, measles, typhoid fever, hookworm, tapeworm, trypanosomiasis (sleeping sickness), yaws, syphilis, leprosy, and elephantiasis infected slaver decks.[3] Mortality rates were appalling. Over the course of the trade, an estimated 13.3 per cent of Africans transported on British ships died before disembarkation (see Table 1.1). And, as Thomas Clarkson calculated in 1788, and Stephen Behrendt in 1997, crew deaths on British ships stood at 18.4 per cent in the 1780s.[4] In short, as Richard Sheridan expressed it, slave ships were 'pesthouses in which epidemics raged beyond the capacity of the surgeons to effect a cure'.[5]

Although there was no legal requirement to do so until the Dolben Act of 1788, virtually all British slave ships carried surgeons, and most of these men had received some degree of medical training. As van Manen has noted, it is tempting to think of these sea surgeons as poorly qualified, inept men, whose 'medicines and treatments did the slaves more harm than good.'[6] Yet, as Figure 9.1 illustrates, there was a marked decline in mortality on British ships after 1750. The 'head money' paid to eighteenth-century surgeons (who commonly received one shilling for each captive delivered into port), no doubt played some part here: keeping captives healthy was in the self-interest of the ship's doctor.[7] As several scholars have argued, however, mortality decline after 1750 also appears to reflect improving understandings of disease prevention, and the ability of slave ship surgeons to harness that new knowledge.[8]

As Figure 9.1 indicates, the Dolben Act of 1788 might also be argued to have played some part in improving the life chances of captive cargoes: death rates dropped very

Materializing the Middle Passage: A Historical Archaeology of British Slave Shipping, 1680–1807. Jane Webster,
Oxford University Press. © Jane Webster 2023. DOI: 10.1093/oso/9780199214594.003.0009

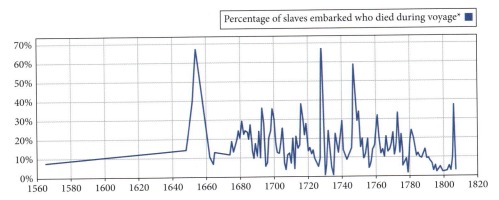

Figure 9.1 Mortality rates among captives on British vessels over time—imputed estimate. (TSTD data set, https://www.slavevoyages.org/voyages/Neg0nOcp (accessed 22 October 2022)).
Note: * = imputed

markedly after it was passed. As discussed in Chapter 5, the Act aimed to lessen overcrowding by limiting the number of captives a ship could carry to 200 per ton burthen; but, surprising though it might seem, the extent to which this change improved the life chances of captive Africans after 1788 is a much-debated issue.[9] What is clear, however, is that the Dolben Act obliged slave ships to carry surgeons, and that these men were required to pass a qualifying examination. Slave ship surgeons were also instructed to keep a log of deaths and their causes. Finally, the Act provided a further financial incentive by stipulating that, on vessels with less than two deaths per hundred captives, surgeons would receive a £50 bonus.

Difference Embodied: Race, Medicine, and the Black Body

Medical regimes on board slave ships reflected both contemporary discourses concerning the transmission of disease, and awareness within the merchant marine of the Royal Navy's approach to combatting sickness and preserving health. As explored in Chapter 3, sailors moved frequently between naval vessels and merchant ships, and some very influential naval surgeons (including Thomas Trotter) had spent time on slave ships.[10] Gilbert Blane's *Observations on the Diseases Incident to Seamen*, published by a leading naval reformer at the height of the slave trade in 1785, provides an excellent snapshot of naval 'best practice' and will be referred to several times below. But Blane, writing about British seamen, had nothing to say on perceived differences between the black body and the white, which also fundamentally informed medical regimes on slave ships. In the mid-eighteenth century, just as Britain emerged as the leading global transporter of African captives (as discussed in Chapter 2), a new conception of race began to appear in contemporary discourse. Until this point, understandings of human difference had been influenced by monogenism—an idea made popular through the writings of Buffon and other naturalists.[11] Monogenic theory was based on the biblical account of human origins, and hence on the belief that the entire human race was descended from Adam and Eve. It is fascinating to note in this context that the first African man and woman to be taken on board a slave ship were by common practice dubbed 'Adam' and 'Eve'. Thomas Smith, a Scottish sailor on board *Ann Galley* in 1762, noted that the first captive to be boarded was given the name Adam: the man would later go on to lead an attempted insurrection.[12] James Arnold, who had served as surgeon's mate on the *Alexander* in 1785, noted that 'it is usual on board the slave ships to give the appellation of Adam and Eve to the first man and woman that are brought on board' (**HCSP 69: 50**), and Samuel Gamble gave the name Adam to the first male slave to board his vessel (*Sandown* **1793–4: 64**). Monogenists held that observable differences, such as colour and susceptibility to certain diseases, and perceived differences (in intellect and physical endurance, for example) were the result of 'degenerative' environmental factors and, to varying degrees, cultural factors such as diet and custom. In this sense, the human body was malleable: it could be acted upon by the environment in which it found itself. Blackness was not thought to be entirely hereditary: the skin of white men moving to warmer climates would darken, and their descendants would no longer be white.[13]

In the later eighteenth century, monogenism began to give way to polygenism: the understanding that human differences can be explained only in terms of multiple sets of 'first parents'.[14] For polygenists, bodily differences were fixed rather than malleable, and were the result of ancestry rather than environmental stimuli. Complexion, for polygenists, was the most visible marker of a mass of inherent, and inherited, 'char-acteristics'—from hair texture and facial features to a supposedly stronger odour and a weak brain—which together were perceived to make up the 'African' constitution. Late-eighteenth-century polygenic theory has interesting antecedents in the work of individuals with a close knowledge of the slave trade, one of whom was the naval surgeon John Atkins. In 1721–2, Atkins made a voyage to the Guinea coast as part of a mission to protect merchant slavers from the predation of pirates.[15] He was one of the earliest British proponents of polygenic theory, stating in 1734 that, 'tho' a little heterodox, I am persuaded the black and white race have, *ab origine*, sprung from different-coloured first parents'.[16] This understanding directly informed the section of Atkins's popular handbook *The Navy-Surgeon* discussing yaws, sleeping sickness, and other diseases believed by the author to be unique to the African constitution.[17] As Saakwa-Mente expresses it: 'handbooks such as *The Navy-Surgeon*, because they circulated among a specialized audience of mobile medical professionals and were popular enough to have been reprinted in several editions, may have played a particu-lar role in the increasing circulation of the new racial ideas.'[18] By mid-century, certainly, it was common to see well-known naval surgeons, including James Lind, advocating the use of Africans (preferably from the Guinea coast) for hard labour on shore in the West Indies. Unlike British mariners, it was argued, men from Guinea were tolerant of the heat and seemingly immune to yellow fever.[19]

It was against this backdrop of changing ideas about the human body that Parliament began the first sustained investigation into conditions on slaving voyages,

286 MATERIALIZING THE MIDDLE PASSAGE

in 1788–92. In this context, Roxann Wheeler has argued that the slave trade debates were 'a catalyst that resulted in the honing of rationales about human difference, or the questioning of them'.[20] As Wheeler has shown, a complex symbiosis developed between emergent notions of racial difference and Parliament's 1788–92 deliberations, and the fact that the slave trade became the subject of sustained public interest in the very decade in which the contours of racial thought were beginning to be firmly mapped out in British society certainly had some important implications for the slave shipping business.[21] I will return to this point below, with particular reference to discourse and practice surrounding heat tolerance.

Preliminaries on the African Coast

Branding

Branding, involving the use of a hot iron to mark the skin for life, was introduced into the slave trade by the Portuguese.[22] Until the decline of the RAC (that is, until *c*.1720), British captives were usually branded before they were taken on board slave ships, in order to differentiate them from captives enslaved by the monopoly companies of other nations.[23] Branding has a long history as a form of punishment in European societies, but, as Keefer has noted, it has always had a stigmatic and negative association when applied to humans, and was reserved for those who were never envisioned as future members of society.[24] All of the Africans carried by Thomas Phillips on the RAC vessel *Hannibal* were branded 'in the breast, or shoulder, with a hot iron, having the letter of the ship's name on it' (*Hannibal* **1693–4: 218**). The naval surgeon John Atkins noted during his 1721 voyage to Guinea that company slaves were branded with the initials DY (for 'Duke of York'; the head of the RAC, and the future King James II).[25] British ships contracted by *asiento* to carrying slaves to Spanish colonies were required to brand them on entry to the Americas. At a large sale of Africans on 10 October 1717 in Santiago de Cuba, the British corvette *Neptune* placed on sale eighty-six African slaves described as 'pieces of the Indies'. All were branded with the *Real Asiento* brand, made on the right side of their breasts. The symbol reproduced a royal crown topped by a small cross.[26]

The early independent traders appear to have continued the practice of branding: in 1724–5, Thomas Hodgson, surgeon on *Katherine Galley* (owned by Humphry Mortice and captained by William Snelgrave), noted captive deaths in a ledger in which the 'marke of each slave' was also recorded. Captives who had passed between vessels owned by Mortice bore more than one brand mark: twenty-one captives on *Katherine Galley* were marked I.G., indicating that they had spent some time on *Italian Gally*, captained by John Dagge for Mortice.[27] Branding was not generally employed by the private syndicates that came to dominate the British trade in the later eighteenth century, but it did continue in other quarters. The French trader Theodore Canot noted that,

[t]wo days before embarkation, the head of every male and female is neatly shaved; and if the cargo belong to several owners each man's *brand* is impressed on the body of his respective negro. This operation is performed with pieces of silver wire, or small irons fashioned into the merchant's initials, heated just hot enough to blister without burning the skin. When the entire cargo is the venture of but one proprietor, the branding is always dispensed with.[28]

Most captives were (re)branded upon purchase in the Caribbean, and upon any change of ownership thereafter, so the mark of a branding iron was not uniquely a signifier of a saltwater crossing. But, for those who were branded on or before boarding slavers, some part of the ship that carried them into slavery was indelibly etched upon their bodies.

'A great slavery': The Preliminary Medical Examination of Captives

One of the most important duties of the slaver surgeon was to prevent infectious diseases such as smallpox and venereal disease from entering his ship. This necessitated vigilant inspection of each new captive before he or she was accepted on board. In his manual for Guinea surgeons, T. Aubrey cautioned in 1729:

I hold it absolutely necessary that you visit all the slaves, before you suffer them to be bought, because in this affair your own reputation, as well as the owner's interest lies at stake. Sometimes the men have gonorrhoeas, or ulcers in the rectum, or fistulas, and the women ulcers in the neck of the matrix, which they will hide from you, (if you be not careful) merely out of fear of those who bring them on board.[29]

Examinations were carried out either before a slave was purchased, or at the point of embarkation. The procedure, which directly foreshadowed the similar bodily scrutiny that captives who survived the voyage would endure on the auction block, was intimate, intrusive, and humiliating.[30] From the perspective of British sailors, however, the inconvenience was all their own. As Thomas Phillips put it:

our greatest care of all is to buy none that are pox'd, lest they should infect the rest aboard; for tho' we separate the men and women aboard by partitions and bulkheads, to prevent quarrels and wranglings among them, yet do what we can they will come together, and that distemper which they call the yaws, is very common here...therefore our surgeon is forc'd to examine the privities of both men and women with the nicest scrutiny, which is a great slavery, but what can't be omitted.

(*Hannibal* 1693–4: 218)

By the time this intrusive examination took place—and perhaps long before that, right at the point of capture—Africans had been stripped of their clothing. I have reserved discussion of this point until Chapter 10, where a case will be made that not all captives were left *entirely* naked following this act of symbolic debasement. Some may even have retained small items of personal adornment—things that crossed the ocean with them. For present purposes, it is simply necessary to note that most African captives were indeed stripped by their captors. Prurience, and an active appreciation that enforced nakedness divested individuals of identity and status, informed this practice equally; but so too did contemporary attitudes to disease prevention. Numerous witnesses attest to the widespread understanding that captives' clothing harboured 'vermin' and worse. As Henry Smeathman reasoned (*Oeconomy c.1775: 9*): 'The men would have an opportunity of concealing knives and dangerous things, if they had any sort of cloaths, and the whole would get full of vermin and dirt.' The British navy, in this context, had a similar understanding regarding sailor's clothing.[31] Gilbert Blane counselled naval commanders in 1785 that 'the clothes of men are as dangerous a vehicle of infection as their persons', advocating that the best way to prevent the spread of infectious diseases as seamen moved from one vessel to another was by 'stripping and washing their bodies, cutting off their hair and destroying all their clothes before they are allowed to mix with the ship's company in which they are going to enter'.[32] James Lind similarly counselled that 'polluted rags' were a material cause of ship fevers: indeed, he regarded the near-nakedness of Africans on Guinea ships as the material factor in their ability to resist fever.[33] A similar logic appears to have operated on slaving vessels, but only with reference to their captive Africans.

Different Bodies: Observing African Bodily Modification

Somatic distance rendered the enslaved readily identifiable to seventeenth- and eighteenth-century British observers: simply put, slaves were black. But the bodies that surgeons inspected were different from their own in other ways. Many captives had undergone procedures such as scarification, dental modification, nose, lip, and lobe piercing, and circumcision—signifiers of identity that inscribed the body for life. Dental modification was practised by many West African communities, for example, with members of both sexes undergoing painful procedures that were carried out for largely aesthetic reasons, but in some areas also marked the onset of puberty.[34] In the later seventeenth century, Thomas Phillips noted of Africans on the Liberian Coast that 'all their teeth I observed are pointed at the ends as sharp as bodkins' (*Hannibal* **1693–4: 197**). Some hundred years later, in 1796, the physician George Pinckard visited a slaver newly arrived at Bridgetown, Barbados, noting of its captives that 'some had their teeth out, or filed to sharp points'.[35] It is impossible to quantify exactly how many of the Africans boarding slave ships had modified teeth, not least because the frequency of such practices varied considerably in time and space, but in the British colonies the practice was universally acknowledged as a marker of African birth. Practices certainly varied over time. Some of the first Africans to be transported on Portuguese slave ships were taken to Portugal itself, and more than 60 per cent of the

158 African bodies recovered from an urban dump at Valle da Garafia (Algarve), in use from the fifteenth to seventeenth centuries, exhibited dental modification.[36] Yet Handler's analysis of some 7,500 eighteenth-century runaway slave advertisements from Georgia, Maryland, South Carolina, and North Carolina found only 60 references to dental modification.[37] More recently available digitized advertisement databases contain additional examples, but these collections similarly indicate that in the eighteenth century the proportion of runaways with modified teeth was never very high.[38] The same was true of scarification, which involved the creation of indelible patterns on one (or all) of the face, torso, thighs, and arms by means of small incisions or scalding. Scarification was widely practised across West and Central Africa throughout the period of the slave trade and was particularly common in regions favoured by British slave ships, including Senegambia, Ghana, and Nigeria. The practice served various purposes: denoting social status, familial connections, belief systems, and aesthetics, and also signalling the transition to adulthood.[39] The anthropologist Marla Berns's account of *Hleeta* (scarifying) among the Ga'anda of north-eastern Nigeria, based on fieldwork conducted in 1980–2, offers important insights into the practice among one modern West African people, and foregrounds its role in the transmission and re-enforcement of sociocultural values, marking the gradual transition of females from childhood to adulthood and marriageability. This is a status, as Berns notes, that is 'paid for in pain', and whose significance lies, not only in the final composite, but in the carefully phased alteration of the body, which allows for discrete units of design to remain isolated for extended periods.[40]

Scarification was practised throughout the era of the slave trade, and its outcomes observed by a multitude of European commentators, slave traders among them. Writing in the later seventeenth century, John Barbot described the scarified bodies he observed at various points on the African coast. He considered the marks to be the result of scalding, rather than cutting, the skin, saying of natives of Sierra Leone, for example, that they 'always have their ears adorned with a few trinkets, and they have incised marks on the face made with a hot iron'.[41] Barbot comments similarly on the wife of the King of Sestro (Liberia):

> I was never able to understand how she could have her skin raised up in patterns on many parts of her body, on her arms and legs, and about her middle...many other black women were similarly pinked all over from the head to the feet, which created the oddest effect conceivable. They make these patterns on themselves with hot irons.[42]

In the early nineteenth century, Hugh Crow similarly recorded in his memoir (*Kitty's* 1807–8: 199) that 'the Eboes and Brechés [the Nigerian Igbo, and their upper caste] are tattooed with their country and family marks. The national tattoo of the commonality consists of small thickly placed perpendicular incisions, or cuts on each temple.'

Many of the male Africans on board slave ships will have been circumcised. Circumcision was performed widely in West and Central Africa and for a variety of reasons: as a birth practice; a rite of passage; a symbol of reaching adulthood; a sign of tribal affiliation, or a protection against sexual activity prior to marriage. Male circumcision was not unfamiliar to European commentators and is occasionally noted by slave ship sailors and other white observers. Thus, Phillips (**Hannibal 1693–4: 214**) recorded that circumcision was practised on the Alampo coast, while, in his 1750 study of the natural history of Barbados, Griffith Hughes noted that the 'Whiddaw and Angola negroes' imported into the island were 'generally circumcised'.[43] Female circumcision was also practised historically in many of the countries involved in the slave trade, and still is, in the twenty-first century, in twenty-eight countries around the world.[44] In his account of the Guinea coast, William Bosman commented that, in the Kingdom of Benin, '[e]ight or fourteen Days, or sometimes longer after the Birth of their Children, both Males and Females are Circumcised; the former are hereby bereft of their Prepuce, and the latter of a small Portion of their Clitoris'.[45] None of the slave ship surgeons whose work is considered in this book makes reference to female circumcision, but many must have observed its physical outcome. As already noted, surgeons carefully inspected the genitalia of captives in order to identify sufferers of yaws, and in the *Guinea Man's Vade Mecum* Thomas Aubrey details treatments for ulcers in the pudenda and the internal parts of the labia.[46] The most usual form of circumcision found on the bodies of female captives in the slave trade will have been clitoridectomy, which involves the removal of the prepuce of the clitoris or part of the clitoris: this is the practice described by Bosman, above. It is possible that clitoridectomy was not immediately apparent, or intelligible, to the ships' surgeons inspecting captives.[47] Perhaps, because clitoridectomy was not noted as impacting directly upon the health of female captives, genital modification was simply considered an irrelevance in the context of discourse concerning the slave trade.

It is a point of some interest that, despite copious evidence that they must have witnessed the physical outcomes of such practices, slave ship surgeons and masters very rarely refer to captives' dental modification, scarification, or circumcision in their written or parliamentary accounts, and never in the context of the Middle Passage. Yet it is surely likely that the observation of such technologies actively enhanced the perception that the African body was constitutionally different, and required differential medical treatment from that of the European. Certainly, where scarification is discussed in eighteenth-century literature, it is employed to evidence both the exotic 'otherness' and the savagery of Africans. Thus, in his 1752 work *Crito: Or, a Dialogue on Beauty*, Joseph Spence singled out scarification in discussing the relativity of beauty in human thinking:

> In some of the most military nations of Africa, no man is reckoned handsome that has not five or six scars on his face. This custom might, possibly, at first, be introduced among them, to make them lest afraid of wounds in that part, in battle; but, however that was, it grew at last to have so great a share of their idea of beauty, that they now cut and slash the faces of their poor little infants.[48]

Some pro-slavery eighteenth-century commentators actively singled out scarification in emphasizing that the marks on saltwater bodies were the product of African savagery and had not been inflicted upon captives by their new masters. Thus Gilbert Francklyn commented that

> it is possible, that persons from Europe, totally ignorant of Negroes, and the manner of treating them, when they have been seen with their African or country marks on their faces, might suppose them to be scars, indented by their masters; as some of these national marks are very deeply impressed.[49]

While few British slave ship surgeons commented on scarification in writing or in parliamentary testimonies, the practice was, without doubt, clearly understood to offer perspectives on identity and place of origin.[50] One proof of this point is the fact that the patterns of scars on the faces and bodies of 'receptives' were carefully recorded in the Registers of Liberated Africans that were maintained once the Royal Navy began intercepting the slave ships of other nations after 1808. These register entries are detailed enough, in some cases, to pinpoint the birth region of the owner. The boy Cando, whose markings are shown in Figure 9.2 was liberated on 21 July 1814 from the Portuguese/Brazilian schooner *Maria Josefa*. His facial markings correlate with marks identified as belonging to Hausa living in central Sudan.[51]

I will return to scarification in the concluding chapter, where the possible New World impact of these indelible markings, carried into the Americas on captive bodies, is further discussed.

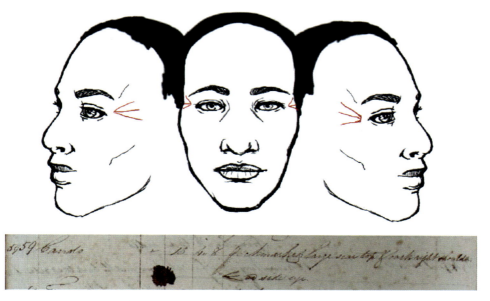

Figure 9.2 Katrina Keefer's reconstruction of the markings of Recaptive 5959 (Register of Liberated Africans 1814–15. Sierra Leone Public Archives/ Katrina Keefer.

292 MATERIALIZING THE MIDDLE PASSAGE

Dealing with the Sick in Africa

Medical Equipment

As slave ships lay off the African coast, some of those on board inevitably began to sicken. What were the tools of the Guinea surgeon's trade in combatting their illnesses? For the early seventeenth century, John Woodall's extraordinary treatise *The Surgeon's Mate* (a lengthy discourse on the proper contents of a sea surgeon's medical chest) furnishes an excellent glimpse into the material world of the 'barber-surgeons' of that era.[52] Woodall was a former surgeon general to the East India Company, and advised naval sea surgeons to carry a vast array of instruments including knives, razors, lancets, scissors, saws, a mallet and chisel, forceps, needles, probes, syringes, specula (ani, oris, linguae), and a wide range of materials used in two of the most common medical practices of the day: blistering and bleeding. The generally better-trained eighteenth-century sea surgeons travelled with wooden chests, usually fashioned from mahogany, containing their implements and store of medicines. These chests were often rather elaborate and were carefully designed to hold a variety of glass bottles and medical equipment. A chest advertised at £2 7s. in a 1793 book of prices was described as

> [t]wo foot long, fifteen inches wide and twenty inches deep, folding wings, the top to lift up; in the top of the carcase are places for twelve quart bottles and twenty-four pint ditto, twelve of which are seen in front by shap'd holes; underneath ditto are nine drawers, the four top drawers have a slider in each, the bottom drawers the whole length fitted up for six gallipots, two sets of pestles & mortars, pallet knife &c; in the right wings are places for sixteen pint bottles, a slider over the bottom drawer to run in the carcase, the slider lin'd with cloth.[53]

The example shown in Figure 9.3 is equally elaborate.

A urethral syringe and mortar and pestle, recovered from *Queen Anne's Revenge* (formerly *La Concorde de Nantes*), are of French manufacture and were probably part of the medical kit of the former slaver's surgeons, conscripted into piracy when Blackbeard captured the ship (Figure 9.4).[54] Other medical finds from the *Queen Anne's Revenge* wreck site include faience apothecary jars, pump clysters (used in delivering medical enemas), a blood porringer, and two apothecary weight sets.[55] The *Henrietta Marie* wreck site yielded a tooth extractor—essentially a set of iron forceps.[56] Several glass medicine bottles were recovered from the wreck of *Fredensborg*, and five white earthenware albarelli (jars) used to hold unguents or medicinal powders were found on the Saint-Quay-Portrieux wreck site.[57] The parliamentary testimony of Captain James Fraser suggests that, on later eighteenth-century voyages at least, a sum of money was allotted for medicines, with the surgeon himself deciding how that money should be spent (**HCSP 71: 29**). Some sense of the expense incurred may be gained from the account book of the Liverpool-based *Lottery*, owned by Thomas Leyland.

Figure 9.3 Medical chest belonging to the naval surgeon Sir Benjamin Outram (1774–1856) National Maritime Museum, Greenwich, TOA0130.

Figure 9.4 Left: urethral syringe (used in treating venereal disease). Right: apothecary's mortar and pestle from the *Queen Anne's Revenge* (formerly the slaver *La Concorde de Nantes*) wreck site.

On a 1798 voyage to the Bight of Biafra, £22 15*s*. 10*d*. was spent on medicines and a further £3 10*s*. 0*d*. on surgical instruments. The surgeon, John Tebay, was paid 6 guineas per month and had the lucrative right to 2 privilege slaves, who together were estimated to be worth £184 4*s*. 6*d*. Tebay did not survive the voyage, however: the cost of his funeral (£5 15*s*. 5*d*.) is also recorded, as is the £14 spent on his coffin.[58]

294   MATERIALIZING THE MIDDLE PASSAGE

Despite their cost, the quality of medical supplies was not always assured: William Dineley, surgeon on *Recovery*, wrote to the ship's owner James Rodgers in 1791 complaining bitterly that the apothecary had fitted out his medical chest 'in a most scandalous manner, his Tartar Emetic and many more of his medicines are worth nothing'.[59] Like many of the medicines employed *c*.1680–1807, Tartar Emetic (antimony potassium tartrate) was mineral-based. It was used to induce vomiting. Mercurous chloride (Hg2Cl2), extracted from cinnabar (mercury ore), was another common purgative. It was also mixed into unguents to form a topical application for syphilis and gonorrhoea, and utilized, with opium and quinine, in treating tetanus.[60] Other common medicines were extracted from plants: rhubarb, penny royal, opiates, linseed, camomile, and peppermint are all examples here, used variously as carminatives, purgatives, diuretics, and emetics, mostly for the supposed purpose of balancing the humours (fluids) within the body.[61] A very high percentage of plant-based medicines—from opiates to rhubarb—was obtained from India and the Far East. Opiates were commonly employed as analgesics; as is evident from his 1729 handbook for Guinea surgeons, T. Aubrey relied heavily on Thomas Sydenham's proprietary laudanum-based opium tincture, invented in the 1660s. The laxative qualities of Chinese rhubarb had been understood for centuries, and by the early eighteenth century the British East India Company was importing 10,000 lb of rhubarb root each year.[62] Samuel Gamble (*Sandown* 1793–4: 7) records carrying a bag of calamine (ZnCO3)—a native zinc carbonate that, when mixed with lard, was effective in treating insect bites.

Many other popular medicines of the late seventeenth and eighteenth centuries were imported into Britain from far-flung places impacted by both European colonialism and the slave trade. Plant-based medicines in this category included sarsaparilla, senna, and cinchona.[63] Sarsaparilla root was obtained from Central America. A tonic made from sarsaparilla soaked in brandy was widely traded along the Guinea coast, and was favoured by both Europeans and Africans.[64] The root was mainly used to treat syphilis and other venereal diseases, and in purifying the blood. T. Aubrey also recommended sarsaparilla-based 'ptysans' (infusions) in treating yaws.[65] Slave ship crews routinely succumbed to malaria on the African coast, and this and other tropical fevers were treated using the bark of the cinchona tree, again native to South America. Often known as Peruvian bark or Jesuits' bark, cinchona (we know it today as raw quinine) was perhaps the most important of the plant remedies discovered in the Americas and was widely used by English physicians from the 1680s, when the Portuguese physician to Catherine of Bragança, the wife of Charles II, became the first person in England to use cinchona to control tropical fevers. Evidently a man of some entrepreneurial flair, Fernando Mendes subsequently began exporting a quinine solution to Portugal, calling it Águas da Inglaterra ('Waters of England').[66] Britain lacked a colonial base in South America, but several substitutes for cinchona were identified in the British Caribbean in the eighteenth century.[67]

Local herbal equivalents of some European medicines were readily available in West Africa. They included Gum Arabic, plantain leaf, Guinea pepper (melagueta), and palm oil. The extent to which English surgeons employed these resources is difficult to determine. Some scholars have suggested that cultural chauvinism limited European engagement with African medical practices.[68] Others, however, have begun to show that the use of African materials was far more extensive than was once thought, and was nested in a broader Atlantic world medical complex.[69] Kathleen Murphy's work on the London-based apothecary and naturalist James Petiver (c.1665–1718) has already been discussed in Chapter 8. Her analysis demonstrates that, by the late seventeenth century, British naturalists were not only familiar with specimens from distant West Africa but were able to obtain them via networks of acquaintances with links to the slave trade. Petiver's 'Catalogue of Some Guinea-Plants' (published in 1697) described the uses, primarily medical, for forty plants indigenous to West Africa. Many of these were collected on Petiver's behalf by John Smyth, minister at the RAC's fort at Cape Coast, who evidently understood the medicinal value of these plants and communicated that information to the apothecary.[70] The catalogue carefully described the appearance and location of selected West African plants and offered guidance on the preparation of simples (botanical medicines) based upon them. In other words, as Murphy has argued, the catalogue provided Europeans visiting West Africa with a practical medical guide.[71] Thus a surgeon on African shores, familiar with Petiver's communications with the Royal Society, might have appreciated that the plant known locally as *ambettuway* could be used in inducing an appetite in a sick person, and had leaves the 'Shape and Roughness...like our *Common Elm*'.[72] But knowledge need not always have translated into use. As Timothy Walker has noted, for example, Portuguese doctors in eighteenth-century Angola largely eschewed African medicinal plants, even though they drew extensively upon indigenous knowledge, and plants, from Brazil.[73]

Ships' surgeons would certainly have been well practised in performing two of the most popular interventions of the period: bloodletting and blistering. The former was considered to rebalance the humours, and therefore to be beneficial for many ailments. The primary method was to cut open a vein (venesection), usually in the inner elbow. Surgeons carried small 'pocket' lancets that could be used for this purpose. A more localized form of bloodletting involved a western form of scarification: scraping the skin with a cube-shaped brass box containing multiple small knives, followed by cupping, which involved drawing the blood by placing a dome-shaped glass vessel over the skin, and extracting the air by suction. The blood was then released using a lancet. See Figure 9.5 for an example of some of this equipment.

Blistering involved burning the skin with an acidic preparation in order to draw malevolent humours to the surface. Cantharadin, an irritant extracted from Spanish Fly (also known as the 'blister beetle'), was commonly used for this purpose on ships. In a 1785 text designed to aid the many merchant ships sailing to the West Indies without a surgeon on board, Dr William Chamberlaine provided the following instructions on the preparation of vesicant (blister) plasters using Spanish Fly: 'To make a blister, cut a piece of leather, linen or even brown paper, of the size you would have the blister, spread it with blistering plaister...and sprinkle some of the fly in fine powder upon it; pressing it down a little, that it may not rub off.'[74]

Figure 9.5 Cupping instruments in leather case, London, England, 1801–1. Science Museum, London, A606733.

The precise medical interventions of surgeons on slave ships are difficult to reconstruct, but it can be stated at once that—in treating the white body—surgeons aimed to remedy imbalances in the humours. Bloodletting, purgatives, sweating cures, and purging via laxatives and clysters were all used to meet this basic aim; operations were a last resort.[75] Very little physical evidence survives regarding the latter, though a surgeon's saw recovered from the *Henrietta Marie* provides a graphic reminder of the realities of surgery in an age before anesthetics.[76] The textual sources provide a little more evidence. John Burnet, a surgeon on the South Sea Company's *Wiltshire*, whose botanical collecting activities are noted in Chapter 8, gave James Petiver 'An Abortive Negroe near full grown' and three polyps 'taken out of the hands of two Negroes', most likely obtained from captive Africans under his care.[77] The doctor on *Sandown* 'amputated a man's finger that was begun to mortify, having been bit by another slave' (*Sandown* 1793–4: 103).[78] Thomas Trotter stitched surgical sutures into the throat of a captive who had attempted to take his own life on *Brooks* in 1784 (**HCSP 73: 82**). Curious as to the sudden death of an apparently robust captive, Alexander Falconbridge was carrying enough equipment to undertake a post-mortem examination during the Middle Passage of *Emilia* in 1786 (**HCSP 72: 589**). Working by candlelight on deck, out of the sight of the slaves confined below, he says he 'opened the thorax and abdomen, and found them a healthy state; I therefore concluded he must have been suffocated or died for want of fresh air'. Falconbridge is the only contemporary witness to refer to such a procedure, and it is clear from his account that the ship's master, James Fraser, was anxious that the Africans on board knew nothing about it. This was presumably because many captives harbored suspicions that their fate was to be eaten, and the sight of a white man slicing open a black cadaver would have instigated widespread panic.

The textual evidence also reveals that medical equipment was not always employed to heal. While corporal punishment was generally meted out to both captives and crew by a ship's captain and his first mate, some surgeons were obliged—or sought—to take a part in such procedures. The one contemporary reference to a slave ship surgeon's use of a lancet, for example, discusses it as an instrument of torture. The ringleaders of an attempted rebellion on *Pearl* (1759) were punished as follows: 'six of them were tied up on one side of the long-boat and six on the other. In this situation the surgeon took out his lancet, and deliberately streaked them down their backs. Having afterwards rubbed brine into the gashes, he left them. And they were taken down and confined below' (*Substance* **1789**: 24).[79] James Morley, a sailor on seven slaving voyages, told Thomas Clarkson he had seen both surgeons and surgeons' mates beating sick slaves who would not take food, 'sometimes with the tails of the cat, at others with the butt end of it' (*Substance* **1789**: 2). As ship's officers, surgeons could also exercise considerable power over ordinary seamen if so minded, and so indulged by their captain. Several of the sailors who spoke to Thomas Clarkson on the fact-finding mission preserved as *Substance of the Evidence* singled out surgeons, alongside captains and mates, as perpetrators of acts of violence against themselves and their shipmates. Thus James Towne, carpenter on *Sally* (1768), recounted the beating meted out to Edward Hilton by the ship's first mate and surgeon. The latter used his cane to strike Hilton, resulting in the loss of the sailor's eye (*Substance,* **1789**: 57).

Berthing the Sick on Board

Space was ever at a premium on slave ships, so berthing the sick presented significant logistical problems. The ships' surgeon was generally able to claim a little space below decks for ailing sailors, but sick captives were isolated elsewhere, and often in an ad hoc fashion. John Barbot (*Treatment* **1712**: 781) followed the French practice of employing a 'lazaretto, under the fore-castle, a room reserved for a sort of hospital, where they [the slaves] were carefully look'd after'. The rationale here was that the ships' surgeon could not himself tolerate the conditions on the slave deck: 'Being out of the crowd the surgeons had more conveniency and time to administer proper remedies, which they cannot do leisurely between decks because of the great heat that is their continually, which is sometimes so excessive, that the surgeons would faint away, and the candles would not burn.' Barbot also cautioned against employing the ship's longboat as an open-air hospital, which would suggest that this was the preferred option on some slavers (*Treatment* **1712**: 782). Housed on or above the deck, and covered by nothing more than a canvas, the longboat will have made a poor 'hospital'. As those on board his ship fell prey to sickness, Newton (*Argyle* **1750–1**: 49) 'cleared one side of the boys'

298 MATERIALIZING THE MIDDLE PASSAGE

room for a hospital, having the melancholy appearance of a sickly ship'. As Captain Bowen, master of *Russel* (1776), reported to Thomas Clarkson (*Substance* 1789: 45), very few ships in the late-eighteenth-century slave trade had designated sick berths.[80] Wherever they were placed, little attention was paid to the comfort of ailing captives. On Alexander Falconbridge's voyages on Bristol ships in the 1780s (*Account* 1788: 28), sick Africans were isolated 'under the half deck, where they lie on bare planks. By this means, those who are emaciated frequently have their skin, and even their flesh, entirely rubbed off, by the motion of the ship, from the prominent parts of the shoulders, elbows and hips.'

Coastal Deaths: Malaria and Yellow Fever among Slave Ship Crews

Captives and crews tended to succumb to different diseases, at different stages in the cycle of the slaving voyage. Sailors were largely isolated from the patterns of disease prevalent among Africans, and commonly died on the African coast, or in the early stages of the Middle Passage, having contracted yellow fever or malaria while on shore.[81] Both were endemic to coastal communities in many parts of West Africa, and the slave trade played a part (though not a unique one) in carrying them to the Americas.[82] Sailors new to the region had no immunity to insect-borne fevers and were thus highly likely to contract them. Men were regularly sent to shore: as noted in Chapter 5, one of the first tasks in Africa was to cut timber for a temporary structure, known as the 'house', which would be built on the main deck to shelter captives, as the 'slave decks' were being erected. As we have seen, James Stanfield (*Observations* 1788: 15–16) regarded the fabrication of the 'house' as one of the greatest causes of crew deaths, stating:

> This enclosure helps the stagnation of air and is, in that point of view, dreadful: but it is more fatal in the act of its preparation. I know nothing more destructive than the business of cutting wood and bamboe, for the purpose of erecting and thatching this structure. The process is generally by the river-side. The faces and bodies of the poor seamen are exposed to the fervour of a burning sun, for a covering would be insupportable. They are immersed up to the waist in mud and slime; pestered by snakes, worms and venomous reptiles; tormented by muskitoes, and a thousand assailing insects; their feet slip from under them at every stroke, and their relentless officers do not allow a moments intermission from the painful task.

Africa killed sailors, and, as Table 9.1 demonstrates, Samuel Gamble's *Sandown* crew was especially hard-hit, with almost the entirety falling sick in the months following their arrival in the Îles de Los (Guinea). Gamble's first port of call on sighting land in West Africa (27 May 1793) was Cape Verde. Eight days later the master noted that the majority of his crew, until this point in good health, were suffering from 'blind Biles' (*Sandown* 1793–4: 38).[83] It is probable that Gamble is here describing malaria, the

Table 9.1 Crew deaths on Samuel Gamble's *Sandown*, 1793–4

Date	Location	Crew deaths	Extracts from Gamble's journal
4 June 1793			'Great part of the Ship's company bad with blind Biles two in the Doctors list. Feverish'
18 July 1793			'From the first of our arrival [4 June 1793] till the middle of July the whole Ships crew continued very healthy, when a general complaint made its appearance all about in the course of two nights, sixteen were down with raging fever…send on shore all the Sick that were fit to remove'
20 July 1793			'18 in the Doctors list, some very dangerously ill and delirious'
30 July 1793	African coast	James McKie, second mate	
31 July 1793			'17 on the Doctors list out of 21 our number'
4 August 1793			'Some of the people dangerously ill …The Doctor Blister'd Thos Roufleys Back and Legs'
5 August 1793	African coast	Thomas Roufley Humphry Sullivan	
7 August 1793	African coast	Charles McLean	
10 August 1793			'Carpenter and Cooper very poorly, which the Doctor has Blister'd'
15 August 1793			'The Carpenter the Doctor Blister'd on his shoulder being much afraid of him loosing the use of his left arm'
20 August 1793			'Ships Company rather better, but their squal'd immassiated appearance points up to me, a faint idea of the resurrection of the Dead'
21 August 1793			'Ships crew worse, some that was getting Well again taken with a relapse. All our Per[uvian] Bark near expended'
22 August 1793			'I find myself very feverish Squamish and sick today this being the third attach since I came into the river'
4 September 1793			'From the 23rd of Augt to this 4th September…confin'd by a sever shake of the Fever and Ague, which [h]as reduc'd me very much, Ships crew not a bit better, some of them so immassiated and reduced that their nighest and most dearest friends would scarcely know them,

Continued

300 MATERIALIZING THE MIDDLE PASSAGE

Table 9.1 *Continued*

Date	Location	Crew deaths	Extracts from Gamble's journal
			even the very tone of the Voice is quite alter'd.'
5 September 1793			'Ships crew no better, all down but the Doctor, and me who am very weak'
15 September 1793			'Ships company begin to be bad with the flux'
23 September 1793	African coast	Peter Frazer	'after a tedious illness of eleven Weeks'
12 October 1793	African coast	Marshall-Fair, carpenter	
31 October 1793	African coast	James Rutherford	
25 November 1793			'Ships Company very weakly. Cooper dangerously ill'
11 December 1793	African coast	James Ronald, cooper	
13 December 1793			'Fever and Ague rages very much both on board and on shore'
20 December 1793	African coast		
2 February 1794			
22 February 1794	Middle Passage	John Cameron, Chief Mate	'of the dropsy and a Complication of other Disorders, not having had Six Weeks good Health since we left London'

Source: summarized from Mouser (2002).

incubation period for which ranged from 7–14 days. Malaria is caused by *Plasmodium* parasites and is spread to humans through the bites of infected *Anopheles* mosquitoes. The result is a fever characterized by periodic shaking, chills, and headaches, followed by nausea, vomiting, diarrhoea, and a high temperature. Recovery is a slow process, and malaria is recurrent: it is clear from Table 9.1 that Gamble himself was a sufferer. As its name suggests, malaria was regarded as miasma-borne: contact with 'bad air' (*mal aria*) was understood to cause an inflammation of the constitution, making a person susceptible to fevers. Malaria was treated with 'Peruvian bark' (cinchona or quinine), which, ingested in large quantities, can cause temporary blindness: hence Gamble's use of the phrase 'blind Biles'. Although ships' surgeons recognized that cinchona could be used to open pores and break a fever, they did not understand it as having pharmaceutical properties that killed malaria parasites. As a result, cinchona was rarely taken in effective curative doses until the late nineteenth century.[84]

After a first wave of sickness on the coast, *Sandown*'s crew appear to have entered remission, and until mid-July seem to have been in reasonable health. But, on 18 July 1793, Gamble reported that sixteen of his men had been struck down with a 'raging fever'. This was certainly yellow fever, the incubation period for which is between three and ten days. Yellow fever is caused by a virus transmitted by mosquitoes of the genus

Aedes, particularly *Aedes aegypti*. Endemic to coastal West Africa, yellow fever has three distinct stages, set out in detail by James Clark in a 1797 treatise on the disease as observed in Dominica. The first stage involved fever, a desire to vomit, and severe pain in the back and forehead. The second stage involved nose bleeding, hiccupping, and restlessness. The third included massive (and ever-increasing) quantities of black vomit that resembled coffee grounds, violent hiccupping, and tar-like stools.[85] Like many infectious diseases, yellow fever was regarded as the product of noxious air—in this case the ethers emanating from tropical land. As Gamble (*Sandown* **1793–4: 54**) mused: 'How is it possible that men who have breath'd in so pure and healthy a climate as our own, can bear the inclemency of such a tainted atmosphere?' Yellow fever was commonly, and ineffectually, treated by phlebotomy (bloodletting) and blistering, carried out to restore a perceived imbalance in the body's internal fluids.

Detailed accounts of the medical procedures used to treat slave ship crews are unfortunately a rarity.[86] In his 1729 handbook for would-be 'sea-surgeons' in the Guinea trade, however, T. Aubrey provides numerous examples of his treatment of ailing sailors in the years 1718 and 1719. Aubrey was not himself a slave ship surgeon; he was employed in the British trading post at Calabar on the Nigerian coast. But he was often called out to ships, or treated sailors brought to shore, and documents nine case studies relating to the crew of the Bristol-registered *Peterborough*, most of whom were treated for 'fevers' or dysentery.[87] Thus Joseph Booth, mariner, succumbed to 'putrid fever' on 29 December 1717 and was restored to health by bleeding, a lengthy series of plant-based purgatives, and tisanes of pearl barley, violets, rose leaves, liquorice root, raisins, citrus, and water.[88] Joseph Skibb, carpenter's mate, having returned from an eight-day trip upriver with a similar fever, was treated by bleeding, a purgative of Tartar Emetic and—because he was delirious—Thomas Sydenham's popular proprietary tincture of opium. Skibb was subsequently blistered, and after a further ten days' treatment along similar lines began to recover.[89] Thomas Watkins, mariner, was treated for what would appear to be the white flux, using purgatives alongside draughts containing cinnamon and opium tincture to combat his griping pains.[90]

Sickness Out at Sea

As slave ships made their way out into the Atlantic, a new range of challenges began to present themselves to the medical men attempting to keep captive cargoes alive. The first of these concerned conditions on the slave deck, where captives would now spend most of their time.

Combatting—or Not Combatting—Overheating

As first explored in Chapter 5, ventilation measures on board slave ships were inadequate. Looking back on his 1783 voyage as surgeon on *Brooks*, Thomas Trotter would recall:

The rooms are imperfectly aired by gratings above, and small scuttles in the side of the ship, which they are obliged to shut at sea, and the gratings are covered with tarpaulings when it blows hard or in rainy weather. The temperature in these apartments, when nearly full, was about 100° of Farenheit's scale.[91]

The few crew members who ventured below decks found these temperatures insupportable. Gilbert Blane advocated that scuttles should be cut in the sides of naval frigates sailing to the West Indies, or the 'heat between decks is almost insupportable'.[92] Conditions on slave decks were far worse. Alexander Falconbridge (*Account* 1788: 25) noted:

During the voyages I made, I was frequently a witness to the fatal effects of this exclusion of fresh air. I will give one instance, as it serves to convey some idea, though a very faint one, of the sufferings of those unhappy beings... Some wet and blowing weather having occasioned the port-holes to be shut, and the grating to be covered, fluxes and fevers among the negroes ensued... I frequently went down among them, till at length their apartments became so extremely hot, as to be only sufferable for a very short time.

Trotter's parliamentary testimony of 1793 is especially useful here. On being asked 'Did the slaves appear to suffer from the want of fresh air?' he replied (**HCSP 73: 85**):

Yes; I have seen their breaths heaving, and observed them draw their breath with all those laborious and anxious efforts for life, which we observe in expiring animals... I have also seen them, when the tarpaulins were, through ignorance or inadvertently, thrown over the gratings, attempting to heave them up, and crying out 'Kickeraboo, Kickeraboo',[93] which signifies, we are dying; on removing the tarpaulins and gratings, I have seen them fly to the hatchway with all the signs of terror and dread of suffocation; many of them, whom I have seen in a dying state, have recovered, on being brought immediately under the hatchway, or on the deck, for fresh air, but others were irrecoverably lost, whom I had every reason to believe were suffocated, having shewn no previous sign of indisposition.

Yet as shown in Chapter 5, very few slave ships carried ventilators. It is instructive at this point to ask why, and the 1788–92 parliamentary inquiries may hold the answer to this puzzle. It is no coincidence here that Parliament began to take evidence on conditions on slave ships at precisely the time that the notion of separate 'racial' constitutions was taking a firm hold in eighteenth-century medical discourse, and, as Roxann Wheeler has argued, while race was not a central component of the slave trade debates of the 1780s, the 'African' constitution was nevertheless explored in a variety of ways in both the pro- and anti-slavery literature, and in particular by Parliament.[94] Bodies whose inherited characteristic were 'fixed' were bodies that could be quantified: difference, in other words, could now be measured. From the safe distance offered by the House of

Commons, the slave ship rapidly became a locus in which African bodily tolerances were deemed quantifiable.[95] What were the limits of heat tolerance for black bodies, for example? Parliamentary speakers asked this question repeatedly, but many of these counsels and committee members framed it in a particular way. As discussed below, a central strategy in parliamentary questioning was to encourage witnesses to differentiate explicitly between the constitutions of African and European bodies: the new understandings of racial difference clearly informed this line of questioning, and many responses to it.

It has controversially been hypothesized that a superior ability to regulate heat (a disputed advantage known as 'thermotolerance') helped African captives to endure conditions on board slave ships. As long ago as 1968, Philip Curtin, the great pioneer in the study of slave ship epidemiology, dismissed this idea as 'pseudo-scientific racism'.[96] Yet thermotolerance has been revisited more recently by geneticists exploring the so-called African gene hypothesis, which posits that a gene increasing the ability of the body to retain salt and water may have been beneficial for survival during the transports of slaves from West Africa to America.[97] Today, however, in regions where salt intake is high, the same 'African gene' may instead cause salt-sensitive hypertension (high blood pressure). The scientific merits of the African gene hypothesis are much disputed today.[98] Even so, a 1725 engraving entitled *An Englishman Tastes the Sweat of an African* (Figure 9.6) perhaps suggests that eighteenth-century slave purchasers perceived the saltiness of African sweat to provide some index to the chances of a captive surviving the Middle Passage.[99] The text (translated) accompanying the numbering on the upper image states: '1. Negroes displayed for sale in a public market. 2. A Negro slave being examined before being purchased. 3. An Englishman licking the Negro's chin to confirm his age, and to discover from the taste of his sweat that he is not sick. 4. Negro Slave wearing the mark of slavery on his arm.'

Certainly, by the 1780s, thermotolerance was regularly advanced as a feature of the racially constructed 'African' constitution. Heat tolerance was among the many 'fixed' characteristics of blacks listed by Thomas Jefferson, for example, in 1787, and, in his view, it was related explicitly to profuse sweating: 'They secrete less by the kidneys, and more by the glands of the skin, which gives them a very strong and disagreeable odour. This greater degree of transpiration renders them more tolerant of heat, and less so of cold, than the whites.'[100] If Africans were heat tolerant, so too of course were the people carried away from Africa, and some of the witnesses questioned by Parliament in 1788–92 made extraordinary claims for saltwater bodies in this regard (Box 9.1).

These claims (all made by supporters of the trade) beggar belief today. Given that numerous slave ship surgeons, including Alexander Falconbridge and Thomas Trotter, had testified in these same hearings not only to their own inability to withstand conditions below decks on a slaver, but to the severe impact of these temperatures on captives, one might imagine that Parliament might also have questioned these claims in the late 1780s. Yet the repeated suggestion that African bodies fared better in the heat were barely challenged, even though ventilation and lavation were consistently argued by naval reformers to be the best means of preventing the spread of a wide variety of diseases that, at the time, were perceived to be miasmatic, or airborne. It was in this context, as discussed in Chapter 5, that Sir William Dolben's 1788 bill to regulate the slave trade initially proposed that two ventilators be installed on every

Figure 9.6 An illustration in *Le Commerce de l'Amerique par Marseille* (1764: ii). The original copper engraving was made by Serge Daget in 1725. John Carter Brown Library. (Courtesy of the John Carter Brown Library).

Box 9.1 Claims made in Parliament concerning African Thermotolerance

What number of feet in length, and inches in breadth, is a negro supposed to occupy?

Warmth is so acceptable to negroes that when a ship has only half its complement of cargo on board, those Negroes then there lay as close to each other, by choice, as afterwards is a case of necessity. (Robert Norris, **HCSP 68: 6**)

Whether it is usual for the Negroes to complain of heat, in consequence of the manner in which they are stowed?

They have occasionally complained of heat... but more generally they complain of cold, and desire the windsails to be removed. (Robert Norris, **HCSP 68: 13**)

Do you mean that solar, or animal heat or both, is that sort of heat which you said was a luxury to Africans?

Both. They frequently desire to have a part of the gratings covered at night. (Robert Norris **HCSP 68: 19**)

Are they as subject to suffocation from heat as Europeans are?

By no means. Being used to a warm climate, heat is more agreeable to their feelings; and I have found them complain more of cold than heat during the passage, and had occasionally fire pans to keep them warm. (James Penny, **HCSP 68: 39**)

Do not the slaves oftener complain of cold than of heat in the middle passage?

They do—and we sometimes, when we think it too cold for them, put them below, and even there they beg to have part of the tarpaulin laid over them. (William Littleton, **HCSP 68: 295**)

Do the slaves bear the heat between the decks better than the Europeans?

They complain often of cold, when between the decks, which is a proof they can bear the heat better than the white people—they can often sleep exposed to the heat of the sun without finding any inconvenience from it. (James Fraser, **HCSP 71: 31**)

Did you ever know any slaves suffocated from the tarpaulins being laid over the gratings through ignorance or inattention?

Slaves are always ready to call to the people on deck to put the tarpaulin up or down, as they find themselves either too hot or too cold. (Clement Noble, **HCSP 73: 111**)

Will you state how large it [the space between the two rows of captives on the slave deck] was to the best of your recollection?

In some places perhaps a foot, and in some more, and in some less. Sometimes, when the weather is cool or cold, they will lay as near the side as they can. (Clement Noble, **HCSP 73: 118**)

306 MATERIALIZING THE MIDDLE PASSAGE

slave ship. This proposal was not enshrined in legislation, neither in 1788 nor in the many subsequent amendments to the Dolben Act, however. Why not? Because Parliament had firmly persuaded itself that African bodies were 'different', and no such measure needed to be taken. In this case, as with deliberations over spatial allocation discussed in Chapter 5, measurement and quantification were employed, not to end slave trading, but to define minimum 'standards' of passage. Given 'enough' air to breathe, and 'enough' space to lie down in, African captives crossed the Atlantic on British ships as they had always done. They would continue to do so until 1807, when it was finally accepted that 'enough' could never be enough.

Middle Passage Deaths

> what the smallpox spar'd the flux swept off, to our great regret after all our pains and care to give them their messes in due order and season, keeping their lodgings as clean and sweet as possible, and enduring so much misery and stench for so long among a parcel of creatures nastier than swine; and after all our expectations to be defeated by their mortality.
>
> (Phillips, *Hannibal* 1693–4: 237)

Most crew deaths tended to occur on the African coast. In contrast, dysentery was responsible for the great majority of deaths among captives, with most people dying either as their increasingly crowded ships lay off the African coast trading for captives, or during the Middle Passage. Newton's voyage on the *Argyle* in 1750–1 provides an excellent illustration of this pattern. Newton carefully recorded all deaths on the ship, and, as Table 9.2 demonstrates, his crew remained healthy until arrival in the Sherboro River estuary (Sierra Leone), at which point several of the men who had been sent either to shore, or upriver in the longboat to trade for slaves, contracted 'fever'. Newton's captives, in contrast, died largely from 'the flux' (dysentery), which raged through the slave decks on three occasions: twice while the ship was still in Africa and once again during the Middle Passage. Yet only one sailor died during the Atlantic crossing (of fever contracted in Africa). Having survived his stay in West Africa, Newton's surgeon succumbed to fever upon arrival in the Caribbean.

Battling the Bloody Flux

> The deck, that is, the floor of their rooms, was so covered with the blood and mucus which had proceeded from them in consequence of the flux, that it resembled a slaughter-house.
>
> (Falconbridge, *Account* 1788: 25)

TECHNOLOGIES OF THE BODY 307

Table 9.2 Sickness and death on *Duke of Argyle*, 1750–1

Date	Location	African deaths	Crew deaths	Extracts from Newton's journal
18 December 1750	African coast		Edward Lawson	'came out of the longboat when he was last on board ill with a fever; this is the 7th day since he was taken'
7 January 1751	African coast		William Pucket	None
9 January 1751	African coast	No. 11 (woman)		'having been ailing some time…she was taken with a lethargic disorder, which they seldom recover from'
11 January 1751	African coast		Andrew Corrigall, Carpenter	'having been ill 10 days of a nervous fever'
11 January 1751				'Having so many sick, am afraid shall not be able to keep our boats going'
12 January 1751				'Putt a boy on shoar (No. 27) very bad with a flux. This day another of our people taken ill with a violent bloody flux, have now 5 whites not able to help themselves'
13 January 1751	African coast	No. 6 (man)		'10 days ill of an obstinate flux'
16 January 1751				'The doctor having been ill these two days, borrowed captain Anyon's to visit our sick people'
17 January 1751				'Mr Bridson had a relapse of his fever with a swelling and inflammation in his face. The cook and 2 small slaves were likewise taken with fevers about the same time'
20 January 1751	African coast		John Bridson, First Mate	'after sustaining the most violent fever I have ever seen 3 days'
26 January 1751				'Had another white man taken ill today, and one that was upon the recovery relapsed'
3 February 1751	African coast	No. 27 (boy)		'Flux' (see 12 January 1751)
13 February 1751	African coast	No. 66 (boy)		'Taken ill with a violent flux'
23 February 1751	African coast	No. 33 (man)		'a fortnight ill of a flux, which has baffled all our medicines'
13 March 1751				'Mr Marshall was taken of a fever on Sunday morning, was afterwards better, but today relapsed again. Having likewise 2 slaves ill of the same disorder'
28 March 1751				'Longboat returns: Mr Hamilton excused his long stay on account of a

Continued

308 MATERIALIZING THE MIDDLE PASSAGE

Table 9.2 *Continued*

Date	Location	African deaths	Crew deaths	Extracts from Newton's journal
				general sickness which seized them in St Paul's River...two are extremely ill, one indeed seems at the point of death'
29 March 1751	African coast		Thomas Bridson, Ship's Apprentice	'general sickness' (see 17 January 1751)
6 April 1751	African coast	No. 110 (man boy)		'Buryed a man boy (No. 110) the only one we have lost the 2nd time the flux has been among us. We have about 12 ill but all I hope recovering'
18 April 1751	African coast	No. 127 (woman)		'of a flux'
21 April 1751	African coast	No. 70 (woman)		'flux'
21 April 1751				'The season advancing fast and, I am afraid sickness too; for we have almost every day one or more taken with a flux'
24 April 1751	African coast	No. 92 (girl)		'very ill of a flux'
1 May 1751	African coast	No. 12 (girl)		'of a flux and fever'
12 May 1751	African coast	No. 101		'of a fever'
20 May 1751	African coast	No. 113 (man). No. 129 (girl)		'long ill of a flux'
21 May 1751	African coast	Woman girl		'of a fever which destroyed her in five days'
21 May 1751				'The doctor was taken ill yesterday and is now worse with a fever and vomiting.'
23 May 1751	African coast	No. 34 (man)		None
7 June 1751	Middle Passage		Gideon Meacham	'came ill out of the longboat, the 28th March, of a fever which he recovered from, but has been otherwise declining ever since'
12 June 1751	Middle Passage	No. 84 (man)		'of a flux'
13 June 1751	Middle Passage	No. 47 (woman)		'Know not what she died of for she has not been properly alive since she first came on board'
20 June 1751	Middle Passage	No. 140 (man) No. 170 (boy)		'of a flux' 'of the gravel and stoppage of urine'
24 June 1751	Middle Passage	No. 158 (boy)		'of a flux'
28 June 1751	Middle Passage	No. 172 (girl)		'of a flux'

29 June 1751	Middle Passage	No. 2 (man)		'of a flux he has sustained about 3 months'
1 July 1751	Middle Passage	No. 36 (man)		'of a flux'
2 July 1751–13 August 1751				No log entries while the ship was in the Caribbean
17 August 1751	Homeward voyage		Robert Arthur, Surgeon	'of a fever which seized him a few days before we left St John's.'

Source: summarized from Martin and Spurrell (1962).

Two kinds of flux were distinguished in the early modern period: one 'white' and the other 'bloody'. Phillips's *Hannibal* was plagued by the former (***Hannibal* 1693–4: 252**); 'The distemper which my men as well as the Blacks mostly died of, was the white flux, which was so violent and so inveterate that no medicine would in the least check it ... I cannot imagine what should cause it in them so suddenly.' Writing from São Tomé at the end of his long stay in Africa, Phillips wearily informed his RAC superiors on 25 August 1694:

> This day with the help of God I do intend to set sail to Barbados ... I have lost in all every way 56 negroes. I question not but God send m[e] well to Barbados to deliver 600 negroes, have had many sick of the smallpox but [only] four dead of it, the flux is the ruining distemper. I have had a fever, a touch of a fever and ague here but thank God it is over.[101]

Phillips might have been feeling better, but, by the time *Hannibal* arrived in Barbados, only 372 of his captives were alive. Doctors were often among the dead, of course, leaving the care of the sick in the hands of men entirely untrained. Following the death of the doctor and his mate on a 1774–6 voyage, James Stanfield was given control of the medical chest on the grounds that he had 'a knowledge of Latin and a little medical reading' (***Observations* 1788: 34**). The only document at his disposal comprised 'a few remarks on the last stage of the flux, written in a minute or two, by a surgeon at St Thomas's, on a bit of cartridge paper'.

It is likely that the distinction between the white and the bloody flux was based on observation of the principal difference in the symptoms of bacillary and amoebic dysentery. Bacillary dysentery (shigellosis) spreads by an oral–faecal route and has an incubation period of between one and six days. It is not usually life-threatening and is characterized by cramping abdominal pain, fever, and watery (sometimes bloody) diarrhoea. Bloody diarrhoea is, however, a more distinctive characteristic of amoebic dysentery, which is caused by the protozoa *Entamoeba histolytica* and spreads through contaminated food and water. It can persist for weeks, with periods of remission, and without appropriate treatment can be fatal. The incubation period for amoebic

310 MATERIALIZING THE MIDDLE PASSAGE

dysentery is much lengthier—between twenty and ninety days—and on many slave ships it spread through the captives during the Middle Passage. As the Bristol slave ship surgeon Alexander Falconbridge informed Parliament in 1790 (HCSP 72: 337), it was almost impossible to cure a bad case of dysentery: large doses of opium palliated the symptoms, but the sufferer invariably died. Steckel and Jensen's study of the voyage journals that were required of surgeons by the 1788 Dolben Act indicate that most captives died of dysentery, in the middle phase of the Atlantic crossing.[102]

Dysentery was also endemic on the West African coast. John Barbot noted that 'the Bloody flux . . . . sweeps away multitudes of blacks after they have lost all their blood', adding that: 'They fancy this distemper is given by witches and sorcerers.'[103] But local communities of course had far more complex understandings of dysentery than Barbot's ignorance would allow. The healing aetiologies of many West Africa peoples twinned material and occult healing forces, and medicines were understood to be material devices that not only healed bodily ailments but fought off the malicious spirits (Barbot's 'witches and sorcerers') believed to cause illness.[104]

The principal weapons against the flux at sea were not medicines, but cleansing routines: the repeated scraping, scrubbing, washing, and fumigation of the slave decks. These activities were not undertaken because it was understood that cleanliness inhibited the transmission of infectious diseases, nor even because the decks were swimming in faeces, mucus, and blood; timbers were scrubbed because the appalling smell below decks was assumed to contain poisonous vapours, which, if eradicated, would reduce the incidence of disease.[105] Microbes and parasites had not yet been discovered, and, prior to the emergence of the germ theory of disease in the early nineteenth century, 'miasmas' (noxious vapours) emanating from decomposing matter were regarded as the primary cause of illness. This is why Phillips (*Hannibal* 1693–4: 230) ensured that 'the negroes scrape the decks where they lodge every morning very clean to eschew any distempers that may engender from filth and nastiness'.

Sailors' testimonies make repeated reference to this cleansing regime, which was a regular part of the daily routine once a ship began to fill with captives. In the late seventeenth century, Africans seem to have been involved in this task, as noted above by Phillips, and also by John Barbot (*Treatment* 1712: 779), who remarked:

> We are very nice in keeping the places where the slaves lie clean and neat, appointing some of the ships' crew to do that office constantly, and several of the slaves themselves to be assistant to them in that employment; and thrice a week we perfume betwixt decks with a quality of good vinegar in pails, and red-hot iron bullets in them, to expel the bad air, after the place has been well wash'd and scrubb'd with brooms: after which, the deck is clean'd with cold vinegar.

The deck timbers, as Barbot noted, were constantly damp as a result of their repeated washing (*Treatment* 1712: 779).

By the eighteenth century, fumigation and cleaning appear to have been tasked entirely to the crew. This may possibly reflect a growing awareness of the relationship between cleanliness, health, and profit. Cleanliness, as Haines and Shlomowitz put it, was by now widely understood to be 'the handmaiden of commerce' at sea.[106] As Niels van Manen has persuasively argued, the later eighteenth century brought a marked shift, across Europe, in attitudes to disease prevention (also called 'hygiene' or 'dietetics'). Reformers such as Jean Noel Halle, who argued that effective disease avoidance depended upon collective hygiene, began to influence approaches to public sanitation. In turn, these changes in attitude seem to have impacted upon preventative medicine at sea. Gilbert Blane's 1785 advice to captains and surgeons of naval ships was that they should

> '[f]umigate frequently with fires of wood sprinkled with pitch or rosin, carried about between decks in a pot or moveable grate, or in a tub with shot in it, when the ports can be opened; or, if the weather will not admit of this, to burn gun-powder wetted with vinegar. The sick berth should be occasionally washed all over with vinegar.[107]

Similarly, the regular 'purification' of slave decks was carefully noted by many slave ship captains from the 1750s.

Following the first African death on the *Duke of Argyle* (**Argyle** 1750–1: 29 and see Table 9.2), Newton's men 'scraped the rooms then smoked the ship with tar, tobacco and brimstone for two hours and afterwards washed with vinegar'. The action was repeated four weeks later. Vinegar simmered to the point of evaporation, and burnt tar, tobacco, and brimstone (sulphur) were the substances commonly employed in purging the stench of captivity.[108] On Samuel Gamble's *Sandown*, so many of the crew fell sick on the African coast that, well before any captives were boarded, local *grumetes* were regularly employed in 'scraping and washing betwixt decks' and 'smoking the decks with tobacco' (**Sandown** 1793–4: 54, 55).[109] 'Scraping' involved scouring faeces, mucus, blood, and vomit from the bare timbers on which the captives lay. The most detailed description of this task is to be found in the parliamentary testimony of James Fraser, master of numerous Bristol voyages in the 1770s and 1780s (**HCSP 71: 30**):

> We generally have a canvas hose, that leads the water from the head pumps down between the decks, which are usually scrubbed with bricks and sand—and afterwards washed clean, and swabbed as dry as possible and frequently we burn tobacco, brimstone or any other thing that we judge proper to sweeten the rooms—there are several fire-pans placed at different parts between the deck, with strong fires in them, which generally dry between decks perfectly in the space of an hour.[110]

Scrubbing brushes will have been a common sight on all slave ships, employed for this and other tasks. The cargo list of the Dutch ship *Groot Prooyen* (1790) included thirteen dozen brooms and six dozen scrubbing brushes.[111] A hardwood scrubbing brush with horsehair bristles was from the wreck of the Danish slaver

Figure 9.7 Scrubbing brush (16.2 × 6.0 cm) from the *Fredensborg* wreck site. Aust-Agder Museum. (Photo: Karl Ragnar Gjertsen, KUBEN Museum and Archive).

Fredensborg (Figure 9.7) and a similar brush back was found on the Saint-Quay-Portrieux wreck site.[112]

Humble artefacts like these materialize a diurnal task that crews loathed and resented in equal measure: James Stanfield (***Observations*** 1788: 16) commented in 1788 that, in his view, one of the primary causes of crew deaths was 'the inconceivably shocking task of scraping the contagious blood and filth, at every opportunity, from the places where the slaves lie'. Ecroyde Claxton, former surgeon on *Young Hero*, told Parliament in 1791 that the flux had spread so widely among the Africans on his ship in 1788 that the sick were kept on the open deck, lying on a sail that had been spread out beneath them, which quickly became covered in mucus and blood (HCSP 82: 34):

> The sailors which had to clean them, from the disagreeableness of the task, became angry with them for an action which they must have known was involuntary and used inhumanely to beat them, either with their hands or with a cat, which made the slaves so fearful of committing this involuntary action, that when they did perceive that they had done it, they immediately, perhaps from some natural tendency to ease themselves, crept to the tub, and there sat straining upon it in such a manner, as from their debilitated state and violent straining, to produce a prolapsus ani, which it was entirely impossible to cure.

As the experienced mate Mr Janverin reported to Thomas Clarkson (***Substance*** 1789: 64), 'such as were not able to clear themselves lay in their own filth until the morning, and such as were so ill as not to be moved (their dirt being just scrubbed up about them) lay till they became better, or till they died'.[113]

Treating the Pox: Discourse and Practice

Dysentery may have been the primary killer of captive Afrians, but it was far less feared by surgeons than was the 'pox'—a name given to various infections that manifested themselves primarily through eruptions on the skin. One of these was smallpox; another was yaws. Smallpox (*Variola*) is a particularly lethal viral infection, so named because of the pus-filled blisters ('pocks') that form all over the body. Present in both Europe and Africa prior to the slave trade, smallpox was carried to the Americas following the Spanish conquest of the Caribbean. Conditions in Africa and on the Middle Passage favoured transmission of this infection, and the regular arrival of slave ships was an important means by which smallpox epidemics spread repeatedly through the Caribbean and South America.[114] The presence of smallpox on a ship certainly deterred African traders from doing business with it: William James told Parliament that, having accepted on board *Britannia* a small girl with smallpox in 1769, the master, James Bruce, concealed her in an empty water puncheon in the hold lest traders be deterred from visiting the ship. The infection spread rapidly through the vessel (**HCSP 69: 138**)

> and the situation became such as no pen nor language is able to describe. The sick berths were incapable of containing all that were ill. Those only could be admitted to them, who were so bad as not to be capable of moving. There they lay in one mass of scab and corruption, frequently sticking to each other and the decks, till they were separated to be thrown into the sea.[115]

Yaws is a chronic bacterial infection caused by a spirochaete bacterium, *Treponema pertenu*. It is found in areas of warm, humid, tropic forest, and spreads through person-to-person contact, entering the system through cuts in the skin. A large ulcer forms at the point of infection, and multiple other ulcers appear on the body. This initial skin lesion typically heals after three to six months, but joint pains, bone pains, fatigue, and new skin lesions may appear five or more years later. In the seventeenth and eighteenth centuries, yaws was assumed to be a venereal disease, because the symptoms are similar to those of syphilis (*Treponema pallidum pallidum*). The latter originated in the Americas, where it was known as the 'great pox'. Many white observers equated yaws with syphilis, assuming therefore an African origin for the great pox too. In 1732, the venereologist Daniel Turner claimed that syphilis was 'brought from Guinea in Africa, where it...is there called by the name of yaws', and that it 'hath since grown up with us, as a just punishment (some say) for that barbarous practice, of trafficking or making merchandize with our fellow-creatures'.[116] The Guinea surgeon T. Aubrey, who dedicated his own 1729 book to Daniel Turner,

314 MATERIALIZING THE MIDDLE PASSAGE

equated yaws with gonorrhoea. He attributed three in four deaths of captives on slave ships to the 'yaws flux', or inveterate Diarrhoeas, which 'come from the relicks of an old Pox, which is what they call the Yaws, and when such a Diarrhoea seises them they are sure to dye'.[117] Aubrey was one of many white observers who regarded yaws as an outcome of African promiscuity, devoting several pages of *The Guinea Man's Vade Mecum* to describing its transmission by concubines.[118]

There is considerable evidence to suggest that, by the eighteenth century at least, Africans were employing variolation (inoculation) against both yaws and smallpox. Inoculation involves inserting micro-organisms into the skin to prevent disease—a technique first introduced to Europe at the beginning of the eighteenth century. It is not clear whether Europeans adopted inoculation from Africans, or vice versa. As Roberts has noted, variolation is not unlike ritual incision, a common characteristic of West African medicine, and European observers may have confused the two. Alternately, inoculation may have appeared in West Africa only after European merchants began inoculating their slaves in the eighteenth century.[119] What is certain is that England faced severe smallpox epidemics in the first two decades of the 1700s, stimulating considerable interest in (and debate about) the merits of inoculation, and in this context the RAC initiated an inquiry, among its slaves in Gambia, Sierra Leone, and the Gold Coast, into local medicinal plants that might be used to combat diseases. Experiments with inoculation were certainly conducted at this time, and, twenty years further on, the technique was successfully used on a plantation in St Kitts.[120] Slave ship surgeons were certainly inoculating against smallpox by the later 1700s. In 1777, the brig *Joshua* embarked 184 captives at the Îles de Los (Guinea). The hundredth was noted to have smallpox and was returned to shore, but two weeks later smallpox appeared on the slave deck, and every captive on board was inoculated. The captain later reported that only 7 of 143 captives were lost.[121] As William James recounted to Thomas Clarkson (**Substance** 1789: 15), *Britannia*, trading for captives at Calabar in 1768, was less fortunate in this respect: despite inoculation, smallpox decimated the ship: 230 of 450 captives died.[122] Saltwater captives certainly took their knowledge of inoculation with them to the Americas. It is clear from Robert Norris's memoir of the reign of Bossa Ahadee (though not from the ship's logbook) that variolation was employed twice on *Unity* after smallpox appeared among the captives (**Unity** 1769–71).[123] In his 1793 *History* of the British West Indies, Bryan Edwards wrote that children from the Gold Coast were inoculated against yaws, citing evidence provided by a saltwater slave:

> Clara, a most faithful well-disposed woman, who was brought from the Gold Coast to Jamaica the latter end of 1784, relates, that she was born in a village near Anamaboo ... She informed me also, in answer to some other inquiries, of a remarkable fact (i.e.), that the natives of the Gold Coast give their children the yaws, (a frightful disorder) by *inoculation*; and she described the manner of performing the operation to be making an incision in the thigh, and putting in some of the infectious matter. I asked her what benefit they expected from this practice?

TECHNOLOGIES OF THE BODY   315

She answered, that by this means their infants had the disorder slightly, and recovered speedily, whereas by catching it at a later time in life, the disease, she said '*got into the bone*', that was her expression.[124]

T. Aubrey's handbook for Guinea trade surgeons ended with four chapters devoted to Africans, two of which are entirely concerned with yaws, and one with diet. Aubrey set out in chapter XIII a purgative method for curing yaws: one that advocated adding substances to heated brandy to cheat unwilling captives into taking their medicine ('for they love hot liquors').[125] He regarded most of the illnesses that presented themselves upon the slave decks (flux included) as best left untreated, however:

> Abundance of these poor creatures are lost on board ships to the great prejudice of the owners and scandal of the surgeon, merely thro' the surgeon's ignorance, because he knows not what they are afflicted with, but supposing it to be a fever, bleeds and purges, or vomits them, and so casts them into an incurable Diarrhoea...when, if he had spared himself the trouble of doing anything for them, but left all to nature, they might have recovered...for alas! When they are in the woods sick of these diseases, they take nothing but cold water and suck oranges, and yet recover.[126]

Not for most captives, then, the bloodletting, reagents, and blister-plasters so favoured in the treatment of the sailors. As Falconbridge noted (**HCSP 72: 302**), bandages and plasters were in any case quickly removed by captives: 'If plaisters be applied, they are very soon displaced by the friction of the ship; and when bandages are used the negroes very soon take them off, and appropriate them to other purposes.' Even where bleeding and medicines were used in the treatment of slaves, their efficacy (such as it was) was impeded by carelessness, as James Morley told Thomas Clarkson (**Substance 1789: 75**):

> It is but too common for the surgeon's mates to be ignorant and to neglect them... He has seen them also cutting and slashing the slaves at the time of bleeding them, and not yet sufficiently skilful to fetch the blood from the proper place...when they give them medicines they have given it in such a careless manner, as if they were regardless whether they took them or not. Mr Morley has stood, and seen them take the pannekin or tin vessel, in which the medicine was, and drive the edge of it between their teeth. Most of the medicine went over their faces. They have then cursed them for being sulky, though the poor creatures have been gasping for life at the time, and have been lying in their own blood and excrement.

To recover and strengthen itself in the era of the slave trade, balance had to be restored to the (European) body by making matter flow: pus, blood, and sweat had to be drawn out by the surgeon, and their presence was regarded as a positive sign of recovery.[127] All that flowed from captive Africans, in contrast, was considered contagion and filth,

316   MATERIALIZING THE MIDDLE PASSAGE

only to be expunged through the weary, diurnal rituals of fumigation and scraping that were the business, not of the ship's surgeon, but of its mariners. While these deeply resented cleaning regimes were imposed in an effort to clear the slave decks of human effluvia, the hold and bilge of any slaver—and particularly one decimated by the bloody flux—must have remained unimaginably fetid. The stench of faeces, sickness, and death oozed from every timber of a slave ship as it crossed the ocean—a transcript of slave shipping that cannot be captured today, but that clearly lived on in the memories, and testimonies, of those who experienced it at first hand.

'Melancholia': Displacement Embodied

Many Africans were described by ships' captains and surgeons as suffering from 'melancholia', 'lethargy', or 'sulkiness'. Late-eighteenth-century surgeons' journals make frequent reference to all three as causes of African deaths. Thus Joseph Buckham, surgeon on *James* in 1788–9, recorded the deaths of fifteen captives, the majority from dysentery but two 'of a lethargy' and one of 'sulkiness' (**HCSP 67: 281**). These conditions mystified British sailors (as Newton's comment on the death of a slave from a lethargic disorder in Table 9.1 indicates), but they were symptomatic of a profound, trauma-induced depression that was probably exacerbated by salt depletion and extreme dehydration.[128] Many captains (and surgeons) held that melancholia was the principal cause of sickness among captive Africans.[129] It was even seen by some surgeons as a cause of dysentery, because those who refused sustenance became debilitated and succumbed to the flux. Thus, in 1790, Isaac Wilson, former principal surgeon on the ship *Elizabeth*, told Parliament that he regarded melancholia as 'one great cause' of deaths, including suicides, on slave ships (**HCSP 72: 87**).

Most white observers regarded melancholia as a baffling and contemptible malaise. An exception here was the Spanish surgeon Franciso Barrera y Domingo, whose extraordinary treatise on slave medicine in Cuba (written in 1797–8) included a detailed account of the effects of 'nostalgia', which he understood to be a pathological form of patriotic love, on recently imported African slaves. Barrera defined 'nostalgia of the Negroes' as 'a melancholic sadness that attacks them suddenly without delirium, furore or fever, born out of a strong aversion to anything that could distract them from their fantasies, unless it is the return to their beloved patria'.[130] Today, we would think of this sadness as a profound homesickness.[131] Domingo also recognized that many Africans had been affected by 'nostalgia' during their Middle Passage, suggesting that exposure to the supposed higher atmospheric pressure on slave ships, alongside the humiliations suffered daily at the hands of their captors, induced a severe form of this sickness, resulting in some cases in suicide. Ramesh Mallipeddi has persuasively suggested that the 'fixed melancholy' that so many white observers noted was both a symptom of emotional distress—an embodied response to dispossession—and a weapon in the armoury of captive resistance; the latter is a topic pursued in more depth in Chapter 11.[132]

Disposing of the Dead

Sailors dying in African waters could be interred on land, but only in places where burial rights had been granted to foreign ships or trading companies. Thus, Captain Shirley, master of *Hannibal's* sister ship *East Indian Merchant*, was buried at the RAC's fort at Accra in 1694. The ship fired guns at half-minute intervals as the corpse was rowed to shore, and Phillips served as a pall bearer (**Hannibal 1693–4: 212**). Samuel Gamble (**Sandown 1793: 56**) was obliged to pay a duty of fifteen iron bars to bury any seaman who died while *Sandown* lay moored at Kacundy on the Rio Nunez: he would pay this duty many times. Left-over timbers from the supply brought out to construct temporary slave decks were sometimes employed in burying the dead. As crewmen of the Danish slaver *Fredensborg* died off the Gold Coast, Captain Ferentz sent to the shore at Fort Christanborg 'planks from Westervig' from which to fashion their coffins.[133] In such ways, the trees of home, brought out to Africa to build the ship's slave decks, enveloped white bodies interred in foreign soil. Falconbridge (**Account 1788: 52**) stated that at Bonny the bodies of sailors were interred in shallow graves on a sandy point a short distance from the town, but that the sand was often washed away, leaving the bodies prey to sharks.

The remains of African captives who died as ships lay at anchor were quickly disposed of at sea. There was no impetus to invest crew time and labour in burying captives on land, because huge numbers of sharks, attracted by the scent of death, circled vessels constantly. West African sharks, and their appetites, both fascinated and terrified European sailors. Observing 'shirks' off the Sierra Leone coast in 1720, John Atkins noted: 'their voracity refuses nothing: canvas, ropeyarns, bones, blanketing &c. I have frequently seen them seize a corpse as soon as it was committed to sea; tearing and devouring that, and the hammock that shrouded it, without suffering it once to sink, tho; a great weight of ballast in it.'[134] The corpses discussed here, wrapped in their own hammocks, were those of sailors. The Dutch merchant William Bosman described sharks observed on the Gold Coast at the end of the seventeenth century, but in this case devouring the remains of captives:

> When dead slaves are thrown over-board, I have sometimes, not without horror, seen the dismal rapaciousness of these animals; four or five of them together shoot to the bottom under the ship to tear the dead corps to pieces; at each bite an arm, a leg, or the head is snapt off; and before you can tell twenty, they have sometimes divided the body amongst them so nicely, that not the least particle is left; nay, not so much as any of the entrails . . . they devour human bodies; which, I am apt to think, they relish very well, since, when our ships depart from those places, they sometimes follow them for three weeks or a month, waiting for more slaves to be thrown over-board.[135]

318 MATERIALIZING THE MIDDLE PASSAGE

Almost a hundred years later, Falconbridge (*Account* **1788: 52**) wrote similarly of the incredible numbers of sharks circling the slavers at Bonny, and devouring the black bodies regularly thrown overboard.

Once beyond coastal waters, the remains of deceased captives were simply pitched over the side. Sailors were similarly committed to the sea but were usually dispatched with some formality. When Thomas Phillip's younger brother died on board *Hannibal*, an elaborate ceremony was conducted:

> Our pinnace being hoisted out, he was lower'd into her and myself, my doctor and purser went in to bury him, the colours of my own ship and the *East India Merchant* being lower'd half mast down, our trumpets and drums sounding as is customary upon such melancholy occasions. We row'd the corpse about quarter of a mile from the ship to seaward; and the prayers of the church being read, I help'd to commit his body to the deep, which was the last office lay in my power to do for my dear brother. The Hannibal fired sixteen guns at half minute distance of time, which was the number of years he had lived in this uncertain world, and the *East India Merchant* fir'd ten guns. (*Hannibal* **1693–4: 196**)

Phillips's brother was a man of some standing, of course: the remains of ordinary seamen were usually sewn up in a piece of canvas, or a hammock, weighted down with ballast in the hope that the body would sink before the sharks took it, and tipped into the sea following a short prayer.[136] In his written testimony concerning the 1787 voyage of *Ruby*, the surgeon James Arnold recorded (**HCSP 69: 131**) that a seaman who died as a result of neglect on the part of the captain and first mate was hastily sewn up into a hammock, taken from a sick sailor, and pitched over the side. There were occasions where no formalities were observed at all: so many sailors died on *Florida* in 1714 that the dead were thrown overboard during the night, lest the captives observed the reduced strength of the crew and attempted rebellion.[137]

The possessions of dead seamen were not jettisoned with them, but were generally auctioned at the mainmast, and thereby acquired by other members of the crew. As discussed in Chapter 8, many sailors made or dictated wills at sea. Table 9.2 contains extracts from the wills of some of the ordinary seamen on *Hannibal*, *Don Carlos*, and *Henrietta Marie*. As these wills show, foremastmen had few possessions, but honoured their family relationships and, where they had none, found 'family' in their fellow crewmen. In Chapters 11 and 12, I will make the case, building on scholarship extending from Mintz and Price to the present, that captive Africans forged fictive kin networks on slave ships. In their own way, and for entirely different reasons, these dying British sailors, who had spent much of their adult lives without the support of their birth families, had done something very similar.

Box 9.2 'I give and bequeath': Extracts from Wills made on *Hannibal*, *Don Carlos*, and *Henrietta Marie*

I Thomas Mead now belonging to the shipp Hanniball Thomas Phillips Commander being very sick and weak but of sound and perfect memory... appoint William Jordan and Paul Pyne my executors in trust for the use of my wife Elizabeth Mead in London having by a former will made her my sole executrix of all my worldly estate... and for the said executors' trouble I leave each of them a ring of a guiney value. In witness thereof I have hereunto set my hand and seale. (Thomas Mead, *Hannibal*, 15 September 1694)[1]

I William Walker belonging to the shipp Hanniball lately arrived from Guiney in the Bay of Carlisle now riding at anchor do make my last will and testament... Imprimis I give and devise unto my well-beloved mother by name Mary Gallop ten pounds sterling to buy her a suit of mourning. Item I give unto Mr Joseph Thompson as satisfaction for his dutiful care over me for residing in his house the sum of thirty shillings per week agreed upon. Item I give unto Thomas Pinford my chest and clothes as my loving shipmate. (William Walker, *Hannibal*, 17 November 1694)[2]

I Richard Sergeant mariner chief mate of the ship Don Carlos now residing at anchor in the harbour of Port Royall whereof is at present master William Easterson... give devise and bequeath to my daughter Elizabeth Sergeant in the City of London the sum of five pounds... to buy her new mourning. Item I give devise and bequeath all my personal weall and estate in the Kingdom of England to John [?] of the City of London... I give devise and bequeath all my weall and personal estates whatsoever in the island of Jamaica to Lawrence Galdy of the City of London merchant and his brother Lewis Galdy of Port Royall. (Richard Sergeant, *Don Carlos*, 23 May 1701)[3]

Peter Christopherson Batchelor a Dane then one of the seamen or mariners on board the Ship Henrietta Maria [*sic*] then sick of the sickness whereof he died on board the said ship the seventeenth day of the said month and being then of sound and perfect mind and memory and with an intent to make his last will and testament did utter and declare these or the like words following viz. Speaking to Claes Johnson his countryman and messmate then present. All that I have in the world or have due I give and leave unto you. (Peter Christopherson, *Henrietta Marie*, 26 December 1698)[4]

[1] TNA: PROB 11/426/380.
[2] TNA: PROB 11/426/345.
[3] TNA: PROB 11/471/470.
[4] This will was made during *Henrietta Marie*'s 1697 voyage (TSTD 15131). TNA: PROB 11/449/39. For a second will relating to this voyage, made prior to departure by John Scorch on 18 October 1697, see TNA: PROB 11/447/267.

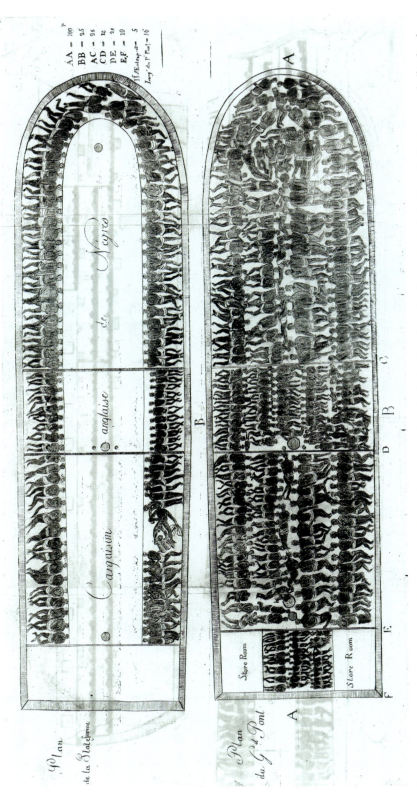

Figure 9.8 Detail from Résumé du Témoignage Donné Devant un Comité de la Chambre des Communes de la Grande Bretagne et de l'Irelande, Touchant la Traite des Negres (1814), showing a woman giving birth on a British slave ship. (Diagram of the Decks of a Slave Ship, 1814, *Slavery Images: A Visual Record of the African Slave Trade and Slave Life in the Early African Diaspora*, http://www.slaveryimages.org/s/slaveryimages/item/2004 (accessed 30 March 2023)).

Conclusion: Children of the Salt Water

Finally, after so much discussion of sickness and death, it remains to consider the slave ship as a place of birth, both actual and metaphorical. Children were certainly born frequently on slave ships. Some will have been conceived before the capture of their mothers, but, given the length of many voyages, it is beyond doubt that some of the infants delivered on slave ships were fathered by sailors; and the ways in which slaver crews gained access to captive women are considered in more detail in Chapter 10. Figure 9.8, a visualisation from a condensation of Clarkson's 1808 *History* of the abolition movement addressed to the Congress of Vienna in 1814, shows an infant being delivered on the bare boards of the 'women's room' of a slave ship. This baby was, literally, a child of the Middle Passage. Is there a way for archaeologists to identify these literal offspring of the salt water in the Americas? No, there is not: but, as explored in my concluding chapter, the science of bioarchaeology is beginning to make it possible for us to identify, from their skeletal remains, some of those who had crossed the Atlantic on slave ships—a 'genomic turn' that is transforming how we, as archaeologists, reconstruct African identities in the Americas.[138]

What of birth in a metaphorical sense? Many years ago, as discussed in Chapter 1, Mintz and Price suggested that the Middle Passage was a place of birth—the site in which 'shipmates' forged the lasting, dyadic relationships from which African-American culture was born.[139] This is a position that many Africanist scholars have vociferously contested in recent years, as also explored in Chapter 1. I agree that it is not advisable to overextend the metaphor of birth in discussing the Middle Passage, yet, as I set out in Chapter 1, I also consider the slave ship to be a site of displacement in which much was lost, but in which creativity and newness were also present. Perhaps *genesis* is a better word to employ here than birth? Not because of the genomic turn, nor because captains in the British trade, in creating their own 'Adams' and 'Eves', framed themselves as gods of human trafficking and creators of 'human cargoes'—though that is a discursive practice requiring acknowledgement and analysis. Rather, 'genesis' seems an appropriate term, because (like creolization theory itself) it articulates the *process* of coming into being. But *what* was coming into being as slave ships made their way across the Atlantic? That question is explored in depth, and with reference to several current areas of academic enquiry—including work by linguists on the genesis of pidgin and creole languages, the historical archaeology of ethnogenesis in the diaspora, and the genomic turn in bioarchaeological science—in the remaining chapters of this book.

Notes

1. They also ate and drank, were raped, had sex, were subject to corporal punishment and torture, and in some cases self-harmed or committed suicide. These themes are explored in Chapters 10 and 11. Latrines, 'necessary tubs', and the disposal of bodily waste are also considered in Chapter 10.
2. Sheridan (1985: 109).
3. Sheridan (1985: 115).

322 MATERIALIZING THE MIDDLE PASSAGE

4. **HCSP 69: 142–202**. Clarkson presented evidence drawn from muster rolls for Liverpool and Bristol ships for 1786–7. He examined rolls for eighty-eight Liverpool slavers (3,170 men sailed, 642 died), and for twenty-four Bristol ships (910 men sailed, 216 died). On an average ship, with a crew of thirty-eight, there were seven crew deaths (18.4%). Behrendt (1997) analysed data from 1,709 Liverpool voyages between 1780 and 1807. In all, 10,439 of 55,778 men died on these voyages—a death rate of 17.8%. But, when deaths recorded on slavers that did not return to England are also recorded, the rate rises to 18.4% (Behrendt 1997: 54). This is exactly the death rate calculated by Clarkson.
5. Sheridan (1981: 617).
6. Van Manen (2006: 133).
7. See Behrendt (1990: 94 and n. 45) on 'head money' paid to slave ship surgeons.
8. This argument is advanced, e.g., by Haines and Shlomowitz (2000).
9. Klein et al. (2001: 103), for example, argue that 'tighter' packing as measured by slaves per ton had no statistically significant influence on mortality; while Steckel and Jensen (1986) suggest that overcrowding increased the risk of gastrointestinal diseases during the Middle Passage. Scholarship on the relationship between 'tight packing' and mortality are usefully reviewed by Duquette (2014): his own analysis, based on a statistical analysis of 2,167 British voyages in TSTD, finds a correlation between slave crowding and mortality. Solar and Duquette's revision (2017) of TSTD calculations of vessel tonnages, however, suggests a more limited relationship between crowding and mortality.
10. Trotter (1786) drew repeatedly on his experiences on the slaver *Brooks*.
11. The first six volumes of Buffon's *Histoire naturelle* were translated into English for the first time in 1775–6.
12. Smith (1813: 13, 18). *Anne Galley*: TSTD 75063.
13. Charters (2012: 216–17).
14. Saakwa-Mante (1999: 30–1).
15. Later published as Atkins (1735).
16. Atkins (1735: 39). Saakwa-Mente (1999) provides a very detailed reading of Atkins's polygenism.
17. Atkins (1734: 18–21).
18. Saakwa-Mente (1999: 48).
19. Lind (1768: 134); see Charters (2012: 227–9) for a discussion of Lind, and of military surgeons, in this context.
20. Wheeler (2000: 241).
21. Swaminathan (2016: 106–10) also explores the concept of race in anti-slavery texts in this period, arguing that 'white' was increasingly constructed as a category (rather than a colour) in abolitionist discourse—the 'white' character being inherently superior to the 'black'.
22. The Portuguese introduced branding in the 1440s: see Thomas (1997: 394).
23. Keefer (2019: 7).
24. Keefer (2019: 5).
25. Atkins (1735: 97).
26. Ferreira and La Rosa (2015: 48–9).
27. Mitchell (2020: 165–6), citing Hodgson, 'Account of what Slaves Died or Was Lost by Accident Onboard the Katharine Galley', in Mortice Papers, reel 3, vol. 5. *Katherine Galley* is TSTD 76407, and *Italian Gally* TSTD 76401.
28. Cowley (1928: 104).
29. Aubrey (1729: 118).
30. As discussed by Mustakeem (2016: 46).
31. Rodger (1988: 107).
32. Blane (1785: 2, 6).
33. Lind (1774: 317).

34. Handler (1994: 114).
35. Pinckard (1806: 230). This passage also mentions scarification: 'Many of them had marks upon their skin which appeared to have been made with a cutting instrument. These, we learned, were distinctive to the nation to which they belonged.'
36. The earliest deposits here date to the fifteenth century and the latest to the seventeenth. The most common form of modification comprised excision: see Rufino (2014: 14).
37. Handler (1994: 117), employing Windley (1983).
38. For Jamaica, for example, see Chambers (2013). There are only 16 references to 'filed' teeth in the 740 advertisements collated by Chambers.
39. Keefer (2013: 541).
40. Berns (1988: 53).
41. Hair et al. (1992: i. 186).
42. Hair et al. (1992: i. 270–1).
43. Hughes (1750: 14, n. 17).
44. Watson (2005) provides an overview of the practice.
45. Bosman (1705: 444).
46. Aubrey (1729: 124).
47. Watson (2005: 426).
48. Spence (1752: 49–50).
49. Francklyn (1789: 195).
50. Keefer (2013: 541) notes that scarification was never used in Africa to denote ethnicity, but it was frequently interpreted in that light.
51. *Maria Josefa:* TSTD 7523. Image and information kindly supplied by Katrina Keefer. The Registers of Liberated Africans are a source of considerable academic interest at present: see, e.g., Nwokeji and Eltis (2002a,b), Keefer (2013), Lovejoy (2016), and Anderson and Lovejoy (2020).
52. Woodall (1617).
53. London Society of Cabinet-Makers (1793: 250).
54. Wilde-Ramsing and Ewen (2012: 125); Carnes-McNaughton (2016: 38).
55. The full range of medical finds from *Queen Anne's Revenge* is detailed by Carnes-McNaughton (2016).
56. For more details on the tooth extractor from *Henrietta Marie*, see https://sketchfab.com/3d-models/henrietta-marie-tooth-extractor-86081122-05943d8f78dd4c0292216afb6b9dbcd5 (accessed 2 September 2022).
57. The medicine bottles from *Fredensborg* are noted in Svalesen (2000: 180). For the Saint-Quay-Portrieux finds, see Herry (2004: 100).
58. Boog Watson (1969: 208); Sheridan (1981: 611). The voyage of *Lottery* is TSTD 82379.
59. Sheridan (1985: 113) citing TNA: Rogers Papers, Chancery C. 107/5, Box No. 2, No. 25. The *Recovery* voyage is TSTD 18115.
60. See Walker (2015) for a detailed study of the uses of mercury in eighteenth-century Portuguese Angola. Walker draws here on a treatise written in 1799 by José Pinto de Azeredo, an Edinburgh-trained Brazilian physician with almost a decade's experience of colonial medical practice in Luanda, a pivotal point in the Portuguese slave trade.
61. The discussion here draws extensively on Roberts (2011). An excess, or deficiency, of fluids (bile, phlegm, and blood) was deemed to cause ill health.
62. Monahan (2013: 231). The quantity imported increased considerably over time, peaking in 1768 at 67,764 lb.
63. Wallis (2012: 31, table 4).
64. Hair et al. (1992: ii. 560); Roberts (2011: 496). On the re-export of sarsparilla and other imported drugs, see Wallis (2012).
65. Aubrey (1729: 122).

324 MATERIALIZING THE MIDDLE PASSAGE

66. Walker (2013: 27).
67. These alternatives are discussed by Chakrabarti (2010).
68. Roberts (2011) argues that a conceptual gulf inhibited 'medical exchange' between Africans and Europeans on the Gold Coast. Trade and colonial expansion impacted considerably upon the quantity and range of drugs imported into England from overseas (as discussed by Wallis 2012), but most of these drugs came from the East Indies and China.
69. See Schiebinger (2018) for the notion of an Atlantic World medical complex.
70. Murphy (2013: 667).
71. Murphy (2013: 668).
72. Petiver (1697: 678).
73. Walker (2016: 13).
74. Chamberlaine (1785: 6).
75. The four humours, or fluids, of the body comprised blood, phlegm, and yellow and black bile. Imbalances in these were thought to be the cause of most diseases: see Bruin (2009: 27). Bruin's discussion of the work of the surgeons of the Dutch East India Company is a valuable addition to recent work on eighteenth-century European medical practice in the wider world.
76. Moore (1989: 161).
77. Murphy (2020: 271).
78. This was not a successful operation: Gamble records that the man died later the same day (*Sandown* 1793–4: 103).
79. Testimony of Mr Thompson, concerning his voyage on *Pearl*: TSTD 90812.
80. See Table 3.4: Bowen's only named voyage was as master of the London ship *Russel*: TSTD 77184.
81. Steckel and Jensen (1986: 64); naval crews were plagued by the bloody flux in the West Indies, but the pattern of slaving voyages was such that malaria and yellow fever tended to strike crews first, shortly after arrival in Africa.
82. Malaria was hyperendemic in coastal areas of western Africa, where people were ordinarily infected as children. Those who survived had a limited immunity to further symptoms but could act as hosts. Yellow fever either kills the victim within 5–7 days or results in rapid recovery and lifelong immunity, which prevents the individual from acting again as a host: Steckel and Jensen (1986: 63).
83. See also Mouser (2002: 38, n. 148).
84. Roberts (2011: 493).
85. Clark (1797: 6–16).
86. The surgeons logbooks required by law after 1788 note crew ailments, but rarely mention details concerning treatment. For an analysis of causes of crew mortality based on ninety-two surgeons' logs in the House of Lords Records Office and the National Archives (sixty of which contain information on crew deaths), see Steckel and Jensen (1986).
87. TSTD 16193. Aubrey also treated sailors from *Parnel Gally* (TSTD 16191), *Ferrand Gally* (TSTD 75842), *Higginson* (TSTD 75837), and *Betty* (TSTD 76589), all of which visited the Calabar coast in 1717–18.
88. Aubrey (1729: 30–3).
89. Aubrey (1729: 33–6).
90. Aubrey (1729: 78–9).
91. Trotter (1786: 31).
92. Blane (1785: 4).
93. The possible origins of kekrebu/kickeraboo are discussed in Chapter 10.
94. Wheeler (2000: 253).
95. This is not to suggest a linear relationship between polygenism and the pro-slavery lobby. As explored by Kitson (2004), the relationship between polygenism, slavery, and anti-slavery, as it emerged in the later eighteenth century, was far from linear. Both theories were connected with overlapping religious and political debates, and several leading abolitionists, including Thomas Clarkson, were monogenists.

96. Curtin (1968: 194). See also Curtin (1992).
97. Wilson and Grim (1991); Moskovitz (1996).
98. Lujan and DiCarlo (2018: 414) have recently made a strong case that 'the slavery hypertension hypothesis provides a rationale for treating African-Americans as a group that had been genetically altered and transformed ... [and] supports our tribal bias for an African-American inferiority that is innately pathological'.
99. Moskovitz (1996: 9). Licking the chin also helped traders to determine the presence of stubble, and hence the likely age of a male captive: Law (2004: 141).
100. Jefferson (1787: 231).
101. Law (2006: pt 3, no. 1397).
102. Steckel and Jensen (1986): based on an analysis of ninety-two surgeons' journals from 1792–6.
103. Churchill and Churchill (1732: v. 18; passage omitted from Hair et al. 1992).
104. Roberts (2011: 483).
105. Lavation and ventilation of closed quarters (such as slave decks) are discussed by Riley (1987: 129–31).
106. Haines and Shlomowitz (2000: 275).
107. Blane (1785: 4).
108. Behrendt (1997: 64) suggests that coal tar, which became available via a new process invented in 1781 and was used to protect ships' timbers, may also have killed bacteria, reducing the risk of dysentery, malaria, and yellow fever.
109. *Sandown* received this treatment on 30 July 1793, 2 August 1793, 3 August 1793, 9 August 1793, 19 August 1793, 22 August 1793, and 13 September 1793. The first captive came aboard on 15 September 1793.
110. See also the testimony of Captain William Littleton, **HCSP 68: 294.**
111. Van Manen (2006: 165).
112. Herry (2004: 103).
113. For Janverin's career as a mate, see Table 3.4.
114. See, e.g., Alden and Miller (1987) on smallpox in Brazil.
115. This testimony concerns TSTD 17717.
116. Turner (1732: 6–7).
117. Aubrey (1729: 106).
118. Aubrey (1729: 110–12).
119. Roberts (2011: 488).
120. Stewart (1985: 61–9).
121. Boog Watson (1969: 205). The voyage is TSTD 92447: *Joshua* was a Liverpool-registered ship owned by John Dobson.
122. This voyage is TSTD 17693.
123. Norris (1789: 117–18). I am indebted to Lisa Lindsay for pointing out that the ship in question (unnamed in Norris 1789) must have been *Unity*.
124. Edwards (1793: ii. 62–3).
125. Aubrey (1729: 121).
126. Aubrey (1729: 107).
127. Duden (1991: 17).
128. As proposed by Kiple and Higgins (1989).
129. See Mallipeddi (2014) for a detailed discussion of eighteenth-century discourse on 'melancholy' in the context of slaving voyages.
130. Denis (2005: 183), citing Barrerra, *Reflexiones Historico Fisico Naturales Medico Quirurgicas.*
131. See Mallipeddi (2014: 236–7) on the emergence of the notion of homesickness in European discourse. Mallipeddi also details the appearance of this concept (framed as 'dejection') in the parliamentary testimonies of the late eighteenth century (2014: 239–40, 243–5).

326 MATERIALIZING THE MIDDLE PASSAGE

132. Mallipeddi (2014: 247).

133. Svalesen (2000: 91).

134. Atkins (1735: 46). The presence of sharks in waters frequented by slave ships is discussed by Rediker 2008.

135. Bosman (1705: 281–2).

136. Earle (1998: 141). See also Smith (1813: 17), discussing the death of sailors in Africa at the time of the 1762 voyage in *Anne Galley*. He says: 'when person a dies on board a ship here their hammock is rolled round about them with a bag of sand made fast to it in order to sink the body, and they are thrown immediately into the sea.'

137. Voyage account of the ship *Florida*, Captain Samuel Paine, 1714–1716, BL Add. MS 39946, 12–13, cited in Tattersfield (1991, 26–7). This voyage is TSTD 75489. The London-based *Florida* purchased captives in Calabar and sold them in Antigua.

138. The phrase 'genomic turn' is taken from Abel and Schroeder 2020.

139. Mintz and Price (1992: 44).

10

Discipline and Punish

A Material History of Middle Passage Practice

As any British slave ship drew away from the African coast, its crew initiated the routines that, for some three hundred years, facilitated the shipping of captive Africans across the Atlantic. By the height of the British trade, as evidenced repeatedly in the parliamentary inquiry testimonies of 1788–92, those routines, and their associated assemblages, had standardized to an extraordinary degree. Throughout the eighteenth century, widely shared modalities operated throughout the British trade, having developed as sailors moved from ship to ship, as masters progressed through multiple captaincies to vessel ownership, and as vessel owners built up collaborative partnerships and syndicates. The outcome was an assemblage of practice evidenced in many of the primary sources central to this book. Chapter 10 draws on those sources to materialize the daily routines on a British slaving voyage as made on a day of fair weather (that is, one on which captives were not locked below) between 1760 and 1787—the period for which the documentary record is fullest.[1] Chapter 11 revisits the same sources, but approaches them from a different perspective, exploring the ways in which Africans understood, and challenged, these same modalities.

In writing this chapter I have naturally drawn on the work of some of the many documentary historians who share my interest in Middle Passage experiences. The present enquiry has a very specific focus, however, on the diurnal regimes of the British slaving voyage, and the ways in which material things mediated and shaped the daily encounters between captives and crews. Every chapter in this book is an exercise, as Martin Hall puts it, in marrying 'words and things'.[2] In the present case, Henry Smeathman's *Oeconomy c.1775* has been a particularly useful textual source on the everyday materiality of the slaving voyage, because the author was unfamiliar with life at sea and provides points of detail on topics—and objects—rarely discussed by sailors. Summary accounts directly concerned with the treatment of slaves, including those of the captains John Barbot (*Treatment* 1712) and John Newton (*Thoughts* 1788) and surgeon Alexander Falconbridge (*Account* 1788) are also key sources here, alongside numerous 1788–92 parliamentary testimonies. Clarkson's *Substance* 1789 has been excavated repeatedly below, because it documents the experiences of ordinary seamen, rather than their officers. Clarkson's famous wooden chest (already discussed in Chapter 8) originally held illustrative samples of several of the items routinely used to discipline and punish both slave ship captives and sailors. All but one of these artefacts is now lost, but Clarkson provided a detailed description of them in his 1808 *History*, and, as will become clear, these absent objects are particularly important to the

Materializing the Middle Passage: A Historical Archaeology of British Slave Shipping, 1680–1807. Jane Webster, Oxford University Press. © Jane Webster 2023. DOI: 10.1093/oso/9780199214594.003.0010

328 MATERIALIZING THE MIDDLE PASSAGE

narrative woven here.[3] Objects recovered during wreck excavations provide further data, not simply illustrating aspects of the textual accounts but yielding information not to be found in any documentary source.

Slave Ships, Prisons, and Convict Transportation

From the perspective of crews, the slave ship was a site for the confinement of others, in which the behaviour and daily life of the incarcerated could be regulated through routines of subsistence, surveillance, discipline, and punishment that had accrued through the practice of generations of sailors over time, but that also drew on the methodologies of the prison system.[4] Following Foucault, 'discipline' is employed in this chapter to refer to 'methods which made possible the meticulous control of the operations of the body, which assured the constant subjection of its forces and imposed upon them a relation of docility-utility'.[5] Foucault in fact regarded slavery as pure coercion, violently appropriating the body (subjecting it to torture, for example) in a way that the 'disciplines' that gave rise to the prison system did not.[6] But the enslaved were not, of course, coerced entirely through physical violence, in the way that Foucault's problematic characterization of slavery implies. Equally, some of the disciplinary punishments used in British prisons and indeed on its ships (flogging, for example) continued to be centred firmly on the body. The slave ship, I will argue here, was a site in which both 'discipline' and violence were present, and in which captives enduring the Middle Passage were exposed to a range of technologies of surveillance and control—including the bell, the fetter, and the whip—central both to carceral institutions in Britain and to the plantation regimes they would shortly encounter in the Caribbean.

In this context, it is not difficult to appreciate why, as it developed in the later eighteenth century, the penal transportation system would be directly informed by practices current in the slave trade. Transportation, initially to the Americas, became the foremost criminal punishment during the eighteenth century, with the British colonies receiving an estimated 30,000–50,000 felons between 1718 and 1775. The two Bristol firms shipping nearly all the convicts sent from the west of England to Maryland from the 1750s to 1775 were also closely involved in slave shipping.[7] Emma Christopher has explored the very close ties between slave shipping and penal transportation to Australia, which commenced in 1788—the year the parliamentary inquires into slavery began.[8] The ships of the notorious Second Fleet bearing convicts to Australia in 1790 were contracted from the partnership of Calvert, Camden, and King, which was also responsible for fifty-three slaving voyages between 1784 and 1807. Both Calvert and King were former slave ship captains.[9] Moreover, convicts were sometimes transported to West Africa on outbound slave ships: Calvert and King's *Recovery* was one of these vessels. The master, Donald Trail, later captained the Second Fleet's *Neptune*.[10]

The discourse and practice of slave shipping was thus closely allied with that of both the prison system and convict transportation. Yet, as argued in Chapter 1, the slave ship was not simply a floating prison: it was a locus for creolizing encounters impacting on all those on board. As will become clear in what follows, captains and crews on slavers developed some understanding of African foodways, harpooned exotic fish, ate yams, and flavoured their food with melegueta pepper (which, as shown in Chapter 8, was also widely used in domestic consumption at home). Their captives, meanwhile, ate from wooden bowls and spoons fashioned by ships' carpenters and smoked (slave-grown) Virginian tobacco from kaolin pipes made in England. These material encounters were never in any sense equitable, but they resulted in outcomes that outlived the Middle Passage itself. Fully to appreciate these complex, sometimes intangible, legacies, it is necessary to develop a firm understanding of the daily regime, and the everyday materiality, of the slaver at sea. That enquiry necessarily begins with a fundamental aspect of the intersection between words and things during every Middle Passage: the logistics of communication between captives whose languages may not always have been mutually intelligible, and between sailors and their captive cargoes.

Pidgins, Creoles, and 'Ship English'

Scholarly opinion as to the linguistic (and ethnic) homogeneity of 'human cargoes' has vacillated considerably since Mintz and Price posited that 'initial aggregates of slaves in particular New World enterprises did not constitute speech communities' and therefore lacked mutual intelligibility.[11] In the 1990s, John Thornton influentially argued that, while language should not be used as a sole measure of cultural identity (in either Africa or the Americas), West and Central Africa at the time of the slave trade could nevertheless be divided into seven culturally distinct subgroups on the basis, primarily, of the languages spoken within each.[12] Further, Thornton argued (*contra* Mintz and Price) that ethnic 'randomization did not occur with the Middle Passage', with ships drawing their entire cargo from only one or two ports.[13] As a result, Thornton suggested, the slave trade effectively replicated, in the Americas, the cultural groupings that already existed in Africa.[14] This argument inspired an entire generation of Africanist historians, and, while Thornton himself was careful not to over-equate linguistic and cultural homogeneity, his work informed an understanding among some historians of the Middle Passage and the diaspora that the majority of the Africans sharing a voyage could, in fact, generally understand one another.[15] Latterly, the pendulum has begun to swing again, with scholars drawing new attention to inter-African language acquisition on both the long overland marches made by many captives to the coast, and during the Middle Passage. Alexander Byrd, for example, has used Olaudah Equiano's *Interesting Narrative* in arguing that 'the language spoken by any particular enslaved African in the Americas was not necessarily their native language but a language bequeathed them by the vagaries and demands of their captivity'.[16]

With reference to linguistic exchanges between Africans and sailors, it is clear from documentary sources that, although some experienced captains acquired a considerable command of local languages during protracted trade negotiations, few seamen had such opportunities. There were some exceptions to this rule, of course: James Towne, carpenter, noted that on his first voyage to West Africa he picked up the local language to the point he understood it 'nearly as well as English' (**HCSP 82: 21**).

330 MATERIALIZING THE MIDDLE PASSAGE

Henry Ellison, who made voyages to the Gambia from a very young age, could speak Mandingo (**HCSP 73: 381**). But examples like these are a rarity, and it seems unlikely that many ordinary seamen acquired proficiency in African tongues.[17] It is equally unlikely that many African captives were proficient in English. Brutality spoke a silent language all of its own, of course, but the Middle Passage was by no means lacking in commands, in words for things, or (to borrow from Foucault again), in *taxonomy*.[18] Indeed, the linguistic encounters taking place on slave ships exemplified, and articulated, the broader complexities of cultural exchange in the salt water.

Slave Ship 'Jargon'

> The Officers call out Messie Messie—on which the poor creatures form themselves into Messes of ten.
>
> (Smeathman, *Oeconomy c.*1775: 5)

> I have also seen them, when the tarpaulins were, through ignorance or inadvertently, thrown over the gratings, attempting to heave them up, and crying out 'Kickeraboo, Kickeraboo', which figures we are dying.
>
> (Testimony of Thomas Trotter, **HCSP 73: 85**)

> In every cargo whatever, so far as my obervation extents, there are always a few got from the district adjoining to the Beach—these, from a long intercourse with Europeans in general, speak English pretty well—the most of those know the language of the adjoining country on their back, and those again the language of others still further back—by which means we come to the complaints of the Negroes, through the mouths of three, four or five interpreters.
>
> (Testimony of John Knox, **HCSP 68: 107**)

These brief observations by Henry Smeathman (passenger), Thomas Trotter (surgeon), and John Knox (captain) together capture the linguistic complexity of the slave ship. The first shows captives responding to a version of the English maritime idiom 'mess', denoting a group of people who eat together regularly. These captives have acquired at least one word of the 'Ship English' spoken by slaver crews, and understand that, when they hear it, they are about to be fed. Conversely, the passage from Trotter reveals his own understanding of the meaning of a Fante term. Trotter probably gained this knowledge from the local interpreter, mentioned elsewhere in his parliamentary testimony, who had been engaged when *Brooks* arrived on the Gold Coast.[19] 'Kickeraboo' was in fact first recorded in English by John Atkins, on a slaving voyage made in 1721: it appears in his list of 'Some Negrish Words' as *kickatavoo*.[20] No doubt uttered many times on slave ships, 'kickeraboo' subsequently migrated into Caribbean creole, and is possibly also the basis for the English colloquialism 'kick the bucket'.[21] In the third of these extracts, taken from John Knox's parliamentary testimony, the captain was evidently eager to assure listeners that captives were well treated on his ships; even so,

Knox's account of the tortuous route by which the sick eventually communicated their needs to the ship's surgeon probably comes very close to the complex realities of Middle Passage communication, and in particular to what appears to have been a heavy reliance on 'unofficial' interpreters, drawn from the body captive.

Chapter 7 of this book focused on the trade goods used in acquiring human captives. Barter was, of course, facilitated by communication using words as well as things, and a large body of work is now available on the pidgin (contact) languages that developed along the West African coast following the arrival of the first Portuguese traders in the fifteenth century.[22] Portuguese influenced the lexicon of many of the earliest pidgins in the region, but English, and specifically maritime English, played an important part here too.[23] Linguists have long argued that the 'Ship English' spoken by British sailors informed the lexicon of many West African pidgins.[24] Sally Delgado's recently published book on sailors' speech in the early colonial Caribbean is an important contributor to that body of work. The role of Ship English in West African pidgin development has received less attention, but, in her discussion of African-born sailors involved in the slave trade, Emma Christopher noted that the *grumetes* hired by many slavers on the African coast developed a 'hybrid form of European language'.[25] Picking up on her point, Ray Costello employed the phrase 'ship's creole' in describing such hybrids.[26] But creole languages emerged only as pidgins—the contact languages initially facilitating trade—became mother tongues for subsequent generations. There is certainly some very good eighteenth-century evidence for developed English–African creole languages on the African coast. For example, a group of letters concerning the slave trade at Old Calabar between 1760 and 1789, and the diary of the Efik trader Antera Duke (1785–8), provide detailed evidence concerning an English-based creole language spoken, and written, by both English slave merchants and their African partners.[27] I suggest that a better descriptor for the form of communication employed on slaving vessels is not 'creole', nor even 'pidgin', but *pre*-pidgin (also known as jargon).[28] Neither pre-pidgin nor jargon is a pejorative term: they simply denote initial linguistic interactions in transcultural contexts. On board slave ships, vocabulary drawn from sailors' Ship English mingled with elements of the African languages (and the European language-based creoles) spoken by captives. Augmented by gestures and sign language, and mediated on the African coast by local interpreters, these voyage jargons—each one unique, yet also contributing to the broader process of linguistic exchange emerging over multiple Middle Passages—crossed the Atlantic to the New World, where they contributed to the emergent creoles of the port societies and settlements of the Caribbean and North America.[29] Put another way, the Middle Passage was a site of language acquisition, and what was learned was not lost: as Delgado argues, while there is much work to be done in this field, there is now enough evidence to posit 'a potential Ship Pidgin as one of the pre-existing forms that were available to the transported workers of plantation and port speech communities'.[30]

The anti-slavery patrol vessel *Black Joke*, a little of which survives in the form of a snuffbox crafted from its timbers (Figure 10.1), is particularly important to the consideration of communication between sailors and captive Africans. In 1829, a

Figure 10.1 Snuffbox made from the timbers of HMS *Black Joke*. The lid shows a view of the ship fully rigged. National Maritime Museum, ZBA 2435.4.

fascinating entry was made in the ship's logbook as it cruised African waters under the command of Lieutenant Henry Downes.[31] This entry took the form of a word list in the Aku (here, 'Accou') language used by Hausa and Ijo captives carried away from Ouidah and Badagry (Box 10.1).[32] Alongside the attempted transcriptions of 'Accou' words, the compiler provided English glosses—work undertaken with the aid of an African interpreter.[33] The majority of the words and phrases in this list describe the daily routines at sea with which the present chapter is also concerned: eating, drinking, use of latrines, sickness, washing, and so on. Some entries take the form of brief sentences that the receptives on HMS *Black Joke* might have used in their efforts to communicate basic needs ('*I* want to eat', '*I* have finished'). The translated African voice is at a reductive minimum here, of course, heard only in the words a sailor would regard as important, not the many other words expressing bewilderment, fear, and pain which the speaker might also have uttered in his or her native tongue. Other phrases are in the imperative mood ('go and wash', 'silence', 'hold your tongue') and are clearly English commands translated into Aku. Finally, a handful of terms, such as 'roundhouse' and 'Boatswain', reveal the ship itself in translation. The *Black Joke* word list was not created on a slave ship, but it perfectly captures the dynamics of communication and—through its deployment of imperatives in particular—reveals the use of language as a tool in the management by English speakers of Africans caught up in the slave trade. Much the same commands will have been issued to captives on British slavers, in one language or another, from the moment they embarked.

Whether through coastal trade pidgin, creole languages, or the use of interpreters, Europeans and their African trading partners were generally able to conduct the business of slave trading effectively. But captives often transported over long

Box 10.1 'Accou Language, used by slaves from the Kingdoms of Haysa and Hio, generally taken in vessels from Ouidah and Badagry' (Extract from Logbook of HMS *Sybille* and HMS *Black Joke* (1827–9)

Ah-way	Go and wash
Sa-bi Sa-bi	quick, quickly
Moh-wey	I have washed
Aa-tang	I have finish'd
Luo.si	I don't want
A.bi.pa.mi	I want to eat
A.noo	my belly's sick
E-na	fire
A.gui	wood for fire
O.fiy.mo.ti	I want aguadiente
Ah.ba.do	corn
Lo.do	wait a little
Mai shou	roundhouse
Elai	land
Foo foo	wind
Ganjar	Boatswain
Oto	plenty, enough
Ah dakay	silence
Ahea dah ca oo	silence or you'll get punish'd
Callee callee	hold your tongue
Manjar, manjar	eat
Moulatoo	I want to make water

Source: Extract from the Logbook of HMS *Sybille* and HMS *Black Joke* (1827–9), National Maritime Museum LOG N/41.

distances to the coast, frequently lacked sustained familiarity with trade pidgins and, although often multilingual, spoke a variety of dialects that were not in all cases mutually intelligible. Linguistic mediation was required, and, during a ship's often lengthy stay on the coast, local interpreters played a crucial role in facilitating communication between the crew and recently acquired captives, inculcating a new lexicon of surveillance and discipline as they did so. In his travel memoir, William Snelgrave, who captained fourteen slaving voyages between 1701 and 1730, set out exactly how he used interpreters to lay down the 'ground rules' of the Middle Passage as he saw them:

When we purchase grown people, I acquaint them by the interpreter, 'That now they are become my Property, I think fit to let them know what they are bought for, that they may be easy in their Minds: (For these poor People are generally under terrible

Apprehensions upon their being bought by white Men, many being afraid that we design to eat them, which, I have been told, is a story much credited by the island Negroes;) So after informing them, that they are bought to till the Ground in our Country, with several other Matters; I then acquaint them, how they are to behave themselves on board, towards the white Men; that if any one abuses them, they are to complain to the Linguist, who is to inform me of it, and I will do them Justice: But if they make a Disturbance, or offer to strike a white Man, they must expect to be severely punished.'[34]

For obvious reasons, the local linguists employed by slave ships generally did not accompany those vessels to the Americas. Recognizing the problems this caused for the Middle Passage, the Portuguese adopted a system whereby free and enslaved African sailors were employed as interpreters throughout a voyage.[35] A woman named Rodney, the property of the owners of the Bristol slaver *Alfred*, was sent out with the ship from England to act as interpreter on its 1786 voyage, but this is the only example of its kind that I have found for the British trade.[36] Virtually every statement concerning hired 'linguists' or interpreters in testimonies about British slavers is made with reference to vessels still on the African coast. Robert Norris provides explicit evidence in this regard, explaining to Parliament (**HCSP 68: 12**) that a man and wife incarcerated on the same ship could 'speak to each other but seldom, and that in the hearing of an interpreter if there be one on board, while the vessel remains on the coast'.[37]

The absence of 'official' interpreters during the Middle Passage of British ships deserves greater consideration. While Africans may have begun to navigate a handful of English commands, effective communication between crews and captives will have been near-impossible using English alone: the very existence of the *Black Joke* word list in Box 10.1 underscores this point. Equally, Africans must have been aware of the strategic advantages to be gained by speaking together in tongues that remained unintelligible to their captors. Caribbean newspaper advertisements requesting the return of 'new Negroes' (that is, Africans recently arrived on slave ships) very frequently note that these individuals spoke very little or no English, and it is highly likely that, both on slave ships and in the initial stages of their life in the Americas, many captives actively resisted acquiring English.[38] But others will have acquired some level of English, and, once the coastal linguists were dismissed, it is probable that captains sought to identify all those on board with some command of both African languages and English. In fact, it is easy to point to a range of ways in which such people might have been found, and their skills exploited. First, British vessels often hired black sailors, some of whom will have spoken African languages or English-based pidgins or creoles.[39] In 1721, the RAC requested that every company ship carry 'two or three negroes' to England or the West Indies to train as sailors: they will have acquired the language at the same time.[40] I come back to these bilingual black sailors, many of whom were cooks, in discussing foodways below. Second, some captives boarding ships will inevitably have known more English than others, and these people could have been employed, willingly or unwillingly, as Middle Passage interpreters and informants. In his parliamentary testimony concerning his voyage on *Emilia*, Alexander Falconbridge referred to 'Cape Mount Jack', a captive who at embarkation 'spoke very little English' but 'in process of time he learn'd more.' (**HCSP 72: 294**).[41] Falconbridge does not specify whether Jack was used as an interpreter, but other captives with some command of English were given a similar role on board other ships. Looking back on a slaving voyage he had made as a youth of 17, William Butterworth recalled that on board *Hudibras* in 1786—7 was a boy who

> was the property of Mr Jolly [surgeon on *Hudibras*'s tender, *Preston*] and was coming to England, as a present to that gentleman's mother: as she resided in Bristol, the name of that city was given to the boy. He was made interpreter between our captain and the other slaves, and was employed to persuade them to come up on deck, two at a time, which he found great difficulty in effecting.[42]

John Ash, 12 years old, the Angolan 'servant to Captain John Ash' who was baptized in Liverpool on 7 November 1781, appears three years later on the muster roll of *Hector*, commanded by Captain Ash and making another voyage to Angola.[43] Boys like these—the 'privilege' slaves of ship's officers—may well have doubled as personal attendants and interpreters at sea. Many slave ships also found room for (paying) Englishmen leaving Africa for the Caribbean or England. These passengers included fort employees, or adventurers like the naturalist Henry Smeathman—men who probably had some knowledge of African languages or coastal creoles. By the late eighteenth century, finally, slave ship captains frequently cemented valued trading partnerships by transporting the children of their African and Eurafrican traders to England.[44] In 1767, for example, Ambrose Lace took the son of the Calabar trader Robin John Otto Ephraim to Liverpool and paid for two years of schooling for the boy.[45] Robin John arrived in England via Antigua, on Lace's ship *Edgar*. He was one of numerous free African children to make a Middle Passage crossing in this way. The exact number is unknown, but in 1788 Robert Norris, James Penny, and John Matthews, the three Liverpool delegates speaking for the slave trade in the parliamentary inquiries, presented written evidence (**HCSP 69: 83–6**) in which they estimated that some fifty African-born children were being educated in Liverpool alone at that time. They noted also that many African adults and children made shorter visits to England, returning with 'the favourite Captain to whose care they have been entrusted'. In addition, they reported, Fante sailors were regularly hired to make up crew numbers on slave ships leaving the Gold Coast and returned home on their ship's next voyage.[46] This account suggests that a significant number of African children, and indeed Fante sailors, could potentially have facilitated communication during the Middle Passage.

One way or another, then, African-language-based linguistic interaction continued during the Middle Passage of many British ships. And every voyage involved some degree of relexification, as captives and crews encountered each other's words for both actions and things.

Sailors' Calls-and-Responses

Sailors regularly sang, and some played the fiddle or other instruments (Figure 10.2). Songs from the folk tradition and the musical theatre were popular off-duty entertainments, and arduous collective tasks such as hauling on ropes and cables were accomplished to the rhythm of calls-and-responses.[47]

Work songs were only one way in which call-and-response was embedded in the diurnal rhythms of the ship, as Smeathman's description of a routine employed by the watches on his Middle Passage crossing suggests (*Oeconomy c.*1775: 10):

> Sometimes the watch use the following method. The officer upon the Quarter Deck calls out *Look out a Midships there*, which one of the watch takes up on the main Deck and calls out, *Look out forward there*. The man on the forecastle returns, *Look out Aft there*. On which the whole watch answer together Ay! Ay!

Antiphonal call and response was also a fundamental characteristic of the soundscape in many parts of West Africa, and also among people of colour in the Americas.[48] Captives certainly sang on slave ships, either out of choice, or because they were compelled to do so, and it is striking how often parliamentary testimonies reveal that African singing elicited an emotional response from sailors. Ecroyde Claxton, who sailed as surgeon on *Young Hero* in 1788, was asked in 1791 if the captives on his ship amused themselves by singing. He responded:

> I believe they very seldom amuse themselves by it—they were ordered to sing by the captain, but they were songs of sad lamentations. The words of the songs used by them were, Madda! Madda! Yiera! Yiera! Bemini! Bemini! Madda! Aufera! That is to say, they were all sick and by and by they should be no more. (**HCSP 82, 36**)

Three years after making his voyage, Claxton could remember exactly what sorrow sounded like, though it had been voiced in a language he did not speak. Thomas Trotter was so affected by the 'howling melancholy kind of noise, something expressive of extreme anguish', made by captives on *Brooks* during the night that he asked his interpreter to enquire into the cause (**HCSP 73: 86**). She informed him that 'it was occasioned by finding themselves in a slave room, after dreaming that they had been in their own country among their friends and relations'.[49] Not all listeners were as receptive as Claxton and Trotter. George Pinckard, hearing the singing of a group of Africans on the deck of a slave ship in Carlisle Bay, Jamaica, in 1796, observed that their song 'was a wild yell, devoid of all softness and harmony and loudly chanted in harsh monotony'.[50] This sort of reaction reveals the inability of many white observers to hear music in timbres that clashed rather than blended, or employed dissonance and repetition.[51]

Few English listeners on slavers, however attentive, will have appreciated that Africans used these sorrow songs to affirm their identities and to pass information

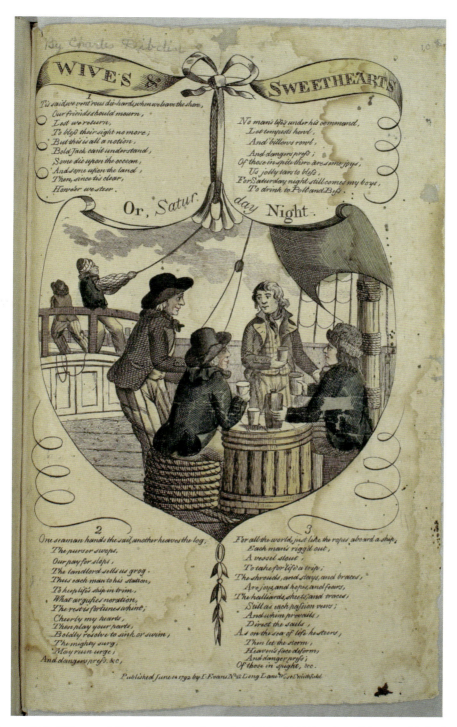

Figure 10.2 *Wives and Sweethearts, or Saturday Night* (1792): a broadsheet published in London by John Evans. The depiction of sailors toasting the health of their loved ones is accompanied by the lyrics from the song, written by Charles Didbin for *Whim of the Moment* in 1788. (*American Antiquarian Society*).

338   MATERIALIZING THE MIDDLE PASSAGE

to each other. I will return to this point in Chapter 11. For the present, a final observation may be offered concerning the impact of musical exchanges upon British sailors serving on slavers. The call-and-response sea shanty—a form of maritime work song that emerged in the early nineteenth century—clearly owes an enormous debt to the singing of free and enslaved black stevedores and sailors labouring in Atlantic ports.[52] Yet, as early as 1743, as Linebaugh and Rediker point out, a group of seamen were court-martialled for singing a 'negro song'.[53] It does not seem unreasonable to suggest that the shanty form might also owe something to the eighteenth-century slave ship and specifically to the moments at which the hauling cries of sailors and the lamentations of captive Africans converged, and resonated, during the Middle Passage.

A Middle Passage Day

The labour of the majority of sailors was generally undertaken in shifts, or watches. On naval vessels, the ship's company was divided into two watches. Each worked in four-hour shifts, and also took one of the two-hour 'dog watches' from four until eight in the evening, meaning that no member of the crew (the senior officers, and specialists such as the carpenter and cook excepted) slept for more than four hours at a time.[54] The timing of watches on slave ships remains unclear, but the daylight hours provided the greatest security challenges to crews, and adult captives were invariably incarcerated below decks between sunset and sunrise. It seems likely, therefore, that the entirety of the able-bodied crew was present on deck during the daylight hours, with a rota in place for a night watch made up of fewer men. Whatever the case, it is likely that, as in the navy, one of the officers of the watch would be charged with timekeeping, using a half-hour sandglass for this purpose. As the sand ran out, the glass would be turned and a bronze or brass bell, suspended on the half- or quarterdeck, would toll the progress of the watch.[55] A single ring of the bell marked the first half-hour of a watch; eight bells called its end.

The slave ship day began relatively late: most slavers preferred to keep their captives below decks for as much time as possible. Let us imagine for this voyage that at 8.00 a.m. the ship's bell was struck eight times, announcing the end of the night watch. The Africans on board may already have been familiar with the sound of a bell ringing, though in other contexts. The face of a Portuguese man, cast in relief on the front of the Edo bell shown in Figure 10.3), reminds us (as discussed in Chapter 6), that in the Kingdom of Benin and elsewhere in West Africa, European sailors were associated with the realm of the dead. Their images were believed to facilitate communication with the supernatural and were thought to be particularly suitable for bells, like this one, associated with ancestral altars. But whether familiar with bells or not, all captives will quickly have come to see that the ringing of the slave ship's bell marked the passage of time and a change of crew.

The day being fair, with the seas moderate and little threat of a downpour or high winds, the master gave orders for the Africans to be brought up on deck. The windsails

Figure 10.3 Brass bell from the Benin Kingdom, dating from the sixteenth or seventeenth century. Metropolitan Museum of Art, 1991.17.85.

were raised from the gratings on the slave deck, and the bunch of keys that opened the ship's many padlocks was brought out.[56] The door of the barricado was secured, and the guns surmounting it manned. These armaments may have included swivel guns and blunderbusses, or 'boat guns' like the four in place on Newton's *Argyle*, mounted on the barricado or inserted into loopholes (*Argyle* 1750–1: 44). Figure 10.4 illustrates the type of swivel gun commonly employed on both naval vessels and slave ships in the later eighteenth century. Research by the Mariners' Museum suggests this gun, found buried in sand near the mouth of Harris Creek on the Back River, Hampton, in 1925 comes from the naval tender *Liberty*, driven aground in a hurricane in 1775. Among the fragments of armaments brought up from the Saint-Quay-Portrieux wreck (a possible slaver) was part of a 'duck-foot' pistol, which could fire five shots simultaneously in different directions.[57] It would have been an ideal weapon for a barricado. The small arms chests were also opened at this point, and the weapons distributed. With all armaments in place, the women's room was unlocked, and the bolts securing the bars on the grated hatchways leading down to the men's room (and any separate boys' room) were drawn. At that moment, most of the crew, excepting the first mate, boatswain, and perhaps

Figure 10.4 Swivel gun (*c*.1750–1770), possibly from the naval tender *Liberty*, wrecked in 1775. Mariners' Museum and Park, 1935.0029.000001A.

also the surgeon, retreated either to the barricaded quarterdeck or (on some ships) the forecastle.[58]

The barricado door was understood by all those crewing a slaver to be the weakest point in their ship's defences. As the Dane Paul Erdmann Isert noted:

> it is established policy that it is better to let a European be killed than to allow the Blacks to gain control of that door, since they could then make their way to the stern of the ship, which is full of weapons hanging there. It would then be a simple task for them to become masters of the ship.[59]

Given such fears, it is easy to see why the barricado door remained locked for much of the day and was also heavily defended. Only a handful of sailors would pass through it as the day progressed. Henry Smeathman's essay is particularly useful in exploring the routine adopted to protect this structure (*Oeconomy c*.1775: 3–4):

> Before or when the men come on deck two Sentries mount guard upon a stage behind the barricade at the top, with musquets and bayonets; where they over look the whole deck; and one at the door of the Barricado with a naked cutlass. This man officiates as porter to the door. When anyone before the partition knocks, he opens a little door to know what he wants and passes the business aft. If the person knocking wants to come aft, the Centinel shuts the small door and bolts it, and then opens the larger one, which is yet so little you must stoop to go through.

DISCIPLINE AND PUNISH 341

Where there is a necessity for greater caution, the centinel does not open the little door, but opens a little loop hole close to the door, through which he can peep and demand who knocks.

With most of the ship's company safe behind the barricado, a handful of sailors now descended to the women's room, whips in hand, moving the occupants towards either the quarterdeck staircase, or a ladder let down through the grating at the fore end of the women's room. Women climbing the stairs, passing the officer's quarters in steerage as they did so, encountered children emerging onto the same stairway. As explored via Robert Norris's detailed testimony in Chapter 5, these small boys and girls had spent the night on the floors of the officers' cabins. Women and girls who had been 'sharing' officers' cots took the same route to the upper deck. The older children billeted on the upper deck left the sleeping places that, as also discussed in Chapter 5, they had been obliged to share with the off-duty sailors. These youngsters may have descended from an elevated platform or crawled out of the spaces under the booms. On some ships they would have been sent to the quarterdeck to join the women and girls. On others, the older boys among them were moved to the forecastle or placed with the male captives on the upper deck.

Despite the heat and filth of the women's room, the locked door and grating had shielded its occupants from sexual violence overnight. In 1796, sailors on the Rhode Island slaver *Mary* attempted to break into the women's room at night, but such actions incurred severe penalties, because they threatened the security of the ship, and they appear to have been rare.[60] From the moment the door opened, however, the female captives became the prey of the crew. The timber barricado structured a social setting in which women and small children were confined on the quarterdeck, day after day, with the greater part of the ship's crew. It is possible that the universal practice of segregating males from females was adopted expressly to provide crews with unfettered access to women, but in my view this is unlikely. Several other factors appear to have been at work here too. First, and crucially, *male* captives were isolated to lessen the threat they posed to their captors; the resultant separation of women was a by-product of that process. Although there is little direct evidence to support this suggestion, it is also likely that slave shipping praxis was informed by the patriarchal construction of gender in the penal system, wherein the incarcerated were routinely separated by gender, and where male warders exerted control over both men and women.[61] Numerous contemporary commentators offer the rationale that gender segregation prevented 'quarrels' among captives. These comments should not be dismissed, given the extremes to which individuals were pushed, but a revealing statement from Thomas Phillips (**Hannibal** 1693–4: 218) suggests that an erroneous belief that profit-sapping 'African' diseases might be transmitted between captives also played a part here.[62] As Phillips put it: 'tho' we separate the men and women aboard by partitions and bulkheads, to prevent quarrels and wranglings among them, yet do what we can they will come together, and that distemper which they call the yaws, is very common here.' Whatever the rationale,

342   MATERIALIZING THE MIDDLE PASSAGE

the segregation of women put them directly in the path of ships' crews and exposed them daily to sexual violence.

The Female Ordeal

> When the women and girls are taken on board a ship, naked, trembling, terrified, perhaps almost exhausted with cold, fatigue and hunger, they are often exposed to the wanton rudeness of white savages ... In imagination, the prey is divided, upon the spot, and only reserved till opportunity offers. Where resistance or refusal, would be utterly in vain, even the solicitation of consent is seldom thought of.
>
> (Newton, *Thoughts* 1788: 105)

Rape was undoubtedly a rite of (middle) passage for many female captives on slavers.[63] But British social *mores* ensured that, even in abolitionist tracts describing the brutalities of a slaving voyage, sexual violence was generally discussed in brief, euphemistic terms. Thus, although James Stanfield spared his readers little concerning the brutalities meted out to both captives and crew on his 1774–6 voyage, he withheld the details of an act 'practiced by the captain on an unfortunate female slave, of the age of eight or nine' (*Observations* 1788: 33). Some suggestions can be made as to where, when, and by whom, girls like this were most at risk of predation, but it is important to preface this assessment by emphasizing that many of the 'women' discussed in sailor's testimonies were children. Slave shippers worked hard to persuade themselves and others that African girls could be considered adult women from puberty, if not before. Inexplicably, many modern scholars still seem prepared to accept that proposition.[64] Yet in the period 1680–1730 the RAC regarded all captives *over 10 years old* as adults.[65] Thereafter, traders began to employ stature as a differential measure—quite literally— in the designation of child and adult captives.[66] Multiple testimonies in the 1788–92 parliamentary inquiry data demonstrate that, by the 1760s, male captives over 4 feet 4 inches were universally regarded as adults. The 1788 Dolben Act, which again stipulated that any male African over 4 feet 4 inches (132 centimetres) was to be considered an adult, simply turned common practice into law.[67] In the UK today, 4 feet 4 inches is the average height of an 8-year-old girl or a 10-year-old boy. British children were certainly smaller in the eighteenth century: Pietsch's analysis of the Marine Society's records for boys who joined the navy during the Seven Years War (1756–63) indicates an average height of 4 feet 4 inches for a boy aged 13.[68] This revealing statistic perhaps goes some way to explaining why 4 feet 4 inches was the figure used to determine 'adult' male status in the slave trade: the same height, that is to say, of the oldest of the 'boys' entering the navy and the merchant marine, who were similarly deemed to be on the cusp of adulthood. Even so, it seems beyond contestation that a significant proportion of the African 'women' to whom sailors referred in their sea logs, memoirs, and witness testimonies had not reached sexual maturity. It follows, too, that some of the 'girls' in these same sources will have been pre-pubescent.[69] Children, as well as adults, were victims of rape and sexual assault on slave ships.

In both the navy and the merchant marine, the female presence on board a ship at sea was not only a rarity; it was superstitiously regarded as a guarantee of bad luck. In this, as in so many other things, slave ships were different: from the moment Africans began to be boarded, women and girls, separated from their male kin and friends, naked, and extraordinarily vulnerable, were a constant presence. Careful reading of the contemporary sources nevertheless indicates that British slave ship sailors understood there to be certain rules governing 'access' to these females.[70] Those rules were structured with reference to the command hierarchy of the ship, and also echoed the 'chivalric' codes informing the treatment of women in military or naval engagements, as exemplified in Smeathman's comment (*Oeconomy c.1775: 8*) that the 'handsome young women are generally under the protection of the Captain, officers and passengers'. As a passenger, Smeathman may well have been extending such 'protection' himself. He also appears to have satisfied himself that the reason that officers 'were obliged to coax' small girls into the cabins rather than the women's room was to defend these children because the older women beat them (*Oecomony c.1775: 8*). Officers expected access to captive females, therefore, and were easily able to obtain it. As Alexander Falconbridge (*Account 1788: 24*) noted: 'The officers are permitted to indulge their passions among them at pleasure, and sometimes are guilty of such brutal excesses as disgrace human nature.'

Captains had their own cabins, and it was to the privacy of these that women and girls would be taken. The written testimony that James Arnold submitted to Parliament in 1788 reports that, a woman slave having been purchased by Joseph Williams, Captain of *Ruby*: 'he sent for her, and ordered her to come by herself; he attempted to sleep with her in the cabin, but on refusing to comply with his desires, she was very severely beaten by him and sent below' (**HCSP 69: 126**). Arnold continues: 'It was the general practice with the Captain [of *Ruby*], on the receipt of a woman slave, to send for her into his cabin for the same purposes, and he has seen several who refused his attempts beaten in the same manner.' Did ordinary sailors have the same 'rights' of access to black women and girls? The answer to this question depended on a number of variables. John Newton's journal entry concerning the rape of a pregnant woman during the 1752–3 voyage of *African* is instructive here:

> William Cooney seduced a woman slave down into the room and lay with her brute like in view of the whole quarterdeck, for which I put him in irons. I hope this has been the first affair of the kind on board and I am determined to keep it quiet if possible. If anything happens to the woman I shall impute it to him, for she was big with child. Her number is 83.[71]

Newton's censure was in part driven by economic considerations: sexual violence resulting in injury might decrease the profit to be made from a captive. Even so, this entry suggests that, on some ships at least, ordinary sailors who 'seduced' captive

344   MATERIALIZING THE MIDDLE PASSAGE

women faced punishment if caught. In this, as in so many aspects of the slave ship's regime, the personal moral code of the captain, and his ability to impose his will on the crew, played a key part. This much is evidenced, for the Dutch trade at least, in a revealing statement made by the crew of the *Haast U Langzaam*, testifying against the actions of the ship's first mate during a voyage to Cape Lahou and the Gold Coast in 1765. The men note that, at Cape Lahou,

> the aforementioned first mate was with the captain and asked for a woman or whore for every sailor, which the captain refused. At this the first mate said it would be for the good of the slaves, and that he had seen it with other captains. The captain answered that he had never made it his habit, and that he would not permit it.[72]

John Newton would not permit it either: he was a god-fearing man, requiring the crew of *African* to observe the Sabbath and trying to play, in his own words, 'the part of a minister to abt. twenty-five people'.[73] Practice varied widely, however, as indicated by Alexander Falconbridge's statement that '[o]n board *some* ships, the common sailors are *allowed* to have intercourse with such of the black women whose consent they can procure' (*Account* 1788: 23–4; emphasis added). But, whatever the ship, the 'opportunity' to which Newton referred above would generally have presented itself to ordinary seamen during the daylight hours, and in the women's room below the quarterdeck. On most ships this room remained unlocked throughout the day, largely because the half- or quarterdeck was so crowded. It would be there, out of sight of the ship's officers, that women and girls would generally be targeted by men like William Cooney. On the quarterdeck itself, however, women were also vulnerable to sexual assault. This point is brought out particularly well in a nineteenth-century lithograph of the main deck of a slaver, by Prexetat Oursel (Figure 10.5). Here, separated by the barricado from the male captives crowded in the waist of the ship, women—naked to the waist, but wearing fabric wrappers around their hips—are being groped by the fully-clothed sailors with whom they share the chaotic quarterdeck.

Oursel was a trained marine draughtsman who had several opportunities to observe slave ships at close hand. He served in the French navy from 1801 until 1813, and an account of his life published in 1887 includes extracts from a journal maintained during two years (1807–8) spent chasing down foreign 'prizes'.[74] One of these was a Portuguese slaver, captured on 31 December 1807.[75] His *Transport des Nègres* is an especially valuable realization, not only for its depiction of the treatment of captive women, but for the detail with which key features of the slaving vessel and its routines are shown. Several features of this lithograph are of particular interest to the present chapter, as will become apparent below. Note the chimney of the 'slave hearth', which is housed in a roofed structure built up against the barricado. Large containers of food are being ferried through an aperture in this defence and handed to the male captives. The group of women in the foreground are 'messmates', sharing a meal from a large bowl set on top of an object that some scholars suggest is a mortar, used for pounding grain.[76]

Figure 10.5 *Transport des Nègres dans les Colonies.* Lithograph by Pretextat Oursel, second quarter of the nineteenth century. Musée des Beaux-Arts, Chartres.

346 MATERIALIZING THE MIDDLE PASSAGE

The Iron Regime: Shackles and Deck Chains

As the morning progressed, male captives and older boys were brought up from their rooms, but in a more controlled way than had been the case with the women and children. Males ascended their ladder in pairs, one couple at a time. Each pair was joined at the ankle by shackle or leg irons, usually fitted soon after embarkation. Shackles could be found on every naval and merchant ship from at least the early seventeenth century, being routinely employed in disciplining petty offenders, or restraining those who threatened order. They were also used in convict transportation.[77] In the 1690s, the decade in which Thomas Phillips commanded the RAC's *Hannibal*, it was not unusual to find male captives on slave ships unchained while on deck. Indeed, Captain Shirley, master of *Hannibal's* sister ship *East Indian Merchant*, drew on his knowledge of African belief systems to mitigate the threat this practice might pose: Philips (**Hannibal 1693–4: 224**) reported that Shirley 'used to make his negroes aboard take the *Fatish* that they would not swim ashore and run away and then he would let them out of irons'. The 'fetish' that Shirley concocted was made of English beer, with the addition of aloes to make it bitter. Phillips himself, in his own words, 'put more dependence upon my shackles'. In this, he was not alone: by the late eighteenth century, male captives were often constrained, not only by ankle shackles, but by deck and mess chains.[78]

As they came up into the daylight, the bolts on the shackles coupling the male captives would be carefully inspected. Smeathman (**Oeconomy c.1775: 3**) records this routine in some detail, noting that the boatswain was required to

> examine the men night and morning to see that they have not cut or filed their irons or got loose, on which account they are not suffered to come up at pleasure, but are compelled to come singly or in pairs up a scuttle in the gratings, which will not admit of more at a time.

Their irons having been inspected, each pair of male captives joined the two lines of men beginning to form on the deck. A length of chain, bolted down to the deck timbers at several points, was passed through a ring on their shackles. This additional form of restraint, known as a deck chain, was employed on many later eighteenth-century ships. Alexander Falconbridge mentioned such chains in 1788, and made their purpose clear (**Account 1788: 21**):

> Their irons being examined, a long chain, which is locked to a ring-bolt hole, fixed in the deck, is run through the rings of the shackles of the men, and then locked to another ring-bolt, fixed also in the deck. By this means, fifty or sixty, and sometimes more, are fastened to one chain, in order to prevent them from rising, or endeavouring to escape.

Deck chains are not mentioned in the earliest British accounts, but were certainly in use by the time John Newton was captaining slaving vessels in the 1750s: he recalled them in his 1788 memoir (*Thoughts* **1788: 103**). Smeathman (*Oeconomy c.1775: 2–3*) indicates that two such chains were used, one each side of the deck, adding that 'the ends of the chains are put through a small hole in the bottom of the barricado and locked upon the quarter-deck'.[79]

The hundreds of restraints required by slavers were purchased from British ironmongers—many of them also foundry operators—whose varied stock included everything from dog collars to hoes and armaments. Thus, prior to sailing from London, Samuel Gamble had received on board *Sandown*: 'Sundry stores from Mount & Johnstons [*sic*] ironmongers, mapping desk, 4 cartridge guns 2 swivells, big iron handcuffs, neck chains & collars, mess and deck chains, slave hearth [hearth] and furnace' (*Sandown* **1793–4: 7**).[80] Shackles and chains were referenced repeatedly in the testimonies collated during the parliamentary inquiries of 1788–92, a factor that no doubt informed Thomas Clarkson's decision to purchase examples of both ankle and wrist shackles in 1787 (Figure 10.6). Both sets were fastened by means of padlocked bolts—a technological advance on the iron wedges in use a century earlier.

The wreck of the slaver *Henrietta Marie* provides considerable insights into the use of shackles during the Middle Passage. Components from 81 double shackles, enough to restrain more than 160 people, were recovered from the wreck site. They comprised paired, U-shaped shackles known as bilboes, which were fitted over the ankles or wrists.[81] The right ankle or wrist of one person was coupled to the left ankle or wrist of another in a metal bond that, for many captives, would endure for the entire crossing. The basic design comprised two U-shaped 'bracelets' looped on to a bolt fashioned from iron round-stock. At one end of the bolt was a forged head and at the other a pierced slot. The head served as a stop to keep the loops from sliding over the end of the bolt. The same effect was achieved at the other end by hammering an iron wedge tightly into the slot, locking the shackles, and thus the captives, to the bolt and each other.[82] As noted in Chapter 7, the stamped iron bars in *Henrietta Marie*'s cargo of trade goods were provided by the ironmonger Anthony Tournay. His business associate Ambrose Crowley, whose vast ironworks in Swalwell (Tyne & Wear) made slave restraints for the RAC, may have provided the shackles.[83]

While the shackles from *Henrietta Marie* were made to one design, slight stylistic variations suggest that they were the work of numerous artisans—men labouring in British foundries to curtail the freedom of others imprisoned on faraway ships. One of the restraints from *Henrietta Marie* was seized with cord; this had been wound around the metal, presumably during the crossing, in order to prevent chafing of the captives' skin.[84] Figure 10.7 illustrates a very similar cord-wrapped shackle from the *Queen Anne's Revenge* wreck site.[85]

The practice of cord-wrapping is nowhere mentioned in the textual record but may have been very common: the constant motion of the sea, allied with the combined weight of the shackle, bolt, and chain (which Robert Norris put at 'a pound or a pound and two ounces' (**HCSP 68: 13**)) meant that abrasions and infections were common on wrists and ankles. Some of the restraints recovered from *Henrietta Marie* were diminutive, leading Corey Malcom to suggest that they had been used to shackle either the wrists of small adults, or the ankles of juveniles.[86] A hundred years later, sailors giving evidence to Parliament were uniformly emphatic that women and children were not shackled on British ships. The evidence from *Henrietta Marie* suggests that, in 1700 at least, that might not have been the case.

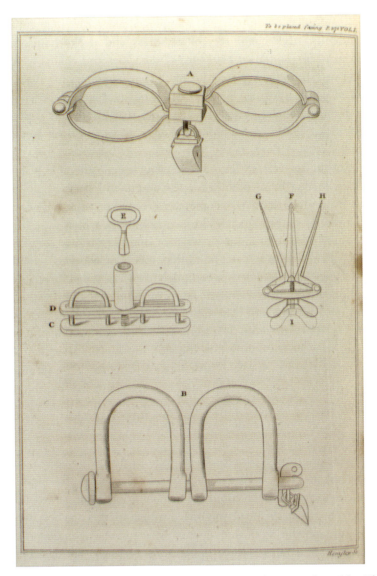

Figure 10.6 Items of restraint, punishment, and force-feeding, purchased by Thomas Clarkson in Liverpool. (A) shackles for the wrists, (B) shackles for the ankles, (C–E) components of thumbscrews, (F–I) components of a speculum oris. Illustrated in Clarkson (1808: i, between pp. 374 and 375).

Figure 10.7 Cord-wrapped shackle from the *Queen Anne's Revenge* wreck site.

With the able-bodied captives all now on deck, the ship's surgeon ventured below to traverse the various 'rooms' and note overnight deaths or additions to his sick list. In the men's room, this might mean separating the living from the dead to whom they were still shackled. Next, he attended to ailing crew and captives, the latter confined in whatever space has been set aside as a 'hospital.' Some of the watch began the lengthy daily routine of scraping clean the faeces, urine, blood, and vomit that had accumulated on the slave decks overnight. This loathed regime has been discussed, as has the work of the surgeon, in Chapter 9. Other men were detailed to the maintenance of the ship. Sun, salt, wind, and rain battered the hull, deck timbers, sails, masts, spars, and rigging day after day; all required near-constant attention. As Rodger put it with reference to the Georgian navy, 'maintenance and repair was the common occupation of the ship's company—the seamen working on the rigging, the carpenter and his crew on the hull and spars, the sailmaker and crew on the sails and the armourer, who acted as the ship's blacksmith, on ironwork'.[87] Sails also had to be furled and unfurled regularly, as changes in wind force and direction required, obliging the ship's 'topmen' to walk out onto the yards, or scramble up through the rigging. For the remainder of the on-duty crew, the principal work of the forenoon watch was to feed the captives.

Middle Passage Foodways

For both captives and crews, the social organization of foodways on board slave ships followed long-established maritime practice, whereby crews were divided into messes: groups of sailors, organized according to rank, who ate and drank together regularly. Crewmen on slavers certainly ate with regular messmates. Barker noted that each mess on *Thetis* was given one piece of meat daily on the Middle Passage, 'which according to the custom of Guinea voyages should be chosen by each mess in their turn' (**Thetis 1754–5: 14**). On the journey to Africa, slaver crews ate familiar foods laden before the voyage began. Samuel Gamble noted down carefully his receipt of 41 tierces beef, 20 barrels of pork, 19 firkins of butter, 50 kegs of tripe, 221 barbaroons (rum-laced fruit cakes), 20 barrels of white bread and 15 more of flour, a puncheon of rum 'for ship's use', 1 ton of potatoes, and 2 firkins of barley (**Sandown 1793-4: 2–14**). The astonishing quantity of tripe presumably offered a thrifty solution to the daily ration of meat that, from 1789, slavers were obliged to provide by law (see Box 10.2). Once on the African coast, the crew's diet expanded considerably. Fish was readily available (see Figure 10.8 for its acquisition) and provisioning details were also sent to shore to

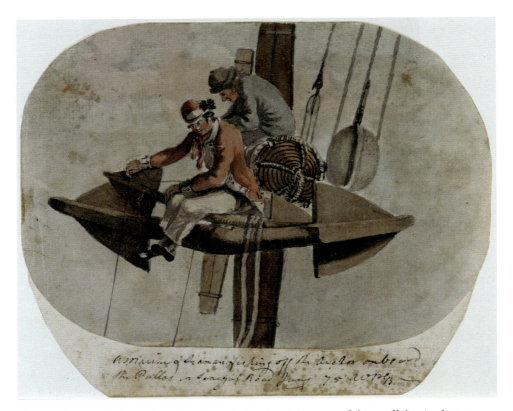

Figure 10.8 Gabriel Bray's watercolour *A Marine & Seaman fishing off the Anchor on board the Pallas in Senegal Road, Jany 75* shows two men from HMS *Pallas* catching fish off the port anchor. National Maritime Museum, PAJ2013.

capitalize on an abundance of fresh foods. Among the many things Gamble and his crew ate in Africa were bonito and porpoise, caught with the ship's fish spear and harpoon; 'fresh stock' (that is, cattle, sheep, goats, pigs, and fowls, including capons),[88] and cucumbers, picked and then pickled by the crew. Gamble himself dined handsomely on shellfish, crabs, turtle eggs, and roasted fowls while on shore (*Sandown* 1793–4: 38, 60, 63, 70–3).

For much of the period discussed in this book, no designated living or eating spaces were reserved for ordinary seamen during the Middle Passage.[89] Meals were taken on the quarterdeck, using durable utensils such as the pewter plates, scarred with knife marks, found on the *Henrietta Marie* wreck site.[90] In the seventeenth century, cutlery was often individually owned: a case containing a silver handled knife, fork, and spoon, belonging to John Barbot, was tossed overboard by a monkey he had acquired in Boutroe.[91] Captains and their officers usually ate in a wardroom set aside for them (presumably below the quarterdeck), using much finer tableware. The officers on *Fredensborg* dined from a Staffordshire stoneware service (Figure 10.9), supped coffee from Chinese export porcelain coffee cups, and took their tea from a Wedgwood Egyptian-style teapot.[92] Tea appears to have been taken with some formality on certain slave ships: the pathologically vicious master under whom James Stanfield served was supplied with a large tea-kettle full of water every morning and evening (*Observations* 1788: 13). A surviving receipt concerning wallpaper for the cabin on the Liverpool ship *Badger* provides a further hint that slave ship captains were not without their domestic comforts.[93]

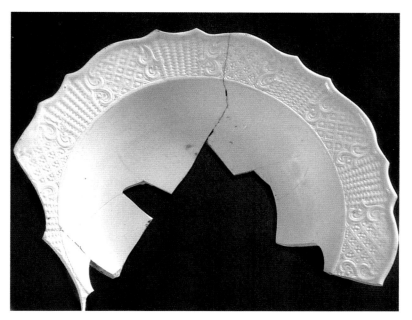

Figure 10.9 Mid-eighteenth-century salt-glazed stoneware dish with moulded border recovered from the wreck of *Fredensborg*. Aust-Agder Museum.

352 MATERIALIZING THE MIDDLE PASSAGE

The cooks on seventeenth- and eighteenth-century merchant vessels employed a rudimentary brick-lined hearth upon which was set a riveted copper boiler or 'kettle' (an example can be seen in Figure 10.10).[94] The usual fuel for hearths was wood, but coal was also employed.[95] Both oven bricks and beech firewood were found on the *Fredensborg* wreck site—the wood evidently the remainder of a stock carried all the way to Africa from Denmark, only to be wrecked a year later off the coast of Norway.[96] A single hearth was generally enough to prepare food for a merchant vessel's crew, but by the time of its departure from Africa a slaver was carrying hundreds of captives, all of whom would need regular meals throughout an average nine weeks at sea. A second hearth was set up on many slavers for this purpose. In 1699, James Barbot noted that the commander of the Fort at Gross-Friedrichsburg had sent *Albion* 'some of his bricklayers, to set up our copper aboard, for our slaves'.[97] Thomas Phillips similarly refers to the 'large copper furnace' used in preparing meals for the Africans on board his ship (*Hannibal* 1693–4: 229), and, in the months prior to sailing from Dartmouth in 1700, *Daniel and Henry* acquired its 'grain kettle' in Rotterdam (*Daniel* 1700: 23). For purposes of access and crew safety, these large 'slave hearths' were always positioned aft of the barricado. Describing the construction of such a hearth on the frigate-built *Argyle*, Newton references what must have been the optimum spot on a twin-masted ship, noting that the crew 'sheathed [with metal] the forepart of the mainmast and the deck between it and the barricado in order to set up the furnace'. In the shelter of the barricado, therefore, a little fore of the crowded quarterdeck, the cook produced two meals a day for the ship's captives.[98] Newton's slave 'furnace' of the 1750s was clearly brick-lined, but, in the 1790s, Samuel Gamble employed on *Sandown* an iron 'slave hearth and furnace' purchased from the London ironmonger Mount and Johnson (*Sandown* 1793–4: 7). In 1780, Alexander Brodie had designed and patented for the Royal Navy a free-standing wrought iron cookstove, which incorporated a tray and firebox.[99] Slavers would have neither need nor space for Brodie's huge stoves, but Gamble's journal suggests some level of adoption of the use of iron equipment.[100]

Two copper kettles have been recovered from the wreck of *Henrietta Marie*. The larger, with a capacity of almost exactly one-half of a cubic yard, will have held the single course, starch-based meals fed to Africans. This cauldron lacks handles and comprises a vast single chamber: based on its dimensions, the capacity was calculated to be about 321.71 litres—enough to cater for at least 300 captives.[101] Slave furnaces were taken down on arrival in the Americas; when excavated, the larger copper from *Henrietta Marie* was found to contain a mass of concreted chains, probably the ones used to hang it over the heat source, stored inside it for the return voyage.[102] The smaller cauldron with two chambers, one of exactly one cubic foot, and the other one and a half cubic feet, was almost certainly used to prepare food for the crew. The twin handles perhaps suggest that it too was suspended on chains above an open fire. This cauldron was probably used in cooking for the crew, perhaps on a small hearth dedicated to their needs. Smeathman (*Oeconomy c.*1775: 5) described such a 'cub

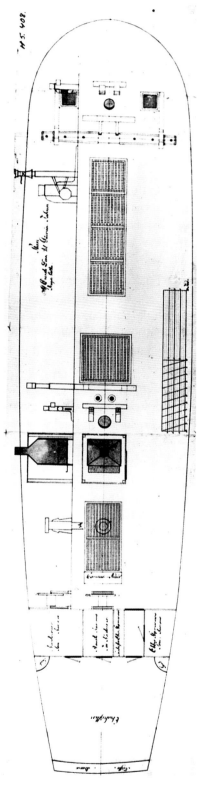

Figure 10.10 Photograph of a deck plan of the Danish ship *Rio Volta* (Danish National Archives) showing, in both plan view and section, the position and appearance of key components of the upper deck, including (at the centre) the cooking stove. *Rio Volta* was constructed in 1777 and made four slaving voyages. Neg. A.3457, M/S Museet for Søfart, Maritime Museum of Denmark.

354 MATERIALIZING THE MIDDLE PASSAGE

house, or little hutch, which contains a fire place, where he [the cook] boils, roasts, broils and fricassees after a fashion for the Captain's Table and the crew'.

As their excavator has suggested, the two cauldrons from *Henrietta Marie* are powerful manifestations of oppression and inequality.[103] They indicate that food preparation was not simply differentiated on board slave ships; it was segregated. Documentary evidence indicates that the same may be said for food consumption: while some foodstuffs, such as stockfish and yams, were consumed by both captives and crews during the Middle Passage, they were eaten in different places, at different times, and using different utensils. And some foodstuffs, such as the livestock penned in cages adjoining the latrines used by captives on the upper deck of *Marie-Séraphique* (see Figure 5.6), were no doubt consumed principally by the ship's officers. At the same time, however, the larger copper from *Henrietta Marie*, ideally suited to preparing the 'one-pot' meals with a high-starch, low-meat content eaten throughout much of West Africa, suggests some engagement by ships' crews with African foodways.[104]

To explore this point further, it is necessary to turn to the food provided for captives during the Middle Passage. The documentary evidence for the provisioning of British slave ships is particularly rich in this respect. Voyage logs, memoirs, and data collated during the parliamentary inquiries all point to a remarkably consistent regime that was established well before 1700 and persisted until the abolition of the British trade in 1807. Bulky foods that kept well—flour, grains, oatmeal, dried peas and beans (particularly fava beans, known as 'horse beans'), salted meat, and fish—were all purchased before the voyage began and were consumed on all three legs of the voyage. But additional protein- and carbohydrate-rich foods, used primarily but not exclusively to feed captives, were also sourced on the African coast. The exact proportion of locally grown foods employed on British slavers is currently a subject of some debate. But there is broad agreement that over the eighteenth century the proportion of the foods taken on board in Europe for captive use increased, while the quantity of African-grown foods declined considerably.[105] British ships appear to have been more reliant upon African foods than other European vessels, and, as is clear from documentary sources, African foodways practices were acknowledged, and enacted, by British slaver crews.[106]

Slave ships acquired what was available locally, so vessels leaving Upper Guinea (including Newton's *Argyle* and Gamble's *Sandown*) were laden with the 'red' rice (*O. glaberrima*) widely cultivated in the region.[107] Ships leaving Lower Guinea (including *Daniel and Henry* and *Fredensborg*) bought maize, sorghum (known as 'Guinea corn'), or millet. Yams and plantains were purchased in huge quantities by ships visiting the Niger Delta.[108] While local foodways dictated what was available, it was widely recognized that captives were more likely to remain healthy if their diet was based on familiar foods. In 1693, Thomas Phillips described the staple foods used on *Hannibal*: vast quantities of horse beans, brought out from England, were dished up alongside 'dabbadabb'—a maize-based porridge made from finely ground grain, boiled with water and dressed with salt, melegueta pepper, and palm oil. Phillips carried out mills, made of iron, in which the maize (he called it Indian corn) would be ground (*Hannibal* 1693–4: 229). Melegueta was widely used in provisioning slavers.

Phillips bought '1000 weight of it at 1 iron bar' on the River Sino, noting that '[t]he reason of our buying this pepper is to give it our negroes in their messes to keep them from the flux and dry belly-ach' (*Hannibal* 1693–4: 195). Dabbadab was described again, a generation later, by John Atkins, who, having sailed with the RAC to Gambia in 1721, also recommended horse beans, rice, Indian corn, and farine as commodious and cheap options for captives. He noted that '[o]ne or other is boild on board at constant times, twice a day, into a Dab-a-Dab (sometimes with meat in it)'.[109] Writing in 1788, Alexander Falconbridge noted that the diet of the African captives on Bristol ships of this period still chiefly comprised boiled horse beans, yams, and rice alongside 'slabber sauce' (presumably a corruption of 'Dab-a-Dab') made from palm-oil, flour, water, and pepper (*Account* 1788: 21).

The preparation of foods for captives brought crews into contact with African foodways in a variety of ways. Sometimes, these encounters were mediated by black cooks. Men of African birth or descent from all parts of the Atlantic world signed on for slaving voyages.[110] But a disproportionate number shipped as cooks, perhaps suggesting that slavers actively sought cooks with an assumed familiarity (by virtue of their colour) with African foodways. Black cooks were present on numerous voyages central to this book. They include George Yorke, on *Daniel and Henry* (*Daniel* 1700: 54); the unnamed cook on Falconbridge's *Alexander* voyage (**HCSP 72**: 343), and James Atkins, on *Sandown* (*Sandown* 1793–4: 16). Others, noted in parliamentary testimonies, include a black Portuguese cook on *Little Pearl* (**HCSP 69**: 135) and the unnamed sailor on *Juno* who was beaten repeatedly with the 'rice-stir' that he used in preparing meals for the ship's captives (*Substance* 1789: 16).[111] Cooks and captains certainly developed a considerable understanding of African food-preparation techniques. In 1694, Thomas Phillips bought some 'cancy-stones' for use on *Hannibal*. He was clearly well acquainted with the production of cancy (or kenkey) bread, noting (*Hannibal* 1693–4: 221) that, at Ouidah,

> they place the cancy stone, which is smooth and broad, shelving in a frame; then put on it thirty or forty grains of Indian corn after it has lain some time soaking in water, then with the rubber (which is a small stone big enough for one to grasp in his hand) they bruise the corn, and continue rubbing it till it is reduc'd to a meal. Of the said meal temper'd with water they make round lumps like dumplins, which they boil in an earthern crock or bake over the fire on an iron or stone.[112]

In his parliamentary testimony, Robert Heatley (**HCSP 69**: 123) noted that sailors were occasionally employed in preparing the provisions laid in for the Middle Passage:

> which provision consists of Guinea-corn, rice and cuss-cuss—the latter is prepared by beating the corn into flour, granulating it in shallow baskets, putting it into earthen cullenders, over an iron pot with water kept boiling, slopt close round with paste, to be done in the steam, and is either eat immediately, with pouring gravy made from flesh, fish or fowl, or dried in the sun and put in casks for the voyage.

A number of witness accounts suggest that captives assisted in food preparation. The 'cancy-stones' acquired by Phillips were 'for our slaves to grind their corn upon' (*Hannibal* 1693–4: 202), for example. Thomas Smith appears to have been referring to women assisting the cook on *Squirrel* in 1763, in his statement that, as the horse beans are being prepared for breakfast, 'the Black Women use broad sticks, which they turn round, licking them with their fingers, and calling out *Suffie, suffie Grand*' to announce the meal is ready.[113] Smeathman notes that the cook on his vessel was aided by 'three or four or half a dozen black wenches pounding, washing and boiling in an immense large cauldron' (*Oeconomy c.*1775: 5). In a letter to his patron Dru Drury, describing a slave ship in the rains of the African coast, Smeathman also referred to 'women slaves in the one part beating rice in wooden mortars to cleanse it for cooking'.[114] An entry in the journal from the ship *Mary* in 1796 similarly records women pounding rice and grinding corn for corn cakes.[115] A painting of *Fredensborg (II)* dating to 1788 depicts two women on the ship's quarterdeck pounding grain in a mortar (see Figure 5.20). This image, as Judith Carney emphasizes, not only provides visual confirmation of the fragmentary textual evidence suggesting African women were obliged to prepare grain on board slavers but underscores the way in which slave ship praxis replicated the gendered organization of such work in West Africa.[116] A sandstone mortar was found on the wreck site of *Fredensborg II*'s sister ship and is illustrated in Figure 10.11. The captain's journal reveals that three such stones were in use, facilitating the preparation of meals based almost entirely on beans and millet.[117] His terminology is instructive: the excavated example, worn by the action of a rounded grinding stone, bears closer resemblance to Phillips's 'cancy-stones' than to the mortar-and-pestle arrangement

Figure 10.11 A sandstone mortar (400 × 250 × 230 mm) found on the *Fredensborg* wreck site. Aust-Agder Museum.

depicted on *Fredensborg II*. Two grindstones were also recovered from the wreck of the Danish *Havmanden*, discussed in Chapter 4.[118]

Black-eyed peas, pearl millet, sorghum, rice, yams, and other foods eaten on board slavers became the staples of the New World diet of the enslaved.[119] Judith Carney, creator of the influential 'black-rice' hypothesis that credits enslaved saltwater Africans with the establishment of rice production in the Americas, has asserted that 'the slave ship served as the vessel by which African plants arrived in the Americas'.[120] The extent to which the slave ship should be regarded as the *primary* conveyor of African foods to the Americas is a much-debated topic at present.[121] But Carney is right to raise the possibility that grains capable of germination might have been transported—covertly or otherwise—on the bodies of disembarking captives. While an oral tradition from Brazil that rice was imported into Maranhão hidden in the hair of a female captive is the sole relevant source to that effect, beads, amulets, and other objects occasionally entered the Americas on captive bodies (as discussed in Chapter 11), and it not impossible that grains and seeds may sometimes have arrived that way too.[122] On balance, however, the recent suggestion that African rice was carried to the Americas 'not by slaves but by slavers' seems a sensible middle ground in a contentious debate.[123]

Sailors also shared in the foods acquired on the African coast. Before 1789, when slave ships were finally obliged by law to supply crews with adequate rations, seamen were often poorly supplied with meat, and thus relied upon the staples fed to captives. Robert Barker reported that rice, yams, and beans were the 'chief support' of the crew during his Middle Passage, supplementing a meagre allowance of two ounces of meat per day and four pounds of bread weekly (*Thetis* 1754–5: 22). The detailed articles of agreement between masters, officers, and men appended to 29 Geo. 3 c. 66 in 1789 (Box 10.2) indicate that, while home-sourced foods were preferred options, the better-fed sailors of the later eighteenth century were still required to eat rice, yams, pulses, and so on when those familiar foods ran out.[124]

In the dying days of the British slave trade, the crew and captives alike on Hugh Crow's *Kitty's Amelia* were fed on a broth made of dried shrimps mixed with flour and palm oil (*Kitty's* 1807–8: 146). In common with their captives, crews also regularly consumed melegueta pepper, which was obtained by grinding the seed of the plant and was, as noted in Chapter 8, prized in Britain both for its pungent taste and as a flavouring (and supposed strengthening agent) for beer and gin.[125]

Captives, like crews, were fed in messes. As John Knox explained to Parliament (HCSP 68: 178): 'The negroes on board an African ship are classed into tens, each of which classes mess by themselves, by which means not one can be overlooked, as they sit in a circle.' This process of arranging captives in groups of ten at mealtimes was as old as the slave trade itself: it was mentioned in 1594 by the Italian adventurer 1594 Francesco Carletti, in his account of his slave-trading voyage to the Cape Verde islands.[126] Almost two hundred years later, a very similar scene was captured in 1771 by an unnamed artist, depicting a mealtime on the second voyage of the French slaver *Marie-Séraphique* (Figure 10.12).

358 MATERIALIZING THE MIDDLE PASSAGE

> **Box 10.2 Extract from Schedule A appended to 29 Geo. 3 c. 66 (1789), An Act to continue, for a limited Time, and amend an Act, made in the last Session of Parliament, intituled, An Act to regulate, for a limited Time, the shipping and carrying Slaves in British Vessels from the Coast of Africa**
>
> The said Master does further agree and engage with the said Officers, Mariners, Seamen, Seafaring men, Landsmen and Boys, that they shall be daily and regularly supplied with good wholesome Victuals, and a portion of Wine or Sprits, as hereafter specified: the said provisions to be issued and dressed in the usual manner in which it is done on Board His Majesty's Ships of War, and served out to the Ship's Company in the Manner following, videlicet,
>
> > Sunday—one Pound and a Half of Beef, containing Sixteen ounces to the Pound, and a Pint of Flour
> >
> > Monday—one Pound of Pork, containing Sixteen ounces to the Pound, and half a Pint of Pease
> >
> > Tuesday—one Pint of Oatmeal and Two Ounces of Butter, and Four Ounces of Cheese; or, one Pound of Stock Fish, with One Eighth of a Pint of Oil, and Quarter of a Pint of Vinegar, in lieu of Butter and Cheese
> >
> > Wednesday—The same as Monday
> >
> > Thursday—The same as Sunday
> >
> > Friday—The same as Tuesday
> >
> > Saturday—The same as Monday
>
> Each person, besides, to have Six Pounds of bread per Week, and a Quarter of a Pint of Spirits, or Half a Pint of Wine, together with [blank] of Water, per Day, of the Voyage. In lieu of Pease and Oatmeal may be served Rice, Indian Corn, Yams, or Calavances.

This unique image shows captives, arranged in groups of ten, seated around circular containers holding the food each unit would share. The male captives are, of course, eating fore of the barricado, separated from the women and children, who are being fed on the quarterdeck. Food was generally distributed in this way in the morning and late afternoon, the process usually being overseen by the ship's first or second mate.[127] As second mate on *Neptune*, for example, John Ashley Hall was tasked with supervising the distribution of meals to women and children on the quarterdeck and roundhouse (poop) (HCSP 72: 253). As Phillips noted on *Hannibal*:

> they are fed twice a day, at 10 in the morning and 4 in the evening ... they are divided into messes of ten each for the easier and better order in serving them ... The men are all fed upon the main deck and forecastle, that we may have them all under command of our arms from the quarter-deck ... the women eat upon the quarter-deck with us,

Figure 10.12 Colorized version of an archived copy of *Vue du navire la Marie-Séraphique de Nantes au moment de repas des captives. 2e voyage a Loangue 1771*. The original painting is privately owned. Collection Dauvergne, Plate No. 9912, National Maritime Museum, France.

and the boys and girls upon the poop; after they are once divided into messes, and appointed their places, they will readily run there in good order of themselves afterwards. (*Hannibal* 1693–4: 229)

By the mid-eighteenth century, the range of 'irons' in use on British ships had grown considerably, and their impact on mealtimes bears consideration. Thomas Smith, who joined the slaver *Squirrel* after the loss of his first ship, *Ann Galley*, in an insurrection in 1763, indicates that on this ship male captives were weighted down by a combination of chains and shackles that secured them *permanently* in groups of ten. He says that the male captives were 'loaded with heavy shackles of iron, and every ten are chained together fast at the necks, hands and feet'. They eat together, 'ten in number', and at night, when one man wants to use the necessary tub, 'all the rest upon the chain, ten in

360 MATERIALIZING THE MIDDLE PASSAGE

number, went along with them'.[128] This is the sole reference I have found to such a process, and so many testimonies refer to males being shackled in pairs, not tens, that Smith's memory may be at fault here.[129] A generation later, however, *Sandown* was certainly carrying 'mess chains' (*Sandown* 1793–4: 7), again suggesting than captives were bound together in groups of ten (the standard number of people in a maritime 'mess'). But it is also possible that mess chains were used *only* at mealtimes, with captives being released from the deck chain and immediately resecured using shorter lengths of chain that bound one mess of ten men together, for the purpose of eating. Different vessels may well have used their 'irons' in a variety of ways, but, however they were employed, mess chains must surely have joined captives together at the ankle, not the wrist. Smeathman (*Oeconomy c.*1775: 5) certainly appears to indicate that, on his later eighteenth-century crossing, men were not chained at the wrist at mealtimes. This passage also demonstrates that captives being shipped from Sierra Leone (many of whom will have been Muslims) went to some lengths to maintain their cultural preference for eating with the right hand:

> A boy slave or two, then march amongst them with a bucket of water and a small can, and pour a little into the right hand of everyone as they sit, which they wash by moving their thumb and finger, without any assistance from their left hand, as it is never used in feeding... this done, instead of a Towel they snap their fingers, and giving their hands a shake at the same time leave the wind to dry them, and rest them upon their knees, without making any use of them until their victuals is served.[130]

Mealtimes obliged Africans to eat unfamiliar foods alongside those they knew well. Falconbridge noted that most despised horse beans so much that, 'unless they are narrowly watched, when fed upon deck, they will throw them overboard, or in each other's faces when they quarrel (*Account* 1788: 22).[131] Captives were also expected to use a range of unfamiliar wooden artefacts, including buckets or tubs, smaller bowls, and spoons. John Barbot (*Treatment* 1712: 781) noted: 'We distributed them [meals] by ten in a mess, about a small flat tub, made for that use by our coopers, in which their victuals were served.' These tubs, known as 'crews', were to be found on British ships throughout the trade. As *Sandown* neared Africa in May 1793, Gamble's cooper James Ronald was set to work making crews, for example (*Sandown* 1793–4: 29). Alexander Falconbridge noted that food was served to captives 'in tubs, about the size of a small water-bucket' (*Account* 1788: 22) and Robert Heatley (*HCSP* 69: 123) described such tubs as containing three full gallons. Thomas Smith also mentions crews, describing them as 'similar to a bucket, without lugs'.[132] While the sharing of food by group seated around a central vessel was something with which most African captives will have been entirely familiar, the expectation that a spoon should be used to convey food to the mouth was not. Clearly regarding the widespread African custom of eating with the hand as a signifier of all things primitive, European slavers seem to have drawn considerable satisfaction from the notion that the Middle Passage introduced captive Africans to the spoon. Barbot (*Treatment* 1712: 781) noted that each person in a mess had 'a little wooden spoon to feed himself handsomely, and more cleanly than with their fingers, so that they were well pleased with it'. James Fraser, Alexander Falconbridge, and Hugh Crow all mention these utensils too; but, reading between the lines of certain of their comments, one can see that these little spoons—an alien foodways technology for most Africans—were rarely used as intended. Thus, Falconbridge (*Account* 1788: 22) notes that 'they feed themselves with wooden spoons. These they soon lose, and when they are not allowed others, they feed themselves with their hands.'[133] Smeathman (*Oeconomy c.*1775: 6) makes very careful (and, as ever, patronizing) observations about eating, which on his ship did not involve spoons, but instead followed African practices closely:

> The oldest Slave in the Mess[,] for they are accustomed to pay great respect to Age, divides the little morsel of fish very equally among them. This they generally lay on one side as a bon bouche as children hoard the raisins in a plum pudding, and dipping their hands into the tub with great decorum, take up about the quantity of a spoonful more or less, which turning and squeezing in their fingers till it is cool and compact they convey it to their mouths and eat with apparent satisfaction.

Drinking water (and on occasion spirits) were also distributed to captives at mealtimes: in fact, these were probably the only occasions on which water was readily available. The range of utensils used in water distribution varied over time. Barbot remarked early in the eighteenth century: 'At each meal we allow'd every slave a full coco-nut shell of water, and from time to time a dram of brandy, to strengthen their stomachs' (*Treatment* 1712: 781). By the later eighteenth century, water was issued in long-handled pannekins, as noted in several of the 1788–92 testimonies.[134] Falconbridge similarly referenced the use of pannekins, noting: 'Their allowance of water is about half a pint each at every meal. It is handed round in a bucket or watering pail and given to each negroe with a pannekin: a small utensil with a straight handle somewhat similar to a sauce boat' (*Account* 1788: 22).

The pannekin facilitated careful control of the quantity of water consumed by captives. Although every slave ship's hold was crammed with puncheons of water, filled immediately before leaving Africa, its consumption was a perennial source of anxiety for captains. There were numerous reasons for this: the length of the Middle Passage might be longer than anticipated; barrels leaked, and only constant maintenance by the cooper could limit losses; and water quality decreased markedly as a voyage lengthened, sometimes to the point where it was too foul to drink. The quantity of water given to Africans—often no more than a pint or two a day—was entirely insufficient, particularly since these people were confined in stifling holds overnight. The water available to ship's crews was also severely restricted, and on many later eighteenth-century vessels a singular strategy was employed to limit usage. A scuttlebutt (a water barrel with a hole cut in the top) was available on the quarter-deck, but the ordinary seamen were forced to suck the water out of it using a gun barrel; and that was stored at the top of the main mast. To drink necessitated climbing the mast to obtain the gun barrel, and then ascending again to put it back. As multiple

362 MATERIALIZING THE MIDDLE PASSAGE

testimonies in *Substance of the Evidence* indicate, sailors greatly resented this routine, which led to considerable hardship: sick or injured men could not manage the climb, and comrades were not allowed to fetch water for them.[135] The ultimate outcome of the use of pannekins and gun barrels was that the vast majority of those making the Middle Passage were surrounded by water, but chronically dehydrated.

Technologies for Force-Feeding

On every slave ship, some captives would refuse food. Many were too sick to eat, or simply had no appetite: trauma, inadequate drinking water, and the dehydrating effect of a repetitive diet based on dried, salty ingredients contributed directly to sickness and depression, leading in turn to a loss of appetite. For others, the refusal to eat was an active choice. Whatever the cause or motivation, all refusals of food were met with severe reprisals, and, just as there was a widely shared routine for the feeding of human captives, there was a common strategy for force-feeding them.

Numerous documented technologies were employed to compel Africans to eat. Falconbridge (*Account* **1788**: 23) drew attention to one of these practices:

> Upon the negroes refusing to take sustenance, I have seen coals of fire, glowing hot, put on a shovel, and placed so near their lips as to scorch and burn them. And this has been accompanied with threats, of forcing them to swallow the coals, if they any longer persist in refusing to eat.

Mr Thompson, who sailed on the slaver *Pearl* in 1759, mentions the use of a horn to pour nutrients down captive throats, and Mr Towne, who served on two Liverpool ships, recalled both a 'hard stick kept on purpose' for forcing open the mouth, and the use of thumbscrews for the 'more obdurate' (*Substance* **1789**: 53).[136] But the artefact most often employed in obliging captives to eat was the speculum oris, a pair of dividers with a screw mechanism, used to force the jaws apart so that food could then be funnelled into the throat. Thomas Clarkson bought both a thumbscrew and a speculum oris on his fact-finding tour to Liverpool—purchases that emphasize the extent to which these implements had become embodied in the technologies of the slave ship by the later 1700s (see Figure 10.6).[137] Clarkson's acquisitions were kept in the wooden chest that he employed in Parliament in 1788 and were subsequently illustrated and described in forensic detail in his 1808 *History*:

> I also bought a thumb-screw in this shop. The thumbs are put into this instrument through the two circular holes at the top of it. By turning a key, a bar rises up by means of a screw from C to D, and the pressure upon them becomes painful. By turning it further you may make the blood start from the ends of them. By taking the key away, as at E, you leave the tortured person in agony... At the same place I bought another instrument which I saw. It was called a speculum oris. The dotted

lines in the figure on the right hand of the screw, represent it when shut, the black lines when open. It is opened, as at G H, by a screw below with a knob at the end of it. This instrument is known among surgeons, having been invented to assist them in wrenching open the mouth as in the case of a locked jaw. But it had got into use in this trade. On asking the seller of the instruments, on what occasion it was used there, he replied, that the slaves were frequently so sulky, as to shut their mouths against all sustenance, and this with a determination to die; and that it was necessary their mouths should be forced open to throw in nutriment, that they who had purchased them might incur no loss by their death.[138]

The speculum oris was not always successfully employed: in 1790, Isaac Wilson described the case of a captive who died after eleven days without food, both a speculum oris (whose points were 'too obtuse to enter') and a bolus knife having been used in vain to force him to eat (**HCSP 72: 280**). The refusal of food sometimes resulted in acts of exceptional cruelty on the part of sailors, as evidenced in Isaac Parker's parliamentary testimony regarding the torture of a baby 'who took sulk and would not eat' on board the Liverpool slaver *Black Joke* in 1764.[139]

Latrines and Washing: Personal Hygiene

The daily logistics of human waste disposal on slave ships were formidable: hundreds of people were crammed together in a confined space, every one of them needing to urinate and defecate regularly. On ordinary merchantmen, crews made use of pissdales (urinals), 'seats-of-ease' (timber-built privy holes with draining sluices), and sometimes semi-cylindrical privies or 'roundhouses'.[140] On many ships, rows of simple latrines known as 'heads' were built out over the stem on either side of the bow, while more private facilities for the officers were located in the quarter galleries, at the stern of the vessel: lead tubing from a stern gallery seat of ease was recovered from shipwreck C31CR314 (which may be the former slaver *Queen Anne's Revenge*).[141] On slave ships, where crews and captives were segregated whenever possible, separate latrines were provided fore of the barricado for male captives, and on the quarterdeck for females and children. Documentary evidence regarding these facilities is limited, but there are some hints regarding their form. Phillips (**Hannibal 1693–4: 229**) said:

> When they have occasion to ease nature, they are permitted by the centinels to come up, and go to the conveniency which is provided for that purpose, on each side of the ship, each of which will contain a dozen of them at once, and have broad ladders to ascend them with the greater ease.

A similar, segregated arrangement is evident in Jean-René Lhermitte's plan of the French slaver *Marie-Séraphique* (1769), which depicts a row of timber-cut latrine holes fore of the barricado. This facility, adjacent to the pen in which livestock were housed, was clearly only for use by the male captives (see Figure 5.6).[142] Most men, as evidenced above, were not only fettered but also attached via their shackles to a long deck chain looped through many other sets of restraints. It is thus likely that the latrines were available to them only at mealtimes, when the deck chains were unlocked, and smaller groups formed for the purpose of eating.

Latrines were available on the quarterdeck too, but it is entirely unlikely that the female captives and crew shared these facilities. On eighteenth-century British ships, women certainly appear to have been provided with a separate facility. During *Argyle*'s metamorphosis from merchant ship to slave ship, Newton ordered his carpenter to create a dedicated space for the ablutions of female captives, noting: 'The carpenter finished the men's room and began to build a place for the women to wash, etc. between the main chains and the barricado' (**Argyle 1750–1, 20**). The space Newton refers to here seems to have been located on *Argyle*'s quarterdeck, amidst the strengthened ropes (shrouds) that supported the main mast. James Towne, similarly, referred to a 'women's necessary' positioned on the quarterdeck of the slaver *Peggy* (**Substance 1789: 57**).[143] On other ships, the women's latrine, like that of the men, projected over the side of the vessel (as seen in the latrines aft of the barricado in Figure 5.6). A boxlike construction visible beside the longboat on the painting of *Fredensborg II* (see Figure 5.8) was one such facility, and a similar facility was built on the Dutch ship *Unity*.[144] It is a point of some interest that female captives—their bodies otherwise continually exposed to the gaze of the crew—were provided with secluded latrines and washing areas: the practice points to some underlying sensibility concerning 'privacy' for females (including captive women) during ablutions.

How often were bodies washed on slave ships? Sailors rarely washed themselves when their vessel was in open waters: opportunities to do so were very limited, and, as noted earlier, fresh water was often in short supply. Soap was ineffective in salt water, but it was in any case a luxury unaffordable by most. Clothing was generally washed and disinfected at sea in salt water mixed with chamberlye (urine).[145] But what of the slaver's captives? The Africans emerging blinking into the sunlight from below decks at 8.00 a.m. were undoubtedly filthy: slave decks were awash with sweat, faeces, urine, blood, and vomit. African bodies were sometimes washed on British slave ships, but it is very difficult to gauge how often that happened, because none of the seventeenth-century ship's logs or narratives employed in this book discuss the washing of captive bodies, and the eighteenth-century references are both sporadic and contradictory. In his handbook for the Guinea surgeon, Aubrey expressed disapproval of the shipboard practice of forcing captives 'into a tub of cold water every day, and pouring the water over their heads by bucketsful', suggesting that bathing was a frequent occurrence.[146] Yet, while Newton's log (**Argyle 1750–1, 56**) records the washing of captives with fresh water during the Middle Passage, this entry appears some eight months after the first of his captives had been boarded, and at a time when bad weather had obliged him to keep them in their 'rooms' for several days. Four days later, as flux appeared to be taking hold on the slave decks, the captives were washed again. The action was repeated after a further eight days, as the ship neared land in the Caribbean. Newton recorded the minutiae of *Argyle*'s routines carefully, yet these are his only references to washing captives. It is possible that he recorded only the occasions on which all the Africans on board were washed; but Samuel Gamble, who kept an equally detailed log on *Sandown*, made no reference at all to washing.

In the accounts just mentioned, sailors were clearly dousing captives with water. The extent to which captives had opportunities to wash themselves is even harder to gauge. Newton, as seen above, had ordered his carpenter to create a dedicated space in which his female captives could 'wash, etc.' (*Argyle* 1750–1, 20). Smeathman refers similarly to a 'scaffold built on the side of the half deck' for the same purpose, adding that 'the woman and girls are generally washing half the day' in this secluded space, while 'the boys do the same on the forecastle' (*Oeconomy c.*1775: 6). The textual sources are silent regarding how captive women managed menstrual blood loss, but, unless they were provided with rags or clouts, 'washing' will have been the only way for them to remove blood from their bodies—one reason perhaps that so much time was devoted to this activity.[147] According to the parliamentary testimony of James Fraser, male captives were given tubs of washing water in poor weather but, when on deck, were encouraged to sluice themselves under the ship's head pump (**HCSP 71: 26–7**).[148] The pumps were located in the well space at the bottom of the ship, and drew up the water that had collected in the bilges (the cavities between the sides and the keel), which on most ships was discharged into the sea. On Fraser's ships, however, the water was instead emptied over the captives' heads. It will have been far from fresh, comprising a toxic blend of seawater that had leaked slowly through the ship's timbers, human waste, dirty water used in cleansing the decks, and much else-all having percolated from the main deck, slave deck, and hold down into the bilges. Smeathman noted that, on *Elizabeth*, water was simply hoisted up over the side to enable men to wash, every day in the afternoon (*Oeconomy c.*1775: 6). Some years later, Hugh Crow (*Kitty's* 1807–8: 147) suggests a much more regular washing regime on the *Kitty's Amelia*. Caution is needed here because Crow was firmly convinced—and aimed to convince others—that his slave ships were floating hotels—but, if his testimony is to be believed, considerable attention appears to have been paid to the personal hygiene of captives in the final years of the British trade:

> On their coming on deck, about 8 o'clock in the morning, water was provided to wash their hands and faces, a mixture of lime juice to cleanse their mouths, towels to wipe with, and chew sticks to clean their teeth. These are generally pieces of young branches of the common lime, or of the citron of sweet lime tree, the skin of which is smooth, green, and pleasantly aromatic. They are used about the thickness of a quill, and the end being chewed, the white, fine fibre of the wood soon forms a brush, with which the teeth may be effectually cleaned by rubbing them up and down ... About eleven, if the day were fine, they washed their bodies all over, and after wiping themselves dry were allowed to use palm oil, their favourite cosmetic.

Captives thus appear to have washed, or to have been washed, at certain points in their crossing. As numerous testimonies reveal, their heads were also shaved. As soon as

Argyle put out to sea on its crossing to the Caribbean, Newton noted: 'Began yesterday to shave them all and this morning finished' (*Argyle* 1750–1: 56). He does not refer to this process again, however. A handful of references are also made to head shaving in the parliamentary testimonies of 1788–92. Again, caution is necessary, because most of these comments were made by pro-slavery lobbyists, who were keen to evidence the 'care' given to captives. Robert Norris, for example, reported (**HCSP 68: 4**) that on his ships Africans 'were kept clean shaved, and every attention is paid to their heads, that there be no vermin lodged there'. To lure potential buyers, captives were certainly tidied up immediately before sale—a routine that often involved washing, the application of palm oil to the body, and shaving of the hair. It was not necessarily the case that these actions were performed by sailors, however: John Stedman stated that, before disembarkation, Africans newly arrived in Surinam shaved each other's heads using a broken bottle, creating patterns in the form of moons and stars. He also notes that some of these people were sent ashore for sale 'decorated with pieces of cotton to serve as fig-leaves, arm bands, beads etc.'.[149] These adornments are all captured in one of the illustrations made by William Blake for Stedman's text (Figure 10.13). In Blake's picture, a group of implausibly healthy-looking Africans are disembarking a slave ship. The women are wearing wrappers, and two have beads around their necks. Two individuals (a man and a woman) also have shaved and patterned hair. Blake did not *witness* the scene he illustrates, of course; and he does not acknowledge another section in Stedman's *Narrative*, which paints a very different picture of newly arrived Africans just landed from a Guinea ship. There, the captives are emaciated 'scarcely animated automatons', who are compared by the author to 'walking skeletons covered over with a piece of tanned leather'.[150] Mintz and Price have cited Stedman's account of head shaving as evidence for the 'irrepressible cultural vitality' of those enduring the Middle Passage, and the working-out of new cultural subsystems in the course of the voyage.[151] The passage is also of interest for the simple, but astonishing, point that the captives on this ship were allowed access to broken glass. This and other shaving equipment such as razors could be used for self-harm, and turned into weapons: during an uprising on board the Danish slaver *Christiansborg* in 1787, one captive slashed Paul Erdmann Isert across the temple with 'a razor he has seized from another who was in the process of shaving him when the rebellion began'.[152]

With the work of feeding completed, most of the crew spent the afternoon attending to the routine maintenance demanded by the ship. Some of the African women and girls on board may have been involved in preparing food for the next meal; others had the opportunity to wash. With some mobility allowed them, many female captives sought safety in numbers, congregating in groups and avoiding isolation, particularly if they ventured into the women's room below deck. Because the textual sources are silent on the matter, it is extremely difficult to visualize the small children, and particularly those without kin, also sharing the quarterdeck. For the male captives chained on the foredeck, much of the period between one meal and the next (which would be taken at around 4 p.m.) was a time of inaction. But at some point in the afternoon most captives, whatever their age and gender, will have been obliged to take exercise.

Figure 10.13 Group of Negroes as Imported to be Sold for Slaves (1796). Print of an engraving by William Blake for John Stedman (1796). Victoria & Albert Museum, E.1215E-1886.

368 MATERIALIZING THE MIDDLE PASSAGE

Enforced Exercise

On many ships, the afternoon was likely to be taken up in part with the ship's 'dance'. This was the widely used gloss for the process by which captives were forced to take exercise: a 'gruesome form of callisthenics to keep the slavers' shipment from atrophying', as Richard Cullen Rath memorably puts it.[153] Writing in the 1690s, Phillips (*Hannibal* 1693–4: 230) made the earliest documented reference to this routine on a British ship, stating that: 'We often at sea in the evenings would let the slaves come up into the sun to air themselves, and make them jump and dance for an hour or two to our bag-pipes, harp, and fiddle, by which exercise to preserve them in health.' Almost one hundred years later, James Arnold, surgeon on three voyages in the 1780s, described a regime that had by this time clearly become more formalized (**HCSP 69: 127**):

> It was the business of the chief mate to dance the men, and of himself and the second mate to dance the women. The men could only jump and rattle their chains but the women . . . were driven in one among another. The words which were learnt them to pronounce, and which they were compelled to sing while they were dancing, were 'Messe, Messe, Mackarida' (that is) 'good living or messing well among white men'.

Another surgeon, Thomas Trotter, described the process on *Brooks*'s 1783–4 voyage:

> I believe the practice of dancing them is very general in all ships; but in ours it was not practiced till their health made it absolutely necessary that they should be allowed some exercise; the men, who were confined in irons, were ordered to stand up, and to make what motion they could, making a lane at the same time for those who were out of irons to dance round the deck, with all those awkward gestures and motions which they call dancing. Some of them, who did not seem to relish the exercise, were compelled to do it by the lash of the cat; but many of them refused to do it, even with this mode of punishment in a severe degree. (**HCSP 73: 87**)

In the earlier testimonies, references to the equipment used in 'dancing' captives concern European-made instruments, with fiddles (violins) being most frequently mentioned. Among the crew of *Hannibal*, as the passage from Phillips above indicates, were numbered a bagpiper, harper, and fiddler (*Hannibal* 1693–4: 230) John Newton also employed a fiddler (*Argyle* 1750–1: 2). By the later eighteenth century, as several testimonies indicate, African instruments were also present on slavers, and were being played by captives themselves: what is much less clear, however, is the extent to which these instruments were being used in the process of forced exercise. Falconbridge (*Account* 1789: 23) is the only witness to suggest what seem to be African instruments, played by captives themselves, being used in enforced exercise. He states: 'Their musick, upon these occasions [enforced exercise] consists of a drum, sometimes with only one head; and when that is worn out they do not scruple to make use of the bottom of one of the tubs.' Ships belonging to the Dutch West India Company were certainly given special orders to acquire West African drums.[154] British vessels undoubtedly made similar purchases: Robert Norris, for example, notes that on his ships captives were supplied with 'musical instruments of their country' (**HCSP 86: 4: see also 69: 119**), and James Penny made a very similar point regarding the provision of instruments on his ships (**HCSP 69: 117**). On his visit to a slaver newly arrived in Jamaica in 1796, George Pinckard witnessed Africans being 'made to exercise', and encouraged, by the music of 'their beloved banjar'—a stringed precursor to the banjo, demonstrably of African origin.[155] But when and by whom were these instruments generally used? It is striking that, with the single exception of the passage from Falconbridge above, African drums tend to be mentioned not in relation to forced exercise, but in describing captives 'entertaining' themselves at other times in the ship's day. Thus, Henry Smeathman refers to two distinct episodes of 'dancing' in his account of a day on a slaver: the first (*Oeconomy c.*1775: 6) during the forenoon and the second (*Oeconomy c.*1775: 7) after the second meal of the day, and involving the use of a drum. I will return to this important point in Chapter 11. For the present, it is only necessary to note that the slave ship gave Africans 'mid-Atlantic exposure' to European stringed instruments, such as the fiddle and lute, which had counterparts in their homelands.[156] Following the 1739 Stono revolt (when a new slave code was produced prohibiting the use of drums and horns), numbers of enslaved fiddlers increased steadily in South Carolina and Georgia. As Rath notes, it is very difficult to determine where and how these individuals learnt to play the violin.[157] The fiddle remained the instrument of choice among British sailors throughout the eighteenth century, and many saltwater captives will first have seen this instrument in use during the Middle Passage. Bowed instruments were unfamiliar to many West Africans but were prevalent among the Mende people of Sierra Leone region, whose 'shiplike' lutes, discussed in Chapter 6, may be of relevance in this context.[158] While I am entirely in agreement with Homi Bhabha's argument that colonial encounters cannot be understood simply in terms of the mutual 'recognition' of similarities, it is important to acknowledge points of potentially creative elision between the material worlds of captives and crews where one glimpses them, and bowed instruments may represent one of those instances.[159]

The voyage also gave European sailors (musicians included) exposure to *African* instruments and performances. In his analysis of black dance in eighteenth-century London, King-Dorset has suggested that the form of jig known as the sailors' hornpipe, which became popular at precisely the moment the slave trade expanded, incorporates movements that closely resemble African dance, perhaps introduced into the jig repertoire by black sailors, or by the captives enduring the Middle Passage 'dance'.[160] Katrina Thompson has similarly positioned music as a creolizing force on board slave ships, arguing that, 'as multi-cultural groups of Africans danced to the European-based fiddle and the transnational white sailors danced to the beat of an African drum, their customs were merging and developing into syncretic music and dance that would contribute to the foundation of culture and entertainment in the New World'.[161]

370   MATERIALIZING THE MIDDLE PASSAGE

Technologies of Discipline and Punishment: The Cat

Those who refused to dance, like those who refused to eat, faced the whip. Isaac Land has rightly suggested that the eighteenth-century British public 'construed both sailors and slaves as inhabitants of the imperial periphery with the bodies of adults but the minds of children...flogging was seen as appropriate for both'.[162] Yet, if there is one setting where this observation does not generally hold true, it is the slave ship. The human body remained 'the major target of penal repression' (as Foucault put it) throughout much of the period considered in this book, and flogging was certainly a mainstay of corporal punishment in the navy.[163] For offences ranging from mutiny to theft, the whip was one among several technologies employed by naval officers to discipline sailors: other options included 'starting' (beating with a rope's end) and 'gagging' (inserting a metal or wooden rod in the mouth).[164] On slave ships, however, flogging tended to be reserved for captives. There were, of course, exceptions to this rule, with James Towne remembering Captain Scrogham of *Lilly* flogging one of his crew in Charleston harbour. Having exhausted himself, Scrogham 'made the men slaves come up from the main deck and assist him in the butchery which he had begun' (***Substance*** 1789: 59). *Lilly* had reached its destination and was thus at a lesser risk of insurrection; even so, forcing black captives to flog a white body traversed a line that masters in greater command of their tempers than Scogham rarely crossed.[165] During the Middle Passage itself, references to seamen being flogged—by anyone—are relatively rare. This is not to suggest that ordinary seamen avoided corporal punishment: rather, on board slavers, a clear punishment 'hierarchy' appears to have operated in an effort to maintain a corporeal distinction between captives and crews.[166] Blacks were flogged, while the most cited corporal punishments for seamen, meted out by the ship's captain or his officers for a wide variety of real or imagined offences, comprised 'starting', beating, and kicking. Mr Towne (***Substance*** 1789: 58) mentions African-grown canes, 'which captains of Guineamen cause to be procured for the purpose of beating seamen'; Falconbridge referred similarly to the use of bamboo (***Account*** 1788: 40). Short lengths of heavy rope were frequently used in 'starting' seamen who were perceived to be lazy or negligent. Mr Henderson of the *Tryal* (1767) was knocked down and beaten with a tail block (a wooden block wrapped with rope) when he attempted to bring water to a sick man (***Substance*** 1789: 21), and a sailor on *Pearl* (1759) was beaten by the captain with 'a two-inch and a half rope at the end of which he had made an overhang knot himself, to increase the weight of the blows' (***Substance*** 1789: 24). Many similar rope beatings are recorded in the testimonies given to Thomas Clarkson in *Substance of the Evidence*. This is perhaps why he acquired the thick, knotted rope—still in his wooden chest today—with which Edward Robe, master of the Bristol slaver *Alfred*, had beaten (and killed) seaman Charles Horseler. I will return to this, and other artefacts collected by Clarkson, at the end of this chapter.

Sailors could also be beaten with the fists, kicked, or clapped in irons. Ship's carpenter Robert Barker, so badly mistreated by the first mate and surgeon on board

Thetis in 1754 that he was blinded, was shackled to a ring-bolt on the deck for five weeks on short rations; his assistant Henry Curry was beaten and kicked to death (***Thetis** 1754–5*: 19, 22–3). In the case of Africans, however, the disciplinary tool employed by sailors was almost always the whip. The slave ship, as Mustakeem puts it, was 'a central conduit for how bondage unfolded' in the Americas, and her point is particularly pertinent with reference to flogging: put simply, the principal form of corporal punishment employed on slave ships was also widely favoured in disciplining plantation slaves throughout the British Caribbean.[167] Slaver captives could be flogged for a variety of reasons and non-reasons: because they refused to eat or 'dance', because they attempted to jump overboard, or because they were implicated in collective acts of insurrection. Women were not spared the whip and could also be flogged for additional reasons: because they refused an officer's sexual advances, or because they were perceived to be 'sulky'.[168] For most infractions, then, the whip was the artefact of choice. The type used on slavers was usually the cat o' nine tails, also employed by the navy, and expressly designed to cause horrific physical damage. It generally comprised nine separate lengths of cord or leather line, each one knotted to inflict greater injury to the naked back (Figure 10.14). Henry Ellison recalled that David Wilson, the mate of the slaver *Briton*, using a wire cat in the 1760s: the use of it drove six captives to throw themselves overboard (**HCSP 73**: 374).

Figure 10.14 Nineteenth-century naval cat o' nine tails with a wooden handle, wrapped in green baize. Each of the nine rope tails has a single knot at the end. National Maritime Museum, Greenwich, TOA0066.

372 MATERIALIZING THE MIDDLE PASSAGE

In both the navy and the merchant marine, floggings were carried out in front of all on board. In the navy, the sailor was stripped to the waist, fastened to a wooden grating at the ankles and wrist, and lashed in view of the assembled ship's company.[169] The flogging of a slave ship captive tended to be conducted along similar lines, and with a similar semiotic purpose: the bloody rite, and the permanently scarred back that was its outcome, were intended to provide a durable lesson for the Africans forced to watch it. There were some, rare, exceptions to the rule of the public spectacle of ritualized violence 'exorcizing the idea of freedom out of the slave'.[170] James Stanfield served under a sadistic, voyeuristic captain who, too ill to leave his cabin, had those who were to be flogged tied to his bed (*Observations* 1788: 27): 'their faces almost met his, and there he lay, enjoying their agonizing screams while their flesh was lacerated without mercy.' This was the punishment meted out to a woman who knocked over a necessary tub, and to the sailor commanded to whip her—the captain deeming the man's efforts too lenient (*Observations* 1788: 32).

Smoking

By the eighteenth century, if not before, efforts were made to provide all captives with substances and objects to 'divert' them during the hours of inaction between the first meal of the day and the next. Alleviating boredom, it was calculated, promoted well-being, and lessened the threat of unrest.

From at least the seventeenth century, pipes and tobacco were issued to captives on European slave ships. The frequency of such distributions varied considerably, however. John Barbot (*Treatment* 1712: 780) noted that 'we allowed each of them between meals a handful of Indian wheat and Mandioca, and now and then short pipes and tobacco to smoke upon deck by turns, and some cocoa-nuts'. Tobacco is an American cultigen, but it was widely employed by the Portuguese and Dutch in trading for slaves, and its use was well established in some parts of West Africa (including Sierra Leone and Ghana) by the early seventeenth century.[171] Almost four thousand European white clay tobacco pipe fragments were recovered from Portuguese and Dutch contexts at Elmina, for example.[172] Barbot's reference to the distribution of *short* pipes on his ships is particularly interesting: in the Dutch trade, *korte piipen* (short pipes) were produced for use on board slave ships, and Barbot's comment indicates that this idea was picked up by other nations.[173] As David Calvocoressi has noted with reference to Ghana, when local communities began to make tobacco pipes, they developed a form into which a detachable hollow wooden tube or reed stem could be inserted. This was because the coarser clays available locally were not suited to producing the long, thin, clay stems found on European imports. In time, European manufacturers began to copy the local forms, trying to meet local tastes. A short-stemmed pipe found at Adandzi (Ghana), impressed with the name of the French firm Duméril-Leurs and with a bowl in the head of a Classical figure, is a rare surviving example of this dialogue.[174] The *Fredensborg* wreck site produced many small pipes, European in form, but with short clay stems. Most were produced in Drammen, Norway, at the factory of Jacob Boy.[175]

The practice of distributing tobacco to adult captives continued throughout the eighteenth century and appears by that time to have become a weekly occurrence during the Middle Passage. Norris notes rather vaguely (**HCSP 68: 4**) that captives were supplied with 'the little luxuries of pipes and tobacco, and a dram occasionally', but other commentators are more precise. Snelgrave recorded that pipes and tobacco were distributed every Monday morning on his ships, for example.[176] In 1753, on the Danish *Guinea Company's Cron Prindz Christian* (later rechristened *Fredensborg*), captives were given one pipe per week, along with 1/8 of a pound of tobacco.[177] It seems likely that on British ships tobacco was similarly provided in greater quantities than could be consumed in one day. Smeathman (*Oeconomy c.1775: 9*) notes that on his Middle Passage crossing captives wore a 'little bag in which they kept their pepper and salt and their allowance of Tobacco'. I explore the implications of this important comment in Chapter 11.

'Some little games'

In 1790, Captain James Fraser told Parliament that the Africans on his ships had 'frequent amusements peculiar to their own country, such as some little games with stones or shells' (**HCSP 71: 28**). Robert Norris similarly stated (**HCSP 69: 119**) that 'the various implements of playing at their sundry games of chance are furnished them'. Several other parliamentary witnesses mention captives playing 'games of chance', and Handler has suggested that these were games in the wari family (all played with stones, beads, or shells).[178] The material requirements of wari are usually a wooden board (with hollowed-out cups) and 36–48 counters or tokens.[179] Fraser's 'stones or shells' might conceivably have been part of wari sets given to captives to enable them to 'amuse' themselves; but a wari board is easily extemporized, as are the playing pieces. Many small things were scattered about slave ships that crews would never consider as weapons: unsold cowries, stray beads, small bones from food waste, and so on. There were other uses to which 'stones or shells' might be put of course, as discussed in Chapter 11.

Stringing Beads

The complex history of the European trade bead, and its embeddedness in West African traditions of bodily adornment, has already been explored in Chapter 7. It was noted there that many of the women boarding slave ships will have worn European-made glass beads. Smeathman (*Oeconomy c.1775: 9*) suggests that they were allowed to keep them, stating: 'If the women and girls have a few strings of beads around them, they are permitted: glass and polished stones cannot

374   MATERIALIZING THE MIDDLE PASSAGE

accommodate much dirt.' Smeathman's comment (alongside that concerning tobacco pouches, above) directly challenges the notion that slave ship captives were naked throughout their ordeal at sea. This is one of several fragments of evidence leading some scholars today to the view that, covertly or overtly, captives could sometimes retain personal possessions during the Middle Passage. The use Africans might have made of such objects at sea is explored in Chapter 11. For the present, it needs simply to be observed that trade beads were also distributed to female captives *during* the crossing for the purpose, as Falconbridge put it, of 'affording them some diversion' (*Account* **1788: 23**). Several parliamentary testimonies mention this practice. Robert Norris, for example, remarked (**HCSP 68: 4**): 'the women and girls amuse themselves with arranging fanciful ornaments for their persons with beads, which they are plentifully supplied with.'[180] Smeathman suggests a further rationale for the practice (*Oeconomy c.1775: 9*):

> Sometimes beads are given out to them to string to their fancy; it amuses them and decorates them better for the market. Instead of a Table, a cushion, or a peg to work at, they tie one end of the string to their great toes, which is a substitute for a third hand on many occasions.

This distribution of 'recreational' beads is not mentioned by seventeenth-century commentators, perhaps suggesting that bead distribution may have been a later innovation.[181] It is noteworthy, however, that the seed beads recovered from the *Henrietta Marie* (discussed in Chapter 7) are not recorded on the ship's cargo inventory, which mentions only tubular beads. Perhaps the cheaper seed forms were never intended for trade, but were for use by the ship's female captives? As noted in discussing Figure 10.13, John Stedman recorded in 1796 that some captives leaving a slave ship in Surinam (those who were the captain's property, or private venture) were sent ashore 'decorated with pieces of cotton to serve as fig-leaves, arm bands, beads etc'.[182] Boarding a Liverpool slave ship in Carlisle Bay (Barbados) in the same year, William Dyott similarly observed the females wearing glass beads around their necks. The master informed him that 'the chief employment, and indeed amusement, they had was in new-stringing their beads, and that they very frequently broke the string on purpose to set them to work'.[183] I return to beads in Chapters 11 and 12, in considering the part that trade beads carried onto slave ships, or acquired during the slaving voyage, may have played in the future lives of saltwater captives.

Captive Labourers

On every slaver, a handful of Africans spent their days differently from the rest. In the seventeenth and early eighteenth centuries, RAC ships routinely purchased captives on the Windward and Gold Coasts for use as 'guardians' over captives who would later be acquired on the Slave Coast.[184] The most detailed reference to this practice appears in Thomas Phillips's account of the voyage of *Hannibal*, where he notes:

> we have some 30 or 40 Gold Coast negroes, which we buy, and are procur'd us there by our factors, to make guardians and overseers of the Whidaw negroes, and sleep among them to keep them from quarrelling, and in order, as well, to give us notice, if they can discover any caballing or plotting amongst them ... When we constitute a guardian, we give him a cat of nine tails as a badge of his office, which he is not a little proud of and will exercise with great authority.   (*Hannibal* **1693–4: 229**)

David Eltis has suggested that the use of guardians was so deeply embedded in RAC practice that 'it is likely that nearly all the male slaves that Slave Coast-bound ships obtained from the Ivory and Gold coasts west of Cape Coast Castle, as well as many of those from the vicinty of the Castle itself, were used as guardians for slaves from the Bight of Biafra'.[185] A similar tactic was employed elsewhere, too, with captives from Sherboro supervising others from the Bight of Biafra, and Gold Coast purhases playing a similar role on ships embarking captives in the Gambia.

The private traders do not appear to have adopted the 'guardian' principle, which therefore declined in parallel with the fortunes of the RAC, but, as considered in Chapter 11, there is some evidence to suggest that 'boys' were subsequently targeted as potential sources of information on resistance planned by adult captives. Children could more easily be intimidated into giving up information, of course, but it is also important to acknowledge that isolated, traumatized youngsters, separated from their kin and from adult role models, may have found it difficult to forge bonds with the African men on board. James Arnold noted, in this context, that it was not unusual for boys 'to insult the men who, being in irons, cannot easily pursue and punish them for it'. A male captive on *Ruby* pinched a boy who 'had been very active in tormenting' him: the boy was very severely flogged by the master (**HCSP 69: 126**). In the absence of African role models, some boys may have begun to identify with their captors. As Lovejoy remarked, concerning the assimilation of isolated children entering the Spanish Americas: 'Anyone who gained or imposed their cultural views and taboos on these isolated children obviously affected the rest of their lives.'[186] For many months at sea, looking down from the forecastle or quarterdeck, boys witnessed daily the deliberate physical humiliation of adults with whom they had very little interaction. It is not difficult to see why, when these confused and frightened children overheard the things that African adults were planning to do, they occasionally informed their captors. At the same time, however, as considered in Chapter 11, the liminal status of these unshackled boys created discursive transparencies that could also be exploited to African advantage.

There were many other categories of captive labourer on a slave ship. In the seventeenth century, at least, Africans scraped and cleaned the slave decks, as discussed in Chapter 9. Women might assist in food preparation. Some captives were employed as personal 'servants' to the officers. On John Barbot's ships (*Treatment* **1712: 780**), for example, several 'little fine boys' attended upon the officers. The young women who had been singled out to service the sexual demands of officers regularly laboured in a domestic capacity for these men too, washing their clothes, and in some cases even looking after their children. The Captain of *Ruby* subjected his 'mistress' to a severe beating when she accidently tore the shirt of his son, with whom she had been playing (**HCSP 69: 126**). On some ships, those male captives who were not perceived to pose a threat remained unchained on deck, and James Fraser referred (**HCSP 71: 45**) to one man wearing 'a frock coat and a pair of trowsers, which he had received from some of the sailors for washing and mending their clothes'. Perhaps the 'new negro' runaway found in North Carolina wearing nothing but an old blue sailor's jacket had acquired that item in a similar way.[187] On some voyages large numbers of sailors were 'pressed' by the navy, or the ship's company decimated through illness. In such cases, captives took on the tasks of ordinary seamen. When *Benson* arrived in Barbados in 1788, Captain John Ashley Hall recalled, all but two of the men handing the sails aloft were slaves (**HCSP 72: 233**).[188] On Hugh Crow's *Mary*, which lost several men to impressment in 1805, some male captives were even trained to use the ship's cannon and small arms.[189] George Pinckard noted that in late-eighteenth-century Barbados:

> The captains of the Guineamen often relieve their ships' company for the duty of the boat, by training some of their black cargo to the use of the oar. Indeed so useful do many of the negroes become, during the passage, and the time they are detained on board, that their assistance is of much service in working the vessel. We occasionally see the master of a slave ship rowed ashore by four of his naked Africans, who appear as dexterous, in the management of the boat, as if they had been for years accustomed to it.[190]

Given the extent to which canoes were employed in coastal West Africa, it is likely that these men were indeed accustomed to sailing; but, by the end of the Middle Passage, they had also gained additional experience working the smaller boats of European sailing vessels. In the Caribbean, captives who had acquired sailing skills would fetch a good price, because they could be hired out to other ships, and for harbour work.[191]

As mentioned in Chapter 3, it was customary for vessel owners to grant masters, surgeons, and mates the right to buy one or two captives to be transported to the Americas at the owning group's expense, then to sell these people for personal profit upon arrival. No doubt all the captains and surgeons whose testimonies are recorded in this book, including Alexander Falconbridge, Thomas Trotter, and others who testified against the trade in Parliament, gained additional income from 'privilege' or 'venture' slaves.[192] Venture Smith, one of the first African-Americans to have his Middle Passage experience published, was the 'private venture' of Robertson Mumford, steward of the vessel on which he was shipped to the New World.[193] Writing in 1712, John Barbot (*Treatment* 1712: 783) counselled against allowing masters a right to those he dubbed 'licence-slaves', wryly observing that 'the captain's slaves never die since there are not ten masters in fifty who scruple to make good their own out of the cargo'. But he also noted that licensed captives tended to be better accommodated and fed than others, and were often 'train'd up aboard, to be carpenters, coopers, and cooks, so as to sell for double the price of other slaves in America, because of their skill'. The majority of privilege slaves were adult men, because the profit from the sale of 'prime' males was generally higher, and because they would be put to work alongside an all-male crew. Some were 'apprenticed' to specialists such as the ship's armourer or carpenter. Many Africans were already skilled in iron and woodworking. While the part that the slave trade played in the transfer of African iron technology to the Americas is now widely recognized, it remains very difficult to assess the extent to which English armourers and African metallurgists labouring together on slave ships informed each other's practice in mid-Atlantic.[194] What can be said with certainty, as explored in Chapter 11, is that many captives understood the properties of iron perfectly and brought that knowledge to bear on the shackles and bolts used to restrain them. It is certain, finally, that some privilege slaves were carried to England to become the 'servants' of slave ship officers. The burial register for St John's Church, Liverpool, records the deaths of three unnamed black 'servants' of Capt. Penny between 1786 and 1788—surely the James Penny appearing before Parliament in a pro-slavery capacity in the latter year. These are just three among many records concerning the baptisms or deaths of black 'servants' of eighteenth-century Liverpool ships' captains; clearly, the black attendant doubled as a walking advertisement for the successful career of a master of both ships and men.[195]

The captive labourers of the Middle Passage are an intriguing group. Most will have perceived that their differential standing might bring some small personal benefits: a cloth wrapper perhaps, or a share of a sailor's food allowance. The distance between that understanding and the seemingly eager embrace of the emblems of domination that Thomas Phillips attributed to the Gold Coast 'guardians' on *Hannibal* (above) is enormous, but it would be a mistake to assume that even these apparently eager adopters of the 'badge of office' of the slave ship—the cat o' nine tails—necessarily prefigured what Kamau Brathwaite called the 'mimic men' of the Caribbean: the closest imitators of the external elements of white culture.[196] For Brathwaite, parodic imitation was a tragic outcome of the conditions under which creolization took place; but, as more recent scholars have argued, it also opened up insurgent spaces.[197] Every time they obliged men of colour to wield the cat, fire weapons, and climb rigging, crews undermined the social hierarchy of the slave ship; and, as explored in Chapter 11, captives quickly recognized and exploited the subversive possibilities arising as the wooden world of the slaver was turned upside down.

The Second Meal of the Day, and Its Aftermath

Sunset came early in African and Caribbean waters, and it was necessary to feed the captives for a second time before nightfall. Around 4.00 p.m. the mealtime routine of the morning was repeated. The same lengthy procedures were run through once again: the deck chains were unlocked, the Africans organized into messes, food and water

378 MATERIALIZING THE MIDDLE PASSAGE

distributed, and access to the latrines organized and overseen. On some ships, the brief period between this evening meal and sunset seems to have been devoted to 'diversions' of one form or another. To many an eighteenth-century white mind, the spectacle of otherness in bondage offered considerable diversion, as this revealing passage from Smeathman (*Oeconomy c.1775*: 7) indicates:

> The officers and seamen having dined, the Captain treats the slaves, he delivers by his seamen a biscuit or two to each man, or stands on the barricade and pitches them around, and they show their dexterity, catching like monkeys. The women have theirs likewise delivered to them aft of the barricado, but the boys are drawn up on the main deck and handfuls of broken biscuit thrown amongst them to scramble for, which produces a deal of amusement for the time, whilst the women are entertained in the same manner by the girls. After this a drum or an empty cask or tub is introduced; while one beats, another sings, and all the rest dance or join in chorus; and those who signalise themselves most stand a chance for the best drams of Rum or brandy sometimes of Bitters.

For women and girls, the period before sunset must have been an especially difficult time. Still on deck, they were now hemmed around by men downing a toxic cocktail of boredom, spirits, and lust. A particular point of note in Smeathman's account is the reference to drumming and dancing, here taking place long after the enforced exercise that the captives on his crossing had been obliged to undergo much earlier in the day. This second, and very different, form of slave ship 'dance' is considered in Chapter 11.

As the daylight began to wane, the crew initiated a routine that reversed the iron regime of the morning, releasing the male captives from the deck chains, checking carefully that their shackles had not been tampered with, and supervising the return of the men to the slave deck. Smeathman (*Oeconomy c.1775*: 9) noted that, as the deck chains were unlocked on *Elizabeth*, male captives came forward two by two, their shackles were examined, and a check was made that 'they did not carry anything below with them that they may cut their irons or enable them to do any mischief'. The women and girls were directed below, and their stowage similarly supervised. The smallest children were ushered towards steerage, where they would sleep on the floor of the officers' cabins. On the main slave decks, stowage was a complex business, usually overseen by a mate or boatswain, and, as ever, involved the threat of the cat. In the eighteenth century, as evidenced in Chapter 5, adults were crammed together on the slave decks with a pitiful allocation of axial space; only 14–18 inches each, and Alexander Falconbridge noted that, as a result, it was impossible for them to turn or shift with ease.

On some ships, as also noted in Chapter 5, those captives who were not in irons were arranged 'spoonwise' (nested together on their side) with their neighbours. The people directed to crawl under the platform ringing the slave deck, or forced to scramble onto it, would have 'headroom' (space to sit up in) of only 2 feet.

With the stowage of the captives completed, sailors retreated from the slave decks. The gratings to each of those rooms were secured, and the barricado door(s) opened for the first time that day. Smeathman recorded this moment in the Middle

Passage diurnal routine, stating: 'the barricado doors are thrown open and the captain and all the hands walk forward and where they please to stretch their legs' (*Oeconomy c.*1775: 10). It was only with the captives secured below that the crew were able to move freely about the upper deck, and they savoured the moment when it came.

This was the time of day when European musical instruments were most likely to be played for the benefit of crews. It has already been noted that among the sailors on *Hannibal* were numbered a bagpiper, harper, and fiddler (*Hannibal* 1693–4: 230), while John Newton also employed a fiddler (*Argyle* 1750–1: 2). These musicians were not there solely to entertain their shipmates; they were employed in 'dancing' the captives. Music was, however, an important part of maritime life, and an expected recreational activity.[198] Waged musicians played the instruments favoured in their home nations: in the British trade, the fiddle was common; in the French, the accordion.[199] Familiar tunes will have been requested by the sailors, perhaps accompanied by singing and dancing. As the evening progressed, men might also fall to traditional maritime pursuits, such as carving, decorative knotwork, or shellwork (as seen in Chapter 8). Alcohol, whether as part of the crew's weekly food ration, private supplies, or for sale on board, was often available. Games of chance were played, songs were sung, and music was made. For the crew, this was a brief period of leisure.

A Middle Passage Night

At 8.00 p.m. the bell rang out and the night watch began, with a handful of the crew keeping a vigil for part or all of the night. The majority bagged whatever space was available to sleep in, often sharing it with children who could not be accommodated on the floors of the officers' cabins.[200] As the ship pitched and rolled on the ocean, adult captives (and 'boys') sweated in the stifling darkness of their rooms. Pre-nineteenth-century visual representations of these spaces are rare, but Jean-René Lhermitte's illustration of the slave deck on the French ship *Marie-Séraphique* provides a unique glimpse of the spaces, and conditions, below decks on an eighteenth-century slave ship (Figure 10.15). A small number of captives, all afforded slightly more space, are lying on, and covered by, cloth. This suggests that the slave deck doubled as a hospital space. Some of the captives in the women's room also appear to be wearing strings of beads or cowries—a point of some significance in terms of the discussion of beads above.

To return to British ships, it is difficult to determine whether drinking water was available to captives at night. William Littleton told Parliament that '[t]hey have it [water] if they call for it—they have generally something to hold water in amongst them below, and we pour it through the gratings through a funnel' (**HCSP 68: 230**). But this is the sole reference I have found to such a practice among the parliamentary evidence. On most vessels, naked bodies lay on bare timbers, chaffed constantly by contact with damp, rough, and—within a short space of time, filthy—planking. British ships did not follow the Portuguese practice of carrying out 'course thick mats' to serve as bedding for the captives (**Barbot, *Treatment* 1712: 779**). The mass of bodies crowded

Figure 10.15 Plan of the slave deck of *Marie-Séraphique* made by Jean-René Lhermitte in 1770. Château des ducs de Bretagne, Nantes.

together constrained freedom of movement considerably. With no latrines accessible below decks, captives were supplied with wooden 'necessary' tubs, constructed by the ship's cooper. A detailed description of these tubs and their use was provided by Alexander Falconbridge (*Account* 1788: 20):

> In each of the apartments are placed three or four large buckets, of a conical form, being near two feet in diameter at the bottom, and only one foot at the top, and in depth about twenty-eight inches; to which, when necessary, the negroes have recourse. It often happens that those who are placed at a distance from the buckets, in endeavouring to get to them, tumble over their companions, in consequence of being shackled...prevented from getting to the tubs, they desist from the attempt; and as the necessities of nature are not to be repelled, ease themselves as they lie. This becomes a fresh source of broils and disturbances...the nuisance arising from these circumstances is not infrequently increased by the tubs being much too small for the purpose intended, and their being usually emptied but once every day.

It is almost certainly the case that slave decks were unlit. Robert Norris—the sole person to suggest otherwise—assured Parliament that lamps were kept burning on the slave decks at night (**HCSP 68: 4**), but it is impossible to credit that anything flammable would have been left unattended in such a space. The slave rooms were foul places, but they were also sites of resistance, because here, uniquely, captives were generally unobserved by the crew. Sailors might on rare occasions attempt to break into a women's room under the cover of darkness, but few seamen would venture voluntarily into the men's room at night: witness testimonies are very clear on this point. Amidst 'the shrieks of the women, and the groans of the dying', as Equiano put it, and the arguments that erupted as people pushed to the limit of physical and mental tolerance fought for space and air, conversations were held, social bonds forged, and voices raised in collective lament or discussion.[201] Thomas Trotter, Alexander Falconbridge and others, as evidenced above, were all affected by the songs of sorrow and loss emanating from the slave rooms at night. But they were not aware that songs and shouts were key means by which the men and women on board, segregated in rooms separated by stout timber partitions, could communicate with each other at night. One way or another, information could be passed and, in some cases, insurrections plotted. And the cover of night also brought opportunities to those captives—the young 'mistresses' of the officers, the boys sleeping on the main deck, the sick—for whom the darkness brought enhanced, unwatched, mobility. Discussion of these points is reserved for Chapter 11.

Disciplinary Artefacts: Clarkson's Chest Revisited

It remains, finally, to step away from the diurnal regime of the Middle Passage to reflect upon an assemblage that has appeared repeatedly in this chapter: Thomas Clarkson's chest. The contents of Divisions 1–3 of the box—the 'productions of

382 MATERIALIZING THE MIDDLE PASSAGE

Africa'—were considered in Chapter 8. But Division 4 contained something very different: British-made exemplars of the technologies of surveillance and discipline employed on slavers. These included the shackles and speculum oris discussed above (and illustrated in Figure 10.6) and the rope with which Charles Horseler was 'started' (beaten) to death by the master of *Alfred* in 1786.[202] That rope is still in the chest today, along with a second artefact from *Alfred*: an ivory trade token inscribed on the obverse: 'Sold the Alfred 30 slaves. West India of Grandy Bonney a good trader and an honest man.' The reverse states: 'The gift of Captain John Trousdall [*sic*] to young West India of Grandy Bonney.'[203]

The inclusion in the chest of these 'objects of gruesome fascination, to be held, fingered and fantasised in the hands of leading parliamentarians', as Marcus Wood puts it, might at first seem incongruous, given that its contents are otherwise illustrative of the resources, and manufactures, of West Africa[204] But, as explored in Chapter 8, Clarkson lived in an era in which the exotica of other countries were routinely collected and displayed by the social elite. Like Hans Sloane before him, he built up an African collection that incorporated botanical specimens, ethnographic items, and also artefacts used in the punishment of those caught up in the slave trade— a point brought out beautifully in the work of James Delbourgo.[205] Sloane's *Natural History*, as Delbourgo notes, contained a minute description of the punishment of Jamaican slaves much repeated, and condemned, by abolitionists. Sloane was supposedly neither 'for' or 'against' slavery: Clarkson was, of course, vehemently against. Why, then, did he collect the artefacts found in Division 4 of his chest?

This box was not the only visual propaganda tool that Clarkson and SEAST designed to further the aim of abolition: it was one-third of a tryptic, whose other panels comprised the *Brooks* placard discussed in Chapter 5 and the equally famous 'Am I not a Man and a Brother?' seal designed and manufactured at Josiah Wedgwood's Etruria factory.[206] In my view, Clarkson regarded Division 4 of the chest as doing closely interrelated work to the now better-known *Brooks* placard.[207] As shown in Chapter 5, SEAST's visualization of *Brooks* was based on measurements collected by the Royal Navy at the behest of Parliament, and presented in **HCSP 67**.[208] That volume also contained the collated data on imports from Africa outlined in Chapter 7. Much like the *Brooks* placard, then, the chest gave material expression to a mass of information concerning the slave trade—all of it collated for use by the Privy Council Committee in 1788. The chest was an aid specifically designed to encourage the committee members to visualize two unseen worlds conjured repeatedly in the parliamentary inquiry process: a distant continent overflowing with exotic timbers, cloth, spices, and handicrafts, *and* the brutal wooden world of the slave ship. The former found material expression in Divisions 1–3 of Clarkson's cabinet of curiosities; the latter in the *Brooks* placard and Division 4 of the same chest. Though only one of the objects of discipline and punishment acquired by Clarkson survives today, their acquisition, use, and subsequent description in the 1808 *History* wove a complex statement in the new discourse of abolition that Clarkson was attempting to develop in the late 1780s; a discourse upon which this chapter—and this book—has repeatedly drawn.

Conclusion

In his seminal discussion of the creolization process in Jamaica, Edward Kamau Brathwaite influentially argued that the creolization of saltwater Africans began with 'seasoning'; the 'period of one to three years, when the slaves were branded, given a new name, and put under the apprenticeship of creolized slaves. During this period the slave would learn the rudiments of his new language and be initiated into the work routines that awaited him.'[209] As this chapter has shown, many of these 'seasoning' processes were in fact initiated in the weeks and months during which Africans were incarcerated on slave ships. During the Middle Passage, and in the protracted period before the crossing began, rudiments of a new language were encountered by men, women, and children who from the perspective of their captors were already nameless chattels. 'Saltwater' Africans encountered at sea an assemblage of practice they would come to know all too well after disembarkation, from the whip and the shackle to segregated quarters and an architecture ensuring near-constant surveillance during the daylight hours. Some captives—the officers' privilege slaves, cabin boys, and female 'favourites' among them—had served unwilling apprenticeships that had familiarized them with new working practices and new understandings of their own bodies as both possessions and weapons. Many captives, as noted in Chapter 9, had also been branded; some of them more than once. The striking parallels between plantation surveillance and punishment routines and those employed on slavers are not matters of coincidence. The praxis of the Middle Passage made possible the successful control and transportation of captives far superior, in numerical terms, to the small crews who shipped them—a point that plantation owners cannot fail to have appreciated. Yet, while the slave ship may rightly be regarded as an institution sharing many operational practices with contemporary corrective institutions such as the prison and the work-house, its routines were repeatedly challenged by many of those on board. That story is taken up in Chapter 11.

Notes

1. Most of the voyages described by witnesses in the context of the parliamentary inquiries of 1788–92 were made between 1760 and 1787. Diurnal regimes in fact changed very little between 1680 and 1807, but I am careful throughout to draw attention to such changes as did occur, and to their import. In describing the spaces of the slave ship (such as the slave decks and 'rooms') in this chapter, I draw on the evidence set out, and referenced, in Chapter 5.
2. Hall (2000: 16).
3. Clarkson (1808: ii. 14–16).
4. For recent archaeological work on institutional sites, see Casella (2007), Piddock (2007), and Beisaw and Gibb (2009). To date, the slave ship has not been explicitly considered as an 'institutional site', but many of its practices echoed those of terrestrial carceral institutions, as this chapter explores.
5. Foucault (1977: 137).

384 MATERIALIZING THE MIDDLE PASSAGE

6. Foucault (1977: 137).
7. Morgan (1985) discusses the Bristol firms Sedgley, Hilhouse, & Randolph, and Stevenson, Randolph & Cheston, which shipped nearly all the convicts sent from the west of England to Maryland from the 1750s to 1775. The interrelated partners in these firms were also involved, often collaboratively, in slave shipping (TSTD 17312, 17336, 17360, 13390, 17660, 17662, 17665).
8. Christopher (2007).
9. Calvert: TSTD 76097; King: seven voyages including *Surry*, TSTD 78078.
10. See Christopher (2007: 111–12). The work of the Centre for the Study of the Legacies of British Slavery, https://www.ucl.ac.uk/lbs/ (accessed 15 May 2023) has stimulated a new interest in the links between colonial settlement in Australia and the slave trade. See Arnott (2022) for an illuminating analysis of the ways in which slavery permeated the life and approach to colonization of James Stirling, the first governor of Western Australia.
11. Mintz and Price (1992: 20–1).
12. Thornton (1998: 185–6).
13. Thornton (1998: 192).
14. Thornton (1998: 195).
15. With reference to the Middle Passage, see, e.g., Rediker (2007: 117–18, 277). But Rediker also makes an excellent case for some of this intelligibility being the result of the acquisition of pidgin languages or 'maritime tongues' prior to capture.
16. Byrd (2008: 249, and (on Equiano's Middle Passage) 22–6). Equiano (1789: 59) states that he acquired 'two or three different tongues' on his journey through the Biafran interior.
17. Delgado (2019) suggests that African language skills could also be viewed with suspicion: in 1722, William Child was accused of inciting a revolt on board a slave ship because he had been talking to the captives at night, in the Angolan language.
18. Taxonomy is used here in the sense of classificatory systems; and with reference to the historical relationship between taxonomy, nomenclature, and order as explored in Foucault (1989).
19. Trotter notes (**HCSP 73: 86**) that he asked the 'woman who had been my interpreter in the latter part of the voyage' of *Brooks* to determine the cause of a howling noise coming from the hold and 'she discovered it to be owing to their having dreamt they were in their own country, and finding themselves when awake, in the hold of a slave ship'.
20. Atkins (1735: 60); for discussion, see Huber (1999: 23–44), who plausibly suggests that, despite being noted down by Atkins in Liberia, *kickatavoo* can be traced back to Fante, the language of the Gold Coast (where Atkins spend some months in 1721–2). See Hancock (1985) for a discussion of the phonetically similar Krio word *kekerebu*. Krio is the English-lexified creole spoken in Sierra Leone.
21. Hancock (1985: 282).
22. A pidgin as a compressed language arising from contact between two or more groups with no common language under the conditions of trade, slavery, or colonization: Holm (2000: 1).
23. On the Portuguese influence, see, e.g., Huber (1999: 14–30) on the origins of Ghanaian Pidgin. The first documented reference to 'creole' in a linguistic context appeared in 1685 with reference to speakers of a mixed Portuguese/West African language in the Gambia: Baker and Mühlhäusler (2007: 85). The word list of the 'Old Calabar' language provided by Barbot (Hair et al. 1992: ii. 678, 704, n. 23) contains a number of words clearly of Portuguese origin, alongside various African languages including Efik and some Bantu languages: see also Huber (1999: 22–3).
24. 'Ship English' is defined by Hancock (1986: 86) as a situation-specific register of English 'having no single regional source in Britain, which the Africans first heard on their shores'. See also Hancock (1976), Bailey and Ross (1988), Linebaugh and Rediker (2000: 152–4), and, for a more detailed treatment, Delgado (2019). Delgado (2013) also provides a fascinating study of Pirate English.
25. Christopher (2006: 144).

DISCIPLINE AND PUNISH   385

26. Costello (2012: 15).
27. See Lovejoy and Richardson (2001) for the former and Behrendt et al. (2010) for the latter.
28. A jargon or pre-pidgin has relatively unstable structure, is composed of a limited vocabulary, and is frequently augmented by gestures and sign language: Mühlhäusler (1986: 5).
29. Den Besten et al. (1994: 91–4) are among the scholars who regard the transference of English nautical jargon into Atlantic creoles as occurring through a combination of factors on both the African coast and during the Middle Passage. Linebaugh and Rediker (2000: 153–4) argue that Ship English was one of the four main input sources to Atlantic Pidgins, along with Cant, Sabir (Portuguese-based *Lingua Franca*), and grammatical constructions drawn from West African languages.
30. Delgado (2019: 290).
31. National Maritime Museum LOG/N/41. HMS *Black Joke*, commanded by Lieutenant Henry Downes, was the tender for HMS *Sybille*, commanded by Commodore Francis Augustus Collier. Together, they were involved in the capture of sixteen slaving vessels. *Black Joke* was itself the former slave ship *Henriqueta*, captured by the Royal Navy in September 1827. I am very grateful to Michael Graham-Stewart for bringing this document to my attention.
32. The West Africa squadron was based in Sierra Leone, where 'Aku' was a term used by liberated Africans to designate Yoruba speakers. See Northrup (2013: 28–32, and especially table 1.1). Most of the words in this list appear to be of Yoruba origin.
33. African interpreters were used extensively by the Mixed Courts convened for the suppression of the trade and regularly interviewed recaptives on board ships; others aided the British West African Squadron in its patrols: see Graden (2011: 398–406) for discussion of their work.
34. Snelgrave (1734: 163). His voyages were TSTD 41593, 21306, 21221, 21231, 21232, 25657, 76003, 76389, 76397, 76398, 76399, 76497, 75248, and 76316.
35. These men remained on board throughout the voyage. See Candido (2010) for a consideration of enslaved African seamen on Portuguese ships.
36. Clarkson (1808: i. 396–407). Rodney's argument with sailor Peter Green led to the latter's death at the hands of the captain. This was one of two crew deaths on *Alfred*, both of which were investigated by Clarkson. The second death (that of Charles Horseler) is discussed later in this chapter.
37. For other references to the use of African interpreters on the coast, see Wilson, **HCSP 72: 285**; Falconbridge, **HCSP 72: 300, 307**; and Trotter, **HCSP 73: 86**. It is not coincidental that both Trotter and Falconbridge were surgeons: ships' doctors will have made more use of interpreters than most.
38. All of the Jamaican 'new negroes' documented in Chambers (2013) are noted as having no English, or very poor English. As Gomez (1998: 170–5) has observed, many plantation slaves may actively have refused to learn the language of their masters. Others, as White and White (2005: 77) discuss, picked up English with facility and speed during their first few years on the plantations.
39. Behrendt (2007: 78) estimates that, by the end of the British trade, 3% of all sailors on slave ships were black mariners from Africa, Atlantic islands, West Indies, or America. By 1803, black men also filled approximately 18% of American seamen's jobs: Bolster (1997: 6). On black sailors in the slave trade, see Bolster (1997) with Christopher (2006: 51–90) and Costello (2012).
40. In 1721, the RAC requested that 'two or three negroes between 16 and 20 years of age' be put on board all company ships headed to or from England and the West Indies (RAC to Robert Plunkett and Abraham Knox, TNA: T 70/60). RAC correspondence containing these and similar requests is detailed in Sparks (2014: 190–1, 289, n. 11).
41. This man was clearly already known to James Fraser, *Emilia*'s captain. This, and his name, suggest he was a coastal resident acquainted with English-based trade pidgin.
42. Butterworth (1823: 109).

386 MATERIALIZING THE MIDDLE PASSAGE

43. Behrendt and Hurley (2017: 891), citing TNA: BT 98/44, 243. TSTD 81770.
44. For Senegambia, see Brooks (2003: 298–9). See also Lovejoy and Richardson (2001: 96–7) for similar arrangements at Old Calabar, and Sparks (2014: 44–50) for the Gold Coast.
45. Lovejoy and Richardson (2001: 96): this information is revealed in a letter sent from Lace to Ephraim Robin John in 1773.
46. See Lovejoy and Richardson (2001: 96–7) for a discussion of this written submission, and of other examples of African children receiving an English education.
47. Hugill (1961) has shown that the modern (hallyard and capstan) shanty forms are a nineteenth-century development, but also that work songs and hauling cries were employed on merchant ships long before this date.
48. White and White (2005: 20–37); see also Rath (2003: 8–9).
49. Falconbridge (**HCSP 72: 307**) was similarly informed by an interpreter at Bonny that, in singing, captives were 'lamenting the loss of their country and friends'.
50. Pinckard (1806: 231).
51. White and White (2005: 35).
52. The earliest reporting of a song identified with the shantying tradition occurred in 1811: Hugill (1961: 8). On the relationship between shanties and African-American/African–Caribbean work songs, see Abrahams (1974: 7–21) and Hugill (1961: 7–8).
53. Linebaugh and Rediker (2000: 167).
54. See McDermott 2000, 24–5 on 'idlers': specialist sailors who did not stand watches.
55. A half-hour sandglass was used to keep time: Rodger (1988: 39).
56. The loss of one such bunch of keys on *Ruby* in 1787 was blamed on the crew: it was thought that someone had stolen the keys to trade on shore as ornaments. All of the sailors' sea chests were searched, and then broken up for firewood: **HCSP 69: 134** (testimony of James Arnold).
57. Herry (2004: 99).
58. According to Frazer (**HCSP 71: 29**), the chief mate and the boatswain remained with the male slaves on the main deck during the day.
59. Axelrod Wisnes (2007: 312).
60. Donnan (1930–5: iii. 374). This voyage is not in TSTD.
61. Spencer-Wood (2009: 33–4, 36–7).
62. For a discussion of violent altercations between captives during the Middle Passage, especially during mealtimes and below decks, see Byrd (2008: 44–6).
63. Mustakeem (2016: 88).
64. Lovejoy (2006b: 198–9) rightly points out that the 'designation of slaves as "children" is often unclear' but adds that 'it is sometimes assumed to be pre-pubescent, and hence roughly before age 13–14 and certainly before mid-teens.' Laslett (1971) has estimated that in early modern England the average age of girls at menarche was 14, but that this rose at some point in the eighteenth century.
65. See https://www.slavevoyages.org/voyage/about#methodology/age-categories/5/en/ (accessed September 2022). This practice means, of course, that the number of children imputed to have been carried on RAC ships is likely to be a considerable underestimate.
66. In 1750, for example, John Newton (*Argyle* **1550: 41**) noted that he had 'exchanged with Captain Williams No. 60, 61; 2 small boys (of 3 ft 4 in) for a girl (4 ft 3 in) and No. 80, a small boy (3 ft 8 in) for a woman, he being only for small slaves'. Williams was master of the American sloop *Rebecca* (TSTD 27232). As Newton suggests, his captives were all children. James Jones, six years a merchant in the African trade, informed Parliament in 1788 that, while it was an uncommon occurrence, British ships were sometimes sent out to Bonny and New Calabar 'for the purpose of buying boys and girls only' (**HCSP 68: 43**).
67. 28 Geo. III c. 54: 'Provided always, That if there shall be, in any such Ship or Vessel, any more than two fifths Parts of the Slaves who shall be Children, and who shall not exceed four Feet four Inches in Height, then every five such Children (over and above the aforesaid Proportion of two

fifths) shall be deemed and taken to be equal to four of the said Slaves within the true Intent arid Meaning of this Act.'

68. Pietsch (2004: 13).

69. As Lovejoy (2006b: 200) notes, children under 2 (generally classified as infants) remained with their mothers but those aged *c*.2–5 will have presented a particular problem to slave traders, because they were too young to separate from kin or at least adult supervision. It is likely, as he suggests, that fewer children of this age entered the slave trade than did those over 6 or 7. The phrase 'small slaves' was widely used in the eighteenth-century trade and appears to designate children between *c*.6 and 11–13 (the perceived onset of African puberty).

70. Christopher (2006: 189–92) also discusses differential access to the bodies of women on slave ships.

71. Martin and Spurrell (1962: 75). William Cooney (or Cunneigh) is recorded as a foremastman in Newton's list of 'Officers and Seamen belonging to the *African*' (Martin and Spurrell (1962: 65).

72. Testimony against First Mate Cornelis van Kerkhove (signed 13 November 1765), translated at https://eenigheid.slavenhandelmcc.nl/trajecten-van-de-reis-en/thuisreis-en/testimony-against-first-mate-cornelis-van-kerkhove/?lang=en (accessed 2 September 2022).

73. As noted in a letter from Newton to David Jennings: Martin and Spurrell (1962: 84).

74. Veuclin (1887).

75. Oursel names this ship as *Jose & Diligent*, noting the master as 'Isidore Martin Bragues'. This is Isidoro Martins Braga, who captained numerous Portuguese slaving voyages. The earliest of these to appear in TSTD took place in 1812, but it is quite possible that Braga was also the unnamed master of a poorly documented *S. Jose Diligente* (TSTD 51500), which is a better fit for Oursel's timeline.

76. Svalesen (2000: 40–1, 104); Alpern (2013: 45–6) collates documentary references to mortars on board slave ships.

77. Christopher (2007: 110) discusses the use of shackles on the convict transports of the Second Fleet to Australia. These were the same kind of heavy shackle used in shipping slaves.

78. Some variations in practice clearly occurred. Some eighteenth-century commentators report that male captives were not kept in chains once a vessel put out to sea. Thus, Norris (**HCSP 68: 4, 8**) claimed that women and children were never fettered, and men's shackles were removed gradually as voyages proceeded. This was also the position of James Fraser (**HCSP 71: 38**), who reported: 'As soon as the ship was out of sight of land I usually took away their handcuffs, and soon after their leg-irons—I never had the slaves in irons during [the] Middle Passage.' But James Arnold (**HCSP 69: 126**) and many other parliamentary witnesses stated that men remained in fetters throughout the voyage.

79. On ring-bolts and deck chains, see also the testimony of Isaac Wilson, **HCSP 72: 276–7**.

80. Mount & Johnson was an iron merchant and anchorsmith based in Wapping. The business was an early investor in the London Dock Company: see Draper (2008: 437, n. 25).

81. The suggestion that bilboes came to England via the 1588 Armada invasion (Earle 1896: 3) is unsubstantiated, as is the belief that their name derives from that of the Spanish town Bilbao. Bilboes were, however, recovered from the wreck of the Spanish galleon *Senora de Atocha*, lost in 1622, and, as early as 1627, John Smith was advocating the use of 'bilbowes' to punish offenders on British ships: on both of these points, see Malcom (2021: 6).

82. This description is drawn entirely from Malcom's detailed discussion (2021) of the *Henrietta Marie* bilboes.

83. A 1739 inventory of iron goods stored in the Crowley family's Swalwell factory lists some of the many agricultural instruments they produced for the colonial market, alongside 'locks for Negroes necks, shackles, bilboes, port shackles, chains and branding irons' (Charlton 2008: 99–100, citing Suffolk Record Office HA1/G/D/4/12). Over the five-year period from 1706 and 1710, Crowley received £665 from the RAC for ironwork of various kinds: Paul (2014: 137–8).

84. Malcom (2021: 15).

388 MATERIALIZING THE MIDDLE PASSAGE

85. Wilde-Ramsing and Ewen (2012: 127). Two other shackles were also recovered.
86. Malcom (2021: 15).
87. Rodger (1988: 41).
88. Carney (2013: 20–1) notes the claim by a Jesuit priest that guinea fowl arrived in Hispaniola with the first ships carrying slaves there.
89. Until 1789, when 29 Geo. 3 c. 66 (amending the 1788 Dolben Act) stipulated that sleeping accommodation should be available below deck for at least half the crew. Men could presumably also eat in the same space.
90. Moore (1989: 56). Pewter was also part of the trading cargo of *Henrietta Marie* (see Table 7.2), but the letters 'HM' were carved into the back of some of the pewter plates recovered from the wreck, suggesting on-board use.
91. Hair et al. (1992: ii. 474, n. 10), citing an additional passage from Barbot's 1732 text: Churchill and Churchill (1732: v. 212).
92. Svalesen (2000: 179–80).
93. NML: D/DAV/10/29 (TSTD 92536).
94. MacDonald (2014: 105).
95. Gamble's *Sandown* carried '4 chaudrons' (approximately 144 bushels) of coal, presumably used for cooking (***Sandown* 1793–4: 7**).
96. Svalesen (2000: 179).
97. Hair et al. (1992: ii. 344).
98. The 'slave galley' on the Dutch snow *Unity* was positioned rather differently: 'portside, under the forecastle', as noted in the first mate's logbook for 18 December 1761 (Zeeland Archives, MCC Archives, Inv. no. 383, translated at https://eenigheid.slavenhandelmcc.nl/category/days/18-december-1761-en/?lang=en (accessed 2 September 2022)).
99. Horrell (2017: 365).
100. A well-preserved example of a late-eighteenth-century cook stove, bearing some similarity to the Brodie stove, was recently recovered from the *Mardi Gras* shipwreck site in the Gulf of Mexico. See Horrell (2017: 365–7) for the use of Brodie's patent in analysing the *Mardi Gras* shipwreck stove. The unidentified vessel probably belonged to the British or American Navy.
101. Moore and Malcom (2008: 35).
102. Moore and Malcom (2008: 35).
103. Malcom (2000 (no page numbering)) suggests that the cauldrons are evidence for inequality, in that captives and crews were fed in different ways using different equipment.
104. See Ferguson (1992: 94) and Covey and Eisnach (2009: 62) on the 'one-pot' foodway.
105. Eltis (2013) argues that the slave trade boosted West African food production considerably, with produce making up 17% of total exports from the region between 1681 and 1807, and some 67% of that produce being carried away on slave ships. Based on an analysis of RAC account books and similar records from the French and Dutch trade (1681–1807), Dalrymple-Smith and Frankema (2017) revise Eltis's estimate downwards by some 70%. Despite their differences, both Eltis and Dalrymple-Smith and Frankema are broadly agreed that over the eighteenth century the proportion of the required calories and proteins for slaves taken on board in European port cities increased, while the use of African-grown foods declined considerably.
106. Dalrymple-Smith and Frankema (2017: 26) suggest that this was because British slavers had more secure access to local provisions, via their forts, than did other European nations.
107. Newton calculated, after numerous acquisitions, that he had 18,600 lb of rice on board for use on Argyle's *Middle Passage* (***Argyle* 1750–1: 49**). This would need to support 156 captives and the crew. Gamble made a smaller provision, buying 18,774 lb of rice for a cargo of 250 slaves and 20–5 seamen. Mouser estimates that, allowing for some being eaten before departure, this would amount to 1.5 lb per capita consumption daily for 45 days (Mouser 2002: 90). *Daniel and*

Henry shipped 10,000 ears of corn, coconuts, and yams at São Tomé, the final staging post for many ships leaving the Gold Coast (***Daniel* 1700: 119**).

108. Covey and Eisnach (2009: 46–7).
109. Atkins (1735: 171).
110. Behrendt (2007: 78) estimates that black mariners made up 3% of crews in the late British slave trade. For black cooks specifically, see Christopher (2006: 59–61).
111. This information is taken from the evidence of William James. Christopher (2006: 57) suggests that black sailors became 'integral parts of a multiracial crew', but this and other 1788–92 testimonies suggest that black sailors, including cooks, were often singled out for brutality by slave ship captains and others.
112. Phillips was referring to kenkey, a fermented and steamed maize dough still eaten in Ghana and the Caribbean: see Farnsworth and Wilkie (2006: 56).
113. Smith (1813: 31).
114. Coleman (2018: 156), citing an extract from one of Smeathman's letters to Drew Drury, Uppsala University Library, MS D.26.
115. Donnan (1930–5: iii. 376); see also Carney (2001: 146). The ship (TSTD 3661) was on the Gold Coast at this point but had purchased slaves in rice-growing Upper Guinea previously: Eltis et al. (2010: 168).
116. Carney (2007).
117. Svalesen (2000: 112). The 'millet' used on *Fredensborg* may have been sorghum; the two were often confused, as Alpern (2013: 43) emphasizes.
118. Von Arbin, pers. comm.
119. For a full list of African staples supporting the slave trade, see Carney (2013: 17, table 2.2). For a discussion of the starchy porridges of West Africa, also eaten in parts of the American south, see Farnsworth and Wilkie (2006: 56).
120. For the black-rice hypothesis, see Carney (2001). On the role of the slave ship in transporting rice-growing skills, see Carney (2013: 29).
121. See the challenge to the black-rice hypothesis by Eltis et al. (2007, 2010), the responses to this challenge in the 'Question of Black Rice' exchange in the *American Historical Review* (2010). Hawthorne's discussion (2010: 137–72) of rice production in Maranhão, Brazil, treads a persuasive middle ground in this contentious debate, arguing that the rice regime here was a creolized one, merging the skills and understandings of Portuguese planters and slaves sourced from Upper Guinea. As Alpern (2013: 42) notes, the earliest transfers of African rice to the Americas were probably made on vessels taking Portuguese settlers to Brazil.
122. Carney (2001: 154; 2004) discusses the oral tradition that rice arrived in the Americas in captives' hair.
123. Alpern (2013: 43).
124. The foods listed are broadly similar in type and quantity to the standard weekly ration issued to naval crews by the Victualling Board. 'Calavances' are pulses.
125. While numerous commentators (including van Harten 1970: 209) speculate that a bill passed in the reign of George III to prevent the use of melegueta as an adulterant in beer will have led to a collapse in imports of the spice, this Act was not passed until 1809 and related specifically to Ireland (49 Geo. III c. 57).
126. Carletti's account (translated by Malyn Newitt) can be found in Newitt (2010: 157–8).
127. On most British ships, captives were fed at around 10.00 a.m. and 4.00 p.m. Hugh Crow (***Kitty's* 1807: 147**) and James Fraser (**HCSP 71: 27**) also refer to a third meal, midway through the day. Fraser says this 'middle meal' comprised bread and beef, or bread and pork or stock fish or calavances (pulses). He notes that a midday meal not being customary in their own foodways, captives regard this meal as 'an indulgence'. Crow's 'middle mess' comprised bread and coconuts, given out at midday.

390 MATERIALIZING THE MIDDLE PASSAGE

128. Smith (1813: 30, 33).

129. Caution is required with some sections of Smith's account: he suggests, for example, that that male captives on *Squirrel* were routinely circumcised, and also branded; both seem equally unlikely at this point in the British trade.

130. Smeathman is not the only witness to mention handwashing. Falconbridge (*Account* **1788: 40–1**) notes the provision of tubs of water on the quarterdeck for women to wash their hands in.

131. Conversely, Phillips (*Hannibal* **1693–4: 229**) was firmly convinced that his captives liked nothing better than a horse bean: 'these beans the negroes extremely love and desire, beating their breast, eating them, and crying *Pram! Pram!* Which is *Very Good*.'

132. Smith (1813: 30).

133. James Fraser (**HCSP 71: 27**) also refers to provisions being served in wooden vessels called crews and adds 'we generally give each slave a spoon which they very seldom use'. Crow (*Kitty's* **1807: 147**) simply notes that clean spoons were handed out before a meal.

134. Mr Jameson (*Substance* **1789: 14**), who had served on *Britannia* in 1768, said water was provided in a pannekin holding just under half a pint. James Arnold (**HCSP 69: 137**) similarly stated that water was 'served in pannekin of tin, of such dimensions as not to hold quite half a pint'. Henry Ellison (*Substance* **1789: 36**) refers to 'pint pannekins'.

135. For testimonies noting the use of a gun barrel, see *Substance* **1789: 16, 21, 24, 38, 47, 56.**

136. Thumbscrews were also used in extracting confessions from suspected or known 'mutineers'. Having surprised captives attempting to remove their irons on *African's* 1752–3 voyage, Newton 'put the boys in irons and slightly in the thumbscrews to urge them to a full confession' (Martin and Spurrell 1962: 71).

137. The speculum oris had been in use for centuries, but, perhaps as a result of Clarkson's purchase and the testimonies concerning force-feeding that emerged in the parliamentary inquiry process, the speculum oris became well known in abolitionist circles in the 1780s. The disenchanted slave trader in Cowper's satirical poem 'Sweet meat has sour sauce: or, the slave-trader in the dumps' (1788) proposes to sell off a speculum oris, among much else, after the Dolben Act has curtailed his activities. He advertises it thus: 'When a Negro his head from his victuals withdraws, And clenches his teeth and thrusts out his paws, Here's a notable engine to open his jaws, Which nobody can deny.'

138. Clarkson (1808: i. 131).

139. **HCSP 73: 123–5.** The voyage is TSTD 91134. The child suffered and died at the hands of the master, Joseph Pollard.

140. For detailed descriptions, see Simmons (1985: 66–80).

141. Daniel (2009).

142. Guillet (2009: 66).

143.. The voyage is TSTD 91464, in 1760.

144. For *Fredensborg*, see Svalesen (2000: 106). The latrines for the women on board *Unity* were constructed on the day the first African woman was purchased, 10 December 1761, and that for the men erected on the side of the waist two days later (as noted in the first mate's logbook): see https://eenigheid.slavenhandelmcc.nl/category/days/10-december-1761-en/?lang=en (accessed 2 September 2022).

145. Rodger (1988: 107).

146. Aubrey (1729: 131).

147. Rags or clouts (pads of cloth) were the common form of sanitary protection in early modern England: Read (2008: 5).

148. Fraser must have been referring to his male captives at this point, given the location of the head pump at the fore of the ship, where males spent their deck time.

149. Stedman (1796: i. 205).

150. Stedman (1796: i. 200).

151. Mintz and Price (1992: 48).
152. Axelrod Wisnes (2007: 236).
153. Rath (2003: 77).
154. Postma (1990: 233).
155. Pinckard (1806: 230). For the origins of the banjo see Epstein (2003: 10) and Dubois (2016: 109).
156. Epstein (2003: 8, 34).
157. Rath (2003: 90–1).
158. As Rath (2003: 91) notes, however, it is impossible to determine whether the runaway violinists of South Carolina were Mende, and quite probable that they were not.
159. Bhabha (1994: 2).
160. King-Dorset (2008: 72–3).
161. Thompson (2014: 65).
162. Land (2001: 169).
163. Foucault (1977: 8).
164. Land (2001: 175); Byrn (1989: 64–88). Falconbridge (**HCSP 72: 310**) refers to the use of a pump bolt to gag a boatswain who had argued with the mate on one of his voyages.
165. Falconbridge (*Account* **1788: 40**) refers to a sailor being beaten so cruelly with a cat that he leapt overboard.
166. From the 1790s, as Land (2001) discusses, British sailors initiated an aggressive campaign against the use of flogging on ships. This campaign drew an analogy between corporal punishment in the navy and the experience of plantation slavery, arguing that no white person should be treated like a black.
167. Mustakeem (2016: 5).
168. In April 1792, William Wilberforce drew attention in a parliamentary speech to the torture and death of a teenage girl who had refused to 'dance' on John Kimber's ship *Recovery* in 1791 (TSTD 18115). Isaac Cruikshank published an engraving of this atrocity (captioned *The Abolition of the Slave Trade, Or the inhumanity of dealers in human flesh exemplified in Captn. Kimber's treatment of a young Negro girl of 15 for her virgen modesty*) in the same month, and in June Kimber was brought to trial. In the trial documentation, published after Kimber's acquittal, the captain is reported to have stated twice of his victim, during her torture, that 'the bitch is sulky' (Kimber 1792: 34). These events have been influentially reimagined by Saidiya Hartman (2021: 136–72).
169. Byrn (1989: 71–4).
170. Gikandi (2011: 89).
171. Handler (2009a; 2009b: 7–10); DeCorse (2001: 163).
172. DeCorse (2001: 163–7).
173. For discussion of korten pipes, and Dutch sources concerning them, see Handler (2009b: 6).
174. Calvocoressi (1977: 119).
175. Svalesen (2000: 186).
176. Snelgrave (1734: 164).
177. Svalesen (2000: 112).
178. This possibility is explored, and dismissed, by Handler (2009a: 11).
179. Handler (2009a: 11).
180. See also Penny, **HCSP 69: 117**.
181. Handler (2009a: 5) discusses the eighteenth-century testimonies. As he notes, the textual evidence largely dates to the latter part of the century.
182. Stedman (1796: i. 205).
183. Dyott (1907: i. 93–4). See Handler (2009a: 6) on this and other similar examples.
184. For discussion of this practice, and RAC correspondence evidencing it, see Smallwood 2007a.

192 MATERIALIZING THE MIDDLE PASSAGE

185. Eltis (1991: 228).
186. Lovejoy (2006b: 209).
187. Chambers (2013: 86): advertisement in the *Virginia Gazette*, 19 November 1767.
188. This testimony concerns TSTD 80490.
189. Crow (1970 [1830]: 103). See Bolster (1997: 58–60) for additional evidence concerning captives trained as sailors.
190. Pinckard (1806: 326).
191. For a discussion of enslaved ship pilots, some of whom were African born, see Dawson (2013). Bolster (1997: 252, n. 28) calculates that among forty-eight sailors and boatmen noted in runaway slave advertisement from the Chesapeake in 1736–90, 22% were African born.
192. Falconbridge's allocation of a privilege slave on *Emilia* is noted in **HCSP 72: 349–50**.
193. Smith (1798: 13).
194. See, e.g., Goucher (2014) on West African iron-smelting technology in Jamaica.
195. For these and other African-born individuals belonging to Liverpool captains, see Behrendt and Hurley (2017: 891–2). The initial research on Liverpool church registers summarized therein reveals that between 594 and 639 'black' individuals were baptized or buried in Liverpool between 1717 and 1840.
196. Rathwaite (2005 [1971]: 300).
197. Scott (1990: 166–72).
198. Rodger (1988: 44–5).
199. Harms (2002: 33, n. 2).
200. After 1789 (29 Geo. 3 c. 66 Schedule A), slave ship owners were legally obliged to provide their crews with some form of shelter during the Middle Passage—either an awning on the half-deck, space in steerage, or a caulked deck shelter.
201. Equiano (1789: 79).
202. That voyage (TSTD 17984) is discussed several times in Clarkson (1808). Edward Robe (the master) is not named explicitly, but it is clear from Clarkson's manuscript diary that Robe is the man in question (Clarkson's Diary of Travels in the West Country & Wales, 25 June 1787–25 July 1787: St John's College Library, Cambridge).
203. John Trousdale became master of *Alfred* in 1788 following Robe's death in Africa.
204. Wood (2007: 222).
205. Delbourgo (2017: 78–9).
206. See Webster (2009) for further discussion of the Wedgwood seal.
207. For further discussion on the parliamentary history of Clarkson's chest, see Webster (2017).
208. Webster (2009: 318–22).
209. Brathwaite 2005 [1971]: 298.

11

Surviving the Middle Passage

> The goal, after all... is not directly to overthrow or transform a system of domination but rather to survive—today, this week, this season—within it.
>
> (James Scott, *Weapons of the Weak* (1985: 301))

This chapter begins with a consideration of recent scholarship exploring African responses to the Middle Passage. Here, as in the diaspora, responses to domination took many forms, ranging from 'insurrection' (open, collective, aggressive resistance) to the covert, undisclosed actions through which individuals sought to retain their personhood and speak back to power. As first explored in Chapter 6, the slave ship also presented captives with *meta*physical challenges. There is a growing body of evidence suggesting that the captive passage was understood by Africans who experienced it to be witchcraft, or at least a form of spiritual affliction.[1] And, as Stephanie Smallwood has emphasized, 'the very habitat of the ship—the open sea—challenged African cosmologies, for the landless realm of the deep ocean did not figure in precolonial West African societies as a domain of human (as opposed to divine) activity.'[2]

The argument set out below is that scholars of the Middle Passage need to give much greater attention to the physical and metaphysical actions, and the coping strategies, through which Africans challenged the regime of the slave ship: countering domination, but without fatal consequences. In his seminal book *Domination and the Arts of Resistance: Hidden Transcripts*, James Scott employed the term 'infrapolitics' in describing low-profile 'everyday' resistance among early modern subaltern communities, and, in the present chapter, my account of the infrapolitical 'weapons' deployed by Middle Passage captives is directly informed by *Domination and the Arts of Resistance*, and also by Scott's earlier book, *Weapons of the Weak*.[3] I have also taken inspiration from de Certeau's analysis of the mobile tactics of everyday resistance, from Luis Symanski's work on tactics and power relations on sugar plantations in Brazil, and from Johansson and Vinthagen's discussion of the third spaces of Palestinian everyday resistance.[4] As the latter argue, it can be extremely difficult to distinguish confidently between coping mechanisms, survival techniques, and infrapolitical or 'everyday' resistance: and that is precisely why I have adopted the approach taken here.[5] Many of the actions discussed in this chapter can be understood equally as tactical manoeuvres (that is, as active 'resistance', whether overt or covert) or as coping mechanisms in the physical and metaphysical struggle for survival. Many, perhaps, were all of these things at once. But, whatever reading one favours, that judgement is

---

Materializing the Middle Passage: A Historical Archaeology of British Slave Shipping, 1680–1807. Jane Webster, Oxford University Press. © Jane Webster 2023. DOI: 10.1093/oso/9780199214594.003.0011

necessarily based almost entirely on accounts of African actions and motivations as reported, not by captives themselves, but by slave ship crews.

The vast majority of seventeenth- and eighteenth-century accounts of the Middle Passage were produced by white sailors, so in this chapter, more than at any other point in this book, it is necessary to read between the lines of the discourse of the dominant to identify the hidden transcripts of African experience. As discussed in my introductory chapter, James Scott's concept of the hidden transcript—the covert action of ordinary people against the imperatives of those in power—and his methodologies for identifying such 'offstage' actions are central to this book and to this chapter above all. Read with forensic attention, and often against the grain, the public transcripts of enslavers, whether in the diaspora or on board slave ships, reveal important insights into both overt resistance and the undisclosed strategies through which the enslaved resisted domination, or simply found ways to survive. This is true of resistance to slavery in South Africa and the Chesapeake (as explored by Martin Hall, whose work was considered in Chapter 1), and it is equally true of the slave ship, as I aim to show here, in using the testimonies of sailors to uncover the transcripts of African experience during the Middle Passage. While what follows is a text-based analysis, it is also a study of the *material* weapons of the slave ship's 'human cargoes'. As Eleanor Casella has emphasized in her work on nineteenth-century institutional confinement, many strategies for coping with incarceration have an intrinsic materiality.[6] While an archaeologist studying slave shipping does not have the opportunity to excavate material residues to the extent that is possible in terrestrial contexts, aspects of the material culture and material strategies of survival *can* be read out of documentary record, as will become clear below.

At the Extremes of the Spectrum: Insurrection and Suicide

Since the 1960s, a considerable body of work has focused on resistance to slavery across the Americas, with historians and archaeologists alike exploring strategies including collective rebellions or insurrections, flight (running away and the establishment of maroon communities), suicide, and a myriad of generally undisclosed actions including theft, slow working, poisoning, and sabotage. Among scholars of the Middle Passage, however, the form of resistance drawing greatest interest has long been shipboard insurrections, with some recent work also focusing on suicide.[7] Both will be considered here, before turning to infrapolitical actions that (in contrast to insurrection and suicide) generally did not result in loss of life.

Insurrection

In his important book *If We Must Die* Eric Taylor has collated primary sources concerning 493 collective insurrections on European slave ships, 174 of which occurred on British vessels between 1654 and 1807 (Table 11.1).[8] Taken at face value, Taylor's total would suggest that an insurrection occurred once in every sixty of the British voyages included in the TSTD. The many documented plots and conspiracies thwarted in the planning stage are, however, omitted from Taylor's analysis, and indeed from the TSTD data set.[9]

Many shipboard conspiracies and risings are entirely lost to history, recorded only in ships' logs long since destroyed. The true number of shipboard uprisings was undoubtedly far higher than surviving records indicate, therefore. Behrendt, Eltis, and Richardson have estimated that an insurrection was attempted once in every ten voyages; but, if plans and plots thwarted before they could be put into action were counted too, that figure would be even higher.[10] While precise quantification is thus difficult, it can be said with certainly that the fear of insurrection at sea haunted vessel owners and crews in much the same say that it haunted terrestrial plantation owners in the Caribbean and North America. The material expressions of that fear were rather similar too. In the aftermath of major slave rebellions on land, as recent archaeological fieldwork has helped to show, physical changes were often made to plantation land- scapes. Thus, in the aftermath of the 1733–4 rising on St John in the Danish West Indies, planters moved their homes on to higher ground to facilitate better surveillance of their own workforce, and enhance intervisibility between plantations.[11] Similarly, significant architectural and landscape changes occurred on Charleston's urban plant- ations following the thwarted Denmark Vesey rebellion in South Carolina in 1822, with owners relocating slave quarters further from their own homes to reduce the likelihood of attack on their households.[12] On board slave ships, the cognate architec- tural manifestation of the aftermath of successive attempted rebellions was undoubt- edly the barricado—the timber fortification inserted along or to the fore of the quarterdeck of a slaver, cutting the vessel in two. As noted in Chapter 5, this feature is not mentioned in British sources predating 1700 but had become a near-ubiquitous element of slave ships of many nations by the 1750s. Its purpose—the need for which will have been revealed over time, as captives repeatedly breached quarterdecks on

Table 11.1 Documented insurrections on British slaving voyages

Outcome	African coast	Middle Passage	Caribbean coast	Location uncertain	Total
Successful (= freedom for some captives)	44	5	5	5	59
Unsuccessful	49	21	3	10	83
Outcome uncertain	1	0	0	31	32
	94	26	8	46	174

Note: Taylor does not include vessels 'cut off' in Africa (a problematic term that may also refer to attacks from shore), and omits plots discovered before they could be put into action. Nor does he generally include multiple incidents taking place on the same ship. Thus, Robert Norris's *Unity* (1769) appears once in Taylor's catalogue, but the master's logbook records two attempted insurrections, and two additional thwarted actions. All four incidents are discussed in this chapter.

Source: summarizing Taylor (2006: 180–210)

396 MATERIALIZING THE MIDDLE PASSAGE

successive generations of slaving vessels—was to prevent exactly that outcome. The barricado was effectively designed to provide higher ground from which sailors could fire on to Africans surging forward from the waist of the vessel, as shown in a much-reproduced engraving from Carl Wadtsröm's *An Essay on Colonization* (1794), shown in Figure 11.1.[13]

The spectre of insurrection at sea found expression not just in the barricado and the elaborate routines (discussed in Chapter 10) by which sailors crossed it, but also in the practices of the maritime insurance industry. Maritime law employed the concept of 'general average': the idea that losses undertaken to save a vessel and its crew (jettisoning the cargo, for instance) represented a risk shared among all those investing in a voyage.[14] The killing of captives in order to prevent an insurrection on board a slave ship also fell into this category, but in 1781 John Weskett published the first reference work on maritime law, noting the following as standard practice in underwriting slaving voyages:

> Ships and merchandizes from England to the coast of Africa, and at and from thence to our colonies in the West-Indies, &c. are usually insured with the following clause in the policy, viz. 'free from loss or average, by trading in boats, *and also from average occasioned by insurrection of slaves*, if under 10 per cent'.[15]

As James Oldham has noted, the inclusion of slave insurrections in this indemnity clause suggests both that such actions were *expected* on slavers, and that the losses arising from them were proportionally low: in most cases less than 10 per cent of the overall value of the venture.[16] The entire purpose of a general average clause, with its proportionate excess, was to enable underwriters to hedge against small but pernicious claims.[17] What we glimpse from this document, then, is the financial impact of repeated slave ship insurrections. The 10 per cent excess clause noted by Weskett certainly lay at the centre of several appeal cases adjudicated by Lord Mansfield, whose ruling on the *Zong* case was discussed in Chapter 1. One of these concerned the Bristol slaver *Wasp*, impacted by two insurrections in 1783. In the second of these, it was reported:

> Several slaves took to the ship's sides, and hung down in the water by the chains and ropes, some for about a quarter of an hour: three were killed by firing and three were drowned; the rest were taken in, but they were too far gone to be recovered: many of them were desperately bruised; many died in consequence of the wounds they had received from the firing during the mutiny; some from swallowing salt water; some from chagrin at their disappointment, and from abstinence; several of fluxes and fevers; in all to the amount of 55, who died during the course of the voyage.[18]

Wasp had been insured against deaths that were due to rebellion, but, in requesting compensation on the basis that losses exceeded 10 per cent, the owners counted not simply those killed in the rising, but also later deaths from 'abstinence' (starvation) and

Figure 11.1 Colorized reprint of a lithograph from the fold-out sheet ('Plan and sections of a slave ship') included in the cover pocket of Carl Wadström's *An Essay on Colonization*, first published in London in 1794.

398 MATERIALIZING THE MIDDLE PASSAGE

'chagrin'. Mansfield ruled that insurance should be claimable only on captives who died during an insurrection, or shortly thereafter of wounds incurred during the action (that is, mortality as a direct result of 'mutiny').[19] Like the *Zong* case, the *Wasp* hearing foregrounds the extent to which British vessel owners feared, and sought to mitigate, what Jay Coughtry called the spectre of slave revolt.[20] It also foregrounds the struggle in English law to reconcile the chattel status imposed on African captives with the repeated efforts by those people to fight for their freedom, or to end their own lives.

As Table 11.1 demonstrates, insurrections tended to occur mainly during embarkation and while a ship remained in African water, taking on supplies before heading to the open sea.[21] It is easy to understand why: most rebels hoped to survive these actions, and while a ship remained on the African coast, they could entertain a more realistic expectation of reaching the shore and disappearing quietly into the hinterland. Insurrections were far less frequently initiated during the Middle Passage, and those that did occur were rarely successful in the sense of securing the freedom of some of the Africans on board. But that was not always the intended outcome: in the dark waters of the mid-Atlantic—at the point where both land and hope must have seemed furthest from reach—Africans sometimes sought the complete destruction of the ship, its crew, and themselves. Put another way, some Middle Passage insurrections might best be understood as collective suicide bids. There was certainly a close relationship between insurrection and self-destruction on a slave ship: some risings were precipitated by suicides, for example, and in other cases self-destruction was a response to the failure of an insurrection.[22] Following the unsuccessful rebellion on *Wasp* noted above, a number of those involved in the action elected to starve themselves or died, as the master, Richard Bowen, put it, from 'chagrin at disappointment' in the failure of their rising.[23]

I will end this discussion of insurrection with a unique account of an attempted shipboard rebellion: unique because it was written by an African captive, describing his own Middle Passage. As explained in Chapter 3, Ottobah Cuguoano was born on the Gold Coast in 1757 and captured and sold into slavery in 1770. His Atlantic crossing to Grenada is briefly discussed in his *Thoughts and Sentiments on the Evil and Wicked Traffic of the Slavery and Commerce of the Human Species*, published in London in 1787. This account of the Middle Passage is almost entirely devoted to a failed shipboard rebellion. I repeat it here in full because it is so important to the present discussion:

> And when we found ourselves at last taken away, death was more preferable to life, and a plan was concerted among us that we might burn and blow up the ship, and to perish all together in the flames; but we were betrayed by one of our own country-women, who slept with some of the head men of the ship, for it was common for the dirty filthy sailors to take the African women and lie upon their bodies, but the men were chained and pent up in holes. It was the women and boys that were to burn the ship, with the approbation and groans of the rest; though that was prevented, the discovery was likewise a cruel bloody scene.[24]

It was noted above that some rebellions might best be interpreted as collective suicide bids. The plot devised on Cugoano's crossing certainly seems to fall into this category, with the captive body making a collective decision to destroy the ship and themselves. Cugoano also draws attention to the important role that women and boys played in facilitating (but, on occasion, also foiling) shipboard insurrections—a phenomenon that is explored in greater later in this chapter.

Suicide

As early as the 1790s, some abolitionists were making a case that suicide by the enslaved was a principled, heroic, response to tyranny.[25] In modern scholarship on slavery, similarly, suicide has often been framed as the ultimate personal expression of agency.[26] In an important recent study, however, Terri Snyder has questioned that tendency, arguing for a more nuanced approach giving greater attention to the emotional, psychological, and material conditions that fostered self-destruction.[27] I have attempted to follow her advice below. Personally, I find it impossible to write about suicide under the sign of resistance and have elected not to do so here.

It is very difficult to estimate the proportion of captives who died at their own hands, but two important categories of evidence can be used to explore this question. First, deaths by drowning were a regular enough occurrence on slavers to ensure that the question: 'Have you ever known instances of slaves jumping overboard?' was put to almost every sailor appearing before parliamentary committees between 1788 and 1791. The responses indicate that widely shared suicide prevention technologies were deployed to prevent captives killing themselves in this way. On the African coast, both shrouds of netting, and the timber latticework of the makeshift deck 'houses' in which captives were incarcerated as the slave decks were built, inhibited access to the sea (**Falconbridge, *Account* 1788: 198**). Some captives reached the water nevertheless; among them was a man who, almost immediately after boarding, 'forced his way through the network on the larboard side' on one of the ships on which Falconbridge had sailed. The former surgeon supposed that the man was eaten by the sharks that patrolled the waters around slavers on the coast (**Falconbridge, *Account* 1788: 5–6**).

Once out to sea, as mentioned in Chapter 5, half-netting remained in place on the quarterdeck and forecastle, once again to keep women and children away from the side.[28] Netting was not necessary fore of the barricado: the males here were immobilized by deck chains. The latrines were an obvious weak point in the ship's anti-suicide defences, however, as captives clearly observed. On many ships these facilities projected directly over the ocean, and for women, at least, they were also relatively secluded spaces. Here, if anywhere, it might be possible to break through the netting and jump overboard. A female captive drowned having 'got through the necessary' on board *Canterbury* in 1767, for example, and surgeon Ecroyde Claxton recalled Africans on *Young Hero* cutting through two sections of netting that had been lashed together at the point where a necessary tub had been set (**HCSP 82: 35**). Netting would

400 MATERIALIZING THE MIDDLE PASSAGE

be at its weakest where different sections were joined, and the captives mentioned by Claxton had clearly capitalized on the siting of a necessary tub at such a point.

The position of African suicide in British maritime insurance law is a second strand of documentary evidence enabling us to glimpse the extent, and financial impact, of captives taking their own lives. Weskett's *Digest* (1781) notes with reference to slave shipping:

> The insurer takes upon him the risques of the loss, capture, and death of slaves, or any other unavoidable accident to them: but natural death is always understood to be excepted:—by natural death is meant, not only when it happens by disease or sickness, but also when the captive destroys himself through despair, which often happens: but when slaves are killed, or thrown into the sea in order to quell an insurrection on their part, then the insurers must answer.[29]

The legal fiction of (African) suicide as 'natural' death suggests that such losses had in the past impacted significantly on the slave trade, reducing profits for both vessel owners and underwriters. Unsurprisingly, several legal challenges, the *Zong* case among them, were mounted against insurers who had refused to pay out on what they considered 'natural' deaths; but the principle held firm.[30] Later eighteenth-century insurers also refused to underwrite losses incurred by slavers while 'trading in boats'— a term argued to cover both trading expeditions upriver by the ship's boats and also the transportation of captives from shore to ship.[31] This practice surely reflects both the hazards of crossing the bar to waiting slave ships, and the extent to which captives seized opportunities, at these times of transit, to jump into the sea. Similar opportunities occurred at the end of the voyage. In 1803, thirty Igbo captives newly arrived in Savannah were transferred onto a smaller vessel for transhipment; soon after, they succeeded in drowning both the crew and themselves.[32]

It is necessary at this point to pose a very basic question concerning the materiality of African suicides at sea: what were the tools of self-harm?[33] Given that captives were so closely watched, this is an important consideration, the exploration of which foregrounds the extent to which desperation bred grim creativity. On board slave ships, Africans rarely had access to the artefacts—firearms, laudanum, poison—that would ensure a quick death. Starvation and drowning did not require such materials, and this is surely why these are the two most-cited suicide mechanisms in witness accounts. As evidenced in Chapter 9, however, attempted starvation was anticipated and vigorously combatted by crews. Every late-eighteenth-century slaver carried a speculum oris, and, if that failed, the bolus knife, or less clinical technologies of suicide prevention such as hot coals, were deployed. Africans must quickly have understood that they would not be left simply to fade away but would be 'persuaded' to eat by one of these means. As one of Clarkson's witnesses explained (*Substance* 1789: 65):

> Mr Janverin says, that he has frequently seen the slaves refuse sustenance. In all such cases they have been punished. Thumb-screws have sometimes been fixed upon

them: at other times they have been fastened by the arms to the belaying pins of the rails; their bodies have been afterwards stretched out by means of tackles, and in this situation they have been flogged till they have consented to eat, after which they have again refused, when their mouths have been wrenched open by pump-bolts and attempts made to force the food down their throats through a funnel. But almost all exertions of this kind have proved ineffectual, and they have died at last to the disappointment of their enslavers.[34]

A healthy individual can last some three weeks without food, and, while many Africans were undernourished and/or ill at the point of embarkation, starving to death within a regime that employed painful force-feeding methods must have required extraordinary resolve. Witness testimonies are rarely specific concerning suicide by other means, but a handful of accounts refer to hanging or strangulation. Paul Erdmann Isert noted that, on French ships, captives were not allowed loincloths, because it was feared they would hang themselves with these narrow strips of fabric.[35] Yet, as discussed later in this chapter, 'modesty garments' were sometimes given to certain captives on British ships, and such items could have been repurposed for self-harm. Ships also carried vast quantities of rope or yarn, sections of which might be pilfered without the loss being noted by the crew (see Figure 11.2 for examples of ships' ropes).[36] Isaac Wilson (**HCSP 72: 279–80**) served as surgeon on *Elizabeth* in 1788 and recounted two suicides by hanging using stolen rope. In the first case, a woman conveyed a rope below decks, and hanged herself from a batten on the sleeping platform in the women's room. In the second, a woman stole rope yarn and strangled herself using the heavy armourer's vice—which, when not in use, was stored in the women's room—as a counterweight to her own body. Hanging may again be hinted at in Falconbridge's reference to sick captives appropriating their bandages for 'other' uses (*Account 1788; 28*). Certainly, every ship's makeshift sickroom was a potential source of materials for those intent upon suicide. On the Liverpool ship *Ranger* in 1790, a man being treated in the boys' room obtained 'a knife or some other instrument' and turned it upon himself.[37] Thomas Trotter also recounted the attempted suicide of a man in his care on *Brooks* in 1783 (**HCSP 73: 83**). The captive attempted to slash his own throat, by means unstated, and Trotter secured these wounds with sutures. Overnight, the captive ripped out the stitches with his fingernails.

The most cited weapon employed in suicide bids was the sea. It is now well understood that belief systems offering the hope of transmigration and the restoration of identity in the otherworld informed the decisions of some captives to take their own lives.[38] But, as highlighted in Chapter 6, many Africans also believed that the land of the dead was reached only by crossing water. In metaphysical terms, then, the sea was not simply a means to an end (death by drowning); it was a medium by which to 'cross from one world or state of existence to another'.[39] Numerous witness testimonies indicate that captives on board slave ships acted on this understanding. Trading along the Gold Coast and at Ouidah in the 1690s, for example,

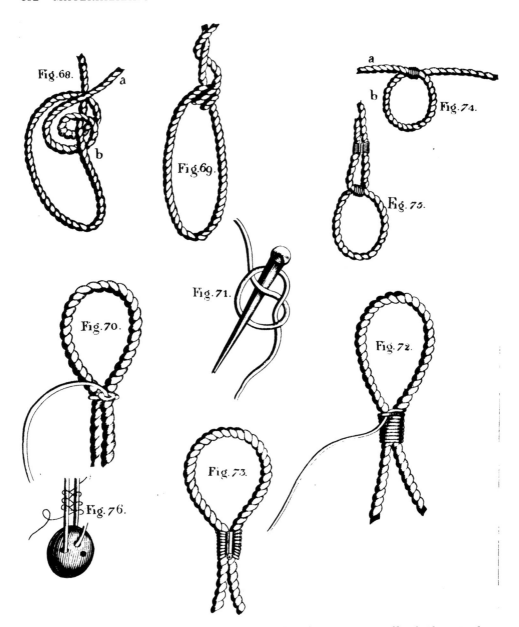

Figure 11.2 Illustration by William Butterworth for *The Young Sea Officer's Sheet Anchor*. From Lever (1808: plate facing p. 9). The central figure (71) includes an iron marlin spike, employed in the seizing process. On Newton's *Argyle*, one of these was stolen and passed down to the slave deck.

Thomas Phillips noted: 'we had about 12 negroes did wilfully drown themselves and others starv'd themselves to death; for 'tis their belief that when they die they return home to their own country and friends again' (*Hannibal* 1693–4: 219). Many years later, recounting details of a voyage on *Young Hero* in 1788, Ecroyde Claxton similarly stated that captives at Bonny believed that by throwing themselves overboard to drown 'they should get back again to their own country'. Having been informed that the way to prevent such attempts was to behead the retrieved corpses of captives who had thrown themselves overboard, Claxton's captain set the ship's cooper to that task, using a hatchet, in sight of all the Africans on board (**HCSP 82: 35**).

Such actions, aided by netting, deck chains, and the vigilance of the crew ensured that deaths through drowning, while far from uncommon, remained proportionally few. As James Towne explained to Thomas Clarkson, several captives on his two slaving voyages made attempts to jump overboard, but he 'never knew any of them succeed, as the crew were constantly employed in watching them' (*Substance* **1789: 53**). From his cargo of almost 700 people in 1694, Thomas Phillips reported twelve drownings (*Hannibal* **1693–4: 219**). Alexander Falconbridge recalled 20 captives jumping overboard from the *Enterprize*, which was carrying more than 500 Africans, in 1787.[40] As discussed earlier, it is questionable whether all such deaths should be framed in terms of resistance; but it is certainly the case that the majority of Africans—those who did *not* seek to destroy themselves by drowning or other means—were also exercising agency, both in choosing life over death, and in refusing to countenance that the only future possible was that offered in the *next* life. It is noteworthy, finally, that drowning and hanging (usually from trees) were the most common forms of suicide among the enslaved in the Americas.[41] Perhaps this was simply because there, as on slavers, the unfree generally lacked access to firearms, laudanum, and other technologies of self-harm. Even so, it is striking how closely the materials of self-destruction utilized by plantation slaves—wood, water, and rope—echo the material world of the captive passage.

Middle Passage Infrapolitics: Resistance below the Line

Most of those enduring the Middle Passage did not commit suicide or attempt aggressive collective action. Instead, captives shifted into what Eleanor Casella, describing coping strategies in nineteenth-century prisons, calls 'an opaque existence'.[42] This opacity in turn made it possible to exploit the small gaps and slippages (or third spaces) within dominance left open by the slave-shipping practices outlined in Chapter 10. In his analysis of resistance by slaves in the antebellum US South—a context in which outright rebellion could not feasibly result in complete overthrow of the social system—James Scott has influentially argued that the enslaved contested the conditions of domination and the abuse of power through low-profile strategies that he collectively dubbed 'infrapolitics'.[43] These strategies, outlined in *Domination and the Arts of Resistance: Hidden Transcripts* (1990), ranged from the cultural 'arts' of dissent (the oral dissemination of subversive folk songs and folk tales, for example) through actions including 'theft, pilfering, feigned ignorance, shirking or careless labour, foot-dragging, secret trade and production for sale, sabotage of crops, livestock, machinery, arson, flight, and so on'.[44] My contention here—and it is one borne out repeatedly in sailors' testimonies—is

404   MATERIALIZING THE MIDDLE PASSAGE

that the slave ship was an initial site in which captive Africans first practised the infrapolitics of resistance to white domination.[45] One way to explore this point is to return to the detailed records maintained by John Newton during his voyages as master of the slavers *Argyle* and *African* in the 1750s. As can be seen in Table 11.2, Newton recorded numerous actions by his captives, ranging from concealment, theft, and sabotage

Table 11.2 Infrapolitical actions on *Duke of Argyle*, 1751 and *African*, 1752–3

Newton's journal	Infrapolitical action
ARGYLE 6 May 1751 At Cape Mount	'The people found 2 knives and a bag of small stones in the men's room.'
26 May 1751 Middle Passage day 3	'A young man, out of irons first on account of a large ulcer, and since for his seeming good behaviour, gave them a large marlin spike down the gratings, but was happily seen by one of the people. They had it in possession about an hour before I mad [*sic*] search for it, in which time they made such good dispatch (being an instrument that made no noise) that this morning I found near 20 of them had broke their irons.'
27 May 1751	'Secured the men's irons again and punished 6 of the ringleaders of the insurrection.'
28 May 1751	'28th Secured the bulkhead in the men's room, for they had started almost every stantient. Their plot was exceedingly well laid, and had they been left alone an hour longer, must have occasioned us a good deal of trouble and damage.'
16 June 1751 Middle Passage day 40	'In the afternoon we were alarmed with a report that some of the men slaves had found means to poyson the water in the scuttle casks upon deck, but upon enquiry found they had only conveyed some of their country fetishes, as they call them, or talismans into one of them, which they had the credulity to suppose must inevitably kill all who drank of it. But if it please god that they make no worse attempts than to charm us to death then it will not much harm us, but it shews their intentions are not wanting.'
AFRICAN 11 December 1752 At Mana	'By the favour of Divine Providence made a timely discovery today that the slaves were forming a plot for an insurrection. Surprised 2 of them attempting to get off their irons, and upon farther search in their rooms, upon the information of 3 of the boys, found some knives, stones, shot, etc. and a cold chisel. Upon enquiry there appeared 8 principally concerned to move in projecting the mischief and 4 boys in supplying them with the above instruments. Put the boys in irons and slightly in the thumbscrews to urge them to a full confession. In the morning examined the men slaves and punished 6 of the principals, put 4 of them in collars.'
23 February 1753 At Sherboro	'The boy slaves impeached the men of an intention to rise upon us. Found 4 principally concerned, punished them with the thumb screws and afterwards put them in neck yokes.'
10 May 1753 Entry in Newton's Diary	'I was at first continually alarmed with their [the male captives] almost desperate attempts to make insurrections upon us ... when most quiet they were always watching for opportunity. However from about the end of February they have behaved more like children in one family than slaves in chains.'

Source: collated from Martin and Spurrell (1962).

through practices we would understand today as conjure, to seeming compliance. Some were clearly the thwarted prelude to collective aggressive action, but others were less obviously so. The actions in Table 11.2 are discussed later in this chapter, but at this point it is important to emphasize that none meets the definition of an 'insurrection' employed by Taylor in *If We Must Die*. We have left behind insurrection here and entered the world of infrapolitics.

A further key point to note with reference to Table 11.2 is that the actions described involved only small numbers of captives. Even in cases of outright insurrection on board slaving vessels, it was rare that *every* African on the ship was involved. To quote Eric Taylor, it would be wrong to imagine all 'enslaved men and women standing shoulder to shoulder, presenting an imposing wall of resistance' as they crossed the Atlantic.[46] It is also important to acknowledge that either voluntarily or under duress—during interrogation, for example—some captives informed against others (as is also clear from Table 11.2). But, as Scott has stressed, the hinterland between complete compliance and outright defiance is vast, and, in placing emphasis on infrapolitics in the remainder of this chapter, it is certainly not my intention to suggest a complete opposition between 'revolutionary' and 'everyday' forms of resistance.[47] As evidenced repeatedly in this chapter (and not least in Table 11.2), these tactics are relational.[48] The tendency of many recent studies to focus on suicide and insurrection—the most extreme challenges to the voyage into slavery—has, however, meant that the experiences of the majority, and the multivariate complexities of their struggle to survive, remain under-explored. My aim in this chapter is simply to afford these complexities the consideration they deserve. For the same reason, I have avoided framing my discussion under what Walter Johnson calls 'the sign of agency'.[49] This is not, of course, because I think agency was impossible in the context of the Middle Passage; rather, it is because I share Johnson's view that, as used in discussing the life experiences of the enslaved, the term has 'become unmoored from the historical experience it is intended to express'. As Johnson argues, it is necessary to look *beneath* the abstractions ('agency' counterpoised against 'power') to uncover what he terms 'a history of bare-life processes and material exchanges so basic that they have escaped the attentions of countless historians of slavery'.[50] In short—though Johnson does not use the term himself—to uncover the history, and contingent intricacies, of infrapolitics.

Drawing inspiration from James Scott's work, I have attempted to identify the 'weapons' of Africans enduring the Middle Passage as they appear in, or can be read out of, the sailors' testimonies first introduced in Chapter 3. The categories identified below are as follows: makeshift weapons created, for the most part, by turning the ship and its iron regime back upon itself; the weaponization of their own bodies by women; the insurgent opportunities created by crews' ambivalent treatment of younger African boys; the African voice and body asserting itself under domination through speech, oral culture, drumming, and dance; and, finally, the spiritual weapons—objects of power intended to protect or harm—created and wielded by those for whom the ship was at once a prison and a 'witch craft.'

Creative Arming

In his analysis of slave ship insurrections, Eric Taylor has helpfully collated primary sources detailing the makeshift weapons used in shipboard insurrections (Table 11.3). As might be expected, most of these were forged from the fabric of the ship itself: timber planking, blocks and billets, metal fittings and implements, and the tools of the carpenter, cooper, and cook figure repeatedly in witness accounts (Figure 11.3). These things were rarely employed directly against sailors, but instead became weapons in the battle against the ship's iron regime: shackles constrained mobility so successfully that, for men, breaking free of these restraints was a necessary first step in any attempted rising or suicide bid. Documentary sources reveal captives prising up the timbers and metal fittings from which the men's room was constructed and using these to force or bludgeon shackle bolts. Just before *Tryal* docked in Barbados (*Substance* **1789: 19**), the captive men used a 'hacked knife and the bar on the men's gratings' to remove their irons. Africans similarly employed pilfered objects that had been smuggled (generally by women or boys) down into the men's room through the latticed hatchways above their heads. The need to 'air' the slave decks meant that the men's room, while locked, was not impenetrable: the marlin spike passed down through the gratings on Newton's *Argyle* (see Table 11.2 and Figure 11.2) is a reminder of this point. Thomas Trotter, surgeon on *Brooks* in 1783, recalled an attempt by male captives to saw off their irons, using an 'old knife, notched for the purpose' (**HCSP 73: 87**). It had been passed to them through one of the gratings above their room, the latticework of which made it impossible to seal off that space completely at night. On some ships, male captives identified and forced open a second weak point on the slave deck: the scuttle giving access into the hold from the men's room. Scuttles were always bolted and padlocked, but, as James Arnold attested concerning an insurrection on the Bristol ship *Ruby* in 1787, captives could sometimes find ways to force the locks (**HCSP 69: 133**). On *Ann Galley*, an uprising that would result in the successful capture of the ship by its captives, a premeditated uprising began when 'a Negro boy that we had on board, catched hold of the cook's hatchet, and went with it in his hand, away unnoticed through the Barakheada (barricado) door in among the slaves'. The first action of the male captives was to break open their irons, apparently using the hatchet for that purpose: 'on one of the guns they laid their irons and opened the forelock of them.'[51]

Some of these attempts to create makeshift weapons and force locks must have worked: a measure of success in this regard is the repeated checking of the male captives' chains, especially at the start of the ship's day, as outlined in Chapter 10. From the perspective of slaver crews, the moment at which male captives emerged on to the deck from below was a particularly dangerous one. The men's room was a no-go area for the crew at night, and there were real possibilities that some captives may have broken free of their shackles while unobserved. To minimize potential danger, captives were made to climb the ladder up to the main deck slowly, two by two. But without sailors stationed below to limit the flow of bodies, it was only as captives reached the open air that the integrity of their shackles could be checked. African men clearly

Figure 11.3 Potential weapons: trade card of the London plane-maker John Jennion, who made a range of tools for carpenters, joiners, and coopers. British Museum Heal, 118.8.

identified a window of opportunity here, repeatedly making attempts to break open iron restraints while below. Ten days after leaving Africa in March 1794, Samuel Gamble (*Sandown* 1793–4: 103) discovered a captive hidden in the hold—an incident that led him to check the irons of the other male captives. Several of these restraints proved unfit for purpose.

Any heavy metal object could be redeployed by captives: John Smith, the mate on *Ruby,* unwisely 'went down with a lanthorn to quiet them [the men]' at night. The lantern was wrenched from his hand, and he was beaten with it, narrowly escaping

408 MATERIALIZING THE MIDDLE PASSAGE

Table 11.3 Weapons used by captives, with the numbers of times each is mentioned in documentary sources

Weaponry	No. of examples	Tools and utensils	No. of examples	Miscellaneous	No. of examples
Small arms*	33	Axes	8	Pieces of wood[†]	19
Swords/cutlasses/ sabres	10	Hammers	3	Bars/pieces of iron	11
Knives	11	Carpenters' tools	2	Shackles/ chains	7
Ships' guns	2	Cooking utensils	2	Food bowls	2
Lances	1	Files	2	Oars	2
Pikes	1	Hatchets	2	Boiling water	1
Razors	2	Buckets	1		
		Coopers' tools	1		
		Hand spikes	1		
		Scissors	1		
		Shovels	1		
		Sledgehammers	1		

* Small arms include blunderbusses, guns, muskets, pistols, rifles, ammunition, gun powder, and items referred to simply as 'arms'.
[†] Pieces of wood include billets, firewood, logs, planks, staves, axe handles, blocks, and boards.
Source: after Taylor (2006: 96, table 1).

with his life (**HCSP 69: 133**). Most of the things later used as weapons had first to be pilfered and concealed, and in this context one of most important insurgent spaces of the slave ship was that created by *lack* of space. On most slavers, the tools of the ship's carpenter, cooper, and armourer presented an obvious security risk: they were variously heavy, edged, bladed, pointed, and sharp. Among the eighteenth-century carpentry tools recovered from the wreck of the British brig *Betsy*, for example, were components of the adze or axe, bevel, hammer, and gimlet.[52] That captives attempted to secure tools and other implements used about the vessel on a daily basis is evident from John Barbot's comment (*Treatment* 1712: 779): 'we use to visit them daily, narrowly searching every corner between decks, to see whether they have not found means to gather any pieces of iron, or wood, or knives about the ship, notwithstanding the great care we take, not to leave any tools or nails.' On naval vessels, carpenters were provided with storerooms for both lumber and the chests containing their many tools.[53] On the French slaver *Marie-Séraphique*, the carpenter's tools were stored in a small, locked room in the storage zone between the bulkheads separating the men's and women's rooms (see Figure 10.15). On a later eighteenth-century British ship, that space would generally be used as a boys' room or hospital, and it is not at all clear where the carpenters, armourers, and coopers serving on British vessels stored their implements. Certainly, the presence of an armourer's vice in the women's room of *Elizabeth* (discussed above) is one hint that secure spaces were few. Every ship needed a powder magazine, but its whereabouts on British vessels is generally unclear.[54]

Small arms were generally locked into wooden chests. Newton carried six arms chests on *Argyle*, for example, storing them in the men's room until it began to fill with captives (*Argyle* 1750–1: 22); where he kept them thereafter is not stated, but, during the day, some small arms must have been kept within easy reach of the crew on the quarterdeck. Thomas Phillips notes as much for **Hannibal** (1693–4: 219): 'we have a chest of small arms, ready loaden and prim'd, constantly lying at hand upon the quarter-deck, together with some granada shells [grenades]; and two of our quarter-deck guns, pointing on the deck thence.' At night, arms chests were probably stored in the captain's cabin, but this was often shared with women and children. Surgeons had lockable medicine and instrument chests, but in the gloom and chaos of the ship's hospital spaces it will have been impossible to keep a constant watch on the where-abouts of all their sharp implements. Space was so short on the Middle Passage that unsold trade goods were often stored in barrels on the slave decks. James Arnold told Parliament that, during the rising on *Ruby* in 1787 mentioned earlier, male captives armed themselves from a cask of trade knives stored in their room for want of space (**HCSP 69: 133**). Other kinds of knife were present on every slaver. Most crewmen carried pocket-knives, both for use in their work and for eating: an attempted revolt on *Fredensborg*, discovered by an African seaman named Aye, centred on a plot to seize the sailors' knives while they were eating.[55] Mealtimes provided captives with other potential weapons, as William Snelgrave's often-cited account of an insurrection on *Ferrers Galley* in 1722 makes abundantly clear. The master had unwisely taken to crossing the barricado and personally distributing pepper and oil to the male captives during mealtimes. They beat him to death with 'the little Tubs out of which they eat their boiled Rice'.[56]

An excellent glimpse of the range of makeshift weapons employed during an insurrection can be found in John Casseneuve's account of events on *Don* Carlos (**James Barbot Jnr, *Don Carlos* 1700: 513**), four days after departing from Cabinda on 1 January 1701:

> About one in the afternoon, after dinner, we according to custom, caused them, one by one, to go down between decks, to have each his pint of water; most of them were yet above deck, many of them provided with knives, which we had indiscreetly given them two or three days before, as not suspecting the least attempt of this nature from them; others had pieces of iron they had torn off from our fore-castle door, as having premeditated a revolt, and seeing all the ship's company, at best but weak and many quite sick; they had also broken off the shackles from several of their companions feet, which served them, as well as billets they had provided themselves with, and all other things they could lay hands on, which they imagin'd might be of use in their enterprize.

Captain James Fletcher, reporting an insurrection on *Hope* off Cape Coast in 1776, similarly noted that the male captives 'threw staves, billets of wood etc.' in their effort to break down, or get over, the barricado.[57] As the sailor Robert Barker noted in his account of his own mistreatment aboard *Thetis*, necessity was the parent of invention for the desperate. In danger of starving to death, he found a source of food:

ripping up part of the forecastle flooring, I soon got into the hold, where I found a way to a bread butt, when drawing the staple with an old scraper and shackle bolt, I took out some bread, and then drove the staple tight in the same holes it was in before, to prevent suspicion.   (**Barker**, *Thetis* **1754–5: 28**)

The ship's weaponry—from the small arms handed out to sailors, to the carriage and/or swivel guns mounted on the barricado, to the ship's gunpowder supply—could also be turned on crews. On most ships, it might be expected that some captives would be acquainted with small arms and know how to deploy them: the ship's larger, mounted, guns will perhaps have been less familiar, but, as first noted in Chapter 6, coastal West Africans built up considerable practical knowledge of sailing ships, their smaller boats, and their weapons, including swivel guns. Certainly, Africans on the London-based *Clare Galley* succeeding in 'making themselves Masters of the Gunpowder and Fire Arms' during a successful insurrection in 1729.[58] A second successful rising, this time on the Liverpool ship *Ann* in 1750, again involved the male captives gaining access to the powder and arms.[59] By the later eighteenth century, this kind of familiarity with ships' armaments can only have increased: war canoes in some parts of West Africa were by now armed with small brass or iron cannon made in Europe.[60] Whether through sickness or impressment, slavers were often chronically undermanned, and, as evidenced in Chapter 10, some ships put captives to work as sailors. Hugh Crow trained a captive on *Will* in the use of artillery in 1789, and on *Mary*, which had lost men to impressment in 1805, some of the male captives were again trained to use the ship's cannon and small arms.[61] Such practices opened spaces that might be exploited by Africans. In 1750, an insurrection on *King David* of Bristol was initiated by fifteen captives whose English-speaking leader built up an exceptionally close relationship with the captain. Perhaps, reading between the lines of the report below, this was a physical relationship, hidden behind the cabin door. Whatever the case, the man and his comrades were never chained, and appear to have had considerable freedom of movement around the vessel. It was reported that:

As the Chief of these Slaves spoke very good English, he often convers'd with the Captain in his Cabbin, where all the Arms were loaded, and consulting with his Comrades, knowing the small Strength of the white men, they at once flew to the Cabin, and secured the Arms in a few Minutes, kill'd the Captain and five of the People.[62]

The Weapons of Women—and Girls

Were they all confined between decks at night during the voyage? They were, a few women excepted.
(Question put to Isaac Wilson, with his answer, **HCSP 72: 274**)

Taylor has rightly observed that attempted insurrections tended to 'rely on slaves who gained privileged positions or unusual access on board'.[63] An example of an African man with access to the captain's cabin on *King David* has just been noted, but the two key groups of captives gaining 'privileged positions' were young women and (as discussed later) boys. In the past as still today, incarcerated women were subjected to gender-differentiated forms of discipline and control.[64] In the context of the slave trade, white sailors simply expected African women to be more passive than men, and their surveillance was managed with reference to that expectation. As John Newton put it, 'from the Women there is no danger of insurrection, and they are carefully kept from the men' (*Thoughts* 1788: 12). Accordingly, it was not a regular practice to shackle females on British ships, and there are no references at all in parliamentary witness testimonies to the use of deck chains to constrain the movement of women.[65] While on deck, then, women and girls generally had greater freedom of movement than did adult males.[66] Moreover, on many British ships the women's room below decks remained open to both female captives and crew throughout the day. This provided sailors with opportunities and spaces for rape, but also gave women chances to access the cabins, cooking hearth, and other places in which the physical weapons of resistance such as small arms and knives might be sought. In a planned insurrection on *Hudibras*, women with access to cooking areas sought to seize 'the cook's knives, forks, axe, and other implements' for use as weapons (**Butterworth, *Hudibras* 1786–7: 123**).

Captive women were also able to use their own bodies as sites of resistance. Sailors' descriptions of African women and girls were often framed in the language of desire: they singled out the 'young sprightly maidens' (**John Barbot, *Treatment* 1712: 780**), the 'handsome' women (**Smeathman, *Oeconomy c.*1775: 8**), and so on. William Butterworth was only sixteen at the time of his voyage (*Hudibras* 1786–7), but, writing about the ship's female captives decades later, he peppered his narrative with an entire thesaurus of terms for female beauty. African females who drew the white male gaze understood that they could make small, material improvements to their circumstances by submitting to sex with sailors, and some did so. Smeathman noted, in this context, that on some ships 'every seaman has his Favourite, with whom he shares his hammock and his allowance' (*Oeconomy c.*1775: 8). He also remarked that some women were provided by their 'gallants' with fathoms or strips of cloth to use as modesty garments (*Oeconomy c.*1775: 9): these cloths might well have served as places of concealment for small objects. Female 'favourites' also carried out domestic tasks, washing clothes and serving food. The young girl selected as the 'favourite mistress' of Joseph Williams, Master of *Ruby*, had been living in his cabin for five or six months when, in 1787, he beat her severely for ripping a shirt. The fact that the garment belonged to Williams's son, and that the girl and his own child were playing together at the time, is instructive of the extent to which she had become embedded in the daily life of the master. Her age is unclear, but it will be recalled from Chapter 10 that those designated as 'girls' on slavers were often pre-pubescent.

Whatever their ages, female 'favourites' were key figures in insurrection plans, risking and sacrificing their persons to the cause of embodied resistance.[67] In exploring

412   MATERIALIZING THE MIDDLE PASSAGE

this point, it is necessary to return to the captain of *Ruby*, first encountered via the surgeon James Arnold's testimony in Chapter 10. It will be recalled that, a young woman having recently been embarked, Joseph Williams 'sent for her, and ordered her to come by herself; He attempted to sleep with her in the Cabin, but on refusing to comply with his desires, she was very severely beaten by him and sent below' (HCSP 69: 126). If African women refused sex, it would seem, Williams beat them: but does not appear to have raped them. Arnold's phrasing, like Smeathman's above, suggests that ship's officers wanted to persuade themselves that the 'handsome' African women they had singled out as sexual 'partners' had *freely* consented to their demands. The expectation that black women were, or should be, both submissive and willing was undoubtedly informed by the widespread stereotyping of African females as libidinous, and also by the complex fusion of disgust and desire that is so evident in the contemporary writing of Jamaican planters like Edward Long.[68] But, one way or another, some captains undoubtedly lowered their guard where their 'favourites' were concerned. How can one know this? Because these 'women of the cabin, having sacrific[ed] themselves sexually to move into a position of power on board the ship', as Taylor puts it, appear in a succession of eighteenth-century accounts of insurrections on slavers.[69] In many of these accounts, they come into focus pilfering and passing on objects to which they alone had access. John Atkins describes an attempted slave mutiny on the *Robert* of Bristol in 1721, as told to him by Captain Harding of that ship.[70] The insurrection was masterminded by a man named Tomba, aided by a few other men and a woman 'who, being more at large, was to watch for the proper opportunity'. One night, she was able to tell Tomba that only five of the crew remained on deck. She also passed a hammer to him, through the grating over the men's room. Given her mobility at night, and her access to one of the carpenter's tools, this unnamed woman must have been 'sharing' the cabin of the captain or another officer. That may be why, when the rising failed, she suffered what even Atkins was moved to call a cruel death: hoisted up by her thumbs, whipped, and slashed with knives.[71] A young woman caught smuggling gunpowder through a hole in the bulkhead separating the men's room and women's room on *Industry* in 1729 was similarly made a bloody example to the rest.[72] Thomas Trotter, surgeon on *Brooks* in 1783, recalled an attempt by male captives to saw off their irons using a knife brought to them 'by a woman who lived in the cabin' (HCSP 73: 87). A woman 'who lay in the cabbin' also played a leading role in a revolt on *Delight* in 1770, helping the male captives to locate the ship's arms chest: she was possibly the only African on board who knew its precise whereabouts.[73] On the Liverpool ship *Thomas* in 1797, two or three women, evidently not locked into the women's room with the rest, having noted

> that the armourer had incautiously left the arms chest open, got into the after-hatchway, and conveyed all the arms which they could find through the bulkheads to the male slaves, about two hundred of whom immediately ran up the forescuttles and put to death all of the crew who came their way.[74]

In all of these cases, the third space was literally embodied, as African females capitalized upon the slippage between a gender-differentiated system of surveillance and control, and sailors' desire for the women and girls in their charge.[75]

The (white, male) perception that African women would submit quietly to sexual demands, and to the voyage itself, was thus frequently proven wrong. Individually or collectively, women not only pilfered objects and transmitted information; they fought back physically. Henry Ellison (**HCSP 73: 375**) described the death of a woman on *Nightingale* 'whom we used to call the boatswain over the others'. She was able— through continuing recognition of her pre-captivity social standing, perhaps—to 'quiet' the women around her. It is unclear whether she took this role upon herself, or indeed whether she expected differential treatment for doing so. But, reading this passage carefully, one sees a woman long used to wielding authority and commanding respect. Her sense of self-worth remained undiminished in extremity: having somehow 'disobliged' the second mate, she was struck with a cat and reacted with fury. She fought back, only to be struck again. Ellison goes on to say that, 'when she found she could not have her revenge' on the mate, she sprung several feet in the air and dropped down dead (**HCSP 73: 369**). A second female 'boatswain' is described by William Butterworth in his account of the voyage of *Hudibras* in 1786–7. Appointed by the master as 'superintendent of her countrymen—and given a dress to wear as a badge of her authority—she played a leading part in planning the second rebellion attempted on this ship (**Butterworth, *Hudibras* 1786–7: 120**). The role that groups of women played in fighting for freedom can also be glimpsed from the log of Norris (*Unity* 1769–71). Although he did not care to reveal as much in his parliamentary testimony, Norris faced open resistance many times on that crossing. Unusually, these were mid-ocean actions. *Unity* cleared São Tome for Jamaica on 28 April 1770. Some five weeks later, on 4 June, Norris noted in his log: 'Put 40 men in arms for plotting an insurrection.' On 6 June: 'The slaves made an insurrection which was soon quelled with the loss of two women'—wording possibly suggesting that this rising was initiated by females. On 23 June, the death of a girl appears to have precipitated a further uprising later the same day. On 26 June, some captives managed to break free of their shackles, but were apprehended; and finally, on 27 June:

> The slaves attempted to force up the gratings in the Night with a design to murder the whites or drown themselves, but were prevented by the watch. In the morning they confessed their intention and that the women as well as the men were determined if disappointed of cutting off the whites, to jump overboard but in case of being prevented by their irons were resolved as their last resource to burn the ship. Their obstinacy put me under the Necessity of shooting the Ring Leader.

Note that the gender of this leader is not specified here, and there is no a priori reason to assume the instigator was a man.[76]

Liminal Boys: The Slave Ship's Mobile Males

It was noted in Chapter 10 that eighteenth-century slave traders generally distinguished between adults and children on the basis of stature, with 4 feet 4 inches being the uniformly accepted height at which, from the perspective of the slave trade, male African adulthood began. Coincidentally (or perhaps not), the mid-eighteenth century also saw the emergence of a dedicated 'boys' room' below decks on British ships. It is not entirely clear when these boys' rooms first came in to use, but one was certainly constructed on Newton's *Argyle* in 1750—the earliest reference I have identified to such a space.[77] As evidenced in Chapter 5, parliamentary testimonies suggest that similar rooms were in use on some, but not all, British slave ships by the 1760s and were widely used on larger vessels after 1780. These new spaces were positioned between the women's room and the men's room and were demarcated by transverse partitions or 'bulkheads'. It is possible that the intention of ship owners was to create a buffer zone to hamper communication, and prevent the transmission of materials, between adult men and women, who had previously been divided from each other only by a single timber bulkhead. But there is also much to suggest that boys between the approximate ages of 6 or 7 and 12 presented slaver crews with a singular conundrum. These pre-pubescent children were perceived to be too old to be housed with females, yet too young to require shackles, or to be placed in the men's room overnight.[78] Whether or not the boys' room emerged in response to this problem, the complex attitude of crews to the male children in their midst certainly created significant opportunities for adult captives.

The girl child rarely appears *as* a child in British accounts of slaving voyages.[79] In the minds and testimonies of most sailors, African women and girls were bracketed both practically (confined to the 'women's room' and quarterdeck) and conceptually: females of all ages were sexualized commodities. African boys, in contrast, stand out in numerous witness accounts as able to roam the decks and to run, play, and even pilfer things. It is not clear why, but crews allowed African boys considerable freedom of movement, and supervised them less closely, than any other category of captive. Perhaps the presence on board of (white) male children—the ship's own 'boys'— informed this process in some way? Whatever the case, unshackled African male children could be found in one of three places during daylight hours on deck. Depending on the vessel's form, these were: with the females on the quarterdeck, on the forecastle (if the vessel was frigate-built); or in the waist of the ship, among the men. Practice varied, but on later eighteenth-century British ships boys usually seem to have spent much of their day among the chained men, fore of the barricado. As Robert Heatley put it in his parliamentary testimony concerning his experiences on ships in the Gambia: 'The slave, if a man, is put on irons on the main deck; if a boy he is put on the main deck loose; if a woman or girl they are placed (without irons) on the quarter deck' (**HCSP 69: 31**). Unlike adult males and all females, while on the upper deck boys could move freely from stern to aft, as far as the barricado itself. As a result, they could ferry information, perhaps shouting it over the palisade, between males and females.

Thomas Trotter, for example, recalled that on *Brooks* 'intercourse between the husbands and wives was carried betwixt them by the boys which ran about the decks'.[80] William Butterworth recalled that, on *Hudibras*, boys ferried messages backwards and forwards between men and women planning an insurrection (*Hudibras* 1786–7: 120). Trotter recalled that boys 'played a sort of game, which they called slave-taking, or bush-fighting, and I have seen them perform all the manoeuvres such as leaping, sallying retreating and all the other gestures made use of in bush fighting' (HCSP 73: 83–4). Trotter recounted this information to support his contention that children without kin had generally been kidnapped. His statement also, of course, reveals psychologically traumatized youngsters attempting to process their experiences, and again foregrounds the point that boys were allowed considerable freedom of moment. This enhanced mobility sometimes made it possible for boys to steal things. Henderson recorded that, on *Tryal* in 1768, '[t]he slave boys, who are loose about the ship, very often steal a portion of [the sailors'] provisions as the seamen have no place of security to put them a small chest only being allowed to four of five men' (*Substance* 1789: 20). Testimonies like this help to explain why, while they are sometimes noted as 'informing' against captives planning insurrections, boys also played an active role in the planning stages of collective risings. On Newton's *African* (as shown in Table 11.2) four boys were found to have supplied men planning an action against the crew with 'knives, stones, shot, etc. and a cold chisel'—items they can only have acquired by moving about the ship largely unobserved. On *New Britannia* in 1773, carpenter's tools intended to be used in a planned insurrection were conveyed on board 'by some of the black boys', though how is not clear.[81] In an insurrection planned on *Fredensborg*, a boy was to act as a go-between, passing information from the women to the men concerning the crew's movements. Male African children, caught in the conceptual slippage between adulthood and childhood (as understood by British sailors), and inhabiting the between-spaces of the vessel at night, occupied a uniquely liminal space on the British slave ship: adult Africans clearly observed, and utilized, the singular between-ness of the boy child.

The Voice under Domination: Oral Communication between Captives

Chapter 10 began with a consideration of the logistics of communication between crews and captives, and it was argued there that, while slave ships were settings in which nascent, English-based 'jargons' emerged, new language acquisition was nevertheless limited. As Gomez has argued for the plantations, it seems likely many captives may have refused to make any effort to learn the language of their domination during the Middle Passage; and it is easy to appreciate the strategic advantages that, in the babel of the slave ship, continued use of African languages must have offered.[82] Multiple witness accounts certainly reveal what Scott calls the 'voice under domination'.[83] In the testimonies of the white men crewing slavers, African voices can be heard loudly and clearly, telling 'the history of their lives and their separation from their friends and

416   MATERIALIZING THE MIDDLE PASSAGE

country' (as James Arnold put it in his parliamentary testimony (HCSP 69: 127)). Captives were sometimes forced to sing and dance, as considered in Chapter 10, but, as Mallipeddi persuasively argues, it would be incorrect to see such performances 'entirely as by-products of coercive power'.[84] Lamentations, songs, and storytelling expressed, and affirmed, both individual and collective identities.

The cohesive power of oral performance is evidenced in William Butterworth's description of the use of call-and-response on his own slaving voyage (*Hudibras* **1786–7: 92–4**). A woman he describes as 'an oracle of literature', who was clearly esteemed by her fellow captives, sometimes sang and performed what Butterworth calls 'slow airs' on the quarterdeck:

> The other females would gather around her in circles, arranged according to age, the youngest forming the innermost ring. The woman herself took centre stage: her attitude, kneeling, nearly prostate, with hands stretched forth and placed upon the deck, and her head resting in her hands. In this posture she delivered her orations; the other females joining in responses, or a kind of chorus, at the close of particular sentences.

Butterworth understood enough to be moved by these collective performances, even though he had no proficiency in the language in which they were conducted. Though the possibility is difficult to evidence, it is surely likely that voices raised in song, or employing call-and-response, as in Butterworth's narrative, may sometimes have transmitted information, messages, and signals facilitating insurrection.

Call-and-Response Revisited

In 1768, the Danish botanist Paul Erdman Isert, a paying passenger on the Dutch Fregat *Christiansborg*, was badly injured in a shipboard insurrection. Isert was not a sailor and (much like Henry Smeathman, another paying passenger on a slave ship) noted details that experienced sailors would not have felt the need to record. Among those details is the African voice, both stilled and raised, at the onset of an uprising taking place on the day after *Christiansborg* departed from the Gold Coast:

> Because there is always a great tumult with such a number of people, I noticed that it had suddenly become extremely quiet. Since most of the crew were below eating, I decided to go to the bow of the ship to see if everyone was at his post, in case the Blacks had some kind of rebellion in mind. When I had reached about midships the door of the bulwark was opened, because the first mate intended to come out to join me. But at the same moment there arose from all of the male slaves a shriek of the most horrifying tone that one can imagine. It resembled the one I had heard at an earlier time, when they were going to attack in battle. Hearing this cry, all the men, who were usually seated, stood up. Some of them hit me on the head with the hand irons with which they were chained together, so that I immediately fell to the deck.[85]

SURVIVING THE MIDDLE PASSAGE   417

I am aware of only one British witness account similarly referencing the use of the voice in the context of insurrection. It can be found in Mr Thompson's interview with Thomas Clarkson for *Substance of the Evidence*, where the sailor recounts the moment at which a rising began on *Pearl*. The captives having been brought up unto the main deck for breakfast, 'one of them pronounced a certain African word, he with the rest of them flew to different parts of the ship' (*Substance* **1789: 23**).[86] But, if one listens very carefully to other testimonies, and particularly to the following statement by Mr Janverin, it is possible to hear captives traversing, with their voices, the physical barriers that divided men from women on board slavers: 'They frequently sing, *the men and women answering one another* but what is the substance of their songs *Mr Janverin cannot say*' (*Substance* **1789: 65**; emphasis added). Call-and-response opened lines of mutual support and communication: it could also be employed to articulate ideas that, as Janverin's testimony again makes clear, remained hidden from white listeners. The insurgent possibilities of call-and-response begin to emerge here; but how was such communication possible at all, in a fortress of sturdy bulkheads? While the documentary sources are not entirely consistent in this regard, there is much to suggest that neither the barricado on the main deck, nor the bulkheads dividing the rooms on the slave deck below it, were wholly effective in blocking out sound. The barricado was constructed from pine, a wood that tends to produce knot holes. These, the loopholes through which guns could be directed, and the periodic opening and closing of the doorway and hatches built into the structure, facilitated the transmission of sound. The same features may also have allowed intervisibility, although witnesses say very little on this point. Issac makes the sole explicit reference, to my knowledge, to the ability of captives to see through holes in a barricado. Discussing the torture of a small child by Joshua Pollard, master on *Black Joke*, Parker says (**HCSP 73: 124**) that the (male) captives saw what was happening 'through the barricado, looking through the crevices; they made a great murmuring and did not seem to like it'.

The struggle to provide 'enough' air below decks was a constant in the slave trade, as explored in Chapters 5 and 9, and obliged the industry to modify merchant ships, sometimes to the detriment of security. On later eighteenth-century ships the bulkheads separating the slave rooms below decks do not appear to have been sheer walls of planking but were 'grating bulkheads', constructed from latticed timbers in an effort to improve airflow from aft to stern on the slave decks. On each one of the nine ships that Captain Parrey measured for Parliament in 1788, 'grating bulkheads' (4 inches thick in each case) separated the rooms of the men, women, and boys below decks. The size of the bulkhead apertures is nowhere stated, but, because crews will have done everything possible to prevent the movement of materials between rooms, they are likely to have been very small (much like those shown on the 'grating-fashioned' top in Figure 11.4). Even so, some hints can be found that 'grating bulkheads' facilitated African communication. Referring to captives planning the second of two insurrections on *Hudibras*, Butterworth noted (*Hudibras* **1786–7: 120**): 'Correspondence on the subject was carried out through the medium of the boys which prevented the necessity of shouting from the two extremities of the ship: though one of the females, vulgarly called

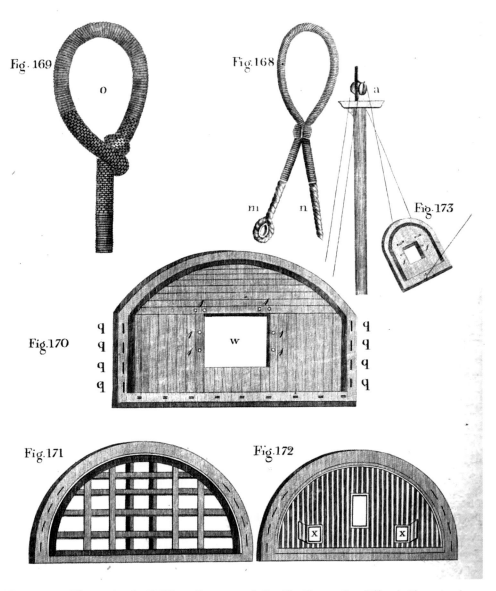

Figure 11.4 Illustration by William Butterworth for *The Young Sea Officer's Sheet Anchor*. From Lever (1808: plate facing p. 23), showing a D-shaped, 'grating-fashioned' top.

Boatswain Bess, frequently violated this rule by calling out to the men.' With freedom of movement on the main deck, these boys may simply have shouted over the barricado. Marcus Rediker takes Butterworth to mean that they carried whispered messages *below* decks, running back and forth between the bulkheads on either side of their apartment. While the memoir is not in fact explicit on this point, the suggestion is a plausible one.[87] Elsewhere, Butterworth (**Hudibras** 1786–7: 131–2) refers less ambiguously to a rumour moving through the three apartments below deck:

'like a train of gunpowder, ignited at one end [the women's room], it ran through the apartment of the boys, to that of the men, the great magazine of suppressed discontent'.

Gratings were also located above each of the slave rooms. As evidenced in Chapter 5, these were virtually the only mechanism by which fresh air could be funnelled below, sometimes with the assistance of windsails. As indicated by the many references to sailors on watch hearing the songs and laments emanating from the slave decks at night, sound travelled upwards and outwards through these gratings. Some testimonies point to the ability of male and female captives to communicate with each other this way; shouting above the not inconsiderable noise of the sails, creaking timbers, clanking pumps, wind, and waves, yet still being heard. Recalling the aftermath of the first failed insurrection on *Hudibras* for example, William Butterworth described the shouted recriminations that passed from the men to the women as they were locked below: conversations which were also overheard by the crew (*Hudibras* 1786–7: 111).

In 1688, a musician named Baptiste attended an event in Jamaica at which many black musicians were gathered. Hans Sloane asked him to 'take the words they sung and set them to music'. As Richard Rath has shown in an exceptionally nuanced discussion, Baptiste went much further, skilfully transcribing the rhythm and melody of three songs, 'Angola', 'Papa', and 'Koromanti', using European (staff) notation.[88] Subsequently reproduced in Sloane's 1707 *Voyage*, this is the earliest known transcription of African–Caribbean music. The song 'Angola' incorporates a call ('Hoba-Ognion') and a response ('Alla, Alla').[89] It materializes, in the seventeenth-century Caribbean, the African practice of using calls to announce events, summon meetings, and make music.[90] Mr Janverin's testimony in *Substance of the Evidence*, cited above, reveals call-and-response in use on the ships that carried Africans like these to Jamaica. Rath argues persuasively that 'Angola' is the result of negotiation between different soundways, taking place in a situation conditioned by exile.[91] Put another way, it is cultural pidginization in action, uneasily blending musical styles that originated in different parts of West Africa, but each of which nevertheless retains its individual distinctiveness. Thus, the upper register employs melodic traits appropriate to the Akan region of modern Ghana, while the bass register is marked by features of Angolan origin.[92] This is African music, in other words, in the very earliest phases of inter-African creolization. Rath's reminder that, whether it was linguistic or extra-linguistic, creolization was a *two*-phase process that begin with pidginization certainly resonates with the argument set out in Chapter 10 concerning the use of pre-pidgin or 'jargon' on board slave ships. His discussion of 'Angola' also provides an excellent viewpoint from which to look back at African recitation, call-and-response, and dance during the Middle Passage; and it was here, not in Jamaica, that many West Africans initially encountered the unfamiliar musical traditions not only of Europeans, but of other Africans. The process that Rath identifies in 'Angola' could as easily have begun on the Middle Passage as in Jamaica. On slave ships, just as Rath has said of the singing of 'Angola', antiphonal call-and-response 'bound the singer together with the rest of

420   MATERIALIZING THE MIDDLE PASSAGE

the people even though rifts of ethnicity and language conspired to separate them'. In a similar vein, White and White have argued that calls functioned as an alternative communication 'whenever groups of newly arrived slaves were kept together'.[93] Their point was made with reference to the Americas, but, as the numerous witness testimonies cited here and in Chapter 10 indicate, it is equally applicable to the slave ship.

The Slave Ship's Dance(s) Revisited

In tandem with song and story, many West African peoples also cemented social bonds through dance. The performative aspects of the slave ship exercise regime have attracted considerable scholarly interest in this context, particularly since Kamau Brathwaite's celebrated 1973 use of 'limbo' (in the poem 'Caliban') as a metaphor to explore the liminality of the Middle Passage experience: both the dance and the ship, like the limbo of Catholic theology, were located in a between-space somewhere at the edge of hell.[94] In the glossary accompanying *Arrivants*, Brathwaite notes that limbo 'is said to have originated—a necessary therapy—after the experience of the slave-ship decks of the Middle Passage'.[95] The slave ship 'dance' and limbo have subsequently become inextricably entwined in some modern writing, although there is nothing in the contemporary witness testimonies to suggest that the slave ship 'dance' took a specific form—indeed, there is much to indicate that it did not. Sonjah Stanley Niaah, for example, argues that limbo, 'which involves the body moving under a stick, is thought to have emerged out of the lack of space available on the slave ship, necessitating the slaves bending themselves like spiders'—a suggestion that is not substantiated in any contemporary source.[96] Geneviève Fabre and Katrina Thompson offer more historically grounded analyses of the 'dance', arguing that, despite being both physically damaging and actively humiliating, it nevertheless resonated deeply with West and Central African peoples who understood movement to music to be a communal activity creating special bonds. It this way, as Fabre suggests, the 'slave dance' was a step towards the creation of a 'new culture in which still vivid memories of African dance could help bring shape and meaning to the experience of enslavement'.[97]

There were other ways, perhaps, in which dance facilitated African interactions. In discussing the slave ship 'dance' in Chapter 10, it was pointed out that explicit references to the use of African instruments on slave ships do not generally appear in accounts of forced exercise but, rather, are made in passages describing times—often in the hours towards sunset—at which captives were allowed to 'entertain' themselves, using instruments from their homelands. Henry Smeathman, for example, refers to two distinct episodes of 'dancing' in his account of a day on a slaver: the first (*Oeconomy c.*1775: 6) during the forenoon and the second (*Oeconomy c.*1775: 7) after the second meal of the day, and involving the use of 'a drum, or an empty cask, or a tub', played by one of the captives. In allowing Africans familiar instruments (or approximations of them), as Katrina Thompson has recently argued, crews unwittingly helped captives to maintain existing traditions.[98] They also opened insurgent spaces that, while not directly evidenced in sailors' accounts, may be glimpsed in the clear preference shown for the drum during this second 'dance'. Europeans understood from the very beginning of the slave trade that Africans used drums as tools of state, and in religious rituals.[99] Caribbean slave owners were certainly aware that drumming facilitated communication over long distances, even if they were unclear that signal drums 'talked' by imitating the rhythmic and tonal characteristics of speech.[100] Jamaican planters prohibited drums and horns as early as 1688, with Barbados doing the same in 1699. St Kitts passed laws in 1711 and again in 1722 prohibiting slaves from 'communicating at a distance' using drums.[101] Yet drums remained in use on slave ships until the end of the British trade and captives frequently made use of them.

A drum in the founding collection of the British Museum, once belonging to Hans Sloane, may have been used by Africans on board a slaver (Figure 11.5). The manuscript catalogue produced following the purchase of Sloane's collection for the nation in 1753 (a document known as the *Miscellanies*) records that the drum was acquired in Virginia. The entry reads: 'An Indian drum made out of a hollowed tree carved, the top being brac'd with pegs and thongs, w^t the bottom hollow, from Virginia, by Mr Clerk.'[102] It was once believed that a Virginian slave of Asante origin carved the

Figure 11.5 Akan drum acquired by Hans Sloane from a Mr Clerk, in Virginia. British Museum, Am, SLMisc.1368.

422 MATERIALIZING THE MIDDLE PASSAGE

drum in the Americas, but it is now widely accepted on stylistic grounds that it was in fact made in West Africa.[103] While it cannot be proven that Sloane's drum travelled from Ghana to Virginia on board a slave ship, there is a strong likelihood that this is this case.

Like the song 'Angola', this African artefact, collected in Jamaica, sits at the crossroads of multiple diasporas and of multiple creolizing encounters. It is not a literate object, but written upon it, nonetheless, is a story of survival and endurance.

Spiritual Weapons: Small Things of Power

In the earliest years of the slave trade, as established in Chapter 6, the slave ship was embedded in African cosmologies in ways that positioned its crews as coming from the land of the dead, and the voyage as a journey to an 'other' world below, or beyond, the sea. While it would be unwise to overstate the case for an entirely unmodified continuity of such beliefs into the eighteenth century, it is important to emphasize two points here. First, for Africans who had made long, forced journeys to the coast, and who had never encountered the sea, ships, or sailors—but whose communities had long experienced the attritions of the slave trade—those ideas may still have held to some degree true. As John Barnes, a former governor of Senegal, explained to Parliament, 'slaves near the coast...know what to expect, but those from the interior are terrified by not knowing the purpose [of the trade]'.[104] In 1799, similarly, Mungo Park reported that captives he encountered being taken down to the Gambian coast believed firmly that whites purchased Africans for the purpose of eating them.[105] Second, as Diana Paton has argued:

> On forced marches to the African coast, on board slave ships, and in their new Atlantic settings, enslaved people were likely to interpret what had happened and was happening to them as the result of religious malevolence. Even if they did not understand themselves as victims of witchcraft, they were likely to use whatever means were available to protect themselves spiritually in a terrifying world.[106]

The slave ship was a bewildering thing sited in a watery realm that challenged African understandings that human life could not be lived at sea, and in which, as Stephanie Smallwood emphasizes, many of the epistemological tools that captives might otherwise have employed to make sense of their circumstances were disabled.[107] In such a setting, the cultural signifiers of (European) Middle Passage practice were, to appropriate a phrase from Bhabha, 'taken for wonders'.[108] For example, the first sight of the cauldron bubbling over the fire on the ship's 'slave hearth' suggested to many captives that their fate was to be eaten by the crew (as noted in Chapter 6). Confused and disorientated, captives understandably reasoned that to survive the voyage they would need spiritual weaponry: tools able to counter the ship as a witch craft. The objects of power identified later in this section would be marshalled in exactly this way.

In evidencing this point, it is first necessary to make a case that amulets and other talismanic artefacts, worn on the body and understood to protect the wearer from harm, might sometimes be carried on board slavers on the bodies of captives and, in one way or another, retained. I then want to consider how these objects, and others created during the Middle Passage, might have been employed by Africans in malign conjure and other forms of spiritual resistance.

In his important consideration of whether captives were able to transport material things across the Atlantic, Jerome Handler has argued that the chances of retaining small objects such as beads or charms will have been low, because contemporary sources suggest that slaves were stripped of their clothing and any remaining personal effects prior to embarkation.[109] Certainly, it is possible to point to an abundance of documentary evidence suggesting that captives were subject to such treatment. In 1721, for example, William Bosman recorded that 'their Masters strip them of all they have on their Backs so that they come Aboard stark-naked as well Women as well as Men',[110] and John Atkins mentioned that when 'stripped of that poor Clout which covers their Privities (as I know the *Whydahs* generally do) they [enslaved women] will keep squatted all day long on board, to hide them'.[111] But, while it is true that many sources refer to the stripping and subsequent nakedness of captives, this is by no means true of all. For example, numerous commentators refer to loincloths and other forms of 'modesty' garment being worn by (usually female) captives. John Barbot distributed to the women (and some men) on his vessels 'a piece of course cloth to cover them': the captives were obliged to wash these from time to time, to prevent 'vermin' (**Barbot, *Treatment* 1712: 780**). Thomas Smith recorded that, on his 1763 voyage, the captives 'are completely naked, having nothing about them, but their heavy chains, and a little rope-yarn rolled round their middle, on purpose to hold their pipe and tobacco'.[112] Though he did not make a Guinea voyage himself, the sailor William Spavens noted in his 1796 account of his adventures at sea that Africans on Guineamen were 'as naked as our first parents in Paradise, save only a hippen of red given to the women to serve in the place of a fig-leaf covering'.[113]

Testimonies thus differ considerably concerning nakedness. The explanation may lie not simply in differential practices on board slaving vessels but in eighteenth-century understandings of the term nakedness itself. Discussing some of the problems that scholars of African material culture face when drawing on European documentary sources, Adam Jones remarked that 'early sources describe the large quantity of ornaments worn by Africans, yet in the same breath refer to them as "naked"'.[114] Thomas Phillips (***Hannibal*** 1693–4: 188) provides an excellent example here. Phillips noted that, in the Cape Verde islands, '[t]he negroes here go naked, except a cloth about their middles and a roll of linen the women wear about their heads'. Two very instructive witness accounts of the appearance of Africans on board slave ships may be considered with this point in mind. The first is to be found in Henry Smeathman's description of his journey on board *Elizabeth* in 1774 (***Oeconomy*** c.**1775: 8–9**). Writing at the height of the British trade, Smeathman stated:

Before the sun gets low enough to make the weather feel cool, the slaves are to be sent down, for they are all entirely naked, except the grown women, some few of whom, the favourites, are treated by their Gallants with a fathom of cloth to throw round them, and others are allowed a small strip a mere modesty piece which hangs before them from a string which is tied round their waists. Sometimes it is long enough to go under their bodies, and reaches to the string behind where it is again tied.

The second account was made in Barbados in 1806, in the dying years of the British trade. In that year, George Pinckard paid a visit to a newly arrived North American Guineaman docked at Bridgetown. The captives were still on board, and Pinckard wrote of them: 'Both sexes were without apparel, having only a narrow band of blue cloth put around the waist, and brought to fasten before, so as to serve to office of a fig leaf, worn by our first parents in the fruitful garden of Eden.'[115] These accounts provide an important reminder that 'nakedness' was a culturally constructed concept, signifying, for the white observer, cultural lack.[116] For eighteenth-century European observers, clearly, the 'modesty' garments given to some captives did not constitute apparel.

A second observation by Henry Smeathman (*Oeconomy c.1775: 9*) suggests that 'naked' Africans might also be wearing small adornments. He remarks:

The men the boys and the girls are not suffered to have a rag about them except a little bag in which they keep their pepper their salt and their allowance of Tobacco. The men would have an opportunity of concealing knives and dangerous things, if they had any sort of cloaths, and the whole would get full of vermin and dirt. If the women or girls have a few strings of beads round them, they are permitted: glass and polished stones cannot accumulate much dirt.

These items were not necessarily retained personal possessions: as shown in Chapter 10, beads and tobacco were distributed to captives during the Middle Passage. But, if crews regarded the beads and small bags they disseminated on board as permissible accessories, then it seems reasonable to suggest that some of the captives who boarded slavers wearing amulets or strings of beads might have been allowed to retain those things.

The Middle Passage of African Things

Newton Plantation, Barbados, is the most extensively excavated slave burial ground in the Caribbean.[117] Figure 11.6 depicts one of the grave goods of Burial 72, an adult male of around 50 years of age, who was interred in the late 1600s or early 1700s; another example of his possessions, a necklace, was discussed in Chapter 1.[118] This pipe is a short-stemmed, earthenware, elbow variety 'of almost certain West African, and possibly Gold Coast, origin'.[119] As noted in the introduction, several other artefacts from this grave appear to be of African origin, including a bead fashioned from

Figure 11.6 Tobacco pipe from grave B72 Newton Plantation, Barbados. See Figure 1.4 for the necklace from the same grave.

powder-glass, again likely to have been made on the Gold Coast, and a carnelian bead manufactured in Cambay (Gujarat, India) and traded into East, and then West, Africa via the overland Sahara and Sahel trade.[120] Beads from two more of the graves excavated at Newton in 1997–8 are also considered to be African-made.[121] The New York African Burial Ground has also produced two graves with beads of African origin. One example, possibly associated with Burial 434, is a cylindrical powdered-glass example probably produced in Southern Ghana. Eight oblate to donut-shaped, opaque yellow powder-glass beads were also found at the throat of an infant (Burial 226). The baby—his or her sex could not be determined—was interred at some point before c.1735.[122] This is not the only grave hinting at a close association between curated African beads and infant burial. For another example, it is necessary to turn to the Rupert Valley cemetery on Saint Helena.

From the 1820s, the navy's Royal Africa Squadron played an active role in policing the Atlantic, capturing slaving vessels and liberating their captives. In 1840, a Vice Admiralty court was established on the tiny island of St Helena to determine the fate of captured slave ships. In the process, over 26,000 Africans were received at the island's 'Liberated African Establishment'. Some never left; weakened by disease, scurvy, and hunger, an estimated eight thousand Africans died on the island and were buried at the Establishment's receiving centre in Rupert's Valley. In 2007–8, a

426 MATERIALIZING THE MIDDLE PASSAGE

small part of the burial ground here was excavated, uncovering the remains of 325 individuals. These 'liberated Africans' died decades after Britain had abolished its own slave trade. Nevertheless, their grave goods are of great importance in addressing the possibility that some captives were able to retain small, portable artefacts when they boarded slave ships. Some thirteen of the excavated bodies from Rupert Valley were interred with items of personal adornment, and the excavators interpret four of these instances as presenting 'direct evidence for the transportation of pre-enslavement material culture'.[123] Skeleton 279 (a 38–46-year-old woman), buried with an older child, was recorded with 151 glass beads and 2 small cowrie shells. The only diagnostic type among the beads was a 'galet rouge' drawn glass bead of a type made in the seventeenth to nineteenth centuries, but many displayed considerable wear, suggesting they had been in circulation for a long time before burial. The cowries must also have been acquired before arrival in St Helena. The excavators concluded that 'the age and wear of the beads, taken with the incorporation of a culturally significant type of shell, provides compelling evidence that the artefact was worn by the woman through enslavement, embarkation, Middle Passage and her time (however short) within the Rupert Valley depot'.[124] A mature male inhumed with a young adult male was found with 1,732 glass beads, all but 3 loose by his neck, which seem to have formed a single necklace. Some 97 per cent of these beads were the 'galet-rouge' type, and the degree of wear on the beads again suggests considerable age and curation.[125] A bead and horn necklace was also recovered in association with a 2- or 3-year-old child, inhumed with a small iron band near one wrist. One of the five beads making up the necklace was an eighteenth-century Dutch pentagon type, and another red bead can be dated to the seventeenth century. The youngest of the beads in this necklace was at least fifty years old, suggesting the object had been passed down at least one, and perhaps more, generations.[126]

A total of 9,486 of the glass beads from St Helena come from a single context: the base of the coffin of a newborn (or stillborn) infant of 37–38.5 weeks gestation. This was an elaborate burial, the most complex on the site. The child was buried wearing a cap of white cotton gauze, his or her head placed on a pillow, and a small red quilt placed over the body. Two coins were placed over the eyes, and the sole of a single leather shoe lay at the child's head. The beads themselves had clearly once formed a single object: a small rectangular 'mat', 18 centimetres wide. Only five of the beads could be securely identified, and all were of nineteenth-century Bohemian manufacture. It is impossible to be certain whether this bead mat was a transported item, but there are multiple parallels for beaded aprons panels in Zaire, Cameroon, Nigeria, and elsewhere. If the item was a retained one, the implications in terms of the 'stripping' of Africans are considerable: the original item was of some size and could not have been discretely concealed. The excavators suggest, plausibly, that the beads were procured either on the slave ship or within the Rupert Valley depot. The retention of personal possessions was undoubtedly a rare occurrence here: but it was clearly happening. George McHenry, surgeon at Lemon Valley (a second reception depot for recaptives on St Helena), noted that most of the Africans arriving in St Helena were naked, but some had 'their hair neatly plaited and ornamented with strings of beads, and coins and pieces of metal, their necks and arms decked with necklaces and bracelets and with large glittering copper rings around their legs for anklets'.[127] Whatever the case, the excavators argue with reference to the infant burial and two adult burials close to it that the commonality of material culture and the positioning of the graves may well indicate 'a family (or ship family) unit which spent time on St Helena and were buried in close proximity as a result'.[128] For this unit, clearly, trade beads—very possibly acquired on their Middle Passage—held a significance that archaeologists can observe, if not fully understand. Chapter 12 will have more to say on the onward trajectories of saltwater trade beads (whether carried on the body from Africa or acquired during the Middle Passage) in the Americas, and on archaeological readings of these artefacts today.

The Third Space of African 'Nakedness'

The practice of rationing tobacco to captives, allied with Henry Smeathman's reference, noted above, to 'a little bag in which they keep their pepper their salt and their allowance of Tobacco', suggests that, on some vessels, Africans could own (or make) and wear small bags. Thomas Smith's reference to captives wearing 'a little rope-yarn rolled round their middle, on purpose to hold their pipe and tobacco' suggests another way in which items could be worn, and stored, on the body.[129] Similar containers were commonly worn on bodies throughout West Africa, of course—but for very different reasons. The use of protective amulets, phylacteries, and charms was widespread, and these strategic objects were discussed by many seventeenth- and eighteenth-century European visitors to West Africa, most of whom referred to them pejoratively as *gris-gris*.[130] John Barbot described the use of *gris-gris* many times in his writing. He said of the Wolof of the Senegal coast, for example, that

> all over their body, on their head, neck, arms, waist and legs, they have little leather pouches resembling small boxes, either elongated or square. These pieces of leather contain a number of scraps of paper covered with characters in either Moorish or Arabesque script, and given them by the *lyncherins* [byscharyns, or marabouts]. They call these *grigri*. You can hardly credit, Sir, the extent to which these Africans carry their belief in the magical properties of these grigri, properties which operate in all sorts of contingencies . . . one grigri will save them from drowning at sea, and another from being killed in war; another again will give a woman a safe childbirth, another will prevent fires, another heal fevers, and so on.[131]

Sacred objects had many different indigenous names, but among Kongo peoples were (and are) known as *minkisi*: a nineteenth-century example in the form of a ship has already been considered in Chapter 6 (see Figure 6.13).[132] In Kongo thought, *nkisi* (pl. *minkisi*) is a personalized force from the land of the dead that has chosen, or been

Figure 11.7 Left: nineteenth-century Kongo power figure (Nkisi Nkondi) from the Dallas Museum of Art. Right: Minkisi Nkubulu, fashioned from fibres, beads, cloth, and other materials, collected in 1919 from Kingoyi. Museum of World Cultures, Stockholm, 1919.01.1162.

induced, to submit itself to a degree of human control.[133] *Minkisi* are essentially containers, housing relics of the dead and medicines: the act of containment harnesses the forces within, enabling them to achieve a desired end (see Figure 11.7).[134] The containers themselves can range from leaves, shells, packets, and bags to ceramic pots and statuettes, but each houses medicines (*bilongo*) that both embody and direct the spirits. Minerals collected from graves, gullies, and stream beds embody the spirits: white clay (kaolin) is particularly important in this context, because white is the colour of the dead. Spirit-directing materials can include seeds, stones, herbs, sticks, and pieces of crystal.[135] As a large body of work by art historians, documentary historians, and archaeologists has shown, the use of *minkisi* and other types of charm crossed the Atlantic with saltwater slaves. In the Caribbean, for example, aspects of *minkisi* have been retained in the creolized spiritual beliefs of Haitian vodun, and Cuban palo.[136]

Some charms were worn on the body; others took the form of bundles or caches placed under steps, over doors, in the corners of rooms, and in the ground. An excellent example, not least in terms of the gains to be made from marrying words with things, is a cache excavated from the corner of a room in the Carrol House (Annapolis, Maryland) in 1990.[137] It was identified as an object of power via a pioneering methodology employing folklore, oral history, and excavation. Cognate archaeological data from African-American sites were interrogated alongside oral testimonies collected from former slaves by the Works Progress Administration (WPA) in the 1930s.[138] The Carrol House assemblage itself comprised twelve quartz crystals, eight quartz flakes, a transparent colourless faceted glass bead, straight pins, cufflinks, tobacco pipe stem fragments, a polished stone, window glass fragments, bottle glass fragments, bone disks, a 1773 George III Virginia halfpenny, an 1803 Liberty head one cent piece, and broken ceramics, all placed in a deliberately created shallow scoop and covered over by an inverted pearlware bowl fragment. As Leone and

Fry and subsequent scholars have demonstrated, this and other similar assemblages from sites in Annapolis were *minkisi* employed in conjuration practices aiming to protect or heal the maker, but also to overturn the will of the master.[139] Such caches could also be used to harm. As Leone and Fry's examination of the WPA data revealed, the materials used in malign conjure, or 'fixing', were wide-ranging, the commonest being snake dust, bags, and the victim's hair.[140] Fixing items were not usually worn on the body but were placed elsewhere—for example, under doorways or—in cases where harm was to be activated by ingestion—in water, alcohol, and food.[141]

Given the widespread use of charms and amulets both within Africa, and in the diaspora, it is surely extremely likely that they were worn, used, and indeed created during the Middle Passage. The remainder of this section considers evidence supporting that contention. For West and Central Africans, as discussed in Chapter 6, slave ships, their crews, and the Atlantic crossing were bound up cosmologically with witchcraft, the dead, and the journey to an 'other' world. These understandings did not simply fade away at the shoreline: they boarded the vessel in the minds of captives and informed their experiences and actions during the Middle Passage.

Many of the Africans sold to slave ships will have been wearing amulets at the time of their capture. As noted above, most were probably stripped of their remaining personal possessions before, or at the point of, embarkation. But several strands of evidence suggest that this was not invariably the case. First, Jerome Handler draws attention to one report from 1750 in which captives smuggled an amulet on a ship, and a second from Charleston 1804 recording that, when two girls were sold separately, they exchanged 'a string of beads and an amulet' from the neck of one of them.[142] Second, an intriguing find from the wreck site of the Danish slaver *Fredensborg* suggests the presence of an African amulet on a slave ship. *Fredensborg* foundered off Norway on the return leg of a slaving voyage from the Gold Coast (Ghana) to the Danish West Indies. The divers excavating the wreck discovered a single leg bone from a water chevrotain and another from a peacock, lying close to each other on the ocean floor. Both these species are found in West Africa, and it is quite possible that the bones recovered from the wreck derive from an African amulet or personal charm.[143]

As noted above, captives on some later eighteenth-century British ships were given little bags (or the materials to make them) in which to keep tobacco, salt, and pepper. This practice may even have emerged because, as the testimonies above suggest, sailors were so accustomed to seeing amulets and charms on African bodies. Perhaps captives who embarked wearing small bags were allowed to keep them precisely because they could, in the crews' eyes, be repurposed and used for tobacco. Whatever the reason, there was clearly some slippage in the minds of sailors concerning 'permissible' objects on African bodies at sea. To borrow Bhabha's terminology, this was a 'slippage of signification' in the articulation of difference—one that allowed a third space to open up, creating insurgent possibilities for captives themselves.[144] It would not be difficult for captives who had been given 'ration' bags, or the materials to make them, to rework these into *minkisi* using materials found on board. Despite the cleaning regimes detailed in Chapter 9, small things of many kinds evaded the broom and scrubbing

430   MATERIALIZING THE MIDDLE PASSAGE

brush: African soil and seeds had been swept into crevices; stray cowries dropped through the holes in cargo sacks and rolled between the deck timbers; fibres left over from ropemaking found their way into many crannies. Objects could also be pilfered: iron nails and wood splinters could be ripped from bulkheads; animal bone could be picked out and secreted in the mouth as food was scooped up on the hand; and kaolin could be obtained by breaking up the European-made pipes handed out to use with tobacco rations. All of these things, overlooked by the crew, could be repurposed in an effort to protect or harm. Stephan Palmié, one of the most trenchant critics of the concept of cultural creolization, had rightly exhorted scholars of the diaspora not to 'fool ourselves into believing that slavery was a great chance to be creative'.[145] But it was surely a *reason* to be so; and it is not difficult to envisage that, in the darkness of the locked slave rooms, materials enabling individual and collective spiritual resistance could be acquired and repurposed.

Two fascinating recent studies of the use of protective amulets by enslaved persons in Brazil discuss *bolsas de mandinga* ('mandingo bags'), which, quite remarkably, survive in the Inquisition trial records for men of African birth who were arrested for witchcraft in Lisbon in the early 1700s.[146] These bags or packets were made from stitched cloth or folded paper, and their contents included folded sheets of paper (*mandinga* papers) containing words, images, and formulae written in ink and blood. The packets enclosed other materials, in a wide variety of forms. One example, still almost intact, was made in 1704 by an African man who had been sold into the slave trade at Ouidah and was given the name Jacques Viegas. This *bolsa* appears to contain hair, seeds, and cotton.[147] Cécile Fremont's analysis foregrounds the point that these objects of Afro-Atlantic agency were often compiled entirely from *European* esoteric materials, but their potency was in no way perceived to be diminished as a result.[148] In an analysis speaking a similar language to that employed in the present chapter, Matthew Rarey looks beyond the concepts of resistance and cultural continuity to highlight the role of amulets in ensuring the *survival* of the wearer; they are, as he puts it, 'representative of their makers' search for safety and protection in a violent world'.[149] It was noted in Chapter 7, with reference to Neil Norman's work, that Africans who practised *vodun* regarded the acquisition of exogenous artefacts as more than simply an aesthetic imperative: practising what Suzanne Blier calls the 'art of assemblage' ensured the vitality of their religion.[150] In short, while the evidence might not be immediately apparent in sailor's testimonies, it cannot be doubted that Jacques Viegas and many other saltwater Africans fashioned or adapted bolas *during* their Middle Passage, as well as after it.

The extensive use of amulets and other apotropaic artefacts by Brazilian slaves is also highlighted in recent work at Valongo Wharf, the key point of entry for the slave trade to Eastern Brazil between 1799 and 1831.[151] These amulets took a wide variety of forms, comprising or incorporating perforated beads, shells, crystals, bones, coins, and Catholic medals. They were employed, as Tania Lima, Marcos de Souza, and Glaucia Sene argue, to create a protective 'second skin' for people living uncertain lives.[152] One find in particular seems to speak to the slave ship experience: a small, circular, metal container with a hinged lid, engraved with a scene that includes a sailing ship. It contained some 1,200 tiny seed beads.[153]

To support the hypothesis that saltwater captives employed *minkisi*, *bolsas*, and other such protective devices during the Middle Passage, it is necessary to return to Newton's *Argyle* and *African* (see Table 11.2). The 'bag of small stones' found by the crew in the men's room of *Argyle* on 6 May 1751 may have been foraged from crevices on the ship; or may even represent the contents of a charm bag that boarded the slaver around the neck of one of the men and was not forcibly removed. Perhaps we should think here of a mixture of both. On 16 June 1751, Newton noted in his *Argyle* journal that

> we were alarmed with a report that some of the men slaves had found means to poyson the water in the scuttle casks upon deck, but upon enquiry found they had only conveyed some of their country fetishes, as they call them, or talismans into one of them, which they had the credulity to suppose must inevitably kill all who drank of it.

Clearly, his captives had engineered the means to employ malign conjure, placing spiritually charged materials into the drinking water reserved for the crew. Newton felt he and his men had little to fear from the use of such weapons, but in 1764 it was reported in *Lloyd's List* that the captain, doctor, mates, and seventeen crew on the Liverpool ship *Johnson* had been 'poisoned by the Negroes' at Loango.[154] Such instances help to explain why Africans arriving in the Americas were widely believed to 'possess the accumulated wisdom of Old World poisoning techniques'.[155] This understanding also arose from empirical observation of the ability of the African-born to extract lethal substances from plants, and was fuelled by well-publicized trials arising from attempts by the enslaved to poison their masters, or each other.[156] The 1696 Jamaican slave code made the use of poison by enslaved people a capital crime, while, in Virginia, poisoning was the second-most-frequent crime for which enslaved people were prosecuted in the mid-eighteenth century.[157]

Conclusion: Towards the 'Ship Family'

This chapter has focused on the strategies employed by Africans, both individually and collectively, to endure and challenge the Middle Passage. Collective acts of violent resistance certainly occurred on a significant proportion of slaving voyages, but I have argued throughout that greater attention needs to be paid to the infrapolitics of the crossing: to the multitude of small actions through which captives challenged their enforced crossing, without loss of life. I made the point earlier that even 'collective' insurrections were factional, and rarely involved every captive on board a ship. But, as a prelude to my concluding chapter, it is equally important to emphasize that all challenges to the Middle Passage—whether individual or collective—were predicated on mutuality.[158] Suicide was possible only if one's shipmates looked away or remained

432 MATERIALIZING THE MIDDLE PASSAGE

silent; the message disseminated by the drum could be heard only by those willing to pay attention to the drummer. At the other end of spectrum, rebellions were necessarily built on the connections and trust built by groups of captives. The small steps through which such bonds were forged are rarely visible in the documentary record but can occasionally be glimpsed. The three men instigating collective action against the crew on *Ruby* in 1787, for example, had entered into a blood oath—James Arnold called it a 'sangaree'—beforehand (**HCSP 69: 133**). On *Pearl* in 1759, as we have also seen, a single African word, agreed upon in advance and unintelligible to the crew, announced a coordinated uprising (***Substance* 1789: 23**). On board slave ships, mutuality might rarely have resulted in collective insurrections supported by every African present, but it certainly facilitated the creation of new social bonds and obligations. Put another way, to materialize the *repertoires* of everyday resistance on board slave ships is also to uncover *relations* between the actors involved.[159] Moreover, as explored in my concluding chapter, the insurgent legacies of the ship 'family' outlived the slaving voyage itself.

Notes

1. Paton (2012: 245); Sweet (2003: 162–3).
2. Smallwood (2007b: 124). See also Sweet's discussion (2003: 196–7) of Kongolese captives' understandings of the baptism that the Portuguese had obliged them to undergo before boarding slave ships. Many interpreted their baptism as a thing of witchcraft or enchantment, an understanding, interestingly, compounded by the use of salt in the baptismal process.
3. James Scott (1990, 1985).
4. For de Certeau (1984), tactical resistance is mobile in the sense that it is not securely placed anywhere, takes place in enemy territory, and 'is always on the watch for opportunities that must be seized' (de Certeau 1984: p. xix). Symanski's (2012) archaeological analysis is directly inspired by de Certeau. I have found the recent work of Johansson and Vinthagen particularly important in framing my understanding everyday resistance: see, in particular, Johansson and Vinthagen (2020: 126–31, 149–80). I should note, however, that I disagree fundamentally with their argument (Johansson and Vinthagen 2020: 34–9) that Scott positions resistance entirely with reference to politicized class antagonism.
5. Johansson and Vinthagen (2020: 58–61).
6. Casella (2007: 146); and, on the hidden transcripts of resistance (drawing, as in the present analysis, on James Scott 1990), see Casella (2007: 69–71). The present chapter owes much to Casella's approach, and particularly to Casella (2007: 84–143), which focuses on recent archaeological work on institutional confinement in America and shows some of the ways in which a focus on everyday materiality can shed a fresh light on subversive and transformative encounters in prisons and elsewhere.
7. Work on insurrections includes Inikori (1996), Bly (1998), Richardson (2001), Behrendt et al. (2001) (summarizing information concerning 388 risings against ship's crews on voyages recorded in the TSTD data set), Sharafi (2003), Taylor (2006), Bialuschewski (2011), and Warren (2013). On suicides as sea, see Mustakeem (2016: 106–30) and Snyder (2015: 23–45).
8. Taylor (2006: 180–213, Appendix: Chronology of shipboard revolts 1509–1865). The figure for British vessels is slightly lower than the total number of 'slave insurrection' voyage outcomes noted in TSTD, which stands at 178.

SURVIVING THE MIDDLE PASSAGE 433

9. Taylor (2006: 13). Only three 'insurrection planned but thwarted' voyage outcomes are noted in TSTD for British ships. One of these is Newton's *Argyle*. The others are *Rebecca* (TSTD 90768) and *Upton* (90772).

10. Behrendt et al. (2001: 456); see also Richardson (2001: 72). Fourteen instances of insurrection were reported by the twenty-two sailors interviewed by Clarkson for **Substance 1789**.

11. Norton (2013: 135–6, 229–84).

12. Barile (2004: 134–6).

13. Wadström, a Swedish naturalist and colleague of Anders Sparrman, was a leading figure in the British abolition movement. After appearing before the Privy Council in 1789, he communicated by letter an extract from his journal for 22 October 1787, detailing information given to him by a French captain named 'Wignie' concerning three English ships 'cut off' in the River Gambia in that year. His source was probably Louis Vignier des Sables, master of *Marianne* (TSTD 33102), present at Goree (where Wadström states he obtained his information) in 1787. Des Sables may well have provided the information on an insurrection on a French slave ship at Sierra Leone, given in section 471 (pp. 86–7) of Wadström's *Essay*, which also informed this image.

14. On averaging in maritime law, see Baucom (2005: 105–10); Oldham (2007: 308); and Pearson and Richardson (2019: 424–6).

15. Weskett (1781: 11; emphasis added).

16. Oldham (2007: 308).

17. Pearson and Richardson (2019: 425).

18. *Jones* v *Schmoll* Guildhall Tr. Vac. 1785, 130–1. The case is discussed in depth by Oldham (2007). See also Krikler (2007: 34–5).

19. Oldham (2007: 304).

20. Coughtry (1981: 150).

21. Behrendt et al. (2001: 464) determined that, of their sample of 287 shipboard revolts, 154 took place in the embarkation phase, 35 in African waters, and 88 on the Middle Passage.

22. For a discussion of this point, see Snyder (2015: 34–6).

23. Taylor (2006: 166); Snyder (2015: 35).

24. Cugoano (1787: 10).

25. Bell (2012) discusses this movement and its Classical inspiration.

26. For Gomez (1998: 120), suicide was 'perhaps the ultimate act of resistance' for Igbo slaves, because their belief was so strong that death would return them to the land of their birth. Mustakeem (2016: 107) refers to suicide on the Middle Passage as 'the ultimate personal sacrifice'.

27. Snyder (2015: 16–18).

28. See, e.g., the testimony of Isaac Wilson, **HCSP 72: 281**.

29. Weskett (1781: 525).

30. Oldham (2007) also considers *Tatham* v *Hodgson* and *Rhol* v *Parr* (both dating to 1796).

31. Rupprecht (2016: 36).

32. Snyder (2010: 39), citing a letter from William Mein to Pierce Butler, 24 May 1803.

33. A question also explored by Mustakeem (2016: 122–9).

34. Belaying pins were used to fasten off ropes; tackles were formed by reeving ropes through wooden blocks and were employed in hoisting. Pumps drew up water from the lower hull: iron bolts were employed in several ways on the piston-like pumps used on many merchant vessels.

35. Axelrod Wisnes (2007: 233).

36. On the basis that there are few contemporary references to it, Mustakeem (2016: 122) suggests that hanging was the 'rarest form of privatised self-destruction' on slave ships; drowning is certainly the most commonly cited method of suicide, but very few other methods are noted, and hanging is actually the most frequently referenced of those.

434 MATERIALIZING THE MIDDLE PASSAGE

37. The log of *Ranger* discussed in Mustakeem (2016: 106).

38. On Yoruba beliefs, see, e.g., Snyder (2010: 54; 2015: 9–10). But note that some African belief systems condemned suicide: this was the case for the Igbo (see, e.g., Gomez 1998: 133–4). For discussion of religious belief as a factor in the suicide of enslaved persons following the Middle Passage, see Marshall (2004).

39. This point is brought out by Robin Law (2011: 15) in discussing Charles Ball's account of a funeral in South Carolina at which the deceased child of an African born slave was given a miniature canoe in which to 'cross the ocean to his country'. My own treatment of this anecdote can be found at the end of Chapter 6.

40. **HCSP 72: 304**; TSTD 81288.

41. Piersen (1977: 153); Snyder (2010: 54).

42. Casella (2009: 24–5). Casella's analysis of the 'enigma of incarceration' has greatly influenced my own thinking in Chapters 10 and 11.

43. James Scott (1985: 19, 183–4; 1990: 183–201).

44. James Scott (1990: 188). de Certeau (1984: p. xiv) employs the term 'tactical acts' for these small acts that cannot secure independence.

45. The Middle Passage has, of course, been discussed before as a site of resistance, but not with reference to infrapolitics. Taylor (2006: 82–3) regards the slave ship as a site in which 'the long tradition of African American resistance first developed into a coherent and somewhat unified movement'. For Gomez (1998: 13), the Middle Passage was a 'birth canal launching a prolonged struggle between slave holder and enslaved over rights of definition'.

46. Taylor (2006: 106).

47. On the hinterland between compliance and defiance, see James Scott (1990: 136). For discussion of 'revolutionary' and 'everyday' resistance, see Johnson (2003: 116–17). Scott (1990: 291–3) considers the equally mispleading opposition between 'real' and 'token' resistance. Both Johnson and Scott make these comments in critiquing Eugene Genovese's *Roll Jordan Roll* (Genovese 1974).

48. Johansson and Vinthagen (2016: 422–4).

49. Johnson (2003: 114).

50. Johnson (2013: 9). See also Browne (2017: 3–5).

51. Smith (1813: 20).

52. McDermott (2000: 109). Betsy was a collier brig under lease to the navy and was scuppered at Yorktown in 1781.

53. McDermott (2000: 71–2). These storerooms were usually on the orlop deck.

54. Thomas Smith noted that on *Ann Galley*, on which he sailed in 1762, the magazine was 'upon the fore hatchway' (Smith 1813: 22): that it to say, it was in a vulnerable position in the event of an insurrection (as here) in which the captives took control of the vessel forward of the barricado. Even so, the captives did not attempt to break into the magazine on *Ann Galley*.

55. Svalesen (2000: 114).

56. Snelgrave (1734: 190); the voyage is TSTD 75484.

57. Donnan (1930–5: iii. 232). Letter from John Bell to John Fletcher, 15 December 1776. The voyage is TSTD 92534.

58. Donnan (1930–5: iv. 274). *Boston News Letter*, 25 September 1729. The voyage is TSTD 77058.

59. Donnan (1930–5: ii. 486). *Boston Post Boy*, 25 June 1750. The voyage is TSTD 90281.

60. Smith (1970: 526).

61. Crow (1970 [1830]: 72, 103).

62. Donnan (1930–5: ii. 486–7). *Boston Newsletter*, 6 September 1750. The voyage is TSTD 17243.

63. Taylor (2006: 102).

64. See the discussion in Johansson and Vinthagen (2020: 126–8).

65. Behrendt et al. (2001: 460) note in this context that, in the evidence presented before Parliament in 1789–91, three captains and seven sailors stated that women were never shackled in the British slave trade.

66. In his testimony concerning an attempted rising on *Upton* in the Gambia in 1762, Henry Ellison states that 'there were a few women that got out of irons but we found it out time enough to prevent it' (**HCSP 73: 370**). *Contra* Behrendt et al. (2001: 461), this is not the only reference to women in irons in the British parliamentary testimonies: James Arnold's written submission concerning *Ruby* (**HCSP 69: 126**) also mentions it. But it is clear from Arnold's account that the women in question were singled out from the rest: they were chained because they had repeatedly threatened to jump overboard.

67. On embodied resistance by women, see Johansson and Vinthagen (2020: 168–70)—a point that remains underappreciated, as does the role of women in insurrections generally: Richardson (2001: 76).

68. On white power, white desire, and Edward Long see Young (1995: 140–2).

69. Taylor (2006: 92).

70. TSTD 16303, en route from the Gold Coast to Kingston.

71. Atkins (1735: 73).

72. Taylor (2006: 91), citing *Weekly Journal or: The British Gazetteer* (London), 5 July 1729. TSTD 92391.

73. Taylor (2006: 92), citing *Lloyds List*, 15 May 1770. TSTD 91564.

74. Behrendt et al. (2001: 461); Taylor (2006: 91), citing *Lloyds List*, 15 December 1797.

75. Johansson and Vinthagen's illuminating discussion (2020: 168–70) of the female body as a third space in Palestinian resistance has been particularly helpful in structuring the argument presented here.

76. The insurgent women of *Unity* are the central subject of an innovative graphical novel by Hall (2021: see in particular ch. 8).

77. Newton (*Argyle* **1750–1: 49**) refers to clearing one side of the boys' room for use as a hospital.

78. For example, James Arnold (**HCSP 69: 51**) refers to 'boys on board from the age of seven to twelve, who had no relations on board'.

79. The recently rediscovered 'Memoirs' of Florence Hall contains a brief account of a Middle Passage crossing to Jamaica as experienced by an Igbo girl of uncertain age, but clearly still a child. Hall (birth name Akeiso) recalls that, while the men and women were chained, the 'naked children were permitted to walk about the ship' (Browne and Sweet 2016: 216). Hall appears to be referring to *both* boys and girls here, suggesting that girls, as well as boys, experienced greater freedom of movement on some ships.

80. Trotter (**HCSP 73: 98**). Trotter also notes that the boys were 'occasionally, at proper times, allowed to come aft' (referring, presumably, to the quarterdeck). This perhaps suggests that, on *Brooks*, the boys spent the majority of the day with the male captives, but at times were allowed to join the women.

81. Taylor (2006: 89), citing *Gentleman's Magazine* (October 1773), 523; *Virginia Gazette*, 23 December 1773 and 6 *January* 1774.

82. On resistance to English, see Gomez (1998: 176–80).

83. James Scott (1990: 136–7). Scott is referring here to 'rumour, gossip, disguises, linguistic tricks, metaphors, euphemisms, folktales, ritual gestures, anonymity'.

84. Mallipeddi (2014: 242).

85. Axelrod Wisnes (2007: 235). The voyage is TSTD 35052.

86. Wadström (1794: 87) notes the use of a 'signal' to initiate an uprising on a French vessel at Sierra Leone, but it is not clear from the text if this signal was a verbal one.

87. Rediker (2007: 279).

436 MATERIALIZING THE MIDDLE PASSAGE

88. Rath (1993: 2003: 68–85). See also Thornton (1998: 226–8), DuBois (2016: 61–4), and, for a further detailed treatment that at points takes issue with Rath, Lingold (2017). Lingold's plea (2017: 624) that historians should pay greater attention to the musical episodes in colonial travel narratives is especially welcome.
89. For detailed discussion of the possible origins of these words, see Rath (1993: 722–4).
90. On the use of calls by the enslaved in North America, see White and White (2005: 20–37).
91. Rath (1993: 724); Dubois (2016: 63–4).
92. Rath (2003: 74–5).
93. White and White (2005: 20).
94. 'Caliban' appears in 'Islands', the third part of Brathwaite's *The Arrivants: A New World Trilogy*: Brathwaite (1973: 194–5).
95. Brathwaite (1973: 274).
96. Stanley Niaah (2010: 19). See also Stanley Niaah (2010: 344–5) and Fabre (1999: 41–3). For Stanley Niaah, a direct line can be traced from the slave ship to modern Jamaican dance hall.
97. Fabre (1999: 42); Thompson (2014: 613–68).
98. Thompson (2014: 1–3).
99. Rath (2003: 78–80).
100. On the use of signal drumming to mimic speech inflections, see White and White (2005: 20–1).
101. Rath (2003: 79) for these and later laws banning the use of drums and horns by Caribbean slaves.
102. Bassani (2000: 49, no. 194 = *Miscellanies*, no. 1368).
103. This is the view expressed by the British Museum in its online catalogue entry, which describes the drum as being of Akan origin, made in Ghana, https://www.britishmuseum.org/collection/object/E_Am-SLMisc-1368 (accessed 2 September 2022). The drum is made of wood varieties (*Cordia* and *Baphia*) native to Africa, alongside vegetable fibre and deerskin.
104. **HCSP 68: 19.**
105. Park (1799: 360).
106. Paton (2012: 248–9).
107. Smallwood (2007b: 124–5, 129–30).
108. This is the title of Bhabha's influential 1985 paper.
109. Handler (2009a: 5).
110. Bosman (1705: 364).
111. Atkins (1735: 180).
112. Smith (1813: 31).
113. Spavens (1796: 198).
114. Jones (1994: 351).
115. Pinckard (1806: 229).
116. On nakedness as cultural lack, see Gikandi (2011: 211–14).
117. Handler and Lange (1978). Numerous pioneering bioarchaeological analyses have been published, revealing important information on the health of the enslaved population here: Corruccini et al. (1987); Corruccini et al. (1989); Jacobi et al. (1992). Further excavation was undertaken at Newton from 1997–8 and isotope analysis was subsequently performed on the twenty-five skeletons recovered at that time (Schroeder et al. 2009). The results suggest that the majority of the individuals excavated in the 1990s were born on the island, if not the estate itself. Seven individuals, however, yielded oxygen and strontium ratios in their tooth enamel that are consistent with an African origin, strongly suggesting that they were first-generation captives brought to the island with the slave trade. These seven did not all originate from the same part of Africa: the data suggest that they came from at least three different zones, possibly including the Gold Coast and Senegambia.
118. Handler (1997). Other grave goods included bracelets, finger rings, and an iron knife.

SURVIVING THE MIDDLE PASSAGE 437

119. Handler and Norman (2007: 7). The bridge or hook between the bowl and stem is particularly characteristic of excavated pipes from southern and coastal Ghana dating to the later seventeenth century.

120. On the powdered-glass bead, see DeCorse (2000: 7). Handler (2007) considers the two Newton carnelian beads. The second, also from a necklace, was found with Burial B63. These are the only carnelian beads to have been recovered archaeologically from slave cemetery contexts in the New World. Handler (2007: 7) notes that, among some Gold Coast peoples, the bead necklaces worn by priests occasionally contained one long red carnelian bead.

121. MacQuarrie and Pearson (2016: 47), citing unpublished information provided by Raymond Pasquariello. Burial 4 produced 57 beads and Burial 10 a further 74.

122. On the likely Ghanaian origins of the beads associated with Burials 434 and 226, see Bianco et al. (2006: esp. 403–4).

123. MacQuarrie and Pearson (2016: 50).

124. MacQuarrie and Pearson (2016: 58).

125. MacQuarrie and Pearson (2016: 58–9).

126. MacQuarrie and Pearson (2016: 59–60).

127. MacQuarrie and Pearson (2016: 20).

128. MacQuarrie and Pearson (2016: 65).

129. Smith (1813: 31).

130. The terms 'fetish' and *gris-gris* became confused and conflated in European thought and writing. Mitchell (2012) considers European uses of the concept of the fetish in commercial transactions on the African Coast and explores the evolution of (mis)understandings both of the fetish and of African value systems, from the seventeenth to the eighteenth centuries.

131. Hair et al. (1992: i. 85–6). Barbot also discusses the use of amulets in Sierra Leone, stating: they wear fetishes around their necks, stuffed with very nasty and dirty little trifles, to which they are particularly careful to give some food morning and evening, and to decorate with pieces of glass and other fripperies. They wear these fetishes not only around their necks but also on their arms, under their arm-pits, on their chests and legs, and over their heart (Hair et al. 1992: i. 221–2).

132. Another term for amulets, employed in the Portuguese Atlantic world, was *bolsas*: see Fremont (2020).

133. MacGaffey (2000: 37). I have drawn heavily on MacGaffey's detailed discussion of Kongo *minkisi* in this section of my discussion.

134. Biebuyck and Herreman (1996: 248); MacGaffey (2000: 43–4).

135. MacGaffey (2000: 43–50); Thompson (1983: 117–19).

136. The art historian Robert Farris Thompson (1983) famously drew attention to the survival of Angola–Kongo *minkisi* elements in Brazil, the USA, and the Caribbean in his book *Flash of the Spirit*. Chireau (2003) provides a recent analysis of the African American conjuring tradition from a historical perspective. For the Cuban variant of *minkisi* (ngangas), see Palmié (2007: esp. 168–78).

137. Leone and Fry (1999); Leone et al. (2001).

138. This data set is available online: *Born in Slavery Slave Narratives from the Federal Writers' Project, 1936 to 1938*, https://www.loc.gov/collections/slave-narratives-from-the-federal-writers-project-1936-to-1938/ (accessed 22 August 2022).

139. Leone and Fry (1999: 381). See also Galke (2000).

140. Leone et al. (2001: 154–5 and table 9.3).

141. Leone et al. (2001: 156 and table 9.5).

142. Handler (2009a: 16, n. 19).

143. Svalesen (2000: 185–6). The water chevrotain is common to Ghana; the peacock is indigenous to both Asia and the Congo.

438   MATERIALIZING THE MIDDLE PASSAGE

144. Bhabha (1994: 235).
145. Palmié (2007: 194).
146. Rarey (2018); Fremont (2020). For further discussion of the use of protective amulets by enslaved persons in Rio de Janeiro, see Lima et al. (2014).
147. Rarey (2018: 20). These objects do not appear to have been subject to scientific analysis.
148. Fremont (2020).
149. Rarey (2018: 21).
150. Blier (2004); Norman (2009); Rarey (2018: 25–7).
151. Lima et al. (2014). The artefacts were recovered from two dumping areas: one on the lateral edge of the wharf and one in front of it, which will have been used by communities living near the wharf. It is possible that some of the amulets may have arrived on the bodies of captives entering the report, but evidence to support that suggestion is lacking. Whatever the case, this study points to the extensive use of amulets by the mainly Central African slaves living in Rio de Janeiro.
152. Lima et al. (2014: 108).
153. Lima et al. (2014: 111, illustrated in fig. 5 on p. 113).
154. TSTD 90866. *Lloyds List*, 29 June 1764; Taylor (2006: 91, 197). Mustakeem (2016: 100) notes an act of attempted poisoning in relation to the sloop *Dolphin* in 1796, but this incident took place on shore—see Mouser (1978: 259).
155. Chireau (2003: 72).
156. Chireau (2003: 72–5).
157. Paton (2012: 251). As Paton notes, none of these strictures against poisoning explicitly addressed the ritual context in which poison was used, but, given African understandings of poison, it is likely that the behaviour that they attempted to control was in practice undertaken in the context of spiritual work.
158. James Scott (1990: 118). As Johnson (2003: 117) put it: 'Collective resistance is at bottom a process of everyday organization, one that in fact depends upon connections and trust established through everyday actions.'
159. As emphasized by Johansson and Vinthagen (2020: 175–9) in their study of Palestinian *sumūd* (everyday resistance).

12

The Middle Passage Re-membered

A Conclusion in Three More Objects

> The experience of the Middle Passage eluded those who lived it and tried to write about it.
>
> (Diedrich et al. 1999: 19)

In the village cemetery in Wethersfield, Hartford County, Connecticut, there is a gravestone inscribed: 'In memory of Quash Gomer: a Native of Angola in Africa, brought from there in 1748, & died June 6th 1799, Aged 68 years.'[1] Quash Gomer purchased his freedom in 1766 and died a free man, but he never forgot his homeland: it was inscribed on his heart, and ultimately on the stone that marked his final resting place. The voyage that Gomer made from Angola to North America is not acknowledged directly on his gravestone, yet it can be glimpsed, present but not articulated, in his funerary biography. As this book has shown, it *is* possible to materialize many aspects of the Middle Passage of Gomer and the millions who made the same enforced journey, but, in that endeavour, I have needed to draw primarily on the written testimonies of the sailors who crewed slave ships. The *African* Middle Passage certainly emerges from those testimonies, but it does so obliquely, sighted through the mirror of European experiences and voices. Directly voiced African accounts of the voyage into slavery do, of course, exist, but they are few and (as discussed in Chapter 3) tend to be very brief. Why is this so? Is it simply because so few Africans had access to literacy that the majority were not able to make their own, independent textual record? Or were the memories so painful that the majority felt unable to confront their trauma directly? Put another way, did Gomer, and the millions who endured what he did, *want* to remember the voyage into slavery, and if so, when, and how? These are the questions explored in my concluding chapter. I use the term 're-membering' throughout this chapter. It is employed with reference to collective memory work (the re-shaping over time of historical memory) and in the imperative sense, advocated by Johanna Garvey, of 'using history, all of it, of not forgetting but always looking both backwards and forward' to re-member a past that must not be forgotten.[2]

Around 9.5 million Africans survived the Middle Passage, with almost three million of those men, women, and children landing in the Caribbean and North America on British-owned ships (see Table 1.1). Historians, linguists, cultural theorists, anthropologists, and archaeologists have dedicated themselves to proving since the mid twentieth century that the African born did not enter the Americas as *tabula rasa* wiped clean by the traumas of a captive passage but retained what Michael Gomez calls

Materializing the Middle Passage: A Historical Archaeology of British Slave Shipping, 1680–1807. Jane Webster, Oxford University Press. © Jane Webster 2023. DOI: 10.1093/oso/9780199214594.003.0012

440 MATERIALIZING THE MIDDLE PASSAGE

'a psychic attachment and orientation towards Africa'.[3] That attachment, it is universally accepted, was the seed from which diasporic identities bore fruit. But 'Africa' and 'New World' are, of course, *landed* terms: they denote the places where captives' journeys began and ended. The part that the intervening ocean voyage played in memory and identity construction is not well understood, but we do know that both slave owners and American-born slaves tended to regard African birth and the 'saltwater' experience as markers of difference, and even inferiority.[4] The white observer Edward Long, for example, asserted in 1774 that Jamaican-born blacks 'hold the Africans in the utmost contempt, stiling them [*sic*] "salt water Negroes" and "Guiney birds"'.[5] Why should saltwater status be perceived pejoratively? Because, as Smallwood perceptively suggests, newly arrived Africans were an unsettling presence

> in immigrant communities seeking stability and coherence. One could never completely escape the saltwater, for even once an African captive's own middle passage had ended, the communities where that slave's life played out in the colonial Americas continued to be moulded by the rhythm of the ships returning to deposit still more bodies.[6]

In these complex social circumstances, were saltwater Africans more likely to bond with others who had shared their own, or any, crossing? When and why did they acknowledge their Middle Passage? What were the media and strategies employed in doing so? And did some captives prefer not to remember, but to forget?

I begin my analysis of these questions by focusing on the growing body of documentary evidence for the enduring bonds forged between captives on board slave ships. As I will show, painstaking analysis of archival sources by a small group of pioneering historians has uncovered unequivocal evidence that fictive kinships forged at sea were indeed maintained in the diaspora. Yet, as one moves beyond the documentary archives of the New World slaving ports, the African Middle Passage becomes more elusive. Recent work has, however, shown conclusively that, while African discursive oral accounts of the slave trade are rare, ritual practices in many parts of West Africa embody memories of the capture, internal transit, and eventual sale of Africans to European traders.[7] As considered below, African-American and African–Caribbean communities similarly evoke the memory of the Middle Passage through ritual practices, but explicit accounts in other formats are again rare.

Repeating the pattern of the introductory chapter, three artefacts help me to consider why the Middle Passage experience always seems to be just beyond reach for the scholar of the diaspora; glimpsed, but shadowy, and found mainly in ritual contexts. The first of these objects is a book: Olaudah Equiano's *Interesting Narrative*, published in London in 1789 at the height of the parliamentary inquiries that have been a key source of witness testimonies throughout *Materializing the Middle Passage*. The second is an eighteenth-century sketch of the scarification marks visible on the body of an African-born soldier, John Rock, who was serving in a Caribbean regiment at the time the record was made. The third, approached via a consideration of the rapidly growing contribution of bioarchaeology to the study of the Middle Passage, is a string of waist beads recovered from the New York African Burial Ground. I use these three objects to argue that the voyage into slavery informed the social identities of saltwater survivors in complex ways that have been neither fully explored, not adequately acknowledged. I will argue that those strategies are best understood, and most likely to be identified, by framing the African Middle Passage with reference to the theoretical frameworks with which this book began: cultural creolization and the third space.

Materializing the 'Ship Family': Documentary Strategies

> It is time we saw the slave ship as captives did: as a place where individuals died but communities were born.
>
> (Walter Hawthorne 2008: 54)

> three negro fellows, imported this last summer from Africa in the ship *Yanimarew*...it is imagined that they were seen some time ago (along with three others of the same cargo) on Chicahominy, and it is supposed they are still lurking about the skirts of that swamp...
>
> (Runaway slave advertisement, *Virginia Gazette* 13 December 1770)[8]

During his interview with Thomas Clarkson in 1788, Captain James Bowen, Master of *Russell*'s 1786 voyage to Granada, explained that 'among his slaves were many relations who had established such an attachment to each other, as to have been inseparable, and to have partaken of the same food, and to have slept on the same plank during the voyage' (**Substance 1788: 46**). As Markus Rediker explains in his richly detailed discussion of shipmate bonding, these 'relations' were not people who shared the same blood; their kinship had been recently formed, through their shared experience at sea.[9] Similar observations to Bowen's were made by slave owners in the Caribbean. Thus, an abridgment of Bryan Edwards's *History* of the British West Indies, published in 1798, informs the reader that '[t]he man who has been a shipmate with the negro during his passage from Africa becomes his dear and inviolable friend; and even the name Shipmate expresses among them every tender idea of regard'.[10] In 1955, Philip Curtin, one of the earliest champions of the study of the Middle Passage, drew on similar contemporary sources in arguing that, in Jamaica, the shipmate bond 'was considered almost as strong as blood relationship, and it passed from one generation to another—a young man felt that the "shipmate" of his father was his own relative as well'.[11]

When Sidney Mintz and Richard Price published their pioneering study of the origins of African-American culture in 1976, they attempted to uncover these dyadic and group ties by interrogating creole languages. In Suriname, for example, Africans who had crossed the Atlantic together referred to one another as *sippi* (a word derived from 'ship'); in Haiti, *batiment* (French for 'ship') was similarly employed.[12] Mintz and Price drew on this linguistic evidence in arguing that, in 'widely scattered parts of

Afro-America, the "shipmate" relationship became a major principle of social organization and continued for decades or even centuries to shape ongoing social relations'.[13] It was, in fact, with *specific* reference to shipmate bonds that Mintz and Price made their much-criticized comment, discussed in Chapter 1, that 'the development of new social bonds, even before Africans arrived in the New World, already announced the birth of new societies, based on new kinds of principles'.[14] I have argued throughout this book that the Middle Passage experience can best be understood through a creolist lens. So it is a point of some interest here that the twin architects of cultural creolization theory were among the first scholars to recognize shipmate bonds and framed these 'new societies' as the outcome of *pre*-existing identities, meeting in the salt water and creating principles of social organization that would shape ongoing social relations in the Americas. My argument throughout has similarly been that creolization theory, allied with postcolonial understandings of displacement (as explored in Chapter 1), provides a persuasive framework within which to reconcile the old and the new as they met on the voyage into slavery. The ship family was the result of that encounter: at once the product of mid-Atlantic creolization (among Africans themselves) and the creative outcome of displacement.

Some historians are today revisiting the concept of the ship family and developing creative strategies by which to recognize these ties more clearly in New World settings. James Sweet has used archival sources in Cuba to reconstruct the attempted return to Africa, in 1556, of two Jolof slaves, Antônio and Zambo. Convinced that the plan to hire a boat would work, Zambo offered passage home to a 13-year-old girl who had shared his Atlantic crossing five years earlier.[15] Drawing primarily on documentation relating to marriage licences, Herman Bennett has used marriage files (*expedientes matrimoniales*) collated by the Catholic church to show that saltwater Africans in seventeenth-century New Mexico continued to interact with people with whom they had shared the Middle Passage—for example, selecting shipmates to witness their nuptials many years later.[16] Alex Borucki has also used marriage files, in this case to reveal the ways in which common experiences in the slave trade shaped bonds and social networks among Africans in Montevideo between 1768 and 1803.[17] Borucki's analysis of *malungo* (shipmate networks) extends to individuals sharing similar experiences, particularly in terms of procurement zones and shipping routes, and is not limited to those sharing the same crossing from Africa, or even within the intra-American slave trade. Even so, the two most frequently mentioned places where witnesses stated they first met the grooms they were speaking for were on board ships and in previous slave ports.[18] Borucki's overall conclusion is that '[t]ransformations of social networks and identities started well before slave disembarkation in the New World and extended as far back as the inland African slave trade'.[19] James Sweet has similarly drawn attention to the use of *malunga* by Angolan shipmates in Brazil. As he notes, while the word might simply have been employed by adoptive kin in acknowledgement of their shared horror and triumph of surviving the Middle Passage, *malunga* was also a 'symbol of authority, brought from the sea by the original ancestors'—the use of which suggests an awareness by saltwater captives that they were establishing new lineages that nevertheless reflected familiar social structures.[20]

Walter Hawthorne has used a range of archival sources to examine the lives of some of the captives shipped from Lagos in the Bight of Benin in 1821 on the Portuguese slaver *Emilia*.[21] The majority (71 per cent) were Yoruba speakers. Most of the remainder were Hausa. *Emilia* was seized by the British naval vessel *Morgiana* and, having been manumitted and landed in Rio de Janiero as *africanos livres* (free Africans), the former captives were obliged to serve fourteen-year 'apprenticeships', which effectively make them *de facto* slaves. The legal documentation surrounding the efforts of some of these individuals to terminate their apprenticeships suggests they supported each other through a fictive kin network or lineage—a network that drew on and maintained Yoruba understandings of social identity, but that had been shaped collectively by people of different 'nations' on *Emilia* and was maintained in Rio de Janeiro. Eventually, in 1836, sixty-eight individuals identified by Hawthorne as likely survivors from *Emilia*—some of them Yoruba, others Hausa—returned together to Lagos.[22] Jennifer Nelson has undertaken a similar analysis of shipmate bonds between *africanos livres* from the Brazilian slaver *Brilhante*, seized by the British Navy in 1838.[23] A year after being 'apprenticed' to a woman named Anna Maria Honoria, two boys from *Brilhante* ran away on the same day. They were not from the same African 'nation' but had clearly formed a lasting bond.[24] Other *Brilhante* captives were still in contact with each other twelve years after their voyage.[25] Noting that Angolan slaves across Brazil identified their shipmates as *malungo*, Hawthorne suggests that 'shipmates were linked to a real and mythical past and...shared a special bond in the present'.[26]

Hawthorne's and Nelson's work concerns ships seized by the British Navy well after 1807. In the British Caribbean, archival sources concerning 'shipmates' have yet to be systematically collated in this way, but a range of sources, from diaries to newspaper advertisements, provide information about ship families here. For example, an entry in the Jamaican planter Thomas Thistlewood's diary for 1751 records the gift of food and drink to his enslaved mistress Marina, 'to treat the negroes, and especially her shipmates withal at her housewarming'.[27] In 1761, Thistlewood bought a newly arrived 15-year-old Igbo girl called Molia (renamed Coobah) at Savanah la Mar. Between 1770 and 1774 she made fourteen attempts to run away, on one occasion being taken up 'near the cave going to Bluefields, where she says she has a shipmate'.[28] In 1765, Thistlewood purchased ten young captives directly off a slave ship: the continuing relationships between these youths can be pieced together through careful reading of his diary. To give just one example, Jimmy and Phoebe, aged 10 and 12 at the time of purchase, began a sexual relationship almost a decade later, in 1774.[29]

As Michael Mullin was one of the first to argue in the 1990s, newspaper advertisements are a valuable source of information on fictive networks among the enslaved.[30] When slave owners placed notices in the local press concerning their 'runaways', it was sometimes specified that the absconder was a 'new negro' who had recently arrived on a slave ship. On very rare occasions, the vessel was named. A notice placed in the

Cornwall Chronicle (Montego Bay, Jamaica) on 30 November 1776 sought the return of a person carried to Africa on perhaps the best known of all British slave ships, much discussed in this book; a Fante man 'bought out of the ship *Brooks*, Capt Noble, last December'.[31] Most unusually, three advertisements record abscondees who arrived in Jamaica on voyages made by the British slaver *Trusty*.[32] On 18 April 1801, an advertisement was placed in the Jamaican *Royal Gazette* for a 'new negro' who had been purchased out of *Trusty*. The advertiser states that 'it is supposed he will endeavor to find out some of his shipmates'.[33] In October 1803, another advertisement was placed in the *Royal Gazette* for a second 'new negro', this time from the Gold Coast, who had 'signified his intention to returning to his countrymen, on board of the ship *Trusty*'.[34] Finally, on 29 July 1809, two years after the British trade had ended, a Chamba runaway named Jaapa, stated in the Jamaican *Royal Gazette* to have arrived on '*Trusty*, Capt. Crosbie', was said to 'have been seen going to windward and with several shipmates. She was very partial to her shipmates and no doubt had attached herself to some of them.'[35] Jamaican runaway advertisements rarely name vessels in this way, but they do help scholars to glimpse the social bonds that developed during the Middle Passage. Thus, the *Cornwall Chronicle* for 4 February 1782 reports the loss of a 'Negro fellow named JOHN, of the Mundingo [Mandike] country... marked on the left shoulder with I.L.'. William Cunningham, the man's owner, speculates that 'he may be about Duncans, where he has a number of shipmates'. In 1785, a 'new negro man of the Congo country' is reported to have absconded and is 'supposed to be harboured among his shipmates'. The runaway, who had been renamed Hercules, is also identified as one of the cargo of Captain Wise, suggesting that he and his shipmates had made the Middle Passage on the Liverpool ship *Sisters*, which had arrived in Montego Bay from the Windward Coast in May 1784. It was clearly felt to be quite likely that, a year later, these shipmates would have sought each other out.[36] In 1793, some eighteen months after the event, a girl named Moll is reported as run away from an estate in St James, and imagined to be harboured by her former husband, or 'by some of her shipmates'.[37] Moll had been resident in Jamaica for some time, but is again assumed to have sought out the people with whom she shared her Atlantic crossing. And, as in the case of Hercules, it is thought likely by her owner that her shipmates will have harboured her—a decision that would have involved considerable risk. Shortly after Christmas of 1798, Bryan Blake placed a notice in the *Antigua Gazette* concerning a 'new Negro woman who answers to the name of COOK; was just out of a fever, has her country marks on her forehead, [and] wore a wrapper and petticoat of green pennistoun'. Having purchased the woman at a recent sale of captives newly arrived from Africa, Blake fears that 'she is gone into the country with some of her ship-mates' and requests that others who bought slaves at the same sale search for her among their own property.[38] A few weeks earlier on Antigua, a woman 'only a few months from Africa, and answers to her country name, HAAWA', was also thought to have been 'inticed into the country by some of her ship mates'.[39]

The shipmate bonds evident in the work of historians like Hawthorne and in my own analysis of Caribbean newspapers, above, present something of a problem to

Africanist readings of the Middle Passage. Hawthorne has persuasively argued that, in their quest for a reading of the diaspora in which New World social identities are the outcome of continuity, not change, Africanists have been forced to adopt a paradoxical position: 'On the one hand,' he says, these scholars 'recognize that shipmate bonds were lasting and constituted one of the building blocks of a shared American identity. On the other hand, they see shipmate bonds as reinforcing rather than replacing pre-existing identities.'[40] It is, if course, possible to reconcile these views by understanding shipmate bonds as overlapping with relationships based on shared African origins and cultures.[41] Yet, in practice, few scholars seem prepared to adopt that position. Hawthorne's point about the documentary record can be paraphrased with reference to the archaeological one: that is to say, the current focus on continuity—on the African origins of Middle Passage survivors, and on the maintenance of African identities and practices by these individuals and their descendants—has hampered consideration of the slave ship as a crucible for change. The continuing focus on captive origins, and on evidencing those origins, has also led historical archaeologists to overlook the astonishing *slipperiness* of the Middle Passage in New World contexts—its ability somehow to evade capture, to elude explicit articulation. The implications of this point are profound: one simple reason the African Middle Passage may be so hard for historical archaeologists to materialize today is that it was caught, for those who survived it, in a liminal zone somewhere between remembering and forgetting. I pursue this point in the next section, in considering the conundrum that is Olaudah Equiano's Middle Passage.

Repositioning Olaudah Equiano's *The Interesting Narrative*

For two hundred years, Olaudah Equiano has been valorised as *the* African voice of the Middle Passage: one of the few persons of African birth writing in English during the eighteenth century, and one of even fewer to describe his shipboard experience in any detail. By his own account, Equiano was born in Nigeria around 1745, kidnapped for the slave trade at the age of 11, and shipped to the West Indies. His autobiography, *The Interesting Narrative of the Life of Olaudah Equiano, or Gustavus Vassa, the African* was published in London in 1789. The description he provides of an 'Eboe' upbringing has long been shown to be heavily reliant on the published works of commentators on the Guinea coast such as Anthony Benezet and William Snelgrave, but such borrowings were so common in the eighteenth century that they have rarely been argued to suggest that Equiano's account was untrue.[42] But in 1999 Vincent Carretta uncovered a baptismal record and a ship's muster roll suggesting that Equiano was born a slave in South Carolina.[43] This revelation generated intense academic debate concerning the veracity of Equiano's Middle Passage.[44] Reading these debates, it is clear that most scholars *want* Equiano to be speaking truth to power about the slave trade. Even among those prepared to concede the possibility that his account of the Middle Passage is a fiction, Equiano continues to be championed as the curator of the

446 MATERIALIZING THE MIDDLE PASSAGE

shared memories of generations of Africans who *did* make that voyage. To quote Marcus Rediker:

> If he [Equiano] was born in South Carolina he could have known what he knew only by gathering the lore and experience of people who had been born in Africa and had made the dreaded Middle Passage aboard the slave ship. He thus becomes the oral historian, the keeper of the common story, the griot of sorts, of the slave trade, which means that his account is no less faithful to the original experience, only different in its sources and genesis.[45]

For this argument to hold value, it must surely be necessary to demonstrate that Equiano's account curates *African* experiential lore. However, if we compare the famous extract from *Interesting Narrative* (see Box 3.2) with the parliamentary witness testimonies from 1788–92 so central to my own book, a new perspective emerges. Equiano claims to have made the Atlantic crossing as a boy, yet his account replicates the narrative structure, and echoes much of the content, of *adult* male experience on board British vessels, as detailed in the sailors' testimonies with which readers of *Materializing the Middle Passage* will by now be well acquainted. These sources comprise the 1788 parliamentary testimonies set out in Table 3.6, Falconbridge (*Account* **1788**), Newton (***Thoughts* 1788**), and Clarkson (*Substance* **1789**). Thus, the captive boards the slave ship and his health is checked. He is astonished by the appearance of the vessel and fears he will be eaten. He is flogged for not eating and witnesses attempted suicides by drowning. He sees the cruel treatment of sailors, specifically flogging with a rope—an action referenced many times in *Substance of the Evidence* and also materialized in Clarkson's chest via the rope used to flog the sailor Charles Horseler (as discussed in Chapter 10). The heat, filth, and sounds of the slave decks are described in terms very similar to those used by Falconbridge (***Account* 1788: 200–1**) and especially by Newton (***Thoughts* 1788: 110–11**). It is also telling that Equiano does not specify his precise quarters, either above or below decks, and seems entirely unaware of the range of possible accommodations for small boys on board slave ships (as set out in Chapters 5 and 11).[46]

In short, virtually every point of detail of Equiano's Middle Passage narrative had already appeared in print, or was a matter of parliamentary record, by 1789. His account need not be a fiction, even so. The memory of a traumatized child would have been deficient, obliging the writer to look to published sources. Equiano knew many leading British abolitionists, including James Ramsay and Granville Sharp, and was involved in the troubled Sierra Leone resettlement project. He even offered to testify before the Privy Council at the first stage of the parliamentary inquiry process—an offer that was turned down.[47] Equiano then wrote to Lord Hawkesbury expressing his support for trade with Africa: (the letter appears in **HCSP 69: 98–9**) and observed both the Commons and Lords debates on the Dolben Act in June 1788.[48] Seen in this light, his echoing of Clarkson, Falconbridge, and Newton could be rationalized as a necessity (given the deficiencies of a child's memory) and even as a deliberate stratagem, resulting in an account of the Middle Passage carefully modified to appeal to British readers sympathetic to the abolitionist cause. Certainly, as Carretta emphasizes: 'Equiano's fellow abolitionists were calling for precisely the kind of account of Africa and the Middle Passage that he supplied.'[49]

My own view is that Equiano's account is a fiction. What makes it unique—and so important to the concerns of the present chapter—is the author's willingness to articulate what most survivors could or would not. As noted in Chapter 3, African accounts of the crossing are generally brief to the point of terseness. Equiano's London-based contemporary Ottobah Cugoano—the veracity of whose Middle Passage experience has never been questioned—seems to have found it impossible to articulate the horrors of his crossing. Having briefly described his experiences at sea (including an attempted insurrection, discussed in Chapter 11), he notes simply:

> But it would be needless to give a description of all the horrible scenes which we saw, and the base treatment which we met with, in this dreadful captive situation, as the similar cases of thousands, which suffer by this infernal traffic, are well known.[50]

Cugoano wrote these words at exactly the moment that Thomas Clarkson was attempting to bring the Middle Passage to public attention by recording in unflinching detail the horrors witnessed by sailors. As evidenced throughout this book, Clarkson acutely perceived that witness testimonies—opening up the Middle Passage in much the way a bioarchaeologist unlocks the hidden history of a skeleton—would play a key role in undermining the slave trade. Yet he sought those accounts wholly from white men. Yes, he must have calculated that Parliament would decline to question black witnesses, as certainly happened with Equiano; but perhaps Clarkson had also come to understand that the personal and collective trauma of those who had endured the Middle Passage as captives was such that few were willing to confront their experiences in the direct manner needed to produce a detailed narrative account. That is one way, at least, to read Cuguano's comment.[51] Certainly, Equiano notwithstanding, the few Africans in the position to provide a detailed account of the slaving voyage from the perspective of its victims did not generally do so.

I have not offered this critique of Equiano and his acquaintances as a way of suggesting that memories of the Middle Passage were determinedly suppressed or ignored: my point is that few saltwater captives seem to have been willing to confront, or articulate, these memories directly.

John Rock's Scarification: Embodied Memory in the Diaspora

Thus far, I have considered narratives codified in book form, but saltwater experience was written on the body too. As set out in Chapter 9, many captives bore indelible evidence of African birth on their bodies in the form of scarification marks, or dental modification. What impact did these somatic markers of the saltwater experience have

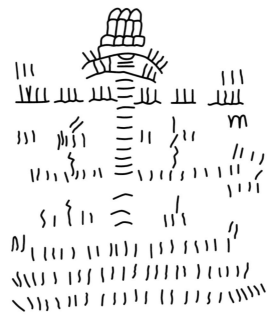

Figure 12.1 The scarification marks of John Rock recorded 18 February 1820, after Mullin (1994: 29).

on material culture, social memory, and ethnogenesis in the diaspora? The second of my three artefacts will be used to address this question. Like so many of the data considered in *Materializing the Middle Passage*, this example is at once 'artefact' and 'text': the scarification marks of John Rock, recorded in a late-eighteenth-century regimental succession register, and existing now only in a primary textual source (Figure 12.1).[52]

Between 1795 and 1838 thousands of Africans—recruited locally, newly purchased from slave ships, or sourced from 'liberated' slaving vessels—were incorporated into new military regiments formed in the Caribbean. Detailed information on the identity of the new recruits was recorded in regimental *Succession and Description* books, which noted each recruit's African village and 'nation' and sometimes, as in John Rock's case, included a sketch of his scarification marks. I suggested in Chapter 9 that, while the testimonies of slave ship sailors contain only the briefest references to scarification marks on the bodies of captive Africans, the careful recording of such marks by the British authorities indicate the strong contemporary understanding among white observers that scarification patterns offered insights into captives' origins. In fact, 'country marks' (like those depicted in Figure 12.2) comprised one of the three principal ways by which colonial whites perceived themselves able to establish an African-born slave's ethnicity—the others being 'looks' (appearance and demeanour) and language or dialect.[53] John Rock's bodily markings were recorded to ensure he could be identified, but also to categorize him ethnically. Scarification was not, in fact, employed as an ethnic marker in Africa, but runaway slave advertisements provide abundant evidence that, in the British West Indies particularly, slave owners perceived

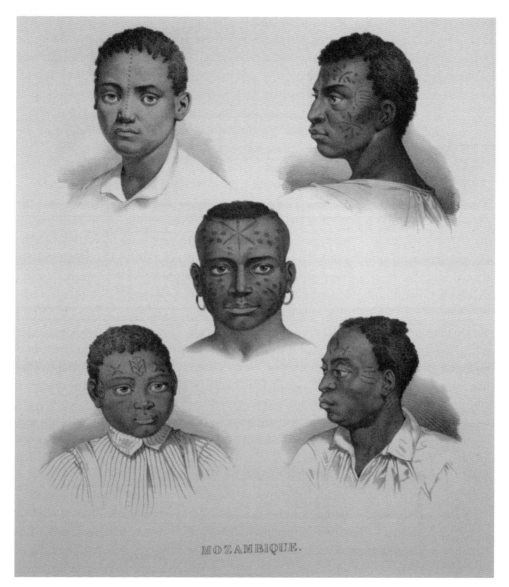

Figure 12.2 Scarification marks on the faces of enslaved Africans from Mozambique, Johann Moritz Rugendas (1835).

clear linkages between specific African 'nations' and particular scarification patterns.[54] For example, slaves with three or four angled and parallel slashes on each cheek or a temple could be confidently identified by Jamaican whites as 'Chamba' (that is, from the Benue River region of Nigeria).[55] Some observers could make even finer distinctions: 'Eboe with marks of Moco'.[56] These ethnonyms—the most commonly employed of which were Coromantee, Mina, Igbo, Angola, Congo, Whydah, Popo, and Mundingo—are not references to specific linguistic or sociocultural groups: they are generic, highly simplified, European abstractions, owing much to the location of the

450   MATERIALIZING THE MIDDLE PASSAGE

primary shipment ports of the slave trade.[57] Yet, as Borucki's work has brilliantly demonstrated, some of the first people to use these terms regularly were diasporic Africans. Borucki makes the important suggestion that the 'early emergence and persistence of umbrella terms such as Angola and Mina throughout the New World, and the constant usage of these terms by African diasporic communities, *suggest that such categories reflected personal experience in the slave trade*'.[58] Here, in other words, we can glimpse saltwater shipmates attempting to bridge ethnic differences in the Americas.

As we read about these indelible marks through registers, runaway slave advertisements, and other documents, we can be virtually certain we are glimpsing the African born. That is because, as Barbara Heath explains it: '[w]hile slave masters noted the presence of "country marks", filed teeth and pierced noses among newly imported, or "salt water" Negroes, scarification, dental modifications and body piercing (with the exception of ears) appear not to have survived even a generation.'[59] This discontinuity demands explanation, particularly since there is no documentary evidence to suggest that bodily modification was explicitly forbidden by slave owners.[60] In a recent study, Paul Lovejoy has argued that scarification disappeared so quickly because it had no part to play in the interface between cultures in the Americas 'other than as a symbol of an African past that no longer had relevance'.[61] It would be hard to find any historical archaeologist today who would accept Lovejoy's argument that the absence of scarification in the Americas is a testimony to the 'social death' of Africans in the diaspora, and in fact, it is possible to envisage several reasons why African-born parents might not wish their creole offspring to bear such marks.[62] Contemporary illustrations and, above all, 'runaway' slave advertisements clearly indicate that white observers drew attention to dental modification and scarification as aspects of a slave's appearance that would actively help to identify an absconder.[63] In addition, scarification was so strongly equated with African birth that it must also have inhibited code-switching—that is, the ability of the enslaved to segue between different aspects of their aggregate identity as situations and contexts demanded.[64] Recent archaeological work has also suggested that, while scarification may have been discontinued on the body, it was not forgotten, and left its mark elsewhere in the material repertoire of the enslaved.

From Bodies to Pipes: Scarified Things?

Anthropological studies have emphasized that West African communities replicate in other media the patterns made on the body, particularly within household spaces. Chapter 9 drew attention to Marla Berns's account of *Hleeta* (scarifying) among the Ga'anda of north-eastern Nigeria. Berns showed that the *Hleeta* designs crafted onto the body to secure the socialization of Ga'anda women were directly and symbolically reinforced through their reproduction on ceramic vessels, tools, compounds, and granaries. Thus, the diamond-shaped, banded *kwardata* motif, cut onto a girl's thighs, was reprised in the decoration of large ritual beer pots used to make bride payments (in alcohol) to the girl's family.[65] Berns is one of several writers to draw attention to the ways in which many sub-Saharan Africans associate pottery with human beings, and replicate body markings on ceramic vessels.[66] Some archaeologists have drawn on this work in arguing that, even though New World slave communities did not employ scarification, the designs found on certain tobacco smoking pipes, and ceramic vessels in the USA and Brazil, replicate African scarification patterns. Matthew Emerson's influential, though also controversial, work on Chesapeake tobacco pipes was an early example here.[67] Emerson argued that some of the designs applied to locally made seventeenth-century tobacco pipes found in plantation contexts in Maryland and Virginia originated in Mali, Ghana, and Nigeria—among them one of the Ga'anda *kwardata* motifs described by Berns in her study of *Hleeta*.[68]

While this suggestion opens up the possibility that scarification marks on saltwater bodies held significance for plantation slaves in the USA, there are attenuating considerations here. First, Berns's account of the *kwardata* was made in the 1980s: whether this mark was in use among Nigerian peoples in the seventeenth century is uncertain. Second, seventeenth-century Virginia and Maryland were not populated entirely by Europeans and Africans: native Americans in both regions very commonly employed bands of diamonds to decorate smoking pipes.[69] Third, the *kwardata* and other symbols found on Ga'anda pottery systematically reinforced the goals of social perpetuation that informed *Hleeta* itself. In contrast, enslaved communities in the Americas did not practise scarification; to paraphrase Smallwood, its presence was isolated to, and dependent upon, the saltwater bodies flowing into the Americas in tune with the unpredictable rhythm of the slave trade itself.[70] This unpredictability, allied with the passage of time, presents significant challenges for those arguing for direct correlations between West African scarification patterns and New World ceramics.

Anthropological work has drawn attention to the impact of the slave trade and subsequent European colonialism upon such practices, and on the role of scarification in identify formation. Ojo's discussion of Yoruba scarification is particularly instructive here. Ojo argues that the expansion of the Oyo empire during the eighteenth century prompted a 'Yorubarization' of different groups with multiple ethnicities. He demonstrates that, by the early nineteenth century, scarification, performed on wives who were not of Yoruba birth, was being actively employed as a symbol of citizenship in this quest for a 'pan-Yoruban' geo-cultural ethnic identity.[71] Ethnogenesis did not wholly take place in the diaspora, in other words: it happened in West Africa too. This point, alongside the startling variety of scarification patterns that Ojo shows to have been employed by some Yoruba in the nineteenth century, provides a reminder that caution is required when attempts are made to map specific scarification patterns onto specific ethnic groups in the diaspora.

A recent study proposing correlations between scarification marks and pottery decorations in Brazil amplifies this point.[72] The authors demonstrate that scarification motifs employed (in Africa) by the Yoruba were replicated on eighteenth- and nineteenth-century ceramic pipes and other artefacts: but, as they also suggest, these symbols had no single, fixed meaning within the diaspora. Motifs changed meaning in Brazil, and were employed fluidly in constructing new ethnic identities, expressed in and through pottery and pipe decoration. Large numbers of Yoruba were imported to Salvador in the later eighteenth and nineteenth centuries, arriving via four slaving ports in the Bight of Benin: Ouidah, Badagry, Porto Novo, and, above all, Lagos. During the nineteenth century, the term 'Nagô' was adopted as a generic descriptor for these Yoruba-speaking peoples.[73] Nagô communities were very strongly bonded and played an important part in the numerous slave rebellions that took place in Salvador. It is likely that the scarification designs re-employed on artefacts here played some part in reinforcing emergent interactive—and resistant—networks among Nagô tobacco workers, not all of whom were of Yoruba origin.[74] Whatever the case, the key point here is that Yoruban scarification marks, as employed in Brazil, took on new, socially inclusive meanings in the context of the emergence of the Nagô 'nation'.

In a second example of recent work from Brazil, in this case by Luis Symanski, a nuanced case is made that, in the later eighteenth and nineteenth centuries, slaves in the Chapada dos Guimaräes region replicated on their ceramics some distinctive scarification patterns employed by the Benguela of Central Angola. The proportion of Benguela in this region was particularly high (57 per cent in the early nineteenth century), and, significantly, many of these individuals were women: in many African societies, pottery-making was the preserve of women. In Brazil, as in the Caribbean, African-born slaves were considered to be of lower status.[75] As a result, scarification (which marked out the body as African) was not practised by those born in Brazil. Symanski's persuasive argument is that markings that could no longer be replicated on the body retained their importance nonetheless, and were both remembered and re-membered in ceramic form:

> Although African slaves were unable to reproduce these symbols on the bodies of their descendants, they could do it on the bodies of their ceramic vessels. When the slaves of Chapada applied African-influenced designs to their pottery, they therefore not only reproduced African-derived aesthetics and systems of beliefs, but also an ideal African body which could no longer be reproduced in their new environment.[76]

The idealized Africa of the displaced in Brazil was, as Symanski notes, 'called Aluanda, an allusion to St Paul Luanda, capital of Angola, and the only African port for [the] slave trade that remained in the collective memory of the African Brazilians'.[77] It was an Africa, in other words, last seen from the deck of the slave ship.

Albeit limited in number, and open to alternative interpretations, studies like those above suggest that the scarification marks present on saltwater bodies might have played greater part in nascent ethnic self-identification in the diaspora than some historians are prepared to allow. It is worth noting in this context that other historians have advanced arguments that resonate with recent archaeological findings. Michael Gomez, for example, influentially suggested for the USA that the importance of scarification diminished over time, as the imposed notion of race obliged enslaved communities to redefine their collective identity in ways less centred on African ethnicities.[78] Even so, my own sense is that Lovejoy's assessment that scarification practices did not survive in the diaspora because they represented an iconography of a *hidden* past has merit with specific reference to the negative perceptions of saltwater slavery with which this analysis began, and which are also central to Symanski's argument concerning the transference of body markings to ceramics.[79] Lovejoy puts it this way: 'In a sense being "creole" meant not having the scarifications of Africa.'[80] I would suggest, more specifically, that lacking the scarifications of Africa signified 'not having experienced the slave ship'.

Bioarchaeology and the Diaspora

Scarification marks were visible to the naked eye and, as argued in Chapter 9, informed slave ship crews' and surgeons' understandings of African bodily difference. Though mariners were entirely unaware of it, their captives carried other equally indelible, but entirely invisible, biological indices of their birthplace in their teeth, bones, and DNA. A brief description of these techniques is necessary before taking a more detailed look at the small group of diasporic individuals who have been identified as African born by such means. First, by determining the isotopic ratios within the tooth enamel and bone collagen of excavated human remains, it is now possible in some archaeological contexts to gain an understanding of a deceased person's region of origin, and subsequent residency. When excavated bodies are subject to this kind of analysis, samples are generally taken from the permanent third molar, representing an enamel development period of 9–13 years of age. Strontium (^{87}Sr/^{88}Sr) values present in the teeth reflect the local geology of the birthplace of a person, incorporated into the body through local food. Oxygen (δ^{18}O) values similarly reflect the localized composition of ground water. Together, these values provide insights into childhood residency, and this makes it possible to determine whether an excavated individual was, or was not, born in Africa.

Second, DNA analysis (discussed in Chapter 2 with reference to recent work on the ancestry of modern populations in the Caribbean) is another rapidly developing science and has been employed on excavated bodies recovered from several sites discussed in this book, including the New York African Burial Ground and Newton Plantation, Barbados. In the 1990s, the New York African Burial Ground project led emerging practice in employing DNA analysis in the study of an African-descendant cemetery population. At this early stage, it was possible to analyse only short stretches of mitochondrial DNA (mtDNA), and the work was also hampered by lack of reference data from Africa, but, as discussed further below, molecular genetic affinities were established for forty-five individuals.[81] With the completion of the Human Genome Project in 2003, and the introduction of microarray technologies and high-throughput sequencing, the 'genomic turn in the reconstruction of African identities', as Sarah Abel and Hannes Schroeder have described it, has picked up even greater speed, and is promising unprecedented insights into the origins of African-descendant populations. But, as Abel and Schroeder also point out, most of these genetic surveys have

454   MATERIALIZING THE MIDDLE PASSAGE

focused on people of European ancestry: individuals of African descent account for only about 3 per cent of the total individuals included in genome-wide association studies.[82]

A third tool employed by archaeologists in determining African birth is dental modification—a characteristic (like scarification) that seventeenth- and eighteenth-century white observers invariably equated with African birth. Individuals with modified teeth were very frequently stated by their owners to be African; to belong to a specific African ethnic group (indicating African birth); or to be 'new negroes' (indicating a recent arrival from a slave ship).[83] Some of the very first Africans carried away from their homelands were taken to Portugal itself, and more than 60 per cent of the 158 bodies recovered from an urban dump at Valle da Garafia (Algarve), in use from the fifteenth to seventeenth centuries, exhibit dental modification.[84] Five of the individuals recovered from the first excavation at Newton Plantation, Barbados, in the 1970s had intentionally modified teeth.[85] Additional fieldwork undertaken from 1997–8 yielded a further twenty-five bodies, two of which also exhibited dental modification.[86] Isotope analysis has subsequently confirmed that both (and five other tested individuals) were African born.[87] In North America, twenty-six of the excavated individuals from the New York African Burial Ground exhibited dental modification.[88] A further 115 examples come from the 'liberated African' burial ground in Rupert's Valley, St Helena.[89] The St Helena dead provide a good deal of information concerning dental modification among nineteenth-century captives shipped from one African region. The TSTD data set demonstrates clearly that most of those enslaved between 1840 and 1867 (the last documented slave voyage) were shipped from Luanda and other Central African ports. While the Rupert Valley dead can thus be stated with some confidence to derive from Central Africa, nineteen separate modification types were present on their teeth—a point that emphasizes the variability of modification practices, even within single African regions. Attempts have been made to map specific modification designs onto named ethnic groups—most notably in the case of the New York African Burial Ground—but the results were inconclusive.[90] Dental modifications cannot be shown to have been region specific, and the most common form noted at Rupert Valley (a simple V-shape made by chipping the maxillary incisors) was used by at least five different ethnic groups in Cameroon and Nigeria alone.[91] The Rupert Valley data do, however, suggest that, in nineteenth–century Luanda at least, dental modification was associated with the onset of puberty: no examples were found on children under 10.[92]

In recent years, DNA testing, isotope analysis, and dental modification have been employed (often in conjunction) to confirm the African birth of a small number of the individuals whose skeletons have been recovered from slavery contexts in the Americas (summarized in Table 12). Newton Plantation, Barbados, offers a good case study in the combined use of these various techniques, as they have evolved over time. The cemetery was first excavated in the 1970s, when more than a hundred skeletons were uncovered.[93] Numerous pioneering bioarchaeological analyses of their teeth and bones have since been published, revealing important information on the health of the Newton Plantation slaves.[94] Further excavation was undertaken at Newton in 1997–8, and isotope analysis was subsequently performed on twenty-five skeletons recovered at that time.[95] The results suggest that the majority of the individuals

Table 12.1 African-born individuals from selected sites in the Americas

Site and approximate dates	No. verified as African born	Probable region of African origin	Reference
Campeche, Mexico 1550–1657	13 isotopic determinations (2012) Work published in 2006 considered 4 cases (all exhibiting dental modification)	Isoptopic determination (2006) suggests the Gold Coast for 3, fourth uncertain	Price et al. (2006) Price et al. (2012: 401, table 2)
Spring Bay Flat Plantation, Saba (Dutch Caribbean) Post-1650	1 (5 teeth from a single individual found in a burial cache)	Isotopic determination	Laffoon et al. (2018)
Zoutsteeg, St Martin Early–mid-1600s	3 (modified teeth)		Schroeder et al. (2014)
New York African Burial Ground 1690–1794	45 (DNA) 26 (modified teeth) 64 in total: 7 examples with both DNA and dental evidence	DNA analysis indicates multiple West African points of origin, and some via the Caribbean; macro-ethnic affiliations with the Fulba, Yoruba, Hausa and Mandinka peoples established for 14 individuals	DNA: Jackson et al. (2009) Teeth: Goodman et al. (2009)
Newton Plantation, Barbados Late seventeenth to nineteenth centuries	7 (modified teeth) 7 (isotopes)	Isotopic determinations: Gold Coast or Senegambia	Teeth: 5 examples from Handler et al. (1982); 2 from Schroeder et al. (2009) Isotopes: Schroeder et al. (2009)
Catedral de Sé de Salvador (San Salvador) 1550s–1856	11	Isotopic determinations—multiple regions of sub-Saharan Africa	Bastos et al. (2016)
Pretos Novos cemetery (Rio de Janeiro) 1769–1830	30	Isotopic determinations—multiple regions of sub-Sarahan Africa	Bastos et al. (2016)
Rupert Valley, St Helena 1840–67	115 (modified teeth)	Luanda, Central Africa	Witkin (2011: 63–72)

Note: The origins of these people have been determined through the presence of dental modification, and/or by isotopic and DNA analysis.

456   MATERIALIZING THE MIDDLE PASSAGE

excavated in the 1990s were born on the island, if not the estate itself. In seven cases, however, oxygen and strontium ratios in the tooth enamel are consistent with an African origin, strongly suggesting that these were first-generation captives brought to the island via the slave trade. These seven men and women did not all originate from the same part of Africa: the data suggest that they came from at least three different zones, possibly including the Gold Coast and Senegambia.

It might be thought that one obvious 'archaeological' way to investigate saltwater identity in the diaspora would be to focus on the material things associated the individuals in Table 12.1. Might not their associated grave goods, for example, reveal information about the owners' continuing relationship with Africa, their Middle Passage, and the people they became in the Americas? In fact, very few of those identified thus far as African born were interred with grave goods. Newton Plantation, Barbados, again provides an example. Some of the dead here were interred with artefacts: the best known of these is the necklace discussed in Chapter 1. Five of the bodies excavated at Newton in the 1970s exhibited dental modification, but their grave goods were meagre: B33 was interred with a complete (European) tobacco pipe, and B35 with a metal belt buckle (perhaps from his clothing), for example. Based on the sparse evidence currently available at Newton and elsewhere, there is very little to suggest that the funerary assemblages of the majority of saltwater captives differentiated them noticeably from others living in slavery in the Americas.[96] But it was so very difficult for the African born to carry personal possessions into the Americas (a point explored in Chapter 11) that it would be most unwise to read very much into this observation. That said, as seen in the discussion of the curated beads at St Helena in Chapter 11, a handful of burials *have* been suggested to yield both artefacts and human bodies of African origin. The last of my three concluding objects comes from one such internment.

An African-Born Woman's Beads

Between 1712 and 1794 an estimated fifteen thousand people were interred in New York's designated 'negro burial ground'. In the 1990s, the remains of more than four hundred of these individuals were uncovered by archaeologists. The string of waist or hip beads in Figure 12.3 was found in the grave of a woman (Burial 340) who was aged between 39 and 65 at death and died before 1735. Her teeth also show evidence of cultural modification, and she is one of the forty-eight individuals from this site whose molecular genetic affinities have since been determined (see Table 12.1). Her DNA indicates macro-ethnic affiliation to the FulBe (Fula), one of the largest ethnic groups in West Africa.[97] While her precise affiliation within this very large ethnic group cannot be determined, it is extremely likely, though not absolutely certain, that she crossed the Atlantic on a slave ship. What part did her voyage play in shaping her identity in the diaspora, and how was the journey remembered in later life? These questions are not at all easy to address.

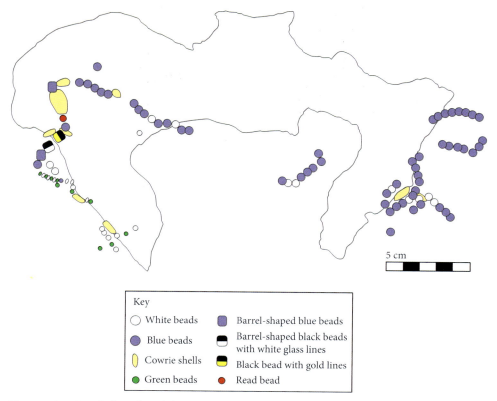

Figure 12.3 Beads found with burial B340, New York African Burial Ground. The beads circle the hips of the deceased woman, whose pelvic bones are shown in grey.
Adapted by Caron Newman from Bianco, DeCorse, and Howson (2006) Fig. 299.

Two bead strings were found in the woman's grave. The first, around her wrist, comprised forty-one beads. The second, seen in Figure 12.3, encircled her hips and incorporated seventy European-made glass beads, another of amber, and seven cowrie shells.[98] The string was positioned on the body in a way that clearly referenced West African practice: women in many regions wore waist or hip beads, as indicators of spirituality, status, and wealth, and to emphasize their figures and procreative roles.[99] Given the DNA and dental evidence indicative of African birth, and the maintenance of African tradition demonstrated by the use and placement of the beads, it is easy to appreciate why scholars of the diaspora regularly refer to Burial 340 and her grave goods as supporting the contention, as Michael Gomez put it, that 'home remained Africa for the African born'.[100]

Several hypotheses may in fact be offered as to why this woman was buried with these beads. Each opens different possibilities concerning her social identity, her Middle Passage, and the part her curated beads played in shaping and materializing an aggregated identity. First, as archaeology lecturers repeatedly remind their students, the dead do not bury themselves. It is possible that the woman was gifted the beads in death, by one of more of the people who interred and revered her. Second, Burial 340 may have accumulated the beads herself—as gifts, through barter, or as market purchases—over the course of a lifetime in North America. She was middle-aged when she died, and if, like many West African females, she had been captured at around the age of puberty, must have accumulated experiences, memories, relationships, offspring, and perhaps also beads, over several decades in North America. A third possibility exists: that some or all of her glass beads may have crossed the ocean with her during the enforced voyage from her homeland.[101] As examined in Chapter 11, Africans could sometimes retain small personal items during the Middle Passage, and some of Burial 340's beads might well fall into this category.[102] But, wherever she acquired them, almost all of her beads had been *manufactured* in Europe. By the time this woman left West Africa, the region had been receiving foreign beads as trade goods for more than two hundred years, and, as shown in Chapter 7, tiny European 'seed' beads were widely employed in bartering for captives and became firmly embedded in African use as a result. The seven cowries from this grave belong to a second category of exogenous material entering Africa through trade. Cowries are regularly framed as exemplifying African practice in the diaspora, but, because the complexities of their circulation do not map easily onto conventional understandings of the triangular trade, they tend, as Stahl has argued, to 'disappear under the particularized surface of African practice'.[103] Yet, as was discussed in my Chapter 1, cowries were not only traded for human captives, but, having entered American ports on slave ships, circulated in local economies and were probably employed as an informal currency.[104]

A fourth option concerning these beads remains to be explored—one not, to date, considered in the archaeological literature on this grave. This is the possibility that the woman in Burial 340 acquired her beads and cowries *during* her Middle Passage. European seed beads and the means to string them were routinely distributed to captive women on boards slave ships, as discussed in Chapter 10. Perry and Woodruff have perceptively suggested that the cowries and other products of the sea found in this and other graves at the New York African Burial Ground may have been associated 'in a multivalent fashion with Africa, the Middle Passage, and the spirits of the ancestors'.[105] But an association with the Middle Passage—actual or conceptual— may as reasonably be posited for Burial 340's *glass* beads. If acquired at sea, these beads must surely have embodied complex and conflicting memories thereafter: a reminder of the traditions of bodily adornment practised in the woman's homeland, acquired during enforced removal from it.

Ultimately, of course, one can only make informed guesses as to what the beads found with Burial 340 reveal about social identity, attachment to homeland, or Middle Passage experience. My point here is that the current tendency among many archaeologists to foreground point of origin (and, thereby, birth ethnicity) in framing the diasporic identities of saltwater slaves means that the multiple subject positions of these individuals in the Americas are insufficiently explored. Moreover, because the New World ethnic identities of the enslaved tend to be conceptualized in terms of African persistence and authenticity—a position on ethnogenesis that Barbara Voss has rightly criticized as 'utopian'—the part that the Middle Passage might have played in shaping the aggregate identities of 'saltwater' captives such as Burial 340, or indeed of her descendants, is very rarely considered.[106] Voss has recently argued that the increasing dependence on bioarchaeology in ethnogenesis research 'unwittingly reinforces racialized models of identity that locate the "truth" of social identity in the body'.[107] Abel and Schroeder have said similarly of DNA analysis that it poses significant challenges in terms of 'translating genetic findings into historically significant terms without reifying the correspondence between genetic and social identities'.[108] To return to Burial 340, reinterred in the renamed New York *African Burial Ground*, it seems clear that the complex life history and aggregated social identity of this woman through her Middle Passage and onward journey through adult life have been subsumed beneath a reading of identity giving primacy to the scientific evidence that points to her African birth—a recovery of her past that can only be regarded as partial.

In his fascinating biography of the banjo, discussed in Chapter 11, Laurent DuBois argued eloquently that the 'first African instrument' was not invented in Africa and is not derived from the traditions of a single African ethnicity. Instead, it is the 'child of the Middle Passage and the bewildering situation of exile and oppression in the plantation world'.[109] Much the same might be said of every saltwater captive, Burial 340 among them, who survived the voyage into slavery. The challenge for archaeologists, of course, is to acknowledge these complexities and to factor in the Middle Passage, alongside homeland and point of embarkation, in analysing the remains and belongings of these African-born, mid-Atlantic creoles whose identities were shaped, in no small part, by the slave ships that carried them from one continent to another.

Re-Membering The Witch Craft: The African Middle Passage Today

Andrew Apter and Lauren Derby's recent collection of papers exploring history and memory in the Atlantic world opens with a passage from the African American dancer Katherine Dunham's ethnographic memoir *Island Possessed*.[110] Detailing her initiation into Haitian vodun in 1936, Dunham describes 'lying on a dirt floor, spoon fashion', tightly interlocked with eight other initiates, on the second of three days of ritual isolation. The woman next to her was invited by the priestess to open herself to the spirt Papa Ghede, and in so doing lost control of her bladder. As she lay on the damp floor, all movement forbidden, waiting for the spirit to enter her own body, Dunham was soaked in her neighbour's urine. The baptismal ritual Dunham experienced marked her transition from *bosal* (outsider) to vodun initiate; and we have already seen that, at the time of the slave trade to Haiti, *bosal/bozal* had another meaning, being a common term in the Spanish Americas for a saltwater slave, newly arrived but unbaptized. Apter and Derby suggest that '[w]hat we glimpse in this extraordinary passage [by Dunham] is nothing less than the Middle Passage, a ritualised palimpsest of the transhipment of slaves, packed "spoon fashion" in the fetid holds of slavers carrying their cargoes to the Americas'.[111]

But this 'glimpse' of the Middle Passage occurs at a considerable distance in time, space, and context from the experiences of the twelve million saltwater captives who personally endured it. Dunham's experience can, of course, be read in many ways. For Apter and Derby, Dunham tugged at a thread of cultural memory stretching, hidden yet unbroken, to the deck of the slave ship. But, for other scholars, these Middle Passage 'memories' are not historical facts in deep storage, but history reworked (or re-membered) in the present by descendant generations, and—as ethnographic objects— by scholars. Certainly, by inserting herself into Haitian ritual, in an effort to cross the emic/etic divide separating the ethnographer from her object, Dunham might today be charged with producing a 'true fiction', or with 'cooking' history by creating a compromised, ethnographic co-production that muddies the waters of Middle Passage memory.[112]

In their work on Afro-Cuban religion, the anthropologists Stephan Palmié and David Brown have drawn attention to a phenomenon that Brown calls the motif of transatlantic 'swallowed stones'. This is the tradition that the Yoruba priests credited with establishing the ifá cult in Cuba had 'swallowed' their orishas' divination signs— the *fundamentos* (foundation) of ifá, including palm nuts and stones—or had tied them around their waists, and carried them across the Atlantic on slave ships.[113] Brown has documented several such stories, one of which concerns Remigio Herrera (better known by the Yoruba name Adechina), who died in 1905 and is celebrated as the African-born *fundamento* (foundation) of the cult of ifá in Cuba. Immediately before his capture, Adechina is said to have 'swallowed his ifa' (in this case sacred nut kernels) which were then defecated, guarded on the slave ship, and reconstituted in Cuba. Tempting though it might have been to draw attention to this belief in my discussion, in Chapter 11, of *minkisi* and other objects of power employed and created on board slave ships, I did not do so. Why not? Because, as ethnographic research has clearly demonstrated, this motif cannot simply be accepted as *bonafide* 'memory' of African experience during the Middle Passage: it is firmly located in the memory work of 1890–1905, the crucial period in which the descent and authority of the *fundamentos* of the ifá cult were established.[114] This is not to suggest that the Middle Passage was lacking in either stones or objects of divinatory power; it is rather to argue, as I did in Chapter 11, that its objects of power should be understood as the contingent product of the African saltwater experience.[115] If the 'swallowed stones' motif is telling us any-thing about the African experience of the Middle Passage, it is that it is surely time to step away from what David Scott called the 'verificationist paradigm' obliging a primary focus on locating a foundational African past and to enter the unique, third space that was the voyage into slavery, and its cultural outcomes.[116]

If we step away from concerns about the *veracity* of Dunham's experience, or that of Adechina, and focus (as archaeologists are inclined to do) on the *context* in which both were articulated, it is surely a point of some significance that, since at least the nineteenth century, and from North America and the Caribbean to West Africa, efforts by descendant communities to remember, or re-member, the slave trade as experienced by their ancestors principally take place in ritual contexts. The growing body of work on this phenomenon has focused largely on recent and current memories of the slave trade within West Africa, but some studies have had a more explicit focus on re-memberings of the Middle Passage in the practices of the living, creole religions of the diaspora, including Santeria, Candomblé, and Vodun.[117] I have already noted that the voyage is re-membered in the initiation rites of Haitian vodun and the 'swallowed stones' of ifá, but it is evoked elsewhere too. Indeed, as Monica Schuler has argued, a survey of Yoruba, West Central African, Fon, and Ewe-inspired initiation rituals in the Caribbean and North America reveals multiple 'episodes resembling the quintessential African slave ship voyage' in which 'melancholic and listless victims enduring head-shaving, fasting and other physical and sensory privations' and experienced incarceration in a hot crowded room while lying on the floor.[118] Katherine Dunham may have inserted herself into a Haitian ritual as an outsider looking in, but in so doing she shared in an embodied form of the memorialization of the slaving voyage that was, and still is, widely practised today. The slave ship itself is occasionally materialized in the rituals of the Americas too: in the boat-shaped shrine dedicated to the Candomblé orixa Oxum in the Casa Branca cult house of Bahia, for example.[119] It is also said to be evoked in the ship-shaped headdresses employed in Jamaican Jonkonnu masquerades in the 1930s, the West African correlates of which were discussed in Chapter 6.[120]

In short, there is much to suggest that Middle Passage memory work is firmly located today in performative rituals, and resides within what Apter and Derby refer to as 'a restricted archive of hidden histories'.[121] But my final argument—the one to which this concluding chapter has been drawing throughout, in its analysis of the evasive quality of the Middle Passage as endured by millions of Africans—is that the journey and its horrors have not *retreated* into that space over time. On the contrary, in researching and writing this book I have come to see that the remembered, and re-membered, voyage into slavery has *always* been located there, in the emic ritual arena in which it was easier to articulate—obliquely and collectively—that which could not readily be voiced directly, or individually.

I want to end by drawing on William van Norman's discussion of the experiences of nineteenth-century Cuban *bozales*—an analysis that provides a possible route to understanding why the memory work of the African Middle Passage has always been situated in the ritual arena.[122] Van Norman proposes that Victor Turner's influential three-stage model for the ritual process—successively separation, a liminal phase, and reincorporation—provides a useful analogue for understanding the transformations experienced by saltwater captives. Captivity (separation from homeland and kin) was followed by the Middle Passage; a liminal ordeal of the most extreme kind, disconnected from time and space. In turn, liminality was succeeded by reinscription, whereby captives emerged with new understandings of culture and identity.[123] As van Norman expressed it, borrowing a metaphor from Bhabha's *Location of Culture*: 'As a stairwell or hallway connects two rooms but is of neither place, so was the voyage.'[124]

This bringing-together of ideas—and of Turner's and Bhabha's understandings of the cultural significance of the between spaces in which, as Turner put it, 'the past has lost its grip and the future has not yet taken definite shape'—speaks powerfully to the themes and concepts underpinning *Materializing the Middle Passage*.[125] In my view, this conjunction elegantly captures, and provides a rationale for, the two essential characteristics of the Middle Passage: its liminality, and its re-membering today primarily through ritual strategies.[126] The *African* Middle Passage is now, and always has been, difficult for the scholar—whether ethnographer, historian, or historical archaeologist—to locate. Why is it so elusive? Because, for the saltwater captives who lived through it and remembered it, just as for their descendants who have successively re-lived and re-membered it, the Middle Passage has always existed in a liminal or third space of creativity—a space somewhere between the imperative to recall and the need to forget.

Notes

1. Gomer's life and gravestone are discussed in Knoblock (2015: 116–17). This is the only gravestone in any New England cemetery to specify the birthplace of an African-born individual.
2. Garvey (1999: 257).
3. Gomez (1998: 14).
4. Smallwood (2007b: 7); Gomez (1998: 168, 189).
5. Long (1774: 410).
6. Smallwood (2007b: 7).
7. On the social memory of the slave trade within West Africa, see Austen (2001), Baum (1999), and Shaw (2002). Baum's seminal work among Diola-speakers in Senegal is an exception to the generalization that discursive oral traditions concerning the slave trade do not survive in West Africa. Shaw's landmark study of divination practices and understandings of witchcraft among Temne-speaking communities in Sierra Leone makes a persuasive case that Temne ritual practices and oral traditions articulate memories of the slave trade.
8. The ship is in fact the Liverpool snow *Yannemerais*: TSTD 91540.
9. Rediker (2007: 263–307, and esp. 305–7).
10. Edwards (1798: 160).
11. Curtin (1955: 26).
12. Mintz and Price (1992: 8, 42–4). Note that, in Costa Rica, shipmates referred to each other as *carabela*, using the Spanish version of the word *caravel* (a small ship): Hawthorne (2008: 73, n. 8).
13. Mintz and Price (1992: 43).
14. Mintz and Price (1992: 44).
15. Sweet (2013: 259).
16. Bennett (2005: 120–5).
17. Borucki (2013); see also Borucki (2015: 57–83).
18. Borucki (2013: 226, 231; 2015: 70).
19. Borucki (2013: 238).
20. Sweet (2003: 33).
21. TSTD 265; discussed in Hawthorne (2008; 2010: 132–3).
22. Hawthorne (2008: 68–70).

THE MIDDLE PASSAGE RE-MEMBERED   463

23. TSTD 1760.
24. Nelson (2015: 361). In all, twelve *Brilhante* captives went on the run, five of them in the same month in 1839. As Nelson suggests, this implies that they may have been working in collaboration.
25. Nelson (2015: 362).
26. Hawthorne (2010: 132).
27. Hall (1989: 18).
28. Hall (1989: 124, 193).
29. Hall (1989: 135); Jones (2007: 96, 101).
30. Mullin (1994: 32 and *passim*).
31. *Cornwall Chronicle*, 30 November 1776. The man, renamed Huntly, had arrived in Jamaica on 12 December 1775: TSTD 92522. Many of the Jamaican advertisements discussed in this section can be found in Chambers (2013) and Mullin (1994).
32. TSTD 83866, master Edward Crosby.
33. This is likely to be TSTD 83862, which arrived at Kingston from Ouidah in March 1801.
34. Probably TSTD 83864, which arrived at Kingston from the Gold Coast and Ouidah in September 1803. The advertisement was placed on 8 October 1803. One month later, a further advertisement was placed regarding a 'New Negro Woman, of the Gold Coast Country', who had also arrived on *Trusty* and must have shared her voyage with this man.
35. Mullin (1994: 32).
36. *Cornwall Chronicle*, 28 October 1785.
37. *Cornwall Chronicle*, 16 December 1793.
38. *Antigua Gazette*, 27 December 1798.
39. *Antigua Gazette*, 28 November 1798.
40. Hawthorne (2008: 56).
41. As sensibly advocated by Borucki (2015: 61). It is also, of course, the argument originally proposed by Mintz and Price.
42. For discussion of these debts, see Ogude (1982), Carretta (2005: 313–15), and McBride (2001: 129–31). For counter-arguments, see Byrd (2006) and Lovejoy (2006a).
43. Carretta (1999). One of these documents (Carretta 1999: 102) is the parish register of St Margaret's church, Westminster, which records the baptism on 9 February 1759 of 'Gustavus Vassa a Black born in Carolina 12 years old'. For further discussion, see Carretta (2003).
44. See, e.g., Byrd (2006), Lovejoy (2006a, 2007), and Caretta (2007). For Equiano's importance as a source on the intercontinental slave trade between the Caribbean and the North American mainland (in which he worked as an enslaved sailor), see O'Malley (2014: 33–4).
45. Rediker (2007: 109).
46. Attempting to reconcile some of the discrepancies in the ages and dates Equiano records in his *Narrative* and the external documentary evidence, Carretta (1999: 100) raised the possibility that the boy may have arrived in Barbados in 1754 on the Liverpool snow *Ogden* (TSTD 90473). If this were the case, Equiano would have been around nine years old. As discussed in Chapters 10 and 11, pre-pubescent boys were deemed too old to be placed in the women's room on British ships of this era and could have spent their nights in several different places, including on temporary elevated decks and in crawl spaces under the booms. By 1754 some British vessels, including Newton's *Duke of Argyle* (see Table 5.4), were also employing boys' rooms. None of these spaces are mentioned in *Interesting Narrative*, where the author states simply that he was 'put down under the decks' (Equiano 1789: 73).
47. Carretta (2005: 264).
48. Carretta (2005: 265–6).
49. Carretta (2007: 116).
50. Cugoano (1787: 10).

464 MATERIALIZING THE MIDDLE PASSAGE

51. Similarly brief references to a Middle Passage crossing to Barbados can be found in Gronniosaw (1770: 16–17), Smith (1798: 13), and in the unpublished, fragmentary 'Memoir of the Life of Florence Hall' discussed by Browne and Sweet (2016). Born in Nigeria, Gronniosaw had been sold into slavery as a child and was bought by a wealthy New York family. He arrived in England in around 1762, and for a time (like Ottoabah Cugoano) was the house 'servant' of Richard Cosway. Gronniosaw's Middle Passage was unusual, in that the boy served as the personal attendant of the master of the Dutch ship on which he was transported. Venture Smith, whose *Narrative* was published in 1798, says only of his Middle Passage crossing to Barbados at the age of 8 that: 'After an ordinary passage, except great mortality by the small pox, which broke out on board, we arrived at the island of Barbadoes: but when we reached it, there were found out of the two hundred and sixty that sailed from Africa, not more than two hundred alive' (Smith 1798: 13). Florence Hall's 'Memoirs', preserved in the papers of the Jamaican plantation owner Robert Johnson, and probably recorded in the early decades of the nineteenth century, contains a slightly more detailed account of a Middle Passage crossing from the Bight of Biafra to Jamaica: this was cited in full in Chapter 3.
52. Mullin (1994: 29, n. 39), citing BNA: PRO, War Office/25/644/, 118.
53. Mullin (1994: 28).
54. Keefer (2013: 541). Ojo's phrase (2008: 370) 'cultural passport' best captures the social significance of scarification among Africans.
55. Mullin (1994: 29).
56. Mullin (1994: 28).
57. Northrup (2000); Torres de Souza and Agostini (2012: 104).
58. Borucki (2013: 238; emphasis added).
59. Heath (1999: 50).
60. Handler et al. (1982: 306).
61. Lovejoy (2010: 99).
62. Lovejoy (2010: 100).
63. See, e.g., Handler (1994: 113–19) and Gomez (1998: 39).
64. Handler et al. (1982: 309), citing Price and Price's discussion (1972: 14) of scarification among the Sarakama of Suriname. Richard Price was, of course, one of the architects of linguistic creolization theory: code-switching is another useful linguistic term from the lexicon of that body of theory.
65. Berns (1988: 68–72).
66. Evidence for such practices is collated in Gosselain (1999).
67. Emerson (1994, 1999), and (*contra*); Mouer et al. (1999). A recent study concerning stoneware vessels made by African-America potters in Edgefield District, South Carolina, has also drawn attention to slash and punctate marks, which, it is argued, 'mimic and suggest West African scarification' (Joseph 2017: see esp. 126–8).
68. Emerson (1999: 60, figs 4.9 and 4.10).
69. Mouer et al. (1999: 105–6).
70. Smallwood (2007b: 7).
71. Ojo (2008: 349, 367–9).
72. Torres de Souza and Agostini (2012).
73. Law (2005: 260).
74. Torres de Souza and Agostini (2012: 110–11).
75. Symanski (2012: 137).
76. Symanski (2012: 137).
77. Symanski (2012: 144).
78. Gomez (1998) argues for the American south, for example, that the affinities and differences between those born in Africa and those born in the Americas became less important in shaping slave identities than a growing sense of a shared African-American identity, the transition between the two being marked by the Denmark Vesey insurrection of 1822.

THE MIDDLE PASSAGE RE-MEMBERED   465

79. Symanski (2012: 137).
80. Lovejoy (2010: 118).
81. Jackson et al. (2009: 90–1, table 7).
82. Abel and Schroeder (2020: 201). For an overview of work undertaken since 2000 on the genetic history of African descendant populations in the Americas, see Fortes-Lima and Verdu (2021).
83. Handler (1994: 116–17).
84. The earliest deposits here date to the fifteenth century and the latest to the seventeenth. The most common form of modification comprised excision: see Rufino (2014: 14).
85. Handler (1994: 117).
86. Schroeder et al. (2009: 559, table 2).
87. Schroeder and Shuler (2006: 6).
88. Goodman et al. (2009: 108, table 12).
89. Witkin (2011: 63–72).
90. Goodman et al. (2009: 107–8).
91. Witkin (2011: 69).
92. Witkin (2011: 68).
93. Handler and Lange (1978).
94. Corruccini et al. (1987), Corruccini et al. (1989); Jacobi et al. (1992).
95. Schroeder et al. (2009).
96. One interesting anomaly is the cache of five disarticulated human teeth (from a single individual) buried in a wooden lockbox with several iron nails, a shell, and assorted isolated animal bones on the Dutch island of Saba. Laffoon et al. (2018) interpret this as a 'burial cache' but other interpretations are possible.
97. Jackson et al. (2009: 91).
98. None of the women's beads is made from powdered glass, but such beads were found with burials 226 and 434: see Bianco et al. (2006: 369). Burial 226 was certainly African born, as evidenced through DNA analysis: Jackson et al. (2009: 91).
99. La Roche (1994: 13–15) provides a summary of bead use in West and Central Africa
100. Gomez (1998: 14). LaRoche (1994: 17) suggested with reference to Burial 340 that her modified teeth and *in situ* waist beads indicate that she 'died and was buried before she had become acculturated'.
101. This was first suggested by LaRoche (1994: 16).
102. Two other adults at NYABG each had a single bead, and twenty-two drawn black beads, again of European manufacture, encircled the hips of a child (Burial 187).
103. Stahl (2015: 74).
104. See Heath (2016) for a detailed analysis of 353 cowries recovered from 55 sites in Virginia, only 8% of which were found in plantation contexts.
105. Perry and Woodruff (2006: 428).
106. Voss (2015: 656).
107. Voss (2015: 663).
108. Abel and Schroeder (2020: 198).
109. Dubois (2016: 52).
110. Dunham (1994).
111. Apter and Derby (2010a: p. xvi).
112. On ethnographic 'true fiction', see Clifford and Marcus (1986: 7); for an important recent study of the 'cooking' of history by anthropologists, see Palmié (2013).
113. Brown (2003: 77–80, 144).
114. Brown (2003: 144); Palmié (2013: 47–8).
115. See also here Palmié's discussion (2010) of the belief that the Cuban Abakuá male secret sodality originated with members of a Calabari Epke society carried to Havana. This excellent empirical

466 MATERIALIZING THE MIDDLE PASSAGE

case study, exploring the 'Middle Passage' of an African institution that was, in effect an Atlantic creole before it even arrived in Cuba, has been particularly helpful in shaping my thinking, both here and in Chapter 1.

116. Scott (1999: 108); Palmié (2013: 33–77 and esp. 46).
117. Examples here, in addition to the numerous papers in Apter and Derby (2010b), include Baum (1999), Shaw (2002), and Schuler (2005). On the place of Middle Passage 'ritual re-enactment' and embodied performance in diasporic North American Christianity, see Woolfork's discussion (2010: 132–58) of *Maafa* commemoration.
118. Schuler (2005: 191).
119. Parés (2010: 74).
120. Nunley (2010: 56).
121. Apter and Derby (2010a: p. xvi).
122. van Norman (2005).
123. This model is set out in Turner (1969).
124. van Norman (2005: 185). The stairwell metaphor is taken from Bhabha (1994: 4).
125. Turner (1992: 132): an introductory comment from a previously unpublished essay, published after Turner's death.
126. For further consideration of the concept of liminality in the work of both Turner and Bhabha, in this case employed in considering postcolonial African identity, see Kalua (2009).

References

A New General Collection of Voyages and Travels, Volume 2 (1745). London: Printed for Thomas Astley.

Abel, Sarah, and Hannes Schroeder (2020). 'From Country Marks to DNA Markers: The Genomic Turn in the Reconstruction of African Identities', *Current Anthropology*, 61, suppl. 22: 198–209.

Abrahams, Roger (1974). *Deep the Water, Shallow the Shore: Three Essays on Shantying in the West Indies*. Austin: University of Texas Press.

Adams, John (1822). *Sketches Taken during Ten Voyages to Africa between the Years 1786 and 1800*. London: Hurst, Robinson and Co.

Adams, Jonathan (2013). *A Maritime Archaeology of Ships: Innovation and Social Change in Late Medieval and Early Modern Europe*. Oxford: Oxbow.

Agorsah, E. Kofi, and Thomas Butler (2008). 'Archaeological Investigation of Historic Kormantse, Ghana: Cultural Identities', *African Diaspora Archaeology Newsletter*, 11/3, Article 1, https://scholarworks.umass.edu/adan/vol11/iss3/1 (accessed 14 June 2022).

Alden, Dauril, and Joseph Miller (1987). 'Out of Africa: The Slave Trade and the Transmission of Smallpox to Brazil, 1560–1831', *Journal of Interdisciplinary History*, 18/2: 195–224.

Allan, David, and Robert Schofield (1980). *Stephen Hales: Scientist and Philanthropist*. London: Scholar Press.

Alpern, Stanley (1995). 'What Africans Got for Their Slaves: A Master List of European Trade Goods', *History in Africa*, 22: 5–43.

Alpern, Stanley (2013). 'Did Enslaved Africans Spark South Carolina's Eighteenth-Century Rice Boom?', in Robert Voeks and John Rashford (eds), *African Ethnobotany in the Americas*. New York: Springer, 35–66.

Alsop John (1990). 'Sea Surgeons, Health and England's Maritime Expansion', *Marnier's Mirror*, 76: 215–22.

Alsop, John (2012). 'Tudor Merchant Seafarers in the Early Guinea Trade', in Cheryl Fury (ed.), *The Social History of English Seamen 1485–1649*. Woodbridge: Boydell Press, 75–116.

Anon. (1773). *Genuine Receipt for Making the Famous Vernis Martin; or, as it is Called by the English, Martin's Copal Varnish*. Paris or ?London: printer not stated.

Anderson, Martha, and Philip Peek (2002). 'Ways of the Rivers: Arts and Environment of the Niger Delta', *African Arts*, 35/1: 12–25.

Anderson, Richard, and Henry Lovejoy (2020) (eds). *Liberated Africans and the Abolition of the Slave Trade 1807–1896*. Woodbridge: Boydell & Brewer.

Appleby, John (1995). '"A Business of Much Difficulty": A London Slaving Venture 1651–1654', *Mariner's Mirror*, 8/1: 3–14.

Apter, Andrew, and Lauren Derby (2010a). 'Introduction', in Andrew Apter and Lauren Derby (eds), *Activating the Past: History and Memory in the Black Atlantic World*. Newcastle: Cambridge Scholars Publishing, pp. xiii–xxxiii.

Apter, Andrew, and Lauren Derby (2010b), (eds). *Activating the Past: History and Memory in the Black Atlantic World*. Newcastle: Cambridge Scholars Publishing.

Arnott, Georgina (2022). 'Slavery, Trade and Settler Colonialism: The Stirling Family and Britain's Empire, c.1730–1840', *Australian Journal of Biography and History*, 6: 51–78.

Atkins, John (1734). *The Navy-Surgeon, or a Practical System of Surgery*. London: printed for Caesar Ward and Richard Chandler.

Atkins, John (1735). *Voyage to Guinea, Brasil and the West Indies: In His Majesty's Ships the Swallow and Weymouth*. London: printed for Caesar Ward and Richard Chandler.

Aubrey, T. (1729). *The Sea Surgeon, or the Guinea Man's Vade Mecum*. London: John Clarke.

Austen, Ralph (2001). 'The Slave Trade as History and Memory: Confrontations of Slaving Voyage Documents and Communal Traditions', *William and Mary Quarterly*, 58/1: 229–44.

468 REFERENCES

Axelrod Wisnes, Selena (2007). *Letters on West Africa and the Slave Trade: Paul Erdmann Isert's Journey to Guinea and the Caribbean Islands in Columbia (1788)*. Legon: Sub-Saharan Publishers.

Babalola, Abidemi Babatunde (2017). 'Ancient History of Technology in West Africa: The Indigenous Glass/Glass Bead Industry and the Society in Early Ile-Ife, Southwest Nigeria', *Journal of Black Studies*, 48/5: 501–27.

Babalola, Abidemi Babatunde, Susan Keech McIntosh, Laure Dussubieux, and Thilo Rehren (2017). 'Ile-Ife and Igbo Olokun in the History of Glass in West Africa', *Antiquity*, 91/357: 732–50.

Bailey, Guy, and Gary Ross (1988). 'The Shape of the Superstrate: Morphosyntactic Features of Ship English', *English World-Wide*, 9/2: 193–212.

Baker, Philip, and Peter Mühlhäusler (2007). 'Creole Linguistics from its Beginnings through Schuchardt to the Present Day', in Charles Stewart (ed.), *Creolization: History, Ethnography, Theory*. Walnut Creek: Left Coast Press, 84–107.

Ball, Charles (1837). *Slavery in the United States: A Narrative of the Life and Adventures of Charles Ball, A Black Man*. New York: John S. Taylor.

Balai, Leo (2011). *Het Slavenschip Leusden. Slavenschepen en de West-Indische Compagnie, 1720-1738*. Zutphen: Walburg Press.

Balai, Leo (2014). *Slave Ship Leusden: A Story of Mutiny, Shipwreck and Murder*. Kindle Edition (2014), https://www.amazon.co.uk/Slave-Ship-Leusden-Mutiny-Shipwreck-ebook/dp/B00J9UMY2O (accessed 27 October 2022).

Ballardie, Margaret (1998). 'Japanning in Seventeenth- and Eighteenth-Century Europe', in Valerie Dorge and F. Carey Howlett (eds), *Painted Wood: History and Conservation*. Los Angles: Getty Publications, 179–85.

Barile, Kerri (2004). 'Hegemony Within the Household: The Perspective from a South Carolina Plantation', in Kerri Barile and Jamie and Brandon (eds), *Household Chores and Household Choices: Theorizing the Domestic Sphere in Historical Archaeology*. Tuscaloosa: University of Alabama Press, 121–137.

Barker, Patrick, and Graeme Henderson (1979). '*James Matthews* Excavation: A Second Interim Report', *International Journal of Nautical Archaeology*, 8: 225–44.

Barker, Robert (1758). *The Unfortunate Shipwright, or, Cruel Captain, being a Faithful Narrative of the Unparalleled Sufferings of Robert Barker, Late Carpenter on Board the Thetis Snow of Bristol; on a Voyage from Thence to the Coast of Guinea and Antigua*. London: printed for and sold by the author.

Barker, Robert (1809). *The Genuine Life of Robert Barker, Dictated by Himself While in a State of Total Darkness*. London: printed by Galbin and Marchant for the author.

Barley, Nigel (1988). *Foreheads of the Dead: An Anthropological View of Kalabari Ancestral Screens*. Washington: Smithsonian Institution Press.

Barley, Nigel (2000). 'West Africa', in John Mack (ed.), *Africa. Arts and Cultures*. London: British Museum Press, 85–123.

Bartlet, John (1764). *Pharmacopaeia Hippiatrica, or, The Gentleman Farrier's Repository of Elegat and Approved Redemdies for the Diseases of Horses*. Eton: J Pole.

Bassani, Ezio (2000). *African Art and Artefacts in European Collections 1400-1800*. Dorchester: British Museum Press.

Bassani, Ezio, William Fagg, Susan Mullin, and Carol Vogel (1988). *Africa and the Renaissance: Art in Ivory*. New York: Centre for African Art.

Bassani, Ezio, and Malcolm McLeod (1985). 'African Material in Early Collections', in Oliver Impey and Arthur MacGregor (eds), *The Origin of Museums: The Cabinets of Curiosities in Sixteenth and Seventeenth Century Europe*. Oxford: Oxford University Press, 245–50.

Bastos, Murilo, Ricardo Santos, Sheila de Souza, Claudia Rodrigues-Carvalho, Robert Tykot, Della Cook, and Roberto Santos (2016). 'Isotopic Study of Geographic Origins and Diet of Enslaved Africans Buried in Two Brazilian Cemeteries', *Journal of Archaeological Science*, 70: 82–90.

Basu, Paul (2011). 'Object Diasporas, Resourcing Communities: Sierra Leonean Collections in the Global Museum-scape', *Museum Anthropology*, 34/1: 28–42.

Baucom, Ian (2005). *Spectres of the Atlantic: Finance Capital, Slavery, and the Philosophy of History*. Durham, NC: Duke University Press.

Baum, Robert (1999). *Shrines of the Slave Trade: Diola Religion and Society in Precolonial Senegambia.* Oxford: Oxford University Press.

Behrendt, Stephen (1990). 'The Captains in the British Slave Trade from 1785–1807', *Transactions of the Historic Society of Lancashire and Cheshire,* 140: 79–140.

Behrendt, Stephen (1997). 'Crew Mortality in the Transatlantic Slave Trade in the Eighteenth Century', in David Eltis and David Richardson (eds), *Routes to Slavery: Direction, Ethnicity and Mortality in the Transatlantic Slave Trade.* London: Frank Cass, 49–71.

Behrendt, Stephen (2001). 'Markets, Transaction Cycles and Profits: Merchant Decision-Making in the British Slave Trade', *William and Mary Quarterly,* 58/1: 171–204.

Behrendt, Stephen (2004). 'Book Reviews', *Slavery & Abolition,* 25/1: 146–7.

Behrendt, Stephen (2007). 'Human Capital in the British Slave Trade', in David Richardson, Suzanne Schwarz, and Anthony Tibbles (eds), *Liverpool and Transatlantic Slavery.* Liverpool: Liverpool University Press, 66–97.

Behrendt, Stephen, David Eltis, and David Richardson (2001). 'The Costs of Coercion: African Agency in the Pre-Modern Atlantic World', *Economic History Review,* 54/3: 454–76.

Behrendt, Stephen, Anthony Latham, and David Northrup (2010). *The Diary of Antera Duke: An Eighteenth-Century Slave Trader.* Oxford: Oxford University Press.

Behrendt, Stephen, and Robert Hurley (2017). 'Liverpool as a Trading Port: Sailors' Residences, African Migrants, Occupational Change and Probated Wealth', *International Journal of Maritime History,* 29/4: 875–910.

Beisaw, April, and James Gibb (2009), (eds). *The Archaeology of Institutional Life.* Tuscaloosa: University of Alabama Press.

Bell, Richard (2012). 'Slave Suicide, Abolition and the Problem of Resistance', *Slavery & Abolition,* 33/4: 525–49.

Bennett, Herman (2005). *Africans in Colonial Mexico.* Bloomington: Indiana University Press.

Berg, Torsten, and Peter Berg (2001). *R. R. Angertstein's Illustrated Travel Diary 1735–1755.* London: Science Museum.

Berlin, Ira (1996). 'From Creole to African: Atlantic Creoles and the Origins of African-American Society in Mainland North America', *William and Mary Quarterly,* 53/2: 251–88.

Berns, Marla (1988). 'Ga'anda Scarification: A Model for Art and Identity', in Arnold Rubin (ed.), *Marks of Civilization: Artistic Transformations of the Human Body.* Los Angeles: Museum of Cultural History, 57–76.

Bethell, Leslie (1966). 'The Mixed Commissions for the Suppression of the Transatlantic Slave Trade in the Nineteenth Century', *Journal of African History,* 7/1: 79–93.

Bhabha, Homi (1985). 'Signs Taken for Wonders: Questions of Ambivalence and Authority under a Tree outside Delhi, May 1817', *Critical Inquiry,* 12/1: 144–65.

Bhabha, Homi (1990). 'The Third Space: Interview with Homi Bhabha', in Jonathon Rutherford (ed.), *Identity: Community, Culture, Divergence.* London: Lawrence & Wishart, 207–21.

Bhabha, Homi (1994). *The Location of Culture.* London: Routledge.

Bianco, Barbara, Christopher DeCorse, and Jean Howson (2006). 'Beads and Other Adornment', in Michael Blakey and Lesley Rankin-Hill (eds), *New York African Burial Ground Archaeology Final Report,* i. Washington: Howard University, 382–418.

Bialuschewski, Arne (2011). 'Anatomy of a Slave Insurrection: The Shipwreck of the *Vautour* on the West Coast of Madagascar in 1725', *French Colonial History,* 12: 87–101.

Biebuyck, Daniel, and Frank Herreman (1996). 'Central Africa', in Tom Phillips (ed.), *Africa: The Art of a Continent.* Munich: Prestel, 251–325.

Biveridge, Fritz (2018). 'Fort Metal Cross: Commercial Epicentre of the British on the Gold Coast', in John Osei-Tutu and Victoria Smith (eds), *Shadows of Empire in West Africa: African Histories and Modernities.* Cham: Palgrave Macmillan, 201–38.

Biveridge, Fritz (2020). 'Archaeological Manifestations of Cross-Cultural Encounters along the Dixcove Coastline, Western Region, Ghana', *Azania: Archaeological Research in Africa,* 55/2: 189–216.

Blackmun, Barbara (1988). 'From Trader to Priest in Two Hundred Years: The Transformation of a Foreign Figure on Benin Ivories', *Art Journal,* 47/2: 128–38.

470   REFERENCES

Blakemore, Richard (2015). 'West Africa in the British Atlantic: Trade, Violence, and Empire', *Itinerario*, 39/2: 299–327.

Blane, Gilbert (1785). *Observations on the Diseases Incident to Seamen*. London: printed by Joseph Cooper.

Blier, Suzanne Preston (1993). 'Imaging Otherness in Ivory: Portrayals of the Portuguese *c.*1492', *Art Bulletin*, 75/3: 375–96.

Blier, Suzanne Preston (2004). 'The Art of Assemblage: Aesthetic Expression and Social Experience in Danhome', *Res: Anthropology and Aesthetics*, 45/1: 186–210.

Bly, Antonio (1998). 'Crossing the Lake of Fire: Slave Resistance during the Middle Passage, 1720–1842', *Journal of Negro History*, 83/3: 178–86.

Boachie-Ansah, James (2008). 'Excavations at Fort Amsterdam, Abandze, Central Region, Ghana', in Timothy Insoll (ed.), *Current Archaeological Research in Ghana*, BAR Series 1874 International. Oxford: Archaeopress, 37–62.

Boachie-Ansah, James (2015). 'Preliminary Report on Excavation at Kormantin No. 1 in the Central Region of Ghana', *Nyame Akuma*, 83 (June): 23–39.

Bolster, W. Jeffrey (1997). *Black Jacks: African American Seamen in the Age of Sail*. Cambridge, MA: Harvard University Press.

Boog Watson, William (1969). 'The Guinea Trade and Some of its Surgeons', *Journal of the Royal College of Surgeons of Edinburgh*, 14/4: 203–14.

Bontick, Frans (1995). 'Les *Mindele*; Hommes d' Étoffes', *Annales Aequatoria*, 16: 135–52.

Borucki, Alex (2013). 'Shipmate Networks and Black Identities in the Marriage Files of Montevideo, 1768–1803', *Hispanic American Historical Review*, 93/2: 205–38.

Borucki, Alex (2015). *From Shipmates to Soldiers. Emerging Identities in the Rio de la Plata*. Albuquerque: University of New Mexico Press.

Borucki, Alex, David Eltis, and David Wheat (2015). 'Atlantic History and the Slave Trade to Spanish America', *American Historical Review*, 120/2: 433–61.

Bosman, Willem (1705). *A New and Accurate Description of the Coast of Guinea*. London: Printed for James Knapton.

Boshoff, Jaco (2018). 'The Search for the Slave Ship *Meermin*: Developing a Methodology for Finding Inter Tidal Shipwrecks', MA dissertation, University of South Africa.

Boys, William (1787). *An Account of the Loss of the Luxborough Galley, by Fire, on her Voyage from Jamaica to London: With the Sufferings of her Crew, in the Year 1727. By William Boys, Second Mate*. London: J. Johnson.

Boudriot, Jean (1984). *Traite et Navrire Négrier*. Paris: Collection Archaéologie Navale Française.

Brathwaite, Edward Kamau (2005 [1971]). *The Development of Creole Society in Jamaica 1770–1820*. 2nd edn, Kingston: Ian Randle Publishers.

Brathwaite, Edward Kamau (1973). *The Arrivants: A New World Trilogy*. Oxford: Oxford University Press.

Brathwaite, Edward Kamau (1981). *Folk Culture of the Slaves in Jamaica*. London: New Beacon Books.

Brooks, George (2003). *Eurafricans in West Africa*. Oxford: James Currey.

Brown, Christopher (2007). 'The British Government and the Slave Trade: Early Parliamentary Enquiries, 1713–83', *Parliamentary History*, 26/2: 27–41.

Brown, David (2003). *Santeria Enthroned: Art, Ritual and Innovation in an Afro-Cuban Religion*. Chicago: University of Chicago Press.

Brown, Vincent (2009). 'Social Death and Political Life in the Study of Slavery', *American Historical Review*, 114/5: 1231–49.

Browne, Randy (2017). *Surviving Slavery in the British Caribbean*. Philadelphia: University of Pennsylvania Press.

Browne, Randy, and John Wood Sweet (2016). 'Florence Hall's "Memoirs": Finding African Women in the Transatlantic Slave Trade', *Slavery & Abolition*, 37/1: 206–21.

Bruin, Iris (2009). *Ships' Surgeons of the Dutch East India Company*. Amsterdam: Leiden University Press.

Buffon, Georges (1779). *Histoire Naturelle des Oisseaux*, vi. Paris: Imprimerie Royale.

Bullman, E. (1789). *The Family Physician; or a Choice Collection of Approved Medicines, for the Cure of Every Disease Incident to the Human Body, with an Appendix of the Preparation of Medicines, Necessary for Private Use.* London: printed for the author.

Bullock, William (1810). *A Companion to Bullock's Museum.* 8th edn, London: Henry Reynell and Son.

Burnside, Madeline (2002). 'The *Henrietta Marie*', in Mariners' Museum, *Captive Passage: The Transatlantic Slave Trade and the Making of the Americas.* Washington: Smithsonian Institution Press, 77–97.

Burstein, Miriam (2020). 'A Forgotten Novel: John Riland's Memoirs of a West-India Planter (1827)', *Slavery & Abolition*, 41/3: 582–98.

Butterworth, William (1823). *Three Years Adventures, of a Minor, in England, Africa, the West Indies, South-Carolina and Georgia.* Leeds: Edward Baines.

Butterworth, William (1831). *Three Years Adventures, of a Minor, in England, Africa, the West Indies, South-Carolina and Georgia.* Leeds: Thos. Inchbold.

Byrd, Alexander (2006). 'Eboe, Country, Nation and Gustavus Vassa's Interesting Narrative', *William & Mary Quarterly* 63/1: 123–48.

Byrd, Alexander (2008). *Captives and Voyagers: Black Migrants across the Eighteenth-Century British Atlantic World.* Baton Rouge: Louisiana State University Press.

Byrn, John (1989). *Crime and Punishment in the Royal Navy: Discipline on the Leeward Islands Station, 1784–1812.* Aldershot: Scolar Press.

Byrne, Sarah, Anne Clarke, Rodney Harrison, and Robin Torrence (2011) (eds). *Unpacking the Collection.* New York: Springer.

Calvocoressi, David (1975a). 'Excavations at Komenda, Ghana', *West African Journal of Archaeology*, 5: 153–64.

Calvocoressi, David (1975b). 'European Trade Pipes in Ghana', *West African Journal of Archaeology*, 5: 195–200.

Calvocoressi, David (1977). 'Excavations at Bantama, near Elmina, Ghana', *West African Journal of Archaeology*, 7: 117–41.

Candido, Mariana (2010). 'Different Slave Journeys: Enslaved African Seamen on Board of Portuguese ships, *c.*1760–1820s', *Slavery & Abolition*, 31/3: 395–409.

Carey, Brycchan (2003). '"The extraordinary Negro": Ignatius Sancho, Joseph Jekyll, and the Problem of Biography', *British Journal for Eighteenth-Century Studies*, 26: 1–14.

Carlos, Ann, and Jamie Brown Kruse (1996). 'The Decline of the Royal African Company: Fringe Firms and the Role of the Charter', *Economic History Review*, 49/2: 291–313.

Carnes-McNaughton, Linda (2016). 'Mariners' Maladies: Examining Medical Equipage from the *Queen Anne's Revenge* Shipwreck', *North Carolina Archaeology*, 65: 28–52.

Carney, Judith (2001). *Black Rice: The African Origins of Rice Cultivation in the Americas.* Cambridge, MA: Harvard University Press.

Carney, Judith (2004). '"With Grains in her Hair": Rice in Colonial Brazil', *Slavery & Abolition*, 25/1: 1–27.

Carney, Judith (2007). 'Out of Africa: Colonial Rice History in the Black Atlantic', in Londa Schiebinger and Claudia Swan (eds), *Colonial Botany: Science, Commerce, and Politics in the Early Modern World.* Philadelphia: University of Pennsylvania Press, 204–20.

Carney, Judith (2013). 'Seeds of Memory: Botanical Memories of the African Diaspora', in Robert Voeks and John Rashford (eds), *African Ethnobotany in the Americas.* New York: Springer, 13–33.

Carretta, Vincent (1999). 'Olaudah Equiano or Gustavus Vassa? New Light on an Eighteenth-Century Question of Identity', *Slavery & Abolition*, 20/3: 96–105.

Carretta, Vincent (2003). 'Questioning the Identity of Olaudah Equiano, or Gustavus Vassa, the African', in Felicity Nussbaum (ed.), *The Global Eighteenth Century.* Baltimore: Johns Hopkins University Press, 226–35.

Carretta, Vincent (2005). *Equiano the African: Biography of a Self-Made Man.* Athens: University of Georgia Press.

Carretta, Vincent (2007). 'Response to Paul Lovejoy's "Autobiography and Memory: Gustavus Vassa, Alias Olaudah Equiano, the African"', *Slavery & Abolition*, 28/1: 115–19.

472   REFERENCES

Carretta, Vincent, and Philip Gould (2001) (eds). *Genius in Bondage: Literature of the Early Black Atlantic*. Kentucky: University Press of Kentucky.

Casella, Eleanor (2007). *The Archaeology of Institutional Confinement*. Gainsville: University Press of Florida.

Casella, Eleanor (2009). 'On the Enigma of Incarceration: Philosophical Approaches to Confinement in the Modern Era', in April Beisaw and James Gibb (eds), *The Archaeology of Institutional Life*. Tuscaloosa: University of Alabama Press, 17–32.

Catsambis, Alexis, Ben Ford, and Donny Hamilton (2013) (eds). *The Oxford Handbook of Maritime Archaeology*. Oxford: Oxford University Press.

de Certeau, Michel (1984). *The Practice of Everyday Life*. Berkeley and Los Angeles: University of California Press.

Chaiklin, Martha (2010). 'Ivory in World History', *History Compass*, 8/6: 530–42.

Chakrabarti, Pratik (2010). 'Empire and Alternatives: Swietenia Febrifuga and the Cinchona Substitutes', *Medical History*, 54/1: 75–94.

Chamberlaine, William (1785). *The West-India Seaman's Medical Directory, for the Use of Such Merchant-Ships Trading to the West-Indies as Carry no Surgeon*. London: Printed and sold by the author.

Chambers, Douglas (1997).'"My Own Nation": Igbo Exiles and the Diaspora', in David Eltis and David Richardson (eds), *Routes to Slavery: Direction, Ethnicity Pand Mortality in the Transatlantic Slave Trade*. London: Frank Cass, 72–97.

Chambers, Douglas (2013) (ed.). *Runaway Slaves in Jamaica (1) Eighteenth Century*, https://ufdc.ufl.edu/AA00021144/00001 (accessed 3 December 2020).

Charlton, John (2008). *Hidden Chains: The Slavery Business and North East England 1600–1865*. Newcastle: Tyne Bridge Publishing.

Charters, Erica (2012). 'Making Bodies Modern: Race, Medicine and the Colonial Soldier in the Mid Eighteenth Century', *Patterns of Prejudice*, 46/3–4: 214–31.

Chireau, Yvonne (2003). *Black Magic: Religion and the African American Conjuring Tradition*. Berkeley and Los Angeles: University of California Press.

Christopher, Emma (2006). *Slave Ship Sailors and their Captive Cargoes, 1730–1807*. New York: Cambridge University Press.

Christopher, Emma (2007). '"The Slave Trade Is Merciful Compared to [This]"; Slave Traders, Convict Transportation and the Abolitionists', in Emma Christopher, Cassandra Pybus, and Marcus Rekider (eds), *Many Middle Passages: Forced Migration and the Making of the Modern World*. Berkeley and Los Angeles: University of California Press, 109–28.

Churchill, Awnsham, and John Churchill (1732). *A Collection of Voyages and Travels*. 6 vols. London: Thomas Osborne.

Clark, James (1797). *A Treatise on the Yellow Fever as it Appeared on the Island of Dominica, in the Years 1793-4-5-6*. London: Printed for J. Murray and S. Highley.

Clarkson, Thomas (1789). *The Substance of the Evidence of Sundry Persons on the Slave-Trade, Collected in the Course of a Tour Made in the Autumn of the Year 1788*. London: James Phillips.

Clarkson, Thomas (1808). *The History of the Rise, Progress, and Accomplishment of the Abolition of the African Slave Trade by the British Parliament*. 2 vols. London: Longman, Hurst, Rees and Orme.

Clifford, Barry (with Paul Perry) (1999). *Expedition Whydah*. New York: Cliff Street Books.

Clifford, James, and George Marcus (1986). *Writing Culture: The Poetics and Politics of Ethnography: A School of American Research Advanced Seminar*. Berkeley and Los Angeles: University of California Press.

Cobbett, William (1816). *Cobbett's Parliamentary History of England: From the Norman Conquest, in 1066 to the Year 1803. Comprising the Period from the Eighth of May 1789, to the Fifteenth of March 1791* (Volume 28). London: Hansard.

Coleman, Deirdre (2007). 'Henry Smeathman and the Natural Economy of Slavery', in Bryccha Carey and Peter Kitson (eds), *Slavery and the Cultures of Abolition*. Cambridge: D. S. Brewer, 130–49.

Coleman, Deirdre (2013). 'Menageries and Museums: John Simons' The Tiger that Swallowed the Boy (2012) and the Lives and Afterlives of Historical Animals', *Animal Studies Journal*, 2/1: 114–32.

Coleman, Deirdre (2018). *Henry Smeathman, the Flycatcher: Natural History, Slavery, and Empire in the Late Eighteenth Century*. Oxford: Oxford University Press.

Coleman, Sarah, Margarita Gleba, and Malika Kraamer (2022). 'From West Africa to Wisbech: Analysing 18th-Century Textiles in Thomas Clarkson's Campaign Chest', *Current Archaeology*, 5 January, https://the-past.com/feature/from-west-africa-to-wisbech-analysing-18th-century-textiles-in-thomas-clarksons-campaign-chest/ (accessed August 2022).

Cook, Gregory (2012). 'The Maritime Archaeology of West Africa in the Atlantic World: Investigations at Elmina, Ghana', Ph.D. dissertation, Syracuse University.

Cook, Gregory (2014). 'Maritime Archaeology in Ghana', in James Anquandah, Benjamin Kankpeyeng, and Wazi Apoh (eds), *Current Perspectives in the Archaeology of Ghana*. Legon: Sub-Saharan Publishers, 109.

Cook, Gregory, Rachel Horlings, and Andrew Pietruszka (2016). 'Maritime Archaeology and the Early Atlantic Trade: Research at Elmina, Ghana', *International Journal of Nautical Archaeology*, 45/2: 370–87.

Coote, Jeremy (2008). 'Mermaids and Mami Wata on Brassware from Old Calabar', in Henry Drewal (ed.), *Sacred Waters: Arts for Mami Wata and Other Divinities in Africa and the Diaspora*. Bloomington: Indiana University Press, 259–75.

Corruccini, Robert, Arthur Aufderheide, Jerome Handler, and Lorenz Wittmers (1987). 'Patterning of Skeletal Lead Content in Barbados Slaves', *Archaeometery*, 29: 233–9.

Corruccini, Robert, Elizabeth Brandon and Jerome Handler (1989). 'Inferring Fertility from Relative Mortality in Historically Controlled Cemetery Remains from Barbados', *American Antiquity*, 54: 609–14.

Costello, Ray (2012). *Black Salt: Seafarers of African Descent on British Ships*. Liverpool: Liverpool University Press.

Cottman, Michael (1999). *Spirit Dive: An African American's Journey to Uncover a Sunken Slave Ship's Past*. New York: Three Rivers Press.

Coughtry, Jay (1981). *The Notorious Triangle: Rhode Island and the African Slave Trade 1700–1807*. Philadelphia: Temple University Press.

Covey, Herbert, and Dwight Eisnach (2009). *What the Slaves Ate: Recollections of African American Foods and Foodways from the Slave Narratives*. Santa Barbara: ABC–CLIO.

Cowley, Malcolm (1928). *Adventures of an African Slaver, Being a True Account of the Life of Captain Theodore Canot, Trader in Gold, Ivory & Slaves on the Coast of Guinea*. New York: A. and C. Boni.

Crow, Hugh (1970 [1830]). *Memoirs of the Late Captain Hugh Crow of Liverpool*. London: Frank Cass.

Cox, Nancy (1990). 'Imagination and Innovation of an Industrial Pioneer: The First Abraham Darby', *Industrial Archaeology Review*, 12/2: 127–44.

Craig, Robert and Rupert Jarvis (1967*). Liverpool Registry of Merchant Ships*. Manchester: Manchester University Press for the Chetham Society.

Crone, Gerald (1937) (ed.). *The Voyages of Cadamosto, and Other Documents on Western Africa in the Second Half of the Fifteenth Century*. London: Printed for the Hakluyt Society.

Cugoano, Ottobah (1787). *Thoughts and Sentiments on the Evil and Wicked Traffic of the Slavery and Commerce of the Human Species, Humbly Submitted to the Inhabitants of Great-Britain, by Ottobah Cugoano, a Native of Africa*. London: s.n.

Cunningham, Neil, and Sean Kingsley (2011). 'A Late 17th-Century Armed Merchant Vessel in the Western Approaches (Site 35F)', *Odyssey Papers*, 23, https://7500393c–b879–4ffa–ae28–f1a2c21e2538.filesusr.com/ugd/be6d77_fd7fb76a860e4370a3e4ed1a285201bb.pdf, (accessed 27 October 2022).

Curtin, Philip (1955). *Two Jamaicas: The Role of Ideas in a Tropical Colony*. Cambridge, MA: Harvard University Press.

Curtin, Philip (1968). 'Epidemiology and the Slave Trade', *Political Science Quarterly*, 83/2: 190–216.

Curtin, Philip (1969). *The Atlantic Slave Trade; A Census*. Madison: University of Wisconsin Press.

474 REFERENCES

Curtin, Philip (1975). *Economic Change in Precolonial Africa: Supplementary Evidence.* Madison: University of Wisconsin Press.

Curtin, Philip (1992). 'The Slavery Hypothesis for Hypertension among African Americans: The Historical Evidence', *American Journal of Public Health*, 82/12: 1681–6.

Dale, Richard (2004). *The First Crash: Lessons from the South Sea Bubble.* Princeton: Princeton University Press.

Dalrymple-Smith, Angus, and Ewout Frankema (2017). 'Slave Ship Provisioning in the Long Eighteenth Century: A Boost to West African Commercial Agriculture?', *European Review of Economic History*, 21/2: 185–235.

Dalzel, Archibald (1793). *The History of Dahomy.* London: T. Spilsbury and Son.

Daniel, Shanna (2009). *The Seat of Ease: Sanitary Facilities from Shipwreck 31CR314, Queen Anne's Revenge Site. Queen Anne's Revenge* Shipwreck Project Research Report and Bulletin Series, QAR–B–09–02, https://www.qaronline.org/media/33/open (accessed 14 December 2022).

Davies, Kenneth (1957). *The Royal African Company.* London: Longmans.

Davis, Ralph (1962). *The Rise of the English Shipping Industry in the Seventeenth and Eighteenth Centuries.* London: Macmillan.

Dawson, Kevin (2013). 'Enslaved Ship Pilots in the Age of Revolutions: Challenging Notions of Race and Slavery between the Boundaries of Land and Sea', *Journal of Social History*, 47/1: 71–100.

Day, Joan (1968). *Technical Terms used in the Brass Mills in the Saltford and Keynsham Area*, https://brassmill.com/linked/1968_-_technical_terms_-_brass_mills_-_day.pdf (accessed 25 November 2022).

Day, Joan (1973). *Bristol Brass: A History of the Industry.* Newton Abbott: David and Charles.

Day, Joan (1988). 'The Bristol Brass Industry: Furnace Structures and Their Associated Remains', *Journal of the Historical Metallurgy Society*, 21/1: 24–41.

Deason, Michael, Antonio Salas, Simon Newman, Vincent Macaulay, Errol Morrison, and Yannis Pitsiladis (2012). 'Interdisciplinary Approach to the Demography of Jamaica', *BMC Evolutionary Biology*, 12/1: 112–24.

DeCorse, Christopher (1989). 'Beads as Chronological Indicators in West African Archaeology: A Re-Examination', *Beads*, 1/1: 41–53.

DeCorse, Christopher (2000). 'An African Bead in New York', *Update: Newsletter of the African Burial Ground and Five Points Projects*, 3/1: 6–7.

DeCorse, Christopher (2001). *An Archaeology of Elmina: Africans and Europeans on the Gold Coast, 1400–1900.* Washington: Smithsonian Institution Press.

DeCorse, Christopher (2016). 'Tools of Empire: Trade, Slaves, and the British Forts of West Africa', in Daniel Maudlin & Bernard Herman (eds), *Building the British Atlantic World: Spaces, Places, and Material Culture, 1600–1850.* Chapel Hill: University of North Carolina Press, 165–87.

DeCorse, Christopher, Liza Gijanto, William Roberts, and Bakary Sanyang (2010). 'An Archaeological Appraisal of Early European Settlement in The Gambia', *Nyame Akuma*, 73: 55–64.

Debien, Gabriel, Marcel Delafosse and Guy Thilmans (1978). 'Journal d'un Voyage de Traite en Guinée, a Cayenne et aux Antilles Fait par Jean Barbot en 1678–1679', *Bulletin de l'Institut Français d'Afrique Noire*, sér. B. *Sciences Humaines*, 40/2: 235–395.

Delbourgo, James (2012). 'Listing People', *Isis*, 103/4: 735–42.

Delbourgo, James (2017). *Collecting the World: Hans Sloane and the Origins of the British Museum.* London: Penguin Books.

Delgado, Sally (2013). 'Pirate English of the Caribbean and Atlantic Trade Routes in the Seventeenth and Eighteenth Centuries: Linguistic Hypotheses Based on Socio-Historical Data', *Acta Linguistica Hafniensia*, 45/2: 151–69.

Delgado, Sally (2019). *Ship English: Sailors' Speech in the Early Colonial Caribbean.* Berlin: Language Science Press.

Den Besten, Hans, Pieter Muysken and Norval Smith (1994). 'Theories Focusing on the European Input', in Jacques Arends, Pieter Muysken and Norval Smith (eds), *Pidgins and Creoles an Introduction.* Amsterdam: John Benjamins, 87–109.

REFERENCES 475

Denham, Woodrow (1981). 'History of Green Monkeys in the West Indies: Part I. Migration from Africa', *Journal of the Barbados Museum and Historical Society*, 36: 210–29.

Denis, Adrián (2005). 'Melancholia, Slavery, and Racial Pathology in Eighteenth-Century Cuba', *Science in Context*, 18/2: 179–99.

Devenish, David (1994). 'The Slave Trade and Thomas Clarkson's *Chest*', *Journal of Museum Ethnography*, 6: 84–9.

Diedrich, Maria, Henry Louis Gates Jnr, and Carl Pedersen (1999). 'Part 1, Voyage through Death', in Maria Diedrich, Henry Louis Gates Jnr, and Carl Pedersen (eds), *Black Imagination and the Middle Passage*. Oxford: Oxford University Press, 17–20.

Diouf, Sylviane (2007). *Dreams of Africa in Alabama: The Slave Ship Clotilda and the Story of the Last Africans Brought to America*. Oxford: Oxford University Press.

Dodds, James, and James Moore (1984). *Building the Wooden Fighting Ship*. New York: Vintage Books.

Donnan, Elizabeth (1930–5). *Documents Illustrative of the History Slave Trade to America*. 4 vols. Washington: Carnegie Institute of Washington.

Don Saltero's Coffee-house (c.1756). *A Catalogue of the Rarities to be Seen at Don Saltero's Coffee House in Chelsea. to Which is Added, a Complete List of the Donors Thereof*. London: J. Oliver.

Dow, George (2002 [1927]). *Slave Ships and Slaving*. New York: Dover Publications.

Drake, B. (1976). 'Continuity and Flexibility in Liverpool's Trade with Africa and the Caribbean', *Business History*, 18/1: 85–97.

Draper, Nicholas (2008). 'The City of London and Slavery: Evidence from the First Dock Companies, 1795–1800', *Economic History Review*, 61/2: 432–66.

Dresser, Madge (2000). 'Squares of Distinction, Webs of Interest: Gentility, Urban Development and the Slave Trade in Bristol c.1673–1820', *Slavery & Abolition*, 21/3: 21–47.

Dresser, Madge (2001). *Slavery Obscured: The Social History of the Slave Trade in an English Provincial Port*. London: Continuum Books.

Dresser, Madge, and Sue Giles (1999) (eds). *Catalogue of the Bristol and the Atlantic Slave Trade Exhibition*. Bristol: Bristol City Museum.

Drewal, Henry (1988a). 'Mermaids, Mirrors, and Snake Charmers: Igbo Mami Wata Shrines', *African Arts*, 21/2: 38–45.

Drewal, Henry (1988b). 'Performing the Other: Mami Wata Worship in Africa', *The Drama Review* 32/2: 160–85.

Drewal, Henry (2008a). 'Introduction: Charting the Voyage', in Henry Drewal (ed.), *Sacred Waters: Arts for Mami Wata and Other Divinities in Africa and the Diaspora*. Bloomington: Indiana University Press, 1–18.

Drewal, Henry (2008b) (ed.). *Sacred Waters: Arts for Mami Wata and Other Divinities in Africa and the Diaspora*. Bloomington: Indiana University Press.

Drewal, Henry (2013). 'Local Transformations, Global Inspirations: The Visual Histories and Cultures of Mami Wata Arts in Africa', in Gitti Salami and Monica Blackmun Visoná (eds), *A Companion to Modern African Art*. Chichester: Wiley-Blackwell, 23–49.

Dubois, Laurent (2016). *The Banjo: America's African Instrument*. Cambridge, MA: Belknap Press of Harvard University Press.

Duden, Barbara (1991). *The Woman beneath the Skin: A Doctor's Patients in Eighteenth–Century Germany*. Cambridge, MA: Harvard University Press.

Dunham, Katherine (1994). *Island Possessed*. Chicago: University of Chicago Press.

Duquette, Nicolas (2014). 'Revealing the Relationship between Ship Crowding and Slave Mortality', *Journal of Economic History*, 74/2: 535–52.

Durkin, Hannah (2020). 'Uncovering the Hidden Lives of Last Clotilda Survivor Matilda McCrear and her Family', *Slavery & Abolition*, 41/3: 431–57.

Dyott, William (1907) (ed.) *Dyott's Diary, 1781–1845: A Selection from the Journal of William Dyott, sometime General in the British Army and Aide-de-camp to His Majesty King George III*. ed. Reginald W. Jeffery. London: Archibald Constable & Co.

Eagleton, Catherine (2013). 'Collecting African Money in Georgian London: Sarah Sophia Banks and her Collection of Coins', *Museum History Journal*, 6/1: 23–38.

Earle, Alice (1896). *Curious Punishments of Bygone Days*. Chicago: H. S. Stone & Co.

476 REFERENCES

Earle, Peter (1998). *Sailors: English Merchant Seamen 1650–1775*. London: Methuen.

Edwards, Bryan (1793). *The History, Civil and Commercial, of the British Colonies in the West Indies*. 2 vols. Dublin: Luke White.

Edwards, Bryan (1798). *The History, Civil and Commercial, of the British Colonies in the West Indies*. London: B. Crosby.

Ehrlich, Martha (1989). 'Early Akan Gold from the Wreck of the *Whydah*', *African Arts*, 22/4: 52–7.

Ehrlich, Martha (2012). 'Two Akan Gold Ornaments from the Wreck of the *Whydah*', *African Arts*, 45/1: 32–41.

Elia, Ricardo (1992). 'The Ethics of Collaboration: Archaeologists and the *Whydah* Project', *Historical Archaeology*, 26/4: 105–17.

Elia, Ricardo (2000). 'US Protection of Underwater Cultural Heritage beyond the Territorial Sea: Problems and Prospects', *International Journal of Nautical Archaeology*, 29/1: 43–56.

Eltis, David (1991). 'Precolonial Western Africa and the Atlantic Economy', in Barbara Solow (ed.), *Slavery and the Rise of the Atlantic System*. Cambridge: Cambridge University, 97–119.

Eltis, David (2000). *The Rise of African Slavery in the Americas*. Cambridge: Cambridge University Press.

Eltis, David (2001). 'The Volume and Structure of the Slave Trade: A Reassessment', *William and Mary Quarterly*, 58/1: 17–46.

Eltis, David (2013). 'The Slave Trade and Commercial Agriculture in an African Context', in Robin Law, Suzanne Schwarz, and Silke Strickrodt (eds), *Commercial Agriculture and the Slave Trade in Atlantic Africa*. Woodbridge: James Currey, 28–53.

Eltis, David, Stephen Behrendt, David Richardson, and Herbert Klein (1999a). *The Trans-Atlantic Slave Trade Database on CD Rom*. Cambridge: Cambridge University Press.

Eltis, David, Stephen Behrendt, David Richardson, and Herbert Klein (1999b). *The Trans-Atlantic Slave Trade Database on CD Rom User Guide*. Cambridge: Cambridge University Press.

Eltis, David, and Stanley Engerman (2000). 'The Importance of Slavery and the Slave Trade to Industrializing Britain', *Journal of Economic History*, 60/1: 123–44.

Eltis, David, and Lawrence Jennings (1988). 'Trade between Western Africa and the Atlantic World in the Pre-Colonial Era', *American Historical Review*, 93/4: 936–59.

Eltis, David, Philip Morgan, and David Richardson (2007). 'Agency and Diaspora in Atlantic History: Reassessing the African Contribution to Rice Cultivation in the Americas', *American Historical Review*, 112/5: 1329–58.

Eltis, David, Philip Morgan, and David Richardson (2010). 'Black, Brown or White? Color-Coding American Commercial Rice Cultivation with Slave Labour', *American Historical Review*, 115/1: 164–71.

Eltis, David, and David Richardson (1997a). 'The "Numbers Game" and Routes to Slavery', in David Eltis and David Richardson (eds), *Routes to Slavery: Direction, Ethnicity and Mortality in the Transatlantic Slave Trade*. London: Frank Cass, 1–15.

Eltis, David, and David Richardson (1997b). 'West Africa and the Transatlantic Slave Trade: New Evidence of Long-Run Trends', in David Eltis and David Richardson (eds), *Routes to Slavery: Direction, Ethnicity and Mortality in the Transatlantic Slave Trade*. London: Frank Cass, 16–35.

Eltis, David, and David Richardson (1997c) (eds). *Routes to Slavery: Direction, Ethnicity and Mortality in the Transatlantic Slave Trade*. London: Frank Cass.

Eltis, David, and David Richardson (2008a). 'A New Assessment of the Transatlantic Slave Trade', in David Eltis and David Richardson (eds), *Extending the Frontiers: Essays on the New Transatlantic Slave Trade Database*. Yale: Yale University Press, 1–60.

Eltis, David, and David Richardson (2008b) (eds). *Extending the Frontiers: Essays on the New Transatlantic Slave Trade Database*. Yale: Yale University Press.

Eltis, David, and David Richardson (2010). *Atlas of the Trans-Atlantic Slave Trade*. London: Yale University Press.

Emerson, Matthew (1999). 'African Inspirations in a New World Art and Artefact: Decorated Pipes from the Chesapeake', in Theresa Singleton (ed.), *I, Too, Am America: Archaeological Studies of African–American Life*. Charlottesville: University Press of Virginia, 47–74.Mul

Enfield, William (1774). *Essay towards the History of Liverpool*. London: Printed for Joseph Johnson.

Engmann, Rachel (2019). 'Preliminary Report on Locally Manufactured Pottery at Christiansborg Castle in Osu, Accra, Ghana', *Post-Medieval Archaeology*, 53/3: 302–8.

Epstein, Dena (2003). *Sinful Tunes and Spirituals: Black Folk Music to the Civil War*. Urbana: University of Illinois Press.

Equiano, Olaudah (1789). *The Interesting Narrative of the Life of Olaudah Equiano, or Gustavus Vassa, the African: Written by Himself*. London: Printed for and sold by the author.

Evans, Chris (2010). *Slave Wales: The Welsh and Atlantic Slavery 1660–1650*. Cardiff: University of Wales Press.

Evans, Chris, and Göran Rydén (2018). '"Voyage Iron:" An Atlantic Slave Trade Currency, its European Origins, and West African Impact', *Past and Present*, 239/1: 41–70.

Ewen, Charles (2006). 'Introduction', in Russell Skowronek and Charles Ewen (eds), *X Marks the Spot: The Archaeology of Piracy*. Gainsville: University Press of Florida, 1–10.

Falconbridge, Alexander (1788). *An Account of the Slave Trade on the Coast of Africa*. London: J. Phillips.

Falconer, William (1769). *An Universal Dictionary of the Marine*. London: printed for T. Cadell.

Farnsworth, Paul, and Laurie Wilkie (2006). 'Fish and Grits: Southern, African and British Influences in Bahamian Foodways', in Helen Regis (ed.), *Caribbean and Southern: Transnational Perspectives on the US South*. Athens: University of Georgia Press, 34–72.

Fabre, Geneviève (1999). 'The Slave Ship Dance', in Maria Diedrich, Henry Louis Gates Jnr, and Carl Pedersen (eds), *Black Imagination and the Middle Passage*. Oxford: Oxford University Press, 33–46.

Fennetaux, Ariane (2009). 'Female Crafts: Women and Bricolage in Late Georgian Britain, 1750–1820', in Maureen Goggin and Beth Fowkes Tobin (eds), *Women and Things, 1750–1950: Gendered Material Strategies*. Aldershot: Ashgate, 91–108.

Feinberg, Harvey, and Marion Johnson (1982). 'The West African Ivory Trade during the Eighteenth Century: The "…and Ivory" Complex', *International Journal of African Historical Studies*, 15/3: 435–53.

Ferguson, Leland (1992). *Uncommon Ground: Archaeology and Early African America, 1650–1800*. Washington: Smithsonian Institution.

Ferreira, Lúcio, and Gabina La Rosa (2015). 'The Archaeology of Slave Branding in Cuba', in Pedro Funari and Charles Orser (eds), *Current Perspectives on the Archaeology of African Slavery in Latin America*. New York: Springer, 45–59.

Findlen, Paula (2013). 'Early Modern Things: Objects in Motion 1500–1800', in Paula Findlen (ed.), *Early Modern Things: Objects and their Histories 1500–1800*. London: Routledge, 3–27.

Focht, Adria (2008). *Blackbeard Sails Again? Conservation of Textiles from the* Queen Anne's Revenge *Shipwreck (31CR314)*. Queen Anne's Revenge Shipwreck Project Conservation Laboratory, https://www.qaronline.org/blackbeard-sails-again-conservation-textiles-queen-annes-revenge-shipwreck/open (accessed 11 November 2022).

Fortes-Lima, Cesar, and Paul Verdu (2021). 'Anthropological Genetics Perspectives on the Transatlantic Slave Trade', *Human Molecular Genetics*, 30, Issue R1: R79–R87.

Fothergill, John (1783). *The Works of John Fothergill M.D.* 3 vols. London: printed for Charles Dilly.

Foucault, Michel (1977). *Discipline and Punish: The Birth of the Prison*, trans. A Sheridan. London: Penguin Books.

Foucault, Michel (1989). *The Order of Things: An Archaeology of the Human Sciences*. London: Routledge.

Fowkes Tobin, Beth (2014). *The Duchess's Shells*. London: Yale University Press.

Francklyn, Gilbert (1789). *An Answer to the Rev. Mr Clarkson's Essay on the Slavery and Commerce of the Human Species, Particularly the African; in a Series of Letters*. London: Logographic Press.

Fraser, Douglas (1972). 'The Fish-Legged Figure in Benin and Yoruba Art', in Douglas Fraser and Herbert Cole (eds), *African Art and Leadership*. Madison: University of Wisconsin Press, 261–94.

Fremont, Cécile (2020). 'Paper, Ink, Vodun, and the Inquisition: Tracing Power, Slavery and Witchcraft in the Early Portuguese Atlantic', *Journal of the American Academy of Religion*, 88/2: 460–504.

Fyfe, Christopher (1964). *Sierra Leone Inheritance*. London: Oxford University Press.

478 REFERENCES

Fyfe, Christoper (2000) (ed.). *Anna Maria Falconbridge: Narrative of Two Voyages to the River Sierra Leone during the Years 1791/1793. With an Account of the Slave Trade on the Coast of Africa by Alexander Falconbridge*. Liverpool: Liverpool University Press.

Galenson, David (1986). *Traders, Planters and Slaves: Market Behaviour in Early English America*. Cambridge: Cambridge University Press.

Galke, Laura (2000). 'Did the Gods of Africa Die? A Re-Examination of a Carroll House Crystal Assemblage', *North American Archaeologist*, 21/1: 19–33.

Garland, Charles, and Herbert Klein (1985). 'The Allotment of Space for Slaves Aboard Eighteenth-Century Slave Ships', *William and Mary Quarterly*, 42/2: 238–48.

Garrard, Timothy (1979). 'Akan Metal Arts', *African Arts*, 13/1: 36–43.

Garrard, Timothy (1980). *Akan Weights and the Gold Trade*. London: Longman.

Garvey, Johanna (1999).'Passages to Identity: Re-Membering the Diaspora in Marshall, Phillips and Cliff', in Maria Diedrich, Henry Louis Gates Jnr, and Carl Pedersen (eds), *Black Imagination and the Middle Passage*. Oxford: Oxford University Press, 255–70.

Genovese, Eugene (1974). *Roll, Jordan, Roll: The World the Slaves Made*. New York: Pantheon Books.

Gerzina, Gretchen (2020). 'The Georgian Life and Modern Afterlife of Dido Elizabeth Belle', in Gretchen Gerzina (ed.), *Britain's Black Past*. Liverpool: Liverpool University Press, 161–78.

Gikandi, Simon (2011). *Slavery and the Culture of Taste*. Princeton: Princeton University Press.

Gilje, Paul (2016). *To Swear Like a Sailor: Maritime Culture in America, 1750–1850*. Cambridge: Cambridge University Press.

Gilroy, Paul (1993). *The Black Atlantic: Modernity and Double Consciousness*. Cambridge MA: Harvard University Press.

Gluckman, Stephen (1998). 'Preliminary Investigations of a Shipwreck, Pumpata Cahuita National Park, Costa Rica', in Lawrence Babits and Hans Tliberg (eds), *Maritime Archaeology*. Boston: Springer, 453–67.

Gomes, Maria, Tânia Casimiro, and Joana Gonçalves (2015). 'A Late 17th-Century Trade Cargo from Ponta do Leme Velho, Sal Island, Cape Verde', *International Journal of Nautical Archaeology*, 44: 160–72.

Gomez, Michael (1998). *Exchanging our Country Marks: The Transformation of African Identities in the Colonial and Antebellum South*. Chapel Hill: University of North Carolina Press.

Goodman, Alan, Joseph Jones, J. Reid, Mark Mack, Michael Blakey, Dula Amarasiriwardena, P. Burton, and D. Coleman (2009). 'Isotopic and Elemental Chemistry of Teeth: Implications for Places of Birth, Forced Migration Patterns, Nutritional Status, and Pollution', in Michael Blakey and Lesley Rankin-Hill (eds), *The New York African Burial Ground Skeletal Biology Final Report*. Washington: Howard University Press, 95–118.

Gore, Charles, and Joseph Nevadomsky (1997). 'Practice and Agency in Mammy Wata Worship in Southern Nigeria', *African Arts*, 30/2: 60–9.

Gosden, Chris, and Chantal Knowles (2020). *Collecting Colonialism: Material Culture and Colonial Change*. Oxford: Berg.

Gosden, Chris, and Yvonne Marshall (1999). 'The Cultural Biography of Objects', *World Archaeology*, 31/2: 169–78.

Gosselain, Olivier (1999). 'In Pots We Trust: The Processing of Clay and Symbols in Sub-Saharan Africa', *Journal of Material Culture*, 4/2: 205–30.

Gott, Suzanne (2002). 'Precious Beads and Sacred Gold: Trade, Transformation, and the Unifying Principle of Generative Nurturance in the Arts of Southern Ghana', Ph.D. dissertation, Indiana University, Bloomington.

Gott, Suzanne (2014). 'Ghana's Glass Beadmaking Arts in Transcultural Dialogues', *African Arts*, 47/1: 10–29.

Goucher, C. (2014). 'Rituals of Iron in the Black Atlantic World', in Akinwumi Ogundiran and Paula Saunders (eds), *Materialities of Ritual in the Black Atlantic*. Bloomington: Indiana University Press, 108–24.

Gould, Richard (2011). *Archaeology and the Social History of Ships*. Cambridge: Cambridge University Press.

Graden, Dale (2011). 'Interpreters, Translators and the Spoken Word in the Nineteenth-Century Transatlantic Slave Trade to Cuba and Brazil', *Ethnohistory*, 58/3: 393–419.

Gronniosaw, Ukawsaw (1770). *A Narrative of the Most Remarkable Particulars in the Life of Albert James Ukawsaw Gronniosaw an African Prince, as Related by Himself*. Bath: W. Gye.

Gualdé, Krysel (2022). *L'Abime: Nantes dans la Traite Atlantique et L'esclavage Colonial*. Nantes: Les Editions Chateau des Ducs de Bretagne.

Guérout, Max (2014). 'Enjeux et perspectives de la fouille des navires négriers', in André Delpuech and Jean-Paul Jacob (eds), *Archéologie de l'esclavage Colonial*. Paris: La Découverte, 129–42.

Guerrero, Saul (2010). 'Venetian Glass Beads and the Slave Trade from Liverpool, 1750–1800', *Beads*, 22/1: 52–70.

Guillet, Bertrand (2009). *La Marie-Séraphique: Navire Négrier*. Nantes: Musée d'Histoire de Nantes, éditions MeMo.

Habib, Imtiaz (2008). *Black Lives in the English Archives 1500–1677*. Aldershot: Ashgate.

Haines, Robin, and Ralph Shlomowitz (2000). 'Explaining the Mortality Decline in the Eighteenth-Century British Slave Trade', *Economic History Review*, 53/2: 262–83.

Hair, Paul (1974). 'Barbot, Dapper, Davity: A Critique of Sources on Sierra Leone and Cape Mount', *History in Africa*, 1: 25–54.

Hair, Paul (1997a). *Africa Encountered: European Contact and Evidence 1450–1700*. Aldershot: Variorum.

Hair, Paul (1997b). 'The Experience of the Sixteenth-Century English Voyages to Guinea', *Mariner's Mirror*, 83/1: 3–13.

Hair, Paul, Adam Jones, and Robin Law (1992) (eds). *Barbot on Guinea: The Writings of Jean Barbot on West Africa 1678–1712*. 2 vols. London: The Hakluyt Society.

Hair, Paul, and James Alsop (1992). *English Seamen and Traders in Guinea, 1553–1565: The New Evidence of their Wills*. Lewiston: E. Mellen Press.

Hakluyt, Richard (1965 [1589]). *The Principal Navigations, Voyages, Traffiques & Discoveries of the English Nation, Made by Sea or Overland to the Remote and Farthest Distant Quarters of the Earth at any Time within the Compass of these 1600 Years*. Cambridge: Cambridge University Press for the Hakluyt Society.

Hales, Stephen (1743). *A Description of Ventilators:... Which was Read Before the Royal Society in May 1741*. London: Richard Manby.

Hales, Stephen (1756). *An Account of a Useful Discovery... and an Account of the Great Benefit of Ventilators... Which were Read before the Royal Society*. London: Richard Manby.

Hall, Douglas (1989). *In Miserable Slavery: Thomas Thistlewood in Jamaica 1750–86*. Barbados: University of West Indies Press.

Hall, Martin (2000). *Archaeology and the Modern World: Colonial Transcripts in South Africa and Chesapeake*. London: Routledge.

Hall, Rebecca (2021). *Wake: The Hidden History of Woman-Led Slave Revolts*. London: Particular Books.

Hall, Stuart (2016). 'Diasporas, or the Logics of Cultural Translation' (Posthumous publication of a keynote address given in 2010), *MATRIZes*, 10/3: 47–58.

Hallett, Robin (1964) (ed.). *Records of the African Association 1788–1831*. London: Thomas Nelson.

Hamann, Nicole (2007). 'Forging an Atlantic World: An Historical Archaeological Investigation of African–European Trade in Metalwares', MA thesis, William & Mary College.

Hamilton, Christopher (2006). 'The Pirate Ship *Whydah*', in Russell Skowronek and Charles Ewen (eds), *X Marks the Spot: The Archaeology of Piracy*. Gainsville: University Press of Florida, 131–59.

Hamilton, Henry (1967). *The English Brass and Copper Industries to 1800*. London: Frank Cass and Co.

Hancock, Ian (1976). 'Nautical Sources of Krio Vocabulary', *Linguistics*, 14/143: 26–36.

Hancock, Ian (1985). 'On the Anglophone Creole Item Kekrebu', *American Speech*, 60/3: 281–3.

Hancock, Ian (1986). 'The Domestic Hypothesis, Diffusion and Componentiality: An Account of Atlantic Anglophone Creole Origins', in Norval Smith and Pieter Muysken (eds), *Substrata versus Universals in Creole Genesis*. Amsterdam: John Benjamins, 71–102.

480 REFERENCES

Handler, Jerome (1994). 'Determining African Birth from Skeletal Remains: A Note on Tooth Mutilation', *Historical Archaeology*, 28/3: 113–19.

Handler Jerome (1997). 'An African-Type Healer/Diviner and his Grave Goods: A Burial from a Plantation Slave Cemetery in Barbados, West Indies', *International Journal of Historical Archaeology*, 1/2: 91–130.

Handler, Jerome (2002). 'Survivors of the Middle Passage: Life Histories of Enslaved Africans in British America', *Slavery & Abolition*, 23/1: 25–56.

Handler, Jerome S. (2007). 'From Cambay in India to Barbados in the Caribbean: Two Unique Beads from a Plantation Slave Cemetery', *African Diaspora Archaeology Newsletter*, 10/1, Article 1, https://scholarworks.umass.edu/adan/vol10/iss1/1 (accessed 04 March 2023).

Handler, Jerome (2009a). 'The Middle Passage and the Material Culture of Captive Africans', *Slavery & Abolition*, 30/1: 1–26.

Handler, Jerome (2009b). 'Aspects of the Atlantic Slave Trade: Smoking Pipes, Tobacco, and the Middle Passage', *African Diaspora Archaeology Newsletter*, 12/2, Article 5, https://scholarworks. umass.edu/adan/vol12/iss2/5/ (accessed 04 March 2023).

Handler, Jerome, and Frederick Lange (1978). *Plantation Slavery in Barbados: An Archaeological and Historical Investigation*. Cambridge, MA: Harvard University Press.

Handler, Jerome, and Neil Norman (2007). 'From West Africa to Barbados: A Rare Pipe from a Plantation Slave Cemetery', *African Diaspora Archaeology Newsletter*, 10/3, Article 2, https://scholarworks.umass.edu/adan/vol10/iss3/2 (accessed 04 March 2023).

Handler, Jerome, Robert Corruccini, and Robert Mutaw (1982). 'Tooth Mutilation in the Caribbean: Evidence from a Slave Burial Population in Barbados', *Journal of Human Evolution*, 11: 297–313.

Harms, Robert (2002). *The Diligent: A Voyage through the Worlds of the Slave Trade*. New York: Basic Books.

Harris, John (1966). 'Copper and Shipping in the Eighteenth Century', *Economic History Review*, 19/3: 550–68.

Harris, Lynn, and Nathan Richards (2018). 'Preliminary Investigations of Two Shipwreck Sites in Cahuita National Park, Costa Rica', *International Journal of Nautical Archaeology*, 47/2: 405–18.

Hart, William (1994). 'Two Early West African Harps in Glasgow', *Journal of the History of Collections*, 6/1: 79–85.

Hart, William (2006). 'Trophies of Grace? The "Art" Collecting Activities of United Brethren in Christ Missionaries in Nineteenth Century Sierra Leone', *African Arts*, 39/2: 14–25.

Hartman, Saidiya (2021). *Lose Your Mother: A Journey along the Atlantic Slave Route*. London: Serpent's Tail.

Hawthorne, Walter (2008). '"Being Now, as it Were, One Family:" Shipmate Bonding on the Slave Vessel *Emilia*, in Rio de Janeiro and throughout the Atlantic World', *Luso-Brazilian Review*, 45/1: 53–77.

Hawthorne, Walter (2010). *From Africa to Brazil: Culture, Identity and an Atlantic Slave Trade 1600–1830*. Cambridge: Cambridge University Press.

Heath, Barbara (1999). 'Buttons, Beads, and Buckles: Contextualizing Adornment within the Bounds of Slavery', in Maria Franklin and Garrett Fesler (eds), *Historical Archaeology, Identity Formation, and the Interpretation of Ethnicity*. Richmond: Dietz Press, 47–69.

Heath, Barbara (2016). 'Cowrie Shells, Global Trade, and Local Exchange: Piecing together the Evidence for Colonial Virginia', *Historical Archaeology*, 50/2: 17–46.

Henderson, Graeme (1975). '*James Matthews* Excavation Summer 1974–5', *Australian Archaeology*, 3: 40–5.

Henderson, Graeme (1976). '*James Matthews* Excavation Summer 1974: Interim Report', *International Journal of Nautical Archaeology*, 5: 245–51.

Henderson, Graeme (1978). 'Four Seasons of Excavation on the *James Matthews* Wreck', in John-Bruce Green (ed.), *Papers from the First Southern Hemisphere Conference on Maritime Archaeology*. Melbourne: Ocean's Society of Australia, 73–9.

Henderson, Graeme (1980). *Unfinished Voyages: Western Australian Shipwrecks 1622–1850*. Nedlands: University of Western Australia Press.

Henderson, Graeme (2008). 'The Wreck of the Ex-Slaver *James Matthews*', *International Journal of Historical Archaeology*, 12/1: 39–52.

Henderson, Graeme, and Myra Stanbury (1983). 'The Excavation of a Collection of Cordage from a Shipwreck Site', *International Journal of Nautical Archaeology*, 12: 15–26.

Henn, Cathryn (2012). 'The Trouble with Treasure: Historic Shipwrecks Discovered in International Waters', *University of Miami International and Comparative Law Review*, 19/2: 142–96.

Herbert, Eugenia (1984). *Red Gold of Africa: Copper in Precolonial History and Culture*. Madison: University of Wisconsin Press.

Herry, Nolwenn (2004). 'Report on Finds from the Saint-Quay-Portrieux Wreck, France', *International Journal of Nautical Archaeology*, 33/1: 96–105.

Herskovits, Melville (1989 [1941]). *The Myth of the Negro Past*. Boston: Beacon Press.

Hicks, Dan (2005). '"Places for Thinking" from Annapolis to Bristol: Situations and Symmetries in "World Historical Archaeologies"', *World Archaeology*, 37/3: 373–91.

Hogendorn, Jan, and Marion Johnson (1986). *The Shell Money of the Slave Trade*. Cambridge: Cambridge University Press.

Holm, John (2000). *An Introduction to Pidgins and Creoles*. Cambridge: Cambridge University Press.

Hopwood, Lisa (2009). 'Glass Trade Beads from an Elmina Shipwreck. More than Pretty Trinkets', MA thesis, University of West Florida.

Hornell, James (1923). 'Survivals of the Use of Oculi in Modern Boats', *Journal of the Royal Anthropological Institute of Great Britain and Ireland*, 53: 289–321.

Horrell, Christopher (2017). 'Analysis of the Mardi Gras Shipwreck Ship's Stove', *Historical Archaeology*, 51/3: 359–78.

Huber, Magnus (1999). *Ghanaian Pidgin English in its West African Context*. Amsterdam: John Benjamins.

Hughes, Griffith (1750). *The Natural History of Barbados: In Ten Books*. London: Printed for the author.

Hugill, Stan (1961). *Shanties from the Seven Seas*. London: Routledge & Keagan Paul.

Hutchinson, William (1794). *A Treatise on Naval Architecture*. 4th edn. Liverpool: T. Billing.

Innes, Joanna (2005). 'Legislation and Public Participation 1760–1830', in David Lemmings (ed.), *The British and their Laws in the Eighteenth Century*. Woodbridge: Boydell Press, 102–32.

Inikori, Joseph (1989). 'Slavery and the Revolution in Cotton Textile Production in England', *Social Science History*, 13/4: 343–79.

Inikori, Joseph (1992). 'Slavery and the Revolution in Cotton Textile Production in England', in Joseph Inikori and Stanley Engerman (eds), *The Atlantic Slave Trade: Effects on Economies, Societies and Peoples in Africa, the Americas, and Europe*. Durham, NC, and London: Duke University Press, 145–82.

Inikori, Joseph (1996). 'Measuring the Unmeasured Hazards of the Atlantic Slave Trade: Documents Relating to the British Trade', *Outre-Mers. Revue d'Histoire*, 83/312: 53–92.

Inikori, Joseph (2002). *Africans and the Industrial Revolution in England: A Study in International Trade and Economic Development*. Cambridge: Cambridge University Press.

Inikori, Joseph (2007). 'Changing Commodity Composition of Imports into West Africa 1650–1850', in James Kwesi Anquandah (ed.), *The Transatlantic Slave Trade: Landmarks, Legacies, Expectations*. Legon: Sub-Saharan Publishers, 57–80.

Insoll. Tim, and Thurstan Shaw (1997). 'Gao and Igbo-Ukwu: Beads, Interregional Trade and Beyond', *African Archaeological Review*, 14/1: 9–23.

Jacobi, Keith, Delia Cook, Robert Corruccini, and Jerome Handler (1992). 'Congenital Syphilis in the Past: Slaves at Newton Plantation, Barbados West Indies', *American Journal of Physical Anthropology*, 89: 145–58.

Jackson, Hazelle (2001). *Shell Houses and Grottoes*. Princes Risborough: Shire Publications.

Jackson, Fatimah, Arion Mayes, Mark Mack, Alain Froment, Shomarka Keita, Richard Kittles, Kenya Shujaa, Michael Blakey, and Lesley Rankin-Hill (2009). 'Origins of the New York African Burial Ground Population: Biological Evidence of Geographical and Macroethnic Affiliations Using Craniometrics, Dental Morphology, and Preliminary Genetic Analyses', in Michael Blakey and

Lesley Rankin-Hill (eds), *Skeletal Biology of the New York African Burial Ground, Part I*. Washington: Howard University Press, 69–94.

Jamieson, Ross (1995). 'Material Culture and Social Death: African-American Burial Practices', *Historical Archaeology*, 29/ 4: 39–58.

Jefferson, Thomas (1787). *Notes on the State of Virginia*. London: John Stockdale.

Jefferess, David (2008). *Postcolonial Resistance: Culture, Liberation, and Transformation*. Toronto: University of Toronto Press.

Jennings, Judith (1997). *The Business of Abolishing the British Slave Trade 1783–1807*. London: Frank Cass.

Johansson, Anna, and Stellan Vinthagen (2016). 'Dimensions of Everyday Resistance: An Analytical Framework', *Critical Sociology*, 42/3: 417–35.

Johansson, Anna, and Stellan Vinthagen (2020). *Conceptualising 'Everyday Resistance': A Transdisciplinary Approach*. London: Routledge.

Johnson, Jessica Marie (2018). 'Markup Bodies: Black [Life] Studies and Slavery [Death] Studies at the Digital Crossroads', *Social Text*, 36/4: 57–79.

Johnson, Samuel (1755–6). *A Dictionary of the English Language*. London: printed by W. Strahan, for J. and P. Knapton et al.

Johnson, Walter (2003). 'On Agency', *Journal of Social History*, 37/1: 113–24.

Johnson, Walter (2013). *River of Dark Dreams: Slavery and Empire in the Cotton Kingdom*. Cambridge, MA: Belknap Press of Harvard University Press.

Johnston, Paul (1993). 'Treasure Salvage, Archaeological Ethics and Maritime Museums', *International Journal of Nautical Archaeology*, 22/1: 53–60.

Jones, Adam (1994). 'Drink Deep, or Taste not: Thoughts on the Use of Early European Records in the Study of African Material Culture', *History in Africa*, 21: 349–70.

Jones, Adam (1995) (ed. and trans.). *West Africa in the Mid-Seventeenth Century: An Anonymous Dutch Manuscript*. Atlanta: African Studies Association.

Joseph, Joe (2017). 'Crosses, Crescents, Slashes, Stars: African-American Potters and Edgefield District Pottery Marks', *Journal of African Diaspora Archaeology and Heritage*, 6/2: 110–32.

Kalua, Fetson (2009). 'Homi Bhabha's Third Space and African Identity', *Journal of African Cultural Studies*, 21/1: 23–32.

Karklins, Karlis (1974). 'Seventeenth Century Dutch Beads', *Historical Archaeology*, 8/1: 64–82.

Karklins, Karlis (1991). 'Beads from the Mid-18th Century Manilla Wreck, Bermuda', *International Journal of Nautical Archaeology*, 20/1: 33–42.

Karklins, Karlis, Laure Dussebieux, and Ron Hancock (2015). 'A 17th Century Glass Bead Factory at Hammersmith Embankment London, England', *Beads*, 27: 16–24.

Keefer, Katrina (2013). 'Scarification and Identity in the Liberated Africans Department Register, 1814–1815', *Canadian Journal of African Studies*, 47/3: 537–53.

Keefer, Katrina (2019). 'Marked by Fire: Brands, Slavery, and Identity', *Slavery & Abolition*, 40/4: 659–81.

Kelly, Kenneth (2001). 'Change and Continuity in Coastal Bénin', in Christopher DeCorse (ed.), *West Africa during the Atlantic Slave Trade: Archaeological Perspectives*. London: University of Leicester Press, 81–100.

Kelly, Kenneth (2004). 'The African Diaspora Starts Here: Historical Archaeology of Coastal West Africa', in Andrew and Paul Lane (eds), *African Historical Archaeologies*. London: Kluwer Academic Press, 219–41.

Kelly, Kenneth (2009). 'Controlling Traders: Slave Coast Strategies at Savi and Ouidah', in Caroline Williams (ed.), *Bridging Early Modern Atlantic Worlds: People, Products, and Practices on the Move*. Farnham: Ashgate Publishing, 151–71.

Kelly, Kenneth (2010). 'Annals of Action; Trade as Power, Trade as Identity', in Alexander Bauer and Anna Agbe-Davies (eds), *Social Archaeologies of Trade and Exchange: Exploring Relationships among People, Places, and Things*. Walnut Creek: Left Coast Press, 99–118.

Kidd, Kenneth, and Martha Kidd (2012). 'A Classification System for Glass Beads for the Use of Field Archaeologists', *Beads: Journal of the Society of Bead Researchers*, 24/1: 39–61.

King-Dorset, Rodreguez (2008). *Black Dance in London, 1730–1850: Innovation, Tradition and Resistance*. London: McFarland & Co.

Kimber, John (1792). *The Trial of Captain John Kimber*. London: William Lane.

Kiple, Kenneth, and Brian Higgins (1989). 'Mortality Caused by Dehydration during the Middle Passage', *Social Science History*, 13/4: 421–37.

Kirby Talley, M., Jnr. (1997). 'Miscreants and Hotentots: Restorers and Restoration Attitudes and Practices in 17th and 18th Century England', *Museum Management and Curatorship*, 16/1: 35–44.

Kitson, Peter (2004). '"Candid Reflections": The Idea of Race in the Debate over the Slave Trade and Slavery in the Late Eighteenth and Early Nineteenth Century', in Brycchan Carey, Markman Ellis, and Sara Salih (eds), *Discourses of Slavery and Abolition*. London: Palgrave Macmillan, 11–25.

Kleij, Piet (2017). 'The Zaanstreek District as a Maritime Industrial Landscape (1500–1800)', in Jerzy Gawronski, Andre van Holk, and Joost Schokkenbroek (eds), *Ships and Maritime Landscapes: Proceedings of the Thirteenth International Symposium on Boat and Ship Archaeology, Amsterdam 2012*. Eelde: Barkhuis Publishing, 69–94.

Klein, Herbert (2010). *The Atlantic Slave Trade*. Cambridge: Cambridge University Press.

Klein, Herbert, and Stanley Engerman (1979). 'A Note on Mortality in the French Slave Trade in the Eighteen Century', in Henry Gemery and Jan Hogendorn (eds), *The Uncommon Market: Essays in the Economic History of the Atlantic Slave Trade*. New York: Academic Press, 239–60.

Klein, Herbert, and Stanley Engerman (1997). 'Long-Term Trends in African Mortality in the Transatlantic Slave Trade', in David Eltis and David Richardson (eds), *Routes to Slavery: Direction, Ethnicity and Mortality in the Transatlantic Slave Trade*. London: Frank Cass, 36–48.

Klein, Herbert, Stanley Engerman, Robin Haines, and Ralph Shlomowitz (2001). 'Transoceanic Mortality: The Slave Trade in Comparative Perspective', *William and Mary Quarterly*, 58/1: 93–118.

Knoblock, Glen (2015). *African American Historic Burial Grounds and Gravesites of New England*. Jefferson: McFarland and Co.

Koleini, Farahnaz, Philippe Colomban, Innocent Pikirayi, and Linda C. Prinsloo (2019). 'Glass Beads, Markers of Ancient Trade in Sub-Saharan Africa: Methodology, State of the Art and Perspectives', *Heritage*, 2/3: 2343–69.

Kraamer, Malika (in press). 'Abolitionism and Kente Cloth: Early Modern West African Textiles in Thomas Clarkson's Chest', in Stephan Hanss and Beatriz Marin Aguilera (eds), *In-Between Textiles, 1400–1800: Weaving Subjectivities and Encounters*. Amsterdam: Amsterdam University Press.

Kriger, Colleen (2006). *Cloth in West African History*. Lanham: Altamira Press.

Kriger, Colleen (2009). '"Guinea Cloth": Production and Consumption of Cotton Textiles in West Africa before and during the West African Slave Trade', in Giorgio Riello and Prasannan Parthasarathi (eds), *The Spinning World: A Global History of Cotton Textiles 1200–1850*. Oxford: Oxford University Press, 105–26.

Krikler, Jeremy (2007). 'The Zong and the Lord Chief Justice', *History Workshop Journal*, 64/1: 29–47.

Laffoon, Jason, Ryan Espersen, and Hayley Mickleburgh (2018). 'The Life History of an Enslaved African: Multiple Isotope Evidence for Forced Childhood Migration from Africa to the Caribbean and Associated Dietary Change', *Archaeometry*, 60/2: 350–65.

Land, Isaac (2001). 'Customs of the Sea: Flogging, Empire, and the "True British Seaman" 1770 to 1870', *Interventions*, 3/2: 169–85.

LaRoche, Cheryl (1994). 'Beads from the African Burial Ground, New York City: A Preliminary Assessment', *Beads*, 6/1: 3–20.

Laslett, Peter (1971). 'Age at Menarche in Europe since the Eighteenth Century', *Journal of Interdisciplinary History*, 2/2: 221–36.

Lavery, Brian (1984). *The Ship of the Line*, ii. *Design, Construction and Fittings*. London: Conway Maritime Press.

Law, Robin (1982). 'Jean Barbot as a Source for the Slave Coast of West Africa', *History in Africa*, 9: 155–73.

484 REFERENCES

Law, Robin (1989). 'The Slave-Trader as Historian: Robert Norris and the History of Dahomey', *History in Africa*, 16: 219–35.

Law, Robin (2004). *Ouidah: The Social History of a West African Slaving 'Port' 1727–1892*. Oxford: James Currey.

Law, Robin (2005). 'Ethnicities of Enslaved Africans in the Diaspora: On the Meanings of "Mina" (Again)', *History in Africa*, 32: 247–67.

Law, Robin (1997–2006) (ed.). *The English in West Africa, 1681–1699: The Local Correspondence of the Royal African Company of England (Part 1: 1681–1683, Part 2: 1685–1688, Part 3: 1691–1699)*. Oxford: Oxford University Press/British Academy.

Law, Robin (2007). 'Book Review. The Memoirs of Captain Hugh Crow: The Life and Times of a Slave Trade Captain', *International Journal of Maritime History*, 19/2: 483–5.

Law, Robin (2011). 'West Africa's Discovery of the Atlantic', *International Journal of African Historical Studies*, 44/1: 1–25.

Law, Robin (2018). 'William's Fort: The English Fort at Ouidah, 1680s–1960s', in John Kwadwo Osei-Tutu (ed.), *Forts, Castles and Society in West Africa: Ghana and Benin, 1450–1960*. Leiden: Brill, 119–47.

Lawler, Andrew (2005). 'Archaeology: Oxford Centre Raises Controversy', *Science*, 25 (February): 1192–3.

Lawrence, Arnold (1963). *Trade Castles and Forts of West Africa*. London: Cape.

Leone, Mark, and Gladys-Marie Fry (1999). 'Conjuring in the Big House Kitchen: An Interpretation of African American Belief Systems Based on the Uses of Archaeology and Folklore Sources', *Journal of American Folklore*, 112/445: 372–403.

Leone, Mark, Gladys-Marie Fry and Timothy Ruppel (2001). 'Spirit Management among Americans of African Descent', in Charles Orser (ed.), *Race and the Archaeology of Identity*. Salt Lake City: University of Utah Press, 143–57.

Lever, Darcy (1808). *The Young Sea Officer's Sheet Anchor*. London: printed for John Richardson.

Lewis, Andrew (2007). 'Martin Dockray and the *Zong*: A Tribute in the Form of a Chronology', *Journal of Legal History*, 28: 357–70.

Lima, Tania Andre, Marcos de Souza, and Glauca Sene (2014). 'Weaving the Second Skin: Protection against Evil among the Valongo Slaves in Nineteenth-Century Rio de Janeiro', *Journal of African Diaspora Archaeology and Heritage*, 3/2: 103–36.

Lind, James (1762). *An Essay on Diseases Incidental to Europeans in Hot Climates*. London: printed for D. Wilson, Strand.

Lind, James (1774). *An Essay on the Most Effectual Means of Preserving the Health of Seamen in the Royal Navy*. London: Printed for D Wilson and G. Nicol in the Strand.

Linebaugh, Peter, and Marcus Rediker (2000). *The Many-Headed Hydra: The Hidden History of the Revolutionary Atlantic*. London: Verso.

Lingold, Mary (2017). 'Peculiar Animations: Listening to Afro-Atlantic Music in Caribbean Travel Narratives', *Early American Literature*, 52/3: 623–50.

London Society of Cabinet-Makers (1793). *The Cabinet-Makers' London Book of Prices, and Designs of Cabinet Work, Calculated for the Convenience of Cabinet Makers in General*. London: London Society of Cabinet-Makers.

Long, Edward (1774). *The History of Jamaica*. London: T. Lowndes.

LoGerfo, James (1973). 'Sir William Dolben and "The Cause of Humanity": The Passage of the Slave Trade Regulation Act of 1788', *Eighteenth-Century Studies*, 6/4: 431–51.

Lovejoy, Henry (2016). 'The Registers of Liberated Africans of the Havana Slave Trade Commission: Implementation and Policy, 1824–1841', *Slavery & Abolition*, 37/1: 23–44.

Lovejoy, Paul (2006a). 'Autobiography and Memory: Gustavus Vassa, Alias Olaudah Equiano, the African', *Slavery & Abolition*, 27/3: 317–47.

Lovejoy, Paul (2006b). 'The Children of Slavery: The Transatlantic Phase', *Slavery & Abolition*, 27/2: 197–217.

Lovejoy, Paul (2007). 'Issues of motivation—Vassa/Equiano and Carretta's Critique of the Evidence', *Slavery & Abolition*, 28/1: 121–5.

Lovejoy, Paul (2010). 'Scarification and the Loss of History in the African Diaspora', in Andrew Apter and Lauren Derby (eds), *Activating the Past: History and Memory in the Black Atlantic World*. Newcastle: Cambridge Scholars Publishing, 99–138.

Lovejoy, Paul, and Vanessa Oliveira (2013). 'An Index to the Slavery and Slave Trade Enquiry: The British Parliamentary House of Commons Sessional Papers, 1788–1792', *History in Africa*, 40/1: 193–255.

Lovejoy, Paul, and David Richardson (1999). 'Trust, Pawnship and Atlantic History: The Institutional Foundations of the Old Calabar Slave Trade', *American Historical* Review, 104/2: 333–55.

Lovejoy, Paul, and David Richardson (2001). 'Letters of the Old Calabar Slave Trade 1760–1789', in Vincent Carretta and Philip Gould (eds), *Genius in Bondage: Literature of the Early Black Atlantic*. Lexington: University Press of Kentucky, 89–115.

Lovejoy, Paul and David Richardson (2004). "This Horrid Hole': Royal Authority, Commerce and Credit at Bonny, 1690–1840', *The Journal of African History*, 45/3: 363–92.

Lujan, Heidi, and Stephen DiCarlo (2018). 'The "African Gene" Theory: It is Time to Stop Teaching and Promoting the Slavery Hypertension Hypothesis', *Advances in Physiology Education*, 42: 412–16.

Lusardi, Wayne (2006). 'The Beaufort Inlet Shipwreck Artifact Assemblage', in Russell Skowronek and Charles Ewen (eds), *X Marks the Spot: The Archaeology of Piracy*. Gainsville: University Press of Florida, 196–218.

Lynn, Martin (1997). *Commerce and Economic Change in West Africa: The Palm Oil Trade in the Nineteenth Century*. Cambridge: Cambridge University Press.

McBride, Dwight (2001). *Impossible Witnesses: Truth, Abolitionism, and Slave Testimony*. New York: New York University Press.

McCarthy, Michael (2005). *Ships' Fastenings: From Sewn Boat to Steam Ship*. College Station: Texas A&M University Press.

McCreery, Cindy (2000). '"True Blue and Black, Brown and Fair": Prints of British Sailors and their Women during the Revolutionary and Napoleonic Wars', *Journal for Eighteenth-Century Studies*, 23/22: 135–52.

McDermott, Brendon (2000). 'English and American Shipboard Carpenters *c.*1725–1825', MA thesis, Texas A & M University.

MacDonald, Janet (2014). *Feeding Nelson's Navy*. Barnsley: Frontline Books.

MacGaffey Wyatt (1974). 'Oral Tradition in Central Africa', *International Journal of African Historical Studies*, 7/3: 417–26.

MacGaffey, Wyatt (1986). *Religion and Society in Central Africa: The BaKongo of Lower Zaire*. Chicago: University of Chicago Press.

MacGaffey, Wyatt (1994). 'Dialogues of the Deaf: Europeans on the Atlantic Coast of Africa', in Stuart B. Schwartz (ed.), *Implicit Understandings: Observing, Reporting and Reflecting on the Encounters between Europeans and Other Peoples in the Early Modern Era*. Cambridge: Cambridge University Press, 249–67.

MacGaffey, Wyatt (2000). 'The Kongo Peoples', in Frank Herreman (ed.), *In the Presence of Sprits: African Art from the National Museum of Ethnography, Lisbon*. Ghent: Snoek-Ducaju and Zoon, 35–75.

MacGaffey, Wyatt (2018). 'A Central African Kingdom: Kongo in 1480', in Koen Bostoen and Inge Brinkman (eds), *The Kongo Kingdom: The Origins, Dynamics and Cosmopolitan Culture of an African Polity*. Cambridge: Cambridge University Press, 42–59.

MacGregor, Arthur (1983). *Tradescant's Rarities: Essays on the Foundation of the Ashmolean Museum 1683*. Oxford: Oxford University Press,

MacGregor, Arthur (2014). 'Patrons and Collectors: Contributors of Zoological Subjects to the Works of George Edwards (1694–1773)'. *Journal of the History of Collections* 26/1: 35–44.

MacGregor, David (1985). *Merchant Sailing Ships: 1775–1815. The Sovereignty of Sail*. London: Conway Maritime Press.

MacQuarrie, Helen, and Andrew Pearson (2016). 'Prize Possessions: Transported Material Culture from the Post-Abolition Enslaved—New Evidence from St Helena', *Slavery & Abolition*, 37/1: 45–72.

Makepeace, Margaret (1989). 'English Traders on the Guinea Coast, 1657–1668: An Analysis of the East India Company Archive', *History in Africa*, 16: 237–84.

Malcom, Corey (2000). 'The Copper Cauldrons aboard the *Henrietta Marie*', repr. *The Navigator: Newsletter of The Mel Fisher Maritime Heritage Society*, 15/2 (2000), https://www.academia.edu/5097911/The_Copper_Cauldrons_of_the_Henrietta_Marie (accessed 23 March 2023).

Malcom, Corey (2003). 'Trade Goods on the *Henrietta Marie* and the Price of Men in 1699–1700', https://www.academia.edu/2056731/Trade_Goods_on_the_Henrietta_Marie_and_the_Price_of_Men_in_1699_1700 (accessed 27 October 2022).

Malcom, Corey (2017). 'Continued Investigations of Sites and Artifacts Believed to Relate to the Pirate–Slaver *Guerrero* and HMS *Nimble*, 2005–2014', https://www.academia.edu/33290259/Continued_Investigations_of_Sites_and_Artifacts_believed_to_relate_to_the_Pirate_Slaver_Guerrero_and_HMS_Nimble_2005_2014 (accessed 23 March 2023).

Malcom, Corey (2021). 'The Iron Restraints of the Slave Ship *Henrietta Marie*. The Mel Fisher Maritime Museum, Occasional Paper 2', https://www.academia.edu/53153698/The_Iron_Restraints_of_the_Slave_Ship_Henrietta_Marie (accessed 29 June 2023).

Mallipeddi, Ramesh (2014). '"A Fixed Melancholy": Migration, Memory, and the Middle Passage', *Eighteenth Century*, 55/2: 235–53.

Mann, Emily (2018). 'Viewed from a Distance: Eighteenth-Century Images of Fortifications on the Coast of West Africa', in John Kwadwo Osei-Tutu and Victoria Smith (eds), *Shadows of Empire in West Africa: African Histories and Modernities*. Cham: Palgrave Macmillan, 107–36.

Manning, Patrick, and Yu Liu (2020). 'Research Note on Captive Atlantic Flows: Estimating Missing Data by Slave-Voyage Routes', *Journal of World-Systems Research*, 26/1: 103–25.

Mark, Peter (2007). 'Towards a Reassessment of the Dating and the Geographical Origins of the Luso-African Ivories, Fifteenth to Seventeenth Centuries', *History in Africa*, 34: 189–21.

Markham, Clement (2010) (ed.). *Journal of Christopher Columbus (during his First Voyage, 1492–93): And Documents Relating the Voyages of John Cabot and Gaspar Corte Real*. Cambridge: Cambridge University Press.

Marshall, Kenneth (2004). 'Powerful and Righteous: The Transatlantic Survival and Cultural Resistance of an Enslaved African Family in Eighteenth-Century New Jersey', *Journal of American Ethnic History*, 23/2: 23–49.

Martin, Bernard, and Mark Spurrell (1962) (eds). *The Journal of a Slave Trader (John Newton) 1750–1754: With Newton's Thoughts upon the African Slave Trade*. London: Epworth Press.

Merkyte, Inga, and Klavs Randsborg (2009). 'Graves from Dahomey: Beliefs, Ritual and Society in Ancient Benin', *Journal of African Archaeology*, 7/1: 55–77.

Merkyte, Inga, and Klavs Randsborg (2012). 'Danish Castles, Forts and Plantations in Ghana: The Archaeological Evidence', *Acta Archaeologia*, 83: 317–22.

Metcalf, George (1987). 'A Microcosm of why Africans Sold Slaves: Akan Consumption Patterns in the 1770s', *Journal of African History*, 28/3: 377–94.

Midlo Hall, Gwendolyn (2005). *Slavery and African Ethnicities in the Americas: Restoring the Links*. Chapel Hill: University of North Carolina Press.

Midlo Hall, Gwendolyn (2010). 'Africa and Africans in the African Diaspora: The Uses of Relational Databases', *American Historical Review*, 115/1: 136–50.

Miller, William, John Callahan, James Craig, and Katherine Whatley (2005). '"Ruling Theories Linger": Questioning the Identity of the Beaufort Inlet Shipwreck: A Discussion', *International Journal of Nautical Archaeology*, 34/1: 339–41.

Minchinton Walter (1979). 'The Triangular Trade Revisited', in Henry Gemery and Jan Hogendorn (eds), *The Uncommon Market: Essays in the Economic History of the Atlantic Slave Trade*. New York: Academic Press, 331–52.

Minchinton, Walter (1989). 'Characteristics of British Slaving Vessels, 1698–1775', *Journal of Interdisciplinary History*, 21/1: 53–81.

Mintz, Sidney, and Richard Price (1976). *An Anthropological Approach to the Study of Afro-American History: A Caribbean Perspective.* Philadelphia: Institute for the Study of Human Issues, *Occasional Paper in Social Change*, Issue 2.

Mintz, Sidney, and Richard Price (1992). *The Birth of African-American Culture: An Anthropological Perspective.* Boston: Beacon Press.

Mitchell, Matthew (2012). 'The Fetish and Intercultural Commerce in Seventeenth-Century West Africa', *Itinerario*, 36/1: 7–21.

Mitchell, Matthew (2020). *The Prince of Slavers: Humphry Morice and the Transformation of Britain's Transatlantic Slave Trade, 1698-1732.* Palgrave Studies in the History of Finance. Cham: Palgrave Macmillan.

Mitchell, Peter (2005). *African Connections: Archaeological Perspectives on Africa and the Wider World.* Walnut Creek: Altamira Press.

Molà, Luca, and Marta Ajmar-Wollheim (2011). 'The Global Renaissance: Cross-Cultural Objects in the Early Modern Period', in Glenn Adamson, Giorgio Riello, and Sarah Teasley (eds), *Global Design History.* London: Routledge, 11–20.

Monroe, J. Cameron (2014). *The Precolonial State in West Africa: Building Power in Dahomey.* Cambridge: Cambridge University Press.

Monahan, Erika (2013). 'Locating Rhubarb: Early Modernity's Relevant Obscurity', in Paula Findlen (ed.), *Early Modern Things: Objects and their Histories 1500-1800.* London: Routledge, 227–51.

Monteith, Archibald (1990). 'Archibald John Monteith: Native Helper and Assistant in the Jamaica Mission at New Carmel', *Callaloo*, 13/1: 102–14.

Moore, David (1997). 'Blackbeard the pirate: historical background and the Beaufort Inlet shipwrecks'. *Tributaries* 7: 31–9.

Moore, David (1989). 'Anatomy of a 17th Century Slave Ship: Historical and Archaeological Investigations of The *Henrietta Marie* 1699', MA thesis, East Carolina University.

Moore, David (1997). Site Report: Historical and Archaeological Investigation of the Shipwreck Henrietta Marie. Mel Fisher Maritime Heritage Society.

Moore, David (2005). 'Technical Comments Relating to "Ruling Theory" and the Identification of the Beaufort Inlet Shipwreck', *International Journal of Nautical Archaeology*, 34/1: 335–9.

Moore, David, and Corey Malcom (2008). 'Seventeenth-Century Vehicle of the Middle Passage: Archaeological and Historical Investigations on the *Henrietta Marie* Shipwreck Site', *International Journal of Historical Archaeology*, 12/1: 20–38.

Morgan, Kenneth (1985). 'The Organization of the Convict Trade to Maryland: Stevenson, Randolph and Cheston, 1768–1775', *William and Mary Quarterly*, 42/2: 201–27.

Morgan, Kenneth (2003). 'James Rogers and the Bristol Slave Trade', *Historical Research*, 76/192: 189–216.

Morgan, Kenneth (2016). 'Building British Atlantic Port Cities: Bristol and Liverpool in the Eighteenth Century', in Daniel Maudlin and Bernard Herman (eds), *Building the British Atlantic World: Spaces, Places and Material Culture 1600-1850.* Chapel Hill: University of North Carolina Press, 212–28.

Morris, Martha (1998). 'The Rise of the English Sailcloth Industry 1565–1643: Coastal Trade Records as an Indicator of Import Substitution', *Mariner's Mirror*, 84/2: 139–51.

Moskovitz, David (1996). 'Hypertension, Thermotolerance and the "African Gene": An Hypothesis', *Clinical and Experimental Hypertension*, 18/1: 1–19.

Mouer, Daniel, Mary Ellen Hodges, Stephen Potter, Susan Henry Renaud, Ivor Noël Hume, Dennis Pogue, Martha McCartney, and Thomas Davidson (1999). 'Colonoware Pottery, Chesapeake Pipes, and "uncritical assumptions"', in Theresa Singleton (ed.), *I, too, am America: Archaeological Studies of African–American Life.* Charlottesville: University Press of Virginia, 83–115.

Mouser, Bruce (1978). 'Voyage of Good Sloop Dolphin to Africa 1795–1796', *American Neptune*, 38/4: 249–61.

Mouser, Bruce (2002) (ed.). *A Slaving Voyage to Africa and Jamaica: The Log of the Sandown, 1793-1794* (Bloomington: Indiana University Press, 2002).

Mühlhäusler, Peter (1986). *Pidgin and Creole Linguistics.* Oxford: Blackwell.

Mullin, Michael (1994). *Africa in America: Slave Acculturation and Resistance in the American South and the British Caribbean, 1736–1831*. Urbana: University of Illinois Press.

Murdoch, Steve (2004). 'John Brown: A Black Female Soldier in the Royal African Company', *World History Connected*, 1/2, https://worldhistoryconnected.press.uillinois.edu/1.2/murdoch.html (accessed 19 November 2022).

Murphy, Kathleen S. (2013). 'Collecting Slave Traders: James Petiver, Natural History, and the British Slave', *William and Mary Quarterly*, 70/4: 637–70.

Murphy, Kathleen (2020). 'James Petiver's "Kind Friends" and "Curious Persons" in the Atlantic World: Commerce, Colonialism and Collecting', *Notes and Records*, 74/2: 259–74.

Mustakeem, Sowande' (2016). *Slavery at Sea: Terror, Sex and Sickness in the Middle Passage*. Urbana: University of Illinois Press.

Navickas, Katrina (2015). *Protest and the Politics of Space and Place 1789–1848*. Manchester: Manchester University Press.

Navickas Katrina (2016). 'Thirdspace? Historians and the Spatial Turn, with a Case Study of Political Graffiti in Late Eighteenth- and Early Nineteenth-Century England', in Sam Griffiths and Alexander von Lünen (eds), *Spatial Cultures: Towards a New Social Morphology of Cities Past and Present*. London: Routledge, 99–107.

Neil, Jeremy (2010). 'Sifting through the Wreckage: an Analysis and Proposed Resolution Concerning the Disposition of Historic Shipwrecks Located in International Waters.' *New York Law School Review* 55 : 895–922.

Nelson, Jennifer (2015). 'Apprentices of Freedom: Atlantic Histories of the Africanos Livres in Mid–Nineteenth Century Rio de Janeiro', *Itinerario*, 39/2: 349–69.

Nelson, Louis (2014). 'Architectures of West African Enslavement', *Buildings & Landscapes: Journal of the Vernacular Architecture Forum*, 21/1: 88–125.

Nevadomsky, Joseph (2008). 'Mammy Wata, Inc.', in Henry Drewal (ed.), *Sacred Waters: Arts for Mami Wata and Other Divinities in Africa and the Diaspora*. Bloomington: Indiana University Press, 351–9.

Newman, Simon, Michael Deason, Yannis Pitsiladis, Antonio Salas, and Vincent Macaulay (2013). 'The West African Ethnicity of the Enslaved in Jamaica', *Slavery & Abolition*, 34/3: 376–400.

Newby-Alexander, Cassandra (2019). 'The Arrival of the First Africans to English North America', *Virginia Magazine of History and Biography*, 127/3: 186–99.

Newitt, Malyn (2010) (ed.). *The Portuguese in West Africa, 1415–1670: A Documentary History*. Cambridge: Cambridge University Press.

Newton, John (1788). *Thoughts upon the African Slave Trade*. London: Printed for J. Buckland in Pater-Noster Row; J. Johnson in St. Paul's Church-Yard; and J. Phillips, in George-Yard.

Norman, Neil (2009). 'Hueda (Whydah) Country and Town: Archaeological Perspectives on the Rise and Collapse of an African Atlantic Kingdom', *International Journal of African Historical Studies*, 2/3: 387–410.

Norman, Neil (2010). 'Feasts in Motion: Archaeological Views of Parades, Ancestral Pageants, and Socio-Political Process in the Hueda Kingdom, 1650–1727 AD', *Journal of World Prehistory*, 23/4: 239–54.

Norman, Neil (2014). 'Slavery Matters and Materiality: Atlantic Items, Political Processes, and the Collapse of the Hueda Kingdom, Benin, West Africa', in Lynn Wilson Marshall (ed.), *The Archaeology of Slavery: A Comparative Approach to Captivity and Coercion*. Southern Illinois University Carbondale Occasional Paper No. 41, Carbondale: Southern Illinois University Press, 215–29.

Norris, Robert (1788). *A Short Account of the African Slave Trade*. Liverpool: printed for Ann Smith's Navigation Shop.

Norris, Robert (1789). *The Memoirs of the Reign of Bossa Ahadee, King of Dahomy*. London: W. Lowndes.

Northrup, David (2000). 'Igbo and Myth Igbo: Culture and Ethnicity in the Atlantic World 1600–1850', *Slavery & Abolition*, 23/3: 1–20.

Northrup, David (2013). 'Identity among Liberated Africans in Sierra Leone', in Jorge Cañizares-Esguerra, Matt Childs, and James Sidbury (eds), *The Black Urban Atlantic in the Age of the Slave Trade*. Philadelphia: University of Pennsylvania Press, 21–40.

Norton, Holly (2013). 'Estate by Estate: The Landscape of the 1733 St Jan Slave Rebellion', Ph.D. thesis, Syracuse University.

Nunley, John (2010). 'Jolly Masquerades of Sierra Leone and the Creole Histories of Atlantic Rim Performance Arts', in Andrew Apter and Lauren Derby (eds), *Activating the Past: History and Memory in the Black Atlantic World*. Newcastle: Cambridge Scholars Publishing, 45–70.

Nussbaum, Felicity (1990). 'Introduction: The Politics of Difference', *Eighteenth-Century Studies*, 23/4: 375–86.

Nwokeji, G. Ugo, and David Eltis (2002a). 'Characteristics of Captives Leaving the Cameroons, 1822–1837', *Journal of African History*, 43/2: 191–210.

Nwokeji, G. Ugo, and David Eltis (2002b). 'The Roots of the African Diaspora: Methodological Considerations in the Analysis of Names in the Liberated African Registers of Sierra Leone and Havana', *History in Africa*, 29: 365–79.

O'Malley, Gregory (2014). *Final Passages: The Intercolonial Slave Trade of British America, 1619–1807*. Chapel Hill: University of North Carolina Press.

Oertling, Thomas (1996). *Ships' Bilge Pumps: A History of Their Development 1500–1900*. College Station: Texas A&M University Press.

Ogude, S.E. (1982). 'Facts into Fiction: Equiano's Narrative Reconsidered', *Research in African Literature*, 13/1: 31–43.

Ogundiran, Akinwumi (2002). 'Of Small Things Remembered: Beads, Cowries, and Cultural Translations of the Atlantic Experience in Yorubaland', *International Journal of African Historical Studies*, 35/2–3: 427–57.

Ojo, Olatunji (2008). 'Beyond Diversity: Women, Scarification, and Yoruba Identity', *History in Africa*, 35: 347–74.

Oldfield, John (2003) (ed.). *The British Transatlantic Slave Trade*, iii. *The Abolitionist Struggle: Opponents of the Slave Trade*. London: Pickering & Chatto.

Oldham, James (1992). *The Mansfield Manuscripts and the Growth of English Law in the Eighteenth Century*. 2 vols. Chapel Hill: University of North Carolina Press.

Oldham, James (2007). 'Insurance Litigation Involving the *Zong* and other British Slave Ships, 1780–1807'. *Journal of Legal History*, 28: 299–318.

Olsen, Carol (1979). 'Stylistic Developments of Ship Figureheads of the United States East Coast', *International Journal of Nautical Archaeology*, 8/4: 321–32.

Osei-Tutu, John Kwadwo (2018). 'Gold Coast Forts and Castles: Key Themes and Perspectives', in John Kwadwo Osei-Tutu (ed.), *Forts, Castles and Society in West Africa: Ghana and Benin, 1450–1960*. Leiden: Brill, 33–6.

Otele, Olivette (2012). 'Bristol, Slavery and the Politics of Representation: The Slave Trade Gallery in the Bristol Museum', *Social Semiotics*, 22/2: 155–72.

Owen, Nicholas (1930) (ed.). *Nicholas Owen. Journal of a Slave Trader*, ed. Eveline Martin. London: Routledge and Sons.

Paley, Ruth, Christina Malcolmson, and Michael Hunter (2010). 'Parliament and Slavery, 1660–c.1710', *Slavery & Abolition*, 31/2: 257–81.

Palmer, Colin (1986). 'The Company Trade and the Numerical Distribution of Slaves to Spanish America, 1703–1739', in Paul Lovejoy (ed.), *Africans in Bondage: Studies in Slavery and the Slave Trade*. Madison: University of Wisconsin Press, 27–42.

Palmer, Colin (2002). 'The Middle Passage', in Mariners' Museum, *Captive Passage: the Transatlantic Slave Trade and the Making of the Americas* Washington DC: Smithsonian Institution Press, 53–75.

Palmié, Stephan (2007). 'Is There a Model in a Muddle? "Creolization" in African Americanist History and Anthropology', in Charles Stewart (ed.), *Creolization: History, Ethnography, Theory*. Walnut Creek: Left Coast Press, 178–200.

Palmié, Stephan (2010). '*Ekpe/Abakuá* in Middle Passage: Time, Space and Units of Analysis in African American Historical Anthropology', in Andrew Apter and Lauren Derby (eds), *Activating* the *Past: History and Memory in the Black Atlantic World*. Newcastle: Cambridge Scholars Publishing, 1–44.

Palmié, Stephan (2013). *The Cooking of History: How Not to Study Afro-Cuban Religion*. Chicago: University of Chicago Press.

Parés, Luis (2010). 'Memories of Slavery in Religious Ritual: Comparing Benin Vodun and Bahian Candomblé', in Andrew Apter and Lauren Derby (eds), *Activating the Past: History and Memory in the Black Atlantic World*. Newcastle: Cambridge Scholars Publishing, 71–97.

Park, Mungo (1799). *Travels in the Interior Districts of Africa*. London: Bulmer and Co.

Paton, Diana (1996). 'Decency, Dependence and the Lash: Gender and the British Debate over Slave Emancipation, 1830–34', *Slavery & Abolition*, 17/3: 163–84.

Paton, Diana (2005). 'Telling Stories about Slavery', *History Workshop Journal*, 59: 251–4.

Paton, Diana (2012). 'Witchcraft, Poison, Law and Atlantic Slavery', *William and Mary Quarterly*, 69/2: 235–64.

Patterson, Orlando (1982). *Slavery and Social Death*. Cambridge, MA: Harvard University Press.

Paul, Helen (2014). 'Suppliers to the Royal African Company and the Royal Navy in the Early Eighteenth Century', in Paul Fynn (ed.), *War, Entrepreneurs and the State*. Leiden: Brill, 131–50.

Pearson, Andrew, Ben Jeffs, Annsofie Witkin, and Helen MacQuarrie (2011). *Infernal Traffic: Excavation of a Liberated African Graveyard in Rupert's Valley, St Helena*, Research Report 169. York: Council for British Archaeology.

Pearson, Robin, and David Richardson (2019). 'Insuring the Transatlantic Slave Trade', *Journal of Economic History*, 79/2: 417–46.

Perry, Warren, and Janet Woodruff (2006). 'Coins, Shells, Pipes, and Other Items', in Michael Blakey and Lesley Rankin-Hill (eds), *New York African Burial Ground Archaeology Final Report*, i. Washington: Howard University, 419–43.

Pettigrew, William (2013). *Freedom's Debt: The Royal African Company and the Politics of the Atlantic Slave Trade, 1672–1752*. Chapel Hill: University of North Carolina Press.

Petiver, James (1697). 'A Catalogue of Some Guinea-Plants with their Native Names and Virtues; Sent to James Petiver, Apothecary and Fellow of the Royal Society; with his Remarks on them. Communicated in a Letter to Dr Hans Sloane', *Philosophical Transactions*, 19: 677–86.

Picton, John (1996). 'West Africa and the Guinea Coast', in Tom Phillips (ed.), *Africa: The Art of a Continent*. Munich: Prestel, 327–477.

Piddock, Susan (2007). *A Space of Their Own: The Archaeology of Nineteenth Century Lunatic Asylums in Britain, South Australia and Tasmania*. New York: Springer.

Piersen, William (1977). 'White Cannibals, Black Martyrs: Fear, Depression, and Religious Faith as Causes of Suicide Among New Slaves'. *The Journal of Negro History* 62/2: 147–159.

Pietruszka, Andrew (2011). 'Artifacts of Exchange: A Multiscalar Approach to Maritime Archaeology at Elmina, Ghana', Ph.D. thesis, Syracuse University, 2011.

Pietsch, Roland (2004). 'Ships' Boys and Youth Culture in Eighteenth-Century Britain: The Navy Recruits of the London Marine Society', *Northern Mariner*, 14/4: 11–124.

Pinckard, George (1806). *Notes on the West Indies*. London: Longman, Hurst, Rees, and Orme.

Plumb, Christopher (2015). *The Georgian Menagerie: Exotic Animals in Eighteenth-Century London*. London: I. B. Tauris.

Polanyi, Karl, and Abraham Rotstein (1966). *Dahomey and the Slave Trade: An Analysis of an Archaic Economy*. Seattle: University of Washington Press.

Porter, R. (1968). 'The Crispe Family and the African Trade in the Seventeenth Century', *Journal of African History*, 9/1: 57–77.

Postma, Johannes (1990). *The Dutch in the Atlantic Slave Trade 1600–1815*. Cambridge: Cambridge University Press.

Poulter, Emma (2011). 'The Real Thing? Souvenir Objects in the West African Collections at the Manchester Museum', *Journal of Material Culture*, 16/3: 265–84.

Price, Douglas, Vera Tiesler, and James Burton (2006). 'Early African Diaspora in Colonial Campeche, Mexico: Strontium Isotopic Evidence', *American Journal of Physical Anthropology*, 130: 485–90.

Price, Douglas, James Burton, Andrea Cucina, Pilar Zabala, Robert Frei, Robert Tykot, and Vera Tiesler (2012). 'Isotopic Studies of Human Skeletal Remains from a Sixteenth to Seventeenth Century AD Churchyard in Campeche, Mexico: Diet, Place of Origin, and Age', *Current Anthropology*, 53/4: 396–433.

Price, Franklin (2016). 'More than Meets the Eye: A Preilinary Report on Artifacts from the Sediment of Site 31CR314, *Queen Anne's Revenge*, An Eighteenth-century Shipwreck off Beaufort Inlet, North Carolina', *Southeastern Archaeology*, 35/2: 155–69.

Price, Richard (2010). 'African Diaspora and Anthropology', in Tejumola Olinayan and James Sweet (eds), *The African Diaspora and the Disciplines*. Bloomington: Indiana University Press, 53–74.

Price, Richard, and Sally Price (1972). 'Kammbá: The Ethnohistory of an Afro-American Art', *Antropologica*, 32: 3–27.

Prideaux Nash, F. C. (1920). 'Extracts from a Slaver's Log', *Mariner's Mirror*, 6: 3–9.

Quilley, Geoff (2000). 'Missing the Boat: The Place of the Maritime in the History of British Visual Culture', *Visual Culture in Britain*, 1/2: 72–92.

Radburn, Nicholas, and David Eltis (2019). 'Visualizing the Middle Passage: The *Brooks* and the Reality of Ship Crowding in the Transatlantic Slave Trade', *Journal of Interdisciplinary History*, 49/4: 533–65.

Randsborg, Klavs, and Inga Merkyte (2009). *Bénin Archaeology: The Ancient Kingdoms*. Oxford: Wiley-Blackwell.

Rarey, Matthew (2018). 'Assemblage, Occlusion, and the Art of Survival in the Black Atlantic', *African Arts*, 51/4: 20–33.

Rath, Richard Cullen (1993). 'African Music in Seventeenth-Century Jamaica: Cultural Transit and Transition', *William and Mary Quarterly*, 50/4: 700–26.

Rath, Richard Cullen (2000). 'Drums and Power: Ways of Creolizing Music in Coastal South Carolina and Georgia, 1730–1790', in Stephen Reinhardt and David Buisseret (eds), *Creolization in the Americas*. College Station: Texas A&M University Press, 99–130.

Rath, Richard Cullen (2003). *How Early America Sounded*. Ithaca, NY: Cornell University Press.

Rath, Richard Cullen (2008). 'Hearing American History', *Journal of American History*, 95/2: 417–31.

Raveux, Olivier (2009). 'The Birth of a New European Industry: L'Indiennage in Seventeenth-Century Marseilles', in Giorgio Riello and Prasannan Parthasarathi (eds), *The Spinning World: A Global History of Cotton Textiles 1200–1850*. Oxford: Oxford University Press, 291–306.

Rawley, James (2003). *London Metropolis of the Slave Trade*. Columbia and London: University of Missouri Press.

Read, Sara (2008). '"Thy Righteousness is but a menstrual clout": Sanitary Practices and Prejudice in Early Modern England', *Early Modern Women*, 3: 1–25.

Rediker, Marcus (2007). *The Slave Ship: A Human History*. London: John Murray.

Rees, Gareth (1971). 'Copper Sheathing: An Example of Technological Diffusion in the English Merchant Fleet', *Journal of Transport History*, 2: 85–94.

Richardson, David (1976). 'Profits in the Liverpool Slave Trade: The Accounts of William Davenport, 1757–1784', in Roger Anstey and Paul Hair (eds), *Liverpool, the African Slave Trade, and Abolition: Essays to Illustrate Current Knowledge and Research*. Liverpool: Historic Society of Lancashire and Cheshire, 60–90.

Richardson, David (1979). 'West African Consumption Patterns and Their Influence in the Eighteenth-Century English Slave Trade', in Henry Gemery and Jan Hogendorn (eds), *The Uncommon Market: Essays in the Economic History of the Atlantic Slave Trade*. New York: Academic Press, 303–30.

Richardson, David (1986). *Bristol, Africa and the Eighteenth-Century Slave Trade to America*, i. *The Years of Expansion 1698–1729*. Bristol: Bristol Record Society.

Richardson, David (1994). 'Liverpool and the English Slave Trade', in Anthony Tibbles (ed.), *Transatlantic Slavery: Against Human Dignity*. London: HMSO, 70–6.

Richardson, David (1996). *Bristol, Africa and the Eighteenth-Century Slave Trade to America*, iv. *The Final Years 1770–1807*. Bristol: Bristol Record Society.

492 REFERENCES

Richardson, David (2001). 'Shipboard Revolts, African Authority and the Atlantic Slave Trade', *William and Mary Quarterly*, 58/1: 69–91.

Richardson, David (2001 [1985]). *The Bristol Slave Traders: A Collective Portrait*. Bristol: Bristol Branch of the Historical Association.

Richardson, David, Suzanne Schwarz, and Anthony Tibbles (2007) (eds). *Liverpool and Transatlantic Slavery*. Liverpool: Liverpool University Press.

Riello Giorgio (2009). 'Things that Shape History: Material Culture and Historical Narrative', in Karen Harvey (ed.), *History and Material Culture*. London: Routledge, 27–50.

Riello, Giorgio (2013). *Cotton: The Fabric that Made the Modern World*. Cambridge: Cambridge University Press.

Riello, Giorgio, and Prasannan Parthasarathi (2011) (eds). *The Spinning World: A Global History of Cotton Textiles, 1200–1850*. Oxford: Oxford University Press.

Riland, John (1827). *Memoirs of a West-India Planter: Published from an Original MS*. London: Hamilton Adams.

Riley, James (1987). *The Eighteenth-Century Campaign to Avoid Disease*. Hampshire: Macmillan Press.

Robbins, Louise (2002). *Elephants, Slaves and Pampered Parrots: Exotic Animals in Eighteenth Century Paris*. Baltimore: John Hopkins University Press.

Roberts, Jonathan (2011). 'Medical Exchange on the Gold Coast during the Seventeenth and Eighteenth Centuries', *Canadian Journal of African Studies*, 45/3: 480–523.

Robinson, Alexandra (2016). '"Citizens of the World": The Earle Family's Lehgorn and Venetian Business 1751–1808', in Felix Brahm and Eve Rosenhaft (eds), *Slavery Hinterland: Transatlantic Slavery and Continental Europe*. Woodbridge: Boydell Press, 45–63.

Robinson, Samuel (1867). *A Sailor Boy's Experience Aboard a Slave Ship in the Beginning of the Present Century*. Hamilton: W. M. Naismith.

Rodger, Nicholas (1988). *The Wooden World: An Anatomy of the Georgian Navy*. London: Fontana Press.

Rodgers, Bradley, Nathan Richards, and Wayne Lusardi (2005). '"Ruling Theories Linger": Questioning the Identity of the Beaufort Inlet Shipwreck', *International Journal of Nautical Archaeology*, 34/1: 24–37.

Rodgers, Silvia (1984). 'Feminine Power at Sea', *Royal Anthropological Institute News*, 64: 2–4.

Rodley, Edward. (2012). 'The Ethics of Exhibiting Salvaged Shipwrecks'. *Curator: The Museum Journal* 55/4: 383-391.

Ross, Doran (1981). 'The Heraldic Lion in Akan Art: a Study of Motif Assimilation in Southern Ghana.' *Metropolitan Museum Journal*: 165–180.

Roulston, Chris (2006). 'Framing Sensibility: The Female Couple in Art and Narrative', *Studies in English Literature 1500–1900*, 46/3: 641–55.

Rufino, Ana (2014). 'Modificações Dentárias Intencionais e Patologia Oral: Estudo de uma Amostra de Escravos Africanos dos Séculos xv–xvii', MA thesis, University of Coimbra, 2014.

Rupprecht, Anita (2016). '"Inherent Vice": Marine Insurance, Slave Ship Rebellion and the Law', *Race & Class*, 57/3: 31–44.

Rugendas, Johann Moritz (1835). *Voyage Pittoresque dans le Bresil*. Paris: Engelmann & Cie.

Saakwa-Mante, Norris (1999). 'Western Medicine and Racial Constitutions: Surgeon John Atkins' Theory of Polygenism and Sleepy Distemper in the 1730s', in Ernst Waltraud and Bernard Harris (eds), *Race, Science and Medicine, 1700–1960*. London: Routledge, 28–57.

Sadler, Nigel (2008). 'The Trouvadore Project: The Search for a Slave Ship and its Cultural Importance', *International Journal of Historical Archaeology*, 12/1: 53–70.

Sahlins, Marshall (1987). *Islands of History*. London: Tavistock Publications.

Sahlins, Marshall (1993). 'Goodbye to Tristes Tropes: Ethnography in the Context of Modern World History', *Journal of Modern History*, 65/1: 1–25.

Sahlins, Marshall (1995). *How 'Natives' Think. About Captain Cook, for Example*. Chicago: Chicago University Press.

Salmons, Jill (1977). 'Mammy Wata', *African Arts*, 10/33: 8–15.

Sanderson, F. E. (1972). 'The Liverpool Delegates and Sir William Dolben's Bill', *Transactions of the Historic Society of Lancashire and Cheshire*, 124: 57–84.

Schiebinger, Londa (2018). 'The Atlantic World Medical Complex', in Paula Findlen (eds), *Empires of Knowledge: Scientific Networks in the Early Modern World*. London: Routledge, 317–41.

Schofield, Maurice (1986). 'Shoes and Ships and Sealing Wax: Eighteenth-Century Lancashire Exports to the Colonies', *Transactions of the Historical Society of Lancashire and Cheshire*, 135: 61–82.

Schroeder, Hannes, and Kristrina Shuler (2006). 'Isotopic Investigations at Newton Plantation, Barbados: A Progress Report'. *African Diaspora Archaeology Newsletter*, 9/3, Article ii (accessed 20 July 2022).

Schroeder, Hannes, Tamsin O'Connell, Jane Evans, Kristina Shuler, and Robert Hedges (2009). 'Trans-Atlantic Slavery: Isotopic Evidence for Forced Migration to Barbados', *American Journal of Physical Anthropology*, 139/4: 547–57.

Schroeder, Hannes, Jay Havister, and T. Douglas Price (2014). 'The Zoutsteeg Three: Three New Cases of African Types of Dental Modification from Saint Martin, Dutch Caribbean', *International Journal of Osteoarchaeology*, 24/6: 688–96.

Schwarz, Suzanne (2015). 'Scottish Surgeons in the Liverpool Slave Trade in the Late Eighteenth and Early Nineteenth Centuries', in Tom Devine (ed.), *Recovering Scotland's Slavery Past: The Caribbean Connection*. Edinburgh: Edinburgh University Press, 145–65.

Schuler, Monica (2005). 'Enslavement, the Slave Voyage, and Astral and Aquatic Journeys in African Diaspora Discourse', in José Curto and Renée Soulodre-La France (eds), *Africa and the Americas: Interconnections during the Slave Trade*. Trenton, NJ: African World Press, 185–214.

Scott, David (1999). *Refashioning Futures: Criticism after Postcoloniality*. Princeton: Princeton University Press.

Scott, David (1991). 'That Event, this Memory: Notes on the Anthropology of African Diasporas in the New World', *Diaspora: A Journal of Transnational Studies*, 1/3: 261–84.

Scott, David (2004). *Conscripts of Modernity: The Tragedy of Colonial Enlightenment*. London: Duke University Press.

Scott, James (1985). *Weapons of the Weak: Everyday Forms of Peasant Resistance*. Yale: Yale University Press.

Scott, James (1990). *Domination and the Arts of Resistance: Hidden Transcripts*. Yale: Yale University Press.

Sharafi, Mitra (2003). 'The Slave Ship Manuscripts of Captain Joseph B. Cook: A Narrative Reconstruction of the Brig *Nancy*'s Voyage of 1793', *Slavery & Abolition*, 24/1: 71–100.

Sharfman, Jonathan, Jaco Boshoff, and Robert Parthesius (2012). 'Maritime and Underwater Cultural Heritage in South Africa: The Development of Relevant Management Strategies in the Historical Maritime Context of the Southern Tip of Africa', *Journal of Maritime Archaeology*, 7/1: 87–109.

Shaw, Rosalind (1997). 'The Production of Witchcraft/Witchcraft as Production: Memory, Modernity, and the Slave Trade in Sierra Leone', *American Ethnologist*, 24/4: 856–76.

Shaw, Rosalind (2002). *Memories of the Slave Trade: Ritual and the Historical Imagination in Sierra Leone*. Chicago: Chicago University Press.

Sheridan, Richard (1981). 'The Guinea Surgeons on the Middle Passage', *International Journal of African Historical Studies*, 14/4: 601–25.

Sheridan, Richard (1985). *Doctors and Slaves: A Medical and Demographic History of Slaves in the British West Indies 1680–1834*. Cambridge: Cambridge University Press.

Shumway, Rebecca (2011). *The Fante and the Transatlantic Slave Trade*. Rochester: University of Rochester Press.

Sidbury, James, and Jorge Cañizares-Esguerra (2011). 'Mapping Ethnogenesis in the Early Modern Atlantic', *William and Mary Quarterly*, 68/2: 181–208.

Silliman, Stephen (2015). 'A Requiem for Hybridity? The Problem with Frankensteins, Purées, and Mules', *Journal of Social Archaeology*, 15/3: 277–98.

Simmons, Joe (1985). 'The Development of External Sanitary Facilities Aboard Ships of the Fifteenth to Nineteenth Centuries', MA thesis, Texas A&M University.

494 REFERENCES

Simms, Tanya, Emanuel Martinez, Kristian Herrera, Marisil Wright, Omar Perez, Michelle Hernandez, Evelyn Ramirez, Quinn McCartney, and Rene J. Herrera (2011). 'Paternal Lineages Signal Distinct Genetic Contributions from British Loyalists and Continental Africans among Different Bahamian Islands', *American Journal of Physical Anthropology*, 146/4: 594–608.

Skinner and Co. (1786). *A Catalogue of the Portland Museum, Lately the Property of the Duchess Dowager of Portland, Deceased*. London: printer not stated.

Skowronek, Russell, and Charles Ewen (2006) (eds). *X Marks the Spot: The Archaeology of Piracy*. Gainsville: University Press of Florida.

Sloane, Hans (1707). *A Voyage to the Islands Madera, Barbados, Nieves, S. Cristophers and Jamaica with the Natural History… of the Last of those Islands*. ii. London: Printed by BM for the Author.

Smallwood, Stephanie (2007a). 'African Guardians, European Slave Ships, and the Changing Dynamics of Power in the Early Modern Atlantic', *William and Mary Quarterly*, 64/4: 679–716.

Smallwood, Stephanie (2007b). *Saltwater Slavery: A Middle Passage from Africa to the American Diaspora*. Cambridge, MA: Harvard University Press.

Smith, Robert (1970). 'The Canoe in West African History', *Journal of African History*, 11/4: 515–33.

Smith, Clifford, and Clarence Maxwell (2002). 'A Bermuda Smuggling Slave Trade: The "Manilla Wreck" Opens Pandora's Box', *Slavery & Abolition*, 23/1: 57–86.

Smith, Thomas (1813). *Narrative of an Unfortunate Voyage to the Coast of Africa. In the Ann Galley of London, David Adam Esq. Commander; with Remarks on the Slave-Trade*. Arbroath: Printed for the author.

Smith, Venture (1798). *A Narrative of the Life and Adventures of Venture, a Native of Africa: But Resident above Sixty Years in the United States of America. Related by Himself*. New London: printed by C. Holt, at the BEE-Office.

Snelgrave, William (1734). *A New Account of Some Parts of Guinea and the Slave Trade*. London: James, John, and Paul Knapton.

Snyder, Terri (2010). 'Suicide, Slavery, and Memory in North America', *The Journal of American History*, 97/1: 39–62.

Snyder, Terri (2015). *The Power to Die: Slavery and Suicide in British North America*. Chicago: University of Chicago Press.

Soja, Edward (1996). *Thirdspace: Journey to Los Angeles and Other Real-and-Imagined Places*. Oxford: Blackwell.

Solar, Peter, and Klas Rönnbäck (2015). 'Copper Sheathing and the British Slave Trade', *Economic History Review*, 68/3: 806–29.

Solar, Peter, and Nicolas Duquette (2017). 'Ship Crowding and Slave Mortality: Missing Observations or Incorrect Measurement?', *Journal of Economic History*, 77/4: 1177–1202.

Sparks, Randy (2014). *Where the Negroes are Masters: An African Port in the Era of the Slave Trade*. Cambridge, MA: Harvard University Press.

Spavens, William (1796). *The Seaman's Narrative: Containing an Account of a Great Variety of Such Incidents as the Author Met with in the Sea Service*. Louth: Printed by Sheardown and Son.

Spence, Joseph (1752). *Crito: Or, a Dialogue on Beauty. By Sir Harry Beaumont*. Dublin: George Faulkner.

Spencer-Wood, Suzanne (2009). 'Feminist Theory and the Historical Archaeology of Institutions', in April Beisaw and James Gibb (eds), *The Archaeology of Institutional Life*. Tuscaloosa: University of Alabama Press, 33–48.

Sprague, Roderick (1985). 'Glass Trade Beads: A Progress Report', *Historical Archaeology*, 19/2: 87–105.

Stahl, Ann (2001). *Making History in Banda. Anthropological Visions of Africa's Past*. Cambridge: Cambridge University Press.

Stahl, Ann (2015). 'Circulations through Worlds Apart: Georgian and Victorian England in an African Mirror', in Richard François (ed.), *Materializing Colonial Encounters*. New York: Springer, 71–94.

Stammers, Michael (1994). '"Guineamen": Some Technical Aspects of Slave Ships', in Anthony Tibbles (ed.), *Transatlantic Slavery: Against Human Dignity*. London: HMSO, 35–40.

Stanley Niaah, Sonjah (2010). *Dance Hall: From Slave Ship to Ghetto*. Ottowa: University of Ottowa Press.

Stanfield, James Field (1788). *Observations on a Guinea Voyage in a Series of Letters Addressed to The Rev. Thomas Clarkson*. London: James Phillips.

Steckel, Richard, and Richard Jensen (1986). 'New Evidence on the Causes of Slave and Crew Mortality in the Atlantic Slave Trade', *Journal of Economic History*, 46/1: 57–77.

Stedman, John (1796). *Narrative, of a Five Years' Expedition, against the Revolted Negroes of Surinam, in Guiana*. 2 vols. London: Printed by J. Johnson.

Steel, David (1794). *The Elements and Practice of Rigging and Seamanship: Illustrated with Engravings*. 2 vols. London: Printed by David Steel.

Steffen, Anka, and Klaus Weber (2016). 'Spinning and Weaving for the Slave Trade: Proto-Industry in Eighteenth-Century Silesia', in Felix Brahm and Eve Rosenhaft (eds), *Slavery Hinterland: Transatlantic Slavery and Continental Europe*. Woodbridge: Boydell Press, 87–107.

Stewart, Charles (2007). 'Creolization: History, Ethnography, Theory', in Charles Stewart (ed.), *Creolization. History, Ethnography, Theory*. Walnut Creek: Left Coast Press, 1–25.

Stewart, Larry (1985). 'The Edge of Utility: Slaves and Smallpox in the Early Eighteenth Century', *Medical History*, 29/1: 54–70.

Stewart-Brown, Ronald (1932). *Liverpool Ships in the Eighteenth Century: Including the King's Ships Built There with Notes on the Principal Shipwrights*. Liverpool: Hodder & Stoughton.

Sweet, James (2003). *Recreating Africa: Culture, Kinship and Religion in the Afro-Portuguese World, 1441–1770*. Chapel Hill: University of North Carolina Press.

Sweet, James (2013). 'Defying Social Death: The Multiple Configurations of African Slave Family in the Atlantic World', *William & Mary Quarterly*, 70/2: 251–72.

Sullivan, George (1994). *Slave Ship: The Story of the Henrietta Marie*. New York: Cobblehill Books.

Svalesen, Leif (1995). 'The Slave *Ship Fredensborg*: History, Shipwreck, and Find', *History in Africa*, 22: 455–8.

Svalesen, Leif (2000). *The Slave Ship* Fredensborg. Kingston Jamaica: Ian Randle.

Svärdskog, Karl-Eric (2005). 'Jenny Lind: The Mystery of Nightingale's Figurehead', *Nautical Research Journal*, 50/4: 221–7.

Swanson, Gail (2010). 'The Wrecking of the Laden Spanish Slave Ship Guerrero off the Florida Keys, in 1827', *African Diaspora Archaeology Newsletter*, 13/3, Article 3, https://scholarworks.umass.edu/adan/vol13/iss3/3 (accessed 24 May 2022).

Swaminathan, Srividhya (2016). *Debating the Slave Trade: Rhetoric of British National Identity, 1759–1815*. London: Routledge.

Sweet, James (2003). *Recreating Africa: Culture, Kinship, and Religion in the Afro–Portuguese World, 1441–1770*. Chapel Hill: University of North Carolina Press.

Sweet, James (2013). 'Defying Social Death: The Multiple Configurations of African Slave Family in the Atlantic World', *William & Mary Quarterly*, 70/2: 251–272.

Symanski, Luís (2012). 'The Place of Strategy and the Spaces of Tactics: Structures, Artifacts, and Power Relations on Sugar Plantations of West Brazil', *Historical Archaeology*, 46/3: 124–48.

Tattersfield, Nigel (1991). *The Forgotten Trade: Comprising the Log of the Daniel and Henry of 1700 and Accounts of the Slave Trade from the Minor Ports of England, 1698–1725*. London: Jonathan Cape.

Taylor, Eric (2006). *If We Must Die: Shipboard Insurrections in the Era of the Atlantic Slave Trade*. Baton Rouge: Louisiana State University Press.

Thomas, Helen (2000). *Romanticism and Slave Narratives: Transatlantic Testimonies*. Cambridge: Cambridge University Press.

Thomas, Hugh (1997). *The Slave Trade*. London: Picador.

Thompson, Robert Farris (1983). *Flash of the Spirit: African and Afro-American Art and Philosophy*. New York: Vintage Books.

Thompson, Katrina (2014). *Ring Shout, Wheel About: The Racial Politics of Music and Dance in North American Slavery*. Urbana: University of Illinois Press.

Thornton, John (1998). *Africa and Africans in the Making of the Atlantic World, 1400–1680*. 2nd edn, New York: Cambridge University Press.

Thornton, John (2003). 'Cannibals, Witches, and Slave Traders in the Atlantic World', *William and Mary Quarterly*, 60/2: 273–94.

Thornton, John (2013). 'Afro-Christian Syncretism in the Kingdom of Kongo', *Journal of African History*, 54: 53–77.

Thornton, John (2018). 'The Origins of Kongo: A Revised Vision', in Koen Bostoen and Inge Brinkman (eds), *The Kongo Kingdom: The Origins, Dynamics and Cosmopolitan Culture of an African Polity*. Cambridge: Cambridge University Press, 17–41.

Tibbles, Anthony (1994) (ed.). *Transatlantic Slavery: Against Human Dignity*. London: HMSO.

Torres de Souza, Marcos, and Camille Agostini (2012). 'Body Marks, Pots and Pipes: Some Correlations between African Scarification and Pottery Decoration in Eighteenth- and Nineteenth-Century Brazil', *Historical Archaeology*, 46/3: 102–23.

Torres de Souza, Marcos, and Luís Symanski (2009). 'Slave Communities and Pottery Variability in Western Brazil: The Plantations of Chapada dos Guimarães', *International Journal of Historical Archaeology*, 13/ 4: 513–48.

Trouillot, Michel-Rolph (2002). 'Culture on the Edges: Caribbean Creolization in Historical Context', in Brian Axel (ed.), *From the Margins: Historical Anthropology and its Futures*. Durham, NC: Duke University Press, 189–210.

Trotter, Thomas (1786). *Observations on the Scurvy*. Edinburgh: printed for Charles Elliott.

Turner, Edith (1992) (ed.). *Blazing the Trail: Way Marks in the Exploration of Symbols. Victor Turner*. Tuscon: University of Arizona Press.

Turner, Daniel (1732). *Siphylis: A Practical Dissertation on the Venereal Disease*. London: Printed for J. Walthoe, R. Wilkin [etc.].

Turner, Phillip, et al. (2020). 'Memorializing the Middle Passage on the Atlantic Seabed in Areas Beyond National Jurisdiction', *Marine Policy*, 122: 104–254.

Turner, Victor (1969). *The Ritual Process: Structure and Anti-Structure*. New York: Aldine de Griyter.

Urban, Kimberly (2017). 'Blackbeard's Beads: Identification and Interpretation of the Beads Recovered from the Shipwreck 31CR314 *Queen Anne's Revenge*', MA thesis, East Carolina University.

Vale, Brian, and Griffith Edwards (2011). *Physician to the Fleet: The Life and Times of Thomas Trotter, 1760–1832*. Woodbridge: Boydell Press.

Van Dantzig, Albert, and Adam Jones (1987). *Pieter de Marees: Description and Historical Account of the Gold Kingdom of Guinea (1602)*. Oxford: Oxford University Press for the British Academy,

Van der Kuyl, Antoinette, and John Dekker (1996). 'St Kitts Green Monkeys Originate from West Africa: Genetic Evidence from Feces', *American Journal of Primatology*, 40/4: 361–4.

Van der Vliet, Jeroen (2017). 'The Curious Case of the *DeWitte Oliphant* of 1755', in Jerzy Gawronski, Andre van Holk, and Joost Schokkenbroek (eds), *Ships and Maritime Landscapes: Proceedings of the Thirteenth International Symposium on Boat and Ship Archaeology, Amsterdam 2012*. Eelde: Barkhuis Publishing, 245–50.

Van Harten, Anton (1970). 'Melegueta Pepper', *Economic Botany*, 24/2: 208–16.

Van Manen, Niels (2006). 'Preventative Medicine in the Dutch Slave Trade 1747–1797', *International Journal of Maritime History*, 18/2: 129–85.

Van Name, Addison (1869–70). 'Contributions to Creole Grammar', *Transactions of the American Philological Association*, 1: 123–67.

Van Norman, William (2005). 'The Process of Cultural Change among Cuban Bozales during the Nineteenth Century', *The Americas*, 62/2: 177–207.

Veuclin, Ernst-Victor (1887). *Aventures d'un Jeune Marin-Dessinateur, Pretextat Oursel, de Bernay 1801–1813*. Bernay: E.-V. Veuclin.

Vlach, John (1991). *By the Work of Their Hands: Studies in Afro-American Folklife*. Charlottesville: University Press of Virginia.

von Arbin, Staffan, and Thomas Bergstrand (2003). *Havmanden—ett Danskt 1600–Talsfartyg*. Uddevalla: Bohusläns Museum, 79–90, https://www.academia.edu/19452396/Havmanden_ett_danskt_1600_talsfartyg_Arkeologisk_efterunders%C3%B6kning_och_v%C3%A5rd (accessed 27 October 2022.

Voss, Barbara (2015). 'What's New? Rethinking Ethnogenesis in the Archaeology of Colonialism', *American Antiquity*, 80/4: 655–70.

Wachsmann, Klaus (1973). 'A "Shiplike" String Instrument from West Africa', *Ethnos*, 1/4: 43–56.

Wadström, Carl (1789). *Observations on the Slave Trade, and a Description of Some Part of the Coast of Guinea, during a Voyage, Made in 1787, and 1788, in Company with Doctor A. Sparrman and Captain Arrehenius*. London: James Phillips.

Wadström, Carl (1794). *An Essay on Colonization, Particularly Applied to the Western Coast of Africa, with Some Free on Cultivation and Commerce*. London: Darton & Harvey.

Waldman, Loren (1965). 'An Unnoticed Aspect of Archibald Dalzel's *The History of Dahomey*', *Journal of African History*, 6/2: 185–92.

Walker, Timothy (2013). 'The Medicines Trade in the Portuguese Atlantic World: Acquisition and Dissemination of Healing Knowledge from Brazil (*c.* 1580–1800)'. *Social History of Medicine*, 26/3: 403–31.

Walker, Timothy (2015). 'Medical Mercury in Early Modern Portuguese Records: Recipes and Methods from Eighteenth-Century Medical Guidebooks', *Asia*, 69/4: 1017–43.

Walker, Timothy (2016) (ed.). *Essays on Some Maladies of Angola (José Pinto de Azeredo 1799*. Dartmouth: Tagus Press.

Wallis, Patrick (2012). 'Exotic Drugs and English Medicine: England's Drug Trade *c.*1550–*c.*1800', *Social History of Medicine*, 25/1: 20–46.

Walvin, James (2001). *Black Ivory: Slavery in the British Empire*. Malden, MA: Blackwell.

Walvin, James (2011). *The Zong: A Massacre, the Law and the End of Slavery*. Yale University Press.

Walvin, James (2017). *Slavery in Small Things: Slavery and Modern Cultural Habits*. Oxford: Wiley-Blackwell.

Warren, Leonora (2013). 'Insurrection at Sea: Violence, the Slave Trade, and the Rhetoric of Abolition', *Atlantic Studies*, 10/2: 197–210.

Watney, Bernard, and Caroline Roberts (1993). 'Liverpool Porcelain Ship Bowls in Blue-and-White', *English Ceramic: Circle Transactions*, 15/1: 1–23.

Watson, Mary (2005). 'Female Circumcision from Africa to the Americas: Slavery to the Present', *Social Science Journal*, 42: 21–37.

Webster, Jane (2007). 'The *Zong* in the Context of the Eighteenth-Century Slave Trade', *Journal of Legal History*, 28: 285–98.

Webster, Jane (2008). 'Slave Ships and Maritime Archaeology: An Overview', *International Journal of Historical Archaeology*, 12/1: 6–19.

Webster, Jane (2009). 'The Unredeemed Object: Displaying Abolitionist Artefacts in 2007', *Slavery & Abolition*, 30/2: 311–25.

Webster, Jane (2015). '"Success to the Dobson": Commemorative Artefacts Depicting 18th-Century British Slave Ships', *Post-Medieval Archaeology*, 49/1: 72–98.

Webster, Jane (2017). 'Collecting for the Cabinet of Freedom: The Parliamentary History of Thomas Clarkson's Chest', *Slavery & Abolition*, 38/1: 135–54.

Weik, Terrance (2014). 'The Archaeology of Ethnogenesis', *Annual Review of Anthropology*, 43: 291–305.

Wellington, Henry, and Rexford Oppong (2018). 'European Fortifications in West Africa as Architectural Containers and Oppressive Contraptions', in John Osei-Tutu and Victoria Smith (eds), *Shadows of Empire in West Africa: African Histories and Modernities*. Cham: Palgrave Macmillan, 239–72.

Wertkin, Gerard (2004) (ed.). *Encyclopaedia of American Folk Art*. London: Routledge.

Weskett, John (1781). *A Complete Digest of the Theory, Laws and Practice of Insurance*. London: Frys, Couchman & Collier).

Wheeler, Roxann (1999). 'Limited Visions of Africa': Geographies of Savagery and Civility in Early Eighteenth-Century Narratives', in James Duncan and Derek Gregory (eds), *Writes of Passage: Reading Travel Writing*. London: Routledge, 14–48.

Wheeler, Roxann (2000). *The Complexion of Race: Categories of Difference in Eighteenth-Century British Culture*. Philadelphia: University of Pennsylvania Press.

White, Shane, and Graham White (1995). 'Slave Hair and African American Culture in the Eighteenth and Nineteenth Centuries', *Journal of Southern History*, 61/1: 45–7.

White, Shane, and Graham White (2005). *The Sounds of Slavery: Discovering African American History through Songs, Sermons, and Speech*. Boston: Beacon Press.

Wilde-Ramsing, Mark (2006). 'The Pirate Ship *Queen Anne's Revenge*', in Russell Skowronek and Charles Ewen (eds), *X Marks the Spot: The Archaeology of Piracy*. Gainsville: University Press of Florida, 160–95.

Wilde-Ramsing, Mark, and Linda Carnes-McNaughton (2016). 'Blackbeard's Queen Anne's Revenge and its French Connection', in Charles Ewen and Russell Skowronek (eds), *Pieces of Eight: More Archaeology of Piracy*. Gainsville: University Press of Florida, 15–56.

Wilde-Ramsing, Mark, and Linda Carnes-McNaughton (2018). *Blackbeard's Sunken Prize. The 300 Year Voyage of Queen Anne's Revenge*. Chapel Hill: University of North Carolina Press.

Wilde-Ramsing, Mark, and Charles Ewen (2012). 'Beyond Reasonable Doubt: A Case for *Queen Anne's Revenge*', *Historical Archaeology*, 46/2: 110–33.

Wilkins, Guy (1955). 'A Catalogue and Historical Account of the Banks Shell Collection', *Bulletin of the British Museum (Natural History)*, 1: 69–119.

Wilkinson, Clive (2004). *The British Navy and the State in the Eighteenth Century*. Woodbridge: Boydell Press.

Williams, David (2000). 'The Shipping of the British Slave Trade in its Final Years, 1798–1807'. *International Journal of Maritime History*, 12/2: 1–25.

Williams, Gomer (1897). *History of the Liverpool Privateers and Letters of Marque, With an Account of the Liverpool Slave Trade, etc.* London: Heinemann.

Wilson, Thomas, and Clarence Grim (1991). 'Biohistory of Slavery and Blood Pressure Differences in Blacks Today. A Hypothesis', *Hypertension*, 17 (suppl. 1): 122–8.

Willett, Frank (1971). *African Art*. London: Thames and Hudson.

Windley, Lathan (1983). *Runaway Slave Advertisements: A Documentary History from the 1730s to 1790*. Westport: Greenwood Press.

Winfield, Rif (2007). *British Warships in the Age of Sail 1714–1792*. Minnesota, Seaworth Publishing.

Witkin, Annsofie (2011).'The Human Skeletal Remains', in Andrew Pearson, Ben Jeffs, Annsofie Witkin, and Helen MacQuarrie (eds), *Infernal Traffic: Excavation of a Liberated African Graveyard in Rupert's Valley, St Helena*, Research Report 169. York: Council for British Archaeology, 57–98.

Wood, Marcus (2000). *Blind Memory: Visual Representations of Slavery in England and America 1780–1865*. London: Routledge.

Wood, Marcus (2002). *Slavery, Empathy and Pornography*. Oxford: Oxford University Press.

Wood, Marcus (2007). 'Packaging Liberty and Marketing the Gift of Freedom: 1807 and the Legacy of Clarkson's Chest', in Stephen Farrell, Melanie Unwin, and James Walvin (eds), *The British Slave Trade: Abolition, Parliament and People*. Edinburgh: Edinburgh University Press, 203–23.

Wood, Marcus (2016). 'Reconfiguring African Trade Beads: The Most Beautiful, Bountiful and Marginalised Sculptural Legacy to have Survived the Middle Passage', in Celeste-Marie Bernier and Hannah Durkin (eds), *Visualising Slavery: Art across the African Diaspora*. Liverpool: Liverpool University Press, 248–73.

Woodall, John (1617). *The Surgeon's Mate, or Military & Domestique Surgery*. London: Printed by Edward Griffin.

Woolfork, Lisa (2010). *Embodying American Slavery in Contemporary Culture*. Urbana: University of Illinois Press.

Young, Robert (1995). *Colonial Desire : Hybridity in Theory, Culture, and Race*. London: Routledge.

Index

Note: Tables, figures, and boxes are indicated by an italic "*t*", "*f*", and "*b*", respectively, following the page number.

For the benefit of digital users, indexed terms that span two pages (e.g., 52–53) may, on occasion, appear on only one of those pages.

Abel, Sarah 453–4, 458–9
Abomey 64–5, 192–3, 235–6
  relief from Palace of Agaja 194*f*
Abomey Plateau Archaeological Project 235
Accra 42, 43*f*, 317
Adams, John 228–30
Adandzi 372–3
Adechina 460
Adélaïde 102*f*, 103, 107–8, 107*f*
Advice, HMS 69
Africa *see* West Africa
Africa 83*t*
African 63–4, 77*t*, 83*t*, 215, 344, 404*f*, 414–15
African Association 272–3
Afro-Portuguese ivories *see under* ivory
Afzelius, Adam 204–5
Agaja, King 192–3, 193*f*, 194*f*
Ajmar-Wollheim, Marta 221–2
Akan
  drums 421*f*
  metalwork 111–12, 191–2, 192*f*, 246–8, 259–60
Aku (Accou) 331–2, 333*b*
Akwete 241–2
Alabama Historical Commission 111
Albion Frigate 32, 58–9, 66*t*, 67, 131*t*, 223–4, 352
alcohol 211, 213–14, 216*t*, 223*t*, 350–1, 361, 379
Alexander 74, 78–9, 83*t*, 284–5, 355
Alfred 334, 370, 381–2
Allada *see* Ardra/Allada
Alsop, James 258–9
Amachree I, King 202–4
Amazon 115
ancestral screens *see under* Kalabari
Andersen, Terry 105*f*
Anderson, John 35–6
Andreo, King 256
Angerstein, Reinhold 218–19, 231
Angola 28*f*, 41*f*, 289–90; *see also* West Central Africa
animals and birds
  collecting 264–71
  trade in 256, 263–4

Ann 198*t*, 410
Ann Galley 171–2, 284–5, 406
Anne 198*t*
Anomabu 42, 43*f*, 45, 218
Antigua 47, 47*t*
Antwerp 245–6
Apsey, Samuel 65
Apter, Andrew 459–61
Arabella 265–7
archaeology *see* bioarchaeology; maritime
  archaeology
Ardra/Allada 192–3, 195, 239
Argyle see Duke of Argyle
Arguin 182–3
Arkwright, Richard 228
arms 211, 215*t*, 216*t*, 226*t*
Arnold, James 78–9, 83*t*
  on Adam and Eve names 284–5
  on dealing with dead crewmen 318
  on sexual violence 343, 411–12
  on slave boys tormenting adult
    slaves 375
  on slaves dancing 368
  on slave insurrections 393–4,
    406–9
  on slave voices 415–16
Aro 46
Arqueonautas 245–6
Arthur, Henry 62
Arthur, Robert 307*t*
Asante 40–2
  drums 421–2
  kente cloth 240–1
Ash, John 335
asiento (contract) *see under* slave trade
Atkins, James 355
Atkins, John 285–6, 317, 330–1, 354–5,
  411–12, 423
Aubrey, Thomas 287, 289–90, 294, 301,
  313–15, 364–5
Aurore 126–8
Aust-Agder Museum, Arendal 106

500   INDEX

Badagry 331–2, 333*b*, 451–2
Badger 260–1
Ball, Charles 206
Bananas Islands 69–70
Banks, Joseph 69–70, 268, 272–3
Banks, Sarah Sophia 272–3
Barbados 31, 33–4, 47–9, 47*t*
Barbot, James 58–9, 66*t*, 67, 137, 223–4, 352
Barbot, James, Jnr 66*t*, 67–9, 187, 188*f*, 214,
    215*t*, 263–4
Barbot, John (Jean) 66–9, 66*t*, 68*f*, 327–8
   on African goldwork 259
   on animal and bird trade 263
   on barricados 169
   on beads 236–8
   on bird trade 263
   on clothing slaves 423
   cutlery 351
   on dysentery 310
   on feeding slaves 360–1
   on female slaves 411
   on hatchways and gratings 137
   on lazarettos 147–8, 297–8
   on licence-slaves 376–7
   on mats 262–3
   on portholes 140–1
   on scarification 289
   on ship cleaning 310
   on slave amulets 427
   on slave boys as servants 375–6
   on slave decks 162–3
   on slave resistance 407–9
   on slaves smoking 372–3
Barbot family 66
Barcklay, Robert 266*t*
Barker, Robert 66*t*, 69, 370–1, 409–10
   on bird trade 264
   on converting ships to slave ships 155
   on food 350–1, 357
Barley, Nigel 202–4, 245–6
Barnes, John 422
Barradas, Esteveo de 244
Barrera y Domingo, Francisco 316–17
Bartar, Edward 266*t*
Bartolozzi, Francesco 91*f*
basket from *São José* wreck 110*f*
baskets and mats 262–3
Bassar 233–4
battery-wares *see* brass
Bauxite 238–9
beads *see* glass beads
Beaulieu, Le 131*t*
Becher, Michael 38–9
Becher & Co. 39
Begho 237–8, 244

Behrendt, Stephen 2*b*, 56, 58, 145, 283, 395–6
Bekinarusibi 202–4, 203*f*
Bell, Mr 77*t*
Bellamy, Samuel 111, 259
Belle, La 224
bells 338, 339*f*
Benezet, Anthony 445–6
Benguela 452
Benin 28*f*, 41*f*, 43*f*, 182–3
   Afro-Portuguese ivories 186*f*, 186
   bells 338, 339*f*
   brass 244
   circumcision 289–90
   fish-figures 188–90
   ivories 186*f*, 186
   Portuguese ships associated with death 185
   textiles 233–4
   see also Bight of Benin
Benin–Denmark Archaeology initiative 235
Bennett, Herman 442–3
Benson 65, 375–6
Berg, J. 143*f*
Berlin, Ira 12
Bermuda 30–1
Bermuda Maritime Museum 115
Bern, Marla 288–9, 450–1
Betsy 407–9
Betty 129*t*, 139*t*
Bhabha, Homi 18, 182, 429–30
bioarchaeology 453–6
Biggs, Mr 242–3, 275–6
Bight of Benin 40, 41*f*, 42*t*, 45, 49, 240–1, 443;
   see also Benin
Bight of Biafra 40, 41*f*, 42*t*, 46, 49, 375; *see also*
   Nigeria
Bini 185
birds *see* animals and birds
Birmingham, brass 246–8
Black Joke 77*t*, 83*t*, 331–2, 332*f*, 333*b*, 363, 417
Blackbeard *see* Teach, Edward
Blake, Bryan 443–4
Blake, William 365–6, 367*f*
Blandford Frigate 39, 149–50, 150*f*, 157–8, 197
Blane, Gilbert 284–5, 287–8, 302, 311
Bohemia, glass beads 219–20, 224–5, 238–9
Bolton 264
Bond, William 266*t*
Bonny 40, 43*f*, 46, 67, 71, 74, 159–60, 159*f*,
   241–2, 401–3
   burial of sailors 317
   sharks 318
   textiles 228–30
Bonville, Thomas 242–3, 275–6
Booth, Joseph 301
Bordeaux 114, 130

INDEX 501

Borucki, Alex 442–3
Bosman, William 289–90, 317, 423
Bossa *see* Tegbesu
Boston 49
botanical specimens 20, 257, 264–71, 266*t*
Bowen, James 77*t*, 297–8, 441
Bowen, Richard 398
Bower, Benjamin and John 227–8, 229*f*
Boy, Jacob 372–3
Boys, William 59
Brackenridge, John 38–9
branding *see under* slaves
brass
   bells 195–6, 338, 339*f*
   gold weights 57*f*, 260
   guns 194–5, 410
   re-use in Africa 20, 244–8
   trade goods 36–7, 116, 202–4, 211–18, 215*t*, 216*t*, 230–3, 231*f*, 233*f*, 245*f*
Brass (Niger Delta), tomb figures 200–1, 200*f*
Brathwaite, Edward Kamau 14, 16–17, 377, 383, 420
Brazil
   against breaking-up of slave ships 114
   amulets 430–1
   ceramics 450–2
   rice imported by slaves 357
   shipmate bonds (*malungo*) 442–3
   slave trade 115
Bray, Gabriel 330*f*
Brecon, Phillips plaque 62
Brick Site wreck 102*f*, 118
Bridson, John 307*t*
Bridson, Thomas 307*t*
Brilhante 443
Bristol
   Baptist Mills 230–1
   brass 230–1, 246–8
   copper 230
   Goldney Hall grotto 270–1
   slave trade 31–2, 34–40, 36*f*, 74–5, 215–18, 276
   transporting convicts 328
Bristol Brass and Copper Company 230–1
Britannia 77*t*, 83*t*, 170–1, 313–14
British East India Company *see* East India Company (EIC)
British Guiana 47*t*
Briton 77*t*, 83*t*
Brodie, Alexander 352
Brooks 59–60, 78–9, 83*t*
   bird trade 264
   broadsheet description (stowage plan) 151–3, 152*f*, 276–7, 382
   creamware jug 79, 80*f*

interpreter 330–1, 336
measurements 129*t*, 139*t*, 150–1
platforms 162
runaways 443–4
slave boys 414–15
slave resistance 406, 411–12
slave suicides 296–7, 401
slaves dancing 368
ventilation, lack of 301–2
Brooks, Joseph, Jnr 153
Brothers 65, 129*t*, 139*t*, 162–3, 198*t*
Brown, Christopher 73
Brown, David 460
Brownlow 63
Bruce, James 313
Bruce, Michael 266*t*
Brüe, André 112–14
Buck, Tom 195–6
Buckham, Joseph 316
Bud 129*t*, 139*t*, 140–1
Bullock, William 267
Bulstrode House grotto 268–9, 270*f*
Burnet, John 265–7, 266*t*, 296–7
Butterworth, William 66*t*, 70–1
   gratings 418*f*
   on call-and-response among slaves 416
   on female slaves 411
   on slave boys' roles 334–5, 414–15, 417–19
   on slave communication 417–19
   on slave resistance and insurrections 413, 417–19
   on slave superintendent 413
   Young Sea Officer's Sheet Anchor 402*f*
Buzzard, HMS 161*f*
Byrd, Alexander 12–13, 16, 329

Cabinda 28*f*, 40
   animals and birds 263–4
   nkisi 205–6, 205*f*
   textiles 214
   trade goods 215*t*
Cadamosto, Alvise 183–5, 262
Calabar 43*f*, 70–1, 194–5, 224, 301; *see also* New Calabar; Old Calabar
calico 225, 227–8, 227*f*
Calvert, Captain 328
Calvocoressi, David 238–9, 372–3
Cambay 10–12
Camden 328
Cameron, John 299*t*
Cameroon 40
Cameroon and Company 65
Campeche 455*t*
Cando 291

502 INDEX

Candomblé 460–1
Cannon Site wreck 102*f*, 118
Canot, Theodore 286–7
Canterbury 77*t*, 399–400
canvas, for sails 134
Cape Coast Castle 31, 42, 43*f*, 45, 64–5, 228–30
captains *see* masters
Carretta, Vincent 87, 445–7
Caribbean
    monkeys 264
    regiments 448–50
    runaways 443–4
    slave trade 27–31, 47, 47*t*, 48*f*
Carletti, Francesco 357
carnelian beads 10–12, 11*f*, 216*t*, 236
Carney, Judith 12–13, 356–7
Carolina 83*t*
carpenters and carpentry tools 55*b*, 56–8, 69,
    155–7, 156*t*, 407–9, 407*f*
Carrol House (Annapolis, MD) 428–9
Carshalton House (Sutton) 268–9
Casa de Guiné 262–3
Casella, Eleanor 394, 403–5
Casseneuve, John 263–4, 409
Castles, John 268–9
cat o' nine tails 370–1, 371*f*; *see also* slaves,
    beaten and flogged
Catherine 77*t*, 83*t*
Caus, Isaac de 268–9
Cavendish 83*t*
Cavendish Bentinck, Margaret *see* Portland,
    Duchess of
ceramics
    decoration based on scarification 450–3
    dish from *Fredensborg* 330*f*
    jug from *Brooks* 79, 80*f*
    pipes 21, 274–5, 328–30, 424–5, 425*f*, 450–2
    and vodun 239–40
Cecilia 266*t*
Ceres 71–2
Chaffers, Richard 8
Chalon, Alfred 257, 258*f*
Chamba 448–50
Chamberlaine, William 295
Chapman, John 259–60
Charles, Thomas 196
Charles I, King of England, Scotland, and
    Ireland 30–1, 220–1, 262
Charles II, King of England, Scotland, and
    Ireland 30–1, 30*f*
Charleston 47–9, 429
Charleston 272–3
Charlotte 71–2
Cheadle Brass Wire Company 246

Chesterfield 272–3
Child, John 266*t*
Chippendale, Haig & Co. 277–8
Chokwe, pendant 218–19, 220*f*
Christiansborg 169, 365–6, 416
Christiansborg *see* Osu
Christianus Quintus 118
Christopher, Emma 328
Christopherson, Peter 319*b*
cinchona *see* quinine
Clare Galley 410
Clark, James 300–1
Clarke, Captain 267
Clarkson, Thomas 39, 73–4, 74*t*, 258*f*, 321,
    327–8, 446–7
    Brooks stowage plan 153
    chest 242–4, 243*f*, 257, 258*f*, 268, 274–8,
        327–8, 381–3
    and Falconbridge 74–5
    ivory trade token 195–6, 381–2
    and Newton 75–6
    on crew deaths on slave ships 283
    on violence against crews 297, 370
    and parliamentary hearings 78–82
    shackles 347, 348*f*
    and Stanfield 76
    Substance of the Evidence 76–8, 77*t*
    thumbscrews and speculum oris 362–3
Claxton, Ecroyde 83*t*
    on netting 160–1, 399–400
    on sickness of slaves 312
    on slave suicide 401–3
    on slaves escaping 160
    on slaves singing 336
cleanliness *see* hygiene and cleanliness
Clevely, John 33*f*
Clifford, Barry 111
Clotilda 103, 111
Coleman, Deirdre 69–70, 268
collecting African exotica 262–3
Collingwood, Luke 6–8
Columbus, Christopher 183, 187
combs 260–1
Compagnie de l'Assentio 107
Compagnie des Indes 116
Compagnie Royale d'Afrique 67
Companion 266*t*
*Company of Adventurers of London Trading to
    Gynney and Bynney* 30–1, 225–6, 262
Company of Merchants Trading to Africa 34–5,
    45, 228
*Company of Royal Adventurers Trading into
    Africa* 30–1
Comte du Norde 83*t*

Concorde de Nantes 112, 224
Cook, Greg 232
Cook, Captain James 181–2, 264–5
Cooke, Mr 266*t*
cooks 355
Coombs, Charles 266*t*
Cooney, William 343
copal 261
Copeland, John 223
copper 230, 244–7
    hull sheathing 132–3
    trade goods 105–6, 115, 213, 218–19, 223*t*
coral 215*t*, 216*t*
Cormantine Castle *see* Kormantin Castle
Coronation 226
Corran, Johnny 241–2
Corran, William 241–2, 248, 267
Corrigall, Andrew 307*t*
Corsican 83*t*
Costello, Ray 331
Coster, Thomas 230
Cosway, Richard 87–8
Cottman, Michael 118–19, 119*f*
cotton 211–14, 215*t*, 216*t*, 217*f*, 225–30, 226*t*, 227*f*, 229*f*; *see also* textiles
Coughtry, Jay 396
Coward, Edward Noll 265, 266*t*
Cowper, William 61, 75–6
cowrie shells 10–12, 11*f*, 64–5, 110*f*, 212–14, 218, 257, 272–4, 273*f*, 457–8, 457*f*; *see also* shells
Cramond, Mr 141
Crane, W. 72*f*
creoles 329–36
creolization 12–18, 321, 328–9, 441–2
crews (buckets) 360–1
crews (ships') *see under* slave ships
Crisp(e), Sir Nicholas 30–1, 220–1, 221*f*, 225–6, 262
Cron Prindz Christian see *Fredensborg*
Crosbie, Captain 443–4
Crosby family 36–7
Crow, Hugh 59, 66*t*, 71–2, 72*f*
    and monkeys 264
    on food and meals 357, 360–1
    on tattoos 289
    on washing 365
    slaves used as crew 375–6, 410
Crow, William 71–2
Crowley, Ambrose 347
Cugoano, Quobna Ottabah 87–90, 398, 447
Cunningham, William 443–4
Curry, Henry 370–1

Curtin, Philip 2*b*, 441
cutlery 351; *see also* spoons

Daget, Serge 304*f*
Dagge, John 286
Dahomey 40, 46, 64–5, 192–5, 193*f*, 194*f*, 235–6
Dakard 274–5
Dalziel/Dalzel, Archibald 83*t*, 194–5
dancing *see under* slaves
Daniel and Henry 32, 61*t*, 62–3, 131*t*
    African cook 355
    cooking and food 352, 354–5
    crews' possessions 259–60
    gold 256–7
    textiles 230
    trade goods 214–15, 216*f*
Daniels, Mr 266*t*
Danish slave trade *see* slave trade, Danish
Danish West India Company 109, 118, 214–15
Danish West-India Guinea Company 105–6, 217*f*
Darby, Abraham 230–1
Dartmouth 32, 62
Davenport, William 215–18, 223
Davis, Ralph 56–7
Deacon, William 223–4, 223*t*
deal planks *see* pine planks
DeCorse, Christopher 233, 237–9
Defiance 266*t*
Delany, Mary 268–9
Delbourgo, James 265, 382
Delgado, Sally 331
Delight 411–12
Delville (Dublin) 268–9
dental modification *see under* West Africa
Denton, William 88*f*
Derby, Lauren 459–61
Diallo, Ayuba Suleiman 265–7
Dick 198*t*
Didbin, Charles 337*f*
Dineley, William 294
Direction des Recherches Archéologiques Subaquatiques et Sous-Mariens (DRASSM) 116
Dixcove 42, 43*f*, 238–9
Dobson 196
Dobson, John 64–5, 195
Dolben, Sir William 78–9, 142
Dolben Act (1788) 78–9
    adults, designation of 342–3
    bonuses for keeping slaves alive 59
    crew sleeping areas 173
    experienced commanders required 58

504 INDEX

Dolben Act (1788) (*cont.*)
  no ventilation requirements 142, 303–6
  slave numbers 40, 153
  slave-to-ton ratios 144–5, 163–4, 256–7
  surgeons required to keep journals 309–10
  surgeons required onboard 55, 283–4
Don Carlos 32, 66*t*, 67–9, 131*t*, 187, 214, 318, 319*b*, 409
Don Francisco 114
Douglas, John 77*t*
Dove, Mr 77*t*
Dover 131*t*
Dover, Thomas 266*t*
Dover-Prize 131*t*
Downes, Henry 331–2
Dragon 259
Drammen 372–3
DRASSM see *Direction des Recherches Archéologiques Subaquatiques et Sous-Mariens*
Dresser, Madge 37–8
Drewal, Henry 183, 188–90, 200
Drury, Dru 69–70, 268, 356–7
DuBois, Laurent 459
Duke, Antera 185, 195–6, 331
Duke of Argyle 34–5, 61*t*, 63–4, 83*t*, 131*t*
  boys' room 168, 414
  deaths on board 306, 307*t*
  deckhouse 159
  defences 338–40, 407–9
  food 354–5
  fumigation 311
  gratings 137
  hearth 352
  modifications made to become slave ship 155, 156*t*
  music-making 338, 368–9
  shaving slaves' heads 365–6
  slave resistance 404*t*, 406, 431
  slave talismans 431
  smaller boats 158
  talismans 431
  trade goods and trading 211, 215
  treating the sick 297–8
  washing area 173, 364–5
Duméril-Leurs 372–3
Dunham, Katherine 459–61
Dutch East India Company 218
Dutch slave trade *see* slave trade, Dutch
Dutch West India Company 108–9, 115, 117–18, 137, 237, 368–9
Dyott, William 374
dysentery 20–1, 306–13
Dyula 234–5

Eagle Gally 77*t*, 83*t*
Eagleton, Catherine 272–4
Earle, Thomas 70–1, 223
East Carolina University 112, 118
East India Company (EIC) 218, 225–6, 226*t*, 272–3, 294
East Indian Merchant 317, 330
Edgar 335
Edo, ivories 186*f*
Edwards, Bryce 314–15, 441
Edwards, George 263–4
Efik 185, 195–6
Elizabeth 69–70, 83*t*, 198*t*, 266*t*, 316, 365, 378, 401, 407–9
Elizabeth I, Queen of England and Ireland 27–9
Elliot, Joseph 150
Ellis, Henry 141
Ellison, Henry 77*t*, 83*t*, 137, 329–30, 413
elm, for keels 128–30
Elmina 40–2, 43*f*, 182–3, 212, 234–5, 247, 262–3
  brass 244–7
  glass beads 237–9
  textiles 240–1
Elmina wreck 108–9, 108*f*
  brass and pewter 233*f*, 245–6, 245*f*
  glass beads 224–5, 237–8
Eltis, David 2*b*, 16, 164, 240, 375, 395–6
Emerson, Matthew 450–1
Emilia 58–60, 74–5, 83*t*, 296–7, 334–5, 443
Engledue, William 271
Enterprize 403
epergne presented to James Penny 82, 86*f*
Equiano, Olaudah 87, 88*f*, 89*b*, 329, 440–1, 445–7
Esterson, William 67–9
Etruria Factory 382
Europa 83*t*
Evans, Chris 230
Evans, David 218–19
Evans, Jenkin 70–1
Evans, John 337*f*
Ewe 234–5, 243

Fabre, Geneviève 420
Fairweather, Patrick 196
Fairy 83*t*
Falconbridge, Alexander 34–5, 59–60, 73–5, 74*t*, 327–8, 446
  on air ports 140–1
  on barricados 168–9
  on crew burials 317
  on deckhouses 160
  on dysentery 306, 309–10
  on force-feeding slaves 362

on language and interpreters 334–5
on netting 159–60
on sharks 318
on slave deaths 296–7, 306
on slave food and meals 354–5, 360–1
on slave music-making 368–9
on slave overcrowding 166*b*
on slave suicides 403
on slaves being given beads 373–4
on slaves jumping off ship 399
on treatment of female slaves 343–4
on treatment of sick slaves 297–8, 315
on ventilation, lack of 144, 302
parliamentary testimony 78–9, 82, 83*t*
post-mortem examination of slave 296–7
privilege slaves 59–60
textiles 242–3, 275–6
Falconbridge, Willliam 75
Falconer, William 137, 142, 197
Fante 234–5, 330–1, 335
Favre, Petitpierre et Compagnie 227*f*
Fazackerly, William 228
Fellowes, Sir John 268–9
Ferentz, Captain 317
Ferrers Galley 407–9
Ferret 83*t*
figureheads *see under* slave ships
Finch Hatton, Elizabeth 7–8, 7*f*
Fisher 65
Fisher, Mel 103–4
fish-figures *see* mermaids and fish-figures
Fitzherbert, John 69
Fletcher, James 409
flogging *see* slaves, beaten and flogged
Florida 318
Flower, Henry 267
Fon 192–3
Formidable 160–1, 161*f*
forowas (ritual vessels) 246, 248
Fort, John 259–60
Fort Amsterdam 42
Fort Metal Cross *see* Dixcove
forts *see under* West Africa
Fothergill, John 69–70, 268
Foucault, Michel 328
Fountain, John 160–1
Fowkes Tobin, Beth 264–5
Fowler, John 35–6
Francklyn, Gilbert 291
furniture *see* houses and furnishings
Fraser, Douglas 188–90
Fraser [Frazer], James (*fl* 1703; surgeon) 266*t*
Fraser, James (*fl* 1772–87; master) 74–5, 78–9,
82, 83*t*, 296–7, 360–1

on heat tolerance of slaves 305*b*
on medicines 292–3
on ship cleaning 311
on slaves being given clothes 335
on slave games 373
on slaves' washing 365
privilege slaves 58–9
Frazer, Peter 299*t*
Fredensborg 19, 101, 102*f*, 103, 105–6
amulet 429
barricado 105*f*, 171
cooking and dining 330, 351–2, 351*f*, 356*f*
crew burials 317
latrines 173
medicine 292–3
model of 105*f*
netting nails 160
pipes and smoking 372–3
scrubbing brush 311–12, 312*f*
shells 271–2
slave resistance 407–9, 414–15
Fredensborg II 126–8, 143*f*, 143, 171, 172*f*,
356–7, 364
Fredericus Quartus 118
Fremont, Cécile 430
French, Martin 38–9
French slave trade *see* slave trade, French
Fry, Gladys-Marie 428–9
Fugger company 245–6

Ga'anda 450–1
Gainsborough, Thomas 91*f*
Galàm 274–5
Gambia 14, 314–15, 375
Gambia Adventurers 31
Gamble, Samuel 65–6, 197
journal 4*f*, 60–1, 61*t*
on African response to figureheads 197
on Anna Maria Falconbridge 75
on barricados 169–70
on cargo and stores 215, 347
on crew burials 317
on crew sickness 298–301, 299*t*
on food and meals 350–1, 354–5, 360–1
on hearths 352
on medicines 294
on naming slave Adam 284–5
on ship cleaning and fumigation 311
on ship's carpenters 157
on slave resistance 406–7
on small boats 158
washing not mentioned 364–5
Garland 83*t*, 198*t*
Garvey, Johanna 439

506 INDEX

Gascoyne 198*t*
Ghana 28*f*, 40, 41*f*, 43*f*
   glass beads 221–2, 222*f*, 237–9, 238*f*
   scarification 288–9, 450–1
   textiles 243
   see also Gold Coast
Gikandi, Simon 162
Gilroy, Paul 1–2
glass beads
   belonging to slaves 10–12, 373–4, 424–7,
     456–9, 457*f*
   ground up and reconstituted 20, 237–8, 238*f*
   manufacture 219–20
   reworked (perforated and abraded) 238–9
   trade goods 104–5, 112–16, 211–25, 216*t*,
     221*f*, 222*f*, 223*t*, 236–40, 247–8
   and Vodun 239–40
   West African 221–2, 222*f*, 233–4, 237, 238*f*
Gluckman, Stephen 118
Goddio, Franck 107
gold 20, 30–1, 61–2, 111–12, 225–6, 244, 246–7,
   256–60
   gold dust 259–60
Gold Coast 40–2, 41*f*, 42*t*, 45, 49, 67–9, 234–5,
   335, 375
   animal and bird trade 263
   beads 236–8, 238*f*
   brass 232, 244–6
   canoes 194–5
   cowrie shells 64–5
   gold 111–12, 225–6
   gold dust 260
   gold weights 57*f*, 191–2, 246–7
   inoculation against yaws 314–15
   ivory 106
   textiles 226, 240–1
   trade goods 214, 232, 262
   see also Ghana; West Africa
gold weights 57*f*, 191–2, 192*f*, 246–8, 260
Golden Age 129*t*, 139*t*
Golden Frigate 162–3
Goldney, Thomas, III 270–1
Gomer, Quash 439
Gomez, Michael 10, 12–13, 415–16, 439–40,
   452–3, 457
Goodwin, Justin 258–9
Goodwood House 268–9
Gosport and Havre Packet 83*t*
Gott, Suzanne 221–2, 238*f*
Gould, James 62
grains of paradise *see* melegueta pepper
Greenfield 218–19
Grenada 47*t*, 74
Grenville, William 277
Greyhound 63

Griffin 67
Griffon, HMS 114
Grimm, Samuel Hieronymus 270*f*
Groeningen 102*f*, 108–9, 232
gromettoes 46
Groot Prooyen 311–12
grottoes, shell 268–71, 270*f*
Guerrero 102*f*, 116
Guillotine 65
Guinea cloth 228–30
Guinea Company 30–1, 225–6
Guinea rods 218–19
guns *see* arms
Gwaton 76

Haast U Langzaam 343–4
Haines, Robin 311
Hair, Paul 258–9
Hales, Stephen 141
Hall 150–1, 151*f*
Hall, Florence 86
Hall, John Ashley 83*t*, 358, 375–6
Hall, Martin 4–6, 327–8, 394
Halle, Jean Noel 311
Hamann, Nicole 232
Handler, Jerome 10–12, 288–9, 373, 423, 429
Hannah 83*t*
Hannibal 31–2, 56, 61–2, 61*t*, 131*t*, 147–8, 201,
   214, 346, 368–9
   animal and bird trade 256, 263
   branding of slaves 286
   bulkheads 165–7
   cooking and meals 352, 354–5, 358–9
   crew burials at sea 318
   crew wills 318, 319*b*
   deaths on board 309
   defences 169
   discovery of a female sailor 201
   dysentery 309
   gender segregation of slaves 341–2
   gold 256–7
   latrines 363
   music 379
   ownership 58–9, 62, 147
   sailors' wills 318, 319*b*
   ship cleaning 310
   ship's defences 407–9
   slave deaths 309
   slave meals 358–9
Harding, Captain 411–12
hardwood 261
harps *see under* Sierra Leone
Harrison, George 153
Hart, William 204–5
Harwich, HMS 63

Hassell, Ralph 218
hats 211, 223*t*, 226, 226*t*
Hausa 291, 331–2, 443
Havannah 227–8
Havmanden 102*f*, 109*f*, 109, 356–7
Hawke 198*t*
Hawkesbury, Lord 446–7
Hawkins, John 27–9
  coat of arms 29*f*
Hawthorne, Walter 13, 441, 443–5
Heath, Barbara 10–12
Heatley, Robert 83*t*, 167, 168*f*, 355, 360–1, 414–15
Hector 196, 335
Henderson, Mr 77*t*, 370, 414–15
Henderson, David 83*t*
Henrietta Marie 19, 101, 102*f*, 103–5, 126–8,
    148–9, 148*f*
  beads 223–4, 374
  copper kettles 352–4
  crew wills 318, 319*b*
  discovery and salvage 103–4
  hull 132–3, 149
  medical equipment 292–3, 296–7
  memorial plaque 118–19, 119*f*
  pewter dishes 232, 351
  sailors' wills 318, 319*b*
  shackles 347–8
  trade goods 223–4, 223*t*
Herbert, Eugenia 244
Herrera, Remigio *see* Adechina
Herskovits, Melville 14
Heywood family 36–7
Hicks, Dan 270–1
Hill, William 62
Hilton, John 277–8, 297
Hoare, Samuel 153
Hobhouse, Isaac 230–1
Hodgson, Thomas 286
Hoffmann, Christian 106
Holland, Thomas 69
Hollschwander, Chris 153–5, 154*f*
Hope 409
Horseler, Charles 370, 381–2
Horwood, Anna Maria 75
House of Commons Sessional Papers
    (HCSP) 78*t*
houses and furnishings 260–1, 270–1
  as trade gifts 196, 261
  see also grottoes
Hudibras 66*t*, 70–1
  slave boys 334–5, 414–15
  slave call-and-response 416
  slave insurrection 411, 417–19
  slave superintendents 413
Hueda 46, 235, 239–40

Hughes, Griffith 289–90
Humphrey, George 268
Hutchinson, William 150, 151*f*
hygiene and cleanliness 310–11

Ibibio, Mami Wata figure 190*f*
ifá (cult) 460
Ife 244
Ife-Ife 237
Igbo 12–13
  olona cloth 241–2, 242*f*
  scarification 289
Igbo Olókun 237
Igbo-Ukwu 236, 240–1, 244
Ijebu-Ode 241–2, 242*f*, 248
Ijo 200, 202–4
Ile-Ife 237
India
  carnelian 10–12
  cotton 213, 215*t*, 216*t*, 217*f*, 218, 223*t*,
    225–6, 228–30, 241
Indiennes de traites 227*f*, 227
Industry 165–7, 411–12
infrapolitics *see* slaves, resistance
Inikori, Joseph 227–8, 230–1
Innes, Joanna 79
inoculation 314–15
insurance, maritime *see* maritime insurance
Intersal Inc. 112
Ipswich, sailcloth production 134
Iris 132–3
iron bars 36–7, 104–5, 213–15, 216*t*, 218,
    223–4, 223*t*, 226*t*
Isert, Paul Erdemann 169, 340, 365–6,
    401, 416
Isle of Man 223
Italian Gally 286
ivory
  Afro-Portuguese ivories 186*f*, 186, 189*f*, 262
  trade gifts and tokens 195–6, 381–2
  trade goods 20, 30–1, 61–2, 106,
    115–16, 202–4, 225–6, 256–7, 259–60,
    264, 275–8
  usage 260–1
Ivory Coast 260, 375
Ivy, Daniel 62
IZIKO (Museums of South Africa) 110–11

Jackson, William 9*f*, 140*f*
Jago, Walter 62–3
Jamaica 47
  creolization 14–16
  Jonkonnu masquerades 460–1
  slave trade 31, 33–4, 47*t*, 49, 74, 439–41
James 316

508　INDEX

James, William 77*t*, 170–1, 313–14
James I, King of England and Ireland, James VI,
　King of Scotland 30–1, 102*f*
James Matthews 102*f*, 114–15, 114*f*, 127*f*, 130,
　134, 138–40
Jamestown 30–1
Jamineau, Daniel 223–4, 223*t*
Jamineau & Rousseau 223
Jane 129*t*, 139*t*, 198*t*
Janverin, Mr 77*t*, 141, 312–13, 400–1, 417
Jason 39
Jefferson, Thomas 303
Jeffreys, Sir Jeffrey 62, 147
Jekyll, Joseph 87
Jemmy 65
Jenkinson, Charles, Baron Hawkesbury (later
　Lord Liverpool) 78
Jennion, John 407*f*
Jensen, Richard 309–10
Jesson, James 265, 266*t*
John, Ephraim Robin *see* Robin John, Ephraim
John, Grandy Robin *see* Robin John, Grandy
John, Otto Ephraim Robin *see* Robin, John, Otto
　Ephraim
John Gally 265, 266*t*
John the Baptist 258–9
Johnson 431
Johnson, Walter 405
Jolly, Mr 334–5
Jonas 27–9
Jones, Adam 423
Jones, George 166*b*
Jones, Thomas 195–6
Joshua 314
journals *see* sea journals
jug depicting *Brooks* 79, 80*f*
Juno 355
Jupiter 83*t*

Kalabari 202–4
　ancestral screens 202–4, 203*f*
　figure of Awomekaso 201
Katherine Galley 286
Keefer, Katrina 286, 291*f*
Kelly, Kenneth 192–3, 235–6, 239
Kendall 266*t*
kente cloth *see under* Asante
King, Captain 328
King David 410
King Pepple 198*t*
King-Dorset, Rodreguez 369
Kiønig, Espen 106
Kip, Jan 44*f*
Kirckwood, John 266*t*

Kitty 129*t*, 139*t*, 140–1, 162–3, 198*t*
Kitty's Amelia 34–5, 66*t*, 71–2, 131*t*, 264,
　357, 365
Klein, Herbert 134–6
knives 214–15, 216*t*, 217*f*, 226*t*
Knox, John 83*t*, 330–1, 357
Komenda 42, 43*f*
Kongo 112, 182–3, 185, 205–6
　minkisi 205–6, 205*f*, 427–8, 428*f*
Kormantin Castle 30–1, 42, 43*f*
Kraamer, Malika 242–3
Kriger, Colleen 212, 240–1

La Rochelle 67
Lace, Ambrose 195–6, 335
Lady Nelson 169
Lagos 443
Lancashire 218
Lancaster 36*f*, 276
Land, Isaac 370
Langton, Bennett 243–4
larch 128–30
Lark 83*t*
Laroche, James 35–6, 38–9
Law, Robin 46, 183, 194, 235–6
Lawson, Edward 307*t*
lead 216*t*
Leeward Islands 47, 49
Leone, Mark 428–9
Leusden 102*f*, 117–18
Lever, Sir Ashton 268
Lever, Darcy 70–1
Leyland, Thomas 292–3
Lhermitte, Jean-René 138*f*, 363–4, 379,
　380*f*
Liberty 338–40, 340*f*
Lilly 77*t*, 370
Lima, Tania 430–1
limbo 420
Lind, James 142, 285, 287–8
Lind, Jenny 200
Lindsay, Dido Belle 7–8, 7*f*
Linebaugh, Peter 336–8
linen, for sails 134
Little Pearl 83*t*, 355
Little Will 132–3
Littleton, William 83*t*, 305*b*, 379–81
Lively 65, 242–3, 275–6
Liverpool
　palm oil 278
　Parrey ship inspection (1788) 126–8, 129*t*,
　　130–2, 137, 139*t*
　porcelain 8
　sails 195

INDEX

shipbuilding 125
silver epergne 86*f*
slave trade 34–7, 36*f*, 40, 46, 63–5, 196, 218, 276
Llangyfelach 230
Lloyd's Register 132–3, 431
Loango 40
Lockwood, Richard 230
London
    Africa House 31
    bird trade 263–4
    Don Saltero's Coffee House 267
    glass beads 219–20, 221*f*
    Holophusikon 268
    slave trade 32, 34–5, 36*f*, 40, 218, 276
Long, Edward 411–12, 439–40
longboats *see under* slave ships
Lord Stanley 125, 126*f*
Lottery 292–3
Louis XIV, King of France 107
Loup Garou wreck 102*f*, 116
Lovejoy, Paul 375, 450, 452–3
Lundberg, Peder Christian 106
Luxborough Galley 33*f*, 59

Mabbot, William 266*t*
MacGaffey, Wyatt 182
McHenry, George 426–7
Mackcersie, Alexander 259
McKie, James 299*t*
McLean, Charles 299*t*
McTaggart, John 74
Makala Kataa 247
Makepeace, Margaret 225
malaria 298–301
Malcolm, Corey 103–4, 347–8
Mali
    scarification designs 450–1
    textiles 240–1
Mallipeddi, Ramesh 316–17, 415–16
Mami Wata 111, 190*f*
Manchester 227–8
Mande 234–5
Manilla Wreck 102*f*, 115, 224–5
manillas 115, 213, 245–6, 245*f*, 248
Mansfield, William Murray, 1st Earl 6–8, 396
Mansong Diara, King 272–3
Marcus 83*t*
Marees, Pieter de 244–5
Maria Josefa 291
Marie-Séraphique 19, 126–8, 170*f*, 359*f*
    barricado 155, 169, 170*f*
    carpenter's tools 407–9
    food and meals 354, 357–8, 359*f*

gratings 137
latrines 363–4
plan of profile, hold, and decks 138*f*
slave deck 379, 380*f*
maritime archaeology 101
maritime insurance 6, 396, 400
maritime law 396–8
Marseilles 227
Marshall-Fair, Mr 157, 299*t*
Martha 198*t*
Martin, David 7*f*
Mary 71–2, 341–2, 375–6, 410
Mason, Mr 266*t*
masters (captains) 45, 55, 57–9, 66, 214
    accommodation 343
    earnings 58–9
    journals 61, 215
    private ventures 58–9
    privilege slaves 58–9, 376–7
Mataró ship model 184*f*
Mathew, Roger 62
mats *see* baskets and mats
Matthews, James 78–9, 82
Matthews, John 83*t*, 166*b*, 335
Mayflower 266*t*
Meacham, Gideon 307*t*
Mead, Thomas 319*b*
medical equipment *see under* surgeons
medicines *see under* surgeons
Mel Fisher Maritime Heritage Society
        (MFMHS) 103–4, 116
Mel Fisher Maritime Museum (MFMM) 104
melegueta pepper 256–7, 261, 354–5, 357
memoirs 66–72
Mende 368–9
mermaids and fish-figures 187–90, 188*f*, 189*f*
Metcalf, George 218
Middleton, Sir Charles 126–8
Midlo Hall, Gwendolyn 12–16
Millar, George 77*t*
Miller, William 38–9
minkisi see under Kongo
Mintz, Sidney 14–17, 318, 321, 329, 365–6, 441–2
Mitchell, Peter 235
Mobile, AL 111
Molà, Luca 221–2
Moneypenny, James 64–5
monogenism 284–5
Monroe, J. Cameron 235–6
Monteith, Archibald John 173
Montserrat 47
Monzolo, Jose 185
Moore, David 103–4, 148–9, 148*f*

510 INDEX

Morgan, Philip 16
Morgiana 443
Morley, James 77*t*, 83*t*, 155, 297, 315
Morley, Matthew 75
mortar from *Fredensborg* 356*f*
Mortice, Humphry 286
Mossuril basket 110*f*
Mount and Johnson 352
Mullin, Michael 443–4
Mumford, Robertson 376–7
Murano, glass beads 219–20, 238–9, 247–8
Murphy, Kathleen 265, 294–5
Murray, William *see* Mansfield, William
    Murray, 1st Earl
Museum of London Archaeology Service
    (MoLAS) 220–1
music-making *see under* slave ships; slaves

Nagô 451–2
Nancy 131*t*
Nantes, printed cotton 227
Nassau 75
National Association of Black Scuba Divers
    (NABS) 118–19
National Museum of African American History
    and Culture (NMAAHC) 110–11
natural history collections 264–71
Navickas, Katrina 18
Ned 196
Nelly 77*t*
Nelson, George 8
Nelson, Jennifer 443
Neptune 83*t*, 198*t*, 286, 328, 358
Nevis 31, 47
New Britannia 414–15
New Buipe 237–8
New Calabar 46, 67, 74, 159–60
New Providence 266*t*
New York 49
    African Burial Ground 424–5, 440–1, 454,
        455*t*, 456–9, 457*f*
Newport 49
Newton, John 34–5, 63–4, 75–6, 327–8, 344, 446
    deckhouse 159
    on boys' room 168, 414
    on crew deaths 306, 307*t*
    on deck chains 346–7
    on female slaves 342, 411
    on food 354–5
    on gratings 137
    on hearths 352
    journal 60–1, 61*t*
    music on board 368–9, 379
    on ship defences 338–40, 407–9

on ship fumigation 311
on ship modifications 155, 156*t*, 162, 246
on slave deaths 306, 307*t*, 316
on slave head shaving 365–6
on slave resistance 403–6, 404*t*, 414–15, 431
on talismans 431
on trade 211, 215
on treatment of female slaves 342–4
on treatment of the sick 297–8
on washing and latrines 173, 364–5
parliamentary testimony 78–9, 83*t*
smaller boats 158
SEAST pamphlet 73–6, 74*t*
Newton Plantation burials 424–5, 454–6, 455*t*
    dental modification 454
    necklace 10–12, 11*f*, 424–5
    pipe 424–5, 425*f*
Nicholls, Henry 196
Nichols, John Bowyer 91*f*
Nicholson 83*t*
Nicholson, Captain 227–8
Nigeria 28*f*, 46
    glass beads 221–2, 236–7
    ivories 186*f*
    Kalabari ancestral screens 202–4, 203*f*
    Mama Wata figure 190*f*
    olona cloth 241–2, 242*f*
    scarification 288–9, 450–1
    see also Bight of Biafra
Nightingale 200, 413
Nixon, Isaac 65
nkisi see Kongo, *minkisi*
Noble, Clement 78–9, 80*f*, 82, 83*t*, 264, 305*b*,
    443–4
Norman, Neil 235–6, 239–40
Norris, Robert 64–5
    cowrie shells 212–13
    journal 61, 61*t*
    melegueta pepper 275–6
    on African-born children of traders 335
    on bulkheads 165–7
    on inoculation 314
    on interpreters 334
    on lighting slave decks 381
    on musical instruments 368–9
    on shackles 347–8
    on slaves having beads 373–4
    on slave head shaving 365–6
    on slave heat tolerance 305*b*
    on slave numbers and overcrowding
        166*b*, 173–4
    on slave resistance 413
    on slaves playing games 373
    on slaves smoking 373

INDEX 511

on sleeping platforms 162–3, 174
on ventilators 142
parliamentary testimony 82, 83*t*
supporting slave trade 78–9, 82
North America
ceramics 450–1
cotton 228
cowrie shells 6, 457*f*
creolization 14–16
food 357
glass beads 220–1
saltwater slaves 6
slave trade 31, 34–5, 47–9, 47*t*, 48*f*, 111
tobacco pipes 450–1
North Carolina Department of Natural and
Cultural Resources (NCDNCR) 112
North Carolina Marine Fisheries 112
Norwegian Maritime Museum, Oslo 106
Nuestra Señora de Atocha 103–4
Nussbaum, Felicity 9–10

oak, for hulls 128–30
Ockiya, King 200
Odyssey Marine Exploration 116
Odyssey site 35F 102*f*, 116, 117*f*, 155–7
Offra 239
Ofiong, Egbo Young 196
Ojo, Olatunji 451
Old Calabar 40, 46, 185, 195–6, 331
Oldham, James 396
olona cloth *see under* Nigeria
opiates 294
Osu (Christiansborg) 42
Ouidah 43*f*, 45–6, 64–5, 133, 192–3, 212,
235–6, 451–2
beads 239
cancy stones 355
cowrie shells 64–5, 214
fort 34–5, 45
language 331–2, 333*b*
textiles 240–1, 243
Oursel, Prexetat 344, 345*f*
Outram, Sir Benjamin, medical chest 293*f*
Owen, Nicholas 271
Owo, ivories 186*f*
Oxford University, Centre for Maritime
Archaeology 107
Oyo 451

Pallas 330*f*
palm oil 202–4, 256–7, 278
Palmié, Stephan 13–14, 429–30, 460
pannekins 361
Park, Mungo 272–4, 422

Parker, Isaac 77*t*, 83*t*, 363, 417
Parrey, Captain 126–8, 129*t*, 130–2, 137, 139*t*,
153, 162–3, 165–7
Paton, Diana 79, 422
Patton, David 266*t*
Pearce, James 39
Pearl 77*t*, 297, 362, 370, 417, 431–2
Peggy 77*t*, 83*t*, 198*t*, 364
Pen Azen wreck 102*f*, 116
pendant with snail disk 218–19, 220*f*
Penny, James 78–9, 82, 83*t*, 86*f*, 141–2, 278,
305*b*, 335, 376–7
pepper, melegueta *see* melegueta pepper
Pepple, King 267
Perry, Warren 458
Perseverance 185
Pery, Colonel John 162–3
Peterborough 301
Petiver, James 265–7, 266*t*, 294–7
pewter 104–5, 214, 215*t*, 216*t*, 223*t*, 233*f*
Philip Stephens 198*t*
Phillips, James 74–6, 152*f*, 153
Phillips, Richard 74–5
Phillips, Thomas 58–9, 61–2
journal 61*t*
on animal and bird trade 256, 263
on bulkheads 165–7
on branding slaves 286
on circumcision 289–90
on cooking and food 352, 354–5
on crew burials and sea commitals 317–18
on dental modification 288–9
on discovery of a female sailor 201
on exercising slaves 368
on feeding slaves 358–9
on gender separation of slaves 165–7, 341–2
on *Hannibal* 147–8, 201
on latrines 363
on medical examination of slaves 287
on shackling slaves 346
on ship cleaning 310
on ship's defences 169, 407–9
on slave deaths 306, 309
on slave suicides 401–3
on slaves as naked 423
on slaves as overseers 374–5
on trade 190–1, 194–5, 214
on vodun 239–40
pidgin 329–36, 419–20
Pietsch, Roland 342–3
Pinckard, George 288–9, 336, 368–9, 375–6, 424
pine planks 155–7, 168
pinnaces *see under* slave ships
Pinney family 36–7

512   INDEX

pipes 21, 235–6, 239–40, 274–5, 328–9, 372–3,
    424–5, 425f, 450–2
pirates 111–12, 130
Pitt, William 78, 277
Pitty and Preedy 86f
Planer, Richard 265, 266t
plant specimens see botanical specimens
Pocock, Nicholas 37–9, 37f, 149, 150f
Pollard, Joshua 417
Polly 77t
polygenism 285
Ponta do Leme Velho wreck 102f, 115, 224–5
Ponton, Mr 77t
Poole 218, 276
Port au Prince 267
Portland, Duchess of 268–9
Porto Novo 451–2
Portuguese slave trade see slave trade,
    Portuguese
Potter, John 196
Price, Richard 14–17, 318, 321, 329, 365–6, 441–2
Prideaux, Walter 60–3, 61t, 214–15, 230,
    259–60
Primrose 258–9
Prince Clause 267
Prince George 266t
Privy Council Committee for Trade and
    Plantations 78, 81
Providence 49
Province of Freedom 75
Pucket, William 307t
punch bowl depicting Lord Stanley 125, 126f

Queen Anne's Revenge 102f, 103, 112–14
  beads 224
  gold 259
  latrine 363
  medical equipment 292–3, 293f
  sails 134
  shackles 347
  site plan 113f
quinine 294, 298–300
Quixote 196

RAC see Royal African Company
racial theories 284–6, 302–3
Radburn, Nicholas 164
Ramsay, James 446–7
Ranger 401
Rarey, Matthew 430
Rath, Richard Cullen 17–18, 368–9, 419–20
Recovery 294, 328
Rediker, Marcus 336–8, 417–19, 441, 446
Registers of Liberated Africans 291

Registration Act (1786) 128, 134–6
Renney, Patrick 59–60
rhubarb 294
Richardson, David 2b, 16, 35–6, 215–18, 395–6
Richey 83t
Riello, Giorgio 225
Rio de Janeiro, Pretos Novos cemetery 455t
Rio Volta 353f
Robe, Edward 370
Robert 411–12
Roberts, Captain 267
Roberts, John 69
Robin John, Ephraim 195–6
Robin John, Grandy 195–6
Robin, John, Otto Ephraim 335
Robinson, Samuel 169
Rock, John 440–1, 447–50, 448f
Rodger, Nicholas 349
Rodgers, James 294
Rodgers, Silvia 197
Rogers, James 35–6, 215–18
Roebuck 267
Ronald, James 299t, 360–1
Rose 129t, 139t
Rose, Joshua 195
Roufley, Thomas 299t
Royal African Company (RAC) 31–2, 218
  10 per cent tax 32, 147
  branding slaves 286
  disease control 314
  flag 146–7
  forts and factories 42–5, 239
  gold 256–7
  ivory 260–1
  language and interpreters 334–5
  shackles 347
  South Sea Company and 33–4
  using slaves as overseers 374–5
  see also Hannibal
Royal Charles 226, 226t
Royal Navy 291, 352, 425–6
Royal Society 264–5
RPM Nautical Foundation 116
Ruby 83t, 318, 343, 375–6, 406–9, 411, 431–2
Rugendas, Johann Moritz 449f
Ruddock, Noblet 35–6
Rugby 78–9
rum see alcohol
Rupert, Prince 30–1
Russel 77t, 297–8, 441
Rutherford, James 299t

Saakwa-Mente, Norris 285
Sahlins, Marshall 181–2, 214

INDEX 513

sailors
  female imposter 201
  fishing 21, 328–9, 350–1, 350*f*
  personal trading 257, 260–74
  shell craft 271–2
  valentines 271–2, 272*f*
  wills 258–9, 318, 319*b*
  see also slave ships, crews
Saint Ann 83*t*
St Helena burials 425–7, 454, 455*t*
St John 395–6
St Kitts 47*t*, 63–4, 314, 420–1
St Vincent 47*t*
Saint-Géran 102*f*, 116
Saint-Quay-Portrieux wreck 102*f*, 116, 155–7,
    292–3, 311–12, 338–40
Sally 77*t*, 83*t*, 297
Salomon 27–9
salt cellars 186*f*, 187, 189*f*, 262
Salter, James 267
Saltford Brass Mill 231*f*, 231
salvage companies 103–4, 112
San Salvador 455*t*
Sancho, Ignatius 87, 91*f*
Sandown 4–5, 4*f*, 34–5, 61*t*, 65–6, 75, 131*t*
  African cook 355
  barricado 169–70
  crew burials 317
  figurehead 197
  food and meals 350–1, 354–5, 360–1
  hearth 352
  medicines and medical care 294, 296–7
  shackles and chains 359–60
  ship cleaning and fumigation 311
  sickness on board 65, 157, 298–301, 299*t*
  slave names 284–5
  slave resistance 406–7
  small boats 158
  stores 347
  trade 215
São Jorge da Mina *see* Elmina
São José 102*f*, 110–11
Sapi, ivories 186, 188–90, 189*f*
Sarah Gally 266*t*
Savi 46, 192–3, 235, 239–40
scarification *see under* West Africa
Schroeder, Hannes 453–4, 458–9
Scots pine 128–30
Scott, David 16
Scott, James 5–6, 393–4, 403–5
Scrogham, Captain 370
scrubbing brushes 311–12, 312*f*
Sea Horse 106–7
sea journals 60–6, 61*t*, 106, 309–10

sea shanties 336–8
SEARCH Inc. 111
Searle 198*t*
seashells *see* shells
SEAST *see* Society for Effecting the Abolition of
    the Slave Trade
Sekondi 42, 43*f*
Sene, Glaucia 430–1
Senegal 28*f*, 41*f*, 240–1, 277–8
Senegambia 41*f*, 42*t*, 194–5, 288–9; *see also*
    Sierra Leone
Sergeant, Richard 319*b*
sexual violence *see under* slaves, women and
    girls
shackles and chains 346–8, 348*f*, 349*f*, 359–60,
    363–4, 378, 406–7
sharks 317–18
Sharp, Granville 75, 446–7
Shaw's Brow china works 8
shells 268–9, 269*f*, 271–2, 272*f*; *see also* cowrie
    shells
Sherboro 375
Sheridan, Richard 283
shipwrecks *see under* slave ships
Shirley, Captain 317, 330
Shlomowitz, Ralph 311
Sierra Leone 30–1, 40, 41*f*, 42–5
  Afro-Portuguese ivories 186
  free black colony 70, 75, 446–7
  harps and bowed instruments 204–5, 204*f*,
    368–9
  medicinal plants 314
  scarification 289
  slave trade 42*t*, 63–4, 215
  textiles 240–1
  tobacco 372–3
  see also Senegambia
Sierra Leone Company 75
Sisters 443–4
Skeen, James 265, 266*t*
Skibb, Joseph 301
Skillin, Simon, Jnr 199*f*
Slave Coast 45
slave ships 1–2, 4*f*, 8, 9*f*, 18–20, 33*f*, 125, 140*f*,
    146–53, 146*f*, 154*f*, 161*f*
  African conceptions and depictions of 181–7,
    186*f*, 191–3, 192*f*, 193*f*, 194*f*, 202–6, 203*f*,
    204*f*, 205*f*
  African crew 334–5, 355
  air ports (portholes) 140–2, 140*f*, 144
  barricado 127*f*, 153–7, 154*f*, 167–71, 168*f*,
    170*f*, 172*f*, 338–41, 395–6, 417
  bell-ringing 338
  bilge pumps 191

514 INDEX

slave ships (*cont.*)
breaking-up of condemned ships 114
bulkheads and rooms 125–6, 147, 155–7, 156*t*, 165–74, 168*f*, 417–19
cargo invoices 215–18
carrack (*nau*) 183, 186*f*
children on board 335
cleaning regimes 310–12, 349
as converted merchant ships 125
cost of 35–6
and creolization 12–17, 21, 321, 328–9
crew, boys as 66
crew accommodation 173–4, 379
crew burials and sea commitals 317–18
crew deaths and sickness 82, 298–301, 299*t*, 306, 307*t*, 312
crew punishment and beatings 370–1
crew shortages 375–6, 410
crews 54–60, 55*b*
daily routine 338–79
deck chains 346
deckhouses 158–60, 159*f*, 298
deck plan 353*f*
defences 130–2, 169–71, 194–5, 338–40, 340*f*, 407–10
eyes painted on prow 184–5
feminization of 197, 201
figureheads 197–202, 198*t*, 199*f*
food and meals 350–62, 350*f*, 351*f*, 356*f*, 358*b*
forecastle barricade 171–3, 172*f*
frigate-built 130–2, 162
forecastles 130–2
fumigation 311
galley-built 130–2
Guineamen nickname 125
hatchways and gratings 137, 139*t*, 141–2, 155, 418*f*, 419
hearths 171–2, 344, 347, 352–4
hull profile 130–2
hull sheathing (coppering) 132–3
insurrection *see under* slaves
journals and logs *see* sea journals
labelled as such on stern 146
lazaretto 147–8, 297–8
longboats 157–8, 297–8
as memorial sites 118–19
music-making 368–9, 379
names of ships 198, 199*t*
netting 156*t*, 160–1, 161*f*, 399–400
owners 6, 35–6, 58–9, 195–6, 198, 215
Parrey ship inspection (Liverpool, 1788) 126–8, 129*t*, 130–2, 137, 139*t*
as pesthouses 283
pinnaces 157–8

quarterdecks 130–2, 155, 160–2, 168, 171–2, 344
repair and replacement 130–2
rigging 133–4, 171–2
sailors' call-and-response 336
sails 133–4, 135*f*, 171–2, 184, 349
ship design and modifications 125–46, 127*f*, 127*f*, 129*t*, 153–74, 156*t*
Ship English and jargon 201–2, 330–6
shipworm damage 132–3
shipwrecks 19, 101, 102*f*, 107*f*, 108*f*, 113*f*, 114*f*
sick berths 297–8
singing and sea shanties 336–8, 337*f*, 379
slave decks and platforms 125–6, 153–7, 154*f*, 162–3
slave numbers and overcrowding 82, 134–6, 136*f*, 144–6, 145*f*, 151–3, 152*f*, 162–5, 166*b*, 283–4, 320*f*, 378, 380*f*
slaves separated by gender and age 127*f*, 155, 168, 168*f*, 169–71, 341–2, 414
slaves transported on and off ships 157–8
tonnage (carrying capacity) 134–7, 136*f*, 145*f*, 147
ventilation and ventilators 140–4, 149, 301–6, 417–19
voyages, numbers and duration of 2*t*
wardroom 351
washing area and latrines 173, 342–6, 379–81
water consumption 361–2
windsails 142–4, 143*f*
yawls 157–8
slave trade, British 27–37
10 per cent tax 32, 62, 104, 147, 223–4
abolition of 39–40, 73, 205–6, 273–4, 277
accounts of, by Africans 86–90
accounts of, by crew members 60–72
accounts of, parliamentary testimony 72–86
African trading partners 194–7
African trading partners' children 335
agents 35–6
asiento (contract) 33, 45, 106–7, 286
and copper industry 230
and disease prevention 287–8
disembarkation points 46–9, 47*t*, 48*f*
goods *see* trade goods
insurance 6, 396, 400
interaction between Europeans and Africans tightly controlled 235
and languages 329–36, 333*b*
legislation 40, 55*b*, 58–9, 78–9, 136, 142, 144–6, 153–5, 163–5, 166*b*, 358*b*
and manufacturing 218–33

INDEX 515

parliamentary inquiries (1788–92) 72–86,
  83*t*, 126–8, 166*b*, 218, 275–8
price of slaves 215
privilege slaves 58–60, 335, 376–7
regulation 40
ship trade vs. fort trade 42–5
South Sea bubble 33–4, 34*f*
and sugar plantations 47
syndicates 35–6
and transportation 328
see also under West Africa
slave trade, Danish 105–6, 109, 118
slave trade, Dutch 31, 47–9, 108–9, 115, 118,
  137, 140–1, 234–5, 343–4, 372–3
slave trade, French 45–6, 107, 116, 141
slave trade, Portuguese 27–9, 40, 115, 218–19,
  288–9, 454
  African responses to Portuguese slavers
    182–7, 186*f*, 194–5, 201–4, 338
  Afro-Portuguese ivories 186*f*, 186, 189*f*, 262
  against breaking-up of slave ships 114
  beads 224–5, 237
  branding 286
  copper and brass 244–6
  cowrie shells 272–3
  creole and pidgin 14, 331
  fortified trading posts 40–2, 234–5
  language and interpreters 331, 334
  manillas 245–6
  medicines 294–5
  and mermaids 187–90, 189*f*
  shipwrecks 110–11, 115
  slave-to-ton rations 144
  sleeping mats 379–81
  textiles 240–1
  tobacco 372–3
slave trade, Spanish 27–9, 31, 33–4, 103–4,
  106–7, 112, 114, 116–18, 286
slaves
  accommodation 127*f*, 155, 162–3, 165–74,
    168*f*
  Adam and Eve naming 284–5
  adults, designation of 342–3
  amulets and charms 423, 427–30
  beads 373–4, 424, 456–9, 457*f*
  beaten and flogged 89*b*, 297, 312, 370–2,
    400–1
  boarding slave ships 158, 160
  branding 286–7
  as cargo 6
  Caribbean regiments, joining 448–50
  circumcision 289–90
  cleaning ships 310, 375–6
  clothing 227–8

as crew members 375–6, 410
dancing 368–70, 420–2
deaths at sea 2*t*, 61–2, 82, 118–19, 132–3, 144,
  283, 284*f*, 306, 307*t*, 317, 396
dehydration 361–2
dental modification 288–9, 454
disease and sickness 20–1, 292–321
DNA analysis 49, 453–6, 455*t*
drums 368–9, 378, 420–2, 421*f*
exercise 368–70
food and meals 354–61, 358*b*, 359*f*, 377–8
force-feeding 348*f*, 362–3, 400–1
head shaving 365–6
insurrection 88–90, 169, 394–9, 395*t*,
  397*f*, 410
jettisoned from ships 6–8
languages and communication 329, 333*b*,
  415–16
medical examination of 287–8, 304*f*
melancholia and lethargy 316–17
metalworking 376–7
music-making 17–18, 368–9, 419–21
Muslims 359–60
naked 287–8, 373–4, 423–4
numbers transported 42*t*
as overseers 374–5
poisoning crew 404*t*, 431
racial theories 284–5, 302–3
resistance (infrapolitics) 403–32, 404*t*
runaways 288–9, 335, 441, 443–4, 448–50
saltwater slaves 1–2, 10–18, 321, 383, 439–40
scarification 288–91, 291*f*, 447–53, 448*f*, 449*f*
seasoning 14, 16–17, 383
shackled 173, 346–8, 348*f*, 349*f*, 359–60,
  363–4, 378
shipmate bonds 441–5
singing 336, 378, 417
smoking 372–3
suicide 398–403, 431–2
thermotolerance 303–6, 305*b*
wari (game) 373
washing 364–5
weapons 406–10, 408*t*
written accounts by slaves 86–90, 89*b*, 376–7
slaves, boys 360, 365, 378, 414–15
  accommodation 82, 127*f*, 165–8, 168*f*, 173–4,
    341, 414
  assimilation 375
  as informers 375, 404*t*
  involvement in insurrections 404*t*, 406,
    414–15
  as messengers 414–15, 417–19
  not shackled 414–15
  as personal attendants 335, 375–6

516 INDEX

slaves, women and girls 147–8, 170–1, 341–6, 345*f*, 366, 378
  accommodation 168*f*, 168, 341–2, 381
  beads 373–4, 424, 457–8
  beaten and flogged 343, 370–1
  call-and-response 416–17
  cooking 356–7
  food and meals 358–9
  girls consider adults at 10 yrs 342–3
  giving birth on ships 320*f*, 321
  involvement in insurrections 88–90, 398–9, 410–14
  naked 423–4
  as personal servants 375–6, 411
  sexual violence 341–4, 411
  shackled 347–8, 414–15
  singing and dancing 368
  suicide 401
  washing space and latrines 173, 364–5
Slave Wrecks Project (SWP) 110–11
Sloane, Sir Hans 262, 265–7, 382, 419–22
Smale, John 185
smallpox 313–14
Smallwood, Stephanie 12–13, 422, 439–40
Smeathman, Henry 66*t*, 69–70, 327–8, 335
  flora and fauna specimens 268
  on barricados 169–71, 340–1, 378–9
  on cooking and dining 352–4, 356–7
  on deck chains 346–7
  on feeding slaves 360–1, 377–8
  on female slaves 343, 411
  on shackling slaves 346, 359–60, 378
  on ship jargon 330
  on ship's watch 336
  on slaves dancing 368–9, 420–1
  on slaves having beads 373–4, 424
  on slaves as naked 287–8, 423–4
  on slaves smoking 373
  on washing facilities 173, 365
Smith, Clifford 115
Smith, John 407–9
Smith, Thomas 284–5, 356–7, 359–61, 423
Smith, Venture 376
Smyth, John 266*t*, 294–5
snail symbolism 218–19
Snelgrave, William 286, 332–4, 407–9, 445–6
snuff box from *Black Joke* 332*f*
Snyder, Terri 399
Society 64–5, 83*t*
Society for Effecting the Abolition of the Slave Trade (SEAST) 39, 73–6, 74*t*, 78–9, 153, 276, 382
Society of Merchant Venturers 69
Solomon, Job ben *see* Diallo, Ayuba Suleiman

song broadsheet (*Wives and Sweethearts, or Saturday Night*) 337*f*
South Sea Company 33–4, 34*f*, 106–7, 265, 266*t*, 268–9
Southwell Frigate 37–9, 37*f*
Souza, Marco de 430–1
Spanish Fly 295
Spanish slave trade *see* slave trade, Spanish
Sparrman, Anders 214–15, 217*f*, 220–1, 222*f*, 248, 274–6
Spavens, William 423
speculum oris 348*f*, 362–3, 400
Spence, Thomas 18, 290
spoons 360–1
Spring Bay Flat Plantation 455*t*
Squirrel 198*t*, 356–7, 359–60
Stahl, Ann 247, 260–1
Stanfield, James 74*t*, 76, 298, 309, 312, 342–3, 351, 372
Stanley Niaah, Sonjah 420
Starke, Thomas 223–4, 223*t*
Steckel, Richard 309–10
Stedman, John 365–6, 367*f*, 374
Steel, David 142–3
stoneware dish from *Fredensborg* 330*f*
Stono revolt 368–9
Sullivan, Humphry 299*t*
supercargoes 55*b*, 57–8, 61, 214–15
surgeons 55, 57–60, 283, 292–301, 349
  blistering 295
  bloodletting 295, 315
  corporal punishment by 297
  earnings 58, 74–5, 283–4
  handbooks 285
  journals 61, 309–10
  medical equipment 292–3, 293*f*, 296*f*, 407–9
  medical examination of slaves 287, 289–90
  medicines 294–5
  private trading 58–9, 258–9
  privilege slaves 59–60, 376–7
  sleeping area 173
Svalesen, Leif 105–6
Swallow 8, 9*f*, 27–9
Swalwell 347
Swansea 247–8
  White Rocks Copper works 230, 246
Swanson, Gail 116
Sweet, James 181, 185, 206, 442–3
Sybille 333*b*
Sydenham, Thomas 294, 301
Symanski, Luis 16, 452
syphilis 294, 313–14
Syracuse University 108–9

Tantumquerry 42, 43f, 160–1
Tarleton family 36–7
Tartar 77t, 83t
Tattersfield, Nigel 62–3
Taylor, Eric 394–5, 405–6, 411–12
Taylor, Henry 103–4
tea 351
Teach, Edward (Blackbeard) 112, 292–3
Teast, Sydenham 275–6
Tebay, John 292–3
Tegbesu (Bossa) 64–5
textiles 36–7, 202–4, 203f, 211–18, 215t, 216t,
      223t, 226, 226t, 233–4; *see also* cotton
thermotolerance 303, 305b
Thetis 34–5, 56, 66t, 69, 131t
   animal and bird trade 264
   crew mistreated 370–1, 409–10
   food 350–1, 357
   ship modifications 155
Thistlewood, Thomas 443
Thomas 411–12
Thomas, Hugh 58
Thompson, Mr 77t, 362, 417
Thompson, Katrina 369, 420
Thornton, John 226, 233–4, 329
thumbscrews 348f, 362–3, 400–1
tobacco 372–3
Togo 40
Toller, William 266t
Tom 83t
tomb figures (Niger Delta) 200f, 200
Torres de Souza, Marcos 16
Touchet, Samuel 228
Tournay, Anthony 223–4, 223t, 347
Town(e), Mr 77t, 362, 370
Towne, James 83t, 297, 329–30, 364, 370, 403
trade beads *see* glass beads
trade goods, African market 20, 104–5, 108–9,
      115, 195, 211, 215t, 216t, 217f
   assortment bargaining 212–14
   and manufacturing 218–33
   see also alcohol; arms; brass; cowrie shells;
      glass beads; iron bars; textiles
trade goods, British market 20, 256
   as collectables 262–3
   flora and fauna specimens 264–71, 266t
   household goods 260–74
   see also animals and birds; gold; ivory;
      melegueta pepper; shells; slaves
Tradescant, John, the elder 262
Trail, Donald 328
Trans-Atlantic Slave Trade Database
      (TSTD) 2b, 16, 40, 46, 49, 103, 133–6
transportation, penal 328

Treasure Salvors Incorporated 103–4
Treaty of Utrecht 32–3
Trial 69
Trotter, Thomas 59–60, 78–9, 82, 83t, 284–5
   on animal and bird trade 264
   on slave boys 414–15
   on slave dancing 368
   on slave languages 330–1, 336
   on slave resistance 406, 411–12
   on slave suicides 296–7, 401
   on ventilation 301–6
   privilege slaves 376–7
Trouillot, Michel-Rolph 17
Trousdale [Trousdall], John 195–6
Trouvadore 102f, 117–18
Trusty 443–4
Tryal 77t, 83t, 370, 406, 414–15
TSTD *see* Trans-Atlantic Slave Trade Database
Tublay, James 267
Tunnell, James 266t
Tunstall, Marmaduke 69–70
Turner, Daniel 313–14
Turner, Victor 461–2

Ughoton *see* Gwato
Unity 61t, 64–5, 83t, 126–8, 131t, 173, 212–13,
      314, 364, 413
Upton 77t, 83t

Valiant 83t
Valle da Garafia 288–9, 454
Valongo Wharf 430–1
Van Manen, Niels 283, 311
Van Norman, William 461–2
variolation 314
Vassa, Gustavus *see* Equiano, Olaudah
Vassall, Samuel 30–1
Vaz Coelho, Antonio 194–5
Velde, William Van de, the Younger 146–7, 146f
Venice, glass beads 219–25, 222f, 237–9
Venus 77t, 83t, 129t, 139t, 162–3
Vernis Martin 261
Vesey, Denmark 395–6
Viegas, Jacques 430
vodun 239–40, 430, 459–61
Voss, Barbara 458–9
voyages *see under* slave ships

Wabshutt, Robert 69, 264
Wadström, Carl 395–6, 397f
Wales, copper industry 230
Walker, James 215
Walker, Sarah 260–1
Walker, Timothy 294–5

518 INDEX

Walker, William 266t, 319b
Walpole, Sir Robert 268-9
Walvin, James 39
Ward, William 150
Warren, Leonora 78
Warwick Castle 77t
Wasp 396-8
Waterlot, Emmanuel-Georges 194f
Watkins, Thomas 301
Watt, William 266t
weapons
  used by sailors *see* slave ships, defences
  used by slaves 406-10, 408t
  as trade goods *see* arms
Wedgwood, Josiah 382
Weskett, John 396, 400
West Africa 28f
  akori (glass beads) 221-2, 237
  akoso (glass beads) 238f
  beads 236-40, 424-5, 456-7
  bells 338, 339f
  bodom (glass beads) 221-2, 222f
  brass 244, 248
  canoes 183, 194-5
  circumcision 289-90
  copper 244
  dental modification 288-9, 454
  food 354-5
  forowas (ritual vessels) 246, 248
  forts 40-5, 43f, 44f, 157-8, 182-3
  iron 233-4
  languages and interpreters 329
  music and songs 419-20
  musical instruments 204-5, 204f, 368-9
  numbers of slaves 42t
  pirogues 195
  pottery 450-1
  scarification 288-91, 291f, 447-53,
    448f, 449f
  slave brokers and traders 194-7
  slave numbers 42t
  slaves ships and traders associated with land
    of the dead and witchcraft 112-14, 181,
    183, 185, 206, 338, 393, 422
  slave ships' figureheads, influence of
    197-202, 200f
  slave trade 27-35, 40-6, 41f, 182-3
  textiles 228-30, 240-4, 242f, 243f
  tobacco and smoking 372-3, 424-5, 425f
  trade goods for West Africa 211

  trade goods from West Africa 256
  trade goods as prestige goods 233-6
  trade goods used in vodun 239-40
  water spirits and fish-figures 188-90, 190f
  see also gold; Gold Coast; ivory
West Central Africa 40, 41f, 42t; *see also* Angola
Western Australia Maritime Museum 114
Wethersfield, CT, cemetery 439
Wheeler, Roxann 285-6, 302-3
Whim 83t
whips 370-1
White, James 195
Whydah 102f, 103, 111-12, 259
Wilberforce, Willliam 39, 75-6, 78-9, 82,
  243-4, 277
Wilbraham 83t
Will 71-2, 198t, 410
William and Sarah 265
Williams, Joseph 343, 411-12
wills *see* sailors, wills
Willson, Robert 223t
Wilson, Isaac 83t, 316, 363, 401, 410
Wiltshire 266t, 296-7
Winchcombe, Thomas 223t
Windward Coast 40, 41f, 42-5, 42t, 49
Wingfield, George 266t
Winneba 42, 43f
Winterbottom, Thomas 204-5
Wise, Captain 443-4
Woburn Abbey 268-9
Wolof 427
wood *see* hardwood
Wood, Marcus 8-10, 118-19, 236, 248, 382
Woodall, John 292
Woodruff, Janet 458
Woods, Joseph 153
Works Progress Administration (WPA) 428-9

Yanimarew 441
Yarmouth, MA 111
yaws 20-1, 287, 294, 313-15
yawls *see under* slave ships
yellow fever 20-1, 298-301
Yorke, George 355
Yoruba 188-90, 233-4, 240-1, 443, 451-2, 460
Young Hero 83t, 312, 336, 399-403

Zoffany, Johann 7-8
Zong 6-8, 39, 400
Zoutsteeg, St Martin 455t